ALSO BY HAZEL ROWLEY

Christina Stead: A Biography

RICHARD WRIGHT

RICHARD WRIGHT

THE LIFE AND TIMES

HAZEL ROWLEY

A John Macrae Book
Henry Holt and Company   New York

Henry Holt and Company, LLC
Publishers since 1866
115 West 18th Street
New York, New York 10011

Henry Holt® is a registered trademark of
Henry Holt and Company, LLC.

Library of Congress Cataloging-in-Publication Data
Rowley, Hazel.
 Richard Wright : the life and times / Hazel Rowley.—1st ed.
  p. cm.
 Includes bibliographical references and index.
 ISBN 0-8050-4776-X
  1. Wright, Richard, 1908–1960. 2. Authors, American—20th century—Biography.
 3. African American authors—Biography. I. Title.

PS3545.R815 Z84 2001   00-054249
813'.52—dc21
[B]

First Edition 2001

Designed by Kelly S. Too

Printed in the United States of America

1 3 5 7 9 10 8 6 4 2

CONTENTS

Richard Wright's papers are in the Beinecke Rare Book and Manuscript Library at Yale University. This winter morning the Old Campus is shrouded in mist. Shadowy figures move between the trees. There is something theatrical about Yale's Gothic stone buildings, with their towers, turrets, and gargoyles. Suddenly the Beinecke Library looms up—a magnificent slab of glistening marble, solid as a tomb. From all over the world, scholars come to this ultramodern building to study the past.

Wright kept everything—drafts of manuscripts, letters, photographs, hotel bills, newspaper cuttings. In 1976, sixteen years after his death, his widow, Ellen Wright, sold his papers to Yale. The collection fills 136 cream-colored boxes.

Wright never came to Yale University—a white privileged world in which he had no place. It is strange to be here poring over his papers: the rough drafts, full of arrows and crossings out; the letters, slightly yellowed now, that he typed while in the South Side of Chicago and in Harlem in the 1930s; his handwritten appointment books; the magnificent photographs he took in Spain and Africa in the 1950s; the rejection letters

("Dear Mr. Wright, We appreciate your thought of the *Saturday Evening Post* in connection with the material we are returning herewith, and regret that it is not quite in line with our present needs"). In the cosseted environment of the reading room, scholars tap away at their laptops. Outside, in the sunken courtyard, snow falls silently.

Gertrude Stein presides over the foyer in Francis Picabia's 1933 oil portrait. She's wearing a Roman-style wrap that leaves one shoulder bare. Beside her, in a painting by Dora Maar, Alice B. Toklas sits at a small table, with Basket, their white poodle, at her feet.

Not only do Stein and Wright have their papers in the Beinecke Library, both these famous American expatriates are buried in the Père Lachaise Cemetery in Paris. Stein was born into a wealthy German-Jewish family in Pennsylvania. Wright, son of a sharecropper, was born in a wooden shack in Mississippi.

In front of the paintings of Stein and Toklas are two tiny upholstered Louis XVI children's armchairs that once belonged to Stein. Alice B. Toklas did the intricate petit point, over a design by their friend Picasso. In Gertrude Stein's apartment, shortly after the Wrights arrived in Paris in 1946, four-year-old Julia Wright was instantly attracted to these chairs and started to play on them. Stein scolded her. They were not for little girls, she said.

RICHARD WRIGHT

1

MISSISSIPPI

Richard Wright's grandparents were slaves. They worked in the cotton trade when Natchez, on the Mississippi, was one of the great cotton ports of the world. There was more wealth in Natchez than in any American city outside New York, and the slave market was the second busiest in the South, after New Orleans.

Wright's maternal grandfather, Richard Wilson, labored in the fields until the early spring of 1865, when he ran away to fight in the Civil War. The eighteen-year-old managed to dodge the Confederate troops and cross the Ohio River into the North. In Cairo, Illinois, he enlisted in the Union navy. He served for three months—from 22 April to 27 July. By then, the war was over. In the South, four million slaves were free.

Full of hope for the future, Wilson returned to Mississippi. According to his grandson, Richard Wilson had been "militantly resentful of slavery," and back in Mississippi, he used to stand armed guard in front of ballot boxes to protect blacks who were voting.[1]

On 26 February 1871, Richard Wilson married Margaret Bolden in the small town of Woodville, in Wilkinson County, Mississippi.[2] Eighteen-year-old "Maggie," as she was known, was small and slight, with deep-set brown eyes and long straight hair. She was so light-skinned that until she opened her mouth and spoke pure Southern Negro dialect, strangers thought she was white. Her grandson Richard Wright believed she was a mixture of Irish, Scottish, and French stock, "in which Negro blood had somewhere and somehow been infused."[3] Like her husband, Maggie was a strong, rebellious, intelligent woman—but illiterate.

The Wilsons settled in Woodville, and according to the 1900 census, Richard worked as a farm laborer. Over the next eighteen years, Richard and Maggie Wilson had nine children—four girls and five boys. Thomas Booker, the eldest son, was born in 1872. The other birth dates are vague. There were no birth records in Mississippi at the time, and the census records are wildly inconsistent. After Cleopatra, Clark, and Charles, Ella was born in 1883. Daughter Maggie arrived in 1886, followed by Edward, Addie (1891), and Lawrence. Around the turn of the century, the family moved to Natchez, living in a wooden house on 20 Woodlawn Avenue, eight blocks from the Mississippi.[4]

By the time Richard Wright came to know his grandfather, the old man was frail, blind in one eye, and suffering from chronic rheumatism. No longer capable of manual work, he was embittered by his long struggle with the Bureau of Pensions. As a war veteran, Wilson was eligible for a disability pension. At first the bureaucrats argued that he had not served for the requisite ninety days.[5] Then they claimed that the name entered on the navy rolls was "Richard Vincent," and there was no evidence that Wilson was the same man. Wilson would dictate yet another letter and send it off. After a time, an official envelope would arrive at the house, and he would ask his grandson to read him the letter. It was always bad news. "I never heard him speak of white people," Richard Wright would recall. "I think he hated them too much to talk of them."[6]

AFTER THE CIVIL WAR, SOUTHERN BLACKS TEMPORARILY ENJOYED NEW LIBERTIES. For the first time, they voted in elections and held political office. They held protests and demonstrations. The prospect of real freedom was in the wind. The backlash was immediate. In 1866 a paramilitary white supremacist organization, the Ku Klux Klan, held its first meeting in Nashville, Tennessee, vowing to preserve the "Southern way of life."

Despite the talk of "forty acres and a mule," Congress did nothing for the former slaves. Soon they were forced into a new system of servitude. The plantations were divided into small farms, worked by sharecroppers. Since the white owner provided the land, tools, and mule, at harvest time the sharecropper had to pay his boss one half or more of the crop as payment. With the remainder, he paid for the food, clothing, and furnishings he had bought throughout the year on credit. If in theory he was free, in reality he was held in bondage by his debts.

By fraud, violence, and intimidation, the progressive Reconstruction governments were gradually overthrown. In 1881 the segregation movement began. In 1896 in *Plessy v. Ferguson*, the Supreme Court of the United States ruled that "separate but equal" was not unconstitutional.

Richard and Maggie Wilson's children, the first generation of Southern blacks to be born free, were still young when the signs "white" and "colored" appeared at bus and railroad stations, public toilets and drinking fountains, theaters and movie houses. Hospitals were segregated. Nurses could only tend their own race. Jails were segregated. Schools and churches were segregated. Trains, buses, and streetcars were segregated. Blacks were not permitted in public libraries, restaurants, rooming houses, saloons, billiard halls, or lunch counters—unless they were expressly for Negroes. Interracial marriage was prohibited. American apartheid was in place. It was called Jim Crow.

Blacks had to act humble, deferential, and cheerful about it. They knew never to contradict a white person—even if they knew that person was wrong. If a black man did not "know his place"—if he came over as "sassy" or "biggity"—he would endanger his own life and put others in the black community at risk.

Teaching was one of the few professions open to black people at that time. Equipped with the most rudimentary literacy skills themselves, several of the Wilson children taught school. Tom began as a teacher, then he made chairs. Edward was a teacher before becoming a Methodist pastor. Ella was sent to teach the children of sharecroppers in a small rural settlement called Cranfield. Her classes were held in the small wooden church. By May, when the thinning, weeding, and chopping time began, many of her pupils would disappear to help their parents in the cotton fields.

Richard Wright's paternal grandfather was Nathaniel Wright. He and his two older brothers worked as slaves on John Rucker's plantation,

about twenty-one miles southeast of Natchez. When Natchez was
occupied by Union forces in July 1863, they left to join the 58th Colored
U.S. Infantry, stationed in the town.[7] But conditions in those makeshift
army camps were appallingly unsanitary and disease was rife. George
and James Wright, both of whom were married, deserted after a few
months. Twenty-one-year-old Nathaniel Wright, still single, stayed on.
He was fortunate to survive the experience.

Wright's paternal grandmother, Laura Calvin, was thought to be
partly Choctaw Indian. She and Nathaniel were married soon after the
war. Nathaniel and his brothers were back working on the same plantation as sharecroppers. The couple had four sons: Solomon, Nathan,
Rias, and George.[8] Before they reached their teens, the boys were
working in the cotton fields.

Ella Wilson was twenty-six when she met Nathan Wright. They married in Natchez on 19 March 1908. Ella was already three months pregnant. Their home was an unpainted log cabin.

Richard Nathaniel Wright, named after his two grandfathers, was
born on 4 September 1908. An untrained black midwife presided over
the birth. It was early autumn. The fields were snowy with cotton lint.
In the backwoods of Adams County, the only trace of the wider world
was the hooting of passing trains. And the arrival, from Mexico, of a
devilish insect called the boll weevil.[9]

Two years later, on 24 September 1910, Ella gave birth to another
boy—Leon Alan. The family went to live in Natchez, with Ella's parents. It was his grandparents' house, on Woodlawn Avenue, that young
Richard Wright almost destroyed. One wintry day, logs were crackling
in the fireplace. The boys' grandmother was ill, and their mother had
told them not to make any noise. Richard, fretful and bored, was standing in front of the fire. It is the dramatic incident with which he begins
his autobiographical narrative, *Black Boy*.

He had an idea. He plucked straws from the broom and added
them to the fire. He tugged the long curtains over so they touched the
darting flames. The fire blazed. Flames leaped to the ceiling. The room
turned bright yellow. Suddenly he was terrified. He ran and cowered
under the house. He heard screams, people running over the floor-
boards above him, the clopping of horse hoofs coming toward the
house, the gongs of fire wagons. His mother rushed about outside, call-

ing him in a shrill, frightened voice. Eventually, his father found him and tugged him from his hiding place.

According to *Black Boy*, it was his mother, not his father, who pulled a branch off an elm tree, stripped off the leaves, and lashed him so hard he lost consciousness. For days afterward he lay in bed with a high fever, screaming at his hallucinations. ("Whenever I tried to sleep I would see huge wobbly white bags, like the full udders of cows, suspended from the ceiling above me.") The doctor apparently said that the boy had to be kept quiet; his life was in danger. "For a long time I was chastened," Wright writes, "whenever I remembered that my mother had come close to killing me."

RICHARD WAS THREE YEARS OLD IN 1911 WHEN THE FAMILY MOVED TO MEMPHIS, Tennessee. Ella told him they would travel upriver on the *Kate Adams*, one of the last of the old steamboats. For days, he plied his mother with questions. Yes, she assured him; it was a big boat. When he set eyes on the *Kate Adams*—a small dirty boat nothing like the gleaming ship he had imagined—he burst into tears. His father distracted him by taking him down to the engine room.

Memphis was a shock to the whole family. They had left rural freedom for a concrete metropolis. Nathan found work as a night porter in a drugstore on Beale Street, and the four of them shared a single bedroom and kitchen in a one-story tenement building. In these cramped quarters, Nathan tried to sleep in the daytime, and the boys were expected to be quiet.

In Memphis, Richard became aware that his parents were arguing a great deal. It seemed to be mostly about food. His father had rigid ideas about cooking. He liked his biscuits to turn out "cherry brown," and complained if they didn't.[10] He disliked vegetables. Richard would invariably wake up in the morning to the sound of his father coming home from work, then his booming voice complaining about Ella's cooking.

Nathan read the Bible on Sundays and prayed, but it did not seem to Richard Wright, looking back, that his father was genuinely religious. Nathan would have liked to be a preacher, but for some reason, he never heard "God's call." He knew it would make God angry if he pretended to be a chosen man when he was not, but he was bitter about his plight. Wright recalls:

> He prayed and brooded, indulged in gloomy monologues that were the despair of my mother and cowed me and my brother to silence. . . . The anxiety that came into my mother's face whenever he complained about his not being "called" made me conceive of it as something dreadful, an event that would leave me and my mother and brother alone in the world.[11]

One morning while Nathan was trying to sleep, the household was distracted by a stray kitten. It was hungry. Richard and Leon fed it some scraps, and it meowed loudly. Nathan came out and complained about the noise. Richard blamed the kitten. Nathan told them to get rid of the damn thing—kill it, whatever. He needed his sleep.

"He said for us to kill the kitten," Richard told his brother. He sensed fun ahead, and a way of getting back at his father. Leon ran away, horrified. Richard found some rope and made a noose. He wrapped it around the kitten's neck and pulled.

His mother swept out of the house, aghast. Richard insisted he had merely been obeying his father. Ella hauled him in front of Nathan, no doubt hoping to see him punished. Nathan bellowed at the boy and turned over to sleep. Ella spent the day torturing her son with talk about death and God's retribution and raging demons. When evening came, he was terrified to go into a room alone. Then she ordered him to go outside and bury the kitten.

> "I can't touch it," I whimpered, feeling that the kitten was staring at me with reproachful eyes.
>
> "Untie it!" she ordered.
>
> Shuddering, I fumbled at the rope and the kitten dropped to the pavement with a thud that echoed in my mind for many days and nights.

His mother stood and watched while Richard dug a shallow grave and put the stiff little body in it. Ella made him repeat after her: "Dear God . . . spare my poor life, even though I did not spare the life of the kitten . . . And while I sleep tonight, do not snatch the breath of life from me." She had Richard weeping with dread.

The arguments between Ella and Nathan were not only about food. Nathan was seeing another woman. Some mornings he did not come home after work. But for the time being, he still brought home money. He sometimes brought the newspaper for his eldest son, who liked to look at the pictures. That spring   it was 1912—Richard was fascinated by the sinking of the *Titanic*.

Nathan stayed away for longer periods, and then did not come home any more. In the 1912 Memphis City Directory, Ella Wright is listed at 336 North Pauline Street; Nathan Wright is not listed at all. At the age of four, Richard discovered hunger. He learned that men could not be trusted, and women by themselves were weak and afraid.

His mother found work as a cook in a white family. It meant leaving the boys by themselves all day. She would come home exhausted and often weep. With no one to confide in but her eldest son, she would talk to him for what seemed like hours. He no longer had a father, she told him, and he must learn to take on the responsibility of the house while she worked.

From now on, five-year-old Richard had to help with the shopping. When Ella showed him the corner store, he felt proud to be so grown up. But the next evening, when his mother came home from work tired and he set out with his basket, he was attacked by a street gang. He ran home scared. His mother sent him off again. The same thing happened again, but this time Ella would not let him inside the house. "I'm going to teach you this night to stand up and fight for yourself," she told him. She gave him a stick to defend himself with. "If you come back into this house without those groceries, I'll whip you!"[12]

When the boys descended on him again, Richard hit out with frenzy. "That night," he writes, "I won the right to the streets of Memphis."[13]

Left alone all day, Richard started to roam. He wandered into a saloon, where the local drunks plied him with alcohol. He began to beg for money. His mother tried everything—beating him, weeping, and praying. "I don't know what I'm going to do with you," she would say.

Sometimes he and his mother enjoyed moments of warm companionship. She read him stories. On Sundays, she helped him decipher words in the newspaper. One day, when she was at work, the man who came to deliver coal taught Richard to count to a hundred. "When my mother returned from her job that night I insisted that she stand still and listen while I counted to one hundred. She was dumfounded."

In Wright's fiction, several of his young male protagonists bask in being ill. That way, they briefly enjoy their mother's devoted care. Then they get well, and their mother leaves them alone in the house again.[14]

RICHARD HAD JUST TURNED SEVEN WHEN HE BEGAN SCHOOL AT THE HOWE Institute, in Memphis, in the fall of 1915. He was scared. The neighboring boys had to coax him inside the building. When the teacher asked him his name and address, he was too frightened to answer.

Around this time, Ella took Nathan to court. The white judge called upon Ella. She stood up, burst into tears, and for a long time could not speak. Eventually she managed to tell the court that her husband had deserted her, was no longer providing money, and that her children were hungry. Then the judge asked Nathan to speak. As his son remembered it years later, Nathan stood up, friendly and smiling, and assured the court he was doing whatever he could. The judge took his word for it.

After that, Nathan Wright completely abandoned his wife and sons. Ella became ill. Richard had to stay home from school to look after her. Then his grandmother arrived, and there was endless worried talk.

One evening, Richard went with his mother to see his father. Later, he would remember standing in a room with a blazing fireplace. They stood in the doorway. His father was standing next to a woman Richard had never seen before. Richard asked his father for money. His father refused. The strange woman said: "Give the boy a nickel."[15] Ella started to weep. The memory would lurk in Wright's mind for years: his father standing next to the strange woman, his laughing face lit by flames.

His grandmother, Maggie Wilson, had to go back home, and the money she brought with her had run out. Ella had no choice but to put her sons into a charitable Memphis orphanage, Settlement House. The adult Wright did not know whether he and his brother stayed there weeks or months. But he would never forget his terror and misery. He and the other children were always hungry, and there was endless whining and squabbling. Worst of all was the feeling that his mother had abandoned him, like everyone else. "During the first days my mother came each night to visit me and my brother, then her visits stopped. I began to wonder if she, too, like my father, had disappeared into the unknown. I was rapidly learning to distrust everything and everybody."[16]

When the director, a thin white woman, asked him to help her in her office, he was overcome, once again, by paralysis. She asked him to blot envelopes with blotting paper, and he wanted to do as he was told, but he could not move his arm. She became impatient and he cried.

One afternoon, he ran away. Night fell. He was lost and scared, and he started to cry. A white policeman came up to him. Richard sobbed that he was trying to find his mother. Then he remembered all the stories he had heard about white people, and grew more frightened. Several hours later at the police station, a white policeman with a friendly face finally got him to speak. Back at the orphanage, the woman director gave him a fierce whipping.

At last—it was the late spring of 1916 or 1917—Ella came to the orphanage and told the boys to pack their things. They were going to their Aunt Maggie in Elaine, Arkansas. On the way, they would stay with their grandparents, who had recently moved to Jackson.

Jackson, Mississippi, was a country town with pretensions. The 1922 Jackson City Directory boasted about its expanding industries, its well-lit, vice-free streets, and the opportunities it offered for education. Colored residents (indicated in the City Directory by a "c" after their names) also paid taxes, but benefited from none of these public services. The streets in the black area were unlit, unpaved, and had poor drainage. In the entire town, there was no public high school for black children.

Wright's grandparents, Maggie and Richard Wilson, lived on Lynch Street, on the west side of town, in a modest two-story wooden house that their son Clark, the carpenter, had bought for them. Richard thought it a grand dwelling. The house had front and back porches, and a staircase with banisters.

His grandmother had become a Seventh Day Adventist, and had moved to Jackson to be near a church. Richard was eight or nine. His grandmother, in her early sixties, was small, thin, and fierce. Behind her round steel glasses, her gaze was unblinking. In her long dresses, high collars, and ruffles, she looked like a prim Victorian woman. But in her own way, she was a thoroughgoing rebel. She never doubted that she was right, and did not hesitate to speak her mind. Unlike her husband's more militant rebelliousness, hers was otherworldly. "She was at war with every particle of reality that ever existed in this world," her grandson would write later.[17]

The Wilsons had a lodger, a young schoolteacher, who was always reading books. Richard was fascinated. One day, he found her on the front porch absorbed as usual, and summoned up the courage to ask what she was reading. The girl hesitated and looked around. "Your grandmother wouldn't like it if I talked to you about novels," she told him.[18] He looked so disappointed that she ended up closing her book and quietly telling him the story of Bluebeard and his seven wives— how Bluebeard slayed six of them and hung them up by their hair. The boy was mesmerized.

The magical moment ended abruptly. In a blaze of fury, Richard's grandmother stepped onto the porch. She shouted at the girl: "I want none of that Devil stuff in my house!" She slapped her grandson across the mouth. "You're going to burn in hell."[19] Shortly afterwards, the young boarder packed her bags.

But she had left a lasting legacy. Richard had discovered the enchanted treasure chest of fiction. "I vowed that as soon as I was old enough I would buy all the novels there were and read them to feed that thirst for violence that was in me, for intrigue, for plotting, for secrecy, for bloody murders."

Their grandfather took the boys fishing in the local creek and showed them around the local sawmill. The boys played hide-and-seek in the house and roamed the fields with the neighboring children. There were blackberry pies (the boys did the picking) and tall glasses of milk. One evening, their mother was sick in bed, and their grandmother supervised them as they bathed. The boys sat in two tubs of water in their bedroom and splashed each other merrily while their grandmother knitted and scolded them. While she was toweling him dry, Richard bent over. Out of his mouth came words he scarcely understood. In an early draft of *Black Boy*, he says "kiss back there." In the published version he says "lick back there." Whatever he said, the meaning was clear, and his grandmother was horrified. She flogged his naked body with the wet towel until he thought she would kill him. He ran screaming to his mother. When Ella found out what had happened, she pursued him with the wet towel herself. Finally, the boy's grandfather stepped in and restrained the women.

Soon after that, Ella and the boys left to join Aunt Maggie in Elaine, Arkansas. At the railway station Richard noticed that there were two separate lines at the ticket window—one with white people and one with black. On the train, he became conscious that their coach had black passengers only, and other coaches carried whites. At his grandmother's house in Jackson, for the first time, he had become conscious of race. When he and Leon had accompanied their grandmother downtown, white people stared at them. Richard had realized that people were baffled by the sight of an old white woman leading two young black boys around. As he found out on that train trip to Arkansas, it was no good asking his mother why his grandmother lived with black people if she was white. Ella told him to stop asking silly questions.

Aunt Maggie and her husband, Silas Hoskins, lived on a wide dusty road, in a white bungalow with a fence around it. Hoskins was older than Maggie and had two children from a previous marriage. They were doing well in Arkansas. Elaine was timber country, and Silas Hoskins owned a saloon that catered to the black workers at the local sawmill.

The dinner table was loaded with food. At first Richard could not believe that his good fortune would last, and he slipped biscuits from the bread platter into his pocket to hoard away for lean times. When his mother washed his clothes, she discovered his petty thieving and scolded him. Richard hid food in other places. It took him a while to break the habit.

He felt unusually free that summer. In the warm early mornings, before the heat of the day, he liked to walk barefoot in the thick dust of the road. A new game was to kill bees by slapping his palms together fast. (He stopped after he was stung.) He liked Aunt Maggie, who powdered her face and painted her lips and was more lively and modern than the other women in the family. She even stood up for him in family arguments. "How come you'all so hard on that boy?" she would ask.[20]

When he had business to do there, Uncle Hoskins sometimes took Richard in his horse and buggy to Helena. Once he terrified the boy by whipping the horse on and heading the buggy out into the Mississippi River. Richard, who could not swim and did not know the water was shallow for a good half-mile, clutched the side of the buggy and screamed. He never trusted his uncle after that.

Hoskins worked in his saloon at night and slept in the day. He did not seem to be bothered by noise. Sometimes Richard would creep into his uncle's room while he slept. He was fascinated by the shiny revolver that lay near his uncle's head. He asked Aunt Maggie about it. Why did Uncle Hoskins sleep next to his gun? She told him that white men had threatened to kill him.

One morning Hoskins did not come home. All day Maggie and Ella worried. Maggie wanted to go to the saloon, but Hoskins had forbidden her to go there. That evening, there were footsteps on the porch. A young black man stood there, twisting his cap. He had been running. "Mr. Hoskins . . . he done been shot. Done been shot by a white man," he breathed.[21] Aunt Maggie screamed and ran out into the night. Ella stumbled after her, pulling her back. "Don't you-all go to that saloon," the boy warned them. "White folks say they'll kill all his kinfolks!"

That same night, under cover of darkness, the women packed their household goods into a farmer's wagon and fled to West Helena. For weeks they cowered in their rented room, scarcely daring to show their faces. There was no funeral. Maggie Hoskins never saw her husband's body. There was no question of her claiming any of his assets.

At the age of eight, Richard Wright had experienced white terror at close hand. His uncle had been murdered for daring to be successful. He had not been subordinate enough. There was no report in the newspapers and no arrests were made. The black community knew what would happen if any of them made a fuss.[22] The culprit may well have been the local sheriff. And the Southern white press generally supported lynching.

As a poet and short story writer in his twenties, Wright would return time and again to the horror of lynching. The poem "Between the World and Me" begins: "And one morning while in the woods I stumbled suddenly upon the thing." The narrator, a black man, enters a grassy clearing and sees white bones, ashes, a ripped shirt, trousers stiff with blood. He observes "torn tree limbs, tiny veins of burnt leaves, and a scorched coil of greasy hemp." Lying around are feathers and traces of tar, butt-ends of cigars, a gin flask, and a lipstick. Filled with icy fear, he imagines the frenzied mob and yelping hounds, and soon, in his mind, he himself is the man being lynched.[23]

The stories in *Uncle Tom's Children* are still today the most gut-wrenching stories of lynch violence in American literature. The black rebel who is shot to death by a white mob in "Long Black Song" is called Silas.

IN APRIL 1945, SOME TWENTY-EIGHT YEARS AFTER THE MURDER OF SILAS HOSKINS, his son Fred Hoskins was sitting in bed next to his wife, reading *Black Boy*. "I could get no further than the part in Chapter 2 where my Father's and Mrs. Maggie's name was mentioned," he wrote to Richard Wright. "I quit, got out of bed and had to write this. I made so much noise on reading it I scared the Wife."[24]

Fred Hoskins, five years older than Richard Wright, was one of two children from Hoskins's first marriage. He was in Natchez with his mother when he heard about the death of his father. They could find out almost nothing. "My grandmother made a trip to Elaine to find out about my father's death," he told Wright. "As you said no one knew where he was buried. If I remember right she was told that my Father was killed because he was to [sic] bigoty and lived to well for a Nigger and was killed by a Deputy Sheriff."

He added that his father liked his drink and liked to gamble. "The mention of my Dad wanting to drive you into the middle of the Miss. River brings back to me the time when he was drunk as usual and drove me to the middle of a pond in Kingston, Miss. and scared me to death."

Wright had had no idea that Silas Hoskins's children were still alive. He wrote back:

> The reason I cannot tell you more about Uncle Hoskins's death is that I was never able to learn any more about it than is contained in *Black Boy*. I asked Aunt Maggie about it time and again and she would never talk. . . . She never wanted to be known among whites or blacks as the widow of a man whom the whites killed. I recall hearing that the whites told her never to say anything about it.[25]

MAGGIE, ELLA, AND THE BOYS WENT BACK TO JACKSON WHILE THEY DECIDED what to do next. But her mother's tyrannical ways and lengthy prayer sessions soon became too much for Maggie. The little group returned to West Helena, Arkansas. While the women worked as cooks in white households, the boys amused themselves. They liked to wade in the sewerage ditch in front of their house, looking for treasures. When the local black children taunted the Jewish storekeeper with anti-Semitic ditties, they joined in. None of the adults tried to stop them.

It took the women a while to realize that they shared the house with a brothel. When Richard started peeping through a crack and the manager of the next-door establishment complained, they moved again. After some time, Aunt Maggie had a new boyfriend. An educated, rebellious fellow, he was in trouble with the police. Anxious whispers between the women suggested to Richard that he had set fire to white people's property. One night, in a big hurry, he and Maggie left for the North. Richard was bereft. The three of them were on their own again.

They were hungry and desperate. Eventually, Ella landed a job in a white doctor's office, which paid the unusually good wage of five dollars a week, and the boys were sent to school. Up till this point—they were now nine and seven—Richard and Leon had never completed a full year of schooling. It was not something that seemed to concern anyone. They could count and read, which made them as educated as most of the adults they encountered.

After school they played with other boys. A favorite game was to fill a large tin can with water, light a fire under it, and insert a stick of wood. They would make believe they were driving trains. As the jets of steam increased, so did their excitement. They would run around the fire, imitating train whistles and bells, calling out things like: "Number five blazing down the line!" "Lawd today!" "The old train's stopping for water!"[26]

On 11 November 1918, Richard was sitting in school when jubilation broke out in the streets outside. Church bells rang out. It was the end of the war. The teacher sent her pupils home. That afternoon, as he mingled with the excited crowds, ten-year-old Richard saw his first airplane. He thought it was a bird. A man in the crowd lifted him on his shoulders. "Boy, remember this. You're seeing man fly."

BLACK SOLDIERS HAD FOUGHT AND DIED IN FRANCE. THEY CAME HOME TO THE South and faced an upsurge of lynchings, more barbaric than ever before. Southern whites, fearing these men had experienced a new freedom in Europe, were eager to remind them of their place. Richard heard the frightened talk around him, and was filled with a dread of white people.

His mother was visibly ailing and it scared Richard badly. She said things like she hoped she would live long enough to see him grow up. One morning, the boys got up to find their mother fully dressed on her bed, unmoving. Frantically they tried to wake her. They shouted "Mama!" Richard shook her. She groaned once or twice. Filled with dread, he ran to fetch the woman next door. A doctor was called. Ella Wright, at the age of thirty five, had suffered a stroke.

She was paralyzed on her left side; she could not talk, and had to be fed. Until her mother, Maggie Wilson, arrived, the neighbors looked after Ella. Richard, embarrassed to be accepting charity from strangers, pretended he was not hungry. When his grandmother finally arrived, she got him to write several letters, by dictation, asking various uncles for money to pay their fare back to Jackson. They packed up again. Ella traveled on a stretcher in the baggage car. Grandmother Wilson said hardly a word to the boys all the way.

Back in Jackson, aunts and uncles arrived whom Richard had never seen before. Maggie came from Detroit, Cleo from Chicago, Thomas, Clark, and Edward from Mississippi, Charles and Addie from Alabama. There were hushed discussions. Richard was scared to go near his mother, who lay in bed, unable to speak, staring vacantly. He would fall asleep to the sound of her groans. He began to sleepwalk. One night an uncle found him wandering in the backyard.

None of the relatives was willing to take on two extra boys. Richard learned, with a pang of envy, that Leon was going with Aunt Maggie to the North. His grandmother asked him which of his other aunts and uncles he would like to go with. He did not want to go with anyone. He wanted to go with Maggie, or else he wanted to stay with his mother. Since his Uncle Clark lived in Greenwood, the closest any of them lived to Jackson, he chose him.

Uncle Clark was a carpenter. His wife, Jodie, also worked. They lived in a neat bungalow. Over dinner that first evening, they decided that Richard would start at his new school the next day. He was given a list of chores to do when he got home. When he had finished, they told him, he should do his homework.

The boy felt no warmth in that house. Aunt Jodie kept correcting his grammar and his manners. And then a family friend called in and let it slip that his small boy had died in that house—in the very bed in which Richard now slept. After that, Richard was haunted by the idea of the dead boy in that bed. Terrified, he begged to sleep in another room. His uncle and aunt said that was ridiculous. Richard, too desperate to sleep, became more and more tense. Eventually he asked his uncle to let him go back to Jackson. His uncle, seeing that the situation was hopeless, put him on the train.

He arrived just as Ella was about to have another operation. When he saw her on the stretcher, being carried into the ambulance, all hope went out of him. "I knew that my mother had gone out of my life; I could feel it."[27] After the operation, she had another stroke. A blood clot had formed on her brain.

One night she called Richard to her and told him she wanted to die; she could not stand the pain. He held her hand and begged her not to talk like that. That terrible night, he realized he no longer felt the pain of pity for his mother. His feelings were frozen.

RICHARD WAS PAINFULLY CONSCIOUS OF LIVING IN HIS GRANDPARENTS' HOUSE uninvited. He was well aware that they were struggling financially. For the next seven years—as long as he lived in that house—the resentment he felt toward his grandmother was complicated by gratitude.

There was barely enough food in the house. The standard breakfast was mush, made from flour and lard, covered with gravy. Dinner was usually "greasy greens"—collard greens that had been boiled with a chunk of lard—and a piece of cornbread. Richard, just like the other members of the household, was always taking bicarbonate of soda for indigestion.

Since he was beholden to the family matriarch, Richard was obliged to submit to her household routine. The day began at sunrise, with prayers. There were prayers at the breakfast table and prayers at the dinner table. Meals were silent: talking at the table was considered sinful. After dinner each family member in turn would read or recite a paragraph from the Bible. On Saturday evenings Richard would accompany his grandmother to the Seventh Day Adventist Church, on the corner of Rose Street and Pascagoula. She went again during the week, but he usually managed to be absolved, on the grounds that he had schoolwork to do.

Occasionally there were all-night services. Ella and her father, the invalids of the house, stayed at home, but Richard was expected to accompany his grandmother. All evening he would squirm on the hard bench. At ten or eleven, his grandmother would pass him a sandwich and allow him to take a nap. "I would awaken at intervals to hear snatches of hymns or prayers," Wright would recall. "Finally Granny would shake me and I would open my eyes and see the sun streaming through stained-glass windows."[28] His grandmother would chide him gently: "While you were sleeping, the Holy Ghost was here."[29]

The Seventh Day Adventist Church was not without appeal for Richard. There were some ceremonies, like the foot-washing ritual, that even as a young boy he found moving. Each member brought a basin and filled it with water, and one after another, every brother and sister had his or her feet washed by another. It was intimate and humbling.

The sermons, told in colorful Old Testament language, could be sufficiently dramatic to make Richard temporarily forget the hard wooden pew. "The elders . . . expounded a gospel clogged with images of vast lakes of eternal fire, of seas vanishing, of valleys of dry bones, of the sun burning to ashes, of the moon turning to blood, of stars falling to the earth, of a wooden staff being transformed into a serpent, of voices speaking out of clouds."[30]

Later in life, Wright liked to boast that as a boy he had taken his religion "neat."[31] Seventh Day Adventists led ascetic, puritanical lives. Unlike the rest of the black community, they worshiped on Saturdays. From Friday sunset to Saturday sunset they were not allowed to perform any physical activity, and this included cooking. They frowned upon dancing, music, card playing, and "worldly" books. Tobacco, alcohol, and coffee were "soul-defiling habits." The Wilsons never ate pork or veal. The only music tolerated in the house was hymn singing. Had Richard hummed one of the blues songs his friends liked to sing, his grandmother would have struck him.[32]

Even as a boy, Richard was confounded by the contradictions he observed in his grandmother. She never refused a hungry beggar who came to the door, but after feeding him, she would ask his religion. Invariably, she would tell him in no uncertain terms that he was headed straight for hell. Sometimes at dusk on the Sabbath she would make the family kneel, and she would say a prayer for the Africans, the Japanese, and Chinese. Yet despite this abstract love of humanity, she had no understanding of the feelings of others and no tolerance for views that differed from hers.

Because he refused to be "saved," Richard was the blight of his grandmother's life. She tried persuasion; she tried coercion. She pointed out to him that one sinner in the house could bring the wrath of God down on the whole house. She even intimated that his mother's illness was due to his lack of faith.

The atmosphere in the house, already tense, became far worse when Addie Wilson returned from the Seventh Day Adventist high school in Huntsville, Alabama, where she had been training as a teacher. Every bit as pious and strong-headed as her mother, she disliked Richard from the start. She was about to start teaching at the local Seventh Day Adventist school, and she insisted that her nephew should go there.

Richard had not gone back to school since the few weeks he spent at his Uncle Clark's, in Greenwood, several months earlier. He was eager to attend the Jim Hill public school down the street. But since his mother as well as his grandmother agreed with Addie about the merits of the religious school over the secular one, he had no choice. In September 1920 he enrolled at the religious school. All grades were crowded into one room, with pupils aged from five to nineteen. Addie was the only teacher.

A novice, she was overzealous about discipline and made no secret of her dislike for her nephew. When by mistake he once called her "Aunt Addie" instead of "Miss Wilson," she was furious with him for showing disrespect in front of the other children. On another occasion she gave him a whipping in class for throwing walnuts on the floor near his desk. He had not done any such thing, but the true culprit did not confess. When she returned from school later that day, Addie approached Richard with a switch in her hand. "You're not going to beat me again," he told her. "I'm going to teach you some manners," she said. But, he protested, she had already beaten him for something he had not even done!

"Why didn't you tell me before?"
"I didn't want to tell tales on other people."
"So you lied, hunh?"

She ordered him to hold out his hand. He refused. If she hit him, he warned her, he would fight her. She hesitated a moment, then struck him with the switch. He opened the kitchen drawer and grabbed a knife. They tussled, ending up on the floor. Hearing the noise, his grandmother hurried into the room. His mother came limping in. Addie rose from the floor and left the room in a rage.

His grandmother wept. His mother wept. "Richard, you are bad, bad," his grandmother railed. "I don't know what I'm going to do with you," his mother wailed. His grandfather told him: "The gallows is at the end of the road you traveling, boy. Just remember that."[33] Addie scarcely talked to him after that incident—neither at the meal table nor in class. "You're not a Wilson; you're a Wright," the women would regularly say to Richard.[34] He wondered whether he really resembled his father, the laughing traitor who had deserted them all.

RICHARD'S FIRST UNINTERRUPTED YEAR OF SCHOOLING WAS THAT SEVENTH DAY Adventist school in Jackson. He hated the strict religious atmosphere and the spineless students, docile in the classroom and strangely brutal in their school-yard games. As the year drew to an end, he announced to the women of the house that he had no intention of going back. He wanted to attend the Jim Hill public school.

His grandmother grudgingly agreed, but the choice of a secular school made her intensify her efforts to save his soul. Richard was twelve now. He had reached the age where he was expected to have a vision, testify, and be baptized. He had been going to church slightly more willingly since he had become infatuated with the elder's wife. She sang in the choir and he stared at her for hours, imagining what it would be like to make love to her. But he still resisted the pressure to be baptized.

The Seventh Day Adventist Church had its annual revival meeting coming up, an event that always generated considerable excitement among the members. His grandmother, his mother, and even Aunt Addie were being unusually kind toward him, and Richard could sense that they held high hopes for his conversion. Not a day passed without one of them begging him to come to God. They warned him that if his soul was not saved, he would burn in the lake of fire. He would come into the house and find his grandmother kneeling in prayer, murmuring his name.

One evening in church—the revival was still to come—the elder preached about Jacob seeing an angel. Richard whispered to his grandmother that if ever he saw an angel, as Jacob had done, he would join the church. She stared at him, then patted his hand. He went back to gazing at the elder's wife.

After the service, his grandmother hurried up to the pulpit and talked to the elder. Soon, the man came over to Wright, smiling. "Your grandmother tells me you saw an angel."[35] Wright, caught unawares, was "speechless with anger."[36] That was not what he had said, he assured the elder; his grandmother had misunderstood. The elder looked crestfallen.

His grandmother, who had been spreading the good news, came up beaming and gave her grandson a hug. A small group was standing around smiling. Wright noticed the elder's wife.

In front of the others, he had to tell his grandmother she had misheard him. When the news sank in, she retreated to the back of the church and stared at him, her black eyes cold and grim in her wrinkled white face. All the way home she would not say a word. In the end, he managed to convince her that he had not deliberately set out to make her look foolish. She wept and urged him to pray harder so that God would come to him. He promised to pray in his room for an hour every day.

He made a genuine effort. He would go to his room, lock the door, and kneel. But his prayers sounded silly to him. He longed to be outside with his friends. One afternoon he found himself passing the time by writing a story. It was about a beautiful Indian maiden who had made some vow. She sat silent and solitary among the "ancient trees," and finally she walked impassively into a stream until the water covered her and she died without a murmur.[37]

Richard was excited by his creation. He knew he could not show it to anyone in his family: stories were "devil's work." Instead, he read it to the young woman who lived next door, swearing her to secrecy. She stopped washing the dishes to listen. When he had finished, she looked at him with a mixture of bewilderment and admiration. Whenever he thought of her reaction, Richard smiled to himself.

———

IN SEPTEMBER 1921, AT THE AGE OF THIRTEEN, HE ENTERED THE JIM HILL PRIMARY school, just up the street. His grandmother and aunt had given up on his soul. These days they treated him coldly. He now had to wash and iron his own clothes. He needed schoolbooks, but his grandmother refused to buy worldly books. The only member of the family who encouraged him was his mother. She urged him to study hard to make up for lost time.

Richard had entered another world. The Jim Hill students belonged to the black middle class—if not in income, at least in their outlook on life. Joe Brown, who would become one of his closest friends, recalls: "Most of our parents were very proud and they dreamed of great things for the futures of their children. Get an education was the byword. The male image of greatness was Booker T. Washington to some, and Dr. W. E. B. Du Bois to others, but our parents always reminded us that there were great people in our race."[38] There were a few black professionals in Jackson—lawyers and doctors, as well as teachers and ministers. They were held up to the students as models.

For the first time, Richard was among boys and girls who cared about their studies. To his astonishment, he was assigned to the fifth grade. He worked hard to keep up, spurred on by the competition. Within a short time, he was promoted to the sixth grade. At home, the women, who had always considered him a professional bad boy, were amazed. He dreamed about studying medicine.

The Jim Hill teachers, whose salaries were a third that of white teachers, were dedicated. They knew that many students would not have the chance to go beyond eighth grade, and they tried to cram in as much as they could while they had the chance. They insisted on good diction and grammar. If the students did not speak standard English in class, they got a whipping.[39]

There were whippings for misbehavior, too. The teachers would usually send them to the principal, Mr. Sam Brinkley. Brinkley would take off his coat and instruct the student to do the same, then he would sit back in his chair, applying the licks with a limb from a rattan tree. "We all knew that after getting a licking from Prof. Brinkley he would get in touch with our parents and we would get another going over," Joe Brown recalled. "Dick was always afraid of what his Grannie might do to him if the word ever got back home."[40]

After school Richard roamed the woods with the boys. They would climb persimmon trees and fill their pockets. They stole watermelons from melon patches. They would raid sweet potato patches and go into the woods and roast them. They sat in the grass and played the "dozens"—a verbal game in which two boys said the most derisive things they could think of—usually sexual—about each other's mothers. They talked about girls and whether they were likely to deliver the goods, and if so, whether they would be any good at it. There was an effeminate boy whom they pelted with sticks and stones and taunted with names.[41] Sometimes there were gang fights. The main weapon was a bow and arrow made out of tree limbs and rubber from car tires, using pebbles or rocks as ammunition. The boys called them "nigger shooters."[42]

Richard's friends rarely set foot in the house. "There was a coldness in Dick's house that kept us away," Joe Brown said later. "We felt that we were always being watched by his Grannie. She was always saying to Dick and Leon, Don't do that, don't do this. What are you boys doing?"[43] Richard never went to his friends' birthday parties. He did not own any smart clothes, and his grandmother would not have given him permission to go anyway. And yet he was accepted in the boys' gangs. Although he excelled in the classroom, he never tried to be a teacher's pet, and he was known for his generosity in helping others.

ONE MORNING WHEN RICHARD WRIGHT WENT INTO THE DINING ROOM FOR HIS bowl of mush and gravy, the atmosphere was tense. His mother looked anxious, and Aunt Addie seemed about to cry. Granny motioned him to his seat, and he bent his head to pray. Only then did he learn what had happened. Grandmother Wilson told God that her husband was ill, and asked Him to heal the patient, if it were His will. A few days later, when Richard came home from school, he was told to go upstairs and say good-bye to his grandfather. "Good-bye son," the old man croaked almost inaudibly. He muttered that God had picked out a seat for him in heaven.

Richard Wilson died on 8 November 1921. There was no weeping. Ella sat in a rocking chair and stared out of the window. Addie looked morose. Grandmother Wilson sent Richard to tell Uncle Tom, her eldest son, who had recently moved to Jackson. Richard ran the whole way, believing his mission to be urgent. His cousin, young Maggie, opened the door and told him that her father was asleep. He bounded to his uncle's bedside and shook him. "Granny says to come at once. Grandpa's dead."[44]

His uncle, who disliked Richard, sat up and stared at him. He told him that was no way to announce a death. "You certainly are a prize fool," he muttered, as he climbed into his trousers. Richard walked home by himself, wondering why, however good his intentions, he always managed to annoy his family.

He was not allowed to go to the funeral. He sat reading the stories in *Flynn's Detective Weekly* until the adults returned from the graveyard. They told him nothing. Later in life, Wright would often wonder about the lack of emotion in his family.

> After I had gone out in the world on my own, many people used to remark about the fact that I was seemingly unemotional. Of course, I was not. I had my emotions. Yet I cannot say that my mother, or my grandmother, or my grandfather was emotional. Most of the time I could not tell what they were thinking or feeling. When I began to write books years later, my friends used to exclaim: "My God, who on earth would have thought you felt like that?" Perhaps, without my knowing it, I, too, had caught some of their spirit.[45]

MOST OF THE OTHER STUDENTS WORKED BEFORE SCHOOL, AFTER SCHOOL, AND on Saturdays. In this way, they earned enough to buy books and clothes. Richard was eager to do the same, but his grandmother refused to let him work on Saturdays. He offered to pay her two-thirds of his wages in board. She refused to be bribed. Their disagreement about the Sabbath became their most serious clash. Richard knew he was being held back by lack of money. His clothes were patched to the point of embarrassing him. Sometimes months passed before he could buy a textbook that the other students were all working from. At lunchtime his friends walked into Mr. Jordan's corner store, across from the school, and ordered one of his delicious sardine and onion sandwiches. Richard had to watch them eat and pretend he was not hungry.

He never let his friends guess how little access he had to a world they took for granted. Any books or magazines other than schoolbooks had to be secreted into the house under his coat, then hidden beneath his pillow. Even with these precautions, books would disappear. He would go to the woodstove in the kitchen, lift up the lid, and there would be the remnants among the ashes. His friends listened to the latest jazz and blues; his grandmother did not permit a radio in the house.

One of his classmates, Jesse Flye, a bright, rebellious young man whose confident clowning in class never ceased to amaze Richard, sensed that he lacked the money for lunch. Jesse was making fifty cents a week selling newspapers sent to him from Chicago, and he encouraged Richard to do the same. He never read the paper, he told Richard, but the fictional stories in the magazine supplement were exciting.

His grandmother gave Richard permission to sell the papers after school. They were aimed at white readers, but the boys sold them in the black community. Richard greedily devoured the pulp fiction in the magazine. Zane Grey's *Riders of the Purple Sage* was being serialized. There were tales about brawny heroes, tales set in faraway cities, and a thrilling story about a scientist who lured his victims into his laboratory, turned on a switch, and they would turn red, black, and blue, then die.

A soft-voiced carpenter who had been buying the paper for some weeks took Richard aside one day and asked whether he knew what he was selling. Did he know that these papers, the *Saturday Blade* and the *Chicago Ledger*, were anti-Negro sheets, preaching the doctrines of the Ku Klux Klan? He pointed to a column that advocated lynching. Richard was aghast. He had had no idea. He gave up the job and learned, soon afterwards, that Jesse Flye had done the same. They were too embarrassed to talk about it.

The summer vacation came, and his friends all had jobs. Since bosses insisted on Saturday work, Richard was unemployed. For weeks, he brooded. Sweaty summer days were punctuated by nothing other than sudden storms. Later that summer, he got a job with a neighbor who was going to the Mississippi delta area to sell insurance policies.

Brother Mance was illiterate, and he wanted Richard to do the paperwork. His wages were the stuff of dreams: five dollars a week.

They made several exhausting trips. Sleeping on shuck mattresses on the floors of shacks, eating salt pork and black-eyed peas, they went from plantation to plantation by train, buggy, or automobile. In shack after shack, Richard would sit at a rickety table and fill out insurance applications by the light of a kerosene lamp. The illiterate sharecropper families were greatly impressed by the "pretty boy" from Jackson who could read and write.[46] He came home with unexpected quantities of money, and the women of the family were impressed. But Brother Mance died later that year, and the job ended.

ELLA WAS STRONGER THESE DAYS, AND RICHARD WAS PLEASED WHEN SHE TALKED of moving into a home of their own. She displayed a new independence from her overbearing mother. She was now attending the Lynch Street Methodist Episcopal Church. Grandmother Wilson was angry about this, but Ella had her own reasons. She desperately wanted Richard to find God. If Seventh Day Adventism was too much for him to swallow, maybe he could accept Methodism.

Richard was relieved to go to the same church as most of his schoolfriends, though after Seventh Day Adventism, he found it hard to take seriously the shouting, moaning, foot stamping, and rolling to the hymns that went on in the black Protestant church.

But soon it was his mother who was putting pressure on him to get himself "saved." She was not alone in this. Even the boys in his gang tried to persuade him to "come to God." And the minister was applying all the pressure he knew how. At that year's Methodist Revival, there were services several evenings in a row. Each time, the minister culled out the "sinners." On the last evening, he asked all those who did not yet belong to the church to stand up. A few remaining rebels stood up. The preacher asked the deacons to talk to them individually about the state of their souls. The deacons sprang up, full of kind words and smiles, and walked toward their charges. Finally, the lost souls were asked to sit together, in the front pew. The hymn singing increased in intensity. Then the preacher asked the boys' mothers to come up to the front. Ella limped to the front, smiling, tears running down her cheeks. She and the other mothers knelt, holding their sons' hands. "Now, I'm asking the first mother who really loves her son to bring him to me for baptism!" the preacher thundered. Ella looked at Richard. "Come, son, let your old mother take you to God," she implored. "I brought you into the world, now let me help to save you." [47]

One by one the rebels gave in to the pressure. By midnight, against his will, Richard found himself shaking hands with the preacher, signing up for baptism the following Sunday. "We young men had been trapped by the community," he would write in *Black Boy*. "The tribe, for its own safety, was asking us to be at one with it."

The price Wright paid for his individualism was a lifelong sense of guilt. It was associated with religion, which in turn was associated with the women in his family, who held their religious beliefs as ferociously as he believed in individual freedom. In order to be the man he wanted to be, he had to reject their views. Ultimately, this meant rejecting the women themselves. It made him feel like a murderer.

WRIGHT WENT TO SUNDAY SCHOOL BECAUSE HIS SCHOOLFRIENDS DID, BUT THE lessons were slow and dull. One or two of the boys regularly fell asleep. They started to play hooky. One spring morning, when the air was scented by magnolias in bloom, a group of boys gathered outside the church and decided it was too nice a day to sit inside. Someone suggested a swim in old man Barrett's water hole. Joking and laughing, they strolled toward the woods. It was a dangerous plan. Barrett, a white man, had sometimes appeared at the swimming hole with his gun and threatened to shoot the "black niggers" if they didn't get out of his pasture.[48]

They reached the water hole and excitedly pulled off their clothes. Robert Ellis remarked that the water looked awfully deep. "I'll beat you in," Richard taunted him. The others joined in. Robert Ellis dived. He did not come to the surface. The boys waited. At first they thought he was playing a trick. Still he did not come up. They were struck by horror. A small group ran off to fetch their parents. One boy started to sob, saying he ought to have gone to Sunday school. Richard was too scared to go home. A week later, Robert Ellis's body drifted to the bank of the white man's water hole.[49]

Years later, Wright would give the swimming-hole scene a different twist in his short story "Big Boy Leaves Home." Four adolescent boys come to the swimming hole. Bobo reminds them that the owner of the property does not allow "niggers" to swim there. The others make fun of his fears. The owner's son appears. He shoots and kills two of the boys. Big Boy, with Bobo's help, wrestle the white man to the ground and shoots him. He and Bobo run. That evening, Big Boy cowers in a clay pit, paralyzed with horror, while Bobo, who has been captured by the mob, is burned with tar and feathers on the hillside. From a distance Big Boy hears the screams, smells the tar, and watches his friend's black body struggle and twist in the firelight. The men and women clamor to see better while Bobo's fingers, ears, and finally his genitals are hacked off as "souvenirs." Once the excitement is over, Big Boy hears one of the men say, "I'll take some of you ladies home in my car."

RICHARD WRIGHT WAS FIFTEEN, IN THE SEVENTH GRADE. MORE THAN EVER, HE needed books and clothes. Some of the boys in his class were wearing their first long pants. He begged his grandmother to let him work on Saturdays. He threatened to give up school if she refused. "See how much I care," she said.

She stood firm. The argument came to a head. If Richard got himself a job on the Sabbath, he could not live under her roof, she told him. He said that in that case, he would leave. She said that was fine with her. He ran to his room, pulled down an old suitcase, and started to toss things in. His grandmother stood in the doorway. Finally she relented. If he wanted to go to hell, she told him, it was up to him.

To his surprise, his mother smiled when he told her he had defied his grandmother. She hobbled over to him and gave him a kiss. As an adult, Wright would comment: "Some fool of an English poet once talked of childhood 'trailing clouds of glory.' He must have been either blind or dumb. I know that there is no stormier period of life than childhood."[50]

2

THE WHISPER
OF LIBERTY

Summer 1923–November 1927

In the summer of 1923 Ella had another stroke. Fourteen-year-old Richard lay in bed at night listening to her groans. Medical help was costly, money was short, and his grandmother decided they would have to share the house to bring in extra income. Her eldest son, Tom, moved in upstairs with his wife and four children. The downstairs living and dining rooms were converted into bedrooms, and the two families used the kitchen in shifts.

The atmosphere in the house degenerated rapidly. There had always been arguments, fights, and emotional storms; Maggie Wilson fought with everyone. She and Addie would shout at each other about points of religious doctrine. Richard, who had made it clear to Addie that he would not suffer beatings from her, now had to assert himself against his Uncle Tom. On one occasion they argued, and his uncle went outside to find himself a switch. Richard flew off to fetch razors. "If you touch me, I'll cut you!" he warned, holding a razor in each hand. His uncle left him alone after that, but not before warning his own children that if he ever caught them talking to the young hoodlum in the house there would be trouble. As much as possible, Richard withdrew into himself. Whole days went by when he spoke to no one except his mother.

He had a series of jobs as a houseboy for white families. By working before school, after school, and all day Saturday—chopping wood, carrying in coal, sweeping the yard, scrubbing floors—he made two dollars a week, with breakfasts and dinners included. It was the first time that he was among white people for any length of time and he was nervous. The coarse language of these poor white families astonished him. And he bitterly resented the way they called him "nigger." He was already worn out by the time he arrived at school, but at least he could purchase the occasional item of clothing on the down-payment system.

THAT SUMMER HE AND HIS FRIENDS JOE BROWN AND PERRY ("CONKEY") BOOKER worked in Bullard's brickyard—ten hours a day, six days a week, for fifty cents a day. Richard was slight of frame (he weighed one hundred pounds), and the work was physically strenuous. First he was a water carrier, which meant lugging pails of water into wet pits of clay for the men to drink, then he worked as a bat boy, loading up cracked bricks into a barrow and dumping them into a pond. He was bitten on his thigh by the boss's savage dog, but the boss merely shrugged. "A dog bite can't hurt a nigger."[1]

In *Black Boy*, Wright described the job as entirely bleak. In a letter to one of Wright's biographers, Constance Webb, Joe Brown recalled some lighter moments. According to him, Dick Wright at one stage drove a dump cart between the loading pit and the hopper into which the clay was dumped. The cart was pulled by a mule. Wright was wary of the mules at first, but the older men showed him how to make them behave. He soon had a favorite called Kate, whom he called sweet names while putting on her harness in the morning. "Dick . . . and Conkey Booker on their way back to the pit for reloads of dirt would have a free for all race with their mules," Brown recalled.[2] Another young man who worked at the brickyard that summer was Bigger Thomas, the daredevil bully whose name Wright would borrow for his famous protagonist in *Native Son*. He and his friends also attended Jim

Hill; tough fellows, they were always in trouble with the teachers. According to Joe Brown, they left Wright alone. They knew he was "real smart," and occasionally he helped them with their lessons.

In September 1924 Richard returned to school for eighth grade. He knew it was likely to be his last year at school. His friends were buying long pants for the vast sum of seventeen to twenty dollars, and he was still in knee pants. No one in his family offered to help him. On the contrary, his grandmother kept hinting it was time for him to be out on his own.

The Jim Hill school did not extend to eighth grade, and Wright, who lived on the west side of the city, now had to get himself to the Smith Robertson Elementary School several miles away in the northeast. There was no public transport. For the first half of the year he walked to school with Essie Lee Ward, who lived with her mother in a small shotgun house on nearby Poindexter Street. Essie Lee, like Richard, was among the more shabbily dressed students in the class—her father had died of TB when she was nine, and her mother cooked in white folks' houses—but she was Richard's chief rival in class. She recalls that Richard was always happy to help her with schoolwork. As they walked to school, he would help her prepare for the day's lessons. Just like the Jim Hill school, discipline was strict. There were smarting hand smacks for students who had not done their homework, and the same punishment for being late. On those occasions when Essie Lee and Richard had to stop and wait for the freight train to pass, they were in trouble. Essie Lee remembers that Wright would put out his hand stoically and say nothing. She used to cry and beg to be spared. The principal, Professor Lanier, would say: "You knew that track was there when you left home."[3]

Later that year, Wright and his friend Joe Brown managed to get themselves old bicycles, and after that they rode together to school. "Some mornings on our way to school, Dick would say 'Let's go through the white neighborhood,'" Brown remembered. "On our route we would stop and go into the garbage cans and find old magazines, newspapers and books to read. Dick loved western stories and funny books, novels and detective stories."[4]

Smith Robertson had fourteen hundred students that year, and the classrooms were crowded. There was no assembly hall or cafeteria, no library or science lab, no gymnasium.[5] But there was a general optimism that things were changing. That year, 1924, a Negro high school was being built in Jackson. It was going to be called the W. H. Lanier High School, after Smith Robertson's principal, W. H. Lanier. For the first time in Jackson history, the current class of eighth grade pupils—Wright and his classmates—would have the chance to continue at a public school. In the past, if students had ambitions to go beyond elementary school, they had to pay to attend the Negro Catholic school. Or else they went to one of the Negro colleges—Jackson, Campbell, or Tougaloo (seven miles north of Jackson)—to do high school work.

Professor Lanier, as he was known (although whites could not bring themselves to call blacks "Mister" or "Miss," educated members of the black community were called "Professor" by whites and blacks alike),[6] was a strict disciplinarian, with a military bent. Every morning he had the students line up in the school yard and march into the building, keeping time with the tolling of the bell. Anyone who fell out of step was subjected to a fifteen-minute routine of marching, halting, and about-facing. Yet Lanier had a soft spot for Richard Wright and encouraged him to do everything he could to stay on at school beyond eighth grade. He would tell him about his son, who was attending a white university in the North. When his boy was in the South, Lanier told Richard, he had to get a white friend to borrow books for him from the public library.

The eighth-grade teacher was Professor O. B. Cobbins, assistant to the principal. Cobbins was knowledgeable and the students respected him, but he was short, physically unimposing, and not good at discipline, and the boys used to tease him. He wore his hair close cut and had a severe cowlick, Joe Brown recalled. Dick Wright and Dick Jordan referred to him privately as "peanut head."

Richard Wright had acquired a reputation as a serious student, hardworking and bright. The teachers respected him. If ever he had to go out of the room, Cobbins called upon Wright to supervise the class. Wright was also known for challenging dubious ideas. Essie Lee remembers an occasion, in the middle of a drought, when Mr. Cobbins asked the class to stand and pray for rain. Richard remained seated. "Why are you sitting?" Cobbins asked. "Didn't you hear me?"

"Yes sir. God has no influence over rain or nature, sir." He risked a whipping. Instead, Cobbins asked him what he thought did cause rain. Richard launched into a scientific explanation. "Water in the rivers and creeks rises by a process of evaporation into the clouds, and when the clouds are full and reach saturation point then rain falls." He got away with it.[7]

If his grandmother ever found out that Richard sometimes stole into the movies, there would have been hell to pay. There were two moving-picture houses in Jackson. The Century Theatre on Capitol Street showed good films—among them the great 1925 silent science-fiction fantasy *The Lost World* and Cecil B. DeMille's *The Ten Commandments*. "We Negroes were only permitted to sit in the buzzard roost," Joe Brown remembered. "We had to go around to the back of the show house, climb the fire escape stairs three flights. There were no toilet facilities."[8] The Alamo, on Farish Street, the center of the black business district, was for "coloreds," but showed mostly low-grade Westerns—many of them starring William S. Hart and Buck Jones, top cowboys of the silent-movie era. Whenever they could, Wright and his friends used to slip inside the Alamo without paying.

One of Wright's after-school jobs that year was to deliver the *Chicago Defender*, the black Chicago weekly. On his route was Jackson College, on Lynch Street. He liked to go there and see the black students strolling around. Sometimes, he and Joe Brown would hang around there in the hope that some friendly students would allow them to shoot a few games of pool. During the football season (there was great rivalry between the two Negro colleges, Jackson and Campbell, both on Lynch Street), Richard and Joe Brown would occasionally carry water buckets for the coaches so they could see the games for free. The president of Jackson College, Mr. Zack G. Hubert, had two sons Wright's age, Zack Jr. and Giles, who used to lend him books.

According to Joe Brown, Richard would talk incessantly about the North. "He would tell us about the news stories he had read in the *Chicago Defender*. How Negroes and white folks could swim together in Lake Michigan and that they sat down beside white women on the street cars and that you could go to the libraries and get any kind of book you wanted to read. He would always say 'I'm gonna leave Mississippi and be long gone up north one of these days.'"[9]

Once, Richard and his friends found poor white boys swimming in Barrett's swimming hole. They hid the white boys' clothing and va-moosed. Joe Brown would recall the tirade they inevitably heard from Richard. "Even though they are poor white trash they can go to Liv-

ingston Park and swim in the public lake, but we Niggers can't. We got
to dive out of trees like black monkeys and swim with the water moc-
casin snakes and bull frogs."[10]

Richard was sixteen, and the girls thought him strikingly handsome.
His classmate, Minnie Farish, remembered that he was always neatly
dressed, with a tie. The sleeves of his jacket were patched at the
elbows, she observed, but he didn't seem to care.[11] She was wrong.

Richard fell in love a couple of times that year. Carlotta Metcalf, who
sat near him in class, was delicate and light-skinned, and he used to
observe her surreptitiously. In the mornings he would watch her walk
into the classroom in her pleated skirt and white, starched middy
blouse with a sailor collar, and try to catch her eye just before she sat
down.

> All the boys used to talk of Carlotta. . . . For some reason or other she
> made boys dream. One day I stood near her on the school ground; we
> were talking and I was happy. A strong wind blew and lifted the black
> curls of her wavy hair and revealed . . . a long, ugly scar. . . . The scar had
> a suggestion of rawness, of violence that made Carlotta vanish, made my
> feeling for her freeze, that made me wonder what on earth I had ever
> seen in her. After that I even avoided looking at her.[12]

Next, he became smitten with Birdie Graves, a shy, quiet girl who
could have passed for white.[13] Richard never knew her at all well; he
adored her from a distance.

> I was in love with something and I did not know what it was. And since I
> did not know, I was always straining towards it. The idea was what drew
> me, fascinated me, lured me. And as soon as the ideal turned into reality,
> I would have none of it. I drew back. I found objections. . . . That was
> the kind of man I was growing into and I knew it. Yet there was nothing,
> seemingly, that I could do about it.[14]

There was one colorful character in their class whom Wright never
got on with. Arthur Leaner had musical talent and he knew how to
make money better than any of the others did. He and his father and
three brothers had a Dixieland jazz band, and they would play at white
people's dances. Back in Jim Hill days, Arthur used to get the students

to put on annual minstrel shows. "There was always an element of resentment between Dick Wright and Leaner," Joe Brown said later. "Dick felt that we were being sold down the river by Arthur's tricky way of using us."[15]

That winter, Leon came back from Detroit. Richard was pleased to see him, but after being apart for six years, the boys were strangers to each other. "It was not long before I felt that the affection shown him by the family was far greater than that which I had ever had from them," Wright would write in *Black Boy*. Leon soon fell in with the rest of the family and started to criticize his brother.

RICHARD WAS KNOWN FOR HIS STORYTELLING SKILLS, AND HIS BEST FRIENDS shared his love of drama. Joe Brown ("Big Mama") and Dick Jordan ("Squilla") enjoyed telling stories, full of colorful detail. Richard would egg them on, asking questions. At night he used to lie in bed and relive his day—what people looked like, what they had said to him, what they actually meant. In effect, he was keeping a journal in his head.[16]

In the spring of 1925, a story by Richard Wright appeared in Jackson's black weekly, the *Southern Register*. Everyone was astounded. At school they did not study literature. They never discussed writing or writers. The students did not know that Negro writers existed. Wright's teachers were as bamboozled as everyone else. What on earth had given him such an idea?

According to Wright, he began the story in class and called it "The Voodoo of Hell's Half Acre." Modeled on the melodramatic pulp fiction he liked to read, it was, he says, about a villainous fellow who was trying to rob a poor widow of her home. Without any encouragement from anyone, he had shown it to the editor of the *Southern Register*, Malcolm Rogers. He was dismayed when Rogers said he could not pay him, but he was very proud of his first publication.

Early issues of the newspaper have not survived, and no copy of the story seems to exist. In the early 1960s, Wright biographer Michel Fabre talked to Tillie Perkins Scott, who had typeset the newspaper in the 1920s. She confirmed that they had published a story of Wright's in the early days of the paper, and she reconstructed the first two paragraphs as well as she could from memory. According to her, the title was simply "Hell's Half Acre," and the narrative began: "Gone are the

days when I attended Jim Hill School." When he was in the sixth
grade, Wright wrote, he and his friend Bigger Thomas used to play
marbles behind Jordan's store. Whenever they were discovered, their
teacher, Mrs. Alice Burnett, would escort them to the principal, Professor S. Brinkley, and he would command them to let their suspenders
down and bare their backs to his hickory switch. The story continued
in this autobiographical vein.[17]

In *Black Boy*, Wright claims that the story gave him nothing but
trouble. His grandmother called it "devil's work." Ella worried that
people would think her son was not serious-minded and this would
put him at risk for finding a job. Addie was horrified that he had used
the word "hell" in the title. Professor Lanier, Wright heard on the
grapevine, had the same objection. Given the autobiographical content, these people probably had objections that Wright failed to
mention.

Wright was now thinking he would like to be a writer. When the
white woman who employed him asked him why he was still going to
school, he was foolish enough to divulge this ambition. Her response
was indignant: "Who on earth put such ideas into your nigger head?"
After that, he kept his dreams to himself.

ANOTHER INSTANCE OF WHITE TERROR HURLED ITSELF ACROSS THE LANDSCAPE.
One of Wright's classmates was a handsome, well-dressed young man
called Carl T. Robinson. His friends called him "Skeet." The Robinsons
lived on Pearl Street, close to the business district—one of the few
streets in Jackson where a sprinkling of affluent Negro families lived
alongside white people.

Richard was walking into town one day, past the Robinsons' house.
To his surprise, Carl was sitting on the porch, looking devastated.
Richard had not yet heard the news: C. T.'s older brother, Ray, had been
killed by whites. He had worked at the Edwards Hotel in town, and
was seeing a white prostitute.[18] It seemed that white men had driven
him down a lonely country road, dragged him out of the car, castrated
him, and finished him off.

Wright turned around and went home. He sat on his own porch and
brooded. This was the second time the "white death" had intruded into
his small world. Once again, the white folks had brutally punished a

black man who had taken a step beyond his perceived station. "The penalty of death awaited me if I made a false move," Wright told himself. "I wondered if it was worthwhile to make any move at all."[19]

He and Carl T. Robinson would choose the more radical path. Robinson would finish high school in Jackson, then study law at Howard University in Washington, D.C. Wright kept in touch with him. "I was to meet C.T. years later and marvel over the titanic change which the death of his brother had wrought in him, how it had altered his entire life, had changed his consciousness," Wright wrote. Robinson became "a strange, silent, ambitious man whose life was dedicated to his people. The South had made one more articulate Negro enemy."[20]

In Wright's 1958 novel, *The Long Dream*, twenty-four-year-old Chris, who works at the West End Hotel and is the hero of all the boys in the neighborhood, is caught in the hotel with a white girl. A white mob deals with him. "Chris died for us," the black undertaker murmurs, as he gazes at the mangled body. He turns to his son: "NEVER LOOK AT A WHITE WOMAN! YOU HEAR?"[21]

THE SCHOOL YEAR ENDED IN MAY 1925. RICHARD WRIGHT WAS AT THE TOP OF THE class. It meant delivering the valedictory speech. Three or four other exemplary students were also asked to speak, including Essie Lee and Dick Jordan. The graduation ceremony was to be held in the newly built auditorium in the city, and whites would be among the audience. "We Negroes had to be on our very best behavior, and not insult the good whites who had given us this rare opportunity," Joe Brown observed.[22]

A few weeks before the ceremony, Lanier called Wright into his office and handed him his speech. "But, professor, I've written my speech already," Wright protested. Lanier looked at him. "You know, we've never had a boy in this school like you before. You've had your way around here. Just how you managed to do it, I don't know. But, listen, take this speech and say it. I know what's best for you."[23]

Wright refused. He wanted to give his own speech. According to the account in *Black Boy*, Lanier threatened that Wright might not graduate. Wright stood firm. "I had been talking to a 'bought' man and he had tried to 'buy' me," Wright wrote harshly. "I felt that I had been dealing with something unclean."

Jordan had accepted his prewritten speech, and the two friends practiced in the woods. Word of Wright's confrontation with the principal spread through the school. His friends told him he was crazy. So did his Uncle Tom, who had contacts among the teachers. Everyone tried to persuade the school's top boy that it was pointless to upset the authorities about such a small matter. Wright argued that it was a matter of principle.

On speech day, the prize students stood in front of a sea of black and white faces. Essie Lee remembers the theme of her prewritten talk: nothing valuable is easily obtained. Wright was terribly nervous and did not speak well. After it was over, some schoolfriends invited him to a party. He refused. He writes in *Black Boy* that he went home, clenching his fists. "To hell with it!" he said to himself.

WRIGHT WOULD BE SEVENTEEN IN A FEW MONTHS, AND HE WAS KEEN TO LEAVE behind the household tensions that made each day a battle. But he needed money to continue in school and he needed money to get away from home. His friends were almost all going on to the new W. H. Lanier High School. A large part of him wished he were doing the same.

In the summer of 1925, while his future was undecided, Wright worked at a series of jobs. He was briefly a porter in a clothing store. After a few days, his boss dismissed him. Other jobs lasted an equally short time. His friend Dick Jordan tried to explain to him that he did not behave right. He was too impatient. His manner was not respectful enough. Nobody could tell him anything. His contempt for the rules showed on his face. Did he want to get killed? No? "Then for God's sake, learn how to live in the South!"[24]

It was not a message Wright was prepared to listen to. By now he had decided that he was alone against the world and things were likely to stay that way. Everyone else had submitted to rules that he himself was not prepared to accept. Jordan tried one last time. "Dick, look, you're black, black, *black*, see? Can't you understand that?"

Jordan was right. With his personality, Richard Wright, as a black man, was a danger to himself. *Deep South*, a 1930s sociological study of race and class, describes the deferential speech and conduct expected of a black person in the South. "It is not enough that he should conform reluctantly to the expected modes of behavior. He must show that he accepts them as proper and right; he must conform willingly and cheerfully."[25]

Dick Jordan worked at a jewelry store on Capitol Street, in the center of the white business district. He told Wright he could get him a job at an optical company on the same street. He would earn five dollars a week. The boss was a Yankee, from Illinois, who had said that he wanted to teach the trade to a black man. But, Jordan insisted, Wright would have to play the game right.

A "Yankee," a common term in the South, indicated a Northerner who was critical of the social arrangements in the South. If a Yankee proved to be a "nigger lover," this made him almost as much of a social outcast as the black people with whom he sympathized.[26] Wright's Yankee boss was a decent fellow, but the men working under him were Southern whites, who resented the presence of a black man in their midst.

For the first month, Wright cleaned and ran errands and learned nothing about the trade. One day he went up to a white employee who was grinding lenses at a machine and asked him questions about the process. After that, the white employees became openly hostile. They called him "nigger"; they made crude jokes about the size of his genitals. One of them insisted that Wright had not called him "Mr." and tried to pick a fight. And after that, a real terror campaign began.

There was nothing the Yankee boss could do. Wright wept in his office. The boss handed him his wages (more than he had earned) and agreed he should try hard to leave the South. "Even for me, it's hard here," he told Wright. "I can do just so much."[27]

Dick Jordan found his friend a job in a drugstore. That did not last either. By now, Wright had become so anxious about his behavior that he had become clumsy. He dropped a jug of syrup on the floor and was sacked after a few days. For weeks he was without a job. He had secretly been hoping to go back to school, and for a few weeks he attended the new W. H. Lanier High School, but he dropped out. He needed to earn money.

Finally he found work at the Edwards Hotel, the place where Ray Robinson had worked as a bellhop. Wright mopped floors and worried that he was not earning money fast enough. He calculated that he would need one hundred dollars to set himself up in a new city. Most of his wages was going on his board at home.

To supplement their meager income, his friends—including Dick Jordan   were stealing from their white employers whenever they had the opportunity. They called him a "dumb nigger" for not doing the same. He retorted that he had no qualms about stealing white property; he *did* have qualms about spending his days in a Southern chain gang.

Jackson College had a storehouse containing cans of preserved fruit. Wright lay in bed at night and wondered if he dared. Meanwhile, at the hotel he was promoted to bellhop. He learned to do as the others did and smuggle liquor to the white prostitutes in the hotel. This brought in a few extra dollars. He also got used to the sight of these women in the nude—on their beds, sitting around the room. If they were alone he would steal a look at them when their backs were turned, as they fetched money from their bags. If they had a white man with them, he assumed a blank expression and showed not the slightest curiosity. He would never forget Ray Robinson's fate.

An opportunity came up to sell tickets at the Alamo, the colored theater on Farish Street. A friend explained that he could make good money if he played the game. The black employees were running a ticket racket, reselling tickets and keeping the money for themselves. But he would have to be utterly discreet.

Wright turned up. The Jewish owner, Abe Lehman, looked at him and said he hoped he could be trusted. Wright reassured him. For the first few days, Lehman watched him carefully. Eventually he went away for hours at a time, and Wright was let into the racket. People handed him their tickets; he gave them to a go-between, and the girl at the counter resold them. In a week, after the profits were divided four ways, he made fifty dollars.

He waded deeper into crime. He broke into a neighbor's house and stole a gun. Using a false name, he pawned it. He and the two Hubert boys, the sons of the president, broke into the storehouse of Jackson College, stole dozens of cans, and sold them to restaurants.[28]

Finally, Wright had enough cash to leave. He bought some new clothes, new shoes, and a cardboard suitcase—all of which he hid carefully at home. He left Jackson on a Saturday night in November 1925. His grandmother and Aunt Addie were at church. His brother was asleep. Uncle Tom and his family were upstairs. He packed his suit-case, strapped his cash around his waist, then put on a shirt, sweater, coat, and hat. Finally, he went to say good-bye to his mother, who was sitting in her rocking chair. Anxiety flooded her face. Had he done something wrong? Was he running away from the police?

He had to leave, he told her. He had put up with the hostility of the family long enough. He would find a job in Memphis, and as soon as possible he would send for her and Leon. She begged him to be quick about it. She was not happy in that house, she told him. He walked the quarter of a mile to the station. Memphis, Tennessee, was still the South—in fact, Memphis was only just over the Mississippi border—but he had heard that things were better there for black people.

He stepped into the colored coach and put his case on the rack. He had recently turned seventeen. As the train hurtled into the darkness, he thought about his mother and his friends and the familiar surround-ings he was leaving behind. He thought about the unknown future ahead. Tears slid down his cheeks. "Ahead the long rails were glinting in the moonlight, stretching away, away to somewhere, somewhere where he could be a man."[29]

SLEEK, BLACK LOCOMOTIVES THUNDER THROUGH THE LANDSCAPES OF RICHARD Wright's Southern fiction, boxcars clinking behind, stack pipes belching smoke, headed for some unknown destination in the North. The mere whistle of a train provokes wistful sighs from Wright's young male pro-tagonists, who know that one way to escape Southern terror is to hoist themselves on top of a passing boxcar, lie flat, and trust that those gleaming rails lead to somewhere better. Those "panting trains" with their "pushing pistons,"[30] yammering roars, and "limp and convulsive halts" carry a promise of manhood and, with it, the whisper of liberty.

It was a cold Sunday morning with faint rays of winter sun when Richard Wright arrived in Memphis, clutching his cardboard suitcase. He walked to Beale Street, the heart of the downtown district, where black folks lived, nefarious for its underworld life as well as its blues. He passed Washburn & Lyle, and remembered that it was the drugstore where his father had worked as a porter some thirteen years earlier. The thought made him nervous. Would he fail in this city, as his father had done? (His father, he had heard, was back sharecropping near

Natchez.) Should he have gone somewhere else? Wasn't this the city where, as a young boy, all his suffering had begun? It did not help that Memphis had a reputation as the murder capital of America.

At the point where Beale Street turned into Beale Avenue, Wright saw a notice about a room in the front window of a frame house.[31] He walked up and down in front of it, hesitating. What sort of a house was it? he wondered. He'd been warned about the pimps, con men, and prostitutes, who could instantly pick naïve newcomers. A woman looked through the window at him, then came out on the doorstep and asked him inside. "Boy, Lord, this ain't no whorehouse," she told him, guessing his dilemma.[32] Mrs. Walls told him that she owned the house, she went to church, and she had a seventeen-year-old daughter. He was safe here.

He was reassured by her friendliness and warmth. It was so different from the guarded coldness of his own family. He could bring alcohol into his room if he liked, she told him. He could bring his girl here. "Do anything you want, but be decent." She invited him to come along with the family to church. He told her he was tired.

He stretched out on his bed for a while, then heard the family coming home from church. Mrs. Walls insisted that he have lunch with her and her daughter, Rosa. She apologized for her husband: Mr. Walls, a carpenter, was working that day.

Wright liked Rosa; she was "young, simple, sweet, and brown."[33] Over lunch, Mrs. Walls declared he would make her an ideal husband. Rosa pretended to be shocked. Afterwards, in the front room, the girl showed him her fifth-grade schoolbooks. She was not good at schoolwork, she told him. Love was the important thing.

Wright, feeling claustrophobic already, went out to get his bearings and look for work. On Main Street, in the city center, a café was advertising for a dishwasher. He went in. He would get ten dollars for the first week, and twelve dollars after that, as well as two meals a day. The money was better than anything he had ever earned before. He was hired for the following evening.

He was pleased with himself. He would be paying three dollars a week for his room; he would eat frugally, and save as much as he could. On his way home, he bought a can of pork and beans, a tin opener, and some cigarettes. For his grandmother, smoking was one of the deadly sins. For him it was a symbol of his new manhood.

He got back to the house and announced he had found a job. Rosa took his coat and discovered the can and the opener in his pocket. He felt humiliated. "My muscles flexed to hit her," he writes in *Black Boy.* Mother and daughter insisted that he share their chicken dinner. Then Mrs. Walls went upstairs, and the two young people repaired to the front room.

Rosa was flirtatious. According to *Black Boy,* she combed his hair. ("You have nice hair," she said. "It's just common nigger hair," I said.) Then she kissed him. He found himself succumbing to the appeal of her curvaceous body. "Let's go to my room," he said. Her mother would not like that, Rosa said. But, she assured him, her mother would not come into the front room. "I kissed and petted her," Wright writes in the published version of *Black Boy.* His first draft was more explicit:

> I had her and pulled away from her with caution to save her from preg-
> nancy. She lay with half-closed, dreamy eyes, breathing gently. She had
> been active, ardent. I looked guiltily around; the house was quiet.
>
> "Mama's sleeping," she said in a soft tone of reproof, a tone that
> asked me not to be afraid.
>
> I began to suspect her. She's had every boy in the block, I said to
> myself. She must have read my thoughts, for she rose and bit my ear,
> then whispered: "It was good. This was my first time."

Clearly it was no more her first time than it was Wright's. But he was worried now, and wished he hadn't done it. She would probably tell her mother, and he would be expected to marry her. Maybe her father would get his shotgun and force him to.

The girl asked if he loved her. She told him she would make a good wife. Wright could hardly believe his ears. "I looked at her and wanted either to laugh or to slap her."[34] He said they should get to know each other better first. She ran out of the room crying.

In the next few days Mrs. Walls tried to persuade him to go with her girl. They would inherit the house, she told him. They could bring up their children here. She even proposed that he try out Rosa to see if he liked her. "Ain't no harm in that." Reeling from the pressure, Wright had no more interest in the girl. Already he was thinking he would have to find another room somewhere.

On Monday evening, he was supposed to start at the café. He had the day to himself. He headed west toward the Mississippi and sat on the bank, watching the boats. Then he wandered around the city. The twelve-story Italianate Renaissance–style Peabody Hotel had just opened, and already had a reputation as one of the finest hotels in the South. Other imposing new buildings were Lowenstein's Department Store, the Cotton Exchange Building, and the Union Planters Bank Building. As he walked around, he had an idea. Perhaps he could find work in an optical company instead of café work. He knew something about the optical business from Jackson, and maybe in this city he would be allowed to learn the trade. He searched in the city directory and found the American Optical Company, located in the American Bank Building on Madison Avenue. Adopting his most confident air, he took the elevator up to the offices on the fifth floor and asked to see the boss.

The manager, John R. Horsley, offered him a job as messenger at ten dollars a week. He warned Wright that as a Negro he could not learn the trade. "That is not our policy."[35] Wright liked the man nevertheless, and though the wages were less than the café job, he thought it more promising than dishwashing. He took it.

He would stay at the American Optical Company for two years, the whole time he was in Memphis. His work started at nine in the morning, but he generally got to the building at eight o'clock, so he could read the Memphis *Commercial Appeal* in the lobby of the bank downstairs. He became friendly with the black men who worked in the building—the porter, elevator operator, and janitors. At lunchtime, when he was not running errands for the white employees in the optical company, making extra money from tips, he joined his friends in their small room overlooking the street. They would joke about the strange ways of the white folks they were working for; they would laugh and talk about going North. Then the lunch hour would end, and it was back to concealing their emotions in the white world.

Not tempted by saloons, shooting craps, or houses of ill repute, Wright was spending as little as possible, saving to bring his mother and brother to Memphis. For breakfast he had a pint of milk and two sweet buns; his lunch was generally a hamburger and a bag of peanuts; and in the evening he would open a can of beans in his room. Occasionally he would go on Saturday night to the Palace Theatre on Beale Street, and hear the dynamic Gertrude Saunders sing the blues.[36] Now that he had broken out of his grandmother's puritanical prison, he responded with visceral excitement to blues and jazz. His other great discovery was secondhand bookstores. He would buy magazines—*Harper's*, the *Atlantic Monthly*, and the *American Mercury*—take them home and read them, then resell them to the book dealer.

One morning in the spring of 1927, Wright read an editorial in the *Commercial Appeal* that savagely attacked H. L. Mencken. Wright knew H. L. Mencken to be the editor of the *American Mercury*. He did not yet know that Mencken was unsparing in his contempt for what he called the "hog wallow politics" of the "benighted South."[37]

Keen to learn more about the man who had provoked such a rabid editorial, Wright decided he would have to follow the example of Professor Lanier's son and gain access to the Memphis Public Library by pretending to pick up books for a white person. He had already been to the library on lunchtime errands to fetch books for others. He knew how the system worked. What he needed was a card so he could borrow books for himself and pretend they were for the card owner. But who would oblige? Who would be prepared to be seen reading Mencken—this man who seemed to enrage Southerners?

He decided on an Irishman who had sometimes asked him to fetch library books. Wright had heard other whites disdainfully call him a "pope lover." Perhaps this man would feel some solidarity for a black who wanted to learn. At the very least, as another outsider, he was unlikely to betray him.

The Irishman hesitated. He nearly always had the maximum number of books out, he explained to Wright. What did he want to read? Mencken? Which book by Mencken? Wright had no idea that Mencken had written more than one book. "It's good of you to want to read," the Irishman told him doubtfully, "but you ought to read the right things."[38] Wright was disheartened. A few days later, the Irishman called him over. He had arranged to take out books on his wife's card; Wright could borrow his. He warned him to be careful. He didn't want to be found out.

Wright did not know the titles of Mencken's books, and he had to think of a way around this problem. He also wanted to be sure that no one would suspect he had written the note himself. He ended up writing: "Madam: Will you please let this nigger boy have some books by H. L. Mencken?" He forged the Irishman's name.

He was nervous when he walked through the door of the Memphis

Public Library at lunchtime. It was a red sandstone building overlooking the Mississippi, with a turret that made it look like a castle. Wright went up to the counter, took off his hat, and stood back while the white people were served. He tried to look as "unbookish" as he could. The librarian had handed him books before, but this time she read the note and looked doubtful. To Wright's relief, she went off and came back with two books. She stamped them. Wright, not daring to look at them, left the building.

When he was safely out of sight of passersby, he stopped to look. One was called *A Book of Prefaces* (he pronounced it "prc-faces"); the other was called *Prejudices*. They were essays, and both books were full of strange names, many of them foreign. Wright was disappointed. Perhaps his daring feat had been a waste of time. But he would delve into the books after work.

> That night in my rented room, while letting the hot water run over my can of pork and beans in the sink, I opened *A Book of Prefaces* and began to read. I was jarred and shocked by the style, the clear, clean, sweeping sentences. Why did he write like that? And how did one write like that? I pictured the man as a raging demon, slashing with his pen, consumed with hate, denouncing everything American, extolling everything European or German, laughing at the weaknesses of people, mocking God, authority. What was this? I stood up, trying to realize what reality lay behind the meaning of the words. . . . Yes, this man was fighting, fighting with words. He was using words as a weapon, using them as one would use a club. Could words be weapons? Well, yes, for here they were. Then, maybe, perhaps, I could use them as a weapon? No. It frightened me. I read on and what amazed me was not what he said, but how on earth anybody had the courage to say it.[39]

The Baltimore journalist and literary critic made laughter into a weapon. He mocked some of the very things that had caused Wright such misery, but whereas Wright had been forced to conceal his opinions, here was Mencken daring to trumpet his. He dismissed the worship of God as sheer buffoonery. His anticlerical statements were shocking even to Wright. As for puritanism—the blight that had almost suffocated Wright during his adolescent years—puritans were simply enemies of life. Young radicals loved Mencken for daring to attack the sacred cows of American society. They relished his assurance, his daring, and the savagery of his disdain. Wright, who was used to being a lonely, dissenting voice, had found an exhilarating mentor.

For the next few years, *A Book of Prefaces* would be Wright's Bible. It was a survey course of European and American literature, given by the most dynamic professor imaginable. Wright did not have access to the catalog at the Memphis library, but Mencken did a lot to make up for that. Like an eagle soaring over the landscape, he examined American society and literature against Europe and the world. He introduced Wright to writers whose names he did not yet know how to pronounce: Dostoyevsky, Flaubert, Maupassant, Nietzsche. And not only did Mencken examine literature against life itself, he was also passionately interested in the craft of writing.

Mencken was a well-known champion of realism. As he saw it, American puritanism had crippled realism in America. It made American writers afraid to be intrepid. In *A Book of Prefaces*, he dismissed *Uncle Tom's Cabin* as a "crude politico-puritan tract."[40] For Fenimore Cooper, Hawthorne, Longfellow, Emerson, and Poe, literature was merely "a hand-maiden to politics or religion." In nineteenth-century American literature, only Whitman had been courageous enough to challenge "the intolerable prudishness and dirty-mindedness of Puritanism." After a century of "infantile romanticizing," Henry James, William Dean Howells, Mark Twain, and Bret Harte had introduced a refreshing element of realism. But they too showed "that timorousness and reticence which are the distinguishing marks of the Puritan."[41]

Among contemporary American writers, Mencken admired Theodore Dreiser, Frank Norris, and Stephen Crane. He liked Upton Sinclair and Sinclair Lewis. Still, he believed, American realist novels had not gone far enough. "They begin to shock once they describe an asthma attack or a steak burning below stairs: they never penetrate beneath the flow of social concealments and urbanities to the passions that actually move men and women to their acts, and the great forces that circumscribe and condition personality."[42]

Mencken had thrown down the gauntlet. As Wright read and reread those essays, leaping up excitedly to pace his Beale Street room, something exploded in his head. Over the next few years, Mencken, more than anyone else, would help him see what he wanted to write and how he wanted to write it. It was Mencken who challenged him to convey the daily reality of being black in America.

WRIGHT WAS EAGER TO READ THE BOOKS MENCKEN ADMIRED SO MUCH. HE forged another note, went back to the library, and took out Sinclair Lewis's *Main Street*. It was the first serious novel he had ever read. It was about white people, and yet it was about the things that haunted him—aspiration, rebellion, and escape. Carol Kennicott's restlessness in a small, philistine Minnesota wheat-town was not unlike his in that stifling Southern environment. When he read *Babbitt* he felt as if the gap between him and his white boss had closed slightly. He could now see that Mr. Horsley represented an American type.

Reading was like a drug. For days he would walk around affected by the mood aroused in him by the fiction he was reading. Sherwood Anderson's stories depicted baffled, groping characters trapped by their situation. Frank Norris's novel *McTeague* portrayed squalid tenement life in San Francisco. Dreiser's novels *Jennie Gerhardt* and *Sister Carrie* made Wright think about his own mother and her suffering.

These books made him want to write himself. He bought paper. He practiced writing sentences. But beyond that, nothing flowed. He told himself that he did not know the world. The men who wrote those books had experience. He despaired. How could he, as a black man with limited horizons, ever hope to get to know white people intimately enough to write about them?

He had to hide the fact that he was reading books. White people, he saw, felt threatened by it. Already people were starting to make comments. "You'll addle your brains if you don't watch out."[43] He developed the habit of wrapping his books in newspaper. That way, those around him would assume he was reading rubbish.

In bleak moments, Wright was painfully aware that the world he aspired to was one he could never reach. He bought a secondhand dictionary and grammar books. It wasn't life alone he needed to know more about; he also had to master the English language. As he ran around day after day on mindless errands, he envied his friends back in Jackson. At the W. H. Lanier High School, they were getting an education that would open their horizons.

He had been in Memphis a year when, in the winter of 1926–27, his mother and brother arrived from Jackson. Wright had found a small apartment at 875 Griffith Place. Leon found work, and they bought furniture on the installment plan. With his mother's hot meals inside him, Wright found himself with more energy.

The three of them shared a dream: to get to the North. Otherwise, Wright's literary ambition separated him from his mother and brother, just as it separated him from everybody else. He had no white friends, and he was equally far removed from educated black people. He did not have the means to aspire to a profession himself. Where *did* his future lie? "My days and nights were one long, quiet, continuously contained dream of terror, tension, and anxiety," he would write in *Black Boy*. "I wondered how long I could bear it."

In May 1927 there was the worst Mississippi River flood in recorded history. Memphis and western Tennessee were under water; so were Mississippi, Louisiana, and southwest Illinois. Newspapers described it as the worst calamity since the Civil War. Half a million people were left homeless and hundreds died. The worst affected were black sharecroppers, living on the low-lying land. Several years later, Wright would write two poignant stories about black families who were victims of the Great Flood.[44]

In the fall of 1927, his Aunt Maggie arrived in Memphis. The man with whom she had fled to Detroit had abandoned her. At the age of forty-one, she was going to have to start over. The family had long discussions about Chicago. They could not afford to all leave at once. It was decided that Maggie and Richard should go ahead.

Wright did not tell his boss he was leaving until a week or so beforehand. He knew that Southern employers felt resentful about the exodus of black people to the North. Black laborers were no longer so easy to come by. For more than a decade, Southern newspapers had been carrying stories aimed at black readers—about deluded Southern Negroes freezing in the North, about race riots in Northern towns. Wright, anxious not to be seen as fleeing the South for better conditions, told his boss that his aunt was taking his sick mother to Chicago and they needed him to accompany them.

The news spread quickly around the building. White employees came up to him, taunting him:

"So you're going north, hunh?"

"Yes, sir. My family's taking me with 'em."

"The North's no good for your people, boy."

"I'll try to get along, sir."

"Don't believe all the stories you hear about the North."

"No, sir. I don't."

. . .

"How're you going to act up there?"

"Just like I act down here, sir."

"Would you speak to a white girl up there?"

"Oh no, sir. I'll act there just like I act here."

"Aw, no, you won't. You'll change. Niggers change when they go north."[45]

Wright desperately hoped he would. That was the point of leaving. He had just turned nineteen. His personal dilemma, though he could not express it to himself, was that in all his years in the South, he had not only learned to fear and hate white people; he also had never encountered a black person who could serve as a model. Never had he heard a black leader speak out against racial injustice. All he had ever experienced—from blacks as well as whites—was pressure to play a submissive black role. The only voices he had ever heard that hinted life could be different were the books he had been reading—all by white writers.

He was hoping to leave the South behind forever. Years later, he realized he could never really do that. The South had formed him and the South had scarred him.

3

THE SOUTH SIDE
OF CHICAGO

November 1927–September 1933

The train heads north, up the Illinois Central. Richard Wright huddles next to the window and looks out at cotton fields, swampland, and small unpainted shacks. The dirt roads gleam in the evening light.

By the time the train crosses the Ohio River it's pitch-dark. Wright has always imagined the waters of the Ohio flashing like quicksilver. When his grandparents were young, this river was the border between slavery and freedom. Sixty-two years after the end of slavery, Southern blacks still see it as the gateway to freedom. Wright has heard of folk kneeling down to pray when their train crosses the river, kissing the ground, and bursting into songs of deliverance—"The Flight Out of Egypt" or "Bound for the Promised Land."

When dawn breaks, cornfields stretch to the horizon. He sees windmills, rusty red barns, huge silos. The train clatters past tidy Illinois towns. He looks at his Aunt Maggie sitting beside him in her shabby hat and coat, and grins.

On these Northern platforms the familiar signs—"For Colored" and "For White"—have disappeared. White people with ruddy cheeks are now climbing into the previously all-black coach. "We look at them guardedly and wonder will they bother us," Richard Wright would write later in *12 Million Black Voices*. "Will they ask us to stand up while they sit down?"

The white people wear clothes that look new and expensive. They do not speak like Wright does, with a slow Southern drawl. Theirs is a fast, clipped Yankee talk that he can scarcely understand. "And the foreigners—Poles, Germans, Swedes, and Italians—we never dreamed that there were so many in the world!"

The outlying suburbs of Chicago look gray and uninviting. Steel and iron mills belch smoke and soot. Finally the train pulls into the Illinois Central terminal. Wright and his aunt step onto the platform. Like the other black travelers from the South, they are apprehensive. "We hug our suitcases, fearful of pickpockets, looking with unrestrained curiosity at the great big brick buildings. We are very reserved, for we have been warned not to act 'green,' that the city people can spot a 'sucker' a mile away."[1]

The big city is frightening. The traffic is chaotic. The buildings are toweringly tall, and new ones are going up everywhere.[2] What a din! Pounding steam shovels and jackhammers make the ground shake. Cars honk their horns; streetcars clatter past on steel tracks.

They wait for a streetcar to take them to Maggie's older sister Cleo Joyner, who lives on the South Side of Chicago. An icy wind blows off Lake Michigan, sweeping around the corner of buildings, howling "like a lost dog in a vast wilderness."[3] In years to come, that wind will blast its way through Wright's Chicago fiction.

They board their first Northern streetcar. His aunt pushes Wright toward a seat next to a white man, who appears not to notice him. The conductor calls out the stops, and Wright cannot understand a word. He turns to his aunt in the seat behind him and catches a frightened look in her eyes. He bites his lip and looks out at the strange city. Should they have come?

He discovers that the South Side is crammed with rotting tenement houses, all inhabited by black people. Aunt Cleo's apartment is a single shabby room she calls a "kitchenette." Her husband, formerly a Southern sharecropper, deserted her in this sprawling metropolis. At fifty-one, she looks old, "beaten by the life of the city."

In 1960, the last year of his life, Richard Wright would tell an interviewer on French radio that nothing in his life, before or since, was as difficult or traumatic as that journey from the South to the North. And yet he was merely one of twelve million Southern blacks who went North during the "Great Migration" between 1916 and 1928. Those trains transported them, overnight, from semifeudal conditions in the rural South to the steel and stone grind of modern industrial capitalism. "Perhaps never in history has a more utterly unprepared folk wanted to go to the city," Wright would comment in *12 Million Black Voices*.

THIS WAS CHICAGO, THE BIG NORTHERN CITY WRIGHT HAD DREAMED ABOUT FOR years. In his youth, so many of the ditties, jokes, and conversations among his friends had been about escape to the North. As young boys, they had gone around singing: "I'm going to shake the dust of the South off my feet," and "Lawd, I'd rather be a lamppost in Chicago than the President of Miss'sippi."

The *Chicago Defender*, the most prominent black weekly in America, was widely read by blacks in the South. Its editor, Robert Abbott, was a black-pride man, and the newspaper ran a vigorous crusade against the racist South. It actively encouraged black migration to the North, its news stories frequently contrasting Southern tyranny with Northern freedom. In the North, wages for blacks could be as much as four times higher than wages in the South, the paper reported. You would not be lynched for running a successful business. You could vote. You could live in a brick house and send your children to school for the whole of the school year and you could sit anywhere you liked on public transport and not be bothered. You did not have to step off the sidewalk if a white came along, or raise your hat, or say "yessir," or wait until all the whites were served first before you could buy your newspaper.

The *Chicago Defender* also printed job advertisements. Chicago, with its steel mills, stockyards, meatpacking plants, and lumberyards, was *the* place for unskilled and menial workers. From the mid-nineteenth century, European immigrants—Irish, German, Scandinavians, Eastern European Jews—had streamed into the city. Since World War I, the new immigrants had been predominantly Southern blacks. In 1916, at the beginning of the Great Migration, there were approximately forty thousand blacks in Chicago. By the time Wright arrived, in 1927, there were more than one hundred thousand. Chicago had become the second largest black city in the United States, after New York.

Chicago was also the most residentially segregated city in the nation. "Why they make us live in one corner of the city?" Bigger Thomas asks in *Native Son*. There were four small pockets of black housing in the city, but 90 percent of Chicago's black population lived in the seven-mile-long black metropolis on the South Side. It had always been hazardous for blacks to move into white areas, but in 1927, the year Wright arrived, the Chicago Real Estate Board came up with a "Model Racial Restrictive Covenant" to protect white areas from black residents. These covenants were legal documents between white home owners who pledged not to rent, lease, or sell their property to "colored persons." The courts enforced them, and transgressors could be sued.

Restrictive covenants were less effective on streets adjacent to the black area, since they were not in the interests of landlords or realtors. The Black Belt (as it was called by University of Chicago sociologists) was expanding street by street, mostly toward the south. As Wright would explain in *12 Million Black Voices*—and the photographs of urban desolation are as eloquent as his text—a black family would move into a previously white street, nearly always to be greeted with violence, then real estate "panic-peddlers" would whip up the fears of the white owners, encouraging them to sell at any price. The realtors would buy the apartment houses for a song, then break them up into one- or two-room "kitchenettes," with a gas burner or charcoal stove in each. Whereas the white tenants might have paid fifty dollars a month for a seven-room apartment, black tenants would now find themselves paying twenty-five dollars a week for one or two rooms. Landlords did nothing toward the upkeep of these houses, and the ramshackle old buildings were allowed to deteriorate until they were eventually condemned. Even then, the city officials rarely demolished them. They knew that would leave the black tenants without any shelter at all.

In order to be able to pay the high rents, whole families would inhabit one room. Where there was an "extra" room, families took in relatives, boarders, and lodgers. (Toilets were usually shared by several families.) The doubling-up and crowding together created the predictable social problems. Disease—scarlet fever, tuberculosis, pneumonia, typhoid, gonorrhea, and syphilis—was seven times higher than anywhere else in the city. So were crime rates, delinquency, and teenage pregnancy. Law enforcement was casual. Black-on-black crime did not particularly interest the police, any more than it interested the newspapers.

The shock that Wright experienced on first arrival was the typical response of black newcomers. When fifteen-year-old Langston Hughes arrived in Chicago in 1917, he was beaten up by a gang of Polish boys and regularly propositioned by whores. In 1931 Horace Cayton and his white wife would arrive from Seattle and were startled to find themselves shunned by white Chicago. Confined by residential restrictions to Chicago's South Side, Cayton wondered dubiously: "Could I feel at home in this fantastic city as crowded as Calcutta, as bizarre as Baghdad?"[4] Arna Bontemps and his family would flee the racial tensions of Alabama during the Scottsboro boys' trial, only to find themselves in the "jungle of Chicago's crime-ridden South Side." Lurching from "revulsion to despair," they learned to hurry home before darkness fell, when "honest people abandoned the streets to predators."[5]

When Wright arrived in November 1927, Prohibition was in full swing, and Mafia gangs terrorized the city. In April that year, the corrupt Republican mayor William Hale Thompson had been voted in for a third term, his campaign expenses paid largely by Al Capone, king of the underworld. "Big Bill" Thompson vigorously courted the black vote and was extremely popular in the traditionally Republican black community. "Innocently, we vote into office men to whom the welfare of our lives is of far less concern than yesterday's baseball score," Wright would write later.[6]

There were plenty of dangers for these Southern country folk trying to make out in the big city. Among them, as Nicholas Lemann writes in *The Promised Land*, was "the constant temptation to fall into the wild life."[7] This is the world Wright vividly conveys in his South Side novel, *Lawd Today!* Within twenty-four hours, his main character, Jake Jackson, a black post office worker who is badly in debt, spends the hundred dollars he has borrowed on gambling, alcohol, and whoring. Finally, a black pimp steals his wallet.

WRIGHT RENTED A ROOM IN THE SAME TENEMENT HOUSE AS HIS AUNT CLEO. Maggie went to stay with friends. The next day, Wright took the street-

car south until he could see no more black faces, then got off and
walked, looking for work. A sign in the window of a delicatessen read:
"Porter Wanted." A stout woman with a thick European accent told him
he would have to wait for her husband, and he realized, with a faint
shock, that they were Jewish, the same people he and his friends used
to taunt when they were young. He got the job and the work proved
easy, but his ears were unaccustomed to European accents and he
often had no idea what his bosses were saying to him. The woman,
particularly, was impatient with him. When he once ventured to ask
her to write something down so he could *see* what she was saying, she
shouted at him that she could not write. He felt humiliated. He had to
be patient with her broken English; why couldn't she be more patient
with him, an outsider from the South? "Only one answer came to my
mind. I was black and she did not care."[8] Later, he realized how wrong
he had been about this Jewish couple, the first white people he had
ever met who treated him like an equal. In this Northern city, the interaction between blacks and whites was utterly perplexing to him.

Black workers were kept out of most skilled jobs. Factory managers
preferred white immigrants. Wright soon learned that the best job for
black male workers—indeed, the only "clerical" job available to them—
was at the Chicago post office. It was an unskilled job, but compara-
tively well paid, and it was possible to be promoted to a permanent
position. The entrance examination involved committing to memory a
"scheme" of nine hundred white cards, with place names and zip code
numbers. An entrance exam was coming up, and Wright studied hard.
He decided he would need two days off work: one for last-minute
preparation, and one to sit the exam. Could he be honest with his
bosses? He chose not to risk it. They might be angry, and he needed his
wages.

For two days he did not turn up to work. Feeling guilty when he
went back, he overcompensated with a tall story about his mother just
having died in Memphis. His bosses did not believe him, and they were
hurt that he was lying to them. In his embarrassment, Wright insisted all
the more fervently that he was telling the truth. He felt like a child. At
the end of the week he collected his wages and never went back. "I
just wanted to go quickly and have them forget that I had ever worked
for them."

While he waited to hear from the post office, he got a job as an errand boy and dishwasher in a North Side café. The hours were long, but the pay, at fifteen dollars a week, was higher than most casual jobs. And in the late afternoons he carried dinner trays to people in the nearby hotel, which brought in tips. This was the place—he writes about it in *Black Boy*—where he discovered that the cook, a tall, red-faced Finnish woman admired for her culinary skills, regularly spat into the pot of soup she had boiling on the stove. Wright did not know what to do. Would the "boss lady" believe him—a black man denouncing a white woman? For weeks he kept the knowledge to himself. When the café employed a young black waitress, he confided in her. They agreed she should tell the boss—a black woman had a better chance of being believed than a black man—and that they were prepared to be fired. In fact, the cook was shown the door.

Wright found the young white waitresses "hard" and "brisk" compared with the women down South, but unlike Southern women, they were "relatively free of the heritage of racial hate." One day, one of them squeezed against him to draw a cup of coffee. She seemed to think nothing of it. Another morning, a waitress came rushing in late, and asked him to tie her apron. For Wright, these moments were seared with significance. He had never before come in close contact with a white woman, and these encounters were "charged with the memory of dread." It was a balm to his taut nerves to discover that in the North not all white women shrank from him as "a creature to be avoided at all costs."[9]

At lunchtime he would sit on a bench in a nearby park. Sometimes two or three of the waitresses joined him. They would smoke cigarettes and chat. After eighteen years in which he had done little more than exchange polite phrases with white people, he found himself listening to these young women talk about their hopes for the future, their home lives, their boyfriends. He was struck by the shallowness of their emotions and their "tawdry dreams" of material acquisition. It seemed to him that black people lived "a truer and deeper life."[10]

Another thought took hold of him as he listened to the chatter of those waitresses. If white Americans were ever going to reach any kind of emotional maturity, they needed to know about Negro lives. He would tell the stories that black people were rarely capable of telling themselves. He would make white readers understand that the differences between black and white folk were not about blood or color. He would try to show that "Negroes are Negroes because they are treated as Negroes."[11]

At other times he worried that these thoughts of his were merely "fantasies of ambition" that prevented him from drowning in a "sea of
· ···· l· ···· ··"[12] Th· ··· ·till i· · ·l·l· ·f ·l··· l· D··· · ····l·, li·· ··l·
existence had been focused on the idea of getting away to the North. There had even been a kind of quiet satisfaction in knowing himself on the outside of Southern life, for he had plans to travel beyond that world. In his mind, Chicago had represented "a place where everything was possible."[13] He had told himself that once in that Northern city, he would go back to school and write books. Now he was there and he was seeing just how finite the possibilities were. He had left behind the racist brutality of the South, but the humiliations of the North were almost harder to bear, because they were more capricious. Chicago had once been known for its unusually fair attitude toward its black citizens, but the vast influx of black peasants unfamiliar with city ways had strained race relations. Southern whites had also come to the North in pursuit of jobs, and they brought their race hatred with them. Never quite knowing what was permitted and what was not, black people in the North were left in a constant state of possible infraction.

It was true that blacks and whites jostled each other on the El and the streetcars; they mingled at ballparks, in retail stores, and in the city's cheaper or chain restaurants; blacks could sit in the public libraries and visit the city's museums. But other places had a rigid color line. Even on Forty-seventh Street, the main commercial strip of Bronzeville, the more pretentious restaurants, nightclubs, and cocktail lounges did not allow blacks inside the door. Many parks and swimming pools across the city were closed to blacks. Even the cool waters of Lake Michigan were often out of bounds. (The 1919 race riots in Chicago were set off when a black boy was stoned by white boys at one of the beaches on the shores of Lake Michigan when he crossed the "imaginary line.") Most hotels were closed to blacks seeking rooms; some movie houses refused to allow blacks on the main floor. Bowling alleys, roller-skating rinks, and public dance halls were segregated. The universities officially accepted black students (Northwestern had forty in a student body of eleven thousand); but they were not allowed in the student café, they could not live in the dorms, they could not use the college pool, and where were the decent jobs for them when they qualified?

In *Lawd Today!* the black postal workers no longer have any illusions about the North: "The only difference between the North and the South is, them guys down there'll kill you, and these up here'll let you starve to death," one says to another. His friend rationalizes: "Well, I'd rather die slow than to die fast!"

WITH TIPS, WRIGHT'S WEEKLY INCOME AT THE CAFÉ CAME TO AROUND TWENTY dollars. He put aside as much as possible. Maggie, who was working as a pieceworker in the garment industry, rented a two-room apartment, and Richard moved in. They decided to summon Ella and Leon from Memphis. For months, Richard shared the windowless rear room with his mother and brother.

The arrangement was bound to cause tension. Wright was almost twenty. In the last couple of years he had enjoyed a measure of autonomy and privacy. For the next nine years he would find himself confined in close quarters with his mother, his aunt—and before long, his grandmother. These women brought with them the values of the Southern black community he had so fervently wanted to escape. "The consciousness of vast sections of our black women lies beyond the boundaries of the modern world," he would write in *12 Million Black Voices.*

In June 1928 he was called for temporary work at the post office. At seventy cents an hour, he came away from the eight-hour shift with $5.60. His spirits soared. With a regular clerical position at the post office, he would be able to spend at least five hours every day reading and writing. The only obstacle was the physical examination. It carried a minimum weight requirement: a male had to weigh 125 pounds or more. Wright weighed 110 pounds. For weeks, he crammed food into himself, buying milk and steak as an investment for the future. To his despair, his weight did not change. A doctor told him it would take time to make up for the years of malnutrition. He failed the physical.

His mother became sick again. Maggie, struggling to bring in money, was incensed by the sight of her nephew reading. She saw it as idleness, which led nowhere. It swelled the electric bill and was not going to help him find a job. Throughout Richard's childhood she had been his sole supporter in the family; now she too was coming around to the idea that he was marked for failure. Doubtless, Wright was taunted with the sorts of comments Bigger Thomas hears from his family in *Native*

Son: "We wouldn't have to live in this garage dump if you had any manhood in you." The bickering became ugly. Finally Wright decided he would put up with it no more; he did not want a reenactment of his domestic life in Jackson. His Aunt Maggie could go her own way.

He managed to get himself reemployed by the North Side café, and though he had no savings whatsoever, he rented a room and a kitchen for the family, and this time asked his Aunt Cleo to join them. "Aunt Sissie," as the family called her, was to stay with them for the duration of Richard's time in Chicago.

Richard and Leon slept in the kitchen, where the smell of cooking never went away. The place was infested with cockroaches and bedbugs, and the more they scrubbed the place and doused it with kerosene and insect powder, the more the vermin seemed to multiply. Wright willed himself away from his dismal surroundings by reading *A Remembrance of Things Past* for hours each night. He was "stupefied by its dazzling magic" and crushed by the thought he could never write about the people in his environment like Proust did.[14]

Writing had become his single aim in life. Without the slightest encouragement from anyone, he devoured books. He studied the writer's craft, sentence by sentence, paragraph by paragraph. Then he covered sheets of paper with his own efforts. Imitating the masters, he tried to construct sentences like theirs. He could see that a good sentence not only conveyed meaning but also the feel of something—the mood. "The lump of butter melted slowly and seeped down the golden grooves of the yam."[15] He was pleased with that sentence. Generally he tore up his pages of writing, swearing to do better in the future.

Leon viewed his brother's reading and writing with "a distant and baffled curiosity."[16] Their mother ignored it. Aunt Cleo would watch Wright for a while as he pored over his books, then shake her head. Their relatives in Chicago, cousins of his mother and aunts, were equally nonplussed. Wright rarely attended family gatherings.

In the spring of 1929 he took the post office physical examination again. This time he met the required weight. For the first time, his situation looked promising. The family moved to a four-room apartment at 4831 Vincennes Avenue. Wright paid fifty dollars a month in rent, more than he had ever paid in his life. He was proud of himself. "At last my mother had a place she could call her own after a fashion."[17]

Like most of the temporary clerks, he was put on the night shift. He and his friends would come stumbling out at 4:30 A.M. Once in a blue moon, Wright would go with them to a "speakeasy" for what they called a "daycap" before going home to sleep. His precious afternoon hours were spent reading—often in the public library uptown. Still using Mencken's *Book of Prefaces* as his guide, he read Chekhov, Turgenev, and Maupassant. He was marked by Stephen Crane's novel *Maggie: A Girl of the Streets*, about an innocent girl in the seedy New York tenement district who briefly becomes a prostitute and finally commits suicide.[18]

How, he asked himself, would Zola, Dreiser, and Crane write about the South Side? He wanted to apply their seemingly impartial naturalistic techniques to depict the daily lives of black people. But he was serving a bewildering apprenticeship, without a guide or fellow writer in sight. Sometimes he felt quite desperate about the chasm between his ambitions and his everyday reality.

THE CHICAGO POST OFFICE WAS THE LARGEST POST OFFICE IN THE WORLD. Because Chicago was a railroad center, and because of its huge mail-order houses (Sears, Roebuck and Montgomery Ward), the city handled a vast quantity of mail. The post office, a huge gray building fourteen stories high, contained a maze of sorting rooms, connected by twenty-seven miles of conveyor belts.

Postal employees liked to say, with mock grandiosity, that they were off "to the office." But the high prestige that the job carried in the black community obscured the unhealthy conditions and sheer drudgery of the work itself. The four central characters in *Lawd Today!*, the novel Wright wrote in the mid-1930s, are postal workers, and Wright paints a desolate picture of the tedium and fatigue, the racket of conveyor belts and canceling machines, the grimy dust that turned the men's spittle black, and the "legion of catfooted spies and stoolpigeons" who snooped on the workers.

In winter the building was cold; in summer it was stiflingly hot. Wright and his fellow mail sorters stood as long as eight hours at a stretch, leaning on the edge of the sorting cases for support, their hands moving endlessly. Their trays of mail were weighed, and stamped with the time, so they could not slack off without losing their jobs.

There was the usual discrimination. Blacks were seldom in supervisory positions, and never over whites. The white workers generally assumed that the post office was a temporary job to pay their way through college until they arrived where they belonged. "We weren't going to be mail clerks all our lives, we weren't going to work among a lot of bums and niggers," says the young narrator in a story called "Post Office Nights," published in the left-wing magazine *The Anvil*.[19] For blacks it was different. One of the characters in *Lawd Today!* remarks: "When a black man gets a job in the Post Office he's done reached the top."

Apart from the pay, the redeeming feature was the company. The post office was a refuge for university students, white and black. While they threw the mail into the designated slots, the workers would talk in low voices, out of the corners of their mouths, so as not to draw attention to themselves. In the post office, for the first time in his life, Wright made friends with white men. There was an Irish fellow he liked, Tim McAulife, who had read many of the same things he had. Together they mocked the world. Politics, they agreed, was full of crooks; businessmen were fools; and revolutionary ideals were naïve. McAulife introduced him to his friends, and within the building they formed a group of "Irish, Jewish and Negro wits who poked fun at government, the masses, statesmen, and political parties."[20] Wright would sometimes sit with white friends in the smoky basement canteen, but this was tacitly frowned upon by most white workers, and regarded as defection by blacks. In general, whites sat at one end of the canteen and talked, and blacks sat at the other, playing bridge—a game Wright learned to master that year. When the men stepped out of the building in the early hours of the morning, they returned to their starkly divided black and white worlds.

Occasionally Wright would go to house-rent parties in the South Side. The admission—a quarter or a half-dollar—helped the occupants pay their landlord. There would be home-brewed beer, spaghetti, pork chitterlings, music, and dancing, and Wright would talk and laugh with Southern girls, nearly all of whom worked as domestic servants in white homes. He could be charming, affable, and funny, but neither in the black community nor in the white community did he ever talk about his passions, concerns, and anxieties. "My face was always a deadpan or a mask of general friendliness."[21]

Wright considered most diversions a loss of precious time. Len

Mallette, a black friend from the post office, once persuaded him to join him for a strip show at the Rialto. Mallette paid. "When we came out, I expected Dick to thank me profusely. Instead, he was irritated by the waste of time. 'I could have been writing,' he said."[22]

In the late afternoon of 24 October 1929, Wright took the El uptown to the post office. When he got out, the newspaper stands carried headlines that blazed: "Stocks Crash. Billions Fade." He was not particularly perturbed. It was white folks who would lose money, he reasoned; blacks had nothing to lose.

Within days, the stock market collapsed. All too soon, Wright would discover that blacks would be among the worst affected by what would become known as the Great Depression. He had hoped to be offered a permanent position at the post office. Now he was told that no new appointments were being made. Soon his contract came to an end. For him, this was an absolute disaster.

He worked again at casual jobs. In the summer of 1930 he was invited back to the post office on a temporary basis. He still harbored hopes for a formal education. Before he could go on to the college studies that really interested him, he needed high school qualifications. He gritted his teeth and enrolled at Hyde Park High School. With special permission from the Board of Education, he was accepted into tenth grade. But it proved impossible after a night at the post office. Tired at school and tired at the post office, he became "as nervous as a dozen starved cats," and had to take sleeping pills to get to sleep at night. The other students were younger than he, white, and wide awake. They rattled off their lessons, making him feel stupid. After a few weeks, he gave it up as hopeless.

His mother became ill again and his Aunt Cleo, a precious wage earner, had a heart attack. Money went on doctors and medicines. Leon developed stomach ulcers—a condition that would often incapacitate him over the years—and the family dispatched him to Toledo, Ohio, where he was to help his Uncle Charles with his gardening job. The women were relying entirely on Richard.

WRIGHT WAS STILL TEARING UP MOST OF HIS WRITING, BUT HE FINISHED A SHORT story called "Superstition." In style and tone it was a skillful imitation of Edgar Allan Poe. The story begins: "Three friends, having done justice,

In leisurely fashion, to a savory, well cooked dinner, and overcome by a delightful lassitude, were enjoying, somewhat languidly, their black coffee and cigars in the sitting room of the apartment." The men settle into their chairs and tell each other stories about events that defy rational explanation. There is an atmosphere of horror and suspense; the language is nineteenth-century American English. Wright was writing about a bourgeois world he had never remotely experienced himself.

He submitted the story to a black magazine, *Abbott's Monthly*, and received an acceptance letter. Jubilant, he wondered whether he could turn out tales for a living. He waited for the check to appear. It did not. The issue of April 1931 appeared, with his story in it, but still there was no check. He visited the editor's office and was promised payment in the mail. None came. Wright resolved never again to write for a magazine without a signed contract.

His Aunt Cleo recovered sufficiently to return to her job. Like her sister Maggie, she was a pieceworker in a garment factory. But Wright was not always working that year. When he was not bringing in an income, he felt guilty if he read a book and guilty for eating the family food. He had little heart for writing.

In the April mayoral election, he was paid to round up votes for "Big Bill" Thompson, the long-standing Republican mayor. Wright had no interest in either candidate—Thompson was corrupt and Anton Cermak was racist—but a job was a job. And not until he accompanied the black precinct captain from door to door did he discover the extent of the electoral rigging. Black folks were paid three dollars to vote for Thompson; others gave their vote in exchange for the right to continue an illicit trade in sex and alcohol. On election day, Wright went into a voting booth, unfolded the ballots he had collected, and scrawled across each one: "I protest this fraud."

Thompson had a huge lead in the black wards, but Cermak was elected mayor. Among the first things he did was to dismiss blacks who held positions on the city council or in the civil service. Ten years of political gains for blacks were undone.

The only source of income Wright could now find was through a distant cousin who worked for a Negro burial society. It involved selling insurance policies on a commission basis, mostly to illiterate young housewives living in the Black Belt. It was a racket that took brutal advantage of ignorance. Wright detested the idea. "If you don't sell them, somebody else will," his cousin argued. "You've got to eat, haven't you?"[23]

Burial societies were one of the few businesses that blacks could own. "The white folks . . . wouldn't touch a black man's dead body even to make money," says Tyree in *The Long Dream*, Wright's 1958 novel about a corrupt black Mississippi funeral parlor business.

Wright visited hundreds of tenements. In one after another, stairways and porches were falling apart, doors hung on one hinge, the plaster was peeling off, windows were broken, roofs leaked, and the plumbing did not work properly. He was disgusted by what he saw and disgusted by the swindles he helped perpetrate. His only form of relief was sex. "Many comely black housewives . . . trying desperately to keep up their insurance payments, were willing to make bargains to escape paying a ten-cent premium."[24]

Wright was keenly aware of the plight of black women, and yet, like most of his male acquaintances, he found himself taking advantage of their helplessness. A passage from an early draft of *Black Boy*, cut from the published version, suggests that his attitude to those he took to bed was not much different from that of the misogynist postal workers in *Lawd Today!* "Occasionally I took up with some Negro girl slut, the extent of such relations growing to fantastic and ludicrous proportions as the years passed."

By paying her ten-cent premium each week, he had a "long, tortured affair" with a young woman with a baby. She did not know who the child's father was. She was not able to read. Her one fantasy was to go to the circus. She pestered Wright. Couldn't he look in the newspapers and find a circus in town? She kept herself and her child by selling herself to men. Wright was jealous of her other men; he despised her ignorance; he hated to think about the lack of meaning in her life; he hated to think about the lack of meaning in his own life, and he despised himself for coming to see her.

In the afternoons, as a break from tramping the streets collecting premiums, he would sometimes wander over to Washington Park, on the edge of the Black Belt. A small crowd of unemployed blacks would stand around listening to the speakers in the Negro forum.[25] Church ministers, Garveyites, and Communists would address the crowd from the small platform under the trees.

Wright admired the Garveyites, whose "Back to Africa" movement was inspired by their eloquent, corpulent, jet-black Jamaican leader, Marcus Garvey. Wright thought the idea of American blacks returning to Africa quite unrealistic, but he liked the dignity of these people who celebrated race pride and blackness, and he liked their passionate rejection of an America that rejected them.

The black Communist speakers made him impatient. In order to resemble Lenin, they turned their shirt collars in to make a V at the front, and turned the visors of their caps backward, tilted upward at the nape of the neck. Instead of talking in the traditional manner of the Southern Negro preacher—slow and incantatory—they adopted fast, clipped Northern speech, and even rolled their *r*'s and mispronounced some words, like the Poles and Russians they heard in the Party.

Wright admired the emphasis they placed on action (some mornings on his way to work, he would pass huge demonstrations of unemployed Negroes), but he could also see that these Marxist radicals alienated many black people. The dramatic way one speaker denounced religion by pointing to the sky and calling on Jesus to strike him dead if he was really up there, then threatening to cut his "fucking beard" and slit his throat, was shocking even to Wright.[26] This was no way to lead a revolution, he told himself.

He came close to real romance with the dark-skinned daughter of a Garveyite. She was a trusting, idealistic woman, and he was sincerely fond of her. She told him she loved him and wanted to marry him. But he could not share her childlike enthusiasms. Nor did he want his own skepticism to destroy her simple faith.

> I liked her because she was simple and direct, because I liked my women as women, women who rested upon their womanhood for their effects, for their expression, for their personality; but life had so led me into the dark bypaths of hope and rebellion that I could only pity her simple goodness, pity the full youth of her heart that wanted to follow me. She lived in the world, and I lived out of it; she lived and I waited; she knew what she wanted and I did not.[27]

His insurance job ended. Hungry Negroes could not afford to worry about their funerals. Wright sold his watch and found cheaper rooms for the family in a condemned building on the corner of St. Lawrence Avenue and Champlain Street. His mother took one look at the place and wept.

The family had managed to procure sheets from the relief authorities. Wright had one suit and two or three shirts, which he washed and ironed himself. One afternoon, he came home with his suit freshly pressed from the cleaners, and hung it near an open window while he took a shower. When he came back, it was gone.[28]

In these almost impossible conditions, he completed his first novel. It was about a black woman he called Myrtle Bolden, who grew up on a plantation in the South, taught school, married, had four children, then went North, where she was abandoned by her husband and eventually died of hunger and neglect. Wright gave her his grandmother's maiden name, Bolden, but it was his mother's life he was thinking about.[29] "Our women are the most circumscribed and tragic objects to be found in our lives," he would write in *12 Million Black Voices*. "They are black, they are women, they are workers."[30]

Then, one day, there was no food in the house. Wright, in despair, tore up his novel and burned it. The next morning he did the thing that shamed him more than anything else: he went to the Cook County Bureau of Public Welfare to plead for bread.

THE DEPRESSION HIT CHICAGO WORSE THAN MOST MAJOR AMERICAN CITIES AND IT affected the South Side worst of all. The hard times would last for eight years—until 1937, the year Wright left for New York.

The first of the banks in the Black Belt closed its doors in July 1930. A month later, every bank in the ghetto was closed, their clients left weeping for their savings. Factories cut back production, and black workers were the first to go. White families could no longer afford to keep their black maids. Evictions were causing havoc throughout the city: in 1931 alone, the Chicago Bailiff's Office threw fourteen hundred unemployed families out of their homes. For most of 1931 and part of 1932, Chicago's public school teachers were not paid; there were no funds in the city treasury.

By the summer of 1932, unemployment had reached an all-time high. It was three times higher in the Black Belt than in any other part of the

city. The presidential election was coming up in November, and throughout the nation, the blame was attributed to the hapless Republican president, Herbert Hoover. On May Day 1932, demonstrators paraded through
the Loop chanting, "We want Hoover— with a rope around his neck."[31]
The black community was also wary of the Democratic candidate
Roosevelt, with his upper-crust accent and Harvard education, whose
running mate was the racist "Cactus Jack" Garner of Texas.

When Richard Wright went to the local relief station and sat for
hours in a crowded room waiting to be interviewed, he suddenly realized he was not alone. His was not an individual failure. Masses of
people were struggling in exactly the same way for exactly the same
reasons. Until then, he had always been cynical about politics. That day
triggered some new thoughts.

Only those who had reached rock bottom were eligible for relief.
The allowance per family for food was a dollar a day. Extras like shoes
or money for medicine might ensue after a caseworker visited the family and verified that it was truly destitute.

In September and October the relief system sent Wright to sweep
the streets. "All day, with a huge broom, I would walk up one street
and down another, pushing my broom, sweeping horse dung, paper,
cigarette butts, dirt into neat heaps. When the trees began to shed their
leaves, I would sweep piles of dry, crackling leaves into big piles."[32]

In December he was called to the post office to help sort the Christmas mail. He met up with his Irish friend again, and they discussed the
economic situation. Wright sensed that his white colleagues had changed.
Their economic problems had made them more aware of social forces
and more sympathetic to blacks. For the first time, he was invited to
their homes.

In January 1933 he was sent to dig ditches in the Cook County Forest
Preserves. "I rode in zero weather for miles in open trucks, then spaded
the frozen earth for eight hours, only to ride home again in the dark, in
an open truck. A strange emotional peace had come to me now. I
knew that my life was cast with the men with whom I worked, slow,
plodding, inarticulate men, workers all."[33]

Franklin D. Roosevelt won the election by a landslide—with very
little support from the black community. In his inaugural address, he
promised to relieve the "dire need" of unemployed Americans and give

a "new deal" to "the forgotten man." He wasted no time in setting up the Federal Emergency Relief Administration. A work relief scheme rather than a dole system, able-bodied unemployed people were put to work for thirteen dollars a week.

When his ditch-digging job ended, Richard Wright turned up at the crowded welfare office on Prairie Street, in the heart of the worst slum area in the ghetto. He was interviewed by Mary Wirth, the assistant supervisor. Her husband was Professor Louis Wirth, the eminent German-born Jewish sociologist at the University of Chicago. She was impressed by the earnest, handsome young man she thought not yet twenty. In fact, he was twenty-four.

Mary Wirth knew one of the directors of medical research at the Michael Reese Hospital, the largest and wealthiest Jewish hospital on the South Side, and she managed to secure Wright a job as an orderly. "I remember talking with him at my desk in the office—worrying about his having to get up at 4:30 A.M. to get to the work which I privately thought a miserable job—and his laughing at me and reassuring me— saying that he was used to it and didn't mind it at all."[34]

She never told Wright that it was the relief agency, not the hospital, that paid him his standard wage of thirteen dollars a week. And he never told her—since he was sincerely grateful for the income—that he *did* mind the job, just as he very much minded his family's desperate predicament. Mary Wirth only saw the smiling face he presented to the world. Privately, he resented the aloof attitude of social workers toward their "clients," and he resented their "pink pills for social ills."[35] Years later, he would comment: "I wished my social worker had given me a sense of pride by telling me what was wrong with the world and what I could do about it, and not, by implication, telling me something that made me feel that I had to knuckle down and take what was coming to me without making a noise about it."[36]

At the hospital Wright scrubbed floors, on his knees, with strong-smelling disinfectants. He fed sick animals and cleaned out their cages. The stench was so foul that at first he felt like retching, but gradually he became used to it. In the mornings he would see tiny human fetuses lying on top of the rotting food in the garbage containers. He and his three black coworkers were expected to eat in the animal room in the basement of the hospital, out of sight of the white patients and their doctors. Across the corridor was the morgue. "While eating you could . . . see corpses being wheeled out to some place down the endless shadowy corridors."[37]

Wright was curious about the experiments going on in the research institute, and occasionally he would ask the doctors questions. He discovered that some of these foreign-born doctors had adopted the racial prejudices of native-born Americans. "If you know too much, boy, your brains might explode," one of them rebuked him.[38]

Each Saturday morning, the city's animal pound delivered a batch of unclaimed dogs to be used in experiments. So that their howling would not disturb the patients, the dogs had to be debarked. Wright's job was to hold them while they were injected with Nembutal, then hold open their jaws while the doctors severed their vocal cords. "When the dogs came to, they would lift their heads to the ceiling and gape in a soundless wail." This image of mute suffering would haunt him.

One freezing winter day, the tedious work routine blew apart. Wright and his black coworkers were taking their lunch as usual, amid the tiers of animal cages, when the bickering between two older men escalated into an all-out fight. One man opened a switchblade knife; the other grabbed an ice pick. One pushed the other against a tier of cages. The whole structure toppled. Cages sprang open. "Rats and mice and dogs and rabbits moved over the floor in wild panic."[39]

The men locked the door and frantically tried to catch the animals. But which cage did they belong in? They had a rough idea how many animals belonged in each cage, but not a clue as to which mice were tubercular and which were cancerous, which dogs were diabetic, or which guinea pigs had been injected with what. By sheer guesswork, they put animals in cages, and replaced the corpses, crushed beneath the cages, with healthy stock from another cage. Then they waited anxiously for the doctors to come in and notice the disaster.

They got away with it. For weeks afterwards, they would joke about the way they had influenced the course of medical research. Wright writes that he "brooded" as to whether he should have gone to the director's office and told him what had happened. But why should he lose his job by acting nobly, he reasoned with himself, when the white hospital staff did not even treat him like a human being? A couple of his fictional characters curb their spontaneous impulse to help white people, for the same reason.

A NEW BRANCH OF THE CHICAGO PUBLIC LIBRARY HAD OPENED IN THE BLACK BELT in January 1932, and Wright now spent a great deal of his free time there. The George Cleveland Hall Library, on Forty-eighth Street and South Michigan Avenue, was a fine Italianate Renaissance–style building in Indiana limestone.[40] The ornate wooden entrance opened into an octagonal rotunda with mirrors, brass ornaments, and dark-oak paneling. The head librarian, Vivian G. Harsh, was a warm, light-skinned woman in her forties. The first black librarian in the Chicago Public Library system, she was committed to building up the "Special Negro Collection" and making the Negro branch into a lively cultural center.[41] By hosting a book review and lecture forum that met every two weeks, she would make the library into one of the leading institutions of the black Chicago Renaissance, in which Wright was to play a key role.

SEVERAL SCENES IN WRIGHT'S FICTION PORTRAY WARM FRIENDSHIP BETWEEN BLACK males. His first novel, *Lawd Today!*, which did not find a publisher until after his death, is a warm and exuberant portrait of black male camaraderie in the South Side. We are shown nothing of this aspect of Wright's life in *Black Boy*.

In 1932 (around the time Wright's grandmother, frail now, came to join them in Chicago), Joe Brown, Wright's friend from Jackson days, arrived in the big city. During the year he stayed in Chicago, he and Wright saw quite a bit of each other. In a long letter to Wright's first biographer, Constance Webb, written in January 1967, Brown provides a glimpse of a quite different Wright—a young man who enjoyed wild pranks, Southern talk, and laughter. Brown lived with his aunt, not far from Wright.

> I lived on Langley Ave, 4700 South. Dick lived on the corner of 46 and Champlain St. Lawrence. His grandmother Mrs. Wilson, Leon his brother, mother and his aunt Sissy lived in a two flat building. The flat was not too far from a 7th Day Adventist Church where his folks attended. Dick seemed to have been the man of the house. And his aunt Sissy, the lady.[42]

When Wright was out of work, Joe would sometimes go with him to the relief station to pick up food rations and food-purchasing stamps. Even Joe Brown was fooled by Wright's brave front about welfare.

Dick was never ashamed of the handouts he and his family were getting from the city and government. He would laugh about the depression that the whole country had gone into, and would say that the poor people were not responsible for their sudden plight and that the U.S. government owed this little ration to us and a lot more from the hang over slavery days. He said he would not sit by with a half loaf of bread under his arm and see his mother and family suffer because of some false pride.

Joe had come to the city to help look after his eight-year-old cousin. His aunt, the boy's mother, worked all day as a pastry cook in a cafeteria; the boy's father had been mysteriously murdered in the city. Wright would sometimes call in, and over home-brewed blue grape wine and occasional "goodies" that Joe's aunt brought home from the cafeteria, the two friends would reminisce about Jackson days and those "damn Southern peckerwoods." They would sometimes get "a little bit woozy," says Joe Brown, but Dick Wright never stayed long. "He would always beat it back home to do some more writing."

Wright showed Joe Brown his pile of writings and the rejection slips he had received from publishers. Joe tried to read bits and pieces, but they were "too far out" for him. Wright also came up, Brown recalls, with a plan for obtaining free books:

Dick and I had a little thing going for a while but we soon got afraid. Dick would use my aunt's address as a member of the Book of Month Club [sic]. The books kept coming and so did the Invoices. I would always get the mail before my aunt would get it, and then I would hide books, bills and letters for Dick to pick up later. This went on for a long time until Dick finally put in for a change of address that didn't exist. We got a little afraid of those final red letter notices and threats of a draft being done on Dick's non-existent bank account.

Occasionally the two young men walked over to Washington Park to listen to the white speakers at the "Bug's Club." Wright, who liked to show off to his impressionable friend, would comment on the female members of the crowd.

> Dick made it his business to meet the highly informed young ladies around our age they were for the most white females in all instances. Dick couldn't some how stomach the Negro girls during this era. He said all they wanted to do was party, party, git high and shack up and make second hand love. Dick was forever in search for some one who could enjoy the things he liked.

Two other former classmates of theirs were in Chicago by then. Dick Jordan had been arrested for stealing from the jewelry store in Jackson where he had worked as a messenger boy. He had jumped bail, fled to Chicago, and changed his name. He was already showing signs of the alcoholism that would kill him prematurely.

Arthur Leaner, the rogue of the old Smith Robertson class, was married with two children. He was temporarily unemployed, and he and his family had been evicted from their home. When Joe Brown and Dick Wright visited him in his Red Cross accommodation, Arthur paced up and down, full of excitable but deadly serious plans for becoming "stinky rich." Wright, who saw it as an enjoyable game, readily joined in. "I was always the silent guy in the party," writes Joe Brown.

Leaner suggested a mail-order business. They would act as spiritual advisers for people with problems—lonely hearts sort of people. Wright suggested they call themselves "The Three Wise Men of the East." Leaner pointed out that they would need to start out with a small outlay of cash. Wright eyed Joe Brown with what Brown called his "stolen under-eyed look." Dick would write the copy for the advertisement, Leaner went on. And they would need a photograph. Brown recalls the discussion:

> We could ask the photographer to slightly over expose the pictures just a little bit so that we would be light skinned and this would give us a foreign look. Dick readily endorsed this idea and then he said we could take 3 big turkish bath towels and wrap it around our heads with a few different twists and then when people see our pictures, they'd never know whether we were Niggers or not. Arthur said to Dick, now we are seeing eye to eye.

The planning had taken five hours, Brown writes, and "the evening had grown old." Arthur went to his icebox, pulled out three bottles of home brew, and they drank to the success of their future venture. Joe Brown and Dick Wright put on their "seedy overcoats," adjusted their earmuffs, and stepped out into the icy night.

> No sooner than Arthur had put the chain on his door, Dick stopped still and said to me: "Big Mama Joe, this is not our home brew."[43]

4

WORDS AS WEAPONS

September 1933–September 1934

On Friday evenings in the autumn of 1933, at the end of his week at the Michael Reese Hospital, Richard Wright would join a group of white post office friends in Abe Aaron's room at the Troy Lane Hotel, on the South Side. They would make potato pancakes or salami sandwiches, drink beer, and talk. At the first meeting Wright was shocked to discover that several of them were members of the Communist Party.

Even his friend Abraham Aaron had joined up. The tall, lanky Aaron had an analytical, skeptical bent of mind, and Wright was amazed that he had fallen for the Party propaganda. Aaron had been brought up in Butler, a small coal-mining town in Pennsylvania, where they were the only Jews in the area, and his father ran a struggling grocery business. Now Aaron was trying to support his studies at the University of Chicago. In exchange for a room, he worked nights as a desk clerk at the Troy Lane.

Abe Aaron was the first person Wright had ever met who wanted to be a writer. He had just had a short story published in the *Anvil*, Jack Conroy's new Midwest magazine for "proletarian writers."[1] Wright told him that he too was trying to be a writer. Aaron urged him to come along to the John Reed Club.

As Aaron explained, the John Reed Club was a national organization of proletarian artists and writers. There were thirty clubs dotted across the country, and the Chicago club had around one hundred members. The Chicago meetings were held on Tuesday evenings, and there were discussions and invited speakers on Saturday evenings. The Chicago club had even launched its own magazine, *Left Front.* Wright protested that the club would not want black members. Aaron assured him he would be most welcome. At a recent gathering of the thirteen John Reed Clubs in the Midwest, the members had resolved to make a greater effort to recruit blacks to the group and to encourage them to take on positions of leadership.

There was nothing Wright longed for more than intellectual companionship and contact with other people who wanted to write. What worried him was the club's association with the Communist Party. John Reed, he learned, was an American journalist who had gone to Russia in 1917 with his wife Louise Bryant, and had written a book, *Ten Days That Shook the World,* about the Bolshevik Revolution. He returned to America and helped establish the U.S. Communist Party in 1919. The following year, he was back in the Soviet Union when he caught typhus and died. As the first American Communist hero, the Russians gave him a state funeral and buried him inside the Kremlin.

Aaron assured Wright that he did not have to be in the Party to be a member of the John Reed Club. Nevertheless, Wright was wary. He doubted that Communists, whom he knew to be predominantly the sons and daughters of foreign-born Jews, could possibly have a sincere interest in Negroes.

One evening in late fall, telling himself he would turn up as an "amused spectator," he took the train to the Loop, and walked to 1475 South Michigan Avenue. He climbed the dark stairway to the second floor. "What on earth of importance could transpire in so dingy a place?" he thought to himself. On the door at the top of the stairs were the words: "The Chicago John Reed Club."

I opened it and stepped into the strangest room I had ever seen. Paper and cigarette butts lay on the floor. A few benches ran along the walls, above which were vivid colors depicting figures of workers carrying streaming banners. The mouths of the workers gaped in wild cries; their legs were sprawled over cities.[2]

The club's executive secretary, Gilbert Rocke, came up and welcomed him.[3] Was he an artist? he asked. "I try to write," was Wright's timid reply. Rocke found him some back issues of the *New Masses*, *International Literature*, and *Left Front* and invited him to join the editorial meeting of *Left Front* currently in progress. Wright hesitated. Rocke propelled him toward the group. All evening, Wright was alert for signs of condescension or hostility. Among these young white artists and writers he encountered nothing but friendliness. He told himself they had been instructed to be friendly to Negroes.

At home, later that evening, he opened the journals. They were different from anything he had ever read. The writers he had read in the *American Mercury* and the *Atlantic Monthly* were generally privileged men, many of whom had been to Harvard or Yale, and who liked to write about things like their travels in Europe. These Communist magazines were about the problems of the common people—workers, farmers, the unemployed. Wright discovered that many of the writers were poor, like him. They had experienced discrimination—as Jews or Irish people, Negroes, women, and as workers. The black poet Langston Hughes appeared regularly in the pages of the national weekly the *New Masses*. There were articles by other black writers. And white writers also seemed interested in race issues. Considerable space was devoted to the notorious trial of the framed Scottsboro boys, in Alabama. Wright told himself excitedly that if these ordinary people had the courage to write about their lives, why couldn't he?

The following week he went back to the club. He read out two poems.[4] Bill Jordan, the editor of *Left Front*, was keen to publish them. Wright was skeptical. "If you're going to publish these scribblings just to recruit me into the party, then nothing doing."[5]

By November Abe Aaron was telling his writer friend Jack Conroy about Wright. "I have some good news for you, Jack. I have a sort of a gang, friends I acquired at the post-office. One of them is a Negro lad about my age. He is writing blank verse. He intends to send some of it to you. . . . I imagine you'll be as wild over it as I am. It's the real thing."[6] Two months later, Aaron wrote again:

Isn't he swell? And he's absolutely self-educated. . . . He also writes short stories. On that score, he considers me a king pin as compared to himself. He sees what luck I am having. So he never submits. Once he did publish a blood and thunder thing in *Abbott's Monthly*. He's heartily ashamed of it. Incidentally, he was cheated out of his check.

In February Abe Aaron lost his room at the Troy Lane Hotel. He told Wright it was due to a change in the management.[8] Years later he divulged the real reason. His boss didn't like a black man coming to the hotel. Aaron protested that the black man was a writer, a serious man, but the following Saturday, after another sociable Friday evening, his boss warned him again. Aaron would not think of asking Wright to stay away; nor would he give in to his boss's racism. The following Friday the group met as usual, and on Saturday Abe Aaron was looking for a place to live. "I would never have told Dick," he remarked in an interview. "He would have been furious that I had lost my job over him."[9]

WRIGHT'S LIFE HAD BEEN TRANSFORMED. HE BECAME ONE OF THE CHICAGO JOHN Reed Club's keenest members. Nearly always he turned up with a poem or piece of prose to read aloud. *Left Front* published two of his poems in February 1934. The *Anvil* published another two in April. In June Wright's long poem "I Have Seen Black Hands" was printed in the *New Masses*.

Wright's poems were angry. Like H. L. Mencken, he was "using words . . . as one would use a club."[10] But these poems had an optimism about the future that was quite new for him. The last stanza of "I Have Seen Black Hands" exploded into revolutionary fervor.

> I am black and I have seen black hands
> Raised in fists of revolt, side by side with the white fists of white workers,
> And some day—and it is only this which sustains me—
> Some day there shall be millions and millions of them,
> On some red day in a burst of fists on a new horizon!

He wrote about workers usurping the places of the capitalists. On paper, at least, he could reverse the power structure. "Rest for the Weary" addressed capitalists with defiant bravado:

You panic stricken guardians of gold
are wise to tremble

. . .

for soon our brawny hands shall
relieve you of all your burdens![11]

In the spring of 1933, the World's Fair opened in Chicago. *Left Front*
pointed out that ever since Chicago had become an international show-
case city, segregation had become worse in its restaurants and on the
beaches.[12]

Around this time, Nelson Algren joined the club. Brought up in
Chicago, a graduate of the University of Illinois, he had just spent several months traveling through the South by boxcar. He was now trying
to write a novel, *Somebody in Boots*, based on his own experiences.
The black character, Dill Doak, strongly resembles Wright. Doak is "an
unusual Negro . . . a man who could not be patronized." He reads a
great deal and is interested in politics. The white protagonist, Cass
McKay, goes with him to Washington Park, where they spread their
coats on the grass among the crowd of black and white workers and
listen to the speakers. Dill Doak suggests a visit to the World's Fair. Cass
becomes aware of the "passing glances" from white people as they
walk. At the fair, they pass a concession where white men are pegging
balls at a slot, and when they hit it, one of the Negroes perched on a
plank in midair gets dumped in a tub of water. Cass notices his companion's "sudden lack of enthusiasm."[13]

In September 1933 Wright gave a talk at the club on "The Literature
of the Negro." In March 1934 he was invited to the Indianapolis John
Reed Club to speak about "Revolutionary Negro Poetry." Later in the
year, the Indianapolis members invited him back to talk about the
poetry of Langston Hughes.

The John Reed Club was Wright's university. On Saturday evenings,
well-known artists, writers, and intellectuals were invited to the club to
speak. The British radical John Strachey, currently touring the U.S.,
talked about the rise of fascism in Europe. Sociologist Professor Louis
Wirth talked about the phenomenon of Jewish ghettoes in American
cities and their impact on the psychological development of the American Jew. Roberta Burgess, who had just traveled to Russia with her
brother Ernest Burgess (another eminent Chicago sociologist), gave a

talk on "Art in the New Russia," illustrated by lantern slides and posters. Jack Conroy, editor of the *Anvil* and author of *The Disinherited*, came from Moberly, Missouri, to talk about "Revolution and the Novel." Maxwell Bodenheim, a maverick New York bohemian originally from Chicago, read poetry. The audience watched incredulously while he kept disappearing to the men's room with a flask, eventually becoming so drunk he could hardly stand up.

Like the Communist Party with which it was associated, the John Reed Club was an unusually international group of people. Most members were Eastern European Jews, and they tended to view America through slightly foreign lenses.[14] The club song was the "Internationale"; members looked outward to the international brotherhood of workers.

It soon became apparent to Wright that there were serious political divisions within the club. Those who were not in the Party begrudged the power and influence of those who were. When one of the artists in the club agreed to paint murals for a government agency, the comrades denounced him as a "class collaborator." A more bitter struggle raged over *Left Front*. The John Reed Club leaders in New York considered the Chicago magazine a waste of time and resources. They wanted members across the country to read the *Daily Worker* and the *New Masses*, published in New York and securely under the Party's thumb. Wright and his *Left Front* colleagues argued hotly for the importance of local magazines. For the time being, the decision was deferred.

A few months after Wright joined the club, a meeting was called to elect a new executive secretary. The position was effectively that of club leader. Wright's name was thrown into the ring. Taken aback, he protested that he was too new to take on such a role. It was after midnight when they ended the interminable discussion and held a secret ballot. The result: Richard Wright was elected. He stood up, nonplussed, and tendered his resignation. The comrades would not hear of it. They assured him the executive board would help him learn the ropes.

Afterwards Wright learned that the voting had been influenced by cynical political rivalry. Since racial equality was one of the Party's central doctrines, no one dared to argue openly against a Negro office-bearer. The non-Communists had voted for Wright as an attempt to break the Communist stranglehold. The Communists had voted for him because they believed they could wield power through him.

Soon after the election, a Party member took Wright aside. If he wanted to continue as leader, he told Wright, he would have to join the Communist Party. It was exactly what Wright had originally feared. But by this time, the John Reed Club meant everything to him. "The club was my first contact with the modern world," he writes in *Black Boy*. He had also come around to the view that Communism was the most effective path to solidarity between workers of all races. Assured by the Party members that his John Reed Club duties as executive secretary would be accepted as his contribution to Party work, he paid his first membership dues.

As leader of the club, Wright was caught between the feuding groups. He tried to steer a middle line. "Trying to please everybody, I pleased nobody."[15]

WRIGHT WAS NOW EXPECTED TO ATTEND COMMUNIST PARTY LOCAL BRANCH MEETings. His unit was the one closest to his place of residence, in the Black Belt. He turned up to find a group of twenty or so—nearly all of them Southern blacks with less than three years of schooling. There were two or three whites.

Wright came in a suit and tie. When he was called upon to introduce himself, he took notes out of his pocket. He told the group that he was executive secretary of the John Reed Club and a writer who had been published in various proletarian literary magazines. He went on in this vein.

After a while a woman giggled. The chairman allowed himself to smile, then the giggling spread around the room. Some struggled to keep deadpan faces.[16] Wright looked around, mortified. Had his report been childish? Had he been too earnest? "I realize that writing is not basic or important," he added uneasily. "But given time, I think I can make a contribution."[17]

"We know you can, comrade," the black organizer said, in a tone Wright found "more patronizing than that of a Southern white man."

The meeting proceeded. Wright felt crushed and furious. Afterwards one of the members explained to him that he had alienated the others with his suit and tie and educated speech. They dismissed him as an "intellectual." Among these working-class Communists, intellectuals were understood to be effete, namby-pamby types who read "bourgeois books" and were therefore "class traitors." Wright was no doubt considered a would-be white man and a "race traitor" as well. It would soon become clear to him that the comrades saw the John Reed Club as a kind of playground for white artists.

WHETHER IT WAS AT THE INSTIGATION OF MARY WIRTH, HIS SOCIAL WORKER, OR whether he arranged it when Professor Louis Wirth came to speak at the John Reed Club, Richard Wright made a visit to the University of Chicago. Louis Wirth, a German Jew, had a particular interest in minority groups, urbanism, and the phenomenon of the ghetto. Wright wanted to ask him for a systematic reading list in sociology—particularly in the area of race relations.

The University of Chicago's sociology department was world famous. It was in Chicago that the discipline of American sociology was established in 1892. The *American Journal of Sociology* was launched from the Chicago department in 1895. Not surprisingly, since it emerged out of a city of immigrant group clusters and one of the main destinations for black migration from the South, "Chicago Sociology" was renowned for its studies of race relations and residential patterns. The first black American sociologists, Charles S. Johnson and E. Franklin Frazier, had trained under the grand old man of Chicago Sociology, Robert E. Park. It was hoped that Horace Cayton and St. Clair Drake would represent a new generation of black sociologists.

When Wright knocked on the door of Wirth's office, he was greeted by Horace Cayton. While pursuing his graduate studies, Cayton was also Louis Wirth's research assistant. A gifted raconteur, Cayton liked to describe his first meeting with Wright. In truth, he probably reconstructed the scene from Wright's memory of the occasion, since elsewhere he admitted he did not remember their first encounter.

> I began showing him the files in the office—I would not say that we were totally statistically oriented at the University at the time, but we were very empirical. We were going out studying every facet of the city. We were discovering the Italian district, the Polish district, the Negro community. We were studying the vast complex of human beings who make up that monster of Chicago, and Dick said: "You've got all of your facts pointed, pinned to the wall like a collector would pin butterflies." I looked at him. He was a poetic little Negro.[18]

Professor Wirth was happy to give Wright a reading list of under-graduate books on sociology. When they met again a few months later, Wirth was astounded by the thoroughness with which Wright had done the reading.[19]

THE MICHAEL REESE HOSPITAL LAID OFF STAFF EARLY IN 1934, AND WRIGHT LOST his job, forcing the family to move again—this time to a cramped, sti-fling attic next to some railway tracks.[20]

Margaret Wilson had recently joined the family, and she was frail these days. Ella was unable to work. Cleo brought in women's wages. Leon was often in Ohio with his Uncle Charles. When he came back to Chicago, he would "get into scrapes," as Wright put it to friends.[21] Fern Gayden, the family's black caseworker, considered Leon mentally dis-turbed.[22]

Despite the burden that fell on him, Wright complained to friends that his mother still treated him like a boy. She worried endlessly about his godlessness. She detested his Communism. Like everyone in the family, she considered his hours and hours of reading and writing a worthless frittering away of time.

The women could not have known much about Wright's sex life, which, from hints he drops in his autobiographical drafts, appears to have been highly active. But they knew enough to consider him a lost soul. Doubtless he did not always come home at night. They knew he had no serious girlfriend and no intention, just yet, of marrying. In Wright's novel *The Outsider*, Cross Damon's deeply religious mother delivers frequent "preachments" about his being "a self-centered liber-tine" with a "lust for pleasure," who is "reaping the wages of sin."[23] In *The Long Dream*, young Fishbelly's mother Emma (a name resembling Ella) endlessly exhorts her son "to turn his back upon the snares of the flesh, and seek the Kingdom of Heaven."[24]

Wright consciously kept an emotional distance from his family. He knew his female relatives intimately. He had shared rooms with them for years. He knew how hard their lives were, how low their income, how unreliable their men, and how important their God. He hated to think about his mother's life, and her complete dependence on him. A recurring pattern in Wright's fiction has the male protagonist steeling himself against the guilt and anguish his mother induces in him. In *Native Son*, Bigger Thomas deliberately represses any tenderness he might feel toward his family:

> He hated his family because he knew that they were suffering and that he was powerless to help them. He knew that the moment he allowed himself to feel to its fullness how they lived, the shame and misery of their lives, he would be swept out of himself with fear and despair. So he held toward them an attitude of iron reserve; he lived with them, but behind a wall, a curtain.[25]

Cross Damon, in *The Outsider*, tries not to think about his mother's vulnerability. "To keep her life from crushing his own, he had slain the sense of her in his heart."[26]

The summer of 1934 was unusually stifling, even by Chicago standards. Wright's grandmother had been ill since the middle of July. In August, the John Reed Club moved to more spacious quarters in the Loop, and the members were busy transporting furniture and painting walls. Around dawn on Wednesday, August 15, Wright was about to go out of the front door to get an early start at the club when he heard a voice calling him weakly. His grandmother had fallen while trying to get to the building's communal bathroom, and she lay crumpled in the hallway, pale and sweating. A yellow-green liquid escaped from her lips. Wright, frightened, called out "Mama! Aunt Cleo!" They came rushing out. He should go, they told him; they could manage. Wright left the house with a feeling of foreboding and spent the day at 505 South State Street, carting tables and benches up the stairs. When he got home, his mother and aunt were sitting quietly at the table, waiting for him.

> "Well," my mother said, "mama's gone."
> "What?" I asked.
> "Mama's gone," my mother repeated.
> "Granny's dead, Richard," my aunt said.[27]

Margaret Wilson died of acute heart failure. The hour of death was marked on her death certificate as 9 A.M. She was born in 1853, but since she did not know the day, her birthday was recorded on her death certificate as 15 August, the date of her death.[28] She was eighty-one.

His grandmother had not really lived, Wright reflected in bed that night.[29] She had merely existed. She had struggled, suffered, and died. Her consciousness was so filled by her religion that her God was more real to her than the world itself. As she saw it, she had borne nine children because it was God's will. If she had brought them up all to adulthood, it was thanks to God.

He thought it ironic that while his slave-born grandmother lay dying, he had left the house to engage in revolutionary work. It symbolized the huge distance that black people had come since the end of slavery. He and his grandmother, though they were related by blood, race, and a common heritage, had belonged to different worlds.

The funeral was held three days later, at the Seventh Day Adventist Church where his grandmother had worshiped. She lay in an open coffin, eyes closed. In death as in life, her thin lips were "tight and grim."

In church, Wright was swept with a violent anger he could barely understand. "I was so angry at the way they dragged the service out, at the manner in which every possible device was used to jerk out more moans and tears, that the joints of my bones seemed to become unhinged."[30] He told himself that he despised these people who murmured that his grandmother was going to Heaven, when he knew—and surely they did too—that she would be "rotting in eternal death." These "wall-eyed yokels" seemed to enjoy the "spectacle of death." They kept "gaping at the family" to see who was weeping and who was not. He did not weep. The scene struck him as "too tragic for tears."[3]

The depth of his emotion was surprising. It was because of his grandmother that he had left home at the age of seventeen. Throughout his childhood she had punished him brutally for what she saw as his consorting with the devil. She had burned his books and whipped him with extreme cruelty. She had worsened their poverty by refusing to let him work on the Sabbath. She had never encouraged him with his schooling. And yet, looking back, Wright was convinced that his grandmother had sincerely loved him. Without her kindness, he would not have been able to remain with his mother. He would not have had those years of schooling in Jackson. He would probably have become a delinquent.

With the death of his grandmother, Wright lost his link to a bygone world. She was the last of his grandparents to die, and with her went the lived experience of slavery, the folklore and myths, the superstitions, prayers, and hopes of his black ancestors in the Old South. He was acutely conscious that this African-American heritage was in danger of being swallowed up without a trace in the steel and stone metropolises of the North.

One day, he vowed to himself, he would write about his grandmother's relationship to religion. He had no desire to mock it. He understood the comfort of religious faith. He knew the strength it gave to the women in his family. He wanted to show "the living inner springs of religious emotion," and why it had such a powerful hold on his people.[31]

THAT SAME MONTH, AUGUST 1934, THE CHICAGO JOHN REED CLUB HOSTED THE Midwest Writers' Congress. There were lengthy discussions as to what the John Reed Club should expect from writers. Wright argued that a revolutionary artist needed to concentrate on producing revolutionary art. The Party members insisted that writers should write for a few hours each day, then devote themselves to Party work and pamphlet writing.

At the congress, *Left Front* was voted out of existence. The Communist faction, who had clearly been briefed, declared that it took club writers away from political action. Wright angrily suggested that they dissolve the entire club while they were at it. He was given a dressing-down for his "defeatism."

One month later, at the Second National John Reed Club Congress, held in Chicago, the club was indeed dissolved. Emotions ran high. There was no consensus as to whether "regionalism" and "proletarian literature" were good things or not. Philip Rahv, who edited the New York club's magazine, the *Partisan Review*, criticized the midwestern delegates for their romanticism about the land. The midwestern writer Meridel Le Sueur got up and explained that local farmers were having their mortgages seized, then burst into tears. Alexander Trachtenberg, a short, dark Russian émigré with a walrus mustache, supported her and was promptly accused of "emotionalism." Wright, bored by the talk that went nowhere, his eyes stinging from the smoke in the room, doodled with a variation of "J. Alfred Prufrock":

> I am tired of all the bitter accusations,
> And recriminations
> And deviations from the line.

The refrain read: "In the union hall the comrades come and go / Discussing the C.I.O."[32]

Near the end of the conference it became clear to Wright that much of the tangled talk was directed from Moscow. Trachtenberg, who ran the Communist publishing house International Publishers in New York and was in constant touch with the Comintern, declared that Moscow had abandoned "proletarianism" the previous month. The Party was now concentrating, he said, on the struggle against fascism. To be effective, there needed to be a broad coalition of American writers on the Left. And they needed to be established writers. Trachtenberg proposed a national organization of writers—the "League of American Writers"—to be based in New York.

Wright argued passionately against the idea. What had happened to the democratic spirit of the John Reed Club? Trachty's proposal sounded thoroughly elitist. What about all the young writers in the club who would not be considered important enough to join the new League of American Writers? It took him a while to realize that no one else was speaking up.

The plan for an American Writers' Congress in New York was published in the *New Masses* in January 1935. With typical strategic skill, the Party voted Richard Wright onto the National Committee, along with the well-known proletarian writer Jack Conroy.

According to the statement in the *New Masses*, the new League of American Writers would "fight against imperialist war and fascism," protest "the imprisonment of revolutionary writers and artists," fight "all forms of Negro discrimination or persecution," and show "solidarity with colonial people in their struggles for freedom."

Richard Wright signed. So did Jack Conroy. So did some sixty other writers and artists across the nation, including Langston Hughes,

Theodore Dreiser, James T. Farrell, and Nelson Algren. Wright was painfully aware that he was signing away the club that had given him opportunities he would never otherwise have had. But he had expressed his disapproval. Now he had no choice. If there was going to be a "League of American Writers," he wanted to be in it.

5

BASTARD INTELLECTUAL

September 1934–Spring 1935

Richard Wright had originally joined the John Reed Club to meet other writers. Ironically, it was when the club was about to dissolve that he found exactly what he was looking for.

In the fall of 1934 he and a few friends in the club formed their own writing workshop. They chose not to meet in the club headquarters, where Party ideology hung heavily in the air and constrained their talk. Instead they met at Lawrence Lipton's rambling house on Rush Street, on the near North Side. The bookish, bohemian surroundings reinforced their first principle: freedom of expression. It was the craft of writing that interested them at these meeting, not politics.

They met weekly, on Wednesday evenings, and discussed a manuscript that had been mimeographed and distributed the week before. They had each made their own editorial comments on the manuscript, and at the end of the evening they passed their copy back to the writer. Looking back later, Wright would remember these workshops as an exhilarating education.

I have never heard an abler group of young writers discuss the work of their fellow writers in the same spirit of humor, good fellowship, and seriousness that characterized that group. Most of my short stories were first read to them, or read by them in the mimeographed form. They would tear them to bits, analyze each line, each paragraph, ruthlessly, without fear or favor. I know of no way in which a writer can more quickly obtain a sense of objectivity about his work than through such a method.[1]

Wright was writing stories about the Jim Crow South—the stories that would become *Uncle Tom's Children*. He also wrote "Between the World and Me" during this time, a poignant poem about a lynching. Nelson Algren, Larry Lipton, and Sam Ross were writing novels—all of which would be published several years later with the help of Wright.[2] Abe Aaron was not among them; he was temporarily back with his family in Butler because of the death of his sister.[3]

Wright was the keenest member of the group. Two years before, he could not have dreamed that such an opportunity would come his way. He was certainly the only black man in the whole of Chicago to sit in a white man's home once a week, among white college graduates, discussing literature. And he was there by his own efforts alone— those hours and hours of reading and "scribbling" that his family thought such an outrageous waste of time. He was not only acquiring writing skills; he was also learning about his future readers. He needed to know how white readers responded to his writing. How much did he need to explain? How could he best convey black speech and idiom?

Wright had gained access to a corner of the white world, but his white friends knew almost nothing about *his* world. He had always been secretive about his home life, even with black friends in Jackson. In the winter of 1934–35 he did not turn up to the writers' workshop for several weeks. The others were perplexed. Could it be that he had stopped coming? Had they offended him? Was he ill? Lawrence Lipton suggested that a couple of them pay him a visit to find out whether anything was wrong. But where did he live? "It dawned on us," says Lipton, "that he had never answered that question, had evaded it in one way or another."[4] Years later, Lipton wrote about his brief encounter with another world:

There was a chill intermittent rain when we set out about noon the next day in a cranky old jalopy we managed to rustle up for the trip. After two or three hours of enquiries in neighboring grocery stores, drug stores, restaurants—no one seemed too eager to divulge such information to a carful of white men, who might be debt collectors for all they knew—we managed to pinpoint a street and find some kids who were willing to lead us to the house.

. . . There was the smell of poverty and decay in the hall. . . . A woman came forward—Richard's mother. I told her I was here with some friends of Dick's, and was he home? You could see fear in her eyes. She hesitated to answer.

. . . Silently, uncertainly, she pointed to what looked like a bedroom door. I knocked and, when there was no answer, I called out to him, telling him the purpose of our visit. Still no answer. Puzzled, I was preparing to leave when the door burst open and Dick was out like a shot, making for the front door and calling back after him, "Let's go, let's go."

I hurried out after him, running a block before I caught up with him and brought him back to where the car was parked. . . .

He was plainly hostile, sullen, resentful, close to tears, but we managed to talk him into stopping at a fish house for a chat. He accepted our explanation but was still reserved: no, he hadn't been ill, he was out of work and didn't have the carfare, he was busy looking for a job. All with a mixture of pride and humiliation.

. . .

It was three weeks before we saw Richard again at our Wednesday night workshops. He never alluded to the incident again and we never mentioned it.[5]

THE RELIEF AUTHORITIES FOUND WORK FOR WRIGHT AS A SUPERVISOR AT THE South Side Boys' Club. Located on Michigan Avenue, it was a club for unemployed youths, aged seven to seventeen, who had been in trouble with the police. Wright described them as "a wild and homeless lot, candidates for the clinics, morgues, prisons, reformatories, and the electric chair of the state's death house."[6] Only a few years older than some of them, Wright sympathized with their rebelliousness. City life

seemed to make these boys even angrier than the rebels he had
known in the South. He speculated that the Northern city gave them
more of "a taunting sense of possible achievement," which made them
more sharply resentful of the reality of the ghetto.[7]

He found their conversations engrossing. These boys had stories
that needed to be told. He listened carefully to their talk and jotted
down phrases. "Their figures of speech were as forceful and colorful as
any ever used by English-speaking people."[8] Growing in his mind was
a fictional character he called "Bigger Thomas," after the angry young
bully he had known in Jackson.

The stated purpose of the South Side Boys' Club was to instruct
"needy colored boys" in "respect for law."[9] Its actual purpose, Wright
could see, was to distract these "Negro Dead End Kids," so they would
be less likely to damage the wealthy white property adjoining the
Black Belt.[10] To this end, the club had the best facilities any black
neighborhood center had ever seen—a gym, swimming pool, game
room, and small library.

Wright resented the club's "dressed-up police work."[11] He was convinced that the wealthy board of trustees did not give a "good goddamn" about the boys. Two of the trustees were active in the Chicago
Real Estate Board's campaign to protect white neighborhoods with
restrictive covenants.[12]

In *Native Son*, the novel he would eventually write about Bigger
Thomas, Wright would show the utter hypocrisy of white philanthropy.
Mr. Dalton, Bigger Thomas's white employer, owns the "South Side Real
Estate Company." A millionaire, his fortune has been amassed from the
exorbitant rents paid by black people for their slum kitchenettes. And
yet he has the reputation of a generous benefactor who gives money to
good causes in the Negro community. "Why, only today I sent a dozen
ping-pong tables to the South Side Boys' Club," he proudly tells Boris
Max, Bigger Thomas's defense lawyer.

"My God, man!" Max exclaims. "Will ping-pong keep men from
murdering?"[13]

THERE WAS ANOTHER ASPECT TO WRIGHT'S CROSSING THE LONG, LONELY BRIDGE
into the white social world: white women found him extremely attractive. He was twenty-six, supremely talented, and highly ambitious. He

was handsome. He had a passionate intensity about him. Two women in the writing workshop, Virginia Scott and Joyce Gourfain, were both enraptured. Virginia Scott, a university graduate in her early thirties, typed up the final copy of two or three of his stories for him to submit to publishers. He would visit her home and read his work aloud to her and her mother. Virginia could see that he was more talented than any of the other writers in the group. It seems that her passion was unrequited.

Wright's first affair with a white woman was almost certainly with Joyce Gourfain. She and her husband, Ed, and their two young children lived in a large house on Kimbark Street in Hyde Park, a few blocks away from the University of Chicago. Ed worked in an advertising agency. Because he made more money than anyone else in their circle of friends, he was known, affectionately, as "the Mogul." Small and slight, he was a similar build to Wright in those days, and Wright acquired one of his cast-off suits. The Gourfains were Communists, and Joyce often complained to Wright that Party duties took time away from the writing and painting she was trying to do.

On Wednesday evenings, before the writing workshop, the Gourfains used to invite Wright to dinner. Ed would put up with endless heated discussions about writers and writing, and then Joyce and Wright would catch the El uptown, braving the bitter wind.

Fern Gayden, the Wright family social worker who was a friend of both Wright and Joyce Gourfain, knew they were lovers. She also knew that Joyce was smitten and Wright was not. It seemed to her that Ed tolerated the affair with good grace.[14]

Joyce Gourfain introduced Wright to Henry James's *The Art of the Novel*—one of the books he would refer to as his "bibles." Joyce was a good critic, and keenly aware of Wright's talent. But Wright liked his women to be beautiful. Joyce was not. Diminutive even in the very high heels she liked to wear, she was plain, her acquaintances point out, with a rather theatrical style of dressing.[15]

Once Joyce Gourfain was walking with Wright in town when they passed her husband's office. On an impulse, she decided to call in. "Are you sure you want me to come up?" Wright asked her. She knew what he meant. For a second, she hesitated. Ed was a junior in the business, and was trying hard to get ahead. Then she thought: "To hell with it."

Wright went with her. "He made it very easy," Gourfain recalls. "He was a very sociable guy."[16]

Wright trusted Joyce Gourfain sufficiently to take her briefly to his home—just long enough for her to notice that the apartment was shabby and cluttered with old ladies' objects—doilies, embroidered things.[17] (Langston Hughes, when he visited the house, was similarly struck by the quantity of objects and "religious chromes" everywhere.)[18] Ella and Cleo disappeared as soon as Wright introduced them. Gourfain thought them terribly timid. She also thought that forty-seven-year-old Ella looked far too old to be Wright's mother.

During the day, Wright would turn up at the Gourfains' house with a bunch of typed paper rolled up in his coat pocket and read Joyce his latest draft. He was working on a grim story about a black man caught in the swollen waters of the flooded Mississippi, trying to get help for his wife, who was about to give birth. At first, Joyce was pleased to offer any helpful advice she could:

> I was impressed until he read his stuff so many times in the house I got sick of it. "Down by the Riverside." He read that, I betcha, twenty times in my house. If a new person was there, if the rest of us had heard it ten times before, out comes the manuscript and we had to hear it again. I got so fed up with it.[19]

It is probable that Joyce Gourfain was a model—one of several, no doubt—for Mary Dalton, the white woman Bigger Thomas would accidentally kill. In May 1940, after *Native Son* was published, Virginia Scott intimated as much in a letter she wrote congratulating Wright. Mary Dalton's insensitivity to Bigger's feelings reminded her, she said, of Joyce Gourfain:

> Maybe you remember that Joyce had several colored girls working for her at different times and that they always ate at the table. As you were there for dinner frequently you may have seen what I did. One of the girls had the same interests and enthusiasms we had and thus had plenty to share with us and talk with us about and didn't at all mind mixing. One other one I saw despised having to be with us, and I sensed some little part of what she felt, of what Bigger felt, and was in agony for her.

But Joyce never seemed to see the difference between the two women!
Yet, certainly her "heart was in the right place."[20]

In 1968 Joyce Gourfain told Horace Cayton she hated *Native Son*
when she read it in 1940. She hated the negative depiction of the white
characters.

IN THE SPRING OF 1935, WHILE HE WAS SEEING JOYCE GOURFAIN, WRIGHT FORMED A
similar friendship—this time platonic—with another white woman.
Jane Newton came from an upper-middle-class, solidly Republican
family in small-town Grand Rapids. Her father, Colonel John C. Emery,
was a banker and former national commander of the American Legion.
A rebellious young woman, Jane finished one semester at the University of Michigan, then dropped out to get married. She moved to New
York, joined the Communist Party, divorced, married again, and divorced
again. Her parents no longer talked to her.

Jane was twenty-six, the same age as Wright, and passionate about
literature. Her third husband, Herbert Newton, was one of the prominent black Communists on the South Side. He had spent two years in
Moscow, studying Marxism-Leninism. Back in the U.S., he had been the
only black member of the "Atlanta Six"—a group of Communists arrested
in Georgia for distributing leaflets that demanded an end to lynching.
In 1930–31 the six were in jail, pending trial. Under the Georgia Insurrection Act, they faced the electric chair if convicted. National protest,
fueled by the Communist Party, had them eventually released on bail.
One of the other members of the "Atlanta Six" was a woman called
Mary Dalton.

As a couple, the Newtons were famous in Chicago. In December
1934 they had been evicted from their home on the South Side. Bailiffs
put the furniture on the snow-covered sidewalk. Communist demonstrators moved the items back into the house. The Newtons were
arrested. When they appeared in front of the Renters' Court, an attorney recognized Jane Newton and told the judge that the young woman
came from a "good family." This complicated things.

Herbert Newton was charged with disorderly conduct and sent to the
county jail. Jane was dispatched for ten days to a psychiatric hospital for

observation, before undergoing a public "sanity hearing." It was clear what the judge thought of a white woman from a good family who turned Communist and married a Negro. The Chicago establishment largely agreed with him. After a cursory examination, one of the hospital's staff physicians told the black *Chicago Defender* that Jane Newton appeared to be a "psychopathic case and suffering from manic depression." He added: "Her Communist sentiments are part of the mania."[21]

At the sanity hearing, Jane Newton was asked questions like: "Do you consider your choice of a Negro man for a husband anti-social?" But the three court physicians agreed that nothing gave them the slightest reason to suspect she was mentally disordered. Indeed, they went so far as to declare her "a brilliant individual."[22]

Wright greatly admired Jane Newton's courage and integrity. He began to drop by. Jane was looking after her young daughter and expecting a second child. She enjoyed the visits of this "fresh-faced," smiling young man. She urged him to read *The Possessed* and *The Brothers Karamazov*. He read his work aloud to her. She never hesitated to say what she thought:

> He had two common expressions, when he listened to criticism: in one, he leaned forward, his mouth a little open, his eyes on the face of the speaker; in the other he drew his shoulders up, lowered his eyes and set his jaw, making him the perfect picture of a person rejecting a proposal and withdrawing to the comfort of his own opinion.[23]

SINCE HIS MEETING WITH LOUIS WIRTH AT THE UNIVERSITY OF CHICAGO, WRIGHT had become an avid reader of psychology and sociology—books that related neurotic behavior and crime to environment. He was struck by the emphasis Chicago Sociology placed on the "life history" approach to subjects like race. These social scientists valued autobiographical narratives told in the individual's own words as a means of analyzing the way attitudes were formed and shaped.

While he was making notes at the South Side Boys' Club, Wright had another idea. Why not write a book about the black Communist leaders he was meeting? They were every bit as intrepid, daredevil, and rebellious as the Bigger Thomases, but their revolt was strategic—

political rather than individual. What had made these men turn to the Communist Party? Wright wondered. What had awakened their interest in social issues? He thought he would write a book of profiles called *Heroes, Red and Black.*

There was, for example, Herbert Newton, whose brush with the electric chair in Georgia had in no way diminished his daring. In Chicago, in the summer of 1932, he had been at a demonstration of black workers protesting an attempt to close a Negro forum in Ellis Park.[24] Before the marchers reached their final destination, Ellis Park, the leaders—David R. Poindexter and Charles Reed—had already been arrested. In the park, Herbert Newton climbed a tree and, with the aid of a megaphone, reminded the workers for fifteen minutes about their right to free speech. *Left Front* reported the incident gleefully.

> The paunchy police, unable to climb to him, endeavored to dislodge him by throwing bricks, but discovered that bricks obeyed the laws of gravity, and landed on their own heads. Finally, when the fire department arrived, Newton descended. Fourteen leaders were arrested. But the fight was on. Since then the park has been open to speakers, and renamed Newton Forum Park by the workers.[25]

The most persuasive and mesmerizing of the Communist orators who regularly spoke in the main Negro Forum in Washington Park was David R. Poindexter. A rebel from the South, he worked at the stockyards. He was always near the front of the demonstrations, and regularly arrested and beaten up by the police. Jane Newton recalled:

> "Dex" . . . was a slim, dark fellow with a volatile disposition and a ready flow of speech, which seemed to have caught Dick's fancy . . . Dex liked to speak on street corners, even in situations where it would be dangerous to do so. (I have seen him in a meeting, his words never stopping until a policeman took him by the collar and cracked his head as if it were an egg.)[26]

Poindexter agreed to be the first of Wright's case studies. Wright hoped to tell Poindexter's story in such a way as to "make his life more intelligible to others than it was to himself."[27] For several weeks he went around to Poindexter's basement apartment on Indiana Avenue. "I'm after the things that made you a Communist," he told him. He listened to Poindexter's reminiscences, writing notes as fast as he could, then went home and typed them up. He was pleased with his idea. He felt he was reclaiming history that would otherwise be lost.

As an adolescent, Poindexter had witnessed the terrifying formation of a lynch mob in Nashville, Tennessee. His account inspired Wright's story "Big Boy Leaves Home," in which Big Boy watches helplessly while his friend Bobo is lynched on the hillside. After his experiences in the Jim Crow South, Poindexter dreamed of going North to organize guns and men, then returning to the South to take vengeance on whites. Instead, while working at various jobs in Chicago and Detroit he came to see white workers as his "class brothers," and he joined the Communist Party.[28]

But Poindexter was already in trouble with the Party. Not a man to submit readily to authority, he regularly stood up at meetings and criticized the leaders. Wright, too, was acquiring the reputation in the Party as a wayward individualist.

One day, Wright was "scribbling furiously" at Poindexter's home when Oliver Law called in.[29] Before rising up through the Communist ranks, Law had spent years in a black regiment in the U.S. Army. He was, Wright writes in *Black Boy*, "tall, taciturn, soldierly." Law looked at Wright's pile of notes and asked what he was doing. Wright told him he was writing a book of biographical sketches about black Communists. Law looked horrified. Wright took the opportunity to tell him he would also like to write about *him*. "I'm not interested," Law snapped.

Wright soon realized that his idea was quite naïve. The black leaders were already wary of him; now they more or less suspected him of espionage. Reluctantly, he gave up the idea. It was a loss for black history. Just over a year later, Oliver Law went to fight in the Spanish civil war. With his years of army training, he became the first black man in American history to become the commander of a mostly white unit, the Lincoln Battalion. He died at the front, in the foothills of Madrid, at the age of thirty-four. In his eulogy, a comrade said: "Some day, the working class of America will properly acknowledge the role this brave Negro Communist played in the fight for freedom."[30]

Today we know almost nothing about Oliver Law. Herbert Newton and David Poindexter, courageous black freedom fighters, have also been forgotten. Wright's rough notes still exist among his papers at Yale University.

SOMETIME AFTER THE TENSE ENCOUNTER WITH OLIVER LAW AT POINDEXTER'S HOME, Wright was in bed with severe chest pains, scarcely able to breathe. Oliver Law turned up at his house and announced that Harry Haywood wanted to see him. Haywood, who had recently arrived from New York, was the new black leader on the South Side.

Wright waited until he had recovered his strength before going to see him. In *Black Boy* he would describe Harry Haywood (he calls him "Buddy Nealson") as short, with "thick lips," a "furtive manner," and a "greasy, sweaty look." An asthmatic, Haywood would "snort at unexpected intervals." Wright disliked him on sight.

Haywood asked him bluntly why he was interviewing David Poindexter. Were they friends? Wright explained that his interest in Poindexter was not political; he was more interested in the details of his Southern upbringing. In fact, he had written a short story based on a lynching episode in Poindexter's childhood. Haywood seemed not to be listening. "We want you to organize a committee against the high cost of living," he told Wright.[31]

Wright protested that he needed all his spare time for writing. Haywood told him that the Party had made its decision. Wright knew what that meant: compliance or expulsion. For the next few weeks he spent several evenings a week discussing housing prices and tabulating the price of groceries with other Communists. He resented every minute of it and longed to be home, writing.

For the next two and a half years, Harry Haywood did more than anyone else to alienate Richard Wright from the Communist Party. He, too, would have made an interesting profile in Wright's projected book. According to his autobiography, *Black Bolshevik*,[32] he quit school in eighth grade. Like Wright, he was fired up by H. L. Mencken's "searing diatribes against WASP cultural idols" in the *American Mercury*, and, like Wright, he had an "excruciatingly monotonous" job at the Chicago Post Office. Ten years older than Wright, he fought in World War I in France, enjoying a brief respite from Jim Crow humiliations, and returned to Chicago in the summer of 1919, in time to witness the worst of the nation's race riots. Three years later he joined the Communist Party, and spent five years at the famous Lenin School in Moscow.

When he came back to Chicago in late 1934, Harry Haywood was eager to prove his credentials. The influence of the Communist Party was growing on the South Side. There had been huge demonstrations of unemployed black workers. More than once, the police had shot into the crowd. In *Black Bolshevik*, Haywood writes that he wanted to strengthen the solidarity between black and white workers. He does not mention his vigorous campaign to rid the South Side Communist branches of "Trotskyists" and "reformers." He was known to have a passion for trials and expulsions. One of his targets was David Poindexter. Another was Richard Wright. To the comrades, he denounced Wright as "a smuggler of reaction," a "petty bourgeois degenerate," and a "bastard intellectual" with an "anti-leadership attitude."[33]

William Patterson, a black Communist lawyer who was in Chicago at the time, admitted later that Haywood was an insensitive leader whose time in Chicago was marked by conflict. Patterson himself had little sympathy for Wright's individualism, but he could see the nature of the clash. "Harry Haywood, then top organizer on the Southside, did not exhibit the slightest appreciation that he was dealing with a sensitive, immature creative genius with whom it was necessary to exercise great patience."[34]

SOON HAYWOOD SUMMONED WRIGHT TO ANOTHER MEETING. THIS TIME THEY were joined by John P. Davis, a black executive from Washington, who was organizing the forthcoming National Negro Congress. A short, swaggering man, Davis made Wright think of Napoleon. They proposed to Wright that he go to Switzerland as a youth delegate. From there he would proceed to the Soviet Union. Wright was dumfounded. It seemed so bizarre that one minute he was starving in the South Side, and the next he was offered a trip abroad, with his fare paid by the Party. The problem was, he did not want to go anywhere as a delegate for the Party. He wanted to see the world through his own eyes—independently. Nor could he abandon his writing just then. The writing workshop was proving an invaluable education, and he was using every spare moment to write. He told them he had writing commitments. There was a silence. Then Davis called him a fool. Wright was furious. "A breath more of anger and I would have driven my fist into his face."[35] As he walked home he made up his mind to leave the Party.

As the Communist leaders saw it, Wright had signed up to work for the revolution, and yet he seemed to think he was too important to do his share. As Wright saw it, he had been terrorized by white racists and persecuted by black levelers for eighteen years in the South, and he was damned if he had come to the North to allow black Communists to bully him.

At the next branch meeting, Wright asked that his membership be dropped from the Party rolls. It was not due to ideological difference, he explained; he simply did not wish to be bound to the Party's directions. Harry Haywood moved that the decision be deferred.

After that, Wright was left alone. In the end, the Party preferred to have him, at least formally, within the ranks. From now on, Wright did not attend branch meetings and he avoided most of his former Party comrades. He found himself missing the "incessant analysis" that went on at meetings, but whenever friends told him about the latest factional fighting, he felt relieved to be out of it. He was lonely, but he had more time for his writing.

One evening, a group of black Communists came to his house. "The party wants you to attend a meeting Sunday," they told him.[36] Wright was bewildered. What was this about? With some prodding, the comrades eventually told him that the Party was going to make an example of David Poindexter, who had proved himself to be an enemy of the working class. Wright felt quite frightened: would this turn into his own trial? But the writer in him was "keenly curious."

He arrived on Sunday afternoon to find Poindexter sitting at a table in the front of the hall, alone. He looked "distraught." Looking around the room, Wright nevertheless felt a pang of nostalgia. These were people with ideals. The whites among them did not hate black people. Some of them had black spouses. How could he not find this group heartwarming? And yet, these people could not accept him. Hardly anyone spoke to him. The leaders gave him hostile glances and looked away. It made him nervous and jumpy. As he saw it, he himself was on trial by proxy.

Poindexter's trial began. Wright observed that it was brilliantly orchestrated. Three hours of speech making took place before the spotlight landed on Poindexter. The first speaker talked about world fascism and the dangers of Germany, Italy, and Japan; the second praised the Soviet Union as the workers' state; the third described the economic disparities within capitalist America; the fourth outlined the plight of Chicago's South Side. The room was electric with a sense of the life-or-death importance of the struggle ahead, and the imperative need for unity and solidarity.

Only then did they hear the charges against the rebel individual among them. The leaders said nothing. It was Poindexter's comrades who got up, one after another, to complain. Finally, Poindexter stood up, broken. "Comrades, I'm guilty of all the charges, all of them."[37]

Wright felt too uncomfortable to stay until the end, even though leaving meetings early was strictly against Party rules. He was acutely conscious of the warning to him in that long afternoon's cathartic performance. He had to admit that he had been filled with emotion by the genuine solidarity in the room. He agreed with everything the speakers had said. He knew that in order to be effective, they had to act as a group. He would always be the "bastard intellectual."[38]

6

CROSSING THE DIVIDE

Chicago: April 1935–May 1937

At the George Cleveland Hall Library, Wright came across Gertrude Stein's collection of novellas, *Three Lives*. He was particularly excited by "Melanctha," a story depicting the anguished love affair of two black characters. Somehow, Stein had managed to capture the musicality, cadence, and rhythm of Southern Negro speech—so much so that Wright felt as if his grandmother was standing again before him.

Gertrude Stein's fractured writing was ridiculed in left-wing circles. So were her "bourgeois" values. When *Everybody's Autobiography* appeared in 1937, Samuel Sillen would proclaim in the *New Masses*: "The mama of dada is going gaga." The criticism worried Wright. Could it be that he was worshipping decadence? He sometimes read his own stories aloud to David Poindexter and his white wife, June. Now, to test the validity of his response, he arranged to read "Melanctha" to a handful of Poindexter's black stockyard worker friends in the Poindexters' front room. Their reaction delighted him. "Enthralled," he writes, "they slapped their thighs, howled, laughed, stomped and interrupted me constantly to comment upon the characters."[1] It reinforced his convic-

tion, frowned upon in Party circles, that contemporary modernist writing was as legitimate as naturalist writing.

Wright loved the more experimental use of language and the technical innovations he discovered in James Joyce, Stein, and the poetry
of T. S. Eliot. He was now writing a novel *Lawd Today!*, a humorous
narrative about four black Chicago postal workers, their working life
and diversions in the South Side. Like James Joyce's *Ulysses* (just published in the United States, after scraping through an obscenity trial),
the action in *Lawd Today!* takes place over twenty-four hours. One of
the postal workers, remarking that white folks could be downright
crazy, tells the others: "I saw in the papers the other day where some
old white woman over in Paris said a rose is a rose is a rose is a rose."
The final section is called "Rats' Alley"—a reference to "The Waste-
land:" "I think we are in rats' alley/Where the dead men lost their
bones."

Lawd Today! contained no heroes, no moral message, none of the
revolutionary optimism of "proletarian literature." Wright was well
aware that the Party would deplore it. But he never intended to be an
ambassador for Communism. Nor did he care to be an ambassador for
black people. Jake Jackson and his friends are blundering, warm fools
who divert themselves with bantering and belly laughs, women, gambling, and bridge. They believe in a whole array of superstitions and
folk remedies; they despise Communists; they firmly believe that "Big
Bill" Thompson, the corrupt white Republican mayor, is on their side;
they boast about deceiving their women; and they lack any pride in the
race. Only toward each other do they show any solidarity.

Never before had a black American writer written so satirically
about life in the black ghetto. *Lawd Today!* is Wright's most modern
novel and some would say his best. The bleakness of the South Side is
relieved by the humor and warmth of the characters. But publishers
were uncomfortable with it.

By March 1935 the manuscript was doing the rounds of publishers.
James Henle, at the Vanguard Press, called in James Farrell as a reader.
Both men thought the novel "extremely promising," but "marred by
repetition and prolixity." James Henle told Wright: "If you will put
some more effort into it I think it very likely that we will want to publish this manuscript."[2] Wright revised the novel on and off for the next

two years. In February 1937 he sent the revised version back to the Vanguard Press. James Henle rejected it. One publisher after another rejected it. Finally Wright abandoned it.

In 1961, a few months after Wright's death, his wife took the manuscript out of a drawer and sent it to Wright's literary agent, Paul Reynolds, and Wright's last publisher, William Targ of World Publishing. The two men dismissed it as an early novel that Wright himself would not have wanted to see published. "It would be a disservice to Richard Wright to publish this work," Bill Targ said. "Wright fails completely to engage our sympathy for any of his characters."[3] Paul Reynolds agreed.

Ellen Wright did not. She wrote to Reynolds:

> I've always tried to be as objective as possible regarding Dick's writing, even though I was his wife. . . . In the case of *Lawd Today!*, far from being a disservice to him in publishing this book as Bill suggests, I feel rather to the contrary. And while it is true that the characters do not come off sympathetically, this should not be, I think, a criterion for the publishability of a book. . . . His style seemed to me taut and poetic (something like that used in *Uncle Tom's Children*), with a wry gallows humour about it.
>
> You suggest that Dick must have had grave doubts about it else he would have submitted it to you. I'm fairly certain I know what happened. He wrote this book when he was still in the grips of the Communist party, and as frequently happened, they tried to control what he wrote, sacrificing truth, even though sordid, to political expediency. To them, the Negro must always be depicted as honest, hardworking, downtrodden, discriminated against, etc, when in truth, the lack of the first two virtues was often the result of being downtrodden and discriminated against.[4]

Ellen Wright persisted in the face of several rejections. Finally, in 1963, the novel was published by Walker & Company. The publisher, mistaking Wright's experimental punctuation for ignorance, painstakingly corrected the style. It also altered or deleted the numerous colloquialisms and obscenities that help make this novel so colorful and modern.[5]

In April 1963 Gwendolyn Brooks, the black poet, reviewed *Lawd*

Today! in the *Chicago Sun-Times*. She admired the "beautiful prose" and the dialogue—"so sharp, so real, you feel that you are hearing it." She thought the comedy "superb" and the horror "chillingly sharp." She added, defensively: "People like Jake are not in the majority. Their portion, I tremblingly estimate, is not even .30 per cent. But they do exist."[6]

James Baldwin, astonished when this novel of Wright's was published posthumously, found himself reassessing Wright's writing career. Wright's interests and stylistic range turned out to be so much more complex than everyone had thought. *Lawd Today!* was "not afflicted with any of the Stalinist garbage . . . of *Native Son*," Baldwin exclaimed. "It in full of niggers! It is full of life! A beautiful book."[7]

WRIGHT MADE HIS FIRST TRIP TO NEW YORK IN APRIL 1935, HITCHHIKING THERE with Chicago friends. The occasion was the first American Writers' Congress, called by the Communist Party to establish the League of American Writers.

Wright was "startled," he writes, by his first glimpse of New York as they came in along the Hudson River. New York seemed so much cleaner and whiter than Chicago. It did not have the factories or smoke pall. The people looked better dressed and walked with purpose. "Could I live here?" he wondered.

He turned up early at Carnegie Hall, where the conference was being held, and asked for accommodation. The conference organizers looked embarrassed. One of them disappeared to make phone calls. Wright felt terribly alone. That evening, he attended the opening session at Mecca Temple and still did not know where he would sleep. The hall was packed. He listened listlessly to the speeches and wondered why he had come. After the session, one of the organizers gave him an address in Greenwich Village. Gratefully, Wright took the slip of paper. It was late at night when he got to the house. A white man opened the door, took one look at him, and shut the door in his face. In the early hours of the morning, a Chicago club member found a bed for him in a friend's kitchen.

The next afternoon, Wright asked directions to Harlem. He walked through streets filled with black people and discovered, to his amazement, that there were almost no hotels for blacks in the area. He spotted a clean-looking hotel, where black people were going in and out.

He went in. To his surprise, a white clerk was sitting behind the desk. Wright hesitated. "I'd like a room." The man looked at him. "Not here." Finally Wright found a bed in the Harlem YMCA at West 135th Street and slept for twelve hours.

At the conference he gave a fervent speech in favor of retaining the John Reed Club, but the vote went overwhelmingly against him. In *Black Boy* he writes: "New York held no further interest and the next morning I left for home."

There are other indications that, despite his depressing experience with accommodation, Wright managed to have a good time in New York. As well as his white friends and acquaintances from Chicago, there were twenty-one black delegates at the congress. America's most famous writers were there. And Wright himself was being talked about as an up-and-coming black writer.[8] Herbert Kline, a Chicago John Reed Club friend who had moved to New York and was now the editor of the New York Communist magazine *New Theatre*, remembers an unusually enjoyable evening with Wright:

> Langston Hughes had invited Dick to a Harlem rent party, and he got us invited too. . . . We were six whites and one black, together taking the subway to a Harlem artist's apartment near 125th Street. . . .
>
> When we arrived we found a grand party going on. Other guests, besides Langston, included . . . various artists, dancers, actors, and musicians.
>
> We had a wonderful time—dancing, singing, gabbing, arguing, drinking wine, beer, some hard stuff, eating—there was plenty of soul food and Jewish delicatessen. During the lively discussions, an idea struck me for a special issue of *New Theatre*.
>
> "Does anyone know of an American magazine publishing a whole issue on Negroes in the theatre arts with talents like the ones assembled in this room?"
>
> Nobody did. But everyone in there responded to the idea, and right then individuals promised some of the articles and poems for our selections. Only Richard Wright didn't complete the one-act play he had pledged. He had to advise us at the last minute that his publisher was pressing him to deliver his novel or void the contract. I always regretted the loss of that play.[9]

Kline's memory was faulty. Langston Hughes was not in New York at the time and had not yet met Wright. Kline does not give the date of the party, but it definitely took place during Wright's 1935 visit to New York. The Negro issue of *New Theatre* came out in July 1935.[10]

Among Wright's papers is a note from his friend Abe Chapman: "We'll be at 'Waiting for Lefty' Sunday afternoon and at 'Awake and Sing' Tuesday night—hope we'll see you there." In all likelihood, Wright went along, for when he got back to Chicago, he wrote to his relief supervisor, Mary Wirth:

> My dear Mrs. Wirth,
>
> I thought you would be interested to know that my trip as a delegate to the American Writers' Congress was successful. I spent about nine days in all in New York City, and followed all the proceedings of the Congress. . . .
>
> I also had time to see some of the plays on Broadway: *Till the Day I Die, Waiting for Lefty, Tobacco Road, Black Pit, Awake and Sing;* etc.[11] The whole thing was enjoyable, and I thank you most heartily for the aid you gave me in this direction.
>
> Sincerely yours,
> Richard Wright[12]

According to his Jackson schoolfriend Essie Lee Ward, who was now living in Chicago with her mother, Wright returned from New York full of excitement about the huge May Day rally in Manhattan.[13] In his story "Fire and Cloud," Wright would describe the euphoria of black and white workers marching together, singing revolutionary songs. His hero says to himself in exulted tones: "Freedom belongs to the strong!" It was something Wright often said himself.[14]

UNTIL NOW, THE COMMUNIST PARTY—AND ITS CULTURAL FRONT, THE JOHN REED Club—had been Wright's sole means of entering the white world. But the Party itself—like the black community—was on the margins of society, an oppositional group, much maligned, and always on the lookout for the Red Squad that regularly arrested its members. Now an opening into a broader world came from none other than the United

States government. It was to provide Wright with paid employment. Moreover, it paid him to write.

In May 1935 Roosevelt set up the Works Progress Administration. Like the Federal Emergency Relief Administration, the WPA was a program of work relief that gave people jobs rather than the dole. The aim was to set people to work on projects that would benefit the country as a whole. The unemployed were to build civic buildings, roads, bridges, and dams.

It was the Federal Arts Project, established two months later, that interested Wright. A subsection of the WPA, it provided jobs for writers, journalists, librarians, teachers, artists, actors, and musicians currently on the relief rolls. The various divisions all aimed to do something for the American people. The Federal Theatre Project would bring performances to people who otherwise never went to the theater. The Arts Project would employ artists to paint murals in public buildings, to make sculptures, and design brochures and posters. WPA orchestras paid new attention to American composers. The Farm Security Administration's historical section would send photographers out to record the desolation of rural America. The writers in the Federal Writers' Project would capture regions of America and the voices of different ethnic groups.

No sooner had the Illinois Writers' Project been formed than Richard Wright was in Mary Wirth's office asking to be put on the rolls. She explained that in order to qualify, employees needed to have had something published. Wright produced his dossier: two published short stories and thirteen published poems. Mrs. Wirth immediately signed him on as a supervisor.

WPA wages were low, so as not to compete with private enterprise, but for most of the younger artists, it was the best salary they had ever enjoyed. Apprentice writers were paid $85 a month, skilled writers $93.50. As a supervisor, Wright's monthly earnings were $125. His relief jobs had paid $50 a month. He and his family left their miserable lodgings at 5636 Grove Avenue and moved to a more spacious apartment at 3743 Indiana Avenue. They would stay there until Wright left Chicago.

The Illinois Writers' Project employed some two hundred writers. Nine were black—a healthier percentage than in any other state.[15]

Wright soon found himself surrounded by friends from the old John Reed Club—Abe Aaron, Sam Ross, Stuart Engstrand, Larry Lipton, Samuel Sillen, and Nelson Algren. (The writing workshop came to a standstill around this time, doubtless due to the distraction of the new job.) Wright was the only one of them to be appointed as a supervisor. And until Arna Bontemps got a job with the Illinois Writers' Project in 1937, Wright was the only black supervisor. In terms of integrated work, he had probably scored the most prestigious job for a black man in the whole of Chicago.

The thirty-hour-week job provided the opportunity to meet other writers, as well as people from all walks of life. The writers went out to research a region, a club, a building, or a social event and produced weekly assignments, four or five pages long. Best of all, the job left them time for their own writing.

Considerable emphasis was placed on worker communities and ethnic groups. But the writers were essentially free to follow their own interests. Sam Ross, a swimming champion and jazz buff, wrote about the culture of swimming and jazz. Abe Aaron, who had worked at the post office, interviewed postal workers and cab drivers. Margaret Walker passed in a short story in Negro dialect. Wright wrote a ten-page essay on "Ethnological Aspects of Chicago's Black Belt," a shorter essay on the Chicago Urban League, and compiled a "Bibliography on the Negro in Chicago."[16] Two other essays describe amusement facilities in the Black Belt.[17]

For the first time in American history, the Federal Writers' Project regarded black life as an integral part of the American experience. Plans were hatched for books on Negro history and folklore. Dozens of WPA writers in the South (nearly all of them white) were sent out to interview more than two thousand former slaves. It was exciting for Wright to see that Negro life was at last being taken seriously. And not just by a group of John Reed Club Communists, but by the American government itself.

ON THE EVENING OF 24 SEPTEMBER 1935, RICHARD WRIGHT WAS AMONG THE throng in a South Side tavern listening to the big fight on the radio. Joe Louis was fighting the white American Max Baer.

Until recently, blacks had been excluded from big league boxing. Twenty-year-old Joe Louis had come into the limelight in June, when he had astonished the world by beating the much taller and heavier Italian giant, Primo Carnera. Max Baer was considered Joe Louis's most serious competition as world heavyweight champion. And young Joe Louis had casually decided to marry his sweetheart just two hours before making his way to New York's Yankee Stadium!

The fight had generated enormous publicity, and the press gave great emphasis to race. Joe Louis was described in the white press as the "jungle killer," the "black panther," and the "brown bomber."[18] In the black community, Wright wrote, Joe Louis represented "all the balked dreams of revenge, all the secretly visualized moments of retaliation."

Joe Louis won. "Good Gawd Almighty! Yes, by Jesus it could be done!" In his first piece of journalism—an essay for the *New Masses* called "Joe Louis Uncovers Dynamite"—Wright captured the wild jubilation that broke out on the South Side, as it did in every black community in the nation.[19]

Two hours after the fight the area between South Parkway and Prairie Avenue on 47th Street was jammed with no less than twenty-five thousand Negroes, joy-mad and moving to they didn't know where. Clasping hands, they formed long writhing snake-lines and wove in and out of traffic. They seeped out of doorways, oozed from alleys, trickled out of tenements, and flowed down the street; a fluid mass of joy. White storekeepers hastily closed their doors against the tidal wave and stood peeping through plate glass with blanched faces.

Wright himself, one of Joe Louis's most ardent fans, was triumphant. In *Lawd Today!* the post office workers recall the fight as they sort mail:

"Lawd, it sure made me feel good all the way down in my guts when old Joe socked Baer."

"I said to myself, let them white folks *chew* that."

. . .

"Just think now . . . He married a gal, goes into the ring the same day, and knocks a guy coocoo!"

———

DURING THE WINTER OF 1935–36, LANGSTON HUGHES VISITED CHICAGO. EVER since reading "I Have Seen Black Hands" in the *New Masses* in the summer of 1934, he had wanted to meet Richard Wright. He and Arna Bontemps, a friend who had just moved to Chicago with his family, tried to look up Wright in the Chicago telephone book, without success. The following weekend, they went to a South Side party, and there he was.

Hughes liked him immediately. As well as their writing, he and Wright had left-wing politics in common. Hughes was not a Party member, but he was a prominent fellow traveler who published frequently in Communist papers. After that first meeting, whenever he visited Chicago, Langston Hughes would drop in to see Wright at his home.

The politically moderate Arna Bontemps was surprised to find Wright a "flaming young Communist." He noticed that Wright did not dance the whole evening. Wright seemed to him a very serious fellow. Soon afterward, Bontemps met Wright again in the downtown Loop district.

> I was standing on the corner waiting for a Cottage Grove streetcar, and he ran across the street and said, "Look here, I have just three cents. I need a nickel to get uptown." This was the Depression and such things were not unusual. I tried to give him a nickel, but he said, "No, I just want two cents." I gave him the two cents, and he said, "I'll bring it to you Friday night."
>
> I thought he was joking, but sure enough, Friday night he came. He walked about two miles to our house and brought the two pennies. After that, every Friday night he used to come over. We'd have dinner and . . . he'd begin reading us some of the stories he had written which later went into *Uncle Tom's Children*.[20]

In person and in their writings, Hughes and Bontemps were far more mild-mannered and "ambassadorial" than Wright cared to be, but he respected these men. The following spring he praised Bontemps's new novel: "In that limited and almost barren field known as the Negro novel, Arna Bontemps's *Black Thunder* fills a yawning gap and fills it competently."[21]

Wright and Bontemps had Seventh Day Adventism in common, and

Wright used to like to discuss it with his friend. Bontemps came from Louisiana (his unusual name was French Creole), where his father had been a lay minister in the Seventh Day Adventist Church. Before coming to Chicago, he had taught at a Seventh Day Adventist black college in Alabama until the white college principal had accused him of subverting the students and ordered him to burn dozens of his books. In an atmosphere of racial tension inflamed by Alabama's long, drawn-out trial of the Scottsboro boys, Bontemps had bundled his wife, children, and books into his dilapidated Ford and fled.

In Chicago, he was again teaching at an Adventist school. He would have preferred not to, but it was the Depression and he had a large family to support and jobs for black professionals were almost impossible to come by. Once again, the school officials were attacking the reading and writing he did outside school hours as "devil's work."

EARLY IN 1936 WRIGHT SUBMITTED HIS LYNCHING STORY, "BIG BOY LEAVES Home," to an anthology of contemporary writing, *The New Caravan*. He received a prompt acceptance letter, with a fifty-dollar check. The anthology was due out in November.[22] It was not a Communist publication; all the other writers were white; the selection was on merit alone. It was Wright's first publication in a book, and it was the first time he had been paid for his writing.

In January his long poem "Transcontinental" was published in the Communist magazine *International Literature*. It was a six-page road-poem, a humorous, sarcastic song to America, which turned Whitman's celebratory "Leaves of Grass" on its head. A typical Wright fantasy, the hitchhikers take over the car, the powerless pushing the powerful to one side.

> HALT
> You shall not pass our begging thumbs
> America is ours
> This car is commandeered
> America is ours
> Take your ringed fingers from the steering wheel
> Take your polished shoe off the gas

We'll drive and let you be the hitch-hiker
We'll show you how to pass 'em up . . .

For the rest of the poem, the workers drive through America, "taking the curves with determination," waving at Manhattan "careening over the miles," passing farms, "vaulting Washington's Monument," and swinging southward, where they defy Jim Crow:

Come on You Negroes Come On
There's room
Not in the back but front seat
We're heading for the highway of Self-Determination

Wright was writing poetry, short stories, and revising his South Side novel, *Lawd Today!* He had also begun another novel, *Tarbaby's Dawn*, set in Jackson, Mississippi, in the 1920s. Tarbaby shares many of Wright's own experiences. Brought up in a fervently religious atmosphere, he is lonely, rebellious, and frequently whipped. He is involved in gang warfare. His mother pressures him until he submits to the ritual of baptism. Finally, he runs away to Memphis, where he wanders up and down Beale Street, feeling lost and bewildered.[23]

AT THE BEGINNING OF JANUARY 1936 WRIGHT WAS TRANSFERRED FROM THE Writers' Project to the Federal Theatre Project, where he worked as a publicity agent for the Negro Theatre.[24] He had not had time to write a play for Herbert Kline's magazine, but he was interested in the theater and believed he would learn a great deal from working with a theater group. That spring he made a trip to New York to see Orson Welles's and John Houseman's all-black production of *Macbeth*. He was dazzled by the colorful costumes and the innovation of the Haitian jungle setting. With the Federal Negro Theatre in Harlem as a model, Wright hoped to generate a lively Negro theater group in Chicago.

Up till then, the Chicago Negro Theatre had been performing standard Negro minstrel shows. Wright persuaded the Federal Theatre administrators to replace the highly conventional director, a white woman, with Charles DeSheim, a talented Jew who had emerged from the radical Group Theater in New York and who shared Wright's taste for contemporary realism. DeSheim had just directed the Chicago production of Clifford Odets's popular left-wing play *Waiting for Lefty*.

Wright proposed to DeSheim that the company mount Paul Green's *Hymn to the Rising Sun*, a grim one-act play about a Southern chain gang. DeSheim readily agreed. The company moved into the Princess Theater, in the Loop. Things looked promising. But Wright hit a snag with the black actors. They thought Green's play denigrating to Negroes. It was neither entertaining nor uplifting, they complained, to act the part of black prisoners whipped and debased on stage. Wright argued that this was realism. One actor said he came from the South and he had never seen a chain gang.

What did they want? Wright demanded angrily. Did they want clowns, mammies, and watermelons? Did they prefer the old minstrel stereotypes? Surely theater should be confrontational! The actors disagreed. "We want a play that will make the public love us," one of them said.[25] Wright, disgusted, told himself that whites were right: "Negroes were children and would never grow up."

From the actors' point of view, Wright was the traitor. First he had chosen a white director, then a white playwright. He had them acting in a play in which Negroes were humiliated. Mammies might be stereotypes, but so were black prisoners. They tried to get DeSheim dismissed in favor of a black director. When Wright stood up for DeSheim, one of the women in the company hissed in his face: "Lawd, Ah sho hates a whiteman's nigger."[26] There was nothing for it: Wright asked the Federal Theatre authorities to transfer him to another section. He ended up in an experimental white company.

The difficulties for the Negro Theatre did not end with Wright's departure. Rehearsals for *Hymn to the Rising Sun* went ahead, with DeSheim continuing as director. On opening night, 14 October 1936, a crowd of some three hundred people stood in front of the Princess Theatre waiting for tickets. The doors did not open. At the final hour, an order had come from the Illinois Federal Theatre director to stop the production. He claimed that the play's "nauseating brutality" would alienate audiences.[27]

The play was never produced in Chicago. DeSheim resigned in protest. The experience reinforced Wright's determination to leave for

New York as soon as he could. Chicago was beginning to feel like a backwater, with a national reputation for conservatism. Earlier that year, a friend, Meyer Levin, had his play *Model Tenement* stopped by the Catholic mayor of Chicago, Ed Kelly. The mayor also banned the play about Georgia sharecroppers that had enjoyed such a sensational run in New York: *Tobacco Road*. In the case of *Hymn to the Rising Sun*, the censorship had come from the Illinois Theatre Project itself. In other cities, the Federal Theatre Project had a reputation for radicalism. Not in Chicago.

In an article called "Hymn to the Sinking Sun," Wright declared that the "heavy hand of reaction" had fallen upon black people in Chicago. "Not in the old, accustomed places such as discrimination in jobs and relief, but in the realm of the theatre and expression." He was incredulous that Chicago, once hailed as the literary capital of the United States, had changed so drastically. "Did these things happen in Chicago—the Chicago of Sandburg, of Dreiser, of Anderson, of Masters?"[28]

In just two years' time, in 1938, the House Un-American Activities Committee (HUAC) would make the Federal Theatre Project one of its first targets. And *Hymn to the Rising Sun* was one of several plays that HUAC would denounce as "Communistic."

THE NATIONAL NEGRO CONGRESS OPENED IN CHICAGO ON 14 FEBRUARY 1936. The president was A. Philip Randolph, head of the nation's first black labor union, the Brotherhood of Sleeping Car Porters. The intention of the three-day congress was to form a black united front, rather like the Communist "Popular Front." There were urgent reasons for black solidarity. When Mussolini had invaded Ethiopia in October 1935, most black Americans had seen it as yet another attempt by whites to destroy blacks.[29] At home, the average income for blacks was one-third to one-half that of whites. In the North almost 50 percent of black families were on relief. In the South there was a lynching every three weeks on average, and Roosevelt, afraid of losing white support in the South, had refused to support the antilynching bill.

On the last day of the congress, Richard Wright chaired a session called "Negro Artists and Writers in the Changing Social Order." The panelists included Langston Hughes and Arna Bontemps. In the *New Masses*, Wright wrote that the congress had generated "new hope" for blacks.[30]

ONE OF THE PEOPLE WHO ATTENDED WRIGHT'S SESSION AT THE NATIONAL NEGRO Congress was young Margaret Walker. After the session, she went up to Langston Hughes and asked whether he would look at her poems. Hughes turned to Wright, who was standing nearby. "If you people really get a writing group together," he told Wright, "don't forget to include this girl."[31]

By May, Margaret Walker was convinced that Wright had forgotten her. But one day she came home to find a penny postcard in her mailbox inviting her to the first meeting of the South Side Writers' Group for black writers. It was to be held at the home of the poet Bob Davis, on the South Side.

Walker describes the evening in her biography of Wright. She was nervous. Before she left home, she fussed endlessly over her clothes. As a straitlaced Southern girl, the daughter of a Methodist preacher, she wore starched cotton print dresses and no lipstick. She was slender and girlish, and with older South Side women she felt foolish and unsophisticated. She left the house, then turned around and went back. "I felt I looked abominable," she writes. Eventually she got there, late. A man was talking, with great energy, about the barrenness of Negro writing. His "pungent epithets" made her draw back in "Sunday school horror." With a shock she realized it was Richard Wright.

After that, the South Side writers' group met on alternate Sunday afternoons in the Abraham Lincoln Center, an important cultural center in the Black Belt. Apart from Wright, the only published writer was Frank Marshall Davis, a journalist at the Associated Negro Press. The previous year, his book of poems, *Black Man's Verse*, had received considerable acclaim.[32] Theodore Ward, from Louisiana, worked at the Federal Theatre Project and was writing a play.

Margaret Walker, at twenty-one, was the youngest in the group. Brought up in New Orleans, in a household full of books and music, she had recently graduated in English literature from Northwestern University and had just secured work with the Federal Writers' Project.

Other members were Marion Perkins (later a sculptor), Marian

Minus, who was studying anthropology at the University of Chicago, and Bob Davis, a poet who became a Hollywood bit actor. Ed Bland, a poet, was killed on the German front in the last months of World War II. Fern Gayden was the Wright family caseworker and a graduate of Northwestern University. Alberta Sims was interested in children's theater.[33]

Wright had the least formal education in the group, and yet he was what Margaret Walker called the "exciting hot center."[34] She was surprised, the first time she read her poetry aloud, to find that he could be kind and encouraging. Frank Marshall Davis paints a similar picture of Wright:

> He was an extrovert, warm and outgoing with an often ribald sense of humor. He was also frank in his opinions, freely expressing what he liked and disliked of the work read before our group. . . . At one meeting he read "Big Boy Leaves Home." . . . When he finished, nobody spoke for several minutes. We were too much moved by his power. Then there was a flood of praise. Frankly I was overwhelmed. We realized this was a major talent, but none of us dreamed how great he would become.[35]

Several of the stories that later went into *Uncle Tom's Children* were exhaustively discussed in that group. There was much talk about an essay Wright was drafting: "Blueprint for Negro Writing." Wright saw it as an important opportunity for the group to formulate and clarify their ideas.

Heavily influenced by Wright, the young black Chicago writers consciously distanced themselves from their Harlem Renaissance predecessors. They agreed that they wanted to write about the "Negro masses" and that their consciousness should be informed by Marxism. But, Wright insisted, Marxism was merely a starting point. "No theory of life can take the place of life."

They embraced "Negro nationalism"—writing about black culture, folklore, religion, and sport—but (Wright was adamant about this) they would not restrict themselves to this. Their literary heritage was European, white American, and Negro.

For the first time in American history, black writers were coming together to discuss their task as black writers. The meetings marked the beginning of what the critic Robert Bone has called the "Chicago

Renaissance"[36]—the extraordinary outpouring of writing from black writers in Chicago between 1935 and 1950.[37] Whereas their Harlem predecessors looked back with nostalgia on their rural Southern past and folk culture, the Chicago writers—with Richard Wright as their "towering figure"—wrote with a new urban toughness, influenced by the Depression and Marxism. As Bone points out, Wright's influence on the Chicago Renaissance continued long after he left that city.

The South Side writers' group broke up just before Wright left Chicago. There were tensions in the group that had less to do with writing than personal rivalries. Everyone knew that Margaret Walker had a crush on Wright.[38] But Wright was attracted to Alberta Sims. He and Ted Ward were both conscious of the considerable charms of Fern Gayden. And in the winter and spring of 1936–37, before she left for New York, Wright was in love with Marian Minus.[39]

IN JULY 1936 WRIGHT WAS TRANSFERRED BACK TO THE ILLINOIS WRITERS' PROJECT. His social world had opened up well beyond the Communist Party. For Wright, the Writers' Project had the huge advantage that writing, not politics, was its raison d'être. As in the Party, the whites were predominantly Jews. Margaret Walker recalls the food served at parties: "salami, bologna, sometimes lox or smoked salmon—and pickles, rye bread and pumpernickel, beer and pretzels."[40]

Frank Marshall Davis occasionally accompanied Wright to Works Progress Administration (WPA) parties. For Davis, even though he had a university degree, it was the first time he had mixed socially with whites. He was intensely relieved, he writes, never once to sniff "the offensive odor of condescension."[41]

Margaret Walker (who did not drink) maintains in her biography of Wright that he "delighted in consuming a great deal."[42] At one party he apparently said to her: "I must have drunk a gallon of beer." In fact, Wright usually drank very moderately, but he liked to shock the puritanical Margaret. Jack Conroy gives a quite different impression of Wright at these parties:

> He sat alone, a good-looking and pleasant-mannered young man but abstracted and aloof from the alcoholically induced merriment about

him. In all the times I saw him, he seldom drank at all and if so sparingly and with no visible effect.[43]

Wright had become good friends with Nelson Algren, an ambitious writer who when he was not in one of his morose moods was an enjoyable companion. Jack Conroy, who had published Wright's early poems in the *Anvil*, continued to be encouraging. From Missouri he wrote to Wright: "It seems to me that you now have a swell chance to get a book published, probably that autobiography of which you sent me a chapter or two."[44] He was most likely referring to Wright's autobiographical essay "The Ethics of Living Jim Crow."

FOR THE PERIOD OF A YEAR, FROM MAY 1936 UNTIL RICHARD WRIGHT LEFT FOR New York in May 1937, Margaret Walker saw quite a bit of him. At first this man had shocked her. Soon she found herself in love with him. She had joined the Illinois Writers' Project in May 1936. She worked at home and Wright worked at the office, but when she came in to submit her weekly assignments, she would walk over to his desk and they would talk. Sometimes they strolled together from the Writers' Project on East Erie Street, the near North Side, to the public library downtown.

Wright recognized Margaret Walker's talent and encouraged her writing. He liked her high spirits and ambition. But he could not return her feelings for him. In many ways she was exactly the sort of woman—Southern, religious, and morally conservative—he was running away from.

Walker was astoundingly naïve about politics and sex. Soon after he met her, Wright spoke at a Midwest Writers' Congress and invited her to come and hear him. The next Sunday, Walker mentioned the congress at the South Side writers' group. Was it a Communist affair? Frank Marshall Davis wanted to know. Walker writes that she had no idea.

I looked at Wright, who only grinned gleefully and said, "Don't look at me!" The whole thing sank in gradually that he was a Communist. I honestly didn't know what Communism or Marxism meant. I had had no courses in sociology, economics, or political science while I was a student in college.[45]

On another occasion, sitting beside Wright's desk at the Writers' Project, she started to peruse something he had just been reading about sexual deviates:

> Quite innocently I asked, to my later embarrassment, the meaning of two words, "cunt" and "pederast." To the first, he looked at me in amazement and said, "You really don't know?" And I shook my head in ignorance. To the second, he turned to Nathan Morris and Jack Scher, and said to Jack, "Jack, Margaret wants to know what a pederast is; tell her." Jack laughed and said, "No, Dick, tell her yourself." But he did not.[46]

According to Walker, Wright asked early on if he could come and visit her at home. She said no. "Don't you take company?" he asked. She said no. "Aren't you old enough?" he mocked her. Eventually she confessed: "I've heard that you like good liquor and bad women." He was astonished. "What lowlife Negro had been badmouthing me?"[47]

It is true that Wright liked to show off to his less sophisticated Southern friends and project himself as somewhat dissipated. He once confessed to Margaret Walker that he was fed up with his "meaningless entanglements" with women.[48] It is not surprising, perhaps, that her hopes were raised.

She was the English major graduate, but he was the tutor. He handed her John Reed's *Ten Days That Shook the World*. He encouraged her to read Karl Marx, Adam Smith, Nietzsche, and John Strachey's *The Coming Struggle for Power*. He gave her a copy of *Madame Bovary*. With his encouragement, she read Stephen Crane, John Dos Passos, and James Farrell's *Studs Lonigan*. She read Chekhov, Gorky, Tolstoy, and Turgenev. They did not always agree. Wright rated Dostoyevsky "the greatest novelist who ever lived." Walker "never felt quite that extravagantly about him." Wright was "ecstatic" about Faulkner's *Sanctuary*; Walker found it "revolting." He loved D. H. Lawrence's *Sons and Lovers*; Walker was not able to appreciate it until she herself became a mother.

Chastely, they would sit in the parlor of Margaret's house and discuss different ways of rendering Southern Negro speech and Southern folklore. Wright was passionately interested in the "dirty dozens"—the ditties he and his friends used to chant in their youth. To him, they were more than merely risqué; they carried a far wider significance. "They jeer at life," he commented. "They leer at what is decent, holy, just, wise, straight, right, and uplifting. I think that it is because, from the Negro's point of view, it is the right, the holy, the just, that crush him in America."[49] His story "Big Boy Leaves Home" opened with one of the boys saying to another: "Yo Mama don wear no drawers." Another boy chimes in: "Ah seena when she pulled em off." There is uproarious laughter.

Walker was writing a novel, *Goose Island*, set among the drug dealers and prostitutes of the Lower North Side, the small black ghetto where she had lived while attending Northwestern University. Early in 1937, after six months at the Illinois Writers' Project, she heard that the authorities were permitting her to work on this novel full-time. This was cause for celebration. To her frustration, Wright was not at work that day. His colleagues informed her that he was at home with a bad cold. She decided to take him some oranges, and asked her sister, Mercedes, to accompany her. Margaret had never been to Dick Wright's house. He always came to hers.

> We found him in the house on Indiana Avenue, in bed and in a room that I could not understand because it had one door and no windows. Imagine my shock when I later realized it was a closet. He was very happy to hear about my good luck, and both of us were embarrassed about the oranges.[50]

She went back to the house on another occasion. Wright was not there, and his Aunt Cleo took the opportunity to say "all kinds of ugly things about him." He was "lowdown," his aunt warned Margaret. "No decent, self-respecting girl would have anything to do with him."[51] It made Margaret wonder. She had heard these things about Wright before.

"MOST OF THE YOUNG ARTISTS AND WRITERS WITH A TINGE OF TALENT FLEE THIS city as if it were on fire," Wright commented about Chicago in June 1936.[52] The literary and political center of the United States was New York. The League of American Writers was based in New York. The publishing houses were in New York. Harlem, the cultural capital of black America, was in New York. Several of his friends had already left.[53] He himself was ready to take flight.

On the home front, Wright was feeling freer. His brother, Leon, who showed some talent as a painter, had just been employed by the Federal Arts Project. After ten years of supporting the family, Wright thought it reasonable that Leon should take over the responsibility for a time.[54] Essie Lee was sympathetic. "Am very glad that Leon staged a come-back so you could get out and give yourself a chance. I don't see how you stood it as long as you did."[55]

In December 1936 Abe Chapman wrote to him. "Can you get out to New York this year. It would be swell having you with us for a while, talking, laughing, paintin' the town red, getting excited together and cooling off, making worlds and destroying worlds, etc. What about it?"[56]

Wright asked for a transfer to the Writers' Project in New York. He assumed his chances were good. "Big Boy Leaves Home" had just appeared in *The New Caravan*, a prestigious anthology of contemporary writing, and had received considerable attention. Everyone agreed he was "going places."[57]

In January 1937 Abe Chapman wrote again. "When you come to New York you must stay with us—we've got a two room place now. So you already have a home in N.Y. . . . All you've got to do is come."[58]

Wright lingered a little longer. He was waiting for his transfer to the New York Writers' Project to come through. Meanwhile, he was having a major impact on the Illinois Writers' Project. His suggestion for a book of essays on Negro life in Illinois had met with considerable interest from Sterling Brown, who headed the Negro Project in Washington.[59] And to Abe Chapman, Wright confessed he was enjoying the delights of a "Negro smile full of Negro sunshine."[60] This was probably Marian Minus, a member of the South Side black writers' group, a graduate of Fisk, and a student of anthropology at the University of Chicago.

Abe Chapman was touched that Wright had confided in him. "With a girl like that you should achieve your 'deep sense of life' you're always hankering after. . . . I hope the sunshine breaks into a permanent glow pervading the *whole* man."[61]

By mid-May 1937 the transfer still had not come through. Marian Minus had left for New York. The second American Writers' Congress was to take place in New York in early June, and Wright was chairing a session. He decided that this was his opportunity. Perhaps it would be easier to arrange the WPA transfer if he was already in New York. Unfortunately, Abe Chapman's offer of accommodation was no longer quite the same.

> We have but one bed at present with no funds to buy another. Herein lies the difficulty and your inability to sleep here. But—we are only two blocks away from a Negro neighborhood—we could get you a room there—to sleep. You could have all your meals with us, spend time at our place—use my desk if you want to write—get meals here—and have friends visit here. How does that sound?[62]

ON THE LAST FRIDAY OF MAY 1937, MARGARET WALKER STOOD IN LINE WITH Richard Wright as they picked up their paychecks from the Illinois Writers' Project. It was Wright's final check. He was leaving for New York that weekend, in a car with friends.

A group of white female employees decided they wanted a good-bye kiss from him. The sight of these "silly, young gushing girls" mobbing Wright with loving farewells was too much for Margaret Walker. She walked off. Wright caught up with her. They got on the El together.

He confessed to her that he felt anxious. He did not have a job yet, and he was leaving with only forty dollars in his pocket. And irony of ironies, he had just been offered a permanent position at the Chicago post office! He was turning down $2,100 per annum—$175 a month. He had sat on his bed in his room, he told Margaret, and thought it over. Then he tore the notice up. He hoped he wasn't making a mistake.

She looked at him. "Would you like to be a postman all your life?"

They laughed. He said he hoped she would come to New York, and soon. She said that for the time being she had to look after her younger sister.

Wright seized both her hands and said good-bye. Margaret was swept by a feeling of utter desolation—"as though something very important and vital and necessary to my life had gone from me and might never come again."[63]

———

THE NEXT DAY WRIGHT LEFT CHICAGO. ONCE AGAIN, HE WAS GIVING HIS MOTHER a hug and heading for broader horizons. Within a decade, he had transformed himself into a confident, educated man, a skilled writer, someone with something to say. His name was already known in left-wing circles throughout the country.

Years later, Nelson Algren would comment:

Richard Wright came to Chicago . . . as a stranger, lived as a stranger, and he left without looking back. . . . Yet his impact upon Chicago has been more enduring than that of any merchant prince, mayor or newspaper owner. For his impact was not upon City Hall but upon the city's conscience; and therefore upon the conscience of humanity.[64]

7

CHANGE OF FORTUNE

New York: June 1937–May 1938

In New York, Wright was plunged back into Party circles. His friends from Chicago who had moved to New York were all committed Communists. The Newtons had just spent several months in the Soviet Union and were now living in Brooklyn, where Herb worked full-time for the Party. Abe Chapman, who lived with his wife Isabelle and daughter Laura in mid-Manhattan, worked for the Party as a cultural adviser. In the first week, Wright used the Chapmans' apartment as his daytime base and slept in Harlem.

The Second American Writers' Congress, from 4–6 June, was organized by the Communist Party. A sense of urgency permeated the sessions. While these writers were meeting in New York, German and Italian planes were helping Franco wreak havoc in Spain. World war was beginning to look unavoidable. As Wright put it in his report on the congress: "The barometer points to storm."[1] Everyone knew that if the combined forces of Franco, Hitler, and Mussolini won the war in Spain, fascists would threaten freedom everywhere.

Ernest Hemingway spoke at the opening session. He and his

companion Martha Gellhorn were just back from Spain where they had been war correspondents. "There is only one way to quell a bully, and that is to thrash him," Hemingway told the audience. If others were beginning to have their doubts about the outcome in Spain, Hemingway appeared to have none.

"Are you for, or are you against Franco and fascism? Are you for, or are you against the legal government and the people of Republican Spain?" the League of American Writers asked its writers in a questionnaire.[2] Some found the questions insulting. Most wrote back earnestly condemning fascism. "Speaking as a Negro Communist writer," Richard Wright replied, "I am wholeheartedly and militantly pro-Loyalist and for the national freedom of the people of Spain." He added that America should be sending arms to help the democratic government of Spain.

Several of Wright's acquaintances were in Spain that summer. Herbert Kline was making a documentary on the front line. Langston Hughes, who spoke fluent Spanish, was reporting on the war for the black press. Oliver Law and Harry Haywood, Wright's old foes in Chicago, were fighting in the Abraham Lincoln Battalion.[3] By July, Oliver Law would be dead.

If the war in Spain united the Left, the Moscow show trials, which had begun in August 1936, were causing deep divisions. The League of American Writers wholeheartedly supported Stalin. Shortly before the writers' congress, Waldo Frank, chairman of the League, expressed disquiet about the trials and was sharply rebuked for his lack of solidarity. James Farrell, already an outspoken anti-Stalinist, told Wright that to him the trials sounded "terribly fishy."[4]

But Wright could not afford to think like that. He needed the Party. He was starting out again in a new city. And as he observed the dark clouds of fascism gather over Europe, he was inclined to believe that the world needed a solid Communist bulwark. Like his friends, he rationalized that if a strong Soviet Union involved some cleaning up of its own backyard, then so be it. The most shocking trial took place early in 1938, when various members of the Bolshevik old guard were accused of ludicrously improbable crimes, and all but one "confessed." All were executed. More than a hundred members of the League of American Writers signed a statement in support of Stalin.[5] Among the signatories were Nelson Algren, Langston Hughes, and Richard Wright.

TO HIS DISMAY, WRIGHT WAS INFORMED THAT HIS TRANSFER FROM THE ILLINOIS Writers' Project to the New York Writers' Project met with a bureaucratic obstacle: he had not been a resident of New York for long enough. From Chicago his brother, Leon, wrote that his employment on the WPA Arts Project was about to end. Wright wrote anxiously to his friend Fern Gayden, the family case worker. "Say, my brother writes me that he's got a 403 [termination of employment form] already. He said that he was going to see you about getting on relief again. I do hope he can get lined up again, because as yet I am not in a position to send him anything."[6]

By the beginning of July, Wright, seriously worried about finances, was obliged to take a job that was not at all what he had in mind when he left Chicago. His Writers' Project supervisor salary in Chicago had been $125 a month. The post office job would have been $175 a month. Now, for $80 a month, he would be working full-time as the Harlem correspondent for the Communist Party newspaper, the *Daily Worker.* New York was more expensive than Chicago, and already he was having to send money back home. "It seems I can never escape my family," he sighed to friends.[7] He might as well have been referring to his Communist family as well.

And yet the Party was more than a useful network: Wright genuinely admired what the Communists were doing. The *Daily Worker* was the only white newspaper in the country to give regular space to black issues, and the only paper to employ black writers on its staff. The Harlem bureau, at 200 West 135th Street, had been established the previous year. It was headed by New York's most prominent black Communist: Ben Davis, Jr.

A tall, athletic Georgian—an ex-football player, like his friend Paul Robeson—Ben Davis, Jr., was a skilled political organizer and orator. He was famous throughout the nation as the black attorney with the Harvard law degree who had defended Angelo Herndon, a Communist from Georgia, sentenced to eighteen to twenty years of hard labor on a Georgia chain gang for leading a peaceful protest march.[8] Like the Scottsboro trial, the case had dragged on year after year. In 1937, due largely to nationwide protests from Communists, labor groups, and church groups on Herndon's behalf, the U.S. Supreme Court finally found the Georgia verdict unconstitutional.

In Harlem, the Communist Party wielded more influence than in any other African-American community in the nation. There were almost one thousand Party members, and new recruits were signing up each day. There had been riots in Harlem in 1935; protesters had boy-cotted white-owned businesses that refused to employ blacks. But nothing had changed. Most restaurants, hotels, saloons, and stores in Harlem were owned by whites, and most of them discriminated against blacks. The housing was as congested as in Chicago's South Side, and rents were higher than in the rest of the city. Harlem did not have a single public high school. (Jackson, Mississippi, had had one for over ten years now.) Tuberculosis was rife. And police brutality was notorious.

In the course of six months—from July 1937 until the end of December 1937—Wright produced forty signed articles on Harlem and dozens of anonymous brief dispatches. He wrote about the pickets at the Italian Consulate to protest the invasion of Ethiopia; protest actions in Harlem against lynching in the South; rallies for the Scottsboro boys, rent strikes, peace parades, concerts, visits from black leaders; Mrs. Roo-sevelt's visit to Harlem; and the memorial service for Milton Herndon (brother of Angelo Herndon), killed on the Spanish front.

His longest piece was a description of a Party meeting at Harlem's Nat Turner Branch (named after the Virginia slave who led the bloodi-est slave rebellion in U.S. history). "Leaving the blare and glare of Lenox Ave, you walk up one flight of stairs and enter an oblong room whose walls are covered with murals depicting the historical struggles of the Negro in America."[9] There were about twenty members, mostly black, he wrote. "There is absolutely no difference between the Negro and white in the Communist Party." Women played an active role in the Party. "As the meeting gets under way you notice that there are no abstractions, no splitting of intellectual hairs." He finished: "These working people may not have polished accents, graceful gestures, etc.; but they have what it takes to build a new world—the ability to ACT and a singleness of VISION."

Writing for the *Daily Worker* gave Wright an opportunity to get to know Harlem, and he had the satisfaction of bringing black issues to the attention of the entire country. But he resented having to write propaganda. He had never admired singleness of vision, and he hated toeing the Party line. Privately, he called it "Stalin's newspaper."[10]

James W. Ford, a major figure in the Harlem branch of the Communist Party, was one of many to be irritated by Wright's attitude. He grumbled several years later. "We sought to put him to writing about pork chops, high rents, crowded houses, child welfare and relief. Wright was dissatisfied with this assignment. . . . He complained to a number of people, never to our committee directly, that he did not want to write for the *Daily Worker*."[11]

According to Ralph Ellison, who shared Wright's skepticism about the Party, Wright was widely regarded with suspicion. He was distrusted not only as an "intellectual" and thus a potential traitor, but as a possible "dark horse" in the race for the Harlem party leadership, a "ringer" who had been sent from Chicago to cause them trouble. Wright had little sense of humor about their undisguised hostility, and this led, as would be expected, to touchy relationships.[12]

Abe Aaron, who had stopped going to Party meetings, wrote to Wright from Chicago that he thought his *Daily Worker* articles "pretty bad." He could see Wright's heart was not in it. "I figured maybe you were hungry, maybe you didn't care, maybe you were hellishly pushed for time. . . . You're no slick journalist with flair for gloss to fit any mood. If you don't feel a thing, you can't write it."[13]

By December Wright was restless. He was a prisoner of the Party; he was living in Harlem,[14] yet another black ghetto; and he was wasting more time on drudgery and earning less for it than he had at any time in the last two and a half years. Ralph Ellison, who had become his closest friend in New York, was briefly back at the family house in Ohio, trying to come to terms with the death of his mother. Wright sympathized—he dreaded the same loss himself. But right now the blight of his life was the *Daily Worker*. "It was not for this that I came to NYC," he told Ellison. "I'm working from 9 A.M. to 9 and 10 P.M. and it's a hard, hard grind. Can't do any work, haven't the time. I am thinking definitely in terms of leaving here, but I don't know when. I seem to be turning my life into newspaper copy from day to day; and when I look into the future it looks no better. I don't want to go back to Chicago, but where else is there?"[15]

Wright's friendship with Ralph Ellison was one of the few pleasures of those first difficult months. Ellison had come to New York the previous year from Tuskegee, the Alabama college famous for its "let's not offend the white folks" policy.[16] It was founded by Booker T. Washington, who had insisted that Negroes, instead of overreaching, should be trained in industrial and agricultural skills. More recently, since Washington's death, the college had branched out to encompass the liberal arts, and Ellison had been majoring in music. His plan had been to earn some money in New York and then go back to Tuskegee to finish his degree. His ultimate goal was to become a composer. Through an introduction from Langston Hughes, he had met Wright a couple of days after Wright arrived in New York. Over the next few months, due to Wright's influence, Ellison's plans would be "fatefully modified."[17]

Ellison was often at the Harlem bureau of the *Daily Worker*. It was partly because he was unemployed, but mostly because he found the company of Richard Wright intensely stimulating. Wright had a small office to himself. He showed Ellison the short stories he kept in his top drawer, and Ellison asked to read them. The two men were soon discussing books, aspects of craft and technique, and the philosophical and political implications of the books they read.

Unlike Wright's more doctrinaire Communist friends, Ellison had an open, inventive mind. Together the two men disparaged the ideological-bound discussions that went on in the "befogged Lenox Avenue" Harlem branch of the Party.[18] They discussed Rousseau's philosophy, Hem's latest book, jazz and blues, Malraux, Stein and T. S. Eliot, white prejudices, the foibles of the black bourgeoisie, and their tastes in what Ellison called "neat looking little ladies."[19]

Both men were Southerners, brought up within segregation, but their backgrounds were very different. Ellison had grown up in Oklahoma City. It was not the Deep South, and he considered himself fortunate to have avoided that hell. His father, a construction foreman who had served in the Philippines, had read widely. (He named his son after Ralph Waldo Emerson.) Like Wright, Ellison lost his father when he was young, but to death, not desertion. His mother was a strong woman who encouraged her sons to read. Ellison was extremely conscious of his higher education, especially when he thought Wright was patronizing him.

But Ellison was seeking a mentor, and for a while Wright was it. To Ellison, who was five years younger, Wright's spirit and sheer daring were exhilarating. Somehow this man from Mississippi radiated a sense of possibility. "He had the kind of confidence that jazzmen have," Ellison said later. "He was well aware of the forces ranked against him, but in his quiet way he was as arrogant in facing up to them as was Louis Armstrong in a fine blaring way."

Early on, Wright suggested that Ellison write a book review for the first issue of *New Challenge*—the new black magazine he was coediting. "To one who had never attempted to write anything, this was the wildest of ideas," Ellison comments. But (he points out) Wright strongly believed there was "an untapped supply of free-floating literary talent . . . in the Negro community."

Wright liked Ellison's review, and pressed him to try his hand at a short story for the following issue. "But I've never even tried to write a story," Ellison protested. "Look," Wright told him, "you talk about these things, you've read a lot, and you've been around. Just put something down and let me see it."

Ellison wrote a story based on his experience of riding freight trains from Oklahoma to Alabama. Wright was enthusiastic and accepted it for the magazine. As it turned out, there would never be a second issue of the magazine, but Ellison had found a new passion.

From May 1937 to the summer of 1940, Ellison was as close to Wright as any man ever came. By the end of that year, Ellison knew he wanted to be a writer. "Workers of the World Must Write!" he wrote to his Mississippi friend.[20]

WRIGHT HIMSELF WAS GETTING NO ENCOURAGEMENT FROM THE LITERARY establishment at all. He had left Chicago thinking it would be easier to find a publisher if he was in New York. Just before he left, he had finished his second novel, *Tarbaby's Dawn*. Now *Lawd Today!* and *Tarbaby's Dawn* were doing the dismal rounds.

Two years before, James Henle at Vanguard Press had encouraged him to revise *Lawd Today!* He now told Wright that the novel caused "more doubt and more debate than any manuscript that has come into this office in a long time." His main concern was that it would not sell. The novel was bleak, and the central protagonist "so unsympathetic."[21] He thought *Tarbaby's Dawn* "a considerable advance on *Lawd Today!*," but he still could not visualize a public for the manuscript.[22]

Wright was to hear the same story time and again. Publishers agreed that his portrayal of black experience was courageous, and doubtless true, but no one wanted to publish the novel. All publishers preferred the more positive *Tarbaby's Dawn* to *Lawd Today!* Saxe Commins, at Random House, called in a third reader for *Tarbaby's Dawn*, but eventually he "very reluctantly" turned it down. "It is remarkable that each of the reports is in complete agreement about the skill with which you picture Negro life in the South," he told Wright. "At the same time the consensus is that such a book would have to overcome almost insurmountable commercial hazards."[23]

Modern Age praised Wright's "graphic realism," but thought the novels "risky" precisely because of this. At Simon & Schuster, the verdict on *Tarbaby's Dawn* was divided, but ultimately the decision was no. "Possibly we are making a mistake," they told Wright.[24] This was cold comfort.

Viking Press was about to publish an anthology of WPA writers, *American Stuff*, and publisher David Zablodowsky thought Wright's contribution, "The Ethics of Living Jim Crow," outstanding. He asked Wright whether he had a novel for him to look at.[25] Wright sent in both manuscripts. Two months later, they were returned. "All the readers very much admired the manuscripts, especially *Tarbaby's Dawn*," Zablodowsky wrote. "They couldn't easily make up their minds about the latter, and finally declined it because they felt that it did not have enough body for a novel with which to introduce a new author."[26]

Wright would come home from a long stint at the *Daily Worker* to find yet another rejection letter in the mail. The next day he would hand-deliver the manuscript to another publisher. He knew the rejections had more to do with the subject matter than with the quality of his writing. It was quite clear to him that readers were more comfortable when he portrayed black characters as victims and martyrs.

Margaret Walker was also aware of this. "I've always felt the stories would go better and quicker than the novels," she tried to console him. "After all it has got to be a mighty unusual white firm to print *Lawd Today!* and don't forget those working conditions in Uncle Sam's Post Office aren't any too wonderful."[27]

Literary agents had been no help. While Wright was still in Chicago, his collection of short stories, *Uncle Tom's Children*, had languished for a year in the exquisite Japanese cabinets of the New York agent John J.

Trounstine.[28] In November 1936 Jack Conroy had put Wright on to his agent, Maxim Lieber.[29] Wright sent him his two novels. But Lieber was even less encouraging than the publishers had been.

Lieber was a Communist. (Several years later it would emerge that he was a spy for the Soviets.) To him, Wright's novels were too experimental, too influenced by modernism, too negative. They lacked the upbeat optimism of social realism. He told Wright bluntly that neither manuscript was "in shape for submission to a publisher."

> It seems to me that you do not have a clear grasp of the technique of a novel, for both these scripts seem to be more like a series of cameos rather than a sequential story. . . . A novel must be tightly woven, each incident must be linked to a succeeding incident.

He was particularly harsh about *Lawd Today!*

> I have a suspicion that you may have been under the influence of Joyce's *Ulysses* in attempting to relate the events in one day in the life of a negro, and while I can see excellent possibilities in such treatment, you have unfortunately not realized any of them. . . . I can see that all of this is due to the fact that you have not yet mastered the art of the novel as distinguished from the art of the short story.[30]

Wright's short stories were now with a third agent, Ann Watkins, who had not been able to place them either.

THAT SUMMER, *STORY* MAGAZINE ANNOUNCED A WRITING COMPETITION. AS Howard Fast writes: "*Story* was the most distinguished magazine of the short story in America at a time when the short story was at its peak as an art form internationally and when American short stories were read and admired the world over."[31] The editors, Martha Foley and Whit Burnett, wanted to see whether the Federal Writers' Project was having any significant effect on American writing. Across the nation, the Writers' Project had employed more than three thousand writers and published some 150 books. What were these writers producing outside working hours?

The competition was open to all writers who had ever been

associated with the Federal Writers' Project. Submissions could be in the form of poetry, drama, or prose—fiction or nonfiction. There was no restriction as to subject, treatment, or length. The first prize was five hundred dollars and publication of the winning manuscript by Story Press in association with Harper & Brothers. The second prize was one hundred dollars. The deadline for entries was 1 September 1937.

Among Wright's friends, there was a flurry of typing. The *Story* offices received more than five hundred submissions. Wright sent in his collection of short stories, *Uncle Tom's Children*. His hopes were raised when that same month Viking Press published *American Stuff* (an anthology of the best work by WPA writers), and several reviewers singled out his autobiographical sketch "The Ethics of Living Jim Crow" for special praise.

Had anyone heard anything yet? Wright asked Abe Aaron in November.

"Haven't heard anything on the Story Mag contest," Aaron wrote back. "Nor has anyone, so far as I know. So bear up. It would be swell hitting the thing, wouldn't it? For me there's very little hope, I know."[32]

APART FROM ALL THE REJECTION LETTERS, THERE WAS ANOTHER BITTER DIS-appointment. Wright had come to New York determined to make *New Challenge* into an outstanding Negro literary quarterly—the first left-wing black magazine in American history.

Dorothy West had founded its predecessor magazine, *Challenge*, in 1934. Her aim had been to revive the dying embers of the Harlem Renaissance. But even the Harlem Renaissance writers had found the magazine "a little prim."[33] Wallace Thurman told her it was "too pink tea and la de da—too high schoolish."[34] West's social conscience had been awakened during the Depression. And her friend Marian Minus— they had known each other in Harlem in the late twenties—had meanwhile been influenced by Wright's South Side writers' group. Minus persuaded West that the magazine must become more left-wing. West had offered Wright and the South Side writers' group a special section in the next issue. Somehow there had been a misunderstanding. It seems to have been compounded by the confusion over Wright's relationship with Marian Minus. In Chicago she allowed Wright to court her. When he arrived in New York, he discovered she was a lesbian.[35]

The day before he left Chicago, Wright told Langston Hughes he would be coming to New York, where he hoped to "help do something with the magazine, *Challenge*."[36]

Dorothy West and Marian Minus have decided to turn the thing left ward, which is the only way it should turn if it is to live. . . . I shall do my very best to get the Party to support it; have it placed for sale in the Workers' Bookstores throughout the Nation; and get as much liberal and White support for it as possible.

Wright had arrived in New York brimming with ideas for the magazine. He hoped to include excerpts from novels in progress. He planned to hold one-act play contests. He wanted to establish an up-to-date book review section. His intention, he told Langston Hughes, was to give the magazine "balls, à la *New Masses*."[37] He seemed to be forgetting his female coeditors.

Within a few days of arriving, he had published a short piece in the *Daily Worker* publicizing the forthcoming magazine.[38] *New Challenge*— edited by Dorothy West, Marian Minus, and himself—was envisaged as the center of a national movement of black writers—something like the John Reed Club.[39]

It was an ambitious idea, and Wright had forgotten that it was not his journal; it was Dorothy West's. The old magazine, *Challenge*, had celebrated writing that Wright deplored. As he saw it, there was no continuity at all between the old magazine and the new one.

Politically and socially, Wright and Dorothy West were poles apart. She came from one of the first black middle-class families of Boston. Her slave-born father had become a successful businessman, and West was brought up to be conscious of her social standing. Eager to become a writer, she had come to New York in 1926, at the age of nineteen. It was the height of the Harlem Renaissance, and the "New Negro" writers of the time—Zora Neale Hurston, Langston Hughes, Countee Cullen, Claude McKay, and Wallace Thurman—viewed her as a kind of little sister. Countee Cullen described her as "a lovable child . . . in spite of [her] terrible yearning towards grownupship and sophistication." Langston Hughes called her "the Kid."[40]

Dorothy West resented Wright from the beginning. She disliked the way he was usurping her magazine and advertising it in the Communist press. She disliked the way the new magazine ridiculed the old one. After a few months, she put her foot down. When *New Challenge* came out in October, the coeditors blazoned on the cover were Dorothy West and Marian Minus. Wright had been demoted to associate editor.[41]

And yet, inside the covers, Wright had had his way. *New Challenge* was left-leaning, hard-hitting, and controversial. The editorial stated: "We are not attempting to restage the 'revolt' and 'renaissance' which grew unsteadily and upon false foundations ten years ago. . . . We want *New Challenge* to be a medium of literary expression for all writers who realize the present need for the realistic depiction of life through the sharp focus of social consciousness." This was Wright, not West.

The issue contained poems by friends of Wright's: Owen Dodson, Sterling Brown, Frank Marshall Davis, Robert Davis, and Margaret Walker. The essays and reviews nearly all underlined the need for a new Negro writing movement with its roots in the experience of the Negro masses. As Professor Alain Locke commented in his review of Claude McKay's autobiography, *A Long Way from Home*, the Harlem Renaissance "should have addressed itself more to the people themselves and less to the gallery of faddist Negrophiles."[42]

The key piece was Wright's "Blueprint for Negro Writing." In it Wright condemned the "parasitic and mannered" writing of the Harlem Renaissance writers, whose patrons were "burnt-out white Bohemians with money." He did not mince words. The Harlem Renaissance writers, he asserted, had "entered the Court of American Public Opinion dressed in the knee-pants of servility, curtsying to show that the Negro was not inferior, that he was human, and that he had a life comparable to that of other people. For the most part these artistic ambassadors were received as though they were French poodles who do clever tricks."

Up till now, Wright argued, Negro writing had been "the voice of the educated Negro pleading with white America for justice." From now on, Negro writers should write for and about the common people. "Blueprint" was also a call for black solidarity. As Wright pointed out, Negro writers had always suffered from isolation. They were not fully integrated into American life; they had been barred from the theater and publishing houses; they were isolated from both white writers and other black writers. They needed to form groups, discuss their ideas, test out their writing on others. They had a long road ahead. There was no time for "malice or jealousy."

The *Daily Worker* called Wright's "Blueprint" a "really important diagnosis" and hailed *New Challenge* as "a magazine of infinite promise."[43] But tension between Dorothy West and Richard Wright came to a head soon after that first issue appeared, with Marian Minus dangling uncomfortably in the middle. Only later did Wright realize the extent of the magazine's financial debts and the women's lack of openness with him. "They kept everything from me so closely that I was in the dark about everything," he told Ellison.[44]

From Dorothy West's point of view, even if the six issues of *Challenge* were undistinguished, she had produced them herself. In 1983, at the age of seventy-six, she still viewed that one and only issue of *New Challenge* as something akin to a raid by Chicago gangsters.

> Today the magazine is considered important. . . . I financed it. I was the editor. I was the everything. When the Chicago group tried to take it away from me, that was the end of the magazine. Leftists . . . The final issue was, I imagine, a very bad issue. Richard Wright wrote not a story, but a treatise—"Blueprint for Black Writing," I think. . . . The magazine's end came about because the Chicago group wanted to take it over. I have a certain strength and I said no. They couldn't do anything without me. So that was the last issue.[45]

MARIAN MINUS'S CONTRIBUTION TO THE ONE AND ONLY ISSUE OF *NEW CHALLENGE* was an admiring review of Zora Neale Hurston's new novel, *Their Eyes Were Watching God*. In a review for the *New Masses*, published the same month, Wright condemned the book. Hurston exemplified the kind of writer he had attacked in "Blueprint."[46]

"Miss Hurston can write," he conceded. But her prose was "cloaked in that facile sensuality that has dogged Negro expression" since its beginnings. Her characters exuded the simple sensuality that whites liked to associate with Negroes. "In the main, her novel is not addressed to the Negro, but to a white audience whose chauvinistic tastes she knows how to satisfy."[47]

When Hurston read *Uncle Tom's Children* a few months later, she would throw equally vehement accusations at Wright. His writing was bleak, negative, and ideological. Where was his pride in the race?

The Hurston-Wright controversy continues to this day.

WRIGHT WAS GOING THROUGH ONE OF HIS "MOPING SPELLS," AS MARGARET Walker called them.[48] For two and a half years he had received one rejection letter after another. He was soon to be thirty. Suddenly and dramatically, his fortunes changed. In mid-December 1937, his residency requirement met, he was finally accepted on to the New York Writers' Project. He and his black colleague Arnold de Mille would take up where the Harlem Renaissance writer Claude McKay had left off, and write about "Black Manhattan."

Far more exciting news came on the very same day—December 15. A letter came from Whit Burnett, organizer of the nationwide *Story* competition. Richard Wright had won! As well as the cash prize of five hundred dollars, *Uncle Tom's Children* would be published the following March—by Harper & Brothers.[49]

Burnett asked Wright not to tell anyone until mid-February 1938 when the winner would be officially announced. For two whole months, Wright had to keep the secret. He did. But he could not help informing some friends that a publisher had expressed interest in *Uncle Tom's Children*.

"Who's bringing out the volume of shorts? And when? Keep me informed," Abe Aaron wrote back on 24 December 1937.[50]

Margaret Walker heard on the day the news became official—14 February 1938. The news had just broken in Chicago, she told him. She heard that morning, just before his letter arrived. "No wonder you are restless, who wouldn't be with such excitement! . . . You still want to go to Mexico I suppose?"[51]

"There's so much I want to do with the money," Wright told an interviewer for the *New York World-Telegram* the following day. "It seems like so much—I never had so much money in my life. And then when I think what I want to do with it, it doesn't seem like much at all." He wanted to go to Mexico. He was interested in the new revolutionary government there. "I'd like to travel a lot, but it mustn't be just traveling. I want to study all the while. Maybe if this book goes over I'll be able to do that."[52]

In the meantime, he told the reporter, he was going to buy a pair of shoes, a new suit or two, an overcoat, and a nice, thick juicy steak.[53]

IT QUICKLY BECAME PUBLIC KNOWLEDGE THAT NOT ALL THE *STORY* COMPETITION judges had favored Wright. The most prestigious judge on the panel, Sinclair Lewis, the man Wright would most like to have impressed, did not like his writing at all.

The official judges had been Sinclair Lewis, Harry Scherman, and Lewis Gannett. Sinclair Lewis, whose books *Main Street* and *Babbitt* had been Wright's first introduction to American literature, had been the first American writer to win the Nobel Prize for literature—in 1930. Harry Scherman was the president of the Book-of-the-Month Club. Lewis Gannett was the literary editor at the *New York Herald Tribune*. The unofficial judges, who seemed to have equal input, were Edward Aswell, publisher at Harper & Brothers, and Whit Burnett and Martha Foley, the husband and wife team who were the editors of *Story* magazine. The six judges narrowed down the possible winners to four: *The Horse* by Meridel Le Sueur, *American Primitive* by Fred Rothermell, *Star Ploughed Under* by Leverett S. Griggs, and *Uncle Tom's Children*. All except Wright's manuscript were novels.

Sinclair Lewis chose Le Sueur's book, followed by Rothermell's. He rated *Uncle Tom's Children* last. He felt strongly about this. "If I were a publisher," he wrote in his report, "I would not for a moment dream of accepting either 'Uncle Tom's Children' or 'Star Ploughed Under' on any terms." Wright's stories left him quite unmoved.

These stories have drama and integrity but they are dreadfully repetitious—the characters are constantly saying the same things over and over—and I suspect that the reader will regard them as essentially false. Lynching is, of course, a dreadful fact; and the fear of lynching a greater one. Yet may it not be that the far greater tragedy of the Negro is not this fear so much as the daily infuriation of being barred out from all sorts of industrial and social competition. Even if this were not true, almost every story dealing sympathetically with the Negro makes it's [sic] climax in a lynching so that the erstwhile horror of that incident has lost much of it's [sic] dramatic value.[54]

All the other judges gave Wright their first vote.[55] Lewis Gannett considered that Wright's manuscript "stood head and shoulders above the rest."[56] Edward Aswell did not hesitate, even though—as the future publisher of these stories—he was slightly concerned about "salability."

SHORTLY AFTER RECEIVING THAT MOMENTOUS LETTER FROM WHIT BURNETT, Richard Wright was ushered into Edward Campbell Aswell's office at Harper & Brothers. Having been told that Aswell was from Nashville, Tennessee, Wright was acutely conscious that he, a Southern black man, was meeting his traditional enemy, a Southern white man. He did not imagine that Aswell would be pleased to have to publish the book, and he fully expected Aswell to condescend to him. He imagined Aswell would probably mumble something about the writing reflecting a "morbid Negro imagination."[57] Aswell noticed his reserve. Years later, he commented to Wright: "In the beginning you had every reason to be suspicious of me and you were."[58]

Despite his formal Southern manner, Aswell was a gentle, kind man. He respected writers. He held out his hand and congratulated Wright heartily. No one had ever managed to capture Southern terror as he had done, he told him. Wright could scarcely believe his ears. By the time he walked out of Aswell's office with a contract and a check, he was sure he was dreaming.

Ed Aswell was thirty-seven, and had been at Harper & Brothers for two years. He was a Harvard graduate, but he was no wealthy Southerner. The son of a draftsman, he had gone to a public high school, then worked as a shoe salesman for five years in Nashville and Chicago in order to pay for his education at Harvard. He had hoped that Harvard would confer on him the status he had lacked in his youth. It did not. Though he graduated magna cum laude, he was never fully accepted in that clubbish New England environment. His resentment was evident in the comments he would contribute to the class of 1926 alumni reports over the decades. He reported to his former classmates that although he respected Harvard's spirit of free inquiry, he had become skeptical about many of Harvard's values. He scorned "pseudo-respectabilities." He disdained most businessmen. He disliked "the kind of blindness that often masquerades as religion."

His fullest comment would be his 1941 class report. He had recently published *Native Son*. Aswell remarked pointedly to his classmates that he had become "increasingly intolerant of intolerance." His publishing life, he explained, had taught him a great deal about *real* learning:

> The best-read man I have ever met, the most thoughtful and courageous, and the one who seemed to me most truly "educated," was not a college professor, nor even a college graduate, but a young Negro, son of an itinerant day-laborer, whose formal education was limited to the grade schools in—of all places—Mississippi. I have often thought that if I, or any of my classmates, had been subjected to one-half the handicaps and injustices that have been his lot since birth, we would have been defeated by life long ago. But he is not defeated. He is, in fact, one of the most powerful and most widely acclaimed novelists of our time.[59]

Aswell's daughter, Mary Aswell Doll, describes her father as "quite conservative politically and rather narrow minded, except when it came to blacks." She believes her father was ashamed of his rather humble Tennessee roots.[60]

Wright would never lose his respect for and gratitude to Ed Aswell. In 1957 he wrote to him: "I would rather die than let you down."[61]

WRIGHT WAS ANXIOUS. HOW WOULD READERS REACT TO *UNCLE TOM'S CHILDREN?* Were the stories really any good? "I wrote my guts into them," he told a reporter. "I only hope they're worth something."[62] He had read the stories so many times he could no longer react to them. He doubted whether anybody else could either.[63]

Margaret Walker had seen this mood before. In Chicago, surrounded by a pile of rejection slips, she had seen him descend into "a furnace of self mortification and agony." Now she urged him: "My dear Dick, for heaven's sake don't despair in the midst of the flames, otherwise I imagine they will consume you. . . . You cannot fail yourself because there are too many who believe in you. I must believe in you in order to believe more fully in myself. So you see it is a selfish business all round."[64]

In the last year of his life, Wright would say to a friend: "I have self-confidence, but I have no self-trust, which is a different thing. I can fight for others, but not for myself. So when I send out a ms, I just sit and chew my nails. I can't help it."[65]

"THESE STORIES BURN LIKE A HOUSE FIRE," WAS LEWIS GANNETT'S COMMENT ON the dust jacket. "They sing as well as sear; and what they have to say is as startling as a race riot." *Uncle Tom's Children* was published on 24 March 1938, with Whit Burnett and Martha Foley, the editors of *Story*, hosting a cocktail party for Wright. The print run was a cautious 550 copies, but by June 1, the book was in its second printing, and by the end of that month, seventeen hundred copies had been sold. These were not large sales, but the book nevertheless caused a splash.

"The U.S. has never had a first-rate Negro novelist. Last week the promise of one appeared," *Time* proclaimed.[66] Fred T. Marsh, in the *New York Herald Tribune*, predicted that *Uncle Tom's Children* would win the Pulitzer Prize.[67] Eleanor Roosevelt, in her "My Day" column in the *New York World-Telegram*, declared the book "beautifully written and so vivid that I had a most unhappy time reading it."[68]

"The South that Mr. Wright renders so vividly is recognizable and true," wrote the black poet Sterling Brown, "and it has not often been within the covers of a book."[69] To Wright's astonishment, even Southern whites admitted that the book painted a true picture. There were, of course, exceptions. Under the heading "A Garbage Can Book," the *Jackson Daily News* dismissed the stories as "nothing more or less than a squawk against lynching."[70]

An element of self-congratulation could be detected among Northern liberals. "Freedom, despite Mr. Wright's evidence to the contrary, is not really dead in America. His own recent history as a writer must prove that," declared the *New York Times Book Review*.[71]

A lone dissenter was Zora Neale Hurston. "Since the author himself is a Negro, his dialect is a puzzling thing," she observed. "One wonders how he arrived at it. Certainly he does not write by ear unless he is tone-deaf." She conceded: "The book contains some beautiful writing." But she was not impressed with its message. "This is a book about hatreds. . . . Not one act of understanding and sympathy comes to pass in the entire work. . . . All the characters in this book are elemental and brutish."[72]

Even today, the violence in Wright's stories is almost unbearable. The white perpetrators are not isolated villains but the white community generally—women as well as men. Wright paints a picture of a Jim Crow South animated by terror. The main characters, who, as the title suggests, are the children and grandchildren of slaves, are officially "free." They do not pretend to like white people, and they are no longer going to cringe before them. As much as they can, they fight back. But in reality, Wright shows that they are far from free. In each of the stories, Wright was exploring a question close to his heart: the question of black manhood. (The characters have names like "Big Boy" and "Mann.") Thirty years before striking black Memphis garbage collectors marched in T-shirts emblazoned with the message "I Am A Man," Wright was asking: How can a black man be a man, if every time he manifests his will he is crushed by white oppressors?

IN JANUARY 1938 WRIGHT HAD TAKEN HIS HARPER & BROTHERS CONTRACT TO Mary Elting Folsom, a Communist acquaintance[73] who worked in the prestigious Paul R. Reynolds literary agency.

She mentioned Wright to her boss, Paul Reynolds, Jr., who said he would like to take him on as a client. Wright was delighted. Three literary agents had had no success with selling his work, and Maxim Lieber had been thoroughly insulting. When Ann Watkins, his last agent, heard that he was moving to Reynolds, she wrote to him that she was "not only personally disappointed" but "a little aggrieved."[74] She did not know yet that the book she had been unable to place was about to win the *Story* prize.

The Paul Reynolds agency was the oldest literary agency in the United States, counting among its past and present clients F. Scott Fitzgerald, George Bernard Shaw, H. G. Wells, P. G. Wodehouse, and Willa Cather. Paul Reynolds, Sr., now seventy-four, still worked in the business, but increasingly his son was taking over.

The Reynoldses were Bostonians, descendants of the famous Paul Revere.[75] Father and son were both tall, lean, and ruggedly handsome. Reynolds, Jr., suffered from being in the shadow of his father and was awkward, with a glacial exterior. When he got to know him better, Wright would write in his journal that Reynolds was "neurotically sensitive" but "good at heart." He added: "He walks like an idiot."[76]

Mary Folsom thought the younger Reynolds "a troubled, unhappy man, and intensely shy with women." When he talked to people in his office, she observed, he never stopped fidgeting. She never told him she was a Communist.[77]

Wright was perfectly aware that Paul Reynolds was politically conservative, but he was to have great respect for him over the years as a literary agent. Reynolds was extremely good at his job. He was an excellent businessman, and he enjoyed driving a hard bargain for his clients. He had a vast network of contacts. He took the reading of manuscripts seriously, commented at length, and said exactly what he thought. From now on, Paul Reynolds, Jr., was a permanent fixture in Richard Wright's literary life.[78]

"OH NO! I WON'T GET SPOILED BY FAME. THERE'S NOT ENOUGH FAME YET TO SPOIL me," Wright replied to a white girlfriend, Henrietta Weigel, who published fiction under the name Henri Weigel.[79]

"I don't write easily or swiftly, but slowly and painfully," he answered Millen Brand, a playwright friend, who had asked him what it felt like to be great. "The moment I start thinking of being a great writer, then I can't write a word. Nothing comes!"[80] In his head he had mapped out writing plans for the next ten years. He was full of ideas and energy. He had no illusions about serious writing; it meant hard work.

He was going every day to the New York Writers' Project, a large loft in the Port Authority Building on Forty-first Street and Eighth Avenue. He was intensely relieved to have extricated himself from Party journalism and pleased to be back working in the bigger, white world.[81] But the job kept him busy. He was writing a chapter on Harlem for the WPA publication *New York Panorama*,[82] while also working for the Negro section of the Project on a book about Negroes in New York.

But the future of the New York Writers' Project did not look good. The WPA administrators in Washington were cutting back the funding. The newly formed House Un-American Activities Committee, the Dies

Committee (named after its Texan head, Martin Dies), had made allegations of Communist infiltration, and there were accusations of lax management. Some writers had already been dismissed; others were being transferred to different projects. In the spring of 1938, the union fought back. For a couple of weeks, Wright was active from morning to night. "We had to hold picket lines, organize delegations and all around raise a lot of hell," he wrote to Henrietta Weigel.[83] The Communist Party wielded considerable influence over the Project. Nevertheless, writers continued to be laid off.

Immediately after its publication, Wright sent a copy of *Uncle Tom's Children* to Henry G. Alsberg, director of the Federal Writers' Project in Washington. He hoped to qualify for "creative work," which would allow him to work full-time on his own writing. At the moment, he was working nights on a new novel, set in Chicago. The main character, Bigger Thomas, was going to be very different from the likable black protagonists in his short stories. He was not going to be a hero.

NOW THAT HE WAS APPROACHING THIRTY AND ESTABLISHING A CAREER AS A writer, Wright thought it time to get married. There was nothing romantic about this decision. His view of marriage was basically that it was a necessary burden. Margaret Walker learned this the hard way. "I'll never forget the way you blew off my head when I told you what I think every man eventually wants and you told me of a woman's conceit," she wrote from Chicago. "I'll never humiliate myself further by breathing such a thing to you."[84]

Nowhere in Wright's fiction is there a positive picture of marriage. His young female characters are keen to marry—largely because they want an economic provider. ("How come gals that way, Bigger?" his younger brother asks Bigger. "Soon's a guy get a good job, they want to marry?") Wright has several young women become pregnant in order to force their boyfriend's hand. The male characters see marriage as inevitable, rather than desirable. For these black men, already struggling in a world pitted against them, women come at a heavy price.

And yet Wright liked women. They liked him. Helen Yglesias, a writer in the Party, met Wright in 1938 and saw quite a bit of him, as a platonic friend, over the next few years. "He was terribly attractive," says Yglesias. "He was one of those men with quite extraordinary charm. Like Ted Hughes. Like Paul Robeson. Women felt an enormous attraction to him."[85]

Little is known about Wright's love life in these years—or, indeed, at any other time. He was an intensely private man. When he first arrived in New York, he occasionally took out Jean Blackwell, a twenty-four-year-old librarian from Baltimore.[86] Blackwell had arrived full of fantasies about the freedom she would encounter in New York and discovered that the only job available to her was in the Negro Division of the New York Public Library.

Wright tried to cheer her up by taking her to the theater. "I got to see many more plays than I ever would have seen at that period, being on my beginning library salary," she says. They saw *Tobacco Road* and *Of Mice and Men*. Blackwell was astonished when, during particularly agonizing moments, Wright beat his chest with his fists. She would have liked to marry him. But he was put off by the class difference. Nearly always on their evenings together there came a point when he would accuse her of being a "bourgeois Negro."

He had several affairs with white women. Nearly all were Jewish and in the Party. One was Henrietta Weigel, a talented writer herself, who worked for the literary agent John Trounstine, where she had first come across Wright's stories. She was married, living on Bleecker Street in the Village, and would invite Wright for drinks or dinner. He would read his work aloud to her. He took her to Brooklyn, to meet Jane Newton. More than once Weigel chided him for being too sensitive about people's reactions to him.

Dhimah Meidman was a modern dancer, divorced, who lived in one of the more genteel streets of Harlem with her mother and baby son. There were other girlfriends—white and black. But when it came to marriage, Wright was more comfortable with the idea of a black woman. Jerre Mangione, the Italian-American writer, remembers a conversation he had with Wright over drinks, after they saw Orson Welles's and John Houseman's memorable production of *Macbeth* in Harlem in 1936. Wright remarked that although he had a number of white friends, some of them women, he would never take a Caucasian wife. According to Mangione, Wright placed considerable emphasis on the "never."[87]

In terms of marriage, Wright was uncomfortably positioned between social classes. He might have been ambitious, light-skinned, and prodigiously talented, but he was a Southerner, the son of a Mississippi sharecropper, with an eighth-grade education and a precarious income. When it came to marrying an educated, young black woman, he was competing with professional men and women in Harlem— lawyers and doctors— many of whom lived in fine apartments in fashionable Strivers' Row and Sugar Hill

Shortly after winning the *Story* competition, he proposed to a middle-class black woman from Brooklyn. When he put the question to her father, he was cruelly rebuked. "That little $500 ain't going to last. How're you going to support my daughter?— I say No!"[88]

It might have been this humiliating rejection that made Wright turn to a more modest marriage proposition: the daughter of his landlady in Harlem. They were already sleeping together, and he warmed to the role of protector. The young woman, Marion Sawyer, had told him about some "unhappy sexual experience" she had had in the past. Now one of the men in the rooming house was pestering her. When Marion was cooking, Wright would chivalrously go the kitchen to ward him off.[89]

According to Jane Newton, Wright found it refreshing that Marion was not one of the gold diggers he was beginning to meet. Neither she nor her mother seemed particularly impressed that he was a published writer, interviewed in the newspapers. It seemed far more important to them that he dressed neatly and did not get drunk or cause trouble.

Wright once brought Marion out to Brooklyn to meet Jane Newton. "She was a slight pale olive-skinned girl, very nervous, hesitant in speech," Newton recalls. "Probably shyness and the fact that Dick pretty well sat her down and then ignored her made it impossible to know much about her from that meeting." Soon afterwards, Jane asked him if he was thinking of marrying Marion. "I guess I will," was the reply.

At the beginning of May 1938, just six weeks after the publication of *Uncle Tom's Children* (and still less time since the disastrous proposal to the young Brooklyn woman), Jane and Herbert Newton were among a small circle of Wright's friends to receive a printed wedding invitation in the mail. The ceremony was to take place on Sunday, 22 May, at the Sawyer residence on West 143rd Street.

After the invitations were sent out, the couple went about obtaining a marriage license. This involved passing a blood test—a Wassermann reaction test for syphilis—from the Board of Health. It was probably

Wright who went to pick up the results a few days later. He learned that Marion's test indicated syphilis with four pluses—the strongest possible reaction. The doctor said he was not able to issue a marriage license.[90]

Wright was appalled. He was quick to suspect that Marion had already known, and was terrified he might have caught the disease himself. When Jane Newton saw him soon afterwards, she was taken aback by Wright's sudden coldness toward the woman he had planned to marry. "He could think of nothing but getting out of that rooming house as soon as possible."[91]

On 11 May 1938, Marion Sawyer was obliged to communicate with Wright by telegram: "I saw the doctor. Marion."[92] She sent the message to 175 Carlton Avenue, Brooklyn. Wright had already moved in with Jane and Herbert Newton. The doctor assured Wright it was congenital syphilis and not active, and though Wright was relieved to hear it, he was scarcely reassured. He asked Ralph Ellison to come with him to make a final break with Marion and her mother. He did not want to face their hysteria on his own, he told his friend.[93] As Ellison recalled later, it was the mother, Mrs. Sawyer, who was the most visibly upset.

On 12 May 1938, the Newtons and other potential wedding guests received a penny postcard announcing that the marriage had been "postponed indefinitely." It was written by Marion, in purple ink.

Wright had installed himself in the Newtons' brownstone house on Carlton Avenue, close to Fort Greene Park. "Am taking the back, large room at the place you saw," he wrote to Henrietta Weigel on June 3. "I'm staying in Brooklyn now for good, that is, as long as I'll be in NY."[94] Weigel was vacationing in Bermuda and finding it dull. "Aw, you shatter my illusions about far away places," he wrote back. "I was thinking that nothing could be better than Bermuda but Heaven. . . . Let me know when you get back and we'll get together. Hunh?"

When Margaret Walker asked about the marriage rumors that had reached her in Chicago, he denied everything.

IN THE LAST SUMMER OF HIS LIFE, RICHARD WRIGHT WAS HAUNTED BY HIS CRUELTY toward Marion Sawyer. At his desk in Normandy, he wrote a whole novel within six weeks. *A Father's Law*, unpublished to this day, is about a black father and son who live in the South Side of Chicago.

The father is a policeman. The son, Tommy, is a student of sociology at the University of Chicago. He has not been the same since he broke off, very abruptly, with his girlfriend, Marie. His parents can't understand the change in him. What they do not yet know is that ever since he and his girlfriend parted ways, he has gone around murdering people –unconsciously hoping to be caught.

Finally he tells his father what happened between him and Marie. They were about to marry. They had their blood tests. Tommy picked up the results. The doctor broke the news: "She's sick, real sick. Son, this girl has four plus syphilis." Tommy left the doctor's office like a blind man. The sun was shining, but he could not see it.

The doctor did the test again, to make sure. Tommy could hardly eat for four days. He was sure about one thing. "I was going to ditch that girl." It was indeed syphilis, but as the doctor explained, it was congenital syphilis, inherited. The woman was in no way responsible, and he could cure it. Tommy muttered: "I don't want her now." He could not bring himself to see her again. The doctor told him she had wept for days.

"The first fear had been a cold one," Tommy told his father. "The second one was as hot as fire. Had I caught syphilis? . . . I felt unclean, polluted, contaminated, poisoned. . . . I went for a Wassermann each month, until the doctor said he would send me to a mental clinic. . . . I sent Marie my savings, told her she could sell the ring." He never saw the girl again. "I just dropped her. . . . It was like killing, Dad."

Several of Wright's male protagonists are so consumed by guilt about something to do with women and mothers and religion that they feel like murderers. They all proceed to commit real murder. Oddly, their actual murders seem to cause them far less guilt.[95]

8

═

GRAPPLING WITH BIGGER

May 1938–February 1939

At the beginning of June 1938 the Writers' Project accepted Wright's transfer to the creative work program. It was effectively a fellowship; he merely had to sign in at the Project once a week. He immediately got down to serious work on his new novel.

Once again, he was attempting something radically different in American race writing. He had no desire to write another *Uncle Tom's Children*, filled with black victims, martyrs, and heroes. "When the reviews of that book began to appear, I realized that I had made an awfully naïve mistake," he would write in his essay "How 'Bigger' Was Born." "I found that I had written a book which even bankers' daughters could read and weep over and feel good about. I swore to myself that if I ever wrote another book, no one would weep over it; that it would be so hard and deep that they would have to face it without the consolation of tears."[1]

His new novel was about a nondescript young hoodlum from Chicago's black ghetto. Bigger Thomas was not likable; he was not going to melt readers' hearts. He was tough, bullying, resentful, and full of fear and hate. Wright was determined to portray Bigger without a drop of sentimentality, without an inch of idealism. By the time he had finished with him, Bigger would be the angriest, most violent antihero ever to have appeared in black American literature. The bankers' daughters were going to flinch this time.

Wright wanted to show that youths like Bigger were not inherently bad, that their intense frustration, hatred, and their crimes were a result of being shut out of American society. As Bigger Thomas explodes to a friend: "We black and they white. They got things and we ain't. They do things and we can't. It's just like living in jail." Wright knew Bigger's yearnings well. In order to show white readers what the world looked like from inside the head of an angry black youth, he would write the book as much as possible from Bigger's point of view.

Wright knew he was taking a huge risk. It took courage after the success of *Uncle Tom's Children*. He had a reputation to lose. While he wrote the first draft of *Native Son*, he repeatedly told friends he did not believe any publisher would accept the novel. Already, two novels of his had been rejected because they did not say what publishers thought readers wanted to read. Before he could put words on paper, he had to consciously shut out the clamor of protesting voices in his head. "See, didn't we tell you all along that niggers are like that?" he could hear whites saying about Bigger Thomas.[2] And blacks would chorus: "But, Mr. Wright, there are so many of us who are not like Bigger! Why don't you portray in your fiction the best traits of our race?" As for the Communists, they were bound to call him "a smuggler of reaction" or "an ideological confusionist."

One of the recurrent images in the novel is blindness. Mr. Dalton, a well-known philanthropist who has made his fortune from real estate in the black ghetto, is morally blind. Mrs. Dalton is physically blind. Their daughter, twenty-three-year-old Mary, precipitates disaster by being blind drunk. On Bigger's first evening in his new chauffeuring job, Mary and her Communist boyfriend, Jan, ask him to drive them to the ghetto. Mary feels like mingling with black people. Embarrassed, Bigger takes them to Ernie's Kitchen Shack.[3] To his horror, Jan and Mary do not let him sit outside in the car; they insist that he join them. Jan orders fried chicken and beer, then a bottle of rum. In the backseat on the way home he and Mary swig from the bottle and pet each other. Jan asks to be dropped off near his home, leaving Mary with Bigger.

When they get home she asks him to help her out of the car. She stumbles loudly on the porch. He helps her into the house and tries to stand her on her feet. Finally he decides he will have to help her upstairs. Half pushing her, half carrying her, he gets her to the top of the stairs, but she is limp and mumbling incoherently. "Goddamn!" Bigger mutters.

He ends up carrying her into her bedroom and lifting her onto her bed. His hands are on her breasts. As if in a dream, he bends down and kisses her. Then the door creaks open. A white blur stands in the doorway. It's Mrs. Dalton, who cannot see. Mary starts to mumble something. Bigger, terrified, holds a pillow over her mouth.

The irony is that he did not want to be in this white woman's bedroom, and he certainly did not intend to murder her. Inevitably and irrevocably, this brief encounter with a white woman will prove fatal for them both.

He thrusts Mary's dead body into the furnace in the basement. In the next few days he writes Mr. Dalton a ransom note. Afraid that she might talk, he murders his girlfriend, Bessie, with a brick. By now, thousands of police are swarming over the ghetto. There's a rooftop chase.

At the end of May 1938, when the novel was still in the planning stages, a case broke in Chicago that was exactly the scenario Wright imagined for Bigger. Robert Nixon, an eighteen-year-old black youth, was caught breaking into a white woman's house. In his terror, he murdered her with a brick. By the end of the day, the white papers were reporting that the "Negro moron" had raped Mrs. Florence Johnson before he bludgeoned her to death.

Wright asked Margaret Walker to send him clippings from the Chicago papers—a task she performed conscientiously for the best part of a year. As Wright had anticipated, the white press did not even pretend to objectivity. Nixon was referred to as a "jungle Negro," a "Negro rapist," a "sex fiend," a "moron slayer." He was repeatedly described as "ape-like." A reporter from the *Chicago Sunday Tribune* observed: "His hunched shoulders and long, sinewy arms that dangle almost to his knees; his out-thrust head and catlike tread all suggest the animal."[4] As Wright states in "How 'Bigger' Was Born," several newspaper items and incidents in *Native Son* were rewrites of Nixon stories from the *Chicago Tribune*.

There was never any doubt how Robert Nixon's life would end. His trial lasted a week. Despite the contradictions in the evidence, the all-white jury was unanimous. In August 1938 Nixon was sentenced to death. The black community was outraged. There were ten reprieves. Finally, in June 1939, Nixon was strapped into the electric chair.[5]

THE DIFFERENCE BETWEEN CHICAGO'S EXCLUSIVE SOUTH SHORE AND THE crowded slums of the South Side could hardly have been more vast, but Wright had always been fascinated by the famous Loeb and Leopold case, which he had read about in Jackson in 1924. Richard Loeb and Nathan Leopold, seventeen- and eighteen-year-old sons of Jewish millionaires, brilliant students at the University of Chicago, had kidnapped a fourteen-year-old boy, bludgeoned his face with a chisel, shoved his naked body into a culvert, burned his clothing in the furnace at Loeb's house, then written his father a ransom letter asking for ten thousand dollars. Because the boys were homosexuals (they were sexual partners), it was widely assumed they had raped the boy before killing him.

The man who defended the young murderers, Clarence Darrow, was the most famous lawyer in the United States at the time. When Wright wrote Bigger's trial scene, Clarence Darrow's *Pleas in Defense of Loeb and Leopold* was on his desk.[6] Darrow, well known as the defender of the poor and weak, had spent a lifetime arguing that crime was the result of poverty and social neglect. Boris Max argues along the same lines.

What intrigued Wright—and everybody else—was that Loeb and Leopold had been raised in the wealthy South Shore area of Chicago and brought up amid vast country estates, governesses, and chauffeurs. Darrow took on their case because he was passionately opposed to capital punishment. Indeed, for these rich white boys, Darrow managed to get a mandatory sentence of execution turned into life imprisonment. In *Native Son*, Boris Max is unable to save the life of Bigger Thomas, a poor black boy.

FROM MAY TO OCTOBER 1938, WRIGHT LIVED WITH THE NEWTON FAMILY IN A large, old brownstone in Fort Greene, Brooklyn. Herbert Newton, busy with Party duties, left the house around 9 A.M. and often did not get home until midnight. Jane was fully occupied with their three children, all under five. Somehow, between the domestic chores and above the hubbub of family life, she managed to enter into endless discussions of *Native Son*.

Later, Wright would fondly recall the "talks, rum, argument, politics, and laughter" of those communal months in Brooklyn.[7] Herbert Newton would drop in, unexpectedly, with comrades from the Party. Herbert's sisters, Dorothy and Gwen, were often on the scene, helping with the children. (Wright had an unreciprocated romantic interest in Gwen.) Jane Newton was easygoing, gregarious, and always ready to grind another lot of coffee beans for new arrivals.

In 1964, in a vividly detailed letter to one of Wright's biographers, Michel Fabre, Jane Newton described what it was like to live that year with Richard Wright and his fictional fantasies.[8] Wright got up early, she says, around 6 A.M.—sometimes earlier at the height of summer. Clutching his lined, yellow legal pad, a fountain pen, and a bottle of ink, he walked to nearby Fort Greene Park. He climbed to the top of the hill, where he sat on a bench, looking down on the brownstones and, in the distance, the ragged tenement houses by the Brooklyn Navy Yard, and filled page after page with his scrawling handwriting.

He returned to the house around 10 A.M., after the domestic chaos had slightly subsided. "It can't have been altogether pleasant," says Jane Newton, "for there were gray days and I remember his coming back wet from having been caught in the rain, but as long as we lived on Carlton Avenue he followed this pattern." By ten, the children had eaten breakfast and were playing in the backyard. Jane would be in the large, light kitchen, "clearing the decks." The kitchen, she says, was where all the household activity took place: meals, conversations over coffee, washing the clothes, ironing, sewing, even bathing the children in washtubs. ("The bath was up two flights and it was impossible to leave the other work to be done just to bathe children.") Sometimes Wright cooked his own breakfast; sometimes Jane cooked it for him. "Whichever way," writes Newton, "the talk began at once." Wright told her what he had written that morning, and they discussed the new developments in the plot. The children would come in and out. ("Sometimes we had rather to shout our opinions to each other across something resembling a bearpit.") After breakfast, Wright would go to his room and type up what he had written that morning.

In the afternoon, he would work, read, go to the Brooklyn Public

Library, or into Manhattan to see people. If he was home, he ate with the children around 5 P.M., and he and Jane Newton would talk while she made dinner. In the evenings, he would disappear to his room or else go out; Jane rarely knew which.

Their arguments were sometimes heated. Jane was shocked that Wright wanted to call the young white woman "Mary Dalton" after the well-known radical who, along with Herb Newton, had been a member of the famous "Atlanta Six." Like Newton, after her narrow escape from the electric chair in Georgia, Dalton had come to Chicago's South Side, where she worked as a Party functionary. "Dick . . . felt very mischievous using her name," says Newton, who thought it "a rather pointless little gesture."

But Jane won the argument about Mary Dalton's dismemberment. In order to fit Mary's body into the furnace, Wright had Bigger severing her head with his jackknife. Newton said that was impossible; he would have to make it a hatchet. Wright didn't want to bring a hatchet into the picture. To prove her point, Newton bought a hen and watched gleefully while Wright, with a newly sharpened kitchen knife, tried to cut its neck over the edge of the kitchen table. He performed the operation halfheartedly, says Newton. "He had . . . little appetite for butchery himself."

One afternoon in midsummer, Wright came into the kitchen, flopped down in a chair, and said: "Jane, I'm going to have to kill Bessie." Jane was horrified. "Oh no, Dick!" She thought it unnecessary in terms of the plot. Nor did she think it would shed new light on Bigger's character. But Wright had decided that the novel had reached a point where something exciting or violent had to happen.

Newton stuck to her view. Wright stuck to his. "I gotta kill her . . . she's gotta go." At this moment, according to Newton, the landlord walked into the kitchen. He was a quiet, young black man who slept upstairs in the room he had lived in since childhood. He overheard Wright's passionate cry and looked rather flustered. He did not seem to be able to remember what he wanted to do in the kitchen, and left. "Dick rocked with laughter as soon as I had closed the door again and enjoyed very much the idea that Mr. Diggs may really have thought that we were discussing an actual murder."

The most serious arguments took place when Wright got to the trial section. Jane Newton thought it overwritten and too didactic; he seemed to her to be cramming his own opinions into the narrative. Wright insisted he could not make these points earlier; he needed to make them, and they were best expressed by Bigger's lawyer. He used to tell her that this might be the last opportunity he would have to get a book published. "He . . . anticipated a storm of protest against his Bigger which might silence him for all time. This was, he said, his chance to say what *he* felt."

They argued about plausibility. It was simply not credible, Jane Newton said, that Bigger's family, his friends, the preacher, the Dalton parents, Bigger's lawyer, and the state attorney would all crowd into Bigger's prison cell. Wright agreed with her, but did not think it mattered. "What I wanted that scene to say to the reader was more important than its surface reality or plausibility," he would write in "How 'Bigger' Was Born."

There was a certain rivalry between them. Jane Newton remembers Wright once bursting out: "Look Jane, what the hell do you know about writing?" Feeling the need to prove herself, she disappeared upstairs to write a story in a couple of hours while he looked after the children. "Dick was grateful when it was done. I made him coffee and took the children upstairs for naps, leaving him to draw his own conclusions about my right to argue with him. He read the story, we talked a little about what I was trying to illustrate in it, I made more coffee and we went back to arguing about *Native Son*."

Jane Newton makes it clear that she felt impatient with Wright at times. She found him stubborn. As a would-be writer herself, she enjoyed the role she played in Wright's creative process, but was irritated that he rarely took her advice. She was astonished that Wright did not know how the story would develop, and saw this as an indication of amateurism. What she also found remarkable (even more so in retrospect) was "the positively public way" in which the novel was composed.

THROUGHOUT THE DOG DAYS OF THE NEW YORK SUMMER, WRIGHT WORKED FURIously. By early October 1938, he was able to send a first draft—576 pages—to Harper & Brothers. His publisher, Ed Aswell, was confident enough about the outcome to give Wright a contract and offer a $250 advance against royalties. He did not like the title *Native Son*, and suggested they both try to think of something "more colorful."

Wright wrote to his agent, Paul Reynolds. "I have reason to believe that they like what I'm doing, so I think that perhaps a little more than $250 can be gotten. If, however, they balk, I'm willing to take whatever you can get."[9] Two days later, Reynolds announced that Aswell had increased the advance to $400.[10]

In the middle of October, Wright submitted an application for a Guggenheim fellowship. He was able to say that he had completed a first draft of a novel dealing with "Negro juvenile delinquency on Chicago's South Side against a background of bad housing, crime, residential segregation, and lack of vocational opportunities." He added that while the narrative was "melodramatic" on the surface, it was a serious portrait of urban Negro experience, and the first of its kind in fiction.[11]

He asked fifteen prominent people, including Eleanor Roosevelt, to write letters of recommendation.[12] Every one of them raved about him in glowing terms. "I go the whole hog for Wright," playwright Clifford Odets declared. Henry G. Alsberg, director of the Federal Writers' Project, thought him "the most promising new writer that the Federal Writers' Project has turned up." Claude Barnett declared him "the most powerful and moving Negro novelist yet to appear in America."

That month, the household was obliged to move. Their landlord, Mr. Diggs, had tuberculosis, and had become too ill to keep up the house payments. Wright and Herb Newton went house-hunting. It was a chore that made the group acutely conscious of its interracial composition. If Jane, a white woman, appeared with her black husband, no landlord would accept them. So the men did the searching, and Jane organized the moving.

The best the men could find in a short time was a cramped apartment over shops on a noisy commercial street in the Bedford Stuyvesant area, at 552 Gates Avenue. When they showed it to Jane, she was dismayed. Wright seemed to gloat over her displeasure: "Why Jane, this is the best the Negro bourgeoisie has!" His comment irritated her. She knew, and so did he, that they could find something more suitable. They both knew that the black bourgeoisie did not live like that. He always talked as if a white person could never know anything about the black community.

The apartment was small, and the children restless. Despite the discomforts, Wright doggedly revised his manuscript. The discussions stopped. Wright—who, according to Jane Newton, "resisted" closeness with the family—kept more of a distance than usual. She points out that he was not good with the children. "He teased them and frightened them and they were never fond of him."

In November the men found a parlor floor and basement arrangement in a large house at 101 Lefferts Place, a short, quiet, tree-lined street. Formerly very fashionable, by now the white residents had moved out.

IT WAS WINTER. WRIGHT WORKED IN HIS BACK PARLOR ROOM FROM SEVEN, EIGHT, or nine in the morning until late at night. In the afternoon, when his mind became blurred, he took a walk. For inspiration, he was rereading Henry James's and H. L. Mencken's literary criticism, Hemingway's stories, Malraux's *Man's Fate*, and an array of detective novels.

"I've worked over some 200 pages and when I look up I see 200 more still waiting," he told his playwright friend Millen Brand in November. "It makes you feel as though you're climbing the Alps, no less."[13] But he was happy.

The Party was pushing Wright forward as its most prominent black writer. *Uncle Tom's Children* had appeared in Russian in *International Literature* and received a highly favorable review in *Pravda*. In Britain, the left-wing publisher Victor Gollancz had asked Paul Robeson to write a foreword to the British edition. At a Communist reception in Wright's honor in Harlem, Wright was hailed as "our new comet."[14] In June he covered Joe Louis's triumphant fight against the Nazi Max Schmeling for the *Daily Worker*.

There were plenty of distractions when Wright wanted them. "He had quite a few girls," says Jane Newton, who particularly remembers a beautiful young black woman, the wife of an undertaker. She and her husband were prominent members of Brooklyn's black social set, but the woman found her husband dull. "She used to visit Dick and they went out together occasionally. . . . She was not, Dick said, 'intellectual' but she was pleasant and gay and tender."[15] There was also Dhimah, the Russian dancer. Jane Newton privately thought her "an awkward homely woman with an affected over-romantic manner."[16]

Wright had many friends and dozens of acquaintances—most of

them in or on the fringes of the Party. He liked to meet white friends over a good Southern meal at Frank's, in Harlem, or for drinks at Café Society, the new and only integrated nightclub in white Manhattan and a popular hangout for progressives of either race. The Jewish owner, Barney Josephson, had given it this name to mock the affluent crowd. Ironically, Café Society quickly acquired its own bohemian chic.

Willard Maas and Marie Menken, whom he got to know on the New York Writers' Project, lived on Montague Street, Brooklyn Heights. Maas was a poet, Menken a painter and budding filmmaker. They were well known for the bohemian parties they held in their garret, with its spectacular views of the Manhattan skyline.[17] Wright enjoyed dinners on their rooftop terrace, listening to Willard's African records and drinking cheap rum. The young poet Norman Rosten was around there one day when Wright read aloud a chapter of *Native Son*. "It had us biting our tongues," Rosten would recall later.[18]

Wright read his work-in-progress to numerous friends. Later, in gratitude, he would dedicate his essay "How 'Bigger' Was Born" to "Abe, Belle, Mannie and Lora." This was Abe and Isabelle Chapman, their baby daughter, Laura, and Abe's brother, Manny, with whom Wright had more or less lived when he first came to New York. The discussions in that household were particularly lively. The two brothers both passionately desired social change, but Abe was a devoted Communist and Manny, a philosopher, believed that radical change would come about through art and religion. To the horror of their Jewish parents, Manny had recently converted to Catholicism.[19]

Sometimes Wright took the A train to Harlem. Ralph Ellison read *Native Son* as it came out of the typewriter. So did Marvel Cooke, a light-skinned journalist at Harlem's *New York Amsterdam News* who lived with her Jamaican husband on Sugar Hill in the same building with W. E. B. Du Bois. Marvel's mother, a wonderful cook, was visiting from Chicago that year, and she doted on Wright. "He used to come by every Saturday night to get some of my mother's hot rolls," Marvel remembered. After dinner he would read to them. "I think I read that first chapter of *Native Son* a million times."[20]

IN NOVEMBER 1938 WRIGHT MADE A TRIP TO CHICAGO. HE ARRIVED ON A SUNDAY, left his bags at his mother's, and hurried around to Margaret Walker's.

She was not home, and her landlady suggested that he wait in the living room. Soon afterwards, Walker returned from church. She writes:

> My landlady said, "There's a surprise for you in the living room." I said, "A surprise for me? What kind of surprise?" I had come in from a bright day outside, and the living room looked dim and shadowy. I squinted my eyes to see, and Wright laughed and said, "Poor little Margaret, she doesn't even know me." I squealed with delight and hugged him, but immediately I felt him freeze, and I knew that his guard was up against my embrace, so I backed away.[21]

They had a quick meal, Walker recalls, and visited Joyce and Ed Gourfain in Hyde Park, then walked down Drexel Boulevard to find a vacant lot Wright could use as an address for the Daltons' house.

The next day, they saw Ulysses S. Keys, a black lawyer involved in the early stages of Nixon's defense. Wright had a list of questions for him about court procedure. They went to Cook County Jail, where Nixon was incarcerated. Wright took photographs. He had thought he might be able to see Nixon, or perhaps even witness an execution. Neither was possible.

He and Walker went together to the Chicago Public Library, and Wright checked out two books on her card. From the elevated railway, Wright took notes on the Indiana Avenue rooftops where Bigger would eventually be captured after a chase across the rooftops. Margaret Walker was doubtful about this melodramatic scene.

"I think it will shock people," Wright told her, "and I love to shock people." Walker recalls: "He grinned gleefully and rubbed his hands together in anticipation, and I couldn't stop laughing."

BACK IN BROOKLYN, WRIGHT WORKED LONG HOURS, REVISING, POLISHING, changing scenes. The ending gave him a lot of trouble. Finally, he decided not to finish with Bigger's execution after all. Two murders were perhaps enough for one book. Instead, he had Bigger saying good-bye to his lawyer, Boris Max, in his cell. Through the barred window Bigger glimpses the "tips of sun-drenched buildings in the Loop." He feels wildly alone. "I never wanted to hurt nobody. That's the truth, Mr. Max." Suddenly he shouts: "I didn't want to kill! . . . But what I killed for, I *am*! . . . I didn't know I was really alive in this world until I felt things hard enough to kill for 'em." Max shrinks from him, horrified.

The opening scene also gave Wright difficulty. "Dick had very sure ideas about what was acceptable in the modern novel," Jane Newton comments. "He felt he could not begin as the Victorians did sometimes, with a quiet description of place or a methodical setting forth of character in expository prose. The action must begin on the first line and proceed like a train."

Soon after Christmas, Ted Ward, an old friend from the black South Side writers' group, came to New York with the Federal Theatre Project. He was part of the cast for *The Swing Mikado*. Earlier that year, his play, *Big White Fog*, had enjoyed a successful season in Chicago. But he was tired of the conservative theater scene in Chicago, and when the household at Lefferts Place urged him to stay on in New York, he moved into a room on the top floor.

Wright gave him *Native Son* to read. "It was, to say the least, the most amazing literary experience of my life," Ward recalled later.[22] He was keen to adapt it for the theater. This provoked excited discussions for the best part of a week, with Ward and Wright acting out parts in the kitchen in front of Jane Newton. They discussed possible actors. Wright thought Ted should act the part of Bigger. According to Jane Newton, this offended Ward, who saw himself as a playwright, not an actor.

Newton believes that Ted Ward was "awfully good for Dick."[23] He was "a voice from home." He had "lived in other places . . . and was much more a man of the world and looked at the matter of writing in a much more methodical way than Dick did." She was well aware of the rivalry between the two men. She remembers one occasion when Ward became furious with Wright for implying that he, Ward, was a lesser writer. She observed that Wright could accept from her any amount of criticism of his novel, but "he wanted unswerving agreement on the matter of the worth of another writer in the house."

One day, Wright burst into the kitchen with a pile of papers. "I've got it!" he told them triumphantly. He had finally found the opening to his novel. He read it to them. It began with an alarm clock going off. "Brrrrrriiiiiinng!" The Thomas family starts to get up. And then they see the rat—a huge black creature. Chaos breaks out. The women leap up on the bed. The boys grab a skillet each. The rat is frenzied; so are they. Finally, Bigger throws his skillet. No sound. He tiptoes forward and peers. "By God, I got 'im," he says. He pounds the rat's head with a shoe. "You sonofabitch!"

By February the final draft was finished. From Chicago, Margaret Walker blasted Wright for not sending back the library books he had borrowed on her card. He returned the books, with a dollar to cover the fines. He told her he had been working for up to fifteen hours a day.

> I never intend to work that long and hard again. If this book is published, then I'll delay getting my next one out, for two reasons: I'm making a new departure and I don't want to kill myself. But I had to get that book out and I wanted it out before the first was forgotten. Rest assured, that if this book is published, you'll *hear* about it. . . . Really, I don't believe that they are going to publish it.[24]

Margaret Walker wrote back: "I can imagine the state you are in now with so many irons in the fire. Tense until you know how the book is going; tense until you hear from the Guggenheim; tense because you're bound to be tired anyway, and I've got a hunch that as usual you're worried about money. Listen, Mister, you'd better relax!"[25]

Early in February 1939, Wright arranged for a young woman to come to the house to type a fair copy for the publisher. When it was finished, Jane Newton says, there was jubilation.

> I remember I had a record of Shostakovich's Prelude in E minor for orchestra and we put it on Dick's phonograph and turned it as loud as we could and played it at the end of a fine evening of drinking and celebrating. The walls *shook*, even in that pretty solid old house![26]

Wright dedicated his novel about a monstrous "native son" who murdered two women to the most significant woman in his life so far. "To my mother, who, when I was a child at her knee, taught me to revere the fanciful and the imaginative."

9

MARRIAGE

February 1939–August 1939

I told you I was going to read your novel last night without realizing
what a monumental piece of work it was," Paul Reynolds, Wright's literary agent, a man sparing with praise, wrote to Wright on 28 February
1939. He had read only a third so far, and wished it had "a little more
humor." But he thought it impressive and predicted it would attract
attention. "What is interesting about your work is that you're writing
realism with regard to the Negro, when in most literature he has been
treated as a comic figure."[1]

Two days later, Reynolds finished the novel. This time he wrote to
Wright more critically. The book had held his interest all the way
through, and he thought Bigger "not only the equal but superior to the
protagonist in Theodore Dreiser's *American Tragedy*." He found the
white characters far less convincing—especially Mary Dalton. "I rather
suspect that the rich Chicago girl is the type that you haven't had much
experience with." The most credible white character, in Reynolds's
view, was Mr. Max. Nevertheless he hoped Wright would cut Max's
twenty-nine-page defense of Bigger "very severely."[2]

The Guggenheim committee members had taken the unusual step

of asking Wright's publisher to let them see the manuscript of *Native Son*. They also asked for reviews of *Uncle Tom's Children*. "I hesitate to tell you all this because it may get your hopes too high," Aswell told Wright in mid-March. "At the moment, at any rate, the situation looks warm."[3]

Two weeks later, the Guggenheim fellowships were announced. There were one thousand applicants and sixty-nine fellowships. Richard Wright was a well-known Communist, and his forthcoming novel was taking on some decidedly risky racial issues, and yet the Guggenheim Foundation awarded him a fellowship.[4] It was worth twenty-five hundred dollars—well over twice Wright's annual salary at the Writers' Project. Jubilant, he wrote to thank all his sponsors.

The news spread fast. From London, where Paul Robeson was acting in *Plant in the Sun*, his wife Eslanda sent congratulations. "It's high time they gave it to a progressive writer!!"[5] Joe Brown, in Mississippi, wanted to know why in the Sam Hill Dick never wrote even a few lines to his old friend "down 'Sippy Way." "Every time I pick up the papers it's Dick Wright, what a man! and it gives me a thrill to know just one guy who has reached the top of the ladder."[6] Gwendolyn Bennett, a Harlem Renaissance writer, wrote to Wright: "Your name being the only Negro's means that on your shoulders rests the burden of proof for all the things we each believe to be right. I know of no abler shoulders on which such a charge could rest."[7]

Wright sent a letter to the Federal Writers' Project, tendering his resignation as of 17 May 1939, when his contract ran out. He thanked the Project for providing him with the chance of a livelihood during the Depression.

He was anxious about giving up the regular income. His brother was ill again, with perforated ulcers, and Wright was once again providing for the family in Chicago. But he also knew that the Writers' Project was in serious jeopardy and his future there by no means secure. The Dies Committee (the precursor to the House Un-American Activities Committee) proclaimed that the Federal Writers' Project and the Federal Theatre Project were "doing more to spread Communist propaganda than the Communist Party itself." One committee member described Wright's autobiographical essay "The Ethics of Living Jim Crow" as "the most filthy thing I have ever seen."[8] The director of the Writers' Project, Henry Alsberg (one of Wright's sponsors for the

Guggenheim), had just been fired and replaced by a conservative. Things did not look good.

Beleaguered as it was, the Communist Party continued to open up opportunities for Wright. In May he received an official invitation from Timofei Rokotov, secretary of the International Union of Revolutionary Writers[9] and publisher of the journal *International Literature*, to spend a year and a half in Moscow as editor of the journal's English edition. Wright knew he could not possibly work with the Moscow apparatchiks breathing down his neck; he wanted very much to go to Russia, but as an independent writer. Moscow's state publishing house, Goslitizdat, had printed two editions of *Uncle Tom's Children* and sold altogether seventy-five thousand copies. He could live quite well off the royalties. But the way the storm clouds were gathering in Europe, he might have to be content for the time being with Mexico.

EDWARD ASWELL HELD THE SAME VIEW AS PAUL REYNOLDS ABOUT BORIS MAX'S courtroom diatribe. It needed cutting. So did some of the newspaper items relating to Bigger. In mid-May, Wright took the manuscript back for revision. He cut some of the newspaper extracts, but hardly shortened Max's speech at all. "You are a fast worker!" Aswell told him in June. "I am glad you were able to cut some of the newspaper items. As for the lawyer's speeches—well, you're the doctor and what you say goes."[10]

Aswell's leniency was remarkable. Most publishing houses were reluctant to produce protest fiction, and they were not keen on Negro subject matter. Gene Saxton, the head of Harper & Brothers, had been reluctant to publish *Native Son*. As Aswell put it later, Saxton "had a rule of thumb gained from his experience, that you can't publish successfully a book about Negroes, or by Negroes."[11] Aswell's enthusiasm for the book had carried the day.

It must have encouraged the team at Harper that Wright was doing so well. His sponsors for the Guggenheim were prominent intellectuals, and the Guggenheim committee itself had been prepared to back *Native Son*. "Fire and Cloud," the final story in *Uncle Tom's Children*, had won second prize in the prestigious O. Henry Awards of 1938, ahead of Steinbeck and Saroyan. This cast a favorable light on Harper, which had published the collection in the first place. Another story,

"Bright and Morning Star," had just been published in the *New Masses* and would soon be one of the selections for Edward J. O'Brien's famous anthology *Best Short Stories for 1939.*

ONE EVENING IN APRIL 1939, AFTER A COMMUNIST EXECUTIVE MEETING, HERBERT Newton brought Ellen Poplowitz home to Lefferts Place for coffee. Ellen was "very pretty . . . quiet and serious," with "a pale very young face framed in dark curls," says Jane Newton.[12] Her real name was Freda, but her Party name was Ellen Douglas, and her friends all called her Ellen. "My memory of it," says Jane Newton, "is that Dick liked her at once and they became friendly very quickly."

Ellen was small, with a pointed girlish face and high cheekbones, and she looked much younger than twenty-six. But her appearance was deceptive. She was the leader of the Fulton Street, Brooklyn, branch of the Communist Party. It was a relatively junior position in the Party hierarchy, but she needed to be a tough, serious, and efficient organizer and an articulate mouthpiece for the local community. It meant attending endless meetings, recruiting new members, checking on absentee comrades, canvassing for more subscribers to the *Daily Worker.* After a day's work as a secretary in an insurance company, Ellen's evenings were filled with Party duties. Several times a week she had to go along to the section office to pick up mail and receive instructions for what to say at the next branch meeting. There were occasional study groups. She was expected to attend major rallies and picket lines.

Ellen Poplowitz had never heard of Richard Wright. But he made an impact on her that evening. "He came bouncing out, effervescent, full of bonhomie, and Jane introduced us," she says. "I thought he was a splendid looking creature. I was immediately attracted to him, but at the time I was all Party, no room for romance or anything. I was a very dedicated person."[13]

Her dedication provided her with the opportunity to see more of Wright. Jane Newton, also a member of the Fulton Street branch, had to baby-sit the children in the evenings and could rarely make it to meetings. From now on, Ellen sometimes delivered Jane's assignments herself. For his part, Wright made an effort to turn up at branch meetings.

In May, the household at Lefferts Place was served notice. Their landlord, a conservative West Indian Negro, did not approve of the "mixing" that went on in the house. Herbert Newton and Wright both tried to reason with him, but he was adamant. Wright and Ted Ward dreamed of hiring a sound truck and blasting out carefully selected calypso songs in front of the landlord's house. (Wright had in mind a song called "Sly Mongoose"; another was about returning to Jamaica.)[14]

This time Wright did not move with the Newtons. Ted Ward had gone to live in the Douglas Hotel, 809 St. Nicholas Avenue in Harlem. Wright decided to take the room next door.[15]

HITLER HAD COMMANDEERED AUSTRIA AND CZECHOSLOVAKIA; MUSSOLINI HAD taken Albania; and the Left was still reeling from Franco's triumph over the freedom fighters when the Third American Writers' Congress took place on the weekend of 2–4 June 1939. At the opening session in Carnegie Hall, Thomas Mann, the exiled German novelist, spoke to a three-thousand-strong audience. At the end of the conference, the audience stood, heads bowed, while Langston Hughes read out a list of forty-five writers around the world who had already sacrificed their lives to the fight against fascism.

During the conference itself, Richard Wright spoke about problems of craft. Langston Hughes gave a heartfelt talk about the difficulty black writers faced in making an income from writing. The kinds of jobs open to white writers—work in publishing houses, magazine and news-paper offices, publicity firms, and radio or motion pictures—were as tightly closed to black American writers as they were to Jews in Nazi Germany, he said, and in their writing itself, there was the thorny prob-lem of subject matter. White publishers liked books about exotic Negroes, naïve Uncle Toms, idyllic Southern plantations, and contented black mammies.[16] Listening to this, Wright must again have wondered to himself whether *Native Son* would have any readers at all.

As if to prove Hughes's point, the movie *Gone With the Wind* was sweeping through the country that year. Wright described it as "the most vicious of Southern anti-Negro slander . . . wrapped in four mil-lion dollars worth of glamour."[17]

———

MARGARET WALKER CAME TO NEW YORK FOR THE WRITERS' CONGRESS. MORE importantly, she wanted to see Dick Wright. Among other things, she was hoping he would help find a publisher for her novel, *Goose Island*. For the last two years, while employed at the Illinois Writers' Project, she had been working on it full-time. She brought the completed manuscript to New York.

It was two years since Wright had left Chicago. Apart from his two brief visits there, he and Margaret had kept in contact by letter. She signed her letters "Yours, Margaret." He signed, as he often did with friends, "As Ever, Dick." His letters were shorter, mostly about his reading and writing. Hers were long and gossipy. She fussed over him: he must try not to be tense; he must remember to wear a coat. She rejoiced over his successes. She wrote about her own literary ambitions. And she told Wright every time someone said something bad about him. She liked to portray herself as his sole defender in the Chicago wilderness.

Wright told her he felt indebted for the trouble she had taken with the newspaper cuttings. (She replied: "I feel grateful to you for many things which I consider of far more intrinsic value than a bunch of newspaper clippings.")[18] But Wright had always felt ambivalent about Margaret Walker. In Chicago he had once asked her why she so often said the opposite of what she actually thought. Wright knew she was in love with him—everyone did, except perhaps Margaret herself.

When she came to New York that summer, Margaret was twenty-three, paper-thin, fragile in health, and prone to what she herself called "hysteria." She was leading a lonely life in Chicago, sharing a room with her sister. She did not have a boyfriend. Eager to be a writer, she modeled herself so closely on Wright that her sister warned her against trying to be "a carbon copy of Dick Wright."

In the year before Wright left Chicago, she liked to see herself as his girlfriend, even though there was never any gesture of physical intimacy from him. Ted Ward once told her that she was "barking up the wrong tree" with Wright. He added—perhaps as a joke, or perhaps in an attempt to turn her attentions elsewhere—that Wright was "a third sex man."[19] She did not understand what he meant at the time, but the seed was planted in her mind. And it stayed.

In 1988 in her biography, *Richard Wright: Daemonic Genius*, seventy-three-year-old Margaret Walker tried to build up a picture of Wright as a homosexual. "He gave the appearance of an almost effete, slightly effeminate personality. He had a pipsqueak voice, small and delicate hands and feet, smooth face with very light beard, and rather fastidious ways or mannerisms. He certainly did not exude a strong maleness or masculinity. Perhaps this is one of the answers to his problems with women. He definitely had problems in that area. . . . There was never any question of marriage or intimate physical relationship between us—not so much as a goodnight kiss, never, not ever."[20]

Back in June 1939, she almost did not make it to New York. She had not been able to organize a car ride, and the train fare was expensive—fifty-four dollars for the round trip. She had to borrow the money and this took so long that she missed the opening evening of the congress. For two weeks, she had been staying up late to finish typing her novel. She writes that the strain and lack of sleep made her "hysterical."[21]

Her train, the super-fast "Pacemaker," left Chicago at 4 P.M. and got into Grand Central Station at nine in the morning on Saturday, 3 June. She saw Dick Wright looking anxiously for her in the crowd. Then he saw her and grinned broadly.

Wright had no sooner taken her bag than she poured out her worries about money to him. He reassured her. He had money and would lend her some. He had made arrangements for her to stay in Marvel and Cecil Cooke's apartment in Sugar Hill, the fashionable section of Harlem. It was ten minutes from where he and Ted Ward were living, at the Douglas Hotel. Margaret wanted to wash and change her clothes. He insisted they take the subway straight to Greenwich Village. Otherwise they would miss the morning session.

They had lunch with some black delegates, including Ralph Ellison. In the afternoon session, Margaret started to nod off. Since Ellison was leaving, Wright asked him to escort her up to Harlem. Wright was beginning to suspect that Margaret had not come for the congress at all. He was excited by it, and wanted to go to every session.

At Marvel Cooke's apartment, Margaret shared a bed with Zelma Velasco, Marvel's younger sister—who also happened to be Ted Ward's girlfriend. (Margaret knew Ted from the South Side writers' group.) Zelma liked to gossip and Zelma had it in for Dick Wright. One evening she told Margaret that they had all been sent invitations to Dick's wedding the previous year, but the wedding had not come off, and she thought he'd let success go to his head—Ted thought so too—and Ted was going to move in with Langston Hughes, which was good because it would be cheaper than the Douglas Hotel and much nicer for Ted.

Margaret Walker's head was still swimming with all this when Wright turned up on Monday morning to take her to breakfast. They talked about his work and hers. He told her he wanted more than anything else to go and live in Paris. Margaret asked whether he knew that Ted Ward was going to move in with Langston Hughes. Wright didn't.

"Well he is, and I'm glad," said Walker. "I was never so mad as when you wrote and said he was staying in the same place you were staying."

"Why?"

"Because it was too damn close," she said.[22] Wright suddenly realized what she was hinting: that he and Ward and Langston Hughes were sexually involved with one another.

That evening Margaret had a complimentary ticket for Robert E. Sherwood's Broadway play *Abe Lincoln in Illinois*. When Zelma saw her all dressed up, she told Margaret she should go and show herself to Dick Wright and ask him to accompany her. Margaret laughed. Zelma insisted. They walked over to the Douglas Hotel, and without announcing themselves, Zelma barged into Ted Ward's room. To Margaret's consternation they found Wright "half sprawled on the bed with his slippers on." Wright did not want to accompany her to the theater. She called him a "louse" and a "lousy bum." She laughed. He did not.

Later that night, when Margaret got back from the theater, Marvel Cooke's apartment was full of people talking and drinking. Wright turned up. He asked Margaret to bring her coat and come with him. He led her to one of the park benches opposite the apartment building, from where they looked down over St. Nicholas Park at the lights of lower Harlem and the Bronx. "I could look at this forever," Margaret said.

"I think the best thing for you to do is pack your things and get out of here the first thing in the morning," Wright told her.

Walker was dumfounded. What had she done? she asked. "What about my novel?"

Her novel no longer concerned him, he said. "This thing has gone on for three years. The relationship between us is at an end."[23]

Again she asked what she had done to provoke this. "Search your conscience and you'll know the answer," he told her. He refused to say more. He said he didn't want any hysterics, and he walked off into the night.

She did not leave the next day. That evening, with Zelma, Marvel Cooke, and Jane Newton as mediators, Ted Ward submitted her to a Communist Party style straightening out session. He accused her of wanting to marry Wright and trying to set herself up as his guardian. She had come between Wright and his friends in the South Side writers' group with her gossip and lies, he said, and she had done exactly the same thing in New York. What did she mean, implying constantly that the men were all having sexual relations with one another? All the rumors she had founded: didn't she realize they all saw right through her?[24]

Before she left New York, Margaret Walker took her novel to Doubleday Doran. On Wednesday, 7 June, at Jane Newton's suggestion, she typed Wright a letter of apology. It was seven pages long. She did not try to justify herself. "Monday night I realized I have gone out of your life. . . . I realize that it all resolves down to this: that I am a rather foolish and giddy girl who rather indiscreetly has talked too much, confided too much in people, and tried too hard to be frank and honest on all occasions in an effort to maintain a friendship which I have valued above all others I have ever known."[25]

Two weeks later, back in Chicago, she sent Wright a note, promising to pay back his ten dollars on her next payday. It was their last communication. She enclosed a last clipping about Robert Nixon. He had just been executed.

MARGARET WALKER'S REPUTATION FOR GOSSIP WAS NOW FIRMLY ESTABLISHED. Langston Hughes sent postcards to a number of friends, including Margaret Walker herself. On them he typed a short poem called "Epic":

> Margaret Walker is a talker
> When she came to town
> What she said put Ted in bed
> And turned Dick upside down.[26]

Fifty years later in her biography of Wright, Margaret Walker stuck to her thesis that Wright had both homosexual and homophobic tendencies, and that he and Ted Ward were sharing each other's beds. In

1991 when Madison Davis Lacy was making a documentary on Wright, he questioned Margaret Walker closely about that day when she and Zelma burst into Ted Ward's room at the Douglas Hotel. Walker admitted the room was so small that the bed was the only place visitors could put themselves.[27]

AMONG WRIGHT'S PAPERS AT YALE IS A NOTE, TYPEWRITTEN AND UNDATED, FROM Ellen Poplowitz. It seems that Wright had asked her for a date on Friday night.

> Dick,
>
> Meeting this Friday at Fulton Street which I must attend.
>
> We're having our party at Jane's this Saturday night and if you are able to make it, I'll see you then.
>
> Ellen

It is a carefully noncommittal note from a busy Communist Party executive. Ellen Wright was discreet; she was also highly practical. She had never been in love before she met Richard Wright. Even then, she says, it was not love at first sight. "No booming heart or anything."[28] Ellen was not an impetuous type.

One evening after a party at the home of a Negro member of their branch, Wright asked Ellen to come for a walk with him. They went up to Harlem and sat in a park. "We talked for hours. We had a wonderful time. We sat on a bench and talked. There was an instant understanding between us," she says.[29] From then on, they saw each other as often as Ellen's Party functions and Wright's own schedule would permit.

Ellen had had relationships with men before. "The Party was ahead of its time in the sexual sense," she says. An Italian boyfriend had wanted to marry her, but she wasn't interested. Her mother was always trying to pair her off with a Jewish doctor or lawyer. "I was bored to death with those guys. We had nothing in common."[30]

A few weeks later, Wright asked Ellen to marry him. It was impetuous. (Ellen did not know that he had already proposed to two others with equal impetuosity.) For Ellen it was bewildering, as well as flattering. She did not know Wright well, and here he was proposing an interracial marriage. Even inside the Party there were mutterings about marriages between black men and white women. Outside the Party, Ellen knew they would be ostracized in many circles. Her mother would be horrified. Ellen herself needed time to examine her feelings.

That summer Wright talked to both Ralph Ellison and Ted Ward about marriage to a white woman, and the problems it could entail.[31] Neither of his friends discouraged him. Ralph was married to a black woman, but he believed in integration. Ted Ward, having broken up with Zelma, was himself courting a white woman, Mary Sangigihan. Ward admitted there were pressures. Black Communist comrades were urging him to break it off. ("Any union between us was bound to create unfavorable reaction among Negro women, thus hurting the progressive movement," Ward wrote to Langston Hughes, now in California.)[32] It did not help matters that Mary was the wife of another black man, Harry Haywood, the ex–Chicago Communist organizer, recently back from Spain.

Jane Newton, confidante to many, was the only one to hear both Ellen and Wright's points of view:

> [Ellen] wanted to marry him and he was very much attached to her, but she couldn't make up her mind to do it because of her family. . . . She told me that she had refused him, but kept wanting to re-consider and felt wrong about it. Dick told me that she had decided she couldn't face her family with a decision to marry him and wanted to wait, to move more slowly, but I gathered that he couldn't wait, that he felt her hesitation reflected on the quality of her feelings for him.[33]

Later that summer, Ellen went upstate New York to Camp Unity, a Communist Party study camp and vacation resort in the Berkshires. While there, she was arrested for distributing leaflets. Nevertheless, in that idyllic rural environment, she had time to reflect. She decided she *did* want to marry Dick Wright. She loved him, she missed him, and she would live with the difficulties. Surely her family would eventually come around. As soon as she was back in New York City, she phoned him excitedly. His voice was cold. He said he did not want to see her. Only by sheer persistence did she persuade him to meet with her. He walked with her from the subway exit to a park bench, and announced that he had met the person with whom he wanted to spend the rest of his life.

Ellen was absolutely crushed. But she knew better than to make a scene. "He was not one for explanations and recriminations," she says. "When a thing is through, it's through."[34]

IN EARLY AUGUST, JANE NEWTON LEFT WITH THE CHILDREN FOR THE COOLER AIR of Martha's Vineyard. A month or so earlier, she had been counseling Ellen Poplowitz about interracial marriage. Now, while she was packing to leave, Wright told her he was back with his dancer girlfriend, Dhimah Meidman.

In late August, Arna Bontemps came to New York for a few days. To Langston Hughes, in California, he wrote: "Ted Ward is in a hot spot, having lost the romantic interest of Zelma Velasco and in turn taken Mary from Harry Heyward [Haywood]. Quite a stew, with lots of cuss words. . . . Boy, Harlem is a pistol! Dick has a new romantic interest, too. Deema, a dancer."[35] There was an unconvincing pencil line through the paragraph, and Bontemps wrote in the margin: "Low gossip."

The gossip was out-of-date. No one had told Bontemps that Dick and Dhimah were already man and wife. Wright was keeping it a tight secret. Evidently he was not ready to proclaim to the world that he had married a white woman and had asked Ellison and Ward to be discreet. On 11 August, a sweltering evening, Ted Ward put on a one-man performance of "Bright and Morning Star" at the Harlem Suitcase Theatre. The following evening, 12 August, Wright married Dhimah in Harlem. It was not until 29 August that Ted Ward wrote to Langston Hughes: "Dick got married. The news hasn't broken yet, but I expect a very hubbub when it does, as his wife is a white woman."[36] It was Langston Hughes, across the country, who broke the news to Bontemps. "Dick married Deema. The ladies of the race, I presume, are raising hell!"[37]

Many Chicago friends did not know for months. Nelson Algren was told the news in December, by Wright's brother. Leon Wright was using a friend's studio near Algren's apartment for his painting. "Glad . . . to hear that you got yourself married," Algren wrote to Wright. "At least your brother Leon has that idea, and I hope he's right. Our heartiest congratulations and may all your troubles be little ones, as they say."[38]

DHIMAH MADE THE MOST OF THE MYSTIQUE OF HER PAST. IN THE DANCE WORLD, it was nothing to be yet another Russian Jew, but to be Egyptian had flair. Dhimah, not able to supply her adopted country with a birth certificate, felt free to invent. Some records give her birthplace as Odessa, Russia; others give it as Cairo, Egypt. On these same records, her date of birth fluctuates from 1900 to 1907.

Her parents, Aaron and Eudice ("Eda") Meidman, were from Odessa. Dhimah was the eldest of three siblings: her brother Sianna (Samuel) was born in Odessa in 1904, and then came Harry. According to a brief job résumé Dhimah once wrote, the family left Russia in 1905.[39] Fleeing from the pogroms, they probably went down to the docks and boarded the first available boat, which happened to be going to Cairo.

In mid-May 1928, the *New York Evening Post* had announced: "A new star burst upon the ever-changing dance firmament last night." In a solo dance recital at the Guild Theatre, Dhimah performed "Madonna," inspired by the paintings of El Greco, and a sequence of dance poems based on the Koran. She danced barefoot, with a simple percussion accompaniment. One critic described "the Egyptian lady" as a "gifted soul."[40] *Dance Magazine* observed: "She seems bent to pour forth life's tragic poetry."[41]

From the beginning, the American Left embraced modern dance. The Communist Party contrasted its revolutionary potential with traditional dance, which it considered bourgeois, effete, and elitist. According to Herbert Kline's Communist magazine *New Theatre*, the "thinking dancer" understood that dance had to be allied with revolutionary ideology.[42] The Workers' Dance League performed at strike meetings and political rallies. Critics in the *New Masses* or *New Theatre* judged the dancers in terms of their social message.

In 1935 Dhimah was invited to Moscow to train a modern dance group.[43] In the Soviet Union she encountered a perplexing paradox: Russian Communists liked traditional ballet; they did not appreciate modern dance at all. Near the beginning of her stay, she wrote an article, "I Dance for Moscow," for *New Theatre*.[44] "The Russians are ardent devotees of the dance," she wrote, and "very curious about new forms." She was hugely impressed to see theaters packed with Red Army men and factory workers, "who only a short number of years ago were freed from the miseries of Tsarist oppression." But as she pointed out, these Russian audiences were used to classical ballet with lavish stage sets, and her stark, barefoot performances caused heated discussions.

She cast it in the best possible light: "As busy as the Soviet people are in their heavy tasks of building a Socialist system, there is nothing that they will accept, no matter how beautifully costumed, how different or even exotic it may be, without understanding, without, if necessary, thorough and satisfactory explanation. It is a new world."

In April 1937, *Dance Magazine* reported that Dhimah was back in New York and would resume her concert activities in the fall. But in the fall there was no mention of Dhimah. She had become pregnant by her current suitor, Bill Wollman, and in December 1937 she gave birth to a son, Peter Wollman.[45]

Wright met Dhimah the following year, at a Communist social function. Dhimah and her mother, Eda, owned a narrow brownstone in Hamilton Terrace in Sugar Hill, Harlem. Dhimah was getting back into dance, and her mother helped with the baby.

Years later, Henrietta Weigel told Michel Fabre that Wright visited her the day before his marriage to Dhimah and admitted he was marrying Dhimah partly to spite Ellen.[46] Others report that he seemed quite dazzled by his Egyptian-Russian girlfriend. Ted Ward said later that "Wright was completely absorbed in [Dhimah], and she seemed deeply attached to him."[47] At the time, Ward wrote to Langston Hughes that Dhimah seemed a "very fine person" and "unusually intelligent and good natured." He believed Dick was going to be happy.[48]

Ralph Ellison was impressed by Dhimah and even more impressed by her small, warm, and energetic mother, Eda, who worked as a seamstress and did all the cooking and sewing for the household and helped looked after Peter, as well as being active in the International Ladies' Garment Workers Union and the Party. Her passion was the theater. She had been an actress in the Yiddish theater in Odessa.

Ellison thought Dhimah "far more sophisticated than Dick." In an interview decades later, he said he would have liked to take Dick aside and urge him: "Man, you have to fall out of love with this woman."[49] But he did not say so at the time.

Whether or not Wright believed he was in love with her, Dhimah represented things to which he aspired: travel, worldliness, and sophistication. Wright was almost thirty-one and highly ambitious. He had just finished a novel that was going to cause a stir. Why not continue to be bold? He had always told himself: "It's my life. I'll see what I can make of it."[50]

Before she went to the Soviet Union, Dhimah had been married to an artist from Philadelphia. She and Wright had to wait for her divorce papers. Two days after the divorce came through, they exchanged vows in the parsonage of the Episcopal Church on 149th Street and Convent Avenue in Harlem.[51] It was the evening of 12 August 1939. The marriage certificate records the groom as thirty and "colored," the bride as thirty-one and "white." Dhimah gave her date of birth as 25 August 1907 and her birthplace as Cairo, Egypt. The witnesses were Ralph Ellison and his wife, Rose.

After the wedding, Wright moved briefly into the Meidmans' house on Hamilton Terrace. Eda wanted to rent out the room on the top floor, and she had placed an advertisement in the *Daily Worker*. Edith Anderson and her husband, eager young Communists, responded. Anderson writes in her memoirs about their visit to the house:

> A statuesque white woman of about thirty answered the door and brought us into the parlor no bigger than an anteroom. In an armchair by a fake marble fireplace sat a Negro man.
>
> "This is my husband, Richard Wright," the woman said, and though her voice was not raised the announcement broke the sound barrier.
>
> We were confronted for the first time not only with a writer who had made the news but with marriage between a black man and a white woman, a handsome white woman, boldly proclaimed. Such a relationship was still mind-boggling to the bumpkins most Americans were in those days, including most Communist Americans. We tried not to stare, that was the best we could do.
>
> In a moment the house-owner, an elderly woman who was Wright's mother-in-law, came in and took us upstairs to see the room. We liked it, paid our deposit, and went away childishly rejoicing; we were going to live in the same house with a wonderful writer![52]

It was not to be. A few days later, Wright, Dhimah, and young Peter—followed shortly afterward by Eda—moved to the Mohegan Colony, near Peekskill, New York, an hour up the Hudson. They were looking after Anna Bushwick's house, a yellow stucco home on Paulding Lane, about a mile from Lake Mohegan. Dhimah and her mother both knew Annie Bushwick, an older woman, Russian-Jewish, who worked in the needle trade and was active in the International Ladies' Garment Workers Union.

It was a marvelous place for Wright to spend some months. The colony, a four-hundred-acre piece of wooded, hilly land that fronted on the lake, was founded in 1923 as an anarchist community. The early settlers had been mostly Russian Jews, but there were also French anarchists, Spaniards, Germans. By the late 1930s, the community was no longer so cohesive. Many of the members had become Communists, and political tensions developed. The colony now comprised anarchists, Communists, ex-Communists, and Zionists.[53]

Wright enjoyed the rural environment. It was good for his writing, as well as for keeping gossip at bay. New York City was only an hour away by train. At weekends he and Dhimah encouraged friends to visit. The colony had a rich concert and lecture program—the profits usually going these days to Jewish refugees. Ted Ward came up and read his theatrical adaptation of "Bright and Morning Star" to the colony. Ralph and Rose Ellison visited. So did Willard Maas and Marie Menken, and Dhimah's brother Harry.

Wright was working extremely hard. His routine was to write five pages or so, have a break and do something else, then write another five. On good days, he managed to fill twenty pages with his sprawling handwriting. In July he had signed a contract for a new novel, with a four-hundred-dollar advance from Harper. It was about a black woman living in Harlem and Brooklyn who decided to pass for white.

Native Son was in galleys, hovering in the wings, due to appear in September. The newspapers were announcing it already.

10

FAME

August 1939–March 1940

Wright told himself he needed a simple, quiet life for writing. "No fireworks."[1] But even in his rural retreat, it was beginning to seem impossible. All summer there had been rumors of a Soviet rapprochement with the Nazis. They were vehemently denied by Earl Browder, leader of the United States Communist Party (CPUSA). How could these "reactionaries" possibly imagine that Soviet Russia would contemplate "joining hands with Hitler?" Browder thundered.[2] Then, on 24 August 1939, Commissar Molotov shook hands with the Nazi diplomat, Joachim von Ribbentrop.

The Nazi-Soviet nonaggression pact caused a mass exodus from the Communist Party. Thomas Mann tendered his resignation as honorary president of the League of American Writers. There would be more departures in November 1939 when the Soviet Union attacked Finland. Wright, Dhimah, and their Party friends echoed the Party line and scorned this "jumping off the train."[3] In an interview in the *Sunday Worker* in February 1940, Wright would pronounce the Nazi-Soviet pact "a great step toward peace."[4]

The same day as that world-shattering handshake, a letter arrived in the mail from Ed Aswell. "An interesting development has occurred which promises very exciting possibilities if it comes off. I want to tell you about it, but please don't base any hopes in it yet. Not to make a further mystery of it, the Book-of-the-Month Club has become very excited about *Native Son*."[5]

The Book-of-the-Month Club, a vast mail-order business based in New York, was the most important book-marketing scheme in the nation. Not only the book club subscribers but everyone who read the newspapers knew of that month's selection. The club wielded an extraordinary influence on the nation's reading habits. If *Native Son* were chosen, Wright would be the first black writer to enjoy club selection. It would bring him vast quantities of readers, sales of a magnitude no writer of his race had enjoyed before, and fame.

When a publishing house sent a galley to the Book-of-the-Month Club, it was processed by three readers. If two of the three marked it as an "A" book, it was sent to the five judges. The Book-of-the-Month Club archives reveal that all three readers were impressed by *Native Son*, but none of them put it in the "A" category. All expressed extreme discomfort with the book. The readers' form asked: "Do you think this should be considered by the judges as a possible book-of-the-month?" Two of the readers said no. Harry S. Scherman put a question mark beside the box. "I don't know how much the public can take," he said.[6] "After the first quarter, I thought I could not go on with the terrible details."

Another reader, Graham Bates, said no, but he added: "I wish a judge might look this book over. Not because there is any chance of its being an 'A' book, the subject will preclude that, but because . . . it has a quality that could not be escaped, and because I reacted to it so strongly that I find myself unable to look through it again to verify first impressions."

The five judges—Henry Seidel Canby, Christopher Morley, William Allen White, Heywood Broun, and Dorothy Canfield Fisher—decided they had better read the novel.[7] They had not made any decision when word reached Aswell that they were "excited" by the book.[8] Above all, they were worried that the book would shock their subscribers. "This was really such a red-hot poker that we weren't sure we were going to manage it," Dorothy Canfield Fisher told an interviewer later.[9] Inevitably, the panel of five saw its role as broader than mere judges of literature. They were acutely aware that they were presiding over contemporary American values.[10]

Aswell told Wright in his letter that Book-of-the-Month selection would mean considerably greater sales, and "a nice sum of money for you." Unfortunately, while the committee made its decision, publication would have to be postponed. The committee's next meeting was not until September, the month *Native Son* had been scheduled to appear. Aswell added:

> And incidentally the Book Club wants to know whether, if they do choose *Native Son*, you would be willing to make some changes in that scene early in the book where Bigger and his friends are sitting in the movie picture theatre. I think you will recognize the scene I mean and will understand why the Book Club finds it objectionable. They are not a particularly squeamish crowd, but that scene, after all, is a bit on the raw side. I daresay you could revise it in a way to suggest what happens rather than to tell it explicitly. Please let me hear about this as soon as possible so that I can convey your answer to the Book Club.[11]

Aswell made light of the request. There is no record of Wright's response. What we do know is that he agreed to the cut. And soon he would find himself agreeing to further changes.

A week later, the word was out. Wright had written a novel that interested the Book-of-the-Month Club. Newspapers talked about the book as a highlight readers could look forward to in the fall. In mid-September, Kit Schryver, a friend who worked at Random House, wrote to Wright. "How are you bearing up under this goddamned torrent of abuse-by worship that the American public can inflict on a hero of the moment? I honestly flinch, but maybe you can ride out the storm."[12]

The judges met in September, but did not come to a decision. They wanted more changes. They cut substantial sections of Max's long, didactic speech in the courtroom. This was something neither Aswell nor Reynolds had managed to get Wright to do, and the cuts did improve the book. But the changes the judges asked for in the early sections of the novel were of a different order. They were not about unnecessary verbiage: they were about censorship. Not only did they alter the tone of the novel, they also changed the dynamics.[13]

The scene that the judges had asked, from the outset, to have cut was a graphic portrayal of masturbation.[14] In the darkened movie theater, Bigger squirms low in his seat and starts "polishing [his] nightstick." His friend Jack notices, laughs, and tells him he will race him to orgasm. In the background the pipe organ is playing; otherwise, Wright leaves little to metaphor.

Wright got rid of any suggestion of masturbation. But the judges did not like the newsreel the boys were watching, which showed Mary Dalton on vacation in Florida, scandalizing the social set by consorting with "a well known radical." What the judges actually disliked, almost certainly, was Bigger's and his friend's reaction to the scene. Mary Dalton was "a hot-looking number," they whispered to each other. Jack said he wished he were down in Florida. Bigger retorted: "You'd be hanging from a tree like a bunch of bananas." The judges wanted the newsreel and the boys' whispered conversation expunged.

Wright wanted to build up a picture of Bigger as a strongly libidinal young man. The judges wanted much of that picture cut. In an essay entitled "Too Honest for His Own Time," the critic Arnold Rampersad comments that the Book-of-the-Month Club changes "almost emasculated Bigger Thomas."[15] What Rampersad does not say is that the judges also dramatically curtailed Mary Dalton's sexual drive. This involved more delicate snipping—a sentence here and there—but the distorting effect on the narrative was even more significant.

After the inebriated dinner in the South Side, Wright had Mary Dalton carrying on with her boyfriend in the backseat of the car. Bigger glances in the rearview mirror and sees Mary lying flat on her back with her boyfriend, Jan, bending over her. He glimpses a "faint sweep of white thigh," then hears them both sigh. He fights off a "stiffening feeling in his loins." After the Book-of-the-Month Club had cut several sentences, all that transpired in the backseat was some kissing. Even the word "spooning" had to go. The white woman had been made to sit up and behave.

In *Native Son*, Wright wanted the issue of rape to loom large, just as it did almost every time a black man was hauled off to jail. The question that hangs over the narrative is what Bigger *might have done* if the white blur—Mary's mother—had not hovered in the doorway. What if Bigger had kept his hands on Mary's breasts?

Wright knew he was playing with fire. Interracial sex was the biggest taboo in American fiction. Built into the American psyche is a scene in which a black man makes his way into the bedroom of a white woman and rapes her. Where Wright came from, black men were lynched for doing nothing more than stirring the embers of this scene in the white imagination.

It was crucial that Wright's readers understood that Mary Dalton desired her black chauffeur every bit as much as he desired her—if not more so. This was the picture Wright had built up. He portrayed Mary Dalton as somewhat easy. It was with playful irony that he called her "Mary," a name we associate with innocence, purity, and virginity.

From the pivotal scene in which Bigger helps the languorous (and decidedly flirtatious) Mary Dalton up the stairs and into her bedroom, the judges wanted these sentences deleted:

> He tightened his arms as his lips pressed tightly against hers and he felt her body moving strongly. The thought and conviction that Jan had had her a lot flashed through his mind. He kissed her again and felt the sharp bones of her hip move in a hard and veritable grind. Her mouth was open and her breath came slow and deep.

In this passage, Mary suddenly makes movements that are not limp at all. Wright intended every detail of her thrusts and grinds. The judges had the white woman's hips stilled. Mary became passive, limp as a rag doll, scarcely conscious. Bigger became the archetypal black beast pawing the sleeping beauty. The white woman was completely absolved from responsibility. Arnold Rampersad argues that the Book-of-the-Month Club changes were "the result, not entirely but in part, of racism—racism that was seldom conscious of itself, that was expressed in subtle, even benign ways, but racism nonetheless."

Why did Wright consent to changes that made Bigger look like a potential black rapist? Did he argue? Did he give in easily? We don't know. But the fact is, he gave in to white pressure. By September 1939, his novel was no longer the same book that had crossed the judges' desk that summer. Bigger looked more guilty; the white woman was back on her traditional pedestal as the inaccessible object of desire.

The judges still hesitated. Altogether, they held up publication for seven months. In November, it was rumored that *Native Son* would be the selection for January. It wasn't. From his desk in the Mohegan Colony, Wright wrote to his friend Willard Maas: "The Book of the Month Club has not yet announced *Native Son*. I don't know what they are waiting on. The book has been completed for almost ten months now and I have still to see it between boards. Curses."[16]

Finally, in January 1940, the judges announced *Native Son* had been chosen for March. To play safe, they made it a dual selection. The other book was *The Trees* by Conrad Richter.

"DOROTHY CANFIELD HAS WRITTEN WHAT SEEMS TO US A VERY GOOD SEND-OFF for *Native Son*," Edward Aswell wrote to Wright in January.[17] Since the book was due to be published in six weeks and had to be rushed to press, he had her introduction typeset without Wright seeing it. "I took the responsibility of saying that I felt pretty sure you would approve. I hope I have not guessed wrong."

Aswell was very pleased to have Canfield Fisher's endorsement for this bombshell of a first novel by his young black author. She was the only woman on the Book-of-the-Month Club selection committee and, by all accounts, she and Henry Seidel Canby were the dominant members. Well known as a Quaker liberal and educational reformer, she was also a popular novelist. Eleanor Roosevelt named her as one of the ten most influential women in the United States.

With her introduction to *Native Son*, Canfield Fisher—more than the other judges—was throwing her reputation behind the novel. It showed courage, and Wright fully recognized that.[18] But the way she introduced the novel to American readers revealed the shadow side of liberalism.

She compared the situation of Bigger Thomas, and Negro youths generally, with that of sheep and rats in scientific experiments set up to examine neurotic behavior in animals. "*Native Son* is the first report in fiction we have had from those who succumb to these distracting crosscurrents of contradictory nerve-impulses, from those whose behaviorpatterns give evidence of the same bewildered, senseless tangle of abnormal nerve-reactions studied in animals by psychologists in laboratory experiments." Canfield Fisher was reducing a powerful novel to the status of a sociological report.

She alluded to the dark, Dostoyevskian depths of human experience plumbed by the novel, then added: "I do not at all mean to imply that *Native Son* as literature is comparable to the masterpieces of Dostoyevsky." Elsewhere she conceded: "The author shows genuine literary skill in the construction of his novel."

After the book came out, Wright wrote to thank Canfield Fisher for her introduction. His tone was lukewarm. "I feel that you did present the material in the book in a light that would make it understood by the American reading public."[19] Did he intend a touch of irony? Wright must have been painfully conscious of the ways in which Canfield Fisher and her colleagues had already mediated between him and his readers.

While the literary public was waiting to read the much publicized *Native Son*, Wright's story "Almos' a Man" was published in *Harper's Bazaar*.[20] "That boy is sure kicking up the dust," Arna Bontemps remarked to Langston Hughes.[21]

IN JANUARY 1940, TWO MONTHS BEFORE PUBLICATION, A CHECK ARRIVED FROM Book-of-the-Month Club advance sales. Wright ordered new suits; he got himself some new ties; and he bought a house in Chicago for three thousand dollars.[22] His mother and Aunt Cleo were going to move into the first-floor apartment (Wright planned to renovate it and add a china closet and toilet), and he would have tenants in the other apartments. The house was on Vincennes Avenue in the ghetto, and he purchased it through his black lawyer friend, Ulysses Keys. Wright, who thought he knew all about the racism of Chicago real estate, was shocked by the way the white "real estate sharks" tried to cheat him.[23]

One morning in late January 1940, Wright caught the train into New York City for a speaking engagement. While he waited on the subway platform at Times Square, he walked over to the newsstand. The papers were full of war in Europe. He stood there wishing he could flee from it all when his attention was caught by a title on the cover of the *American Mercury*: "Life Among the Escapists." The writer was Lawrence Martin, an acquaintance from Chicago days, an academic at Northwestern University and one of the people who had supported his application for a Guggenheim. On the train, Wright read the article with growing excitement. There were two kinds of escapists, according to Lawrence Martin:

> I have no truck with the tribe who escape into art, religion, seduction, booze, business—those who escape inside themselves. We others really beat it: take a train or boat and go far away, to a land as different as possible from wherever we were rooted. We tear the phone from the wall, give the radio to the janitor, cancel the subscription to the *Daily Dopesheet*, kiss the relatives goodbye, and hit for the nearest place where the climate is eternal spring and the cost of living is ceiling zero.[24]

Lawrence Martin and his wife, Sylvia, had left behind traffic jams, college students, and Chicago suburbia and headed for Cuernavaca, just over an hour from Mexico City:

> Man and wife can live fancy here for $100 a month for which amount you can even throw in the inlaws and half a dozen kids. "Fancy" means a large house with grounds, gardens, swimming pool, lime and banana trees, calla lilies growing in the brook, and roses, hibiscus, and bougainvillea rioting all over the place. The house will have four bedrooms, living room, kitchen, two bedrooms, large porch or veranda, and mirador or sun-roof.

Wright wrote to Lawrence Martin the next day:

> Since I saw you last, I took unto myself a wife, a modern dancer; she has a two-year old child (by her former husband, an Englishman). When I returned home, I showed her the article. She went through the roof. At once she suggested that she, the kid, me, her mother and her pianist light out for Mexico. I fell for it. (I don't know if you were laying it on thick or not when you wrote that article, but you painted a picture that is irresistible to one living in a semi-war atmosphere.) Armed with your article, my wife rushes into the city today and phones me later that she booked passage to Mexico for April 5th.[25]

Wright wanted to know whether it would be a problem for an Afro-American to live with a white wife in Cuernavaca. Might Martin be able to secure them a house? If so, he would cable money immediately. Martin had mentioned rents of forty dollars per month for large houses with swimming pools. Wright and Dhimah agreed they could go to fifty dollars. They wanted a two-story house, so they wouldn't disturb each other at work, and a garden. A swimming pool would be nice. How high was Cuernavaca? (Dhimah's mother had a weak heart.) Was it possible to buy eggs, milk, and fresh meat? ("Dhimah wants to know for the sake of the kid.") Dhimah was planning to give dance concerts, and if that failed, she would teach dancing. As for him, he just wanted to "get out of this god-awful country" and write. "Boy, I'm fairly itching to get down there."[26]

Lawrence Martin was encouraging. He would keep an eye out for something in Cuernavaca; he was also visiting Acapulco and would look there. Did Wright speak Spanish? Did he have a car?

No, he did not speak Spanish, Wright wrote back. "Dhimah has been almost everywhere and has the knack of picking up lingos like a dog picks up fleas. I'm afraid that when I come I'll start in with my book and she'll have to lead me around like a blind man."

No, he did not have a car. "Dhimah has been trying to get me to buy one. I don't even know how to drive one. If I picked up one, I'd still have the job of shipping it, learning to drive it, etc. I don't know. It all depends upon how hard she argues whether I get one or not." As far as the house was concerned: "Dhimah says that it would be better to get something for us in Cuernavaca; and then we could look further when we arrive."

On 2 March the *Pittsburgh Courier*, a black newspaper, announced that Wright was thinking of going to Mexico in the spring. "If so, it will be something of a belated honeymoon trip as well, for he was married last summer in New York." It was the first formal announcement of Wright's marriage. The identity of his bride was not revealed. Nor was her skin color.

IN EARLY FEBRUARY 1940, WRIGHT HANDED PAUL REYNOLDS A FIRST DRAFT, 961 pages in all, of his new novel, *Black Hope*. He had been working hard in his rural isolation. "I am aware that this manuscript is in a crude condition," he warned Reynolds, adding that *Native Son* had been in much the same shape when he first handed it to Aswell.[27]

Reynolds did not even show the manuscript to Aswell. He told Wright he wanted this *War and Peace* "cut very severely—perhaps 50 percent."[28] He thought that "one or two of the sex scenes should be toned down as a matter of taste." But he was struck that Wright had made progress with his portrayal of white characters.

Like *Native Son*, *Black Hope* was a mixture of melodrama and realism. Wright was thinking about freedom in relation to race and gender. What did personal freedom mean? Could one be free while compromising one's moral integrity? If blacks were placed in positions that made them dependent, and black women even more so, how far would a highly intelligent, restless black woman be prepared to go to acquire freedom, money, and power? If the economic and social oppression of black people was sanctioned by the law, was it immoral for black people to obtain wealth and power through illegal means?

He proceeded like a philosopher, posing a basic conundrum, then adding another layer. Supposing a black woman had far better opportunities if she passed for a white? Would it be wrong for her to do so? Supposing a wealthy old white man fell in love with her, believing she was white, and proposed marriage to her?

"This is *not* a novel with a 'feminist' theme!" he insisted. But for the first and only time in his fiction, the main character was a woman—a black woman who passed for white. Wright, living with Dhimah and her mother, was becoming aware that white women shared many of the same experiences as black women. He was giving serious thought to the social and psychological conditions in which women lived.

Maud Hampton is twenty-seven, a light-skinned mulatto and graduate of the University of Chicago. The man she loves, twenty-five-year-old Freddie Rogers, is a "tall, brown-skinned, slender young man," who has turned down a lucrative job at the post office in order to write. His fiction depicts "the lives of men and women who had been sucked under in the whirlpool of steel and stone." He's passionate about ideas (he talks animatedly about Malraux's novel *Man's Fate*), politically committed, and imbued with a strong sense of moral integrity. He is always thinking about freedom, the meaning of life, and the meaning of happiness. Freddie is obviously an idealized Richard Wright figure.

Freddie visits Maud in Harlem. He goes out to buy them some ice cream. While he's away Maud squats to the floor, squeezes jelly from a tube into a rubber sac, and inserts a diaphragm. When Freddie returns, they feed each other ice cream from mouth to mouth. What follows is the most tender and ardent love scene in Wright's fiction.

Maud loves Freddie, but wishes he were less concerned with "puny words" and more concerned with making money. Wanting more from life than being a social worker in Harlem, she hatches a radical plan to change her life. She disappears to Brooklyn without a trace and takes arsenic wafers for a month. They make her violently ill, but they lighten her skin.[29] As a white woman, she becomes the housekeeper for a bedridden white millionaire. With his death, Maud inherits a fortune and a position in New York society. But she is not free. She is torn between the lure of power and wealth, her love for Freddie, and her conscience. In the end, she kills herself, leaving her fortune to her black maid and the house to the black Domestic Workers' Union.

SHORTLY BEFORE LEAVING FOR MEXICO, WRIGHT MADE ANOTHER TRIP TO Chicago. It was late February 1940, and for the first time, he traveled by air. "With damp hands and weak knees, I climbed into a huge, sleek, steel plane and flew above the clouds, holding as I sailed onto the flimsy window curtain in order to keep from falling to earth."[30] *Life* magazine paid for his trip. He was the official consultant for a photo-documentary article *Life* intended to run as a tribute to *Native Son.* Wright arrived in the late afternoon, and he and the white photographer from *Life*, Hart Preston, headed straight for the South Side.

Wright had become very interested in photography. On his visit to Chicago the previous September, he and Dhimah had visited Frank Marshall Davis, a keen photographer. Davis took some studio portraits of Wright, and Wright had impetuously bought his twin lens reflex camera.[31]

Wright did not stay with his mother. Horace Cayton had offered the guest room at the Good Shepherd Community Center on South Parkway, which provided educational, social, and recreational facilities for the surrounding black community and was rapidly becoming the favorite Chicago base for visiting black luminaries like Langston Hughes. During those few days, Wright and Cayton formed a friendship that would prove important for both men in the next few years.

Cayton was in his element as director of the Good Shepherd Community Center. He liked people, and he was a good host. As a raconteur there were few, with the exception of Wright, who could rival him. His former wife, Bonnie Hansen, a white woman, recalls: "He was exciting—stimulating—and given to amazing flashes of insight into all sorts of situations—great and small. It just felt good to be with him."[32] The bedrock discrimination they had encountered in Chicago had been a terrible shock to the young couple from Seattle. Accommodation, social interaction, employment—everything posed a problem. When it was discovered that she was married to a black man, Hansen was fired from her job.[33] Eventually the strain proved too much. These days, Cayton was married to Irma, a light-skinned social worker from Georgia.

Cayton was an expert on the South Side. He and his fellow black sociologist St. Clair Drake were undertaking a thorough study of the "black metropolis." With his help—and a bodyguard-chauffeur Cayton managed to organize—the team photographed families in dilapidated hovels, reefer dives, refuges where homeless boys slept on the floor, seedy pool- and dice-shooting rooms. The street urchins marveled at Hart Preston's camera and tripod and jostled each other to hold the flashbulbs. Preston, a lanky six-foot-sixer, attracted almost as much attention as his photographic equipment.[34]

Wright spent time with Ulysses Keys and signed the papers for the house.[35] A few years earlier he could scarcely afford to rent a slum kitchenette. Now he was owner of a large house.

On that trip to Chicago, Wright had lunch with a group of black writer friends—among them the seventy-two-year-old W. E. B. Du Bois, who was visiting from New York. Du Bois wrote about the meeting in his *Amsterdam News* column:

I lunched lately in Chicago with four young men and others. There were Langston Hughes and Arna Bontemps both looking a bit corpulent and yet young; both calm, generous and eager, and working and planning for the wants of the world. There was a new face there—young Richard Wright. A face good, strong and intelligent, Wright is not an accident; he has worked hard. Toward the end Allison Davis dropped by, a bit fine drawn, but always a gentleman and a scholar. One feels a certain sense of relief and confidence in meeting four such sturdy pillars of the day to come. They seemed built for bearing weights on their shoulders; and there are weights to be borne.[36]

THE DAY BEFORE *NATIVE SON* CAME OUT, EDWARD ASWELL WROTE TO WRIGHT:

I should like to be among the first to congratulate you once more on *Native Son*. You know what I think of it, and have always thought of it, but let me be a little more explicit. It is not only a good book, a sincere, straight, and honest book, a courageous book, a powerful and eternally moving book, but in addition to all this, I truly believe, a great book. It is my conviction that its publication will be remembered in years to come as a monumental event.[37]

On the morning of publication, Friday, 1 March 1940, Charles Poore declared in the *New York Times*: "Few other recent novels have been preceded by more advance critical acclamation, or lived up to the expectations they aroused so well."

Saturday Review featured Wright's photograph on the cover. Inside, Jonathan Daniels remarked: "For terror in narrative, utter and compelling, there are few pages in modern American literature which will compare with this story." Critics compared *Native Son* to Steinbeck's *The Grapes of Wrath*, Dreiser's *An American Tragedy*, Dostoyevsky's *Crime and Punishment*. They all agreed the novel was "strong meat."

Book-of-the-Month Club judge Henry Seidel Canby hailed it "the finest novel as yet written by an American Negro."[38] Several critics predicted that Wright would be the first Negro to win a Pulitzer Prize for fiction. "Nobody can doubt that Richard Wright's *Native Son* is as inevitable a choice for next year as *The Grapes of Wrath* was for this," the *New Masses* predicted.

Harper & Brothers had printed 170,000 copies of *Native Son*—an extraordinary print run for a first novel. Within a few days, they reprinted the book. Within a few weeks, *Native Son* had sold more copies than any novel Harper had published in the previous twenty years. From New York to San Francisco, the book soared near the top of the best-seller lists. After three weeks, 215,000 copies had been sold, and the novel was still selling at a rate of two thousand copies a day. *Native Son* was a literary phenomenon.

The Book-of-the-Month Club judges, who had thought they were putting themselves out on a limb, were taken aback by the abundance of praise from all quarters. "With all that anticipation of what we thought was going to be an explosion when it came out, you can imagine how flat we all felt when the first reviews were of unalloyed praise of the power and vigor of this new voice," Dorothy Canfield Fisher said later. "We felt very much like people going upstairs in the dark who think there's one more step than there is!"[39]

"It is a rare and special thing that Wright has done, as no American writer before him," Mike Gold, author of the 1930 best-seller *Jews Without Money*, said in the *Sunday Worker*. "He has written a story on the racial theme without sentimentalizing it. . . . It is no exaggeration to say that at one stroke he has become a national figure. . . . The story of *Native Son* is one that will burn itself on the imagination of this country, I believe, as has no other novel about Negroes since *Uncle Tom's Cabin*."[40] Gold, a prominent New York Communist who had first seen Richard Wright as a "shy unformed Chicago poet" at the Chicago John Reed Club Congress in 1934, considered his transformation to best-selling novelist "one of the literary miracles."

Black critics were mostly positive. The poet and Howard University professor Sterling Brown thought *Native Son* would stir the national conscience if any book could.[41] Ralph Ellison chimed bells in the *New Masses*. "In Wright's *Native Son* we have the first philosophical novel by an American Negro. This work possesses an artistry, penetration of thought, and sheer emotional power that places it into the front rank of American fiction."[42] Ellison hoped that *Native Son* marked the "take-off in a leap" that would see fiction about American Negro life incorporated, at long last, into mainstream American fiction. Didn't it prove that publishers could, after all, accept "honest Negro writing"?

Wright was the first best-selling black writer in American literary history. Nobody wanted to appear sour-faced. At first, it was only in private conversations that the deep ambivalence about the book surfaced. Lillian Johnson was the first black critic to express discontent publicly. "I do not feel that Mr. Wright has written a book that will do anything constructive for his people as a race. I am of the opinion that the book could do a great deal of harm," she wrote in the Baltimore

Afro-American. She hated the way the word "nigger" was used throughout the narrative, and she wished the book had one intelligent colored person in it. Why did Bigger have to desire the white girl, even though he did not like her?[43]

Letters from black readers poured in as a response to Johnson's comments. Some thought the novel an admirable portrayal of conditions in black ghettoes; others dreaded the conclusions white readers would draw. "They will believe him typical of all of us. They so easily lump us into one classification," said one letter writer, who made the point that Bigger was not at all typical "Our record of criminality is . . . usually against ourselves. How often does a colored man go out and kill some white person after brooding over wrongs?"[44]

Langston Hughes read the novel on the train while on tour. He congratulated Wright on "a tremendous performance . . . a really great book which sets a new standard for Negro writers from now on."[45] Privately, he was dismayed by its bleak portrait of black life. The following year, in an essay called "The Need for Heroes," Hughes would proclaim it "the social duty of Negro writers" to show "the deep reservoirs of heroism within the race."[46] He added: "Suppose *Native Son's* Bigger Thomas (excellently drawn as he is) was the sole survivor on the bookshelves of tomorrow?"

Shirley Graham wrote to her mentor and future husband, W. E. B. Du Bois: "Last Sunday's *Times* carried a page on *Native Son.* That book turns my blood to vinegar and makes my heart weep for having borne two sons. They say it is a great book. Why?"[47]

Du Bois was more positive. "It is a great piece of work and the only kind of thing that compels attention just now. Wright too is a nice fellow. I met him in Chicago. I think he will go far."[48]

The controversy about *Native Son* would never die. In 1946, in an article called "It's About Time," Langston Hughes would write pointedly: "It's about time some Negro writer wrote a good novel about *good* Negroes who do *not* come to a bad end. . . . With all of the millions of colored people in America who never murder anybody, or rape or get raped or want to rape, who never lust after white bodies, or cringe before white stupidity . . . With all the millions of normal human, lovable colored folks in the United States, it is about time some Negro writer put some of them into a book."[49]

In the 1980s the young African-American writer David Bradley, brought up to embrace the black pride of the civil rights era, would declare that he hated *Native Son* "with a passion." The novel "was pandering to white expectations," he said. "I myself did not want a nut like Bigger Thomas sitting next to me on a bus or in a schoolroom, and certainly I did not want him moving in next door." In Bradley's view, Richard Wright had "sold his people down the river to make a buck."[50]

But this was in the future. In the spring of 1940, the literary world talked of little else. "What do you think of *Native Son*?" became almost a greeting cry. Three weeks after publication, Richard Wright, his wife Dhimah, her son Peter, and her mother Eudice Meidman sailed out of New York to Mexico.[51]

11

CUERNAVACA

March 1940–June 1940

For years Wright had longed to travel.[1] But he left New York while a storm was breaking around *Native Son*. In Cuernavaca, he would find himself isolated, waiting for the mailman to bring him secondhand news. As a late honeymoon, the trip was a disaster. He and Dhimah had been married seven months when they boarded the SS *Monterey* for Mexico, accompanied by Dhimah's two-year-old son, Peter, and her mother, Eda. Three months later, the marriage would be over.

From the port of Veracruz they took a train due west to Cuernavaca. Lawrence and Sylvia Martin had found them a house for twenty-seven dollars a month. But the Wrights, who had traveled first class and arrived with a set of expensive new suitcases, had not come to Mexico to live frugally. Lawrence Martin remembers:

> *Native Son* had made him a lot of money; the cheap house was not good enough now, and he found an ambitious villa with a swimming pool, where in short order he was playing host to visitors like Mabel Dodge Luhan. He took guitar lessons and Spanish lessons, and soon became

a well-known and liked member of the community, and the only Negro in it.[2]

Within a few days the Wrights found a spacious Spanish colonial-style villa at 62 Madero Street, in the hilly Miraval district. "Cuernavaca is beautiful," Wright told Paul Reynolds. "If I can't work here, then I'll be able to work nowhere. The house I am getting has ten rooms, a huge swimming pool, spacious grounds, flowers everywhere, fruit trees."[3] He was impatient to start concentrated work on *Black Hope.*

In a valley at the foot of blue-colored mountains, Cuernavaca had a climate the tourist brochures described as "eternal spring." The sixteenth-century Palace of Cortés houses a splendid mural by Diego Rivera portraying the conquest of Mexico. The town was packed with American tourists and weekenders from Mexico City. "They crawl everywhere, like ants or bed bugs," Wright complained.[4] As for the local Mexicans, he pronounced them "likable folks, but dull."[5]

He made little progress with his Spanish; there was no incentive. Cuernavaca had a large American colony, and the local Mexicans seemed keen to practice their English. At least, in the privacy of his pool, he was learning to swim. "I can swim now about twenty feet," he told friends, "then I stop and see if the water is still under me and if I'm still on top of it."[6]

One Sunday in April he attended his first bullfight. It was in Mexico City. Langston Hughes, who lived there during his teens, had loved the bullfights. D. H. Lawrence, when he came to Mexico, had been horrified. Wright was dubious. They killed six bulls that day, and at the fifth, he told Ralph Ellison, he had to close his eyes for a moment. He left when they were killing the sixth. "That does not mean that I don't like it, but the first time was just a little too much, with the high altitude in Mexico City."[7]

Over the last six years, Mexico's President Cárdenas had introduced social and educational reform and distributed millions of acres of land to cooperative peasant communities in an attempt to break up the old *hacienda* system. But his socialist government was up against inflation, a soaring population growth, the Catholic Church, and American oil companies. An election was approaching, and political tension was mounting. "It seems that things down here in Mexico might pop off, too,"[8] Wright wrote to Willard Maas.

For a black man, Mexico was a welcome haven. "People of all races and colors live in harmony and without racial prejudices or theories of racial superiority," Wright wrote in the *Atlantic Monthly*.[9] He added that he only ever experienced racism when he came into contact with American tourists or businessmen.

The climate was like Mississippi, he told Joe Brown. He was swimming twice a day, eating lots of fruit, and working. But the days drifted into each other. "Nothing is doing. One becomes bored to death at times. One misses the Gay White Way, the noise and excitement of New York."[10]

Mexico was beautiful but backward. "I wanted to go to Europe," Wright pointed out to Willard Maas. "I'm not yet one of those people who can get excited over primitive people. Maybe the reason is that I'm too primitive myself, I don't know."[11]

He even missed American radio broadcasts. The news from Europe was shocking: the Allies were suffering terrible defeats, and he was relying on outdated English-language newspapers. Like all his Communist friends, Wright still hoped the United States would keep out of the war. He felt no solidarity with England and France—"imperialist powers" who oppressed Negroes and colonial peoples. And he felt strongly that Negroes should not be conned a second time into fighting for someone else's freedom when they did not have their own. He had just written a review of James Weldon Johnson's reissued 1930 classic, *Black Manhattan*, which pointed out the abysmal treatment of blacks during and after the Great War.[12]

Domestic relations at 62 Madero Street were strained. Soon after they arrived, Dhimah was stung by a scorpion when she tried to push it down the bathtub drain. The venom was known to cause paralysis of the respiratory muscles or cardiac failure. "She had to have a powerful injection against lockjaw," Wright told Aswell. "Then she had to have another injection to counteract that one, then six more to overcome the effects of the first ones."[13] They were told that the insect had probably crawled into the bathroom from the creek that flowed through the gorge at the bottom of the property, so they moved farther up the street, away from the river, to 33 Madero. Dhimah had twenty-five injections altogether. But the scorpion was not the only disruption to Wright's work. "Peter yells as much as always, goddamn."[14]

Wright was anxious about his own "native son." "How is old Bigger faring since I left him to stalk the streets of New York?" he asked Willard Maas. "I do hope that people are running up to him to kiss and embrace him, for at bottom he is a good boy, even if he did murder a couple of times."[15]

It was frustrating enough to have to rely on friends for news, but when Ralph Ellison's first two letters did not arrive, Wright feared that other mail was getting lost. Ellison then realized that Wright had not given him the name of the state, Morelos. "No doubt Dhimah must have given you the address," Wright told him. "The workings of a woman's mind is still as much a mystery to me as ever. . . . A kind of natural, primitive functioning."[16]

He was supposed to be writing about the mysterious female species in *Black Hope*, and Ralph Ellison sent him cuttings about the situation of black domestic workers in Brooklyn, but Wright was too distracted to settle down to his new novel. Letters from New York and Chicago informed him that sales of *Native Son* had leveled out at 250,000, and a backlash of criticism had set in.

"Your book is raising a 'fog' as to its sociological contribution," Ulysses Keys wrote from Chicago. "Many favor; many do not. But all read it. (That's important.)"[17] Ellison told Wright he had recently discussed the novel with a bunch of white women. "Spent the evening in a beautiful Village apartment patiently explaining to the nice, if insipid, bitches just why Bigger felt like laying Mary when he had a hand full of breast. They seemed fascinated by that part. . . . The book is like the Bible, it seems to hold *some* kind of satisfaction for all."[18]

What hurt Wright was that it was the Communists who were attacking him most fiercely. In the face of all the negative criticism now coming his way, he decided to write for publication a talk he gave in Harlem in February. "How 'Bigger' Was Born" was his own Henry James–style preface to *Native Son*. In it he wrote about his aims and intentions, and the pressure he had felt *not* to tell the story he wanted to tell.

IN LATE APRIL 1940, RALPH ELLISON WENT TO WASHINGTON, D.C., TO COVER THE Third National Negro Congress for the *New Masses*. From among the crowd of Communist delegates, Ellen Poplowitz came running up to him.[19] "She asked me for your address," Ellison wrote to Wright, "but I stalled in order to ask your opinion; should I give it to her?"

She seems to be living at a high pitch of tension, both nervous and emotional. Made me wish there was something I could do to help her. Someone had told her that you were not happy—which made her the second person to ask me that question. As in the previous instance I replied that I had no reason to suppose that you were not happy. I intend to discover who it is that has raised the question, if you wish; I think it is Jane. Ted was the other to put the question. I told him that I had no interest in the matter and it was dropped. You can see why I suspect Jane, she being the person they both knew in common. I hope I am not doing her an injustice. I hope you'll forgive me for mentioning this, for I have no personal interest in the matter.[20]

Ellison knew how fiercely Wright guarded his private life. What Ellison did not tell his friend was that Ellen had burst into tears and told him she still loved Wright.[21] Nor was he quite as noble as he made out to Wright. Years later, Ellen recalled that Ellison "played his own cards first" and "made a pass" at her. "I was a very pretty young girl," she said. "But Ellison never appealed to me."[22] Four days later, Ellison asked Wright again. "What about Ellen?"

"About Ellen: just let it ride," Wright wrote back. "She's a really mixed up little girl; it's too bad, too."[23]

"YOU WERE A WISE GUY, DICK, FOR GETTING THE HELL OUT OF HERE WHEN YOU did," Ralph Ellison assured him, "for I'm sure you would have had to committ [sic] murder had you stayed. *Native Son* shook the Harlem section to its foundation and some of the rot it has brought up is painful to smell."[24] He and Ted Ward had sat up for six hours one night "trying to explain what fiction is about" to two prominent Harlem Communists, Abner Berry and Ted Bassett. They had little success.

Because Wright was the most prominent black writer in the country and a Communist, the Party was obliged to take his novel seriously, but it could not cover up a powerful ambivalence within the ranks—especially among the black comrades. Ted Ward, an earnest Communist ideologue himself, sent Wright a report on the virulent discussions that were taking place in the Harlem branch:

> They were all for setting up a bureau to which writers like you would have to submit their materials before publishing them. The idea was really stupid, but you would be surprised to know how heated they became when I opposed it. Another thing was that you should be forced to attend meetings and do party work, so that you would learn how not to make such a mistake as *Native Son*.[25]

In April Ben Davis, Jr., wrote a long review in the *Sunday Worker*.[26] He said that Wright had done "a brilliant and courageous job"; the novel was "a terrific indictment of capitalist America," and the Communist Party rejoiced over Wright's "magnificent artistry."[27] But Davis wished there could have been at least one positive Negro character, and he disliked the way Wright made Bigger into a symbol of the Negro people generally. "The average unemployed Negro youth does not become a rapist and a murderer," he argued. Indeed, the typical Negro at a lynch trial was "completely and wholly innocent." Nor did he like Wright's picture of white Communists: all talk rather than action, well-meaning but fundamentally naïve.[28]

Mike Gold at the *Daily Worker* now agreed with Ben Davis that Bigger represented "only a small and hopeless fragment" of the Negro people.[29] Wright wrote long letters to both of them. Bigger was not meant to symbolize all Negroes, he wrote, but any personality, white or black, under stress. He had made Bigger guilty in order to show the "surging forces" in oppressed communities, which could spill out at any time. "I made Mrs. Dalton blind to symbolize how millions today do not realize or admit this!" As for his depiction of Communists, did Party members really think they should be represented in fiction as "white knights charging into the sunset?"[30]

In May there were two scathing reviews in the mainstream press. Burton Rascoe, a white man, wrote in the *American Mercury* that he found the message of *Native Son* "utterly loathsome and utterly insupportable." It seemed to him that the novel was condoning murder and placing the guilt entirely on white people.

In the *Atlantic Monthly*, David L. Cohn[31] accused Wright of inciting hatred of whites in the same way that the Ku Klux Klan stirred up hatred of blacks. *Native Son* was "a blinding and corrosive study in hate." He argued that Jews had suffered far more than Negroes—"even under slavery."[32]

Criticized by the Left and Right alike, Wright had reached the point where he could no longer see degrees of subtleties. "Listen, can you tell any difference between Ben's article and the one in the current issue of the *American Mercury?*" he asked Ellison.[33]

Wright wrote an open reply to David Cohn to be published in the next issue of *Atlantic Monthly.* "Never in the history of these united states did a negro ever tell a jew what I told that jew," he boasted to Ralph Ellison.[34] *Atlantic Monthly* editor Edward Weeks cabled he would have to censor Wright's "trenchant reply" if they did not want to start a holy war.[35]

The censored reply Weeks published nevertheless retained the essence of Wright's criticism. "If the Jew has suffered for two thousand years," Wright wrote, "then it is mainly because of his religion and his other-worldliness and he has only himself to blame."

WRIGHT WAS DISCOVERING THAT WRITER FRIENDS WERE HIGHLY AMBIVALENT about his success. Letters of congratulation usually came with a thinly concealed subtext: "If the boy from Mississippi can do it, why can't I?"

Ellison assured Wright that Ted Ward "has quite a bit more respect for your ideas these days and is fighting tooth and nail for the book."[36] But Wright had never trusted Ward, with whom he had a history of rivalry. Now that the Party had turned against the book, Ward admitted to Wright that he himself had reservations about its political message. "I told the branch that they were not developed enough to teach you anything, but that I felt your trouble was that you had not studied the Theory of the Proletarian Revolution, and that this accounted for the skepticism which colors NS."[37]

"Gee, Dick," Joyce Gourfain had written, "do you make me burn up with envy. I blame it on the kids, but that isn't fair to either you or the kids. For I do know what it takes to write a novel even if I haven't got one written."[38]

Wright had sent Nelson Algren a copy of *Native Son* with a diplomatic inscription: "To My old Friend Nelson Who I believe is still the best writer of good prose in the U.S.A.—Dick."[39] Algren was touched.

He had tried to commit suicide when his first novel did not do as well as he had hoped. Now he was finding it hard to come to terms with *Native Son*—both its anger and its success. He wrote to Wright:

> I'm honestly hit so hard I have to get it off my chest. This isn't by any means a letter of congratulation. I don't feel any need to tell you how well-thought out or how well-sustained it is and all that, you'll hear that all over. . . . What does get me is it's such a threat. I mean a personal threat. At first I felt it was just a challenge, but it's more. You've done a very, very smart thing: I don't think any white person could read it without being either frightened or angry at the end. My own reaction happened to be anger more than anything else. . . . I think too my resentment may have been partly personal: a guy gets sore when he's known another person a while and then learns that the guy really isn't as nice inside as he is out. . . . You've hit me with something you've been holding behind your back all the while.[40]

Margaret Walker's reaction, which Wright never knew about, was the strongest of all. "Oh my god, I almost went to the insane asylum," she told an interviewer later. Someone had told her she was the model for Bessie. The idea haunted her. Now that Wright was no longer speaking to her, she took the view that in order to research the novel, he had used her mercilessly. She also told people he had stolen ideas from her own unpublished novel. She had written about rat catchers, and lo and behold, *Native Son* began with Bigger killing a rat.[41]

> I couldn't function for two weeks. I would go to bed and get up and read some more; I read that book over and over and over again. . . . For days, I wasn't even taking a bath. . . . I had to go to a psychiatrist. . . . I don't think I resented the man's success, because I had always believed in that; I had expected him to succeed. But I didn't expect him to cheapen the relationship by treating me the way he did.

Walker's psychiatrist told her to face the fact that she was in love with Wright and her love was unrequited and she was hurt. Walker dismissed this theory as "inane and illogical."[42]

Wright felt angry about the response from Communists. He was angry with white bigots. And he was angry with black critics. "I really think that

Negroes are to blame for the reactions to NS," he told Nelson Algren. "So few of them have ever tried to [tell] the truth about how they feel. They are shamed, scared, and want to save their pride. Well, in writing that book I just threw shame and fear and pride out of the window."[43]

SPURRED ON BY THE SCANDAL SURROUNDING THE NOVEL, PRODUCERS AND playwrights clamored for the stage and movie rights. Wright was astonished. He was also acutely aware that dramatization was likely to distort the novel, accentuating its more sensational aspects.

Ted Ward asked for the stage rights. Paul Robeson wanted to make *Native Son* his debut as a producer. In mid-May, word came that Orson Welles and John Houseman were interested in the stage production. Orson Welles, the brilliant enfant terrible of the theater and movie world, was currently in Hollywood with John Houseman, working on the movie *Citizen Kane*.

Wright knew Houseman and Welles from their flamboyant WPA production of *Macbeth*. And everyone had heard of Orson Welles. Flattered, he asked Ellison to make discreet inquiries. Ellison was soon able to assure him that Housemen and Welles were "liberal" and "more objective than are the usual showmen."[44]

Wright explained his concerns to Houseman candidly. There had been numerous expressions of interest in the production rights, he told them, and for obvious reasons, he and his agent Paul Reynolds were anxious that the play should be in the best possible hands.

> I realize the limitations of the screen and stage in America. Can such a book be done in a light that presents Bigger Thomas as a *human being*? . . . To be honest, I'm more interested in that than I am in seeing the book on the stage or screen. . . . We have already enough plays and movies showing Negroes in other roles, traditional roles. To screen or stage "Native Son" in the old way means nothing to me. . . . The main idea I tried to get across . . . was this: here is a human being trying to express some of the deepest impulses in all of us through the cramped limits of his life.[45]

Wright had not yet mailed the letter when Irene Lee, Sam Goldwyn's story editor, flew in from Hollywood to put the case for Houseman and Welles. She and Wright talked by his swimming pool. Lee said it would be wiser to put *Native Son* on the stage before they thought about a movie, and there was some latitude in the choice of the person to write the script. Wright mentioned Paul Green, a white dramatist who said he was interested. Lee stressed that Wright himself should have some input. Wright mentioned Ted Ward as a possible choice for Bigger Thomas. Lee was open to suggestions.

Wright added a postscript to Houseman: "I liked Miss Lee's approach to the subject." Houseman replied by return mail.

> Please believe that both Welles and I understand fully the way you feel about your book. At all times the prospect of a dramatization must be a gruesome one to a serious novelist—in the case of "Native Son" the problem is of course an especially delicate one. . . .
>
> We have always, so far, steered clear of dramatization of novels. With your book, however, it seemed to us—both to Welles and me reading it quite independently before discussing it—that here was a story written by you in novel form but capable of extension and development in the dramatic form. . . . Ideally, and rightly treated, "Native Son" is of course a great picture. You know enough of the setup here and of the inevitable inhibitions in the motion picture business to realize that, today, its chances of being shown on the screen in a final form that would give you as an author any pleasure at all are virtually nil.
>
> The theatre, however, in the hands of a few people, is still a free medium in which a serious artist can express himself directly and courageously to his audiences. . . .
>
> I can only say now that if we should produce "Native Son," the more of your help we can have, the more you can transmit to us of the intention and the spirit of your book, the better pleased we shall be.[46]

Paul Green seemed to Wright the best of the prospective scriptwriters. A Southerner, he was the first white American playwright to write sympathetically about black life in the South. In 1927 he had won the Pulitzer Prize for his play *In Abraham's Bosom*, about a rebellious North Carolina black man who dreams of founding a school for black children and ends up shot by a mob. It was Green's brutally realist one-act play about a chain gang, *Hymn to the Rising Sun*, that Wright had wanted to put on in Chicago and that had caused such a ruckus among the actors in the Federal Negro Theatre.

Wright wrote to Green that his offer interested him more than anyone's else's. "But I would very much like to know (if it is not asking too much!) just what you think you can do with the book." He would like to go through the script before it was final; would that be acceptable to Green?[47]

Paul Green suggested a formal collaboration. Could Wright come to Chapel Hill, North Carolina, to work with him for a few weeks? Wright, who was already longing to leave Mexico, decided he would go there in June for an initial discussion. If he and Green could agree on things, he would make quick trips to Chicago and New York, then return to Chapel Hill for a burst of hard work.

The decision came as a relief. He was sick of the isolation in Cuernavaca. He was making no progress whatsoever with *Black Hope*. His wife was driving him mad. His head was still full of *Native Son*. Why not write a play about Bigger, and then move on to something else?

BEFORE HE LEFT, WRIGHT HEARD THAT HERBERT KLINE WAS IN MEXICO TO SHOOT a documentary, with John Steinbeck as scriptwriter. Since his Chicago John Reed Club days, Kline had been editing the New York Communist magazine *New Theatre* and making a reputation for himself as a director of antifascist documentaries. During the Spanish civil war, he had filmed at the Madrid front. When the Nazis invaded Czechoslovakia and Poland, he was there with his movie camera.[48] For some weeks, Kline and his wife, his brother, and his Czech cameraman had been staying in a large villa in Mexico City, inspecting locations for filming and waiting for Steinbeck to turn up.

Steinbeck arrived in late May, having just been awarded the Pulitzer Prize for *The Grapes of Wrath*. There was tension between him and his wife (he was intending to leave her for another woman), and the planning sessions involved considerable quantities of alcohol. Kline recalls:

> We ate together and drank together—even though John would laugh
> and tell me not to drink more than one drink to his three. Richard
> Wright, a long-time friend of my brother Mark and mine from Chicago

days, showed up after his "hit" novel *Native Son*. John liked him, and sometimes this fine writer joined our talk-fests on the film plans.[49]

At the end of May, Wright accompanied the team on a reconnaissance trip into Michoacán. Driving about in a station wagon with Steinbeck and Kline, Wright saw the wretched poverty in the remote Indian villages. Children were dying from colitis and tuberculosis, and the villagers were convinced it was God's will. It was to be the theme of Steinbeck and Kline's prize-winning film, *Forgotten Village.*

WRIGHT'S LETTERS FROM MEXICO REVEAL NOTHING AT ALL ABOUT HIS PERSONAL life. Joe Brown, his old Jackson friend, did not even know Wright had a wife. To Algren, who did know, Wright did not mention Dhimah. When Willard and Marie asked about her, he merely said: "Dhimah is fine; she was ill a little, but all right now." In response to Ellison's hints that he might not be happy, he wrote: "About my being happy I'll have to talk to you about it when I see you." Then he deflected the question as rumor. "I'm getting used to the fact that now anything can and will be said about me. Boy, if I told you some of the things you'd be wild-eyed."[50]

On 15 June 1940 Paris fell. A few days later, Marshal Pétain signed an agreement with the Germans. Now France, Denmark, Norway, the Netherlands, and Belgium were all under German occupation. In the United States, Congress introduced the first compulsory draft in American peacetime history. Registration would begin in October for all men aged between twenty-one and thirty-six. At first, the selection would be by lottery. "I don't want to fight in this war," Wright told friends grimly.[51] Algren joked about flight. "Will you let me know how the landscape looks around Cuernavaca? . . . Lots of big high mountains and long deep caves and nice overhanging rocks and big tall grass?"[52] Both men were among three hundred writers from the League of American Writers to sign an antiwar petition in the *New Masses*.[53]

Wright and Dhimah had been in Mexico eleven weeks when they packed up to go home. Wright left Mexico City on 10 June to make his way by train through Mississippi to North Carolina. There was no question of his traveling in the South with a white wife. And he wanted to be alone. With everything so uncertain—the state of the world and the state of his marriage—he felt a need to journey into his past.

Dhimah, Eda, and Peter returned to New York on 12 June. "Dhimah will look you up when she arrives," Wright told Ralph Ellison.[54] And that was all he said.

DHIMAH ROSE MEIDMAN NEVER TOLD HER SIDE OF THE STORY. SHE LIVED LONG enough to see the publication of two biographies of Richard Wright— by Constance Webb and Michel Fabre—but she did not talk to either biographer.[55]

Dhimah, by all accounts, was a theatrical woman who lived in a cocoon of fantasies. When it came to daily life, she was totally impractical. Unable to cook, she relied on her mother for everything to do with the running of the house. Her son, Peter, describes her as a "sophisticated airhead."[56]

From the beginning, the marriage was under immense pressure. Even in New York, which saw itself as the most liberal city in the United States, interracial relationships carried considerable social opprobrium. In their book *Black Metropolis* (1945), Chicago sociologists Horace Cayton and St. Clair Drake (both of whom had experience of white wives) would have this to say about marriages between black men and white women:

> There is practically no intermarriage within the present-day Negro middle class, which is even more conservative than its white counterpart. . . . Prominent Negroes married to white women are always open to the charge that they have "deserted the race." . . . Communist leaders report that within their circles, although intermarriages are not frowned upon, they have observed Negro women, upon some occasions, voting against measures proposed by certain Negroes who had white wives. . . . In general, it may be observed that when Negro leaders married to white women have found it possible to retain their positions of influence, it has been in spite of their marriage; a white wife never strengthens their position vis à vis Negroes.[57]

With Dhimah came an entire entourage. With Wright came Bigger Thomas. The astounding news that the Book-of-the-Month Club was interested in *Native Son* had come just ten days after the wedding. This was followed by seven months of uncertainty, and then suddenly the couple faced fame and unexpected affluence. There was the euphoria of publication and extravagant praise, and then came biting criticism. The Party, which throughout the 1930s had played such a central role in the lives of Wright and Dhimah, put Wright on trial and pilloried him. Meanwhile, the war in Europe was escalating, and Wright faced the prospect of being sent away to fight in a Jim Crow army.

It is also probable that by the time they went to Mexico Wright had discovered some of Dhimah's pirouettes around the truth. On their marriage certificate, she had given her date of birth as 25 August 1907. This made her thirty-one, a year older than Wright. But her first marriage certificate gives her year of birth as 1901; her social security record gives it as 1902; her death certificate gives it as 1900.[58] The woman Wright married that summer evening in Harlem was not thirty-one, about to turn thirty-two. She was quite possibly thirty-eight.

It is possible that Wright discovered only later that Dhimah's first husband was not the father of her son. Soon after her marriage to Wright, Dhimah quietly informed Bill Wollman that she wanted him to have nothing more to do with his son. According to a letter he wrote her, he had wept and pleaded. She stood firm.[59]

Wright had been married to Dhimah for six months when he went to Chicago, in February 1940 (just before Mexico), and bought a house. On the purchase form he declared himself a bachelor.

FOR SOME TIME WRIGHT HAD WANTED TO "RE-SEE AND RE-FEEL THE SOUTH." IT was thirteen years since he had fled from it to Chicago. He had changed. He was a confident writer now, with money. He looked different. His voice had been modified by his years in the North. Would he be treated just the same as before? Would he react the same way?

He boarded a train in Mexico City, headed for San Antonio, Texas. Dressed in a smart, gray tweed suit, he carried an expensive suitcase, a typewriter, and a satchel full of books. In the carriage with him, as the train clattered through the Mexican countryside, were white Americans, Mexicans, Germans, and Spaniards.

When they reached the town of Brownsville, on the border with Texas, the train stopped. The whites were ushered into one coach and Wright, the only Negro on the train, into another. The conductor motioned some Mexicans into the carriage with Wright, but made them sit at the other end. "Mexicans seemed to hover somewhere between white people and Negroes," Wright observed in an essay he would write about that trip through the South, "How Jim Crow Feels."[60]

To his dismay, the immigration officer confiscated his passport.[61] Then the customs officer came on board and was visibly disconcerted by this black man with a typewriter. Was it his, he wanted to know? Was he a teacher? Wright told him he was a writer. Was he a preacher? the officer asked, ignoring Wright's answer. Then he looked at Wright's satchel. "Say, boy, these books ain't communistic, are they?" He wanted to know where Wright was born. When he heard Mississippi, he smiled. "I knew you was a Southern nigger. You niggers can travel all over the world, but when I see a Southern nigger, I know it."

In San Antonio, Texas, Wright changed trains. All the signs—the waiting rooms, drinking fountains, and public facilities—read "For Whites" and "For Colored." While he stood waiting on the platform, a white man in a wheelchair stared at him brazenly. Eventually the man wheeled up to Wright and fingered his jacket. "Boy, where'd you get that suit?" he asked. "What'd you pay for it?"

From New Orleans, Wright took the train to Natchez, Mississippi. The only blacks allowed in the dining car were Pullman waiters and porters. Wright wanted cigarettes and asked the porter to fetch him a packet. They chatted. The porter told him that in some states, Negroes were not allowed in the dining car at all; in others they had to eat before the whites ate or after the whites were finished; in others they ate at the same time, concealed from view by a cloth screen.

Natchez filled Wright with dismay. Nothing seemed to have changed, except that an alarming number of people from his past had died. Looking at the South with fresh eyes, he could now see what was a well-known fact: the people were the worst fed, housed, and clothed and the most illiterate and diseased in the whole country. He felt numb inside. Not even the "broad, yellow Mississippi" or the "tall, moss-hung oaks" were able to move him.

> Fat pigs wallowed in the filthy front yards of Negro laborers. Sparrows flounced in the dust of gutters. People moved and spoke slowly, as if lacking bodily energy, as if their diets, composed mainly of lard and starch, were deficient in vitamins. The standard diversions of white and black were sex and religion. At night in the narrow alleys was the smell

of burning hair coming from Negro beauty parlors where black women tried to make their hair look like that of white people. There was a persistently sour smell of earth around the backs of houses where dishwater was thrown out of windows, for there was no plumbing. Over the stench of outdoor privies came the sweet scent of magnolias. The cooking was heavy and greasy and stayed in one's stomach for an ungodly number of hours. It rained often and the damp smell of vegetation always hung in the air. By day flies hummed. At night mosquitoes sang.[62]

Two months earlier, the monotony of Natchez life had been disrupted by disaster; the town had been on the front page of the national newspapers. The Negro community had suffered a terrible tragedy. On the evening of 23 April 1940, the young black clarinetist Walter Barnes and his sixteen-piece orchestra from Chicago, one of the nation's best swing bands, had been playing at the Rhythm Club, on St. Catherine Street. The old wooden hall was decorated with Spanish moss, draped from the rafters and beams. As a precaution against gate-crashers, the rear door had been blocked off and the windows crisscrossed with steel bars. Close to midnight, the dancing was in full swing when someone flipped a match. A flash fire erupted. There was a stampede to the front door, and within minutes the air supply in the hall was cut off. There were 209 deaths and just 17 survivors. Every family in town had lost someone. Walter Barnes died. Prominent Negro citizens died; dozens of adolescents died; and several of the children of Natchez became orphans overnight.

Wright would describe that ferocious fire in his 1958 novel *The Long Dream*. He kept close to the facts, except that the Natchez fire was more deadly than his fictional fire, where there were only forty-two deaths. It is another instance where Wright's fiction is less horrifying than the reality on which it was based.

Wright tried to obtain his birth certificate. He knew it would be required for draft registration in October. But in Natchez, he discovered, no birth records had been kept before 1912—neither for whites nor blacks.

He wanted to see his father again. Nathan Wright and his brothers, Solomon, Rias, and George, were working as sharecroppers near Stanton, close to where Wright was born. For the first time, Wright met his half sister, Joanna. She was hoping to become a dancer, and Wright tried, in vain, to persuade her to come North with him. He searched for the cabin where he had been born, but the site was covered with weeds. It had burned down. Nobody knew when.

The reunion with his father was tense. Wright reasoned to himself that it was "continuous association" and "shared ideas" that made people close, "not the myth of blood."[63] In *Black Boy*, he would paint a memorable portrait of his father—"standing alone upon the red clay of a Mississippi plantation, a sharecropper, clad in ragged overalls, holding a muddy hoe in his gnarled, veined hands . . . standing against the sky, smiling toothlessly, his hair whitened, his body bent, his eyes glazed with dim recollection."[64]

Wright could see his own features in his father's face; he could hear an echo of his own voice in his father's. Nevertheless, he writes, "we were forever strangers." He thought about the "simple nakedness" of his father's life. He was scarcely an individual in any real sense of the word, Wright mused. He was simply "a creature of the earth." The city had proved too much for him; he had returned to the peasant existence he knew best—an existence in which "his soul was imprisoned by the slow flow of the seasons, by wind and rain and sun."

Two photographs survive from Wright's June 1940 visit to Natchez. In one of them, Nathan is sitting stiffly against the wooden window of his shack. Self-conscious in front of the camera, an uncertain smile plays on his lips. His hair, cropped close to his scalp, is still black; his back is straight. His eyes are misted with cataracts. In the other, Nathan and three of his brothers stand outside in a semicircle. Richard Wright is in the middle. The sharecroppers are wearing overalls; Richard Wright stands out with his tie, smart trousers and braces, and steel glasses.

In the evening of 19 June, the last of four days in Natchez, Wright passed the time drinking beer in a dingy tavern. The automatic phonograph ground out tunes. Nobody seemed to be listening. Wright felt "numbed and lost." It was past midnight when he boarded the train for Birmingham, Alabama. He was making his way to North Carolina.[65]

The next morning, he wanted breakfast. Not permitted in the dining car himself, he asked the Negro porter to fetch the Negro waiter, and he ordered scrambled eggs, toast, and coffee. An hour passed and the waiter did not return. Wright asked what the problem was. The porter went to the dining car and came back looking uncomfortable. "They awfully busy up there." Wright could tell he was hiding something.

By midday he still had not eaten. The train stopped at a station. He gazed listlessly out of the window and noticed the white soldiers in the next coach get off. Five minutes later, the waiter came hurrying up with his breakfast. "He placed the tray on my knees, and spoke in a low, rushing, almost hysterical voice that told me he did not want me to ask him any questions." Wright pressed him. "It was the white soldiers in the next coach," he told Wright, avoiding his eyes. He would say no more.

The porter eventually told Wright in a frightened whisper: "He was bringing you your breakfast, but them white soldiers wouldn't let him. They said they didn't wanna see no tray taken to the nigger coach. Now, Mister, this is the South. Don't make no trouble for us."

12

BACKSTAGE AND ONSTAGE:
THE DRAMA OF *NATIVE SON*

Summer 1940

In the spring of 1940, Paul Green had walked through the woods on his farm in North Carolina, jotting down a list of the flora he observed (dogwood, plum, hawthorn, huckleberry, willow, buckeye, Judas trees) and musing about that violent, urban novel *Native Son*. "Found it horrifying, brutal and extraordinarily vivid," he noted in his journal. "Reminiscent a bit of 'Crime and Punishment.' Doubt I could do anything with it. However, I feel it's the most vivid writing I've seen by any Negro author in America."[1]

Cheryl Crawford, director of the leftist Group Theater in New York, had asked whether he might be interested in dramatizing it. Green was not tempted until he heard that Orson Welles and John Houseman were likely to get the stage rights for a Broadway production. Then he decided that he would, after all, put in a bid for the dramatization. *Native Son* was not his kind of thing, and in Green's view, Wright's novel was not going to help correct social wrongs or bring about racial harmony. But if he and Wright could collaborate on the dramatization, he wrote to Aswell at Harper, "all matters could be discussed as we went along."[2]

Wright was enthusiastic. Paul Green was the only white playwright to produce serious drama about the Negro experience. He knew his craft. And it appeared that he was not afraid of controversy: his plays had been attacked as much as praised. Wright believed he could "handle a boy like Bigger."[3] He and Green had very different perspectives, but if they worked on the play together, Wright was sure he could impart his own vision, showing the social forces that create a Bigger Thomas.

John Houseman was not at all keen on working with Paul Green. He did not see how Green's moralist religious perspective could possibly be compatible with Wright's angry left-wing vision. He could foresee Paul Green turning a forceful novel into an artistic little drama bristling with pious certitudes, cathartic suffering, and redemption. He also knew that Green was notoriously slow when it came to producing a finished play.

Houseman would have liked Wright to do the dramatization himself, with help from him, but Wright insisted he did not feel competent. "My field is the novel; I know very little about the movies and still less about the stage," he wrote back.[4] Under the circumstances, collaboration seemed the best solution.

Harper & Brothers wanted to publish the play, and offered an advance of one thousand dollars. Wright's agent, Paul Reynolds, suggested a 60 percent–40 percent breakdown, with the greater share going to Wright, as author of the novel. Green wanted 50–50. The final contract gave "the author" (Wright) 55 percent and "the dramatist" (Green) 45 percent. It had an important symbolic significance: Wright was understood to be the dominant partner.

Houseman had arranged to meet Wright and Green in Chapel Hill for preliminary discussions. He drove down from New York with his mother, who was visiting from Europe. Wright arrived by train in nearby Durham, still churned up by his Jim Crow trip through the South. From 20 to 22 June, Paul and Elizabeth Green put the three of them up on their wooded property two miles out of Chapel Hill.

This was still the South. Having Wright stay involved Paul Green briefing each of his Negro employees: A "wonderful Negro writer" is coming . . . and "you just behave yourself, you know."[5] Blacks were not used to serving blacks.

Elizabeth Green, the daughter of a minister, was proud of her husband's boldness when it came to what whites used to refer to in those days as "the Negro problem." It took courage to have black guests staying in the house. "I expected almost any night to wake up and find a cross burning on the front lawn," she said later. "Maybe I was rather disappointed that it didn't happen!"[6]

JOHN HOUSEMAN, LIKE PAUL GREEN, HAD GOOD CREDENTIALS IN AFRICAN-AMERICAN theater. Educated at a British boarding school, in the 1930s he had come to the United States and discovered the theater. During 1935 and 1936, he had successfully codirected the Federal Negro Theatre in Harlem. While working there, he had invited Orson Welles to direct a production. He was taking a risk. Welles was twenty at the time (twelve years younger than Houseman) and a mercurial genius. He had come up with the idea of a nineteenth-century version of *Macbeth*, set in the jungle of Haiti. The first all-Negro production of Shakespeare in American theater history, it proved a triumphant success—in Harlem, on Broadway, and on national tour.[7]

In August 1937, Houseman and Welles established their own repertory theater, called Mercury Theatre. The partnership proved both dazzling and explosive. Welles, as an actor and director, was frenetic, exhilarating, and exhausting. His capacity for work (he would sometimes rehearse for sixteen hours at a time) matched his gargantuan appetite. (His actors would watch incredulously while he devoured a whole chicken.) Houseman managed the administration and budget and wrote the scripts. Both men knew how to coax the best out of people they needed, and were ruthless with those they didn't need.

For a while now, the two men had been ready to go their own way. But then Welles had asked Houseman to help Herman Mankiewicz with the screenplay for *Citizen Kane*. While Houseman was editing the script and trying to keep Mankiewicz sober, he read *Native Son*. He told himself it would make a wonderful play. He also knew that there was only one man who could be relied upon to make it into an electrifying theatrical experience. Welles agreed to work on the play as soon as he finished *Citizen Kane*.

Houseman had come to North Carolina to set things in motion.

I was there when Wright arrived—a surprisingly mild-mannered, round-faced, brown-skinned young man with beautiful eyes. It was only later, when I came to know him better, that I began to sense the deep, almost morbid violence that lay skin-deep below that gentle surface. . . .

I spent a day with him and Green, listening to Paul's ideas for the play. I watched Dick Wright for his reactions: I saw nothing. But my own apprehensions rose sharply. Paul Green was a man who sincerely believed himself free of racial prejudice. . . . Throughout his stay, according to Dick, he could not have been more courteous, thoughtful and hospitable in his treatment of his black guest. But, having granted him social equality, he stopped there. From the first hour of their "discussions" it became clear that he was incapable or unwilling to extend this equality into the professional or creative fields. Whether from his exalted position as veteran playwright and Pulitzer Prize winner or from some innate sense of intellectual and moral superiority (aggravated by Wright's Communist connections), Paul Green's attitude in the collaboration was, first and last, insensitive, condescending and intransigent.[8]

Despite his misgivings, Houseman signed the dramatic rights. The three men told one another they had high hopes for a fine play. The script, they agreed, should be finished by October.

In the late afternoon of Saturday, 22 June, Houseman, his mother, and Richard Wright drove back to New York. In his memoirs, Houseman recalls that Wright seemed rather disturbed about the direction some of Paul Green's reflections were taking. Houseman asked "with some impatience" why he had not spoken up and given him (Houseman) "a chance to provoke a confrontation."[9]

The travelers reached Washington as it was getting dark. They looked for a place to eat. A self-service cafeteria was open in the vicinity of the White House. They had piled their trays high and sat themselves down when the manager came over to their table and informed them that no "coloreds" were allowed. Houseman and his mother, embarrassed, started to argue with the man. Wright quietly headed for the exit with his tray.

The Housemans followed. "It was a warm night, and the three of us sat on the curb and ate our supper while Dick explained to my mother that he was accustomed to this sort of thing which would never change until the entire system was changed."[10]

———

WRIGHT SPENT FOUR DAYS IN NEW YORK. (DHIMAH HAD BEEN BACK, LIVING IN Harlem, for ten days.) He stayed with Jane and Herbert Newton, in Brooklyn, then took the train to Chicago.

"Arna says tell you hello, and that we hope to see you soon," Langston Hughes had written from Chicago, just before Wright left Mexico. "When you come back we will buy a small bottle of rum for you and your wife, and I will drink it."[11]

Wright arrived in Chicago without a wife. Chicago treated him like the prodigal son. Nelson Algren and Jack Conroy threw a party for him at which they launched their magazine, the *New Anvil*.[12] Wright gave his talk, "Why 'Bigger' Was Born," in the Church of the Good Shepherd on the South Side.[13] The church was so crowded that people were sitting in the aisles and standing by the side of the rostrum. Wright was given a standing ovation.[14]

The American Negro Exposition had just opened at the Chicago Coliseum. Wright, an honored guest, autographed copies of *Native Son*.[15] But the exposition was not proving to be the triumphant success it was meant to be. The government funding had fallen into the wrong hands. This was Chicago. Langston Hughes, always out of pocket, was beginning to realize he was not going to be paid for the months of work he had just done. The funds had dried up. Wright, on the other hand, was off to Chapel Hill to work with Pulitzer Prize–Winning playwright Paul Green on a Broadway play to be directed by Orson Welles. Everything seemed to be going well for him.

WRIGHT RETURNED TO CHAPEL HILL ON 8 JULY. HE COULD NOT GO TO THE CAROLINA Inn, where visiting scholars usually stayed. He could not eat in the restaurants next to the university. Paul Green had found him a room in a boardinghouse in the black area between Chapel Hill and the white, working-class, cotton mill district of Carrboro. Just a few streets away from the university, with its handsome old buildings and spreading live oaks, the black district was a different world. The streets were unpaved; the houses were shabby.

Paul Green was Professor of Dramatic Art at the University of North Carolina, and well known on that all-white Southern campus for his progressive views about race. In the past, his hospitality to black scholars had caused rumblings from the locals and reprimands from the university administration.[16] This time he had sought official permission from the university president to have Wright work with him in an office on the university grounds.

It was summer; the campus was quiet. The president hoped the presence of a black man would go almost unnoticed. Green and Wright were allotted space in Bynum Hall, an administrative building that was once the old gymnasium.

Chapel Hill was swelteringly hot that summer of 1940. For days on end, the temperature hovered between 100 and 106 in the shade, and scarcely dropped at night. The two men started out in a room on the southwest corner of Bynum Hall, and were driven out by the heat. For a few days they tried working in Green's log cabin on his farm. But that was less convenient, since Green had to pick Wright up and take him there. Eventually, they were given two rooms in the northeast corner of Bynum Hall, where at least they were not subjected to the afternoon sun. A friend lent them a fan. "So we were enabled to continue," Green wrote in his journal.[17]

Curious faces would look in at the window. Never had anyone in the South seen such a sight. A white man and a black man were sitting across from each other at a long table. On the table were a large typewriter, a pair of horn-rimmed glasses that the white man would sometimes put on for reading (the black man wore steel rims), a book that looked like a novel with handwriting in the margin, a packet of Pall Mall cigarettes, an ashtray half full of stubs, and sundry notebooks and papers. Everywhere there was paper filled with type, crossings out, and bold arrows in black ink. Sometimes the black man would sit at the typewriter and burst into composition, like a bird into song. The white man liked to pace the room, theatrically touching his forehead with the back of his hand as he pondered an idea.[18]

Thirty years later, in the 1970s, Paul Green gave several interviews in which he talked about those weeks with Wright. By then, the civil rights movement had fundamentally changed attitudes toward "blacks," as they were now called. Black students had been admitted to the University of North Carolina. A decade had passed since Wright's premature death. Paul Green was now rather embarrassed about the way he had treated Wright that summer of 1940.

Something I regretted. I never understood it. He called me "Mr Green" and I called him "Dick" or "Richard." What in the heck went on? But anyway that was the relationship, although we felt very close together.[19]

Now when I look back on it—you know, when you have a friend who has died, you say, Jesus, if I'd known he was going to die, I'd have done so different. I would have gone to see him; I would have treated him so differently.[20]

In the 1970s, Green claimed that before he agreed to dramatize *Native Son*, he had written several stipulations into the contract. The first was that he would have the right to "poke some fun" at Communism. "I didn't want to put something on the stage saying that I was behind this thing, Communism."[21] Another was that he would be allowed to make Bigger Thomas partially responsible for his own downfall. "I didn't subscribe to the old familiar whine that 'the reason I'm a dead beat, or I'm mean, or I can't get anywhere in the world is that the world treats me wrong.' No. Every man has something to do with what he becomes."[22]

In all of Green's meticulously kept contracts and correspondence at the University of North Carolina, there is no sign of any such clause. Green also claimed, after Wright had died, that he wrote the whole play himself, but that Wright was "so helpful" that he, Green, insisted on using joint names. He says he once asked Wright to try his hand at writing a scene. It did not work. "It was beautiful, but completely novelistic."[23]

Green's memory was flawed. It was understood from the beginning that the play would be published under joint names. And though Green, as a skilled playwright, almost certainly wrote more, the first draft was a mutual process—both in its conception and in the writing. In an interview given at the time, Wright explained that he and Green met each morning, discussed the content of a scene, then retired to write separately and came together again in the late afternoon to compare notes. "We would both work at a scene until we felt we had packed it with all the necessary action. Mr. Green would then compress it. After that, I would go over it, making sure that the dialogue and imagery were Negro and urban."[24] This picture of their collaboration is reinforced by Ouida Campbell, their secretary, who was often in the room with them, taking notes.

The collaboration was congenial, but Houseman was quite right: it was unequal. It was a play they were writing, and Green was the proven playwright. Green was forty-six; Wright was thirty-one. Green was a Pulitzer Prize winner, a university professor; they were on his territory, he was white. Years later, Paul Green was as adamant as ever about the "rightness" of his views:

> In the novel, as I read it, Bigger Thomas was practically completely a product of his environment: and I wouldn't subscribe to that. A human being has got some responsibility to his own career; and I don't care what Freud says or what the whining people say, you can't put it always on somebody else.[25]

What further complicated the collaboration were the genuine—and major—problems associated with turning the novel into something appropriate for the stage. In the novel, the reader's sympathy with Bigger, such as it is, comes from seeing things through his consciousness. On stage, Bigger would be seen from the outside. The novel had already been described as "melodramatic"; the stage drama could all too easily become sensationalist. Violence that was just tolerable on the page would not be tolerable on stage. And then there was the interracial sex. If a black man fondling the breasts of a white woman was barely acceptable in a novel, a theater audience would be stampeding up the aisles.

The problem was how to solve these issues, given the two men's quite disparate personal philosophies. Paul Green was a Southern gentleman. His speech, as well as his writing, had a biblical ring to it. "The South is acquainted with sin, more than any other part of the country," he told an interviewer in 1960. "We are just full of the drip of human tears." In the same interview, he added: "The love between the Negro and the white is something wonderful to behold in the South."[26]

Green did not share Wright's focus on environmental forces; he thought entirely in terms of individual responsibility. It was the "human soul" that interested him—what he called "the god-like spirit in man."[27] He believed in self-reliance, courage, and righteousness—the founding principles of the American Constitution. His hero was Thomas Jefferson, a fellow Southerner, whom he liked to quote. A favorite was: "A nation can only be as strong and healthy as its citizens are strong and healthy."[28]

Green's passion was Greek tragedy. He liked tragic heroes. Like the Greek playwrights, he believed in catharsis. "The urge to associate with, to help the suffering one, to lift him up, to ease him, brings with it . . . a gained fullness of personality," he once said. "The feeling is pleasurable."[29] His plays about Negroes were tragedies; his black characters victims and martyrs. In the 1930s, Communist critics had criticized him for his "tragic and defeatist attitude towards life."[30] Wright had written cathartic stories once, in *Uncle Tom's Children*, and had sworn never to do so again.

From the beginning, Green set out to soften the impact of *Native Son*. It was a story about hate; he believed in love. He vehemently disapproved of Wright's basic premise: that Bigger Thomas could transcend his circumstances only by an act of violence. He tried to make Bigger more likable. One of his strategies was to make the white woman, Mary Dalton, less likable. In Green's version, her friendliness toward Bigger is less idealism than brassy boredom. His stage directions have her "dressed in a flowing red robe, opened at the bosom."

Green proposed to replace the harsh realism of the murder scene with "the pale cast of dreaming."[31] Instead of having Bigger kill Mary Dalton on stage, he wanted to show Bigger dreaming about the murder afterward. And Green persuaded Wright that one murder was more than enough. "Bessie" (who was now called "Clara," since Green thought too many of the characters had names beginning with "b") throws her arms around Bigger and is destroyed by police gunfire.

The final scene caused endless discussion. Green wanted Bigger to walk toward the execution chamber with straight shoulders and head high—"like a god." That way, Green insisted, Bigger would be a hero and the play would be a tragedy, rather than simply "pathetic."

Miss Ouida Campbell was employed to type up the work-in-progress. Mostly she sat at her typewriter in the small space outside the two office rooms. Some afternoons she was invited behind the closed doors of Bynum 201. A space was cleared for her at the table, and she wrote down dialogue, in shorthand. Well aware that she was privileged to be witnessing literary history, several months later she described the scene for the *Carolina Magazine*:

> Mr. Green—big, tall, with his horn-rimmed glasses, his white suit and the old Panama hat he kept putting on and taking off—was a combination of a Southern Gentleman and a nervous artist as he walked around the little room. Richard Wright . . . sat by the window, smiling often as he talked, dressed in a pink sport shirt and maroon slacks. He had, as always, an air of quiet, assured, self-confidence.
>
> Bigger was their greatest problem. In the novel, Wright had Bigger hating violently, a hate caused by fear. He lived by this hate—it was his only creed. Mr. Green wanted to take some of this hate out of Bigger.[32]

The room, she writes, was filled with an excitement, "tense and suppressed." Mr. Green would walk up and down, smoking one cigarette after another and running his hand through his hair. Mr. Wright would tilt his chair back against the wall, swing his foot, and smile. According to Campbell, the arguments were always affable. "They had an easy, joking, bantering relationship. They rubbed along very smoothly. If there were disagreements, they talked them out and compromised. Or did it Mr. Green's way."[33]

During those weeks, Ouida Campbell saw Bigger Thomas undergo a transformation. He started to say things like "I'm so hungry I could chew me a piece of the Lamb of God." Shortly before his death, he said to his lawyer: "I wanted to be free, to walk wide and free with steps a mile long—over the fields, over the rivers, and straddling the mountains and on—like God." Miss Campbell wondered whether Bigger could survive this tug-of-war:

> At the time the first draft was finished and Wright went back to New York, Bigger Thomas was guilty not only of murder, but of the crime of inconsistency. He was about equally divided: one half Mr. Green's Bigger—sensitive, misguided, puzzled about life in general; and the other half Wright's Bigger—full of hate and fear, cunning, but at the same time looking for an answer to the questions that rise in his mind.[34]

Among Wright's unpublished papers at Yale is a revealing seven-page drama called "The Problem of the Hero."[35] The two characters are called "white man" and "black man." Wright wrote it several months after his sojourn in North Carolina. At the top of the first page, he stated: "The following is not a verbatim report of conversations that took place between Paul Green and me, but an attempt to re-construct the general sense of the central problem we faced in dramatizing my novel, *Native Son*." The play opens with the white man talking:

> WHITE MAN: (graciously but seriously) I wasn't quite satisfied with your novel when I read it, but I liked it. I felt it was the best piece of fiction written by a Negro in America. Now, in dramatizing it, I would like to make your character, Bigger, a hero in the tragic sense. As he stands now, he seems a figure of pathos, more acted upon than acting.

The black man argues that Bigger is not able to determine his own destiny, which is what it takes to make a tragic hero. The white man says: "But there must be heroes!" The black man answers: "There shall be heroes, when men are *free!*" The white man does not like it that Bigger discovers the possibilities of life through "reprehensible deeds, through acts of murder, through evil." He sees Bigger as an "inverted Christ" figure. The black man worries that the play is no longer "true to Negro life." It has become a metaphysical drama. The white man sees Bigger "from the point of view of heroic tragedy." He is convinced that what they want is an "overreaching symbol that heals." "But he's got to be true, credible," the black man protests.

BY MID-AUGUST GREEN AND WRIGHT MANAGED TO PRODUCE WHAT THEY TENTA-tively called "a first rough working draft." Wright had to return to New York. From now on, they agreed, Green would be mainly responsible for the rewriting and polishing, but they would continue their discussions from a distance, and Green would make short trips to New York.

Just before Wright left town, trouble brewed. There are different versions of the story, recalled through the mists of passing years. According to Ouida Campbell, some bohemian university student friends in Chapel Hill threw a party for her—she had just turned nine-teen—and she invited Richard Wright along. Theirs was an easy rela-tionship, says Ouida. "Mr. Wright never flirted with me, but he could charm the ears off a brass monkey."[36] Paul Green seemed to remember that the party was at Ouida's house in Carrboro. Whichever it was, it was a hot night; the doors and windows were open, and the neighbors did not like what they saw.

The day after the party, Paul Green and Wright were putting the finishing touches to their first draft when the phone rang. It was the university chancellor. Paul Green tells the story:

> He said, "This boy you've got here working with you: he's been here four weeks, and . . . you promised me that there wouldn't be any trouble."
>
> I said: "Well, sure, I didn't think there'd be any trouble. What trouble is there now?"
>
> He said: "Well, your cousin . . . he's down here at Eubanks' drugstore, and he's got a pistol, and he's got several men around him, and they're going after Richard Wright. . . . Your secretary gave a party for Richard Wright last night in Carrboro and invited some people. And the folks out there got on to it that she was entertaining a Negro, and they are on the warpath."[37]

Paul Green assured the chancellor that Wright was leaving the following afternoon. "Tomorrow afternoon is a long ways off," the chancellor said.

"What do you want me to do?" Green asked.

"I want you to get him out of town. . . . This thing could get out of hand and give the university a black eye."[38]

Green hurried downtown and found his cousin, an ex-boxer (in some versions Green makes him six feet, six inches), with three or four other "rough-looking fellows." Green took him aside and tried to reason with him, but his cousin's eyes were blazing, he had a pistol in his pocket, and he kept telling Green: "We're going to run him out of town tonight."

> That night (I never told Wright about this) I went and stayed in the cotton patch outside that house where he roomed. I thought well, if there's going to be any trouble, I might as well be in it. I didn't carry a gun or anything; I just went. But nothing happened; nobody ever came. . . . The next day, Wright came in there, shiny and breezy and all.[39]

Wright *did* know about the threats, since years later in Paris he laughed about the episode with an acquaintance from Chapel Hill.[40] Whatever the true facts were, on the afternoon of Monday, 12 August, Wright caught the train for New York as planned.

13

ELLEN POPLOWITZ

New York: August 1940–Summer 1941

After being away from New York for five months, Wright was back with the Newtons, living in a basement apartment in another brown-stone house in Brooklyn.[1] Dhimah had asked Rose and Ralph Ellison to share the upstairs apartment in her mother's townhouse in Harlem. They had been living a few doors away, and for the sake of economy, they moved in. Perhaps Dhimah hoped this might help her get back with Wright. If so, it didn't work. Wright visited her only once. They withdrew to Dhimah's end of the apartment to talk in private, and then Wright left. To Ellison, he seemed very disturbed.[2]

The explanation Wright gave Ellison was that Dhimah had the wrong impression of his wealth; she had spent his money too freely in Mexico.[3] He told Jane Newton that he had a bad time in Mexico, and had not been able to write. He hinted that there had been some angry scenes. Wright had married Dhimah hoping she would teach him sophistication and worldly wisdom, Newton recalled. "He felt after-wards that whatever he had learned had been inordinately expensive and had to do mostly with expenses and temper tantrums."[4]

Wright cut off all communication with Dhimah. He calmed himself by gardening. He bought books on the subject and spent hours in the backyard, planting vegetables and flowers. He wrote the liner notes for the black folksinger Josh White's new album, *Southern Exposure*, pointing out that the blues could be protest songs—"fighting blues" as much as wailing blues and moaning blues. At the beginning of autumn, he sent a note to Ralph Ellison. "Listen, will you do me a favor? Will you ask Dhimah to let you have my things? If she does, will you bring them over to me in a taxi? I'll defray the cost." Dhimah still had his winter coat and his corduroy trousers. And now that he was at last "swinging back into hard work again," he needed his portable table.[5]

According to Ellen Poplowitz, who within seven months would become Wright's second wife, he never spoke about Dhimah. "He was a man who looked ahead. For Dick, finished is finished."[6]

IT WAS A HOT SEPTEMBER EVENING AT THE GOLDEN GATE BALLROOM IN HARLEM. The publicity posters announced: "Two of America's Most Distinguished Artists—Paul Robeson and Richard Wright." The benefit evening was to raise funds for a new black theater group to be directed by Ted Ward, who had been busy for months finding sponsors.[7] The first play scheduled was Ward's *Big White Fog*.

Tickets were twenty-five dollars, a small fortune, and the crowd mostly white. Hazel Scott, a star at Café Society, sang a few bars of Liszt's Second Hungarian Rhapsody, then, to the delight of the crowd, exploded into swing rhythm. Ted Ward spoke briefly about the aims of the Negro Playwright's Company. Richard Wright launched into "Why 'Bigger' Was Born." His talk was too long and serious for a hot swing palace on a sticky night. The audience grew restless.

At last, Paul Robeson came on. He sang "Old Man River," with new revolutionary lyrics, and "Fatherland," a song about the Soviet Union. The applause was thunderous.

WHILE PAUL GREEN WAS REVISING THEIR PLAY, WRIGHT WAS BACK AT WORK ON *Black Hope*. His conception of the novel had changed drastically. He was now more interested in exposing the scandalous exploitation of young black domestic workers by illegal employment agencies in Brooklyn and the Bronx. These agencies brought young women from the South with the lure of free transportation and immediate employ-ment in New York, held them in the city in semicaptivity, and then sent them out as underpaid domestic servants in white households.[8]

Wright collected newspaper cuttings, and talked to social workers and to his friend Marvel Cooke, who at the height of the Depression had written an article about the Bronx "slave market," as it was popu-larly known. The term referred to street corners where black women would stand waiting for white housewives to approach, single them out from the group, and employ them for an hour or two for anything between fifteen and thirty cents an hour.[9]

Accompanied by a stenographer, Wright went along to the Domes-tic Workers' Union in Brooklyn and Harlem to interview women work-ers—young black women who spent their day alone and unprotected in white people's homes. They would not talk when Wright tried to interview them one by one. But when he spoke to them in a group, they spilled out their stories so fast the stenographer could hardly get them down. They told of abuse, humiliation, and underpayment. Wright also sensed a high degree of sexual exploitation, but could not get the girls to open up on that subject.[10]

His notes were piling up. But he was having great difficulty coalesc-ing two very different novels into one.

NATIVE SON WAS DOING EXCEPTIONALLY WELL IN THE SOVIET UNION AND WOULD shortly be out in Denmark, Germany, Spain, Portugal, Switzerland, Sweden, Britain, and Australia. In the U.S., however, sales had tapered off dramatically. At the end of the year, Arna Bontemps wrote to Langston Hughes: "Just read in a *Publishers Weekly*, summarizing 1940 in the book marts, that one of the sensations of the year was the sud-den boom and abrupt decline of *Native Son* as a best-seller. It con-cluded that the boom was due to the novelty of such a book being chosen by Book-of-the-Month and the fade-out followed discovery on part of readers (who thought they were getting a murder thriller) that the book contained a 'political argument.'"[11]

If the disappointment was hard on Wright, financially the three months on the American best-seller lists also took their toll. In 1939 Wright had declared an income of $2,585 to the Internal Revenue

Department. In 1940 his income was $28,019 (approximately $450,000 in today's currency). He found himself in the highest possible tax bracket.

Paul Reynolds suggested to Harper that they spread Wright's royalties over two years, but Aswell dashed that hope. "The Treasury Department regards income due in a given year as taxable in that year, even though it may be actually received in a subsequent year," he told Reynolds. "Since *Native Son* had so much publicity and is so generally known to have been a best-seller, a reporting of reduced royalty earnings might therefore occasion suspicion. In that event, of course, Mr. Wright would not only have to pay the full tax, but might also incur penalties for evasion."[12]

"A large percentage of Wright's earnings went to Uncle Sam," Paul Reynolds writes in his memoir, *The Middle Man*. Indeed, it was the "Wright situation" that made Reynolds think up a way around this injustice. He came up with a different sort of contract with publishers, getting them to pay out authors' royalties over a period of years. "Ultimately the Internal Revenue Department gave its formal blessing to this practice. Today spreading of an author's income over a period of years is almost universal," writes Reynolds.[13] It was an important innovation for writers. But it was too late for Richard Wright. It is one of literary history's ironies that the U.S. government made almost as much out of Wright's protest novel as he did.

WRIGHT WAS REVIEWING BOOKS ON A REGULAR BASIS. HE ENJOYED THE OPPORTUNity to collect his thoughts on a book by writing about it. He was full of praise for Carson McCullers's novel *The Heart Is a Lonely Hunter*. The cover blurb reported that it was her first novel and she was just twenty-two. Wright was curious. How could this white woman have been brought up in the South (which she surely must have been to write this book) and come away with such a profound understanding of black people?

> Miss McCullers's picture . . . is perhaps the most desolate that has so far come from the South. Her quality of despair is unique and individual; and it seems to me more natural and authentic than that of Faulkner.
> . . . To me the most impressive aspect . . . is the astonishing humanity that enables a white writer, for the first time in Southern fiction, to handle

Negro characters with as much ease and justice as those of her own race.[14]

He was less enthusiastic about two autobiographical narratives by two major black intellectuals: *Dusk of Dawn* by W. E. B. Du Bois and *The Big Sea* by Langston Hughes. He wrote that though the men shared the same goal, they represented "two camps of leadership." Du Bois pinned his hopes on an educated black elite—a "talented tenth"—and Langston Hughes looked to the masses. Wright (who identified with neither group) believed that the future lay in "an alliance between the educated Negro and the masses of workers."[15]

Wright dismissed Du Bois as a "conservative," who belonged to the "old school." He asserted: "Du Bois comes from a Puritan New England background, a product of French, Dutch and African blood. His boyhood resembles that of millions of whites."[16]

Langston Hughes played a "double role," Wright said, as a realist and a cultural ambassador.[17] Wright made it clear that he approved of Hughes's realism. It was widely known what he thought of ambassadors. To Wright, the writer's role was to tell the truth, not act as a diplomat.

"The two books are recommended highly for those anxious to examine at close range the tissue and texture of contemporary Negro life. But I think the average reader will finish them with a hunger for something more. . . . What is lacking in the lives of these two men is an effective rationale of action or program." Wright was sounding rather like the Communist critics of *Native Son*.

NOT LONG AFTER WRIGHT MOVED BACK TO BROOKLYN, ELLEN POPLOWITZ DROPPED by—ostensibly to see Jane Newton. Wright was working in his room. He heard her voice and came onto the landing at the top of the stairs and called her name. "It was a really eerie thing," she says. "I knew immediately that my family counted for nothing. . . . I was very excited and we fell into each other's arms and there was no talking after that. The whole thing was settled. . . . I just moved in with Dick right in that house."[18]

They had not seen each other for more than a year. Everything had changed and nothing had changed. Wright had become famous. He was much criticized in the Communist circles that meant everything to Ellen. But she did not hesitate.

For Ellen, it meant a radical break with her family. In the next few weeks, Rose Poplowitz came to the house several times in an attempt to talk some sense into her daughter, but Ellen refused to see her. "She was highly strung," says Ellen, "and very emotional."[19] Rose Poplowitz came around to plead with Jane Newton for support, but she must have realized that hers was a lost cause in that interracial household.

Ellen was twenty-eight and looked scarcely twenty. Small and slim, with dark wavy hair, she had sparkling green eyes and Slavic cheekbones. She had none of Dhimah's worldly sophistication. She had never traveled abroad. Her future husband had to teach her to cook. But she shared with him a love of books, an ease with words, and a strong sense of justice. As her work with the Party showed, she was loyal, committed, efficient, and practical.

The Poplowitz family belonged to that huge wave of immigrants from eastern Europe who in the early years of the twentieth century had boarded ships in Baltic and German ports to escape the pogroms at home. Their Russian, Polish, Ukrainian, and Czech names scrawled on ledger after ledger, in ship after ship, were the first of many marks they were to make on the new country. Yiddish was their native tongue, not English. As Jews, they were treated shabbily in their new country as well. And yet—as Wright and his black friends had not failed to notice—these newcomers soon moved to neighborhoods where black people were not permitted to live. They were employed by businesses that did not employ blacks. Soon they owned and operated small businesses, and with their accumulated income helped each other find jobs.

It was February 1912 when Ellen's father, Isidor David Poplowitz, had boarded the *George Washington* in Bremen and sailed to New York. As soon as he found lodgings and work in the new country, he sent for his wife, Rose, and their two-year-old daughter, Florence. This was his second family.[20] He was forty-one; his wife, Rose, was twenty-four and pregnant.[21] Freda (Ellen) was born in New York's Lower East Side on 3 September 1912. Eighteen months later a son, Moe, was born—known in the new country as Martin. By 1916 the Poplowitz family had left the overcrowded Jewish ghetto on Manhattan's Lower East Side and moved to Brooklyn.

According to Ellen, her parents had no interest in politics. They had little sense of what was going on in Russia. There were no newspapers or books in the house. Her father designed shoes for a shoe manufacturer in Brooklyn. The business flourished, and by the early 1920s he was able to buy a brownstone on Eastern Parkway. The family occupied the parlor floor and basement and rented out the top floor. The girls attended PS 178 on Dean Street, where the pupils were a mixture of Jews and blacks. Then they went to Girls' Commercial High School, a handsome building across from Prospect Park and the Brooklyn Botanical Gardens, where the pupils were mostly Jewish and Italian.

Looking back, Ellen considers her childhood "a bad beginning to life."[22] Her mother, a cold personality, could not read or write. Ellen's father was better educated and a gentle, religious man, but he was a remote figure, old enough to be her grandfather, and busy with his work and the synagogue. Ellen does not remember playing with her older sister or younger brother. Nor does she recall having any friends at school. Her refuge was books.

An independent spirit, Ellen clashed dramatically with her mother. As soon as she graduated from high school, at seventeen, she left home and worked in an insurance agency in east Manhattan. She boarded at the Salvation Army Girls' Home on Thirteenth Street. "The price of my freedom," she says, "was that I had to turn over half my wages to my mother."[23] The Depression had just begun. Times were hard.

In 1930, when she was eighteen, Ellen joined the Communist Party. Already as a high school student she had occasionally attended Party functions. "All my friends were in the Party," she says. "It was my first family." After a few years, she was delivering speeches on street corners. By the late 1930s she was head of the Fulton Street branch, a mixed-race branch. (Fulton Street, in Bedford Stuyvesant, was the demarcation line between the black and white districts.) And in the spring of 1939, Herbert Newton introduced her to Richard Wright.

Richard and Ellen stayed on a few more weeks with the Newtons, then moved together to Harlem. Ellen's sister, Florence, broke off all contact with Ellen. Ellen's father asked his daughter whether she loved the man she intended to marry, and when she said she did, he seemed content. He never met his son-in-law. Ellen's brother, Martin, was the only member of the family to support Ellen's decision.

———

IN NORTH CAROLINA, PAUL GREEN WAS TOYING ENDLESSLY WITH *NATIVE SON*. HE had a reputation in theatrical circles for making constant changes to his scripts and never being able to stick to a schedule. "Directors had a lot of trouble with Paul," says a colleague, "and he with them. He was seldom satisfied with his writing or their staging. . . . In some cases, Paul was asked not to come back to rehearsals."[24]

During the fall, Green came twice to New York, staying at the Hotel Bristol, where he and Wright continued their discussions until the hotel manager told Green there had been complaints about his black friend using the house elevator and forbade any more visits.

The play was supposed to have been finished by October 1940. It was not. Green had made major changes to the draft he and Wright had written that summer, and it was moving further and further toward Green's vision. Wright gave way on important points. "The more I've thought of your idea of ending the play with Bigger killing himself, I like it," he wrote to Green in early October.[25]

It was John Houseman who put his foot down. He did not appreciate the way Green had toned down the realism and lessened the impact. He did not want Bigger to be "godlike." He did not want dream sequences with Negro spirituals in the background. He did not want long reflective dialogues. It was his view that if Green did not like Wright's realism, he should not have undertaken this job in the first place.

He was also heartily sick of Green's dillydallying. He wanted the script finished. Orson Welles had finished shooting *Citizen Kane*; in a matter of weeks he would be ready to start work on *Native Son*. Green was suggesting that the play go into rehearsal while he fixed up the odds and ends. Houseman refused. "Years of bitter experience" had taught him where that led.[26]

Houseman writes in his memoirs that he lay in his raised red velvet bed one morning and reflected that the situation was ridiculous. Paul Green had become an obstacle. On Christmas eve 1940, he sat down and wrote Green a letter. He told him he did not like the murder enacted as a dream scene in a blue haze. "In the novel the killing is a factual, tragic event." He thought Green's latest ending to the play "absurd." It was time he stopped avoiding the violence in Wright's narrative. "I see no reason why anybody would reprieve Bigger, and having been reprieved, his killing of himself, if it proves anything at all, seems to me to prove something entirely different from Wright's conclusion in the novel. As I see it the point was that Bigger *did* find his personal truth (the truth which society had denied him) through violence."

Houseman wanted to start work on the play at the end of January 1941, and he needed a finished script several weeks before that, he told Green. "Wright, I believe, is also upset by the delays and feels that he has lost a great deal of time and does not want the matter to drag on much further. I know how terribly busy you are yourself. What do you think we should do about it?"[27]

Houseman was frankly hoping that Green would opt "out of the picture."[28] Wright, who had gone along with Green's changes, felt like a traitor. But he was sandwiched between two strong-headed men. His agent, Paul Reynolds, who was backing Houseman, tried to reassure Wright about their treatment of Paul Green:

> If he would pull out we could, of course, offer him the choice of having his name fixed to the final draft of the play or left off, as he preferred. The problem is probably going to be one of not offending his pride. I gather that he is a very gentlemanly man and a very nice man but just the same if his feelings got hurt or his pride got hurt he might get up on his ear. . . .
>
> Providing we can work out this headache I don't think you should regret that Green was the choice. I gather from what you have said that he has been valuable from the point of view of stage technique which is what was expected from him and that his defect is his liking for dreams and vagueness and fantasy and that we all of us knew beforehand. If that latter can be eliminated there ought to be a chance for a very successful play.[29]

AFTER A FEW WEEKS IN HARLEM, WRIGHT AND ELLEN HAD MOVED BACK TO THE Bedford Stuyvesant area of Brooklyn. They were living on the second floor of a drafty, old two-family house.[30] In the new year, Wright came down with a nasty bout of grippe. A young woman, Berthe Hibble, who came around to the house to type Wright's still-rough manuscript,

Black Hope, as he dictated it to her from his scarcely legible sprawled longhand, used to complain that her fingers were too numb to type. Wright would go down to the cellar to stoke the furnace, and they laughed about it reminding them of a certain scene in *Native Son*.[31]

Ellen also rented a semifurnished room a few blocks away.[32] While they were waiting for Wright's divorce to come through, Wright wanted her to have a separate address—partly to avoid gossip (with *Native Son* about to open on Broadway, he was in the limelight again) and partly because he wanted to avoid Dhimah charging him with adultery.

Helen Sattler, a young woman who lived in the house where Ellen rented a room, recalls the deep secrecy that surrounded Ellen at the time. A mutual Party friend told Sattler that Ellen had been disowned by her family because of her involvement with a black writer and warned Helen not to ask Ellen any questions. Sattler recalls: "Ellen never mentioned her lover by name, but said he was in the process of getting divorced and she had to stay out of the picture because of possible publicity."[33]

Wright was also hoping that he and Ellen could go abroad, and this, too, had to be kept quiet. The novelist Erskine Caldwell, a member of the Communist Party, was in China and Moscow, reporting on the war. Hemingway had just left for China to report on the Sino-Japanese War for *PM*, the new progressive daily. Wright was frankly envious. "Many white writers learn, study, and broaden themselves by doing jobs of this sort, while most of our Negro writers cling close to the fireside," he wrote to Claude Barnett, head of the Associated Negro Press in Chicago.[34]

He had approached Barnett with a specific suggestion. He wanted to put his novel aside for a while and work as a foreign correspondent for the Negro Press. "I'd like awfully to go to Russia, China, and India and report the war for a three-month period." He added: "I'd appreciate your keeping this matter more or less in confidence until the thing is generally certain and some of the other publicity has died down."

Wright was curious about the lives of other colored people, in other countries. "I would like to get stories of how the brown, red and yellow people are faring, what they are hoping for, and how their attitudes are likely to influence the outcome of the war in Europe," he told Barnett.

Claude Barnett wrote back immediately:

I confess a feeling of deep interest, even thrill, at the proposal which you make. . . . The sort of thing which you propose is closely akin to our whole idea for ANP. It is the sort of job which we ought to be able to do—to give a broad picture of what is happening to black people—both domestically and away. That we do so imperfectly is due to the peculiar wraps and handicaps which seem to beset our folk whatever their line of endeavor.[35]

Barnett and Wright both wrote to the State Department asking for passports for Wright and his "wife." Wright did not tell Barnett he was about to change his wife. He followed the principle that the less he said about his private life the better.

IN JANUARY 1941 WRIGHT PUT ASIDE *BLACK HOPE* FOR SIX MONTHS. THE WPA PHO-tographer Edwin Rosskam had approached him with the suggestion of a photo-documentary book on the history of the American Negro. Rosskam wanted to publish a selection of the remarkable photographs of black life in the Farm Security Administration's historical files in Washington. Wright, it seemed to him, was the ideal man to write the text. Viking Press offered one thousand dollars as an advance, to be divided equally between the two men.

Wright was enthusiastic about the idea. The photographic material would allow him to focus on the story of the Great Migration—that extraordinary historical phenomenon he had experienced personally. He had been wanting for some time to research the social ramifications of that journey from South to North, from country to city, from feudal-ism to industrialism, from community life to urban alienation. And he liked Rosskam, a German-born Jew, who had strong feelings about the oppression of minority groups.

In preparation for writing, Wright read widely: books about the his-tory and economy of the American South, the Southern caste system, and Northern urbanism. In mid-January, as soon as he recovered from his grippe, he went down to Washington to look at the WPA photo-graph files with Ed Rosskam. Decades later, Ed's wife, Louise Rosskam, recalled that Wright's visit was not easy. "Washington . . . was a very segregated city in those days."[36] The only restaurants they could eat in together were Chinese.

Wright and Rosskam went through thousands of photographs by white WPA photographers who had roamed the land during the Depression and captured revealing moments of black life in the South.[37] There were photos of workers bent over in the cotton fields, families dressed up for church, poverty stricken interiors of sharecropper shacks. There were long-suffering faces, gentle faces, faces lost in religious ecstasy.

Wright wrote, as usual, with passion. The narrative became a labor of love. He decided to write in the first person plural—"we"—as if telling the story from the black migrants' own viewpoint. He wanted to give voice to the voiceless. He wanted to transform an impersonal black mass into tangible individuals with emotions of their own. He wanted to make white readers see what that migration experience— from hope to disillusionment—*felt* like.[38]

He did not write with anger this time, but with unusual tenderness. "Our black children are born to us in our one-room shacks, before crackling log fires, with rusty scissors boiling in tin pans, with black plantation midwives hovering near, with pine-knot flames casting shadows upon the wooden walls, with the sound of kettles of water singing over the fires in the hearths." In *12 Million Black Voices*, this nonfictional account of Southerners who move north, Wright's empathy for his own people is more evident than in any of his fiction.

The narrative contained an impassioned plea for understanding and justice. "In the main we are different from other folk in that, when an impulse moves us, when we are caught in the throes of inspiration, when we are moved to better our lot, we do not ask ourselves: 'Can we do it?' but: 'Will they let us do it?' Before we black folk can move, we must first look into the white man's mind to see what is there, to see what he is thinking."

IN LATE JANUARY, JOHN HOUSEMAN DECIDED TO FIX UP PAUL GREEN'S SCRIPT himself. He needed Wright's cooperation for the rewriting. Wright, appalled by the messiness of the situation, agreed. He spent several mornings at Houseman's apartment on West Ninth Street, helping cut what Houseman saw as sentimental and long-winded flab. "It seems that the more we cut the more powerful the play becomes," Wright wrote to Green, as reassuringly as he could.[39]

A week later, Wright sent off another note to North Carolina. This time, he was broaching a delicate subject; it was no longer a question of cutting. "I don't know just how you will like the last scene, but we recast it in terms of the book," he told Green. "It is short, effective, I think, and forms a good conclusion to the play."[40]

Houseman had the curtain dropping with Bigger Thomas awaiting his death, grasping the prison bars and looking straight at the audience, while the lights faded out. Wright knew Green would hate it. He would see this scene as representing Bigger crucified by society. It was exactly the "pathetic" ending he had so adamantly fought against.

ONE MORNING WHEN WRIGHT WAS AROUND AT JOHN HOUSEMAN'S APARTMENT cutting Paul Green's flourishes out of *Native Son*, he heard he had been chosen as the Spingarn Medalist for 1940. It was almost as much of a surprise as the Book-of-the-Month Club selection. The Spingarn Medal, from the National Association for the Advancement of Colored People, was the most prestigious award in the black community. Named after Joel Elias Spingarn, a white man who had served on the NAACP's board of directors and put up the funds, the award was bestowed annually to the "American Negro who has made the highest achievement during the preceding year or years in any honorable field of human endeavor." Previous winners had included W. E. B. Du Bois, James Weldon Johnson, Carter G. Woodson, Mary McLeod Bethune, and the singer Marian Anderson. And now the conservative middle-class black community was hailing Richard Wright, a Communist protest writer.

The Spingarn tribute to Wright described the "powerful depiction in his books, *Uncle Tom's Children* and *Native Son*, of the effect of proscription, segregation and denial of opportunities to the American Negro." It continued: "He has given to Americans who have eyes to see, a picture which must be faced if democracy is to survive."

"Honestly, I'm beginning to feel almost *respectable!*" Wright told his friend Claude Barnett, director of the Associated Negro Press. "I thought I was radical, but the public is catching up with me."[41] Sincerely moved by an acknowledgment he had never expected, he told the black press he felt "a deep sense of responsibility."

I accept this award in the name of my father, a sharecropper on a Mississippi plantation, and in the name of my mother who sacrificed her health on numerous underpaid jobs, and in the name of millions of others like them, whose hope for peace and security reflects the aspirations of the common people everywhere during this period of war and cataclysmic social change.[42]

There were weak protests from the black community. An anonymous reporter for the *Pittsburgh Courier* argued that *Native Son* had done very little for race relations.[43] A handful of letters to black newspapers made the same point. But the fact remains that Richard Wright, the most controversial black writer in American literary history, was being officially acclaimed by black America. Despite some ambivalence toward *Native Son*, the black community was acknowledging that this novel, bought by more than 250,000 Americans, mostly whites, was a groundbreaking moment—a moment of truth—in African-American literature.

ALTHOUGH HE STILL SEETHED ABOUT THE PARTY'S RECEPTION OF *NATIVE SON*, Wright was steeped in Party activities. He spoke at the Writers' School, sponsored by the League of American Writers. He read from *Black Hope* in the League of American Writers' Friday night reading series. He was one of the speakers to pay tribute to Mike Gold at an anniversary function to celebrate Gold's twenty-five years in the labor movement. He was in the American Peace Mobilization group, a member of the Exiled Writers Committee, and a member of the Citizens' Committee to free Earl Browder. (The leader of the American Communist Party was in jail. Officially, it was because he had traveled under a forged passport. Wright was convinced that it was actually because of his opposition to the war).

At a luncheon in Theodore Dreiser's honor, held by the American Council on Soviet Relations, Wright was one of the speakers to introduce Dreiser. On the program, sent to him in advance, the Communist organizer had written: "Dick! We want the tone to be anti-war." Wright called Dreiser "the greatest living humanist in America."[44]

ON 11 FEBRUARY, ORSON WELLES ARRIVED IN NEW YORK, A HURRICANE FROM THE West. A giant of a man with a chubby, boyish face, he was swaggering, domineering, and mesmerizingly intense. He was not particularly interested in the play *Native Son*'s moral message. He cared about dynamic theater. He weighed in immediately on Houseman's side. Long passages of anguished dialogue did not make good theater, he said. He wanted the action to sweep past the audience like a torrent.

In February, after a tortured visit to New York, Paul Green wrote in his journal:

> Struggle with Welles, Hauseman [sic] and Wright to make play come out with some sort of moral responsibility for the individual. . . . "No Negro singing" says Welles. "Too much spiritual stuff in all Negro plays." . . . Also took away dream-murder interpretation. Left wing, left wing, propaganda complete. But since Wright was on their side I yielded. After all, his novel, his characters . . .

Green could not stand up to this coalition, but he did not yield his rights to the printed play. Wright's agent, Paul Reynolds, now saw it as inevitable that there would be two different versions of the play—a printed and a stage version. It was an awkward compromise. Wright knew about it. So did Houseman. Nobody told Orson Welles. Nor was Aswell informed, at Harper & Brothers. Aswell said later: "Had we been consulted about it at the time, we would have objected."[45]

For once, the Mercury Theatre had no trouble attracting funding. Not with the name of Orson Welles—the biggest man in Hollywood—attached to the play. Lionel Stander, a left-wing actor known for his fund-raising skills, easily persuaded the Hollywood investor Bern Bernard to produce fifty-five thousand dollars.

Auditions began on 12 February. The much sought after role of Bigger Thomas went to Canada Lee. A stocky, broad-shouldered former boxer with cauliflower ears and a broken nose, he had played Banquo in Welles's and Houseman's production of *Macbeth*. He was thirty-four, but looked much younger. "It isn't difficult for me to play Bigger Thomas," he told the *New York Herald Tribune*. "I've known guys like Bigger Thomas all my life. . . . I saw some in school and I grew up with some pretty tough guys. Some of them are in jail now and some of them went to the electric chair."[46]

Doris Dudley was selected for the role of Mary Dalton. After a few days, she could not take the pressure from friends and acquaintances and withdrew from the play. It did not help that the newspapers were filled with reports of a trial in Connecticut in which a black butler was accused of raping his white female employer.

Twenty-two-year-old Anne Burr took over the part and made an excellent job of it. "You don't mind getting smothered every night?" the *Brooklyn Eagle* would ask her in June. Burr replied that Desdemona had been taking it for centuries, so she, Mary Dalton, could hardly complain. It was a bit tough going at first, because Canada Lee makes it pretty realistic. There was one dress rehearsal when I thought I was really going to get it!"[47]

To create the atmosphere of the Chicago Black Belt, Orson Welles had the stage framed with dingy yellow brick. Within this outer brick wall, there was a different set for each scene. Welles wanted all scene changes to take place within one minute flat. During these blackouts, the audience would hear the roaring of the furnace or the sirens of police cars while thirty-five stagehands worked at high speed.[48]

In order to have no slackening of the tension, there would be no interval. When the time came, Welles would instruct the ushers not to hand out programs until after the show. He did not want the audience lighting matches to study their programs and spoiling the blackouts at the end of each scene.

"There were deep menacing shadows—a tension felt throughout," one member of the audience would recall later. "When Bigger was cornered—'Come out, you black bastard!'—he cowered, firing straight into the audience, and answering shots and searchlights came from the rear of the theater. Sirens were turned on, increasing the pitch—and the curtain fell."[49]

In the trial scene, the judge was separated from the audience by the railing across the apron of the stage, while the defense attorney, Bigger, and his family sat below in the pit. The staging was as inventive as the sound effects and lighting.

Native Son was Houseman's and Welles's last Mercury production, and their last production as a team. They were more distant from each other these days, and quarreled less. During rehearsals, Houseman found Welles "happy, overbearing and exciting to work with."[50] Their arguments were mostly about money. Welles refused to stint in any way; Houseman, as usual, was more down-to-earth.

They advised Wright to stay away from the theater until the play took shape, but this was precisely the process that interested Wright. He went several times to watch rehearsals. He enjoyed the group's talent and spiritedness. And he was both impressed and horrified by the bearlike Orson Welles, with his boundless energy and raging temper. Rehearsals would go on for hours. Welles was coaxing, encouraging, and fiercely demanding. For the actors it was both exhilarating and exhausting. They were terrified of him, and they worshipped him. "You had to be prepared to take such an enormous amount of guff and madness from him," says Jack Berry, Welles's assistant.[51] Wright told the *World-Telegram*: "One Orson Welles on earth is enough. Two of them would no doubt bring civilization itself to an end."[52]

Everyone associated with the play was conscious that *Native Son* was making history. It was a risk: *Native Son* could open up new opportunities for black actors, or it could cause a backlash. "The Negro has never been given the scope that I'm given in this play," Canada Lee said. "Now things are going to happen."[53] The play was breaking with the standard black caricatures: the primitive African savages, devoted mammies, loyal Uncle Toms, and eye-rolling buffoons. Bigger was a rebel.

The interracial cast was the first since Eugene O'Neill's *All God's Chillun Got Wings* in 1924; of course interracial kissing was unheard of on Broadway. Welles and Houseman were well aware that a light-skinned black woman in the part of Mary Dalton would forestall criticism, but they were keen to set a precedent. Indeed, *Native Son* paved the way for Paul Robeson, just two years later, to kiss his white Desdemona on the Broadway stage.

EARLY IN MARCH, PAUL GREEN WIRED PAUL REYNOLDS: "SINCE I AM UNABLE TO BE in New York at this time, and in order to help *Native Son* towards as complete presentation as possible, I wish Wright to take over the authority as author for the production of the final scene there, and likewise I will take the authority for the published script of the last scene, the rest of the play standing in joint responsibility as is."[54]

Green arrived in New York on Friday, 7 March. He met Wright and Paul Reynolds and signed the Harper & Brothers contract. Then he made his way through heavy snow to the theater. "Rehearsal continued for hours with Welles working terrifically and somewhat playboyishly," he noted in his journal. "Air full of flashlight bulbs." He was interested in Welles's "intense close-up method."

The next morning, Green handed in to Harper the complete proof of the written play, with *his* final scene. Back in North Carolina on Monday, he wrote to Reynolds: "After considering the method—a kind of fierce close-up intensity—which Welles is using in producing the show, I came to the conclusion that the script had best adhere somewhat to that, since the matter of a well-rounded, well constructed play was already through the window. So I limped the ending across the goal line as best I could."[55]

Wright had lost much of the respect he once had for Paul Green. He now saw that Green had always acted as if *he* owned Bigger. On 12 March, two weeks before the play was to open, Wright submitted a piece about their collaboration to Brooks Atkinson, the drama editor of the *New York Times*. Written in the form of a minidrama, Wright called it "The Problem of the Hero."

The first two acts are set in Chapel Hill, six weeks apart. The white man and the black man are "laboring night and day through 105-degree heat." Act III is in a New York hotel three months later. Act IV is in the same hotel one month later. Stage directors indicate that the white man speaks "graciously but seriously," in an "impassioned manner," "with serious profundity," and with "his voice charged with faith." The black man speaks "skeptically but humbly," "earnestly," and "quickly and uneasily." The white man is at all times friendly, condescending, and keeps passionately reassuring the black man that they share the same vision. In Act IV, the white man tells the black man: "The deletions which you have made helped the play enormously, but the heart has been cut out of it. And the additions you have made constitute a message less optimistic than what I had hoped for."

Wright sent a telegram to Paul Green:

Wrote article for NY Times on our collaboration discussing problem of hero in US drama. Gave your views and mine. Tried desperately to be objective and fair. Maybe they wont use it then will publish elsewhere see you over weekend regards

Richard Wright[56]

Green wired back the same afternoon. (He did not tell Wright he had been on the phone to his friend Atkinson.)

> I am sure your article for the Times is a good one, but wonder whether it is wise to make public at this time any past difference of opinion between the authors. Since the published ending is so nearly in line with the stage version except for a little cutting here and there don't you think we had better stand or fall together on the production? . . .
>
> Affectionately, Paul Green

Whether Wright withdrew the piece, or Green prevailed upon Atkinson, or Atkinson himself decided against it, "The Problem of the Hero" was never published.[57]

TWO WEEKS BEFORE *NATIVE SON* WAS DUE TO OPEN ON BROADWAY—THE SAME day that Wright and Green exchanged telegrams about "The Problem of the Hero"—Richard Wright and Ellen were married in the small New Jersey town of Coytesville. The ceremony took place at 9:30 in the evening on Wednesday, 12 March 1941. No family members were present. Wright had told almost no one. He wanted no publicity just now about a second marriage to a white woman.[58]

Wright had not even told Ralph Ellison about the wedding. (Ellison was deeply hurt when he heard.)[59] This time, the witnesses were Ben Davis (evidently Wright had forgiven him for his review of *Native Son*) and Abe Aaron, Wright's old Chicago friend, who was briefly in New York City.

Somehow, the Wrights managed to keep ahead of the gossip. Two weeks after the wedding, the gossip column in the black newspaper *New York Amsterdam Star-News* commented: "The boys in the Stuyvesant sector are anxious to learn the moniker of the nifty-looking chick who is jaunting about with Richard Wright."[60]

GREEN HAD NOT YET SEEN THE NEW ENDING TO THE PLAY. HE CAME TO NEW YORK for the dress rehearsals, planning to stay for the premiere. Houseman, with ill-concealed relish, recalls Green's reaction:

He appeared in the theatre one evening, sat in silence and left without a word after the last scene. The next day, the day of our first preview, we held a meeting: Green, Wright, his agent, Welles and myself. Green insisted that we reinstate his version—particularly the final scene. I told him it was much too late for that and, besides, we had no intention of being parties to the distortion of a work we admired. Richard sat silent beside his agent, who informed us that Green's version (credited to Paul Green and Richard Wright) was already in his publisher's hands. I suggested he get it back and change it to conform to the acting version. Green was furious. When Orson began to howl at him, he got up and left and we never saw him again.[61]

Green's own story, in a 1970 interview, is more or less consistent with Houseman's:

I finally gave up. Wright sided with Welles again. My contract would have protected me; I didn't have to yield, but I said, Richard, it's your book and if you want to end it pathetic, all right. Orson spoke up. He said: "Jesus, here I am beset by General Sherman from the North and they're driving up from the South. How can I do anything?" He had these figures of speech. And so I said, "Well, all right." And so I walked out. I said, "It's yours. Go ahead." So on opening night I didn't go. I just thought I'd let it be Richard's show.[62]

There were last-minute problems. The technicians were not able to execute the scene changes fast enough to satisfy Welles. Opening night was postponed twice, from 17 to 24 March. The troupe was beginning to call the play "Native Grandson."

On the night of the premiere, there was an effusive tossing of verbal bouquets. One of many telegrams was for Houseman and Welles.

Let me thank and congratulate both of you for the energy, talent, speed, and courage which both of you brought to the staging, producing, and directing of Native Son. I have said time and again and I say now that I feel that Native Son has been in the hands of two of the most gallant men in the theatrical world. Good luck always to both of you.

Richard Wright

From a grateful star came: "Thanks for my big chance Orson. I shall live up to your confidence in me. I'll be in there punching till the curtain comes down. Canada Lee."

Others were for Richard Wright: "Dear Dick, This is to thank you for your beautiful play. The director of its first production is very fond of you. Orson."

After the performance, Paul Robeson telegrammed Wright: "You have advanced the cause of your people immeasurably and doubly strengthened your place in American letters. Congratulations and thanks."

That first night, the theater was full. Blacks from Sugar Hill sat beside Communists who sat beside white Park Avenue glitterati. Orson Welles glided down the aisle with his glamorous Mexican actress girlfriend, Dolores del Rio. After every scene, there was vigorous applause. At the end, cheers and shouts produced fifteen curtain calls. Finally, Richard Wright was pressured to make an appearance and a short speech. He graciously thanked everyone involved and expressed regret that Paul Green could not be there.

Brooks Atkinson, in the *New York Times*, called it "the biggest American drama of the season."[63] This was "theatre that tingles with life," he wrote. The *New York World-Telegram* declared: "It proves . . . that Orson Welles, whether you like to admit it or not, is no boy wonder but actually the greatest theatrical director of the modern age."[64] There were murmurs about the Pulitzer Prize for drama. Canada Lee was unanimously hailed as a brilliant new discovery. Even Eslanda Robeson conceded that her husband could not have performed better.[65]

Those less inclined to be swept away by the sheer theatrical brilliance pointed out that the play was a "drastic oversimplification" of Wright's novel and "a considerable garbling of his message."[66]

Paul Green, in North Carolina, was not overjoyed by the play's success. "Native Son, bastard and mutilated as it is, doing well with the public," he wrote in his diary. "Can't get much pleasure out of seeing it succeed since one edge of its truth has been chiseled and blunted off."[67]

He was more gracious when he replied to Paul Reynolds's congratulations. "I feel that in a great many places, Welles saw further into the possibilities of the script than the authors did. The ending is, I think, still weak, whereas it could have almost lifted the audience out of its seat. Still, I think we are all lucky—and we owe a lot to Welles."[68]

Ed Aswell, at Harper & Brothers, had a nightmarish time with all the last-minute changes Paul Green made to the galleys. Nevertheless he managed to rush the production through, so that the book came out a few days after the premiere. When Orson Welles set eyes on the book and saw that it was quite different from the stage play, he bellowed that he wanted his name and that of Mercury Theatre taken off the jacket immediately. Paul Reynolds had some delicate negotiating to perform with Aswell. Finally, Aswell agreed to remake the jacket provided Welles agreed to bear half the cost of the changes.

Box-office sales were less lively than Mercury Theatre had hoped, but still good at around $14,500 a week. Welles told the cast he was sure the play would run for three years, and maybe for five. He had to return to Hollywood, and was tied up with other commitments for at least a year, but he talked of producing *Native Son* as a movie with RKO. They would have to film it in Mexico since it would be impossible to work with an interracial cast in Hollywood. Fox and Metro also expressed interest in the movie rights. The play's financial backers agreed the movie rights were likely to fetch one hundred thousand dollars.

Then, suddenly, after the initial clamor and controversy, interest dropped. The high-cost production relied on substantial box-office takings. The tickets were expensive; audiences fell away. By early June the weekly gross had slipped to $8,500. And after all the excited talk only one definite bid came in for the picture rights: Metro-Goldwyn-Mayer offered twenty-five thousand dollars to shoot the film with an all-white cast. Wright was horrified.

In order to continue, the managers asked the cast to accept a reduction in salaries. Houseman and Welles agreed to work without pay for several weeks. Wright and Green took a 40 percent cut in their royalties. Wright typed three pages of notes called "Blueprint for an Emergency," in which he suggested ways—newspaper publicity, advertising, and patrons—to keep the play on the stage.[69]

By late June, Welles and Houseman decided to close the season. The play had run for fifteen weeks—115 performances. It was a perfectly respectable tally, but the company had suffered a loss of some thirty-six thousand dollars.

Native Son would resume in late summer, in a more economical version directed by Jack Berry. The set was more modest, and the ticket prices lower. The troupe would perform in the major Northern cities and, briefly, below the Mason-Dixon line—in Baltimore and St. Louis—before returning to New York City almost a year later.

In the summer of 1941, Houseman was back on the West Coast when a note arrived from Richard Wright. "If it had not been for your willingness to give so generously of your time, I doubt gravely if *Native Son* would have ever seen the boards of Broadway. It was a little shameful and ridiculous that you could not have gotten public credit for that help, but that would have meant dragging into the open those all-too-touchy relations between Paul Green and me, and I was seeking, above all, to keep any word of dissension out of the public press."[70] This, of course, was not true. It was Paul Green who had been so anxious for the word not to get out.

That year's New York Drama Critics' Circle Award went to Lillian Hellman's *Watch on the Rhine*, a play about an American combating Nazism.[71] The Pulitzer Prize for drama went to Robert E. Sherwood for his anti-Soviet play, *There Shall Be No Night*, about the Russian attack on Finland. The *New Masses* was disgusted by the bias of a committee that awarded the prize to this "war-mongering attack on the Soviet Union."[72]

A year later, when the play was back in New York and once again in the financial doldrums, Paul Green would write to Paul Reynolds: "Well, the chickens come home to roost crippled or not. The murder should have been played as Bigger's nightmare remembrance—as Wright and I first conceived it, and the final scene should have shown Bigger Thomas becoming more of a man. But it's all past now."[73]

14

THE WEATHERCOCK TURNS

April 1941–April 1942

In early April, soon after *Native Son* opened on Broadway, the Wrights took the train to Chicago. *12 Million Black Voices* required photographs of the black urban experience in the North; Works Progress Administration photographers had focused almost exclusively on black rural life in the South. Ed Rosskam and another WPA staff photographer, Russell Lee, were going to spend two weeks in Chicago capturing the South Side on camera.[1]

The photographers worked from dawn to dusk, taking advantage of the early spring sunshine. With Wright's help, the two white men were able to get inside slum kitchenettes, bars, factories, storefront churches. Altogether, they took 420 frames. "Dick Wright really knew that stuff cold," says Edwin Rosskam. "He knew where everybody was, and he knew everybody in the Negro world of Chicago. . . . I don't know if many white men had the opportunity to see it the way we saw it. Man, that was an experience. We did everything from the undertaker to the gangster."[2]

Richard and Ellen stayed in the guest room at the Good Shepherd Community Center, enjoying the warm hospitality of Horace and Irma

Cayton.[3] Wright did not take Ellen to meet his mother, aunt, and brother, who probably did not even know yet about his divorce and remarriage. Many did not. For the time being, Ellen was still calling herself Ellen Poplar. (She mostly used the name "Poplar" rather than "Poplowitz.")

"This morning Ellen and I are cleaning up our correspondence," Wright wrote to Ralph Ellison on 9 April. "We are planning this afternoon to start amassing facts for the book." To help Wright with the text, Cayton showed him the relevant sections of his huge files on Chicago's black community. For several years Cayton and Professor W. Lloyd Warner, a white Chicago sociologist, had been codirecting a study of juvenile delinquency in the South Side. With funding from the WPA and the Julius Rosenwald Foundation, it was the largest research project ever to focus on an American Negro community.

For Wright, the piles of clippings, figures, maps, and graphs amassed by the Chicago sociologists were an inspiration. He took the dry facts and added imagination and poetry. *12 Million Black Voices*, like all Wright's writing, was driven by a passionate desire to bring about change. This was an important difference between him and the Chicago sociologists, who held the view that the good sociologist must be detached and apolitical. In fact, the dean of Chicago Sociology, Robert E. Park, was a conservative, closely associated with the famous black "accommodationist" Booker T. Washington. As the Swedish scholar Gunnar Myrdal would point out in his 1944 book, *An American Dilemma*, Park's writing was underpinned by a do-nothing fatalism.

The seventy-seven-year-old Robert Park was visiting Chicago—he was teaching, these days, at Fisk University in Nashville—and Cayton invited him to the settlement house one evening. Wright wrote later that he walked into the living room to be greeted by "an infirmed, whitehaired old gentleman who insisted, with the aid of his cane, upon rising from his chair to greet me." Wright urged him to remain seated. "I rise in your honor, sir," Dr. Robert Park said in his gruff voice. Then he looked at Wright with his direct gaze: "How in hell did you happen?"[4]

Wright gave a reading at the Good Shepherd Community Center, and the Caytons hosted a party for him. A journalist from the *Pittsburgh Courier* mentioned Wright's "proud, affable little wife."[5] Arna Bontemps reported with bemused bewilderment to Langston Hughes: "Dick had his wife with him this trip. But it was not Deema. Ellen Poplar seems to enjoy that honor at the moment. What happened to

Deema? Wasn't it you who told me he was married to her? Well, any-how, Ellen is a pretty little trick and perhaps the best bet—if one is to judge by looks."[6]

RICHARD WRIGHT AND CLAUDE BARNETT HAD WRITTEN SEPARATELY TO THE STATE Department to request passports for Richard and Ellen Wright. Claude Barnett put his request quite bluntly. "We are writing you to request that passports for visits to Russia, Japan and China be issued to Mr. Wright on the same basis that they are being issued to other distin-guished writers in various areas."[7]

Wright's strategy was to sound as if his travel arrangements were finalized except for the mere matter of a passport. He stated that he would be traveling to the Soviet Union and China as a reporter for the Associated Negro Press, departing from San Francisco on 21 July 1941 on the SS *President Hayes* bound for Vladivostok via Kobe.[8] His wife, Freda Wright, would be accompanying him as his secretary, and they would be staying abroad from three months to a year.

But the State Department did not intend to issue a passport to a black foreign correspondent critical of the American government. Its excuse, paradoxically, was the strictness of recent Soviet regulations that banned American diplomats and journalists from traveling outside Moscow. "The Department . . . does not believe that accredited Ameri-can journalists should be permitted to proceed to the Union of the Soviet Socialist Republics until the Soviet Government is disposed to be more lenient towards the travel of our representatives."[9]

The State Department did not want to promote the Negro press—widely blamed for promoting discontent among Negroes about the segregated armed forces. Since the 1920s, the FBI had been targeting black newspapers, repeatedly charging them with sedition and trying to ban them.

THE PULITZER JUDGES ANNOUNCED IN MAY 1941 THAT THERE WAS NO DESERVING candidate for that year's fiction prize. Wright's *Native Son*, Heming-way's *For Whom the Bell Tolls*, Thomas Wolfe's *You Can't Go Home Again*: none was considered worthy.

The *Philadelphia Record* protested that the "13 distinguished gentlemen" should step down as judges. They were not literary critics, and their decision was nonsensical.[10] The *New Masses* insisted that *Native Son* should have won the prize.

Despite the criticism of *Native Son* within its ranks, the Party rallied to Wright's support. At the Fourth American Writers' Congress in June 1941, the League of American Writers chose *Native Son* as the most distinguished work of fiction written in the past two years. Wright was elected vice president of the league (one of six), Dashiell Hammett was elected president, and Theodore Dreiser honorary president. Wright was still a valued passenger on the Communist train.[11]

By the summer of 1941 all American males under the age of thirty-five were eligible to be drafted (a 1A classification) unless they had dependents or a health problem. "I hope to hell you obtain deferment," Abe Aaron wrote to Wright from his infantry-training battalion in Texas. "From what little I'm able to see and hear, a Negro's life in the army, especially since in all likelihood he'll be sent south for training, is hell. . . . There is not even regular bus service here for Negro soldiers going to Mineral Halls, the nearest town (and what a hell of a town it is)!"[12] Wright was thirty-three, but he could claim two dependents—his wife and his mother. For the moment he was classified as 3A.

The opening session of the Fourth American Writers' Congress, held on 6 June 1941, took the form of an antiwar rally.[13] Wright gave a virulent antiwar speech. "What We Think of Their War" was published in the *New Masses* and widely quoted in newspapers around the nation. By "we" Wright meant fifteen million American Negroes. If blacks were reluctant to support the war, Wright said, it was because their problems were at home, not in Europe. In the South, Negroes were not able to vote, work in industry, or organize. They did not have decent houses or schools. They were lynched and no one was punished. They were discriminated against in the war industries. Why should they fight a racist Hitler in a segregated army that herded them into separate units from their white compatriots? Did the government not care about the morale of the black troops? Nor could Negroes forget how their country had treated black men when they came home from World War I. The recent lynching in Georgia of a young black soldier still in uniform had revived those painful memories.

Two weeks after Wright's much publicized speech, Hitler's armies invaded Russia, shattering the nonaggression pact Hitler had signed with Stalin in 1939. Minutes after the news came over the radio, the phone rang at the home of Franklin Folsom, secretary of the League of American Writers. "What do we do now?" the voice at the other end of the line wanted to know. Folsom writes:

> It was Richard Wright calling. Few people were thrown more off balance than he by the abrupt and violent change on the world scene. . . . I don't recall how I responded to Dick's disturbed inquiry. I was taken as much by surprise as he was.[14]

What the Communist Party did was to perform a dramatic about-face. The "imperial war" rhetoric was dropped overnight. Mother Russia had been attacked by the Nazis; everything had changed. It was now the "people's war." The Party called upon all Americans to help the Soviet Union and Great Britain bring about the defeat of the fascist aggressors. The American Peace Mobilization, a Communist group, quietly changed its name to the American People's Mobilization.

A few days later, Wright boarded a Pullman car for Texas, where he was to receive the Spingarn Medal at the national conference of the NAACP. John Hammond, a white record producer who worked with several black jazz and blues musicians and was on the national board of the NAACP, went with him. He recalls that Wright had originally prepared a speech urging black Americans to stay out of the war at all costs.[15] Before he left for Houston, prominent functionaries of the Communist Party had urged Wright to recast it as a pro-war speech. Wright, after all, was one of the vice presidents of the League of American Writers and a highly visible member of the Party.

A keynote speaker at the NAACP conference in Houston was A. Philip Randolph, the leader of the Brotherhood of Sleeping Car Porters, a man Wright considered "a truly exceptional man."[16] The previous month Randolph had issued a call for ten thousand blacks to march on the White House on 1 July to protest discrimination against blacks in the military and the war industries. The response was tremendous: it was estimated that one hundred thousand blacks stood ready to march. President Roosevelt was horrified. Randolph had stood firm. Now Randolph brought the news that Roosevelt had signed an executive order banning racial discrimination in defense employment after Randolph agreed to postpone the march indefinitely. It was the first executive order on race relations to come from a president since the Emancipation Proclamation. The mood of the conference was buoyant.

The closing night, Friday, 27 June, drew the largest audience of all. The Good Hope Baptist Church in Houston was overflowing. More than eight hundred people stood outside, listening to the speeches through a loudspeaker, as Elmer A. Carter, New York editor of the black magazine *Opportunity*,[17] presented Wright with his medal. "Richard Wright is the first novelist to bear the Negro's message," he told the audience, "to show his resentment of the forces that made him what he was and . . . to a large extent he is."[18]

Wright talked briefly about his own life. He told the audience that he considered it his duty as an artist to say what he thought and felt, regardless of race, policy, party, and creed. It is what he had done in *Native Son*; it is what he pledged to do always.[19] He did not broach the subject of war.

The weathercock had turned. Wright knew that if he was going to remain in the Party, he had to support the war. But this was a pirouette he could not come to terms with. Even if Roosevelt carried out his promise to end discrimination in the war industries, the U.S. military was still segregated. Wright was not prepared to risk his life fighting for freedom abroad when he didn't have it at home. An irreversible gulf had opened between him and the Communist Party.

ELLEN WAS PREGNANT. SHE HAD GIVEN UP HER JOB. FOR TAX PURPOSES WRIGHT was formally paying her a monthly wage of one hundred dollars to be his secretary. It made more sense than paying someone else. Since they were not permitted to leave the country, for the time being they would have to hunker down and make the best of things. They signed a year's lease on a four-room apartment at 11 Revere Place, Brooklyn.

Wright had finished his narrative for the Viking photo-documentary book, *12 Million Black Voices*. Ed Aswell, at Harper, was glad he was getting back to *Black Hope*. "I have been hoping all along that the new novel could be ready in time to publish next spring," he told Wright. "How do you feel about it and what do you think the chances are?"[20]

Wright said he would see what he could do. But when he sat down in his new study he found himself starting an entirely new novel, *The Man Who Lived Underground*. "I have never written anything in my life that stemmed more from sheer inspiration," he would comment later.[21] The inspiration was his grandmother's ardent religious disposition— something he had been wanting to write about for some time.

The novel was also about police brutality toward blacks. Herbert Newton had recently been arrested for leading a picket line protesting the firing of fifteen thousand New York WPA workers. "When we reached the station house I was surrounded by six policemen," Newton told the *New York World-Telegram*. "I was punched in the face and kicked. They hit me on the jaw and I fell over a chair. I was taken into a small room and hit on the back of the head. They jumped up and down on my back while I lay on the floor."[22] The police broke several of his ribs. (His children agree that their father was never the same after that beating. A few years later, at the age of forty-four, he died of a heart attack.) In the *Daily Worker*, Wright spoke out bitterly against the New York police department.[23]

Around this time he read a bizarre story in the magazine *True Detective* about a white man who lived for several months in a hideout in the sewers and would occasionally steal things from aboveground stores by coming up through trapdoors. Sometimes he returned the stolen goods.[24] He worked the story into his new narrative.

The Man Who Lived Underground, reminiscent of the nightmarish world of Franz Kafka, was about an innocent black man haunted by a sense of primal guilt and brutalized by a cruel and arbitrary system of "justice." Wrongly accused of a crime, he hid in the sewers and made occasional forays into the absurd world above ground. Frederic Wertham, Wright's psychiatrist friend, read the novel and sent Wright his response:

> The Freudians talk about the Id
> And bury it below.
> But Richard Wright took off the lid
> And let us see the woe.[25]

Wright was more and more struck by the madness of the forces of repression in the "aboveground" world. In the United States, the very concept of civil liberties was disappearing. He and 150 other pro-Communist writers, teachers, and actors had been publicly condemned by Martin Dies's virulently anti-Communist committee for the statement they had signed in April 1938 in favor of the Moscow trials. Congress had recently passed the Smith Act, which made it a crime to "advocate or encourage the overthrow of the United States government." It was largely aimed at Communists. The punishment was ten years in jail—unless the rebel was an alien, in which case he or she could be deported.

WPA employees now had to sign an affidavit to say they were not Communists. Other institutions and businesses had brought in loyalty oaths. Morris Schappes, a professor of English at the College of the City of New York, had been sentenced to eighteen months in the New York City "tombs" for refusing to name Communist colleagues at his workplace. Wright, outraged by the implications for American democracy, wrote an introduction to Schappes's book, *Letters from the Tombs*. "Many of our officials in America today believe that they are protecting their civilization when they imprison a man for thinking in 'a certain way,'" Wright wrote, "but they are not protecting their civilization. Instead they are destroying its very foundation."[26]

In mid-August 1941, Richard and Ellen went for two weeks to the White Mountains in New Hampshire, where the League of American Writers organized a gathering of writers. Afterwards they spent ten days at Pigeon Cove, enjoying the sea air and rocky inlets of Cape Ann, on the coast of Massachusetts.[27] It was a welcome respite from the endless requests—talks, book reviews, blurbs, reader reports, introductions to books, reading friends' manuscripts—that came Wright's way these days. Ed Rosskam wanted him to spend time promoting *12 Million Black Voices*. Nelson Algren asked him to write an introduction to his novel set in the Polish district of Chicago, *Never Come Morning*. (Wright had recommended the novel to Aswell, who was publishing it. Over the years Wright had read several drafts and made suggestions for changes—all of which had to be done with great tact. Algren was touchy.) Sam Ross, a friend from Chicago Writers' Workshop, had asked him for an honest opinion on his novel about a steel strike; if he liked it, would he use his influence to get it published? Lawrence Lipton had written a novel about anti-Semitism in Chicago, *Brother, the Laugh Is Bitter*. Wright had praised it to Aswell, who was publishing it. Paul Reynolds cautioned Wright against too many commitments. "Your time and energy is limited just as much as the next fellow's is."[28]

Wright was jubilant when Joe Louis won another victory at the end of September. He paid tribute to his hero with the lyrics of a blues song, "King Joe." Count Basie wrote the music, and Paul Robeson, for the first time in his life, sang the blues. Wright was proud of their collaboration. Recorded by John Hammond on the Okeh label, "King Joe" was for sale in mid-November, released on two sides of a ten inch 78 RPM record. The *New York Times* critic thought it "mighty good" jazz.[29] The *New Masses* declared it "swell music to dance to."[30] By mid-January, forty thousand records had been sold.

CLINTON BREWER WAS A THIRTY-SIX-YEAR-OLD BLACK MAN WHO HAD BEEN IN JAIL since the age of seventeen for stabbing his teenage wife to death. He read *Native Son* and wrote to Richard Wright. He said he had been studying harmony and counterpoint by correspondence; it kept him sane. Struck by his letter, Wright went to see Brewer at the New Jersey State Prison at Trenton. The prison band played Brewer's "Stampede in G Minor" for him.

Wright showed the score to Count Basie, who liked it enough to make a recording. Together, Basie, Wright, and John Hammond wrote to the governor of New Jersey on Brewer's behalf. In July, astoundingly, Brewer was granted parole.

Several newspapers carried the story of the murderer who, behind bars, had transformed himself into a musician. They spoke of his bewilderment as he walked around the neon-lit, auto-filled streets of New York after nineteen years shut off from the world in a New Jersey prison. "The other evening he was in the home of Richard Wright," *PM* reported.[31] Brewer was going to be Count Basie's musical arranger. "I have no hesitation in predicting a splendid career for him," Hammond, Basie's recording director, told the press.[32]

Three months later, Brewer stabbed another woman to death when she refused to marry him, and stuffed her body in a clothes closet. "Dick Wright's Bigger Thomas Comes to Life in Clinton Brewer," the *New York Amsterdam News* proclaimed.[33] It was the end of Brewer's splendid career.

It must have been devastating for Wright. But his interest had been aroused by this man. Why this compulsive desire to kill women? Wright had just read Frederic Wertham's book *Dark Legend: A Study in Murder*, a case study of an Italian immigrant youth who had killed his promiscuous mother to save the honor of his dead father. Wright found it "as fascinating as any novel."[34] He wrote to Wertham, a leading New York psychiatrist active in Communist Party circles, and asked whether he would be prepared to see Clinton Brewer and give his expert opinion on his sanity. They went together to see Brewer in prison. Wertham's testimony of insanity saved Brewer from the electric chair.

In 1954 Wright would dedicate his novel *Savage Holiday* to Clinton Brewer. His fictional protagonist, Erskine Fowler, has the same extreme ambivalence toward women. He proposes marriage to his neighbor, Mabel, who is not interested. In a frenzy of resentment, lust, and jealousy, he plunges a butcher's knife again and again into her naked body.

"YOU SHOULD SEE SOME OF THE TIES ELLEN IS KNITTING FOR ME," WRIGHT TOLD his friend Willard Maas one Saturday morning in November. He was talking into his new ediphone. "She has never knitted before, but the slightest hint is all she needs to fly into some masterpiece of tangled whirl and bring it into some artistic order." In her transcription, the typist added modestly at this point: "Oh, pshaw, t'aint nothin'—Ellen."[35]

A few hours later, Wright flew to Washington, D.C., to speak at the National Conference of Negro Youth, leaving Ellen to type up and send off the morning's correspondence. She apologized to Willard for mistakes in her typing. "Dick flew to Washington about an hour ago and I'm so lonely already that my attention to the thing at hand isn't all it should be." Her husband was due to fly home again that evening.

"There's peace and love in our home," Wright wrote proudly.[36] Ellen's pregnancy had brought her mother back into her life. Even if relations between Rose Poplowitz and Wright were strained, it was a relief for Ellen no longer to be cast out of her family. She was compiling a scrapbook of articles about her husband. As her pregnancy advanced, Wright was taking over the housework and cooking. Their happiness was obvious to others. Clair Goll, a poet friend, would inscribe her book *Love Poems*: "To Dick and Ellen, the true lovers."[37]

In 1945, four years into the marriage, Wright would comment in his journal after they came home from a party: "Ellen looked very sweet and beautiful; I have never seen a woman prettier than she no matter where I go. She looks so much younger than all the others, and so little and so pretty."[38]

Arna Bontemps made a visit to New York and was impressed, he wrote to Langston Hughes, by his visit with the Wrights.

Ellen and Dick have a charming, secluded place in Brooklyn, 11 Revere Place, with an unlisted phone. Ellen is otay, didn't you know?[39] Cute, too. Her mother dropped in while I was there—to my surprise. Maybe I shouldn't have been surprised. Dick has a new dictaphone and all the trimmings, and is he going to town? Knocked out his new novel about religious life among Negroes in a couple of months. Written at white heat, as they say, "The Man Who Lived Underground." His "12 Million Black Voices" is going around—advance copies. I got one yesterday. Yours must be on its way. It's a beautiful creation; pictures and text both lyrical. Embree just commented that he thought it was too much on the "wailing wall" side and that it neglects to suggest a way out, but as a "wailing" performance, he says, not even Dubois [sic] has ever wept so beautifully.[40]

12 MILLION BLACK VOICES WAS PUBLISHED IN MID-NOVEMBER 1941.[41] AS WRIGHT explained in his foreword, this was not a book about "those few Negroes who had lifted themselves, through personal strength, talent, or luck, above the lives of their fellow-blacks." Those were "single fishes that leap and flash for a split second above the surface of the sea." He was writing about "that vast, tragic school that swims below in the depths against the current, silently and heavily."[42]

The critics agreed that the story was beautifully conveyed. Wright's sentences were musical and the photographs were magnificent. Ben Davis, Jr., gave the book lavish praise in the *Sunday Worker*.[43]

Some readers wished Wright had presented a more balanced picture, showing the Negro's determination, struggles, and achievements. Beatrice Murphy, in the *Afro-American*, complained that the book was as depressing as *Native Son*.[44] The *New York Times* pointed out that protest books were not meant to resemble a grocer weighing sugar or flower. "Mr. Wright's text is neither 'impartial' nor does it attempt to show 'all sides'; it is a stinging indictment of American attitudes toward the Negro over a period of 300 years."[45]

Wright's poet friend Willard Maas wrote to him: "This is the best, perhaps the only, poetry you have written Dick! It is simple, direct, not untouched by the fire which is your natural speaking voice."[46]

Ralph Ellison found himself weeping when he held the published book in his hands. Ellison had made that journey from South to North. He knew what it felt like. His nerves, too, had been left "peeled and quivering." Following an afternoon reading Wright's narrative and "brooding over the photographs," Ellison sat down and typed the most emotional letter he would ever write to his friend Dick. "I felt so intensely the fire of our common experience when reading *12 Million Black Voices* that I felt the solder of my dicipline [sic] melt and found myself opened up and crying over the painful pattern of remembered things."[47]

Another who was profoundly moved by the book was the young black photographer Gordon Parks. "It became my bible, a big part of my learning, and the inspiration needed to keep my camera moving where it might do the most good."[48]

Three weeks after publication, on Sunday, 7 December 1941, the Japanese bombed Pearl Harbor, the American naval base in Hawaii. The next day Roosevelt declared that America was at war. The *New Masses* sent a message to the White House pledging "all our strength, our loyalty, our lives to the victory over our nation's enemies."[49]

Wright felt sick at heart. "They are asking us to die for a freedom we never had!" he wrote to Joe Brown.[50]

Within months, American literature, art, and filmmaking would be transformed. Protest literature was a thing of the past. The photographic section of the Farm Security Administration—the department responsible for the marvelous photographs in *12 Million Black Voices*—was transferred to the Office of War Information, where photographers were exhorted to boost American spirits.

WRIGHT KNEW WHAT AWAITED HIM IF HE WAS CALLED UP. HE WOULD BE SENT South to a training camp for "coloreds." He would face the humiliation of riding in crowded Jim Crow cars, not being able to buy a cold drink in a Southern town on a boiling hot day, being given the dirtiest and most menial jobs in the armed forces. Ellen, who was five months pregnant, would not be able to visit him down South. And after training, he would be sent abroad, in the dark and dirty bowels of a troop ship, where the black soldiers were housed, taking meals after all the white soldiers had finished their meal shifts, and after all that he might well be killed at the front. After the last war, the black mothers of the Gold Star fighters had been dispatched to France in cattle boats to see the graves of their sons in Flanders. White mothers had sailed on luxury liners.

He turned—for the last time—to the Party. His black comrades Ben Davis and James Ford (who, previously antiwar, were now encouraging blacks to participate) suggested that he apply for work in the Office of War Information.[51] The Party, they told him, had contacts there.

Two weeks after America joined the war, Wright wrote a letter to the Office of War Information. He also wrote to Paul Green in North Carolina. Green was a World War I veteran and a member of the army reserve. In both letters Wright used these same words:

> Though I have been deferred in the draft because of dependents, I am anxious to serve the national democratic cause through my writing if such can be useful in helping us defeat the Axis powers. I feel that I can be of some service in clarifying and popularizing the Administration's war policy and war aims among the Negro people and among the American people as a whole.[52]

He told Green he had added some new lines to the play *Native Son*, now playing in Chicago, to suggest a readiness on the part of the Negro to fight. In the application form for the Office of War Information (which Ben Davis helped him fill out), Wright said he was a patriotic subject wishing to contribute to the war effort, and stated that he was a member of the Communist Party. Ben Davis said he would deliver the form to his contact at the Office of War Information. Wright waited and waited, and never heard a thing. He suspected that Davis and the comrades had decided he was unreliable or too intransigent for the job. The episode left him very bitter about Ben Davis.

ANOTHER OPTION THE WRIGHTS WERE TAKING SERIOUSLY WAS TO GO AND LIVE IN Canada. As with Mexico, they did not need passports to cross that border. Through Willard Maas and Marie Menken, who were currently making a documentary, Wright met some filmmakers who worked for the National Film Board of Canada.[53] They told him about the new director, John Grierson, a Scot who had established documentary film-making in Britain and was now developing the Canadian film industry. They encouraged Wright to apply for work as a scriptwriter.

One of them, Ernest Borneman, wrote to Wright from Canada that he planned to produce a documentary about the small Canadian Negro communities that were once terminals of the Underground Railroad. Would Wright like to collaborate with him?[54]

Wright wasted no time in writing to Grierson. His talent lay in the dramatic treatment of narrative, he told Grierson. One critic had described the text of *12 Million Black Voices* as a "cinematic soundtrack."[55]

Grierson was a progressive who genuinely admired Wright's work. But Wright was the last person he needed on the team just then. The Canadian film board was under pressure to produce wartime propaganda. Wright was known for his outspoken stance against the war. As Grierson told Wright: "Your lips are touched with fire."[56]

IN DECEMBER 1941, JUST AFTER AMERICA JOINED THE WAR, WRIGHT SUBMITTED HIS short novel, *The Man Who Lived Underground*, to Paul Reynolds. Wright was pleased with it. He felt it was more a philosophical novel than a novel about race. "It is the first time I've really tried to step beyond the straight black-white stuff," he told Reynolds.[57]

Reynolds did not like it. Before sending it on to Harper & Brothers, he phoned Aswell to discuss it. Soon afterwards, Ed Aswell rejected it. Reynolds did not send the manuscript anywhere else.

The rejection remains a mystery. Presumably it was because Wright's novel portrayed all too clearly the madness and arbitrary "justice" of the world at a time in which publishers were looking for more rousing stories. *Native Son* had made Harper & Brothers thousands of dollars the previous year. Since then, the play of *Native Son* and the photo-documentary book *12 Million Black Voices* had been highly praised. Why did Aswell and Reynolds insist on repressing this novel?

When the spring 1942 issue of the magazine *Accent* published excerpts, Ralph Ellison wrote to congratulate the editor, Kerker Quinn, on drawing attention to an important new book, the first depiction of Negro religious experience in Negro writing.[58]

Wright's novelist friend Edwin Seaver sent the manuscript to Harry Scherman, director of the Book of the Month Club. "It seems to me that the 'Man Who Lived Underground' is one of the most notable short novels I have ever read," Seaver told Scherman. "Only a great writer could do it. . . . It is a parable of Everyman, a mystery in the religious sense, told in terms of rigorous realism."[59]

Two years later, Edwin Seaver published half the novel—the second half—in his anthology, *Cross Section*. Ever since, *The Man Who Lived Underground* has remained a novella. The complete novel has never been published. And yet critics have consistently regarded the narrative as one of Wright's most powerful.

"FOR GOD'S SAKE, LET'S QUIT. I'VE HAD IT," WRIGHT BURST OUT TO ELLEN ONE spring day in 1942. Recently he had found himself ranting to Ellen more and more often about the Communist Party's "unconditional support" for the war. How dare the comrades urge the black brothers to fight in a Jim Crow army and to donate blood to segregated plasma banks?

There had been an exodus of blacks from the Party. Those who remained had to support black participation in the war. Prominent black leaders toed the line. James W. Ford argued that this was no white man's war. "This is a people's war, and by full participation in its victorious conclusion . . . the Negro people will see the achievement of full historical justice." Paul Robeson declared: "*Because* the Negro people are Jim Crowed, persecuted, denied their full rights, they have an even greater stake in this war than white Americans. . . . That is why every Negro who is loyal to his own people cannot but be 100 percent loyal to America."[60]

By now, Ellen felt the same way as her husband about the Communist Party's attitude to blacks. Her work in a predominantly black branch in Brooklyn had persuaded her that the Party was using the Negro for its own ends. "It was very cynical, the whole business," she said.[61]

These days the black press throughout the nation was more

vociferous about racial discrimination than were the Communists. In February 1942, the *Pittsburgh Courier* initiated the "Double V" slogan, which would become an important rallying cry for blacks during the war. Blacks had to fight for a double victory: against discrimination at home and against fascism abroad.

For the time being, Wright did not want to attract the attention of the War Department by speaking out against the war. These were dangerous and frightening times. Rather than leaving the Communist Party publicly, he simply withdrew from all activities and campaigns. The comrades knew. On 14 October 1942, an FBI agent interviewed somebody who knew Wright. Whoever it was advised that "Richard Wright . . . had split with the party because of his dissatisfaction with the way the Party handled the Negro question."[62]

The break was not easy for Wright. Despite bad moments, the Party had supported him for almost ten years. The Communist Party was one of the very few places in America where blacks and whites mixed. It had provided a path out of the Black Belt. It had offered a barrier against American racism. Years later Wright told Ed Aswell: "My membership in the Communist Party had . . . sort of neutralized the racial problem; when I left the Communist Party I had to face the racial problem with no protecting 'gang' at my side."

IN APRIL 1942, FOUR MONTHS AFTER HARPER & BROTHERS REJECTED *THE MAN WHO Lived Underground*, Wright delivered *Black Hope* to Paul Reynolds. Two years before, Reynolds had asked him to cut it in half. In the meantime, Wright had cut the novel and fundamentally changed it.

Reynolds was still dissatisfied. He typed four pages of detailed comment, suggesting many changes—major and minor. "Anyone reading all this criticism would think I didn't like the novel at all and I can only say with all the emphasis possible that the reverse is true," he told Wright. He said he thought it "a larger and deeper book than *Native Son*." He added: "Many, or perhaps most authors get swelled heads after a big success and their resulting work may be hurt. I think you are inclined to be almost too humble and self-doubting about your own abilities."

Reynolds placed a lot of weight on Wright's new novel:

With *12 Million Black Voices* I had a feeling that the book being a picture book probably wouldn't have a large sale and being non-fiction wouldn't probably affect your career as a writer in any way at all. *Black Hope* is different. If it has a large sale you have a fair chance of being somewhat a fixed star in the publishing firmament. Your books will vary in sales but they should hold up among the class of large sellers say the way a man like Steinbeck does, or A. J. Cronin. If *Black Hope* doesn't sell, you will remain the author of *Native Son* and the trade and the book stores and everybody will think of you in that way. That doesn't mean that another novel later on can't still have a big sale—of course, it can, but it is more difficult.[63]

For the moment, *Black Hope* was still scheduled for October publication. The prospect of tackling it again, making further changes, exhausted Wright in anticipation. And just two days after Reynolds's letter, there was a major distraction on the home front.

15

WARTIME BROOKLYN

April 1942–December 1943

Julia Wright came into the world in the early morning of 15 April 1942. From the Jewish Hospital in Brooklyn her father excitedly phoned friends.[1] During the next few days, Ellen heard a group of nurses gossiping. Somebody had had a *black baby*.[2] It was Ellen's first inkling of what was to come. She was relieved when the week was up and she and Julia could leave.

Wright came with their neighbor Becky Crawford, an older Jewish friend, to take his family home. Years later, Ellen recalled how anxious he was that day. He insisted on holding the baby—he said Ellen was too weak—but he worried about holding her correctly. Then he was unnerved by Becky's constant stream of advice. Becky insisted that Ellen should not have listened to the doctor, who said it was better to use scientifically prepared formula milk rather than breast-feed the baby. Wright thought the doctor probably knew what he was talking about. When they got home, he took out one of the rubber teats he had sterilized beforehand and tried to attach it to the bottle. It flew out of his hand onto the floor. The same thing happened with several others. He got into quite a state. Becky looked triumphant.

Wright's tremendous pride in his child was accompanied by what Ellen describes as "a terribly anxious feeling."[3] Friends noticed it too. "Dick doted on Julia," says Louise Rosskam, adding: "He seemed incredulous that she existed."[4] Constance Webb had a similar impression when she met the Wright family four months later.

Webb was twenty-four, a photographer's model from California, with an ambition to write. The Trinidadian writer and activist C. L. R. James was courting her at that time, and they had been invited to dinner at the Wrights' apartment on Middagh Street, close to the Brooklyn Bridge.[5] It was a warm August evening. Nello, as his friends called C. L. R., rang the bell. Wright opened the door. Webb was taken aback by this handsome man with the luminous skin and dark eyes who seemed boyishly happy to see them. His expression, she thought, was almost "gleeful."[6]

Knowing that Ellen had been a Communist organizer, Webb imagined she would be "opinionated" and "somewhat masculine." She was in for another surprise:

Ellen, a small girl with short curling brown hair came into the room wearing an apron. Her cheeks were flushed and her eyes appeared brown, then green, then yellow-brown, as if reflecting varied emotions. They were extremely alive and her face also held the look of glee, almost conspiratorial, that Wright's held. . . . That evening I thought she was shy. . . . There was an expression of love and interest on her face and pride in her husband. She was quiet for the most part but when she spoke it was quick, incisive and to the point.

Dick and Ellen radiated a happy compatibility. Webb comments: "The electric quality which one noticed immediately upon meeting Wright obviously existed between them as well."

While Ellen was busy in the kitchen—she assured Constance she did not want any help—her young guest had ample opportunity to observe the men together. Dick and Nello were both talkers, and they left her out of the conversation entirely. Nello was tall, thin, and formal-sounding, with his British-Trinidadian accent. Wright's voice, she noticed, had an "extraordinary range"—from high to baritone. When she thought about it later, she realized that Wright talked more than anyone else that evening, but without appearing to dominate the conversation. "Most wonderful was his laugh," Webb writes. "When he laughed, all of him laughed." And everyone else laughed too.

But beneath Wright's surface joviality, Webb thought she could detect a darker, more brooding man. As the evening progressed, she noted that he had rather full eyelids and he used them, at times, to half cover his eyes. She felt he was hiding his emotions.

Before they sat down to dinner, Wright asked if they would like to see Julia, who was now four months old. Down a long hall, past a glimpse of a luxurious-looking bathroom, they found the baby asleep in her cot, lying on her stomach, hands clenched, legs sprawled like a frog:

> I saw that Wright did not want us to approach too near the crib and he nervously and possessively pulled a light blanket up over her body and tucked it under the back of her neck. His actions were strange because we could see that she was perspiring in her sleep but Wright asked Ellen if the window should be closed, walked over to test if there was a draft and had to be reassured that all was well before he and Mr. James returned to the front room. After he left, Ellen smiled faintly and pulled the blanket back down to the middle of Julia's body. I felt the indulgence and love in her face was for Wright as well as for her baby daughter.

Why were there books under the head of the crib? Webb asked. Ellen explained that Dick had thought Julia was coming down with a cold and that the angle might make it easier for her to breathe.

Most surprising of all to Constance Webb were the antique furnishings and luxury trimmings in the apartment—the long dining table, linen cloth and napkins, the gleaming silver, the formal china. "This was a setting not at all common among left intellectuals," she writes. "Most of them disdained the trappings of the 'bourgeoisie,' even when they themselves had grown up in that milieu." The kind of people she knew prided themselves on having apple boxes for bookcases and posters for decorations. The Wrights were different.

"MIDDAGH WAS A WHITE MAN'S STREET IN WHITE BROOKLYN HEIGHTS," SAYS BEN Appel, a writer active in Party circles who lived around the corner and occasionally dropped in to see Wright.[7] The street was elegant and tranquil, with maple trees shading the sidewalks in the summer and the smell of the ocean on windy days. Number 7 was in a row of three-story brownstones. From the upper windows there were views across the East River to the towering peaks of Wall Street, the Statue of Liberty and beyond to the Jersey shore.

When Richard and Ellen Wright had moved into the neighborhood with their two-month-old baby in June 1942, the neighbors complained. Someone threw stones at the window. George Davis's black superintendent, who brought coal to the house and stoked the furnace, refused to work there anymore when he discovered that a black man was living there with his white wife.[8] One did not have to be black or an interracial couple to be unwelcome in Brooklyn Heights. Sol and Frieda Rabkin, who became friends of the Wrights, also had trouble renting an apartment there. One landlord after another would tell them: "We don't rent to Jews."

George Davis, the fiction editor of *Harper's Bazaar*, had lived in the house for two years when he invited the Wrights to join them in the summer of 1942. He had first met Richard Wright in January 1940, through their mutual friend, the poet Willard Maas. George Davis published Wright's story "Almos' a Man" in *Harper's*, and asked him to lunch.[9] A few months later, when Wright's glowing review of Carson McCullers's first novel, *The Heart Is a Lonely Hunter*, appeared in the *New Republic*, Davis wrote him a note:

> My friend Carson McCullers was so deeply touched by your review of her book and is most anxious to meet you. I am sharing a house with McCullers and W. H. Auden in Brooklyn. It is now terribly torn up but we hope soon to have a housewarming and would be delighted if you could come.[10]

Wright and Ellen had met the household. George Davis, a boyish-looking thirty-six-year-old, had published a novel himself in his mid-twenties, but his greatest gift was as a talent scout.[11] He had helped launch the careers of two other young Southerners: Carson McCullers and Truman Capote. An affable homosexual, Davis seemed to know every artist in town. Truman Capote described him as "benevolent and butter-hearted," despite his "guillotine tongue."[12] Anaïs Nin thought him "like an overgrown child, soft, round face, . . . occasionally cynical."[13]

W. H. Auden, the British poet, had come to the United States in 1939 with Christopher Isherwood. He organized the household budget. Carson McCullers, a lanky twenty-three-year-old with huge shining eyes and a Georgian drawl, had just parted from her husband, and was currently in love with a woman. The other resident was Gypsy Rose Lee, the striptease artist. With the help of George Davis, she was writing a novel called *The G-String Murders*.[14]

By the time the Wrights moved in, two years later, the house had become a well-known bohemian landmark in Brooklyn, but it was no longer run communally.[15] The Wrights kept largely to themselves. Oliver Smith, the painter and stage-set designer, occupied the attic rooms; George Davis had the third floor; and Carson McCullers divided her time between Middagh Street and Yaddo, the artists' colony in upstate New York.[16] She had suffered a stroke the previous year and her health was fragile. Her love life, as usual, was in disarray. She and George Davis spent long evenings consoling each other with talk and drink.

As Anaïs Nin wrote in her diary, the house was filled with "old American furniture, oil lamps, brass beds, little coffee tables, old drapes, copper lamps, old cupboards, heavy dining tables of oak, lace doilies, grandfather clocks."[17] One of Davis's passions was antiques. Another was epicurean dinners and good conversation. Around his dinner table and at his parties the Wrights met Leonard Bernstein, Aaron Copland, Salvador Dalí, Kurt Weill, Lotte Lenya, and dozens of other New York and émigré filmmakers, musicians, actors, and writers.[18]

Wright himself was fashionable company these days. Before he moved into the house, McCullers had inscribed his copy of *Reflections in a Golden Eye*: "Dick, I have wanted to see you for a long time, but you are so exclusive."[19] Anaïs Nin was thrilled to meet him. "Richard Wright is handsome, quiet, simple, direct," she wrote in her diary. "His speech is beautiful, modulated and smooth. His ideas clear."[20] She also noticed: "He has finely shaped hands."

Nin was having affairs with Canada Lee, black Broadway star of *Native Son*, and Albert Mangones, a twenty-six-year-old Haitian architect. "I feel a real love for the Negro world," she confided in her diary. "I feel close to them, to their emotional sensitiveness, their sensory awareness, their beauty, the soft velvet of their eyes, the warmth of their smile, the purity of their violence. They are human."[21]

Soon after meeting the Wrights, Nin invited them, along with George Davis, to a party at her Fourteenth Street penthouse. Canada Lee turned up. They sat in circles on the floor, Mangones and his Haitian friends played the drums, and there was dancing. The Wrights were invited back again. This time, a young poet friend of the Wrights, Naomi Replansky, accompanied them. Nin's husband, Ian Hugo, was there. Replansky recalls: "Anaïs Nin fluttered around, fawning on Richard Wright. Her nails were painted a dramatic color—gold or black. She seemed to be desperately hanging onto the remnants of youth."[22] Nin was forty; Replansky was twenty-four.

Nin made another pilgrimage to 7 Middagh Street, accompanied by her Haitian friends. Her aim, she wrote in her journal, was "to serenade Richard Wright."[23] She and her friends wooed him with singing, dancing, drumming. Years later, she commented: "He did not respond fully, and I did not know then that he was mistrustful of our friendship. He did not believe in it."[24]

Nin persisted. She and a Russian poet friend, Irina Aleksander, went back to Brooklyn Heights. This time—Irina insisted—they went without the Haitians and their drums. They sat on the porch with the Wrights and various residents of the house. Irina talked incessantly. Wright said he was disappointed the Haitians had not come. "His disappointment made me aware of mine," Nin wrote, "of my own detachment from talk and cerebral activity."[25]

That evening, Wright told Nin he was unhappy in America and longed to see Europe. He was tired of New York hostesses who invited him because he was successful, then looked hesitant if he turned up with a less successful friend. Eventually he and Ellen, who drank less and retired earlier than the other members of the house, bid the group on the porch good night. Nin wrote in her journal: "Richard Wright is dignified and sensitive. . . . Wright's wife, Ellen, is a handsome, quiet, warm Jewish girl. The evening was lovely."

THE WRIGHTS HAD BARELY SETTLED IN TO BROOKLYN HEIGHTS WHEN, ON 1 JULY 1942, Wright received a notice from the Brooklyn draft board. He had been reclassified "1A" and was to report for his physical examination within ten days.

Wright was convinced it was discrimination. He knew no other married men with children who had been called up. He appealed. His neighbor Becky Crawford wrote to Eleanor Roosevelt on his behalf:[26]

> Richard Wright, the negro writer, who is the author of "Native Son" and "Uncle Tom's Children," has been notified that he has been reclassified in 1A. . . .
>
> He is married to a very fine white woman, has a three month old daughter, supports his invalid mother, also his wife's mother, whose son, her main support, is in the army, stationed at Pearl Harbor, in fact was there when Pearl Harbor was attacked.
>
> He has just finished a rough draft of a novel, and needs more time to complete the finishing touches. It is to be published in the fall.
>
> He is definitely anti-fascist, whole-heartedly for the war, but naturally feels great concern about Jim Crowism in civilian life, the army and the navy. . . .
>
> My understanding has been that the army is not calling married men with children at the present time, as they do not want to break up homes until absolutely necessary. . . . He feels there has been discrimination in his case, because he is a negro, and I'm afraid he is right.
>
> With the justifiable pride the negroes feel in Richard Wright's standing as an American writer, I feel it would have unfortunate repercussions in the whole negro population all over the country, if they felt that an unfair decision was made in his case, especially crucial at this time, when there is so much outspoken and smoldering resentment among negroes as they feel they are good enough to die with, but not live with, the white population.[27]

Wright was granted a ninety-day deferral pending the outcome of his appeal.[28] In the meantime he turned to various influential friends for help in obtaining some sort of writing commission. In his 1971 memoir, *The Middle Man*, Paul Reynolds recalls that Wright phoned him, and Reynolds suggested sandwiches in the reception area of his office. ("In the 1940s it was difficult, sometimes impossible, to find a first-class hotel or restaurant that would serve a Negro guest.")[29] When Wright asked for his help in procuring a writing commission in the army, Reynolds writes that his response was ambivalent:

I told Wright that I would like to leave the reception room, go to my desk, think about the matter alone for ten minutes, and then rejoin him. I was in a quandary. Wright was considered a Communist. However, Russia was our ally and certainly Wright was violently anti-Nazi. The question was whether Wright might get more interested in improving the lot of the Negro soldier than in giving his full efforts to beat the enemy. Would Wright become a troublemaker in the Army? . . . I rejoined Wright and asked him what I should say if someone thought that he would be working for his race rather than implicitly obeying Army orders.

Wright assured Reynolds that his loyalty to his country came before other principles, and that to all intents and purposes he had left the Communist Party. In the end, Reynolds agreed to write a friend of his, Colonel Walter Welles, who was in charge of the army's public relations in New York.

A few days later, Reynolds phoned Wright. He jokingly called him "Lieutenant." It looked as if Welles had managed to pull off a commission for Wright in the Office of War Information in Washington. While Wright waited to hear more definitely, Horace Cayton tried to help the commission along. He wrote to a friend in the War Department in Washington, recommending Wright for a job in the press relations department and assuring him that Wright's "left wing leaning" would not stand in the way of his service to the country. "It would be a terrific waste of his ability to put him in a private's uniform."[30]

Weeks passed and Wright did not hear anything. He decided to sit the Volunteer Officer Entry Examination. The training school lasted six months and was a far more palatable option than training as an enlisted private. Wright hoped that after the training period he would be able to get back to New York and work in public relations or on the staff of an army newspaper. He obtained a copy of the booklet *Practice for the Army Tests* and studied hard, getting friends to help him with the mathematics and algebra.

Whether or not Eleanor Roosevelt had anything to do with it, Wright heard early in October that he had been reclassified as 3A because of his dependents. Soon after, Reynolds had to inform him that the Washington writing commission had not come off after all. "I telephoned the doleful news to Wright, who took it very well," Reynolds writes. "He said that he had expected something to go wrong. He had never believed the Army would accept him."

On 19 December 1942 a letter came from the Volunteer Officer Candidate Board saying that Wright had made the score on the test and his application was favorably considered. The final decision would depend on a physical test and his general suitability for induction. Two weeks later, another letter came: "You have been found to be *not* qualified . . . by the Second Service Command Board of Review." No reason was given.

EVERY TEN DAYS OR SO, IN THE COURSE OF THE AFTERNOON, WRIGHT WOULD make his way to his favorite barbershop on Fulton Street in Brooklyn to get his hair cut. He loved going to that smoky place where his ears were "drenched delightfully by fulsome Negroid speech." It was his "secret grotto," his retreat, his "spiritual haven from New York's terrifying and impersonal vastness."[31] Once inside the door he would forget his tense urban life, the war, the rations, the shortage of butter. Temporarily he could leave behind "the strain of chasing fiction plots." For a mere fifty cents, he could sit incognito and hear ribald black male talk and hilarious belly laughter, unimpeded by listening whites. It took him back to his old days in the South. He would listen to "tall tales of Mississippi River life, stories of black gals seduced under hair-raising circumstances, chronicles of prodigious eating and drinking." Occasionally there would be a "loud smacking of lips as someone took a nip out of a bottle."

Then, sometime in 1942, the Office of War Information published a thick picture booklet called *Negroes and the War*, widely distributed in the nation's black ghettoes.[32] Written to recruit black fighters, it said that Hitler called Negroes "half-apes" and that the Allies were fighting against racism. It pointed out the rapid progress Negroes had made in democratic America. ("We are now fighting shoulder to shoulder with our fellow Americans in the present world conflict.") Celebrating the achievements of Negro Americans in all fields of life, it featured photographs of happy-looking black Americans in cozy homes, at pleasant jobs, and looking handsome in their army uniforms. It focused particularly on Negro "leaders"—artists, scientists, musicians, athletes, writers.

Among them was Richard Wright. The next time he went to the barber-shop, everything had changed:

> When I entered, the talk died. I pulled off my hat, coat, vest, sat and lit a cigarette and waited to enjoy my people, their rolling phrases, their laughs that start at the top of the diaphragm and work their way slowly up the esophagus to explode in prolonged bursts of physical glee. But none came. I grew uneasy. I looked about and could discern no cause for this silence. What was wrong?
>
> Presently a white-coated barber came bashfully over to me with a mysterious periodical in his hand. He spread the pages before my eyes and pointed to an idealized image of my face.
>
> "That's you, ain't?" he asked.
>
> . . . A ceremony commenced. I was introduced all around as a "writer." My hand was shaken. My identity as a so-called "leader" was made known. . . . When I got into the chair, my favorite barber, instead of telling me my weekly joke, began to ask me questions about the Nazis, the Dies Committee, the Japs, General De Gaulle, and the FBI.

The war did the rest. Wright tried other barbershops, but war talk had taken over everywhere he went. The war had stifled "free black laughter, the tall black tale, the black belly-laugh."

IN OCTOBER 1942 A WHITE MAN WHO LIVED IN WASHINGTON SENT A LETTER TO the Secretary of War, calling his attention to certain passages in *12 Million Black Voices*. They could lead to "many forms of sabotage," he wrote, "and result in a general breakdown of morale."[33] He referred to a passage where Wright represented the feelings of radical black nationalists:

> There are some of us who feel our hurts so deeply that we find it impossible to work with whites. . . . Our distrust is so great that we form intensely racial and nationalistic organizations and advocate the establishment of a separate state, a forty-ninth state, in which we black folk would live. . . . There are others of us who feel the need of the protection of a strong nation so keenly that we admire the harsh and imperialistic policies of Japan and ardently hope that the Japanese will assume the leadership of the "darker races."

The Military Intelligence Service forwarded the letter to J. Edgar Hoover, director of the Federal Bureau of Investigation, and Hoover sent a memo (marked "Internal Security—Sedition") to the New York office, asking the Special-Agent-in-Charge to look at the book and all Wright's other writings. "If your inquiry develops information of an affirmative nature, you should of course cause an investigation to be undertaken as to subject's background, inclinations, and current activities."[34]

Throughout the war, the FBI undertook a "concentrated investigation" of Negroes who acted or exhibited sentiments "in a manner inimical to the Nation's war effort."[35] The FBI was highly suspicious of "racialists" who believed in Negro rights, and would remain so throughout the 1950s. From now until the end of his life, Richard Wright would be under constant surveillance from intelligence organizations.

•

RICHARD WRIGHT WAS CONSCIOUS OF BEING FOLLOWED BY THE FBI, SAYS THE poet Naomi Replansky. A friend of both Richard's and Ellen's, she was in love with Wright. During 1943–44 they met occasionally as lovers. One day two men came to her residence in Brooklyn, where she lived with her parents, and asked if she was married. She was convinced they were FBI agents. Wright, when she told him, was upset and angry.

Two Replansky poems that allude to her passion for Wright, "Even the Walls Have Ears" and "Restless Dialogue," are full of the anguish of potential discovery.[36] She was not thinking of the FBI alone.

Wright himself had every reason to want to keep private any occasional affair he had with another woman. He was in love with Ellen, and he did not wish to hurt her. He cared a great deal about being a good father. If the FBI was eager to procure evidence against him, so were his enemies in the Communist Party. There were people in the black community who would be happy to see his interracial marriage fail. Wright was keen to show the world that such a marriage was perfectly normal and not worthy of the comment it constantly aroused. "There're no problems in people of different races marrying and living together," he would write in his journal in January 1945. "The only problems that may arise come from those who look on, and those who look on are usually the ignorant."[37]

Nathan Wright, Natchez, June 1940. *Photograph by Richard Wright. JWJ Collection, Beinecke Library, Yale University. (All photographs in Wright papers appear courtesy of Ellen Wright.)*

Ella Wright, Chicago, 1930s. *Beinecke Library, Yale University.*

Margaret Bolden Wilson, Richard Wright's grandmother. *Beinecke Library, Yale University.*

Graduation class at Smith Robertson, 1925. Richard Wright is in the back row, fifth from left. In front of him is Birdie Graves. Joe Brown is back row, second from right. Essie Lee Davis is in front row, second from left. Minnie Farish is beside her, third from left. Their teacher, Professor Cobbins, is in the second row, on the extreme left. *Courtesy David Bakish.*

Margaret Walker, writer friend in the Chicago days. *Schomburg Collection, New York Public Library.*

Nelson Algren, Chicago writer friend, Paris, 1950s. *Photograph by Stephen Deutch. Courtesy Katherine Deutch Tatlock.*

Edward Aswell: Wright's first and favorite publisher. *Courtesy Mary Aswell Doll.*

Paul Reynolds, Jr., Wright's literary agent. *Photograph by Fabian Bachrach. Courtesy of Robbin Reynolds and Dianne Watkins Stuart.*

Ralph Ellison—one of many whom Wright encouraged. *Courtesy Library of Congress Prints and Photographs Division.*

Jane and Herbert Newton
with Michelle, Carl, and
baby Dolores. In the
backyard at Carlton
Avenue, summer 1937.
*Courtesy Dr. Dolores
Newton.*

Jane Newton.
Courtesy Dr. Dolores Newton.

Dorothy Canfield Fisher,
at home in Vermont.
*Dorothy Canfield Fisher
papers, Special Collections,
University of Vermont
Library.*

Dhimah Rose Meidman and Richard Wright, New York, 1939. *Beinecke
Library, Yale University.*

Paul Green and Richard
Wright working on the play,
Native Son, in Chapel Hill,
North Carolina, July 1940.
*Reprinted with permission
of the News & Observer
of Raleigh, North Carolina,
N.C. Division of Archives
and History.*

Richard and Ellen Wright at home in the early days of their marriage. *Courtesy Beinecke Library, Yale University.*

Wright and Horace R. Cayton studying graphs and charts of Chicago's South Side. Good Shepherd Community Center, April 1941. *Courtesy Vivian G. Harsh Research Collection of Afro-American History and Literature, Chicago Public Library.*

Discussing blues song "King Joe" with Count Basie, October 1941. *ACME Newspictures photograph. Courtesy Bettman/Corbis.*

Naomi's lovers were generally women. Wright was aware of this, she says, and never said anything derogatory about it. She loved this intense, brooding, angry man who was so passionate about writing. She knew she meant less to him, but believed their intellectual companionship was important to him. There is a cautious note from her among Wright's papers. "I'm an insistent dame," she wrote, asking him to meet her one evening soon. "I know you're very busy and I'm asking a lot, but it's important to me."[38]

Naomi, of Polish-Jewish origin, was beautiful, with a slight build and a sensitive sculpted face. Though she was in the Young Communist League, she had little interest in politics. She worked in a factory during the war and wrote poetry whenever she could. Wright was encouraging. In December 1944 he passed her manuscript *Ring Song* to his friend John Woodburn at Little, Brown. He wrote her a reference for a grant. And he was instrumental in getting poems of hers published in Dorothy Norman's magazine *Twice a Year*.[39]

WRIGHT WAS STILL HALFHEARTEDLY REVISING *BLACK HOPE*. IN MARCH 1943 ED Aswell wrote to him that he had heard Wright was "still a free man," and he hoped this meant he was able to work on his novel. "I am very keen about publishing that book."[40] But early in April, Wright made a brief visit to the South. It changed his writing plans.

He went first to Chicago, where Horace Cayton had arranged for him to address the Institute of Psychoanalysis. Wright spoke about the fear and hate that affected the entire life of the Negro. The talk went well. The following evening, the two men boarded a train and headed south to Nashville, Tennessee. The foremost black sociologist in the country, Chicago-trained Charles S. Johnson, had invited them to speak at Fisk University, one of the oldest black campuses in the country.

Wright and Cayton shared a luxurious double compartment in the train. Fisk was footing the bill. As they sped southward, they took off their jackets, put on slippers, and called the porter for ice and soda to mix with the scotch Cayton had brought with him. They sat back, enjoying this rare opportunity for intimate conversation. Cayton's second marriage, to Irma, had just broken up. Feeling mentally fragile, he was thinking of embarking on psychoanalysis. Wright was curious about analysis, and, unlike others, was never mocking. Cayton told him gratefully: "You are one of the few people in this country that I can have a free exchange of ideas with without feeling inhibitions and fears that I am not saying the right thing."[41]

Wright himself had become an avid reader of Freud and psychoanalysis. Ever since meeting Clinton Brewer, he had been fascinated by the psychopathology of crime. He had come to the conclusion that he needed to know something about the abnormal mind in order to understand the "normal" mind. He thought perhaps that he needed to know more about neurosis in order to understand the pathology of racism.

The two men were hoping to coedit a magazine, and much of their talk that evening was about that. They thought they would call it *American Pages*, and aim for white and black readers. In it they planned to publish critical essays on modern American culture and analyze the "Negro problem" in terms that showed the emotional cost of living in America. It would be a popular magazine, a monthly, with no political allegiance. But first they needed financial support. Cayton had good connections with Marshall Field and the Julius Rosenwald Foundation. He would try them.

The train crossed the Mason-Dixon line. Cayton, a Northerner who had taught briefly at Fisk before he had fled from the South in horror, assured a nervous Wright that Nashville was not *too* bad. It was, after all, the Middle South, not the Deep South. And though Tennessee had been the first state to bring in racial segregation, in 1881, there was less fear of violence from whites than in Mississippi, even if the possibility was always in the air.[42] Within Nashville, Fisk was an oasis.[43]

The dinner gong chimed in the corridor. Now in Jim Crow territory, they decided to order a meal in their room. "I don't feel like looking into the faces of a lot of red-faced peckerwoods," Wright agreed. But the next morning, his curiosity took over.

"I knew Dick would goad me into the diner," Cayton wrote later. "I knew he would persist, driven to a new experience in Jim Crow living which he knew would humiliate and infuriate him." Cayton was shaving in the small bathroom when Wright suggested the dining car and he did his best to persuade Wright to call a waiter to their room instead. "God, I don't need to go through everything to know how it feels!"

But Wright had his way. Sure enough they were the last to be seated, and theirs was the table in the hot little space near the pantry. As they sat down the white steward slipped behind them and pulled the curtain around the table, hiding them from view. Cayton wrote later:

As we lingered over coffee, Dick said, "Did you notice that waiter when he talked to the steward!"

"Yeah, sure."

"Poor black devil, his voice went up two octaves and his testicles must have jumped two inches into his stomach."

"Yes, I guess so."

Dick persisted. "He does that to emasculate himself, to make himself more feminine, less masculine, more acceptable to a white man."

It was so obvious, so shockingly true and so graphically stated that I laughed. "Oh hell, don't probe his guts. You're right, but you're spoiling my breakfast," I complained.

They arrived in Nashville in midmorning on Friday, 9 April. Fisk University was a collection of handsome gray brick buildings among magnolia trees, on a hill overlooking the town. Founded in 1866, one year after the end of the Civil War, the first students at Fisk School had been former slaves—adults and children—eager to learn to read. To raise funds for new buildings, a group of young men and women—the "Jubilee Singers"—stepped out on tour, singing old slave songs to white audiences in the North and in Europe. Fisk's first permanent building, beautiful "Jubilee Hall," was built on the proceeds.

Wright was deeply impressed by the university's history and the thousands of songs and historical documents in the Fisk archives. He visualized a movie portraying the singers' dedication and adventures, the humiliations they endured on tour, and their ultimate triumph. In the next few months he wrote an outline and part of a script, but unfortunately it was not an idea that easily found funding.

Fisk's most famous graduate was W. E. B. Du Bois. At the age of seventeen, he had taken the train South from New England. His family was distressed that he wanted to go to the land of former slavery, but he was beginning to feel "lonesome" in New England and wanted to spend time among people of his own color. The Tennessee he came to in 1885 had just introduced segregation. The backdrop to his studies were recurrent lynchings. "No one but a Negro going into the South without previous experience of color caste can have any conception of its barbarism," Du Bois would write in his autobiography.[44]

Richard Wright gave his talk that evening, after attending an organ recital in the Fisk Memorial Chapel. It was daunting. In the South, blacks and whites rarely sat in the same room together. On this occasion, the audience was mixed. The students were black, the faculty members were mostly Northern whites, and whites from the town also attended. In the audience was Robert Park, the grand old man of Chicago sociology who had retired to Fisk, and Charles S. Johnson, the country's preeminent black sociologist.

For days Wright had been stumped by his speech. He knew he had to be careful not to appear *too* anti-Southern. Finally he had decided to talk casually about his own experiences in the South and North. He called the talk: "What I've Been Thinking." When he lived in the South, he had seen everything through Southern eyes; since going North, he had developed new eyes with which to look back at those days. According to Joyce Cooper Arkhurst, a student who was listening that evening, the audience was first confounded, then shocked. Never had they heard anyone talk about racism as Richard Wright was doing.[45]

Halfway through his speech Wright noticed that the audience was "terribly still." Occasionally there would be tense laughter. "It crashed upon me that I was saying things that Negroes were not supposed to say publicly, things that whites had forbidden Negroes to say."[46] Afterwards, a black schoolteacher came up to him. "Goddamn," he said in a low voice, "you're the first man to tell the truth in this town!" A white man told him stiffly: "You've brought the race problem to Nashville."

There was heated discussion. Two weeks later, Charles S. Johnson wrote to thank Wright: "Your visit was about as stimulating and delightful as any event in my academic memory here. You won the blasé students and their slightly bored dons completely, needling them to an amazing animation."[47]

For Wright, the visit to Fisk was a turning point. He had managed to interest a mixed audience with stories from his Southern past. Several years before, his autobiographical sketch "The Ethics of Living Jim Crow" had moved white readers. Why not develop his reminiscences into a book? It would not be autobiography exactly; he wanted to show what it was like to live on the receiving end of racism. This time he would not write about a Bigger Thomas, the self he might have become. This time he would write about himself.

FROM CHICAGO, WRIGHT TELEGRAMMED ELLEN, "ARRIVING THURS MORNING 9.30 Grand Central. Oceans of love for you and Julia. Dick."[48] He got back to New York in time to celebrate Julia's first birthday. Once again he had decided to put *Black Hope* aside.

He thought it would be easy to write about himself. It wasn't. "I found that to tell the truth is the hardest thing on earth," he observed "Harder than fighting in a war, harder than taking part in a revolution." He told potential autobiographers: "You'll find that there are many things that you don't want to admit about yourself. There will surge up in you a strong desire to alter facts, to dress up your feelings."[49] To keep the fresh, anecdotal tone of his Fisk talk, he sometimes spoke into his dictaphone, then typed it later, making changes as he typed.

He was inspired by other writers' thinly fictionalized accounts of their alienated youth. George Moore's *Confessions of a Young Man* portrayed his struggles against the restrictions of his Victorian environment. James Joyce's *The Portrait of the Artist as a Young Man* depicted an Irish youth rebelling against the stifling constraints of religion and bigotry. In *Sons and Lovers* D. H. Lawrence described an artistic young man brought up in a philistine coal-mining town.[50]

Wright's memories were painful: his father abandoning the family; the brutal lashings; the desolation of the orphanage; the poverty, loneliness, and hunger. He wrote about the move to Chicago, the disillusionment of encountering racism in the North, and the dreariness of those Depression years. He tackled the Communist Party: the dream it had once represented for him, and the disillusionment. He called the book *American Hunger.* It was about the hunger—physical and spiritual—felt by black Americans in their own country.

AMERICA WAS NOW FEELING THE WAR. THERE WAS FOOD RATIONING. MAJOR CITIES had an electricity "brownout" at night, in case of bombing raids. The Works Progress Administration, a major source of employment for blacks, was shut down in 1943. Leon Wright, who had a job as an artist in the map division of the Federal Arts Project in Chicago, was once again out of work. The black press was full of the indignities suffered by their fighting men. (During the war years, some two thousand rebellious black men were imprisoned for refusing to comply with the Selective Service Act.)[51] In the summer of 1943 there were race riots in Detroit and Texas. At the beginning of August, when a black soldier was shot by a white policeman in Harlem, a spontaneous mob gathered on 125th Street and proceeded to smash and loot stores, restaurants, and lunch counters. Wright went up to Harlem a couple of days later and walked around among the debris and broken glass. "It was a spontaneous outburst of anger," he told *PM*. He predicted more dangerous clashes to come.[52]

Brooklyn neighbors Sol and Frieda Rabkin were taken by surprise when they went to the Wrights' for dinner a few days later. Sol argued that it was no time to riot in the middle of the war; it served no good purpose; blacks were merely looting and pillaging their own stores. Wright was furious. This riot had been coming a long time, he said.[53] The stores didn't belong to blacks; that was the point. All the stores and businesses that had been looted were owned by whites. The jazz clubs and soul-food restaurants were all owned by whites. Often these places did not even admit black clients. "He was on a tear," Frieda recalls.

AFTER A YEAR IN BROOKLYN HEIGHTS, WRIGHT DECIDED THE HOUSE DID NOT provide the ideal environment for young Julia. They felt a deep affection for George Davis, a gentle, cultured man, but his wild behavior was worrying. He and Carson McCullers used to go on all-night drinking sprees in the sailors' bars on nearby Sands Street, close to the naval yard. Under the bridges, where rats ran wild, Davis would pick up young men. Several times he had come home beaten up. On more than one occasion he had been hospitalized.[54] Carson McCullers was ill much of the time and seemed bent on further destroying herself with alcohol. Wright wrote in his journal: "The more I talk with her the more I feel there is something in her that I cannot like; and she is one person whom I want to like."[55]

In mid-August 1943 the Wrights moved out. (Two years later, most of the brownstones on the street would be pulled down to make way for the Brooklyn-Queens Expressway.) The Wrights would spend the next two years in a six-room apartment in a brick apartment building at 89 Lefferts Place in the Bedford Stuyvesant section of Brooklyn. Wright had lived on that street before, with the Newtons. It was a short, quiet street. Across from their building was a mortuary, Campbell Funeral Parlor. "Many of my neighbors are dead," Wright liked to joke.[56]

RICHARD WRIGHT WROTE *AMERICAN HUNGER* IN SEVEN MONTHS. IT WAS FINISHED just before Christmas 1943, almost four years after *Native Son* had been published to great acclaim. Since then Harper had rejected *The Man Who Lived Underground*, and Wright had not been able to pull *Black Hope* together. He had every reason to feel nervous about this new book, and he did.

He was sure this manuscript would please neither his agent nor his publisher. The war was raging; publishing houses were looking for rousing cheer and proud patriotism. He had ended the book in Chicago in the late 1930s. Pacing the floor of his bleak room, he asked himself: "What had I got out of living in America? . . . My country had shown me no examples of how to live a human life. All my life I had been full of a hunger for a new way to live." In the other room a radio was playing, and a white man's voice "hinted of a coming war that would consume millions of lives." He sat down in front of a piece of paper, vowing to himself that he would hurl words into the darkness; his words would "march" and "fight."

16

A TROUBLINGLY
DELICATE MATTER

December 1943–December 1944

Paul Reynolds read the manuscript of *American Hunger* over Christmas and phoned Wright to say he liked it very much. The cover note he sent to Aswell was unambiguous. "I took the liberty of telling Dick that in my opinion you'd be very interested in it and that I felt confident any publisher would be extremely keen to publish it."[1]

Aswell had been expecting a novel. Nevertheless, it took him only three days to write back: "We certainly want to publish Richard Wright's autobiography."[2] By early February 1944, Harper was already announcing a new book by Richard Wright: *American Hunger*, scheduled to appear in June.

Aswell asked for minor changes. He found the last third of the narrative, about Wright's experiences in the Communist Party in Chicago, slightly tedious and thought Wright should shorten it. To his mind, the ending of the book was too furious and abrupt. He was concerned about libel, and wanted Wright to change the names of all living people, the places he had worked at, the newspapers he had sold, and so on. He asked Wright to cut down the number of times he used the word "tension." And he thought the sex in the Memphis rooming-house scene should be less explicit.

Wright spent two weeks revising the manuscript, but balked when it came to shortening the Chicago section. "Maybe I'm too close to it," he told Aswell. "If you have any concrete ideas as to where something could be weeded out, I'd like very much to hear it."[3] He had tried to strengthen the ending, but it was still negative. "One thing is certain, I cannot step outside of the mood rendered there and say something without its sounding false."

Once again, Aswell accepted Wright's scant revisions. A lawyer went through the manuscript for libel, defamation, and obscenity. Were Wright's parents likely to cause any trouble? she queried. She presumed there was no chance of suit by the cook who spat in the soup? She thought certain passages were likely to provoke the criticism of anti-Semitism. Most of all, she was concerned about Wright's description of the Chicago Communist leader Harry Haywood. Even though Wright had changed his name to Buddy Nealson, the real-life man was readily identifiable by those who knew him, and the portrait was highly libelous.[4]

EARLY IN JANUARY 1944 WRIGHT RECEIVED ANOTHER DRAFT NOTICE AND FEARED he was about to go into the army. On his registration form he wrote a passionate protest statement about fighting in a Jim Crow army.

> In compliance with law, I am reporting for induction into the armed services of my country, under conditions which I consider excruciatingly degrading and humiliating. For 300 years America's national policy toward her suppressed colored population has been postulated upon the assumption that Negroes are an inferior people. I reject that assumption and its application in terms of Jim Crow rules and regulations in the armed forces.
>
> The segregated units and quarters for Negroes in the armed forces violate my instincts and feelings to the degree that I feel that to serve in our armed forces is to fight in defense of such a system and to give my approval to it. And it is to make known my emphatic rejection to that that I make this statement.

I shall, therefore, render military service passively, obeying all orders automatically, strictly observing the letter of the law and obeying all demands made upon me, yet fervently hoping that any military action in which I shall be engaged and which shall extend this loathsome system of racial hate and segregation will fail, even though I shall fall before the fire of the enemy in such engagements.

I make this statement as an individual, speaking for no group or political party, and I stand willing and ready to accept any and all consequences flowing from it. . . . I am weak and the government is strong enough to compel me to do that which is against my will and judgment, but no power on earth can compel me to approve that which I deem unjust and morally fraudulent.[5]

Within a week or so, the Brooklyn Draft Board gave Wright a 4F classification. This disqualified him, at least for the time being, from the armed forces.[6] The reason given was "psychoneurosis." A note in Wright's FBI file reads: "It appeared from Subject's contacts with his Local Board that his interest in the problem of the Negro has become almost an obsession."[7]

THE GALLEY PROOFS OF *AMERICAN HUNGER* WERE READY BY MID-MAY, AND ASWELL sent them off to the Book-of-the-Month Club. Two weeks later, the judges told Aswell they were very interested in the manuscript. In an interview ten years later, Dorothy Canfield Fisher claimed that she and her colleagues selected the book "without any qualms or uncertainties."[8]

Her memory was not good. The fact is, Canfield Fisher and her colleagues liked *some* of the manuscript. They liked the first three hundred pages, the part called "Southern Night," about Wright's formative years in the South. They did not like the last 150 pages, called "The Horror and the Glory," set in Chicago—a passionate indictment of Northern racism and also the Communist Party.

If Wright were prepared to drop the Chicago section, the judges told Aswell, they would consider the part called "Southern Night." They did not like the title *American Hunger*. Clifton Fadiman, who had recently replaced Heywood Broun on the judging panel, came up with the innocuous suggestion: *First Chapter*. They wanted one particularly lewd passage deleted.⁹ And if Wright agreed to end the narrative when he left the South, he would need a new conclusion. Fadiman suggested that he write a kind of summary of his feelings about the Jim Crow South and what it meant to him to be going North. Canfield Fisher wondered if Wright could make his flight from South to North sound more positive. Could he not use the word "hope"?

Perhaps Aswell managed to persuade Wright that "The Horror and the Glory" did not absolutely fit with the first part of the narrative and that the book worked best as a record of childhood and youth. He assured Wright that Harper would incorporate the Chicago section into some future book.¹⁰ Whether or not he hesitated, Wright consented to the shorter book. He agreed that some sort of new ending would be necessary if the book finished earlier. Privately, he had no intention of imbuing it with hope. That went against the whole thrust of his book. Going North had *not* resolved his problems as a black American. Far from it.

Originally the section called "Southern Night" had ended with Wright stepping from the elevator into the street, wondering whether his plan to leave that night for the North was a dream. The stark final sentences read: "This was the culture from which I sprang. This was the terror from which I fled." Now, Wright ended the book on the train heading north. "I was running more away from something than toward something," he wrote. He did insert the word "hope," but not in the upbeat way Canfield Fisher had in mind. "In the main, my hope was merely a kind of self-defense, a conviction that if I did not leave I would perish."

He sent the new ending to Aswell. "I think that this rounds out the first section and also hints at more to come. Now that we've gone to such lengths, I hope this turns out all right and I hope that others think that this fills the bill."¹¹

Four days later, Wright received a closely typed two-page letter from Canfield Fisher.¹² She asked him to explore further his question: "What was it that made me conscious of possibilities?" Wright's answer had been books. Canfield Fisher insisted: weren't they, at least partly, *American* books? "Could it be," she prompted him, "that even from inside the prison of injustice, through the barred windows of that

Bastille of racial oppression, Richard Wright had caught a glimpse of the American flag?"

She hoped Wright would listen to "an elderly woman writing to a young man" about a "troublingly delicate matter." She assured him that some white Americans "have done what they could to lighten the dark stain of racial discrimination in our nation."

> To receive in the closing pages of your book, one word of recognition for this aspiration, if it were possible for you to give such recognition honestly, would hearten all who believe in American ideals. We would never dream of asking it—we were told by our parents and have told our children never to ask for it.

Wright could not bring himself to express gratitude to white Americans. He toyed with some sentences and sent the revised ending back to her with a brief letter. "I fully understand the value of what you are driving at," he told her, "but, frankly, the narrative as it now stands simply will not support a more general or hopeful conclusion. The Negro who flees the South is really a refugee; he is so pinched and straitened in his environment that his leaving is more an avoidance than an embrace." What he had written, he insisted, was "factually right" and "emotionally right."[13]

Canfield Fisher wrote again. "I gather than you cannot bring yourself to use, even once, the word 'American' in speaking of 'the tinge of warmth which came from an unseen light.' . . . Was it only in Russian, and British or French fiction that you found anything to give you tidings from afar that there were human brothers of yours on the globe, who had ideals?" She finished: "I'm dictating this letter in rather a hurry, trying to catch the one mail out from our tiny village and may not be saying exactly what I mean. But I'm sure that with your sensitive ear you can catch the over-tone. I do hope you also catch the over-tone of my unwillingness to say too much about this."[14]

Wright was silent for ten days. Eventually a handwritten note arrived from Canfield Fisher. His silence made her "very uneasy," she confessed. "I'd never forgive myself if (in my own attempt to be honest) I had stepped beyond the line of permissible influence on a younger writer! Don't you put in a single word which is not from your heart!"

She had reason to be worried. Wright was an outspoken man. His public image was that of an uncompromising writer who said exactly what he thought. In one episode after another of *American Hunger*, Wright showed his determined resistance to any kind of individual or group pressure. The Book-of-the-Month Club was occasionally criticized for the enormity of its influence on American reading habits. What if it became known that the judges were not only *selecting* books for Americans, but also *modifying* them?

Her letter crossed with Wright's final draft. For the first time, he used the words "American" and "America"—but not at all as the glowing epithets that Canfield intended. He named some American writers—Dreiser, Masters, Mencken, Anderson, and Lewis—whose critical attitude toward "the straitened American environment" provided him with a "tinge of warmth from an unseen light."

To Aswell he did not conceal his impatience. "Enclosed is yet another copy of the end of the book. I really feel that this ought to do the thing."[15]

The day he heard that the Book-of-the-Month Club had at last voted for his book, Wright sat down and wrote Canfield Fisher a two-and-a-half-page letter. He thanked her for her concern, which he hoped would never die. He told her that as a writer, he was always open to other people's suggestions. When he created Bigger Thomas, he said, he had to steel himself to go against accepted ideas. "The average moral-minded American simply does not want to believe that his attitude toward others can breed personalities so thwarted and twisted."

He added: "I do not think that Negroes will be treated any better in this country until whites themselves realize that there is something dead wrong with the American way of life."[16]

I think it is significant that those American writers who influenced me were all rebels of a sort. Mencken was derived from Nietzsche; Dreiser was derived from Spencer and Marx; Anderson from Chekhov . . . I feel that these men could not have had any means to grasp the problems of our culture had they not availed themselves of the richer springs of thought found elsewhere. . . . (The Carnegie Corporation had to import a Swedish scientist, Gunnar Myrdal, to write the first honest and objective analysis of the Negro in our society.) . . . Personally, I've had to depend mainly upon outside influences for my view of myself and others in America.

Canfield Fisher wrote back: "The final version of your ending comes in, to give me the greatest satisfaction. You have *not* said a word beyond what you really felt and feel—I might have known you'd be incapable of that—the ending is a beautiful piece of writing and deeply full of meaning."[17]

A FEW DAYS LATER, ED ASWELL WIRED CANFIELD FISHER. "TITLE STILL UNSETTLED. Which do you prefer, 'American Hunger' or 'Southern Night' or 'First Chapter'?"[18]

"I prefer 'First Chapter,' " she wrote back, "but I think Wright himself and you should make decision as to title."[19]

Wright disliked "First Chapter"—a colorless title if ever there was one. He liked "Southern Night," the title he had originally given the section. But no one else did. Finally he came up with *Black Boy*. "Now, this is not very original," he told Aswell, "but I think it covers the book. It is honest. Straight. And many people say it to themselves when they see a Negro."[20] Aswell took the precaution of consulting the Book-of-the-Month Club judges. They liked it.

MORE THAN HALF A CENTURY LATER, WHAT ARE WE TO MAKE OF THE WAY THE Book-of-the-Month Club shaped its March 1945 best-seller? Was it censorship? Or was it a courageous promotion of a book that even after pruning remained outspoken? Was it insightful editorial intervention or was it gross interference? It contained elements of all of these things. For years, until Wright's correspondence with Canfield Fisher came to light, everyone assumed it was Ed Aswell who wanted the Chicago section cut. Aswell and Wright may have agreed it was best to leave this rumor undisturbed.

It has often been argued that cutting the Chicago section made *Black Boy* a better work of art. There is no doubt that over the decades the abridged version has been more widely read and better appreciated than the complete narrative would have been, with the flatly narrated account of Communist Party machinations in the Chicago

section. But the shortened *Black Boy* lessened the more serious challenge that Wright had intended in *American Hunger*.

Black Boy has, traditionally, been seen as a story of triumph. Although
Wright avoided the subtitle "autobiography," the narrative has always
carried that status. Readers have seen the abyss between the tormented
protagonist and the best-selling author he became as evidence that the
American Dream is real. This was scarcely the point Wright wanted to
make.

The last talk Richard Wright would ever give, in November 1960, at
the American Church in Paris, was about compromise. It was called
"The Position of the Negro Artist and Intellectual in American Society."
In it, he claimed that "all Negro artists or intellectuals have in them an
inevitable and functional streak of cynicism." It stemmed, he said, from
the Negro intellectual's "dependent status" in American society. "We
know that our artistic projections cannot be sold or favorably regarded
if they clash too violently with the prevailing white norms of the society in which we live." It was a lesson he had learned—twice over—
from the Book-of-the-Month Club.

RUMORS HAD STARTED TO CIRCULATE ABOUT WRIGHT'S FORTHCOMING ESSAY, "I
Tried to Be a Communist," billed to appear in two installments in the
August and September issues of *Atlantic Monthly*.[22] It appeared that
Wright was about to cut his ties, very publicly, with the Communist Party.

On 28 July, in anticipation, Wright issued a press statement from
Paul Reynolds's office. He told the *New York Herald Tribune* he had
left the Communist Party, unofficially, back in 1940. "I had my way of
expressing my conception of Negro experience in my writing. I
thought it would be of value to them. They had their ideas of how I
should react as a Communist. There was an irreconcilable gap." He
was, of course, thinking of the Party's reaction to *Native Son*. He also
pointed out that during the war the Communist position on the American Negro had undergone "a distinct and lamentable regression." Communists, Wright summed up, were "narrow-minded, bigoted, intolerant,
and frightened of new ideas which don't fit into their own."[23]

A telephone conversation tapped by the FBI reveals that Ben Davis,
for one, was horrified by Wright's statement. "It's terrible!" he told his
unidentified Communist friend "It escaped our forces on the paper."[24]

The Party, already nonplussed by the defection of black members during the war, asked Davis to make a statement supporting the Party's position. Ben Davis duly berated Wright for his "wholly unjustifiable attack upon the Communists." Wright had accused the Party of intolerance when it came to his writing, but, Davis pointed out, the Party had not taken an official position on *Native Son*. In a spirit of free discussion, some members had given it the highest praise, and others had rejected it. "However, Wright sulked and chafed at all criticism; and rejected it all," wrote Davis. "Who was intolerant in this case, Wright or the Communists?" Davis called Wright's assertions about the Party's position on Negro rights "ridiculously uniformed."[25]

Wright could not resist answering Ben Davis—indirectly. Horace Cayton, who wrote a regular column in the *Pittsburgh Courier*, agreed that Wright could write the column in his name. Wright's provocative statement was signed by Cayton.

> It is curious that Communists have not yet grappled with Wright's extensive statement of his experiences with them which appeared in the *Atlantic Monthly*, where Wright calls into public question the whole Communist relation to the Negro people in America . . . Beyond the infantile name-calling that Ben Davis, the New York Negro Communist councilman, indulged in in a recent issue of the *Sunday Daily Worker*, there is silence.
>
> One wonders what Communists really believe today about the Negro. Without even an iota of apology, Ben Davis urges Negroes to donate blood to the jim crow blood banks. James Ford, who runs occasionally for the Vice-Presidency of the United States, has been in a fit of prolonged ecstasy over the War Department's film, "The Negro Soldier," a film which seeks, it seems, to create the impression among white people in America that the Negroes do not bitterly resent discrimination and segregation in the armed forces. . . .
>
> When the history of the Communist relationship to the Negro during this war is written . . . Communists will have a lot to answer for.[26]

It provoked a furious rejoinder from Ben Davis, who tried to belittle Horace Cayton and his "world-shaking little typewriter."[27]

Wright's provocative press statement was—as the Communists guessed—a mere appetizer. His *Atlantic Monthly* essay, "I Tried to Be a

Communist" (extracted from the section of *American Hunger* the Book Club had suppressed), described his experiences in Chicago Communist circles—the inside squabbles, the slavish obedience to the Moscow line, the hostility to independent-minded individuals. Wright was so angry that only the libel laws stopped him from naming names. Over the next decade, the disillusioned voices of ex-Communists would become more common—fashionable even. In 1944 this bitter essay by Richard Wright was one of the first.[28]

"In a peculiar sense, life had trapped me in a realm of emotional rejection," Wright had written in his new conclusion to *Black Boy*, when thinking about the effect of the South on his character. It was a perceptive insight into himself. His picture of the Communist Party was not balanced. He wrote with the righteous anger of a betrayed lover.

Wright knew that his essay would have major repercussions. It was well known that leaving the Party—or worse, being expelled—could break people. He did not know which of his Party friends would remain on speaking terms with him or who would turn away when they passed him in the street. He was aware that he would be accused of treachery, cowardice, and treason. (Ted Ward was just one former friend who considered Wright's essay "a piece of despicable betrayal.")[29]

But Wright felt at home in an embattled world. He was delighted to be leaving the Party at a triumphant moment in his career. With *Black Boy* as a Book-of-the-Month Club selection, the Communists would not be able to say, as they liked to: "See, he left us and he is drowning!"[30]

IN MID-AUGUST 1944, WHILE NEW YORK WAS SUFFERING ONE OF THE WORST HEAT-waves on record, Richard, Ellen, and Julia Wright took the train to Canada. They were looking into the possibility of buying a house in the Canadian countryside—"a farm," Wright told a friend, "where perhaps we could, with the help of a farmer tenant, cultivate farm products with a view toward sustaining ourselves."[31]

Even in Montreal, they briefly encountered 100-degree heat. They had booked accommodation on a farm outside Montreal, but when they got there, Ellen found the place "too crummy for living," Wright told Ellison.[32] They left for Ottawa, where Wright went along to see his friends at the Canadian film board, located in an old sawmill by the river. John Grierson, the Scottish director, had just returned from a month in war-torn England and France, but no offer of work was forthcoming.

For almost three weeks the Wrights stayed in a cottage on Lake Meech, in the mountainous Gatineau country, just outside of Ottawa. Wright liked to row two-year-old Julia around on the clear blue lake. They swam and went for walks. "I'll hate to leave here," he told Ed Aswell. "Racoons [sic] come up to the door. Bass can be actually seen in the lake nearby. And all the books I brought along to read are unread."[33]

Black people were rare in Quebec, and Wright was something of an object of curiosity, but he sensed no racial prejudice. He felt comfortable with the Canadians. They seemed to him calmer than Americans, and he was struck by the honesty of the storekeepers. Like the Mexicans, Canadians looked upon the United States with a "cold eye," he wrote to Canfield Fisher. "It is rather startling to hear the nation as a whole discussed in realistic terms by foreigners."[34]

While Wright enjoyed the tranquillity of Gatineau, his article "I Tried to Be a Communist" caused an uproar at home. Ralph Ellison found himself once again sending clippings from the Communist press. Robert Minor (pointing out that Wright described a "Jewish Chap" as having "hanging lips and bulging eyes") accused him of gross anti-Semitism.[35] James Ford, in an article entitled "The Case of Richard Wright: A Disservice to the Negro People," wrote that Wright had never identified with his people; he had always been aloof. ("Wright's shameful manner of writing about Negroes is disgusting and damaging to their dignity.") And now Wright had struck a bargain with those who had "an anti-Communist axe to grind."[36]

Letters and phone calls flooded in. James Farrell, who had been so scathing about the Communist message in *Native Son*, sent congratulations to Wright and hoped they could meet for a talk.[37] George S. Schuyler, the right-wing black journalist, praised Wright in the *Pittsburgh Courier*.[38]

Wright told Ralph Ellison: "Now it is over, I feel a great sense of freedom. I'm greatly relieved. Believe me."[39]

AND THE FBI? HOW DID THE FEDERAL BUREAU OF INVESTIGATION REACT TO THE most prominent black Communist writer in the United States publicly denouncing Communism?

Just before the scandal blew up, an FBI internal memorandum recommended that Wright be put on the Security Index, the list of key individuals considered most dangerous, potentially, to the nation's stability.[40]

After the *Atlantic Monthly* essay appeared, the New York Field Division sent a telegram to J. Edgar Hoover in Washington. Now that Wright had left the Party, they were thinking of a discreet interview with him. A few days later, Hoover wrote back: "It would seem that Wright does not think the Communist Political Association revolutionary enough at the present time with respect to the advancement of the Negro. This should be considered seriously prior to any action on your part."[41] He evidently doubted that Wright would be useful as an informer.

The FBI concluded that a man who had left the Communist Party because it was not militant enough on the Negro question should certainly be on the Security Index. It was agreed that the New York office would stay closely on his case.

"GOSH, WHEN ARE THEY GOING TO BRING OUT *BLACK BOY*?" WRIGHT WAILED AT the end of November 1944.[42] He had submitted the manuscript almost a year previously. Originally, the book was to appear in June. Until the Book-of-the-Month Club decided on the month for selection, the galleys were simply sitting in Aswell's office.

"It is in the lap of the gods," Aswell wrote back early in December. "At the last meeting in November, they selected the book for February. At the meeting this month, they will pick the March book."[43]

In mid-December, the Book-of-the-Month Club judges finally selected *Black Boy* for March 1945. Just as they had done with *Native Son,* they had delayed publication by seven months. Once again, they made it a dual selection—along with Glenway Wescott's novel *Apartment in Athens.*

Dorothy Canfield Fisher would review the book in the February 1945 *Book-of-the-Month Club News.* She went to considerable trouble with the review, eager to promote a book she thought deserving of attention. Richard Wright, she asserted, was "one of the most accomplished and gifted of our younger American authors." She thought it lamentable that he felt caution toward *all* whites—many of whom

were "trying to open the door of decent opportunity to colored people." As if writing a secret message to Wright himself, she had special
praise for the conclusion they had dueled over with such gracious but
stubborn ferocity:

> In the last pages he sweeps his readers out from the concrete and defi-
> nite, with their crushing weight of literal fact, into a spacious realm of
> thought, poetry, beauty, and understanding. . . . He quiets his deeply
> troubled spirit—ours with his—by drawing a long breath under the
> open sky of the universal.

Her words would surely have irritated Wright. He had never
intended his book to quieten anyone's spirit. That was precisely why he
had put his foot down as much as he had, risking Canfield Fisher's disapproval and placing the book's selection in jeopardy.

ONCE AGAIN, THERE WERE BIG REWARDS FOR AGREEING TO MAKE CHANGES.
Wright could anticipate a considerable income early in the new year
from advance sales of *Black Boy,* and Aswell also gave him a seventy-
five-hundred-dollar advance for his next novel, *Black Hope.* This was
quite an increase on the four hundred dollars he had received for
Native Son. The Wrights decided to buy a house.[44] Earlier that year,
their landlord at Lefferts Place had tried to raise the rents dramatically.
Wright had organized a successful rent strike, but he and Ellen had
enough of landlords. Paul Reynolds agreed with him that real estate
was the thing to buy to escape inflation. He also suggested postponing
the *Black Hope* advance payment until the new tax year, even offering
to tide Wright over, if he needed it, with an interest-free personal loan.
Wright did not need the loan, but he appreciated Reynolds's business
acumen and generosity.

Occasionally Wright decided that he was sick of "stone and steel" and
the hectic pace of city life. He and Ellen would go and inspect a piece of
land in the country, and then he would remember his childhood, when
he had been scared and hungry, and he would tell himself he was happier with the anonymity of a big city. Acting on both impulses, he had
put in bids for both a 241-acre farm in northern Vermont and a three-
story brownstone house at 13 Charles Street in Greenwich Village.

"Why should I live in a black belt area and be cheated like all other Negroes are cheated?" he wrote in his journal. "Why cannot I live where there are good schools for Julia, and stores that carry good food at reasonable prices; why should I live in a black belt and pay a premium for being born black! I'll be damned if I'll do it!"[45]

To buy in the Village, he and Ellen had to think up a scheme to get past the vendor, the real estate agents, the banks, the current tenants, and the neighbors. Their lawyer, Jacob Salzman, told them that no bank in Greenwich Village would give a Negro a mortgage, for fear the neighbors would make it unpleasant for the bank. They could not buy the house in Ellen's name: as a couple they were too well known, and a woman purchaser was an object of suspicion anyway. So they set up a corporation—the "Richelieu Company." Wright was the faceless man behind the corporation.

For weeks, he and Ellen were anxious and tense. Would they get away with it? Would they be able to live where they wanted to live?

THE LAST DAY OF THE OLD YEAR, 1944, DISAPPEARED WITH A SPECTACULAR CRASH. Horace Cayton was staying at the Wrights' apartment for a few days, and Wright invited Michael Carter, a sociologist and newspaperman, to join them for lunch. Carter, who worked for the *Brooklyn Eagle,* was the only black journalist in the country to be employed by a white newspaper.[46]

The three men set off to Joe's, the most famous restaurant in downtown Brooklyn. Carter had been there before, with white journalist friends. They wondered a little apprehensively whether they would be segregated.

Wright described the episode later in his journal.[47] They walked in the door and everyone stared. They strolled to a table, trying to look as though they did this every day. The waiter took their order. People continued to stare. "I suppose they're going to say something to the proprietor when they leave. But, fuck 'em."

Wright started to talk to his companions fast and nervously, expounding his "old thesis" that fear was the dominant emotion in Negro life. A woman at a nearby table did not stop gaping. "That white bitch is staring at me . . . as though I were a dog, a cat; and she turns aside only when I stare back at her. If she were young, I'd sicken her by winking; but, hell, she's ugly!" Wright got his table companions to admit they were in a constant state of fear of white people. ("We knew that it was rare for Negroes to admit this simple fact.")

Wright was pleased with his Italian ravioli. They drank martinis. The waiter passed by, frantically busy. While he served a table of whites, he deposited a pile of dirty dishes on the black men's table, near the edge. "All three of us morbidly sensitive niggers saw that. . . . That damn white waiter would not have placed those dishes on any other table but ours."

"I don't like that," Carter said. He pulled at his pipe. He told them he had a mind to push the dishes off the table. Cayton was aghast. Wright half egged him on. "You wouldn't," he said. He added: "I have compulsions like that too, sometimes." Cayton asked Wright what he meant. Carter said: "I'm going to do it, goddamn!" Slowly, surreptitiously, his brown hand pushed the pile of dishes toward the edge. There was an almighty crash. "I had to do it," he said.

The white-faced waiter came running up, appalled. He stared at Carter as long as he dared. "You were careless," Carter said offhandedly. "You balanced them on the edge." The waiter told him excitedly they couldn't have fallen. But he checked himself and picked up the pieces. He did not want to prolong this public spectacle.

"Tell me what you felt," Wright said to Carter after the waiter disappeared.

"Just hate before I pushed 'em," said Carter.

And after?

"Pain in my legs, nausea, fear, tension, but I'm all right."

Wright went home to help Ellen prepare for their New Year's party. The others were joining them later.

17

DAILY LIFE

January 1945–April 1945

For three and a half months, from 1 January to 19 April 1945, Wright kept a journal. Often he made several entries a day. He was restless, nervous. On his desk were advance copies of *Black Boy*, his second Book-of-the-Month Club selection. The publication date was 1 March. It was a deeply personal book, and traditionally black folks kept their business to themselves. How would people respond?

On the first afternoon of the New Year, he had organized a meeting in his Brooklyn apartment with Horace Cayton and St. Clair Drake, both sociologists, and Lawrence Reddick, curator of the Schomburg Center, in Harlem. They were planning a collection of essays called *The Negro Speaks*.[1] That evening, Wright typed in his journal:

> My mind is just about made up that I'm going to stop work on this idea for a Negro symposium. Negroes are so, each and all, caught and held in the vise of their fear about race relations, that they cannot meet and talk to each other. They are like a bunch of worms all tied up together, each seeking to suck nourishment from the other.

St. Clair Drake had insisted that they must write out of a "body of knowledge." He wanted scientific accuracy; he disliked general statements about "the Negro." Wright had protested. Surely one could generalize that the English were a seafaring people? Drake disagreed. Not all Englishmen go to sea. And what was an "Englishman," anyway?

> I stared; I seem to be listening to the talk of an insane man. . . . Finally it became impossible to talk to Drake and it slowly dawned upon me that scientific integrity was not what he was really trying to protect; that he was fighting against a certain view of life that was painful to him as a Negro. . . . It's quite clear that Drake's fierce rejection of art, of intuitive perception, of emotion, is his way of getting away from a hard real world. . . . He wants to dodge what [being] a Negro means.

That evening, Wright took Horace Cayton to meet his friend Dorothy Norman at her house on East Seventieth Street. In the subway he told Cayton that she wrote a regular column in the *New York Post* and edited a journal, *Twice a Year*, which focused on civil liberties and the arts. She was Jewish, wealthy, married, with two children. He had met her the previous year at a party for Theodore Dreiser.

> We arrive and at once poor Horace is floored, for Dorothy's home is rich and beautiful. Dorothy comes in and Horace is startled. Here is beauty and brains. . . . Horace begins to talk; he is excited. . . . He . . . became slightly drunk. He sailed into Dorothy, wanting to know why was she concerned about Negroes, what insecurities did she have?[2]
>   . . . I sat and listened with mounting horror while a Negro asked questions of a rich white woman that no white man would have dared ask. And the white woman, poised and full of wisdom, with a smile and clenched fingers, calmly recited the history of her life. I wanted to yell, Stop!

THE NEXT DAY, ELLEN TOOK JULIA TO NURSERY SCHOOL WHILE WRIGHT STAYED IN bed. His foot was swollen and sore. A new maid came to clean. She

clutched a large Bible. "Ellen and the maid seem not at first to understand each other; I put my two cents in and coddle Ellen into letting the
maid stay, I trush d that black Bible she carried with her."

He roused Cayton, made ham and eggs for breakfast, and they
talked for three hours. After he walked Cayton to the subway, Wright
fetched the afternoon papers from the corner store. A group of Negroes
was discussing the war. The papers were full of the German attacks on
the Western Front. There was talk of the draft being extended to 4Fs.

Ellen brought home a small beef roast. After dinner, they dismantled
the Christmas tree. "Oh, God, won't the Julia baby be disappointed. I
worry about Julia's excessive activity. My little daughter is so tense, so
eager; it stabs me to see her."

IN THE EVENING OF 3 JANUARY, MICHAEL CARTER AND HIS WIFE, EDWINA, CAME
around. Carter showed Wright the profile on him he had just written for
the *Afro-American*. Wright cut a sentence that described his lifestyle as
"lavish." Carter himself admitted it was not true. Wright retorted that
lying seemed to be part of being a journalist.

They found themselves talking about Communism. It was not the
ideas that were wrong, they agreed; it was the people who ran the
show. The Carters, too, had once been close to the Party.

Wright's foot became excruciatingly painful. Everyone in the room
started guessing what it might be. Carter thought it was probably gout.
His wife, who was a nurse, agreed. Maybe he had heart trouble, Carter
suggested. Wright was not amused. Eventually, Carter suggested calling
his own doctor, a Russian Jew. Wright asked whether he was a Party
man. Carter said no. "Thank God!" Wright said.

Ellen was disgusted that Wright should ask such a question. "You
can trust any doctor," she said. "They have ethics." Wright was not convinced. "I always have the feeling that a party doctor might just give me
something to finish me off," he wrote in his journal.

The doctor arrived and everyone stood up to look while he examined Wright's foot. Wright suddenly became irritated. "A man has a right
to see his doctor alone, if he wants it; the doctor said so too. I compromised, letting Ellen remain and telling the rest to get into another room.
They did."

The doctor said the right instep had been bruised—probably by Wright's shoes. He prescribed rest and hot compresses.

ON 4 JANUARY, ELLEN CAME HOME WITH SOME THICK WOOLEN SOCKS SHE HAD managed to find downtown. Wright was delighted. Wool was scarce these days. And they were a bargain—sixty-nine cents a pair.

Salzman phoned to say the Vermont property deal did not appear to be coming off. The owner, Mrs. Watkins, was unable to organize a clear title. She apparently could not prove that her husband, who died fighting in the Spanish civil war, was dead.

Dorothy Norman, a member of the India League of America, was holding an afternoon tea for Mrs. Pandit, the sister of Nehru. Wright was sure he would not like her. "I don't get much out of meeting Easterners," he wrote. "There's something lacking in them." He told himself that Westerners might be tense and neurotic, but Easterners were "bland" and "unsalted."

That evening, at 8 P.M., he was back home, writing in his journal. Dorothy Norman's drawing room had been full of fashionable people— New York artists and intellectuals and Indians.

> The Hindus present were soft, flaccid, with no passion and no drive. They were beautiful, with tinted skins, flowing black hair and indescribable eyes. But beauty does not free people from British rule, and never will. . . .
>
> Tonight I put the question: Why is there not a greater spirit of the West in India? And right off they stared at me. . . . Well, I'm an American; and I'm not ashamed of it. I'm Western to the core, with all of the faults and weaknesses of a Western man. Do you want us to kill? they railed at me. Engage in senseless competition? . . .
>
> I argued back. . . . Can't you see that the great, powerful industrial states set the tone and condition of living in this world? . . . We rebels here do not understand this business of nonviolence. . . . Each and every Indian ought to learn how to make gunpowder in his kitchen just like a girl learning to cook.

WRIGHT HAD PUT ASIDE *BLACK HOPE* AGAIN AND WAS ANXIOUS TO MAKE PROGRESS with a new novel, *The Jackal*, about a gang of Harlem delinquents. He had spent several days in the children's court in Brooklyn, and had visited Wiltwyck School—a facility for wayward Harlem boys at the foot of the Catskills. One of the black psychiatrists there had talked to him at length about the psychology of delinquency. Wright's friend Dr. Frederic Wertham wanted to set up a free psychiatric clinic in Harlem, with a focus on adolescents. Wright was doing his best to help.[3]

January 6:

Times Square is fabulous during the war. Painted women, fur coats! Jostling. Loud talking. Money flowing like water. Crowds in front of movie houses. My eyes catch sight of a black face now and then. And I feel grateful that I'm in the cold, impersonal North where the whites just pass you by and let you alone. . . . There's no place like New York.

On Sunday, 7 January, it was snowing. When Wright went out to fetch the papers he could not see the sky. Samuel Sillen's biting review of Steinbeck's *Cannery Row* in the *Sunday Worker* shocked him. He wondered why people so enjoyed attacking writers who happened to write a bad book.

Perhaps these people wanted once upon a time to write, and failing, they are glad to see what they feel is another failure and then they heap upon that writer's effort all of the hate and scorn they feel for themselves. Seems to me like folks ought to be kind of grateful for the writer who lives in the sweet agony of uncertainty and tries to wring out of himself something for them.

He watched Ellen play hide-and-seek with Julia. The little girl ran off to hide, called to her mother, then a curly head bobbed up, and Julia dissolved in laughter. She liked to hide in dark corners, Wright mused, or cover her head with the quilt. "Perhaps Freud would say that she is trying in play to find the womb."

He worked on *The Jackal*. The snow turned to driving sleet, and he listened to the scraping of shovels as neighbors cleared the sidewalk. He cursed the dinner they went to the previous evening at Ethol and Chef Kossa's house.[4] It left him tired and sapped his energy for writing.

Ralph Ellison phoned to tell him about the racial conflict on board various U.S. convoy ships. He was taking a nap when the phone rang again. It was Rose Poplowitz. As always with her, his voice immediately assumed a "sweet, purring, neutral tone." Ellen told him she always knew when he was speaking to her mother. According to her, he spoke with "false, hearty warmth." But he was firm about his compromises with her.

> Once my mother in law became a little carping about the way we ran our house, and I told Ellen to tell her to go home and stay there. There've never been any arguments between me and her family; I've put our relationship on a simple basis: either they come to the house and behave themselves or they stay away. They prefer to come and behave; as long as that lasts they are welcome, but the moment they cook up any monkey business, they'll get the gate. Ellen and I think of one accord about this. It works; there's peace and love in our home.

THE NEXT DAY, SNOW WAS DEEP ON THE GROUND. THE SKY WAS LEADEN. ELLEN decided not to take Julia to nursery school.

Salzman phoned. Their bid for the house on Charles Street had been turned down for the time being; the vendor wanted cash only. Salzman was trying to arrange a two-thirds cash settlement with a bank. "I'm discouraged," Wright wrote in his journal, "and so is poor little hoping sweet Ellen. I'll have to do something real soon about our moving to the Village. We've been talking about it for too long."

He worked on *The Jackal*, and in between dyed two pairs of woolen socks bright green. "They look rich! I feel proud over having gotten woolen socks at all, proud at having gotten them so cheap, and proud over having successfully dyed them a good, solid color."

An offer came over the phone: five thousand dollars for ghosting Joe Louis's memoirs. "I must say the prospect of meeting and knowing a guy like Joe Louis intrigues me no end. Of course, Paul Reynolds, my agent, would have the heebeegeebees. Shall I do it?"[5]

During the night he enjoyed the drip, drip of melting snow falling from the roof.

January 9:
Seven weeks stand between me and the publication of *Black Boy!*

On 12 January, Wright had lunch on Park Avenue at the house of Marshall Field, the philanthropist and owner of the *Chicago Sun*, reputed to be the world's fifth richest man.[6] In that luxurious Victorian apartment, over cocktails, lunch, and cigars, Wright listened to four hours of inane talk about race issues. The room contained a mixture of black people and white people. Everyone was well-dressed and well-mannered; voices never rose above an acceptable level, and nothing significant was said. He came home filled with the futility of it all.

THROUGHOUT SUNDAY, 14 JANUARY, IT SNOWED. THE FAMILY GOT UP LATE AND had a late breakfast. In the afternoon a twenty-two-year-old Japanese-American woman, Amy Tory, came around. Horace Cayton had asked them to look after her while she was in New York. She told the Wrights that when the Japanese attacked Pearl Harbor, her family was rounded up and sent to a concentration camp. Wright was struck that, though she looked different, she was in every way American.

Amy asked about Horace before she left, asked as innocently as any little love-struck girl would. What could I say? Horace is a man of the world, neurotic, restless; I don't really think that he's capable of being in love with anybody really; and now this innocent, oh so American little sweet Japanese girl wants to know if he will marry her. Well, I talked and talked and tried to explain what sort of man Horace was; I don't think I was successful.

That evening, Ellen went to a movie.

Julia was half-awake, listening to the janitor shoveling snow from in front of the apartment house. . . . I tucked the cover about her dear little head (hell, I must use language like that when talking about my only daughter) and sang out to her, Good Night, and she answered in a sleepy, throaty voice, Gooo-ooo-od Ni-iii-ghttt . . .

Salzman, the lawyer, phoned. Their cash bid of $17,500 for 13 Charles Street had been accepted. But there was a catch. Salzman was able to arrange part of a first mortgage (eight thousand dollars) without revealing Wright's identity to the bank, but he could not organize a second mortgage.

That night, 17 January, Richard and Ellen lay in bed and tried to think of ways to procure a loan of thirty-five hundred dollars. Wright could try to get another advance from Harper, but that would be mortgaging himself to them "hook and nose." He could sell his sales contract on the Chicago property, but that would mean losing a lot of money. He and Ellen were so tense they hardly slept.

The following day, Wright took the subway into Manhattan to see Paul Reynolds. His agent said he would like to be able to lend him the money, but he had a wife and children and what with the war, everything was up in the air. Wright said he would not dream of a personal loan. Reynolds decided that the only way out was to borrow from a bank and put up Wright's contracts with Harper as security. He went out to see his bank manager. Wright waited in the office. He was hungry and did not have any cigarettes. An hour went by.

Eventually Reynolds came back and said he could get a bank loan, but Wright would have to pay it back at the rate of $150 a month. This would reduce his regular income to $290 a month. "Can you live on that?" he asked.

Wright bit his pencil. "I'll risk it."

"Well, you always have extra items coming in," Reynolds said.

Wright signed various papers and felt as if he was signing away his life.

I rush home; it is late now, almost five o'clock. . . . I call Ellen from the street and she comes running down. Julia is playing in the snow with her shovel and she is too busy to know that I'm trying to buy her a house. Ellen comes running and I kiss her, and say, "I got it!" The whole amount? Yes, darling. She is so happy! Yet she gets terribly tense, too. We go upstairs and prepare dinner; poor little Ellen darling is so happy and tense that she is developing a headache. I make her take a couple of aspirins. I too am tense.

January 21:

Good Lord, how my moods do change! This gloomy but sunlit afternoon I've been wondering how I can ditch the literary life and start anew at something else. I've had this yearning many times. . . . I wish I could make films. Or engage in some sort of government work. I know that as long as I live in the United States, I can never change my profession, for I'm regarded fatally as a Negro writer, that is, as a writer whose ancestors were Negroes and therefore the Negro is my special field. . . . Yet, frankly, I don't know what I can do other than write. And I was only this morning thinking of doing a long series of novels. Clearly I want to get out of America; maybe that's why I keep thinking of a new profession, for I know that I could not write in another language. But maybe I'll find a compromise by going to live in a foreign country and writing for the American market.

A LETTER ARRIVED FROM ELLEN'S BROTHER, MARTIN, STATIONED IN PEARL HARBOR, announcing he was going to marry a Japanese girl. Wright was pleased. "The more mixtures the better!" His mother-in-law did not share his view. "She called right after dinner and, although I sat on the other side of the room reading the evening's papers, I could hear her hysterical cries coming wild and metallic over the wires." Rose Poplowitz wanted Ellen to write to her brother and urge him to abandon the idea. Ellen refused.

With all the advance publicity it was now widely known that Wright had married a white woman. A Southern black woman wrote to him that he had set a bad example. He ought to have married a colored woman—"there are all shades among us"—and shared his wealth with his own race.

"I did not marry a white woman," he retorted in his journal on 17 January. "I married the woman I loved. . . . I live but once on this earth and I'll be damned if I'll live according to some narrow and crazy race doctrine."[7]

He got a letter from the editors of *Negro Digest*. They feared they might be "stepping into a hornet's nest," but they had written to a number of leading Negroes married to white women, asking both partners for brief statements on the subject: "Does Interracial Marriage Succeed?"[8]

Wright did not reply. His private life was nobody's business. But he had begun a play, called *Sacrifice*, based on the most famous interracial marriage in Harlem.

The black newspaperman George S. Schuyler had married a Southern belle from Texas. Josephine was known for her view that the white race was "spiritually depleted" and that "America must mate with the Negro to save herself."[9] She had always touted their musically gifted daughter as a genius, a model of "hybrid vigor." At thirteen, Philippa Schuyler was famous throughout black America as a composer and concert pianist. It was also widely known in Harlem that the girl suffered from bad nerves and depression.

Like everyone else, Wright was horrified by the way the white woman seemed to be making her daughter into a sacrificial lamb for her own dubious doctrines. His play would end with the daughter committing suicide.

Horace Cayton wrote to Wright that he had given the subject of intermarriage considerable thought. "I think some of the things that I found out about myself might prove interesting to you in view of the piece you are eventually going to do on Schuyler. . . .You can show the guilt involved in such a marriage on the part of both persons which accounts for the motivation they had to make a genius out of the child."[10]

February 6:

Yesterday I went down to Charles Street and walked several times in front of number 13, where we plan to move. I like the neighborhood but don't know if it will like my black skin. But I'm going to live there, come hell and high water. Why should I not live there?

In the evening, Wright gave a speech at Columbia University. He told himself that the $120 fee would help toward his repayment.

February 7:

Still tired. Oh, why do I work myself into such a lather when I have to make a speech. I used to speak a lot and was not so tense about it. Maybe four or five lectures will make me all right. I hope so.

Wright wrote to his brother, Leon, and mailed him a package of clothes. While in a bookstore, he picked up a copy of Mencken's *Prejudices* and dipped into it again.

I recall, as I read him, the exact spot and time in Memphis when I first read the book. Oh how glad I am that I'm not down there now. I must be a lucky guy, sure. To think that I'm not running errands for some sadistic son of a bitch southern white. . . .

February 14:

Went to Harpers to meet Ed Aswell. I was howled over to see copies of *Black Boy* ready. It is a beautiful book, slender, modern-looking, and with a good binding. It is strange that when reality comes true you cannot think of what to say; the moment fails; the look of things remains the same . . . you strain to feel what it is that you dreamed. . . . At heart I feel it is better to strive than to realize. It seems that I like forlorn hopes and causes.

On 16 February, advance copies of the book were sent out to readers.

I fell asleep thinking that *Black Boy* was out over the land, that people were reading about my life, about how I grew up, about how I felt and feel. It was a strange feeling.

HARPER & BROTHERS HAD SPENT FOURTEEN THOUSAND DOLLARS ON PUBLICITY. A week before publication, there was a cocktail party for Wright at the home of Frank MacGregor, the head of Harper. Everyone predicted the book would do well.

March 1:

Whee, what a tense day! But one really does manage to get through these days. The sun is clear and the sky is high and blue. A change in the weather is welcome. . . .

Well, the house is bought! . . . Ellen came in last night, after I had got ten Little One from the nursery, all tired and tense. She could barely tell me what happened. She was startled at what buying a house meant, the men involved, and how they acted. . . . But she finally said that it was over. We are now the owners of 13 Charles Street, New York City! . . .

Aunt Maggie wrote a special delivery to say that *LIFE* men had been down in Jackson, Miss. all week. But they could not get anything out of the family. She warns me not to come South to see them, as it will not be safe for me. There will no doubt rise against me in the South some wild hate. Hope they don't bother my folks. But what will the folks say when they know what I've written about them.

ON 5 MARCH WRIGHT SPENT THE DAY PREPARING HIMSELF FOR THE LIVE EVENING radio program *The Author Meets the Critics*. The program had a reputation for being something akin to bearbaiting.

The broadcast began with an argument between the two white critics Sterling North and Lewis Gannett. North made the comment that the book displayed exquisite Negro speech rhythms throughout. Gannett said this was "pure nonsense and condescension." North retorted that maybe Gannett did not "know the right kind of Negro." Wright's benevolent rolling laugh covered up the titters from the audience. Then he spoke.

Afterwards, hundreds of letters flooded in to the radio station. Wright probably did not read them all, but one listener, Tanya Kaagan, reflected the common view:

Dear Sir,

I listened with but average interest to Sterling North and Lewis Gannett thinking, "Oh, another book on the Negro-White problem. I know all about it." Then Richard Wright spoke and I realized I had never really understood the problem, nor the Negro, nor ourselves in this connection.

The author was dynamic; all logic without, all fire inside. He completely paled all other speakers. I could not bear for him to be interrupted. Here was courage and daring! Here was truth. He is bound to do great things for he has the gift to inspire. Listening to him, I wanted to know him, to help him, to fight for his people. I want to hear all he has to say and read all he will write. Truly, I cannot wait to read his *Black Boy*.[11]

THE REVIEWS OF *BLACK BOY* WERE GENERALLY POSITIVE. SOME CRITICS FOUND THE book admirably objective and restrained; others thought it lacked balance.

W. E. B. Du Bois, who had praised *Native Son* and *12 Million Black Voices*, found the picture "terribly overdrawn." He thought the young protagonist "a loathsome brat." Why did the Negroes in the book have "almost no redeeming qualities"? Why was there not "a single broad-minded, open-hearted white person in his book"? It seemed to Du Bois that Wright was incapable of empathy—"even with his own parents."[12]

Several reviewers were disconcerted by the book's "bitterness." Horace Cayton commented in Dorothy Norman's journal, *Twice a Year*: "That a Negro should be bitter about his treatment in America shocks white Americans to their moral depth. . . . America is a moral nation and wants to feel that it is good, decent, and fair. To be confronted with the fact that a group of people hate, even though these people have been outraged, creates a feeling of guilt."[13]

In a marvelous tribute, "Richard Wright's Blues," Ralph Ellison suggested that Wright had imbibed the influence of his own culture more than he recognized. His narrative was like the blues. The blues, after all, were "an autobiographical chronicle of personal catastrophe expressed lyrically." He added: "Their attraction lies in this, that they at once express both the agony of life and the possibility of conquering it through sheer toughness of spirit."[14]

BY 10 MARCH WRIGHT WAS SICK AGAIN. IT BEGAN WITH A BAD HEADACHE AND soon became a fever. He called it "grippe." The doctor gave him sulfur (which Wright thought made him even weaker) and told him not to get out of bed in case he caught pneumonia. For days Wright lay in a kind of haze, plagued by a "dragging, gnawing sensation" in the small of his back. Julia was coughing. Ellen was tired, and he dared not call her for help.

The mail was heavy: letters from fans, requests for interviews, requests to speak, invitations to parties, congratulatory letters from friends. (Some were from Communists who had refused to speak to him until now.) Wright also had to write reports on several books for the Book-of-the-Month Club. For a whole week, he did not venture out of the house. Finally, he got up and staggered off for a haircut.

March 19:

Tried to take a nap, but could not sleep. Ellen is working on my scrap-book. I put the roast on to cook. Ellen went for Julia and I cooked the rest of the dinner. . . . Ellen came with Julia and then I felt so sick I could not eat. Ellen thought that I was angry about something. She does not yet realize really that I'm sick, it seems. She thought better of it and was sorry. I was sorry too for my weakness made me raise my voice.

Wright was trying to organize a cottage for the summer. A publisher friend told him about Dr. Frank Safford and his wife, who owned a summer artist colony at Wading River, Long Island. On 3 April, he went to see them.

I found them nice people; we sat and talked and drank. . . . I was tired but I put up a good smile to cover it. Well, it seems that for $200 Ellen and Julia and I can have a cottage for a month, May, and after that we'll have to give it up. I didn't like it, but did not say so. (How odd it is that during the entire day I was facing whites and did not let my true feelings come out.) When I came home and told Ellen about the Saffords' place, she felt like I did about it; did not want to go for just a month.

April 5:

I've never been this weak before in my life. I'm not used to being sick, so I fret. My mind wants to be up and doing and my body cannot respond. That makes me disgusted. I've no experience of being ill.

April 6:

Yesterday I saw in the *NY Post* that I had bought a house in the Village, on Charles Street. Well, it seems like the cat is out of the bag. Wonder if the race issue will rise? Salzman says that I ought to make it public now; guess I will.

April 10:

Mike [Carter] says that he heard that my book has been banned in Mississippi.

April 12: Roosevelt was dead. A massive cerebral hemorrhage. Incredulous, Wright and Ellen tuned in to the radio.

> We are stunned, as though someone we know or who is related to us is dead. One's mind reels when one tries to figure out what changes will be wrought by FDR's death. Went to bed but did not sleep much at all; thinking about Roosevelt.

Only a month before, Wright had talked to Eleanor Roosevelt at a fund-raising tea for Wiltwyck School. "The death of Roosevelt simply knocked all the optimism out of people," he would write to Gertrude Stein in Paris six weeks later.[15]

Life magazine told Wright they would have to postpone their photo-documentary article on *Black Boy* because of the death of the president. They had managed to take photos in Memphis and Jackson and planned a nine-page spread.

> I had been expecting something like that to happen and it did. God-damn. But what man is worthier to have the space than FDR, who really gave me a chance to write books?

THE DRAMAS AT CHARLES STREET WERE NOT OVER. THE WRIGHTS WANTED THE parlor floor and first floor for themselves, which meant evicting those tenants. The top-floor tenants threatened a rent strike. They turned out to be none other than Franklin Folsom and his wife, Mary, staunch Communists who were kind to Wright when he first came to New York. Mary Elting Folsom had introduced him to Paul Reynolds. Franklin Folsom had been the executive secretary of the League of American Writers when Wright was vice president. But Wright's anti-Communist *Atlantic Monthly* essay had changed everything. When Wright inspected the building for the first time, he ran into Folsom on the stairs. His old friend looked the other way.[16]

WRIGHT SAW IN THE *NEW YORK TIMES* A NOTICE ABOUT A FARM IN VERMONT, 220 acres, selling for eighteen hundred dollars. "I think Mrs. Watkins is trying to sell the Vermont stuff right under my eyes, hoping I won't see her do it," he wrote in his journal. He phoned his lawyer, Salzman, to investigate the matter. If it was what he suspected, he wanted to sue.

Today is the Little One's birthday; she is three delightful years old. . . . We are having a birthday party for her and the neighbors' children are coming over. There'll be ice cream and cake and paper toys.

18

PREPARING TO LEAVE

May 1945–May 1946

James Baldwin was twenty years old when he rang the bell to Wright's Brooklyn apartment one evening in May 1945.[1] Small, thin, and frog-eyed, he looked about sixteen. Brought up in the squalor of Harlem, illegitimate, with eight younger half siblings, he had been a boy preacher in a Pentecostal church. These days he was out of what he called "the church racket." He was writing about it in a novel.

Baldwin was intimidated by the black middle class—the people on the hill, as he thought of them. The only black writers he had heard of, apart from Wright, were Langston Hughes and Countee Cullen, and both of them, he knew, lived on Sugar Hill. Richard Wright was differ-ent. Baldwin had just read *Black Boy* and found it immensely liberat-ing. He had read *Uncle Tom's Children* and *Native Son*. He knew that rage and sorrow and murderous bitterness; he knew those tenements, he knew those rats.[2] He had seen Canada Lee's "terrifying stage per-formance of Bigger Thomas." Somehow he imagined that Richard Wright would be like that. He was taken aback, he remembered later, by the figure who greeted him:

His voice was light and even rather sweet, with a Southern melody in it; his body was more round than square, more square than tall; and his grin was more boyish than I had expected, and more diffident. He had a trick, when he greeted me, of saying, "Hey, boy!" with a kind of pleased, surprised expression on his face. It was very friendly, and it was also, faintly, mockingly conspiratorial—as though we were two black boys, in league against the world, and had just managed to spirit away several loads of watermelon.

We sat in the living room and Richard brought out a bottle of bourbon and ice and glasses. Ellen Wright was somewhere in the back with the baby, and made only one brief appearance near the end of the evening. I did not drink in those days, did not know how to drink, and I was terrified that the liquor, on my empty stomach, would have the most disastrous consequences. Richard talked to me or, rather, drew me out on the subject of the novel I was working on then.[3]

In the next few days Wright read the rough draft of Baldwin's novel *Crying Holy* (years later it would become *Go Tell It on the Mountain*) and suggested that he apply for five hundred dollars from the Eugene F. Saxton Trust Fund, recently established at Harper & Brothers to help promising writers. Wright phoned Aswell and put in a good word for him.

In November 1945, the Harper committee was unanimous. From upstate New York, where he had gone to live cheaply and write, Baldwin wrote to thank Wright. "It's one of the most wonderful things that has ever happened to me."[4]

Wright was generous with his help, even though he was besieged these days by requests to read manuscripts. Esther Carlson, the young white woman who introduced him to Baldwin, had read a story at a meeting of writers Wright attended in Greenwich Village earlier that year. A year later, when the story was accepted by the *Atlantic Monthly*, she wrote to him: "I reflected today how you were the first one in my whole life who told me sincerely that I could write."[5]

Chester Himes, who had begun writing in the Ohio State Penitentiary, where he was locked up from age nineteen to twenty-six for armed robbery, had recently arrived in New York. Wright met him in Harlem, at one of Langston Hughes's parties.[6] In November 1945 Wright would write a favorable review of Himes's first novel, *If He*

Hollers Let Him Go, about tensions among black and white shipyard workers.[7] He admired Himes's "honest passion" and "brutal prose." The prose could be jerky at times, but Himes was "tough-minded," with no illusions.

Himes was greatly encouraged by this praise. "It is really warming to a new novelist to learn that the petty jealousies, snipings, bickerings, animosities that have plagued Negro writers are being put aside in this new school which it has fallen your responsibility to head," he thanked Wright.[8]

From Chicago the poet Gwendolyn Brooks was another to write Richard Wright a grateful letter. "Many folks have encouraged me but few of them have gone out of the way to help me as you have. I hope I won't disappoint your faith in me."[9] Wright had done his best to promote her collection of poems *A Street in Bronzeville*. "She is a real poet," he told Aswell. "I'd say that she ought to be helped at all costs."[10] In 1949 Gwendolyn Brooks's collection *Annie Allen* would make her the first black writer to win a Pulitzer Prize.

IN JUNE THERE WAS MORE TURBULENCE IN THE AMERICAN COMMUNIST PARTY. EARL Browder, the man who had led the Party for fifteen years, a popular man, intensely loyal to Stalin, was fired. The first ominous sign was a letter by the French Communist Jacques Duclos, published in a French Communist magazine, which accused Browder of crass "revisionism." Browder had betrayed the principles of Marxist-Leninism, said Duclos. Throughout World War II, he had swung the weight of the Communist Party behind Roosevelt, propping up a capitalist regime.

It was the beginning of a witch-hunt within the CPUSA. Previously loyal members now turned their backs on Browder. They did not want to be accused of "revisionism" themselves. To Wright's disgust, Ben Davis and James W. Ford now said exactly what he, Wright, had been saying throughout the war. Ben Davis, Jr., excoriated Browder for betraying the Negro people by disbanding the Communist Party in the South. James Ford said it had been a bad mistake to tell the Negro people to wait until the end of the war for their democratic rights. Wright was contemptuous. Ben Davis was "corrupt," he told friends.[11] As for James Ford: "He seems to be ready to do the bidding of anyone who rules. He has the soul of a slave, not a man."[12]

———

"BECAUSE OF THE WAR, THIS IS THE CLOSEST I CAN GET TO PARIS," WRIGHT WROTE from Quebec in July.[13] The family was spending a second summer in Canada—this time on the Ile d'Orléans, just down the St. Lawrence River from the city of Quebec. The river had sea tides. Sometimes it looked like a river and sometimes like the ocean. They stayed in an old seignorial manor on the western tip of the island. Wright felt as if he were in seventeenth-century France.

They had left New York on 25 June, eager to escape both the heat and the city's racial tension. In Brooklyn he and Ellen had been taking French lessons twice a week from a young American tutor. Ellen, who had a smattering of French from high school days, was making progress. Wright's was slow, but he promised himself he would take his French studies more seriously when he got back. His affinity with France had been strengthened by two very heartening publishing contracts: Albin Michel was going to publish *Uncle Tom's Children* and *Native Son*, and the prestigious publishing house Gallimard had just accepted *Black Boy*.

The air in Quebec was pure, food was cheap, and there was none of New York's rationing. Milk and cream were plentiful, and sirloin, he told friends back home, was a mere twenty-five cents per pound. ("I'm not trying to torture you; just conveying information.")[14] It was the ideal setting to recover from the strain and illness of the last few months. The Wrights were going early to bed and sleeping long hours.

In that old-European environment, Wright read *A Midsummer Night's Dream* and *Twelfth Night* and fell again under Shakespeare's spell. Parker Tyler's *The Hollywood Hallucination* made him dream once again of writing a movie script that showed whites the truth about Negro life. He had recently bought a thousand-dollar movie camera. When the war ended, he hoped to establish a group of black filmmakers.

The NAACP attorney Charles Hamilton Houston sent him court records about a recent case that reminded him, he told Wright, of *Native Son*. Julius Fisher, a black janitor, had killed a white librarian in Washington, D.C. She had accused him of not cleaning her desk. "You black nigger," she said to him, "that is what they are paying you for." A fury took hold of him, and he slapped her. She screamed and did not stop. "The screaming seemed to have gotten on my nerves," he told the courtroom.[15] To strangle that scream, he killed her. He was sentenced to the electric chair.

"Of course, the woman's scream was what set poor Fisher off," Wright wrote to Houston, thanking him profusely for sending the material. "A white woman's scream to a southern Negro is not just a scream; it is a scream of a woman calling the lynch mob; it is the siren of the police car; it is the bell of the fire-wagons; it is the shrill police whistle; and in a white woman's scream a black man can hear the baying of hounds tracking him down." It was the seed of a short story, "The Man Who Killed a Shadow."[16]

From Mississippi, Joe Brown wrote to congratulate him on *Black Boy*. "That last number you dished out was a honey. Every where I go the peckerwoods are speaking in no nice terms and are they red in the faces, and hot in the breeches; you said a mouthful."[17]

Wright rarely answered letters from friends. For once, he wrote back. "What did Jordan say when he heard that, under the name of Griggs, he had been described in *Black Boy*? Was he angry? . . . Did you see what old Bilbo (The Man) said against me in the U.S. Senate? Boy them crackers don't like me none, it seems."[18]

"The Man"—U.S. Senator Theodore Bilbo from Mississippi—was notorious for wanting to send blacks back to Africa and for opposing antilynching bills.[19] At the end of June, in the U.S. Senate, he had railed against various black leaders and writers—especially Wright and his best-seller *Black Boy*. "It should be removed from the bookstores; its sale should be stopped. It is a damnable lie from beginning to end. . . . The purpose of the book is to plant the seeds of hate in every Negro in America against the white men of the South or against the white race anywhere, for that matter . . . It is the dirtiest, filthiest, lousiest, most obscene piece of writing that I have ever seen in print. . . . But it comes from a Negro, and you cannot expect any better from a person of his type."[20] Bilbo's tirade had been widely quoted in the newspapers.

In Quebec, Wright's energy and inspiration came back to him. He wrote an article on juvenile delinquency in Harlem on behalf of the progressive Wiltwyck School.[21] He wrote a lecture for the forthcoming Breadloaf conference in Vermont. He finished reading the galleys of *Black Metropolis*, Horace Cayton and St. Clair Drake's eight-hundred-page sociological tome about life in the Chicago Black Belt, and wrote an introduction to it—a twenty-five-page cri de coeur that critics uniformly praised.[22]

Wright had confidently told American friends: "There is no race prejudice here, none whatsoever."[23] But when a black American doctor and his wife checked in at an English hotel in Quebec, the white American guests demanded that they not be allowed to eat in the dining room. The management felt obliged to ask the couple to take meals in their room. The couple, hearing that Wright was in town, came to discuss the matter with him. They sued the hotel, but this cost them a thousand dollars. "The Dr. and his wife remain trembling in the hotel, eating or trying to eat in the dining room," Wright wrote to Ellison. "The woman told me that she could not make her food go down; the Dr. says that he lost 3½ pounds from worry and tension."[24]

In early August, the United States dropped atomic bombs on Hiroshima and Nagasaki. "My radio is announcing in French that the war is all over," Wright wrote to Aswell on 12 August. "Hope it is true; there have been many wild rumors."[25] A few days later, he made a brief trip across the border to give a talk at the Breadloaf Writers' Conference in Vermont. The trains were crowded with returning soldiers.

Back in Quebec, the air was heavy and humid and the August flies so thick they could no longer enjoy the porch. Julia had been ill with giant hives, so much so that she had spent two days in hospital. Wright worried about the series of talks his lecture agent had lined up for him between October and February. He was bored with the "bourgeois people" on the island, he told Ralph Ellison, and "itching for the poisoned life of NY again."[26]

In his essay on *Black Boy*, Ellison had described Wright as "a personality agitated to a state of almost manic restlessness."[27] Wright thoroughly agreed. "Why can't I just sit like other people?" he asked himself in his journal. "What is gnawing at my gizzard? Why am I always seeking out new people, new ideas, new points of view? Why can't I rest? God knows that I am a hot and bothered man! Is it because I'm in such contradictory circumstances: a plantation Negro living in New York, a peasant who is an artist of sorts, a Negro married to a white girl, a Communist who cannot stand being a member of the Communist groups, a writer who does not and cannot and will not write as other writers write?"[28] "Ellen keeps saying, Stop saying 'wish' dear. And I can't."[29]

When their return railroad reservations were canceled due to the movements of returning troops, he and Ellen decided to cut their stay short by two weeks. They flew back to New York on 1 September.

TWO WEEKS LATER, THEY MOVED FROM BROOKLYN TO GREENWICH VILLAGE. THEY could not occupy their own house on Charles Street; the tenants' lease allowed them to stay until October, and the tenants were refusing to move. The Wrights' lawyer, Salzman, had been arguing their case in court and was about to institute dispossession proceedings.

Through friends they were able to move into a third-floor apartment in a beaux arts turn-of-the-century apartment building at 82 Washington Place, a block away from Washington Square. For a racially mixed couple, it was a breakthrough. They managed to enroll Julia in the Harriet Johnson Nursery School on Bank Street, which had a very good reputation. She was the only black child at the school.

Black Boy was selling twice as well as *Native Son*. (By the end of the year, sales would exceed half a million.) Harper, due to wartime shortages, had run out of paper. For the next six months, World Publishing took over the rights, until January 1946.[30]

No sooner had Wright moved into the new apartment and cleared his desk of dozens of small tasks than he had to prepare for his grueling lecture tour. His lecture agent, Harold Peat, had organized forty-six lectures between October 1945 and February 1946. Wright detested the idea, but each talk would bring in around $250 to $350, and his gross income from the tour would be $13,300.

"I wonder if that isn't too many and isn't going to wear you out?" Paul Reynolds had asked.[31] But both men saw it as an excellent way for Wright to lighten his financial burden. After all, as they discussed, Wright had to prepare only two lectures; he could deliver the same talk in different places. It might even provide a welcome break from writing.

Before he left on tour, Wright became ill. He was terrified that it was a recurrence of the grippe that had brought him so low in March and April. The doctor prescribed sulfur again. On 8 October he left for Baltimore. By train he traveled to Pennsylvania, to Wisconsin, then Boston, Massachusetts. He was back home for a week with a head cold.

At the end of October, he set out again: Hartford, Connecticut; Newark, New Jersey; Howard University in Washington. He caught his breath for a few days at home, then traveled to Illinois, Iowa, and Minnesota. Speaking at high schools, colleges, synagogues, and women's clubs, he was shocked by the vast ignorance about race in America. He met people of good will who abstractly wanted to do something to help, but they seemed frightened when he made concrete suggestions. The talks were tiring enough, the social mixing worse. Lying on his bed in sundry hotel rooms he told himself that the hinterland was just as Sinclair Lewis described in *Main Street*.[32] He bought six books by Nietzsche and immersed himself in reading whenever he had the chance. In Chicago he stayed with Horace Cayton, and there was a letter from Julia, written in Ellen's hand. "Dear Daddy, I want you to come home soon. And bring me some presents. And I want you to stay in my house."[33]

He was running a fever. Cayton was irritated by what he saw as Wright's hypochondria. He was even more irked by Wright's conquest of a "pretty, blond, white girl." Cayton relates the episode in his autobiography, *Long Old Road*.[34] Wright did not join Cayton at dinner one evening. He said he felt ill. Cayton was convinced he wanted to stay behind with the young woman. The next day, Wright left town. The girl came looking for him. When Cayton told her Wright had left, she burst into tears. He writes: "On some strange impulse I led her through to my apartment and into my bedroom. She didn't utter a word or put up any resistance as I undressed her and took her to bed. I was as flabbergasted as she at my strange behavior." The next day Cayton confessed to his psychoanalyst. Some weeks later, at a party in New York, he confessed to Wright.

From Chicago, Wright went to Columbus, Ohio. The next day, suffering from exhaustion, he took the train back to New York. Ellen and his doctor persuaded him to abandon the tour.

The lecture agent, Harold Peat, let Wright know that he had a wretched time canceling the talks. It involved long-distance calls, apologies, and explanations to distraught organizers. (The scheduled talk in Detroit had already sold more than twelve hundred tickets.) Peat demanded his cut of twenty-nine hundred dollars. Reynolds argued that he could not get commissions on lectures Wright did not deliver. Peat threatened to sue. Reynolds stood firm.

"There is no point in my repeating how badly I feel about the lectures and the way they turned out," Reynolds told Wright. "I had a good deal to do with talking you into doing the lecturing and I think at least your wife feels that I am sort of a black sheep in the matter."[35]

"I gave up my lecture tour for good," Wright told author Carl Van Vechten. "I'm no good at it. I speak well, but it wears me too thin."[36]

The reason Wright was occasionally in contact with Carl Van Vechten, the famous white patron of the Harlem Renaissance, was that Van Vechten had put him in touch with Gertrude Stein. By now, several letters had flowed between Paris and New York. It began when Wright reviewed Stein's latest book, *Wars I Have Seen*, in March that year. The review prompted him to look again at her earlier writing "How odd that this woman who is distrusted by everyone can remind me of the most basic things in my life," he had written in his journal. He thought it had something to do with her living outside America.

> I'd say that one could live and write like that only if one lived in Paris or some out of the way spot where one could claim one's whole soul. And I cannot do that here now. All the more reason why I dream and dream of leaving my native land, to escape the pressure of the superficial things I think I know. That's why I left the South, and now I want to leave the entire country, and some day I will, by God.[37]

Carl Van Vechten had sent Wright's review to Stein. "I didn't expect it to interest me much," he told her. "To my surprise, it is more understanding than any other review of the book that has yet appeared."[38]

Stein liked it a great deal, and asked one of her American GI friends in Paris to find her a book by this young man Richard Wright. He brought her a copy of *Black Boy* from the army library. "I am very enthusiastic," she wrote to Van Vechten, asking him to send her Wright's other books.[39] In April she wrote to Wright herself. She told him she had finished *Black Boy*. "For the first time an American negro writing as a negro about negroes writes not as a negro but as a man. . . . It is the first really creative book written except my own in this period. . . . I wish we might meet, there would be lots to say."[40]

She told Wright that she rarely had contact with Negroes:

> I talk casually with the American soldiers on the streets and we walk and talk together. A great many of them talk about the minorities in America, it is on all their minds, it worries them, they have gotten a perspective on

America being so far away. I myself talking to every level of American soldier have not talked to any American negro, I see them on the street in our quarter, but, in the last war we talked but somehow in this war I do not seem able to say to them hello boys how do you like it as I do to all the others, there have not been any that have come to see me, why not.

Wright wrote her a three-page, chatty letter. He wanted to know: "Is it bad in France now? Is there enough food? Was there much destruction?"[41] He told her he was going to do his best to bring his wife and child to France next year.

In October, he encouraged her to come and lecture in the United States. "The nation feels guilty right now about the Negro and if you came and hammered it home while they feel that way, why they would sit back and take notice."[42]

That same month, Stein told the *Chicago Defender* she had discovered Richard Wright that year.

> I found Wright was the best American writer today. Only one or two creative writers like him come along in a generation. . . . He tells something never told before in a perfectly distinctive way. . . .
>
> The theme is the Negro but the treatment is that of a creative writer. . . . Wright's material doesn't dominate him. With most Negro writers the Negro is on top of the writer.[43]

They were corresponding regularly, Stein said, and she hoped to see Wright in Paris.

IN THE FALL OF 1945 WRIGHT HEARD FROM ANOTHER GREAT AMERICAN MODERNIST writer, William Faulkner:

> Dear Richard Wright:
>
> I have just read *Black Boy*. It needed to be said, and you said it well. Though I am afraid (I am speaking now from the point of view of one who believes that the man who wrote *Native Son* is potentially an artist) it will accomplish little of what it should accomplish, since only

they will be moved and grieved by it who already know and grieve over this situation.

You said it well, as well as it could have been said in this form. Because I think you said it much better in *Native Son*. I hope you will keep on saying it, but I hope you will say it as an artist, as in *Native Son*. I think you will agree that the good lasting stuff comes out of one individual's imagination and sensitivity to and comprehension of the suffering of Everyman, Anyman, not out of the memory of his own grief.[44]

It was evident that some Mississippians were reading *Black Boy*, despite that state's ban on the book. Did Wright send a copy to his family? It is not likely. His father was scarcely literate. His mother and aunt had probably never read a book in their lives, and were not going to start with this one. But Leon Wright read it. In 1967, seven years after Wright's death, Leon Wright wrote to Constance Webb: "I can say that in my opinion my brother's account of events in his autobiography draws a quite honest self-portrait of his personality as I knew him. My impression is that my brother was a born poet, writer and critic, who had great interest in people and personalities. Interest which, it seems to me, often caused him to get into difficulties even as a small child with playmates, parents, his mother's family, friends and acquaintances . . ."[45] Leon Wright admitted that he scarcely knew his brother and that they lived in different worlds. "I went to live with my Aunt Margaret at the age of ten and in later years was with my brother for only brief periods of time, during which I recall he read continuously and seemed to live almost exclusively in a world of books and ideas."

A second letter from Leon Wright hinted that he had been quite upset by *Black Boy*. "I do not find it difficult to believe that the misrepresentations in 'Black Boy' were made for the quite worthy reasons stated in your letter," he told Webb, "but I do feel that my brother should not have found it necessary to make irresponsible statements involving members of the family to aid him in his cause."[46]

He asked Webb to refer to him in her book only by the name of Alan, so that he could "be assured of some degree of privacy here in Chicago." These two letters were the last time Wright scholars heard from Leon Wright. He died in Chicago in 1999, at the age of eighty-nine.

———

"ALL ROADS LEAD TO PARIS," STEIN REMARKED IN HER *AUTOBIOGRAPHY OF ALICE B.*
Toklas. If American writers harbored an expatriate dream, it was about
Paris.

For black Americans, the dream had largely to do with freedom
from race consciousness. "We all wanted to go to Paris," said Countee
Cullen, the poet, who spent a year there in 1928 and returned as often
as he could.[47] Langston Hughes lived in Paris for several months in the
mid-1920s; Horace Cayton was there in the mid-1930s. They were exhil-
arated by the taste of freedom. Paris had a reputation for treating black
visitors like any other visitors, which on the whole meant leaving them
alone. "In Paris one feels free to be an outsider, to watch," James Baldwin would write.[48] For writers, that meant a great deal.

"I hope that Paris will be as so many have said it used to be," Wright
wrote to Gertrude Stein. "Will it?"[49] France had always been Wright's
dream. Zola and Maupassant had been early literary models. He had sat
in his Chicago slum and read Proust. He admired André Malraux, the
man and the writer. These days he was excited about the new philosophy of freedom emerging from France, which had become the new
rage in the Western world. "New York is buzzing over existentialism,"
he told Stein. "It frightens most folks here. Too gloomy, they say."

Gloomy or not, Jean-Paul Sartre's emphasis on freedom, angst, solitude, and commitment had immense appeal in a world that had lived
through the war, the struggles of the Resistance, and the atom bomb.
People wanted to believe, once again, that the individual had power.
Man is free, Sartre proclaimed. In a world without God, man makes
himself.

In France, Jean-Paul Sartre had burst into fame in October 1945
when he gave a talk, "Is Existentialism a Humanism?," at the Club Maintenant in Paris. The lecture theater had been packed. Women had
fainted. The Paris newspapers were full of it. That same month, Sartre
and Simone de Beauvoir launched a new journal, *Les Temps Modernes.*
The first issue contained Richard Wright's story "Fire and Cloud."

Early in 1946 Dorothy Norman invited the German philosophers
Hannah Arendt and Paul Tillich to her house to explain to Wright the
derivation of existentialism. In March, Wright met Jean-Paul Sartre in
Dorothy Norman's drawing room. Wright asked Sartre what he thought

about America and was disappointed that he seemed to be holding himself back.

Sartre certainly told Wright that he had been shocked by the racial discrimination he observed in the United States. "In this land of freedom and equality, there live thirteen million untouchables," he had written after his first visit, the previous year, in *Le Figaro*. "They wait on your table, they polish your shoes, they operate your elevator, they carry your suitcases into your compartment, but they have nothing to do with you, nor you with them."[50]

In April Wright was back in Dorothy Norman's drawing room to meet Albert Camus. He had played an influential role in Gallimard's accepting *Black Boy* for publication. With the help of the philosopher Lionel Abel as interpreter, Wright asked Camus about conditions in France and said he hoped to go there soon. Camus was pleased, but said he hoped Wright would not stay permanently. It seemed to him that blacks had to stay in America and fight. Both Wright and Abel were taken aback by the vehemence of Camus's conviction.[51]

THERE WAS A VAST GULF BETWEEN THE AFFLUENCE OF AMERICA AND THE HARD-ship in Europe. European visitors to the United States all sent food parcels back home. Sartre and his French journalist colleagues arrived looking so shabby that a delegate from the Office of War Information had propelled them down Fifth Avenue and bought them all suits. Albert Camus, on his first evening in Manhattan, had been alarmed by the bright neon lights: he thought the city was on fire. Even Americans were surprised by the new prosperity all around them. "The shop windows are full of new, queer, and modern stuff," Wright informed Gertrude Stein. "The magazines are getting more and more color in them, great big ads about cars and washing machines and fountains and motor boats and typewriters and whiskey and canned goods."[52]

The new abundance would not keep Wright in the country. He and Ellen worried that they might not be able to find healthy food for Julia in France. But Wright had been trying ever since 1939 to get abroad. Now that the war had ended, he was not going to let shortage of food and material deprivations in Europe stop him.

Dorothy Norman was helpful. She suggested that Wright represent her journal, *Twice a Year*, in Paris, establishing contacts for its distribution in Europe, soliciting articles, and reporting back on cultural and political affairs in France. On paper she made him a coeditor. She wrote to the State Department on Wright's behalf.

Wright asked Gaston Gallimard, his French publisher, for a letter. Gertrude Stein put in a word for him at the American embassy in Paris. On 10 March 1945 Wright and Ellen submitted their passport applications. At the end of March Wright wrote to Stein: "The time is about ripe for me to hear one way or the other. They've kept my application long enough for the answer to be yes."[53]

A French journalist, Michel Gordey, came to Wright's Greenwich Village apartment to interview him.[54] When Wright opened the door, Gordey was struck by his kindness and the "soft, intelligent eyes" behind his rimless glasses:

> After a few minutes, I no longer know who is being interviewed, Wright or me. Questions are bandied about. Wright wishes to leave for France in a few weeks and asks me about Paris, about French writers, daily life and problems, about political struggles and intellectual debates on the Left Bank. I realize he knows French literature and is even cognizant of Existentialist squabbles. He is bursting with impatience.[55]

To strengthen Wright's case with the State Department, Gordey arranged for colleagues in Paris to send letters inviting Wright to give lectures. He also spoke to the head of French Cultural Services in New York. This happened to be Claude Lévi-Strauss, the anthropologist.

By April Wright was nervous. He checked with lawyers. Didn't he, as an American citizen, have a legal right to a passport? No, he did not. The State Department had the power to withhold passports at its discretion. He was told that the U.S. government did not want Americans flooding Europe just now. Conditions were bad; food shortages in Europe were serious. The government feared that American citizens could become stranded. Wright was beginning to despair. Could it be that even now, after waiting four years for the war to end, he would not be permitted to leave the country?

On 11 April the State Department asked Wright to submit proof that the French would grant him a visa. Wright rushed to the French embassy. He came away with another document to send to Washington.

Two more weeks passed. The Wrights were booked to leave the following week. They had packed up their apartment, filled their trunks (including 240 pounds of foodstuffs they were entitled to take with them), and still they did not have passports, visas, or tickets.

On 25 April 1946, Claude Lévi-Strauss sent Wright a formal invitation. The French government was inviting him as an official guest, and would pay his fare and his first month's expenses in France.

Wright phoned Washington. The assistant chief of the passport division told him they had not received any documents whatsoever. Wright, incredulous, said he would fly down in person with duplicates. The official told him not to bother. He would mail the passport on Monday, 29 April. Wright said that would be too late. They were due to leave on 1 May.

Wright flew to Washington on Sunday evening, 28 April, and was at the passport office at nine o'clock on Monday morning. He handed the documents over the counter. The official barely looked up. "We don't need those. You hang on to them." Within two hours, Wright had the passports in his hands. Back in New York, he headed straight to the French embassy to get their visas. Then he went to pay the boat passage and pick up their tickets. The ship was leaving on Wednesday.

19

CROSSING THE ATLANTIC

May 1946–January 1947

Richard, Ellen, and Julia Wright left New York on 1 May 1946 on the SS *Brazil*, a battered old cargo boat that had been converted into a troopship during the war and was now a passenger liner. Hardly any of their friends knew they were leaving. They themselves had not known until the last minute. "I felt relieved," Wright wrote, "when my ship sailed past the Statue of Liberty."[1]

The ship was crowded and the service bad, but the sea was calm. Four-year-old Julia was excited and boasted to her parents that she spoke French already. She won a dog-shaped balloon one evening in a competition. Her father observed an American army relief group on board, on its way to help out in Europe. Would it export American attitudes? The whites completely ignored the four blacks in the group, who shared a cabin, sat together, and were not invited to join in the dances on board. Wright visited the men in their cabin and found them "bitter as hell."[2] But the Europeans on the ship seemed far more open. After four days at sea, Wright wrote to Ralph Ellison on ship notepaper: "Already the harsh race lines of America are fading."[3]

They were traveling to the lean, hungry countries where supplies of coal, gas, and electricity were erratic; milk, butter, eggs, and meat were rationed; the coffee ersatz, and houses cold. Reports indicated that things were improving. Janet Flanner had written in her most recent "Letter from Paris" in the *New Yorker*: "Paris is now like a thin, ill, handsome old woman with some natural color flushing her cheeks as she fumbles to her feet."[4]

The ship landed in Le Havre on Thursday, 9 May, in the afternoon. The approach to the harbor, past skeletons of half-sunken freighters and troop ships with their masts jutting out of the water, was their first glimpse of a forlorn, war-torn Europe. It made Wright acutely aware of how much they, in America, had been spared.

They were taken by bus to the station, to connect with the overnight boat-train to Paris. There was rubble everywhere. The French looked poor and hungry. Wright could see the tension between the French civilians and the U.S. soldiers, who were loud and brash and drove their jeeps too fast. Americans abroad seemed worse than those at home.

At the station, he was continually accosted by French men wanting to exchange dollars for francs. He was shocked. He had not expected the black market to be so brazen.

On the train, too agitated to sleep, he pressed his face against the windowpane, trying to make out the landscape through the dark night. In the morning he walked from carriage to carriage and chatted with people. He wished he could speak better French. "I know just enough not to starve in Paris," he had told Gertrude Stein before leaving.[5]

The train was modern and clean. Americans had warned that they would be shocked by the dirtiness of France. Don't expect toilet paper! they had said. Wright was beginning to think these were tall stories.

THE TRAIN PULLED IN TO THE GARE SAINT-LAZARE AROUND SEVEN IN THE MORNING on Friday, 10 May. The sun was just rising and the breeze was fresh. The train had been due at the ungodly hour of 6:30 A.M., but Gertrude Stein had come to meet it. She had been feeling frail recently, but she had put herself out for her new friend. So had Douglas Schneider, from the American embassy, who arrived with two sleek limousines—one for the Wrights and one for their luggage. A man from the French Foreign Office was there. "I felt confused and important and scared," Wright wrote later to Dorothy Norman.[6] It was, indeed, bewildering. First the State Department had tried to prevent his departure, and now the U.S. government was welcoming him to Paris.

Maurice Nadeau, a reporter for *Combat*, the daily newspaper Camus had founded during the Resistance, searched the platform for Richard Wright. Among the swirl of porters and disembarking passengers, many of whom were chewing gum, he could not see any sign of a black man.[7] He imagined he was looking for someone tall and strong, like the GIs he saw striding around the streets of Paris. Most passengers had found their friends by now and were hugging them and crying and slapping each other on the back. Nadeau was about to turn away when he heard "a big, resonant laugh." A man in a wide-brimmed hat and large overcoat was squatting down playing with his small daughter. Nadeau heard him exclaim "Julia!" The big laugh rolled over the platform again, causing people to turn around and look.

Nadeau went up to him. "Mr. Richard Wright?"

"Yes!" the man said, his eyes twinkling behind his metal glasses. Nadeau suddenly felt deeply moved. He had read "Big Boy Leaves Home," the lynch story that had appeared in *L'Arbalète* during the Occupation. In *Les Temps Modernes* he had read "Fire and Cloud." How could this affable, mild-mannered man have emerged from such a nightmarish world?

Nadeau spoke no English, and Wright spoke very little French. With the help of the man from the French Foreign Office, they managed to communicate. "How long are you going to stay in France?" Nadeau asked. "Two months, six months, a year, maybe forever!" That big laugh again. Was the black problem in the United States nearing a solution? Nadeau noticed Wright's quizzical black eyebrows rise and fall. "There is not a black problem in the United States, but a white problem. The blacks now know what they want. . . . The whites don't."

But this was not a good place to talk, Wright told Nadeau. The rest of the group had gone ahead. He swept Julia up in his arms, gave Nadeau a well-meaning pat on the back, and rushed off.

From the car the Wrights saw wrought-iron balconies draped with flags in honor of the first anniversary of V-E—Victory for Europe— Day. Street sellers were selling lily of the valley. The chestnut trees were beginning to drop their red and white spring blossoms. A weak sun lit up the old stone buildings. Barges moved lazily down the river. Years later, Douglas Schneider recalled Wright's initial response to Paris.

> The travelers seemed wide awake, so instead of taking these new friends of mine directly to their hotel on the rue de Vaugirard, we went the long way around, down the Champs Elysées, past the Tuileries on the rue de Rivoli and back along the quais. Richard Wright was sitting next to me, and as we entered the Place de la Concorde, facing the Louvre, and later all along the Left Bank, I heard him exclaim under his breath: "How beautiful! How absolutely beautiful!"[8]

Stein had reserved two rooms at the Trianon Palace Hotel in Saint-Germain-des-Prés. It was close to the Luxembourg Gardens and within walking distance of her apartment at 5, rue Christine. She told Wright that her closest friend, a young American called Christopher Blake, lived in the same hotel with his French boyfriend. It was too early in the morning to introduce them, but Blake would no doubt come and see them later. He was an ex-GI who admired Wright's writing, and if ever Wright needed anything, he should just ask. The Wrights, very conscious of being in a strange new land without being able to understand the language, were grateful.

After Stein had left, Wright went out to explore the nearby streets. "The area teems with tiny book stores, publishing houses, painters' studios and art shops," he observed.[9] Later that morning, the Wrights were unpacking when a redheaded Brooklyn boy, "jittery, nervous . . . speaking a fast furry language," knocked on the door.[10] It was Chris Blake and his friend ("a sickly little French boy whose face repelled me the moment I saw it," Wright told Dorothy Norman later). Blake described himself as an aspiring writer and a royalist.

The next day, in the *Courrier de l'Etudiant*, Blake remarked that Wright should cure his "paranoia about race," and move on to other themes.[11] Wright almost certainly never knew about the article.

That afternoon, Wright went to see Sylvia Beach, on the nearby rue de l'Odéon. She and her bookstore, Shakespeare & Company, were the heart of the 1920s Left Bank expatriate world of Joyce, Hemingway, Stein, and others that Wright had heard and read so much about. He was hoping to distribute *Twice a Year* from her bookshop.

It turned out that Shakespeare & Company no longer existed. Sylvia

Beach, one of the few Americans to stay on in France during the war, had closed her bookshop in 1941, after a German officer told her the books would be confiscated the next day. For eight months she had been interned in a detention camp for British and American women. Her young Jewish assistant had died in Auschwitz. When Paris was liberated, Beach had come out of hiding and returned to her apartment above the bookstore, crammed with boxes of books. But she was tired after her hardships and lacked financial resources. She did not think she would be reopening her bookshop.

"We are between two worlds," Wright told himself.[12]

THE NEXT EVENING, SATURDAY, 11 MAY, WRIGHT WAS LEANING OUT OF THE WINDOW of their hotel room when beneath him the street filled with shouts, laughter, and singing. He went out to see what was happening. The loudspeakers were blaring out music and people of all races, colors, and classes were dancing in the street to celebrate V-E Day. Wright took out his pipe and leaned against a tree to watch.[13]

Then he saw his first black GI. He was giving his arm to a pretty, blond girl and they were about to dance. Wright strolled over to talk to him. The young man, who was from St. Louis, introduced his girl. They were going to get married, he told Wright. Where will you live? Wright asked. The young man did not hesitate. "St. Louis."

Could it be that this fellow did not know? Had he forgotten what it would mean to take this white woman to St. Louis? That it would mean death for him? Since the end of the war, there had been forty-five reported lynchings of ex-servicemen in the South. There had been race riots. As gently as he could, Wright told the young soldier that things were not looking too good at home on the racial front. Didn't he know that?

No, said the soldier.

Wright realized that in two years in France this young man had forgotten. He grinned at the couple a little awkwardly, shook their hands, and said good-bye. As he went back to the hotel, he told himself how easy it was to forget and how necessary it was to remember.

ON SUNDAY, WITH A GENTLE RAIN FALLING ON PARIS, WRIGHT REFLECTED THAT this was a "gentle city."[14] That same afternoon, the *Les Temps Modernes* editorial committee crowded into Jean-Paul Sartre's room in Montparnasse to discuss the next few issues. They were going to devote the August-September 1946 issue to contemporary American writing. Richard Wright would be featured prominently. De Beauvoir, who read English fluently, was currently choosing an extract from Cayton and Drake's *Black Metropolis*. Boris Vian, the twenty-six year-old writer and jazz trumpeter, was going to write about Negro spirituals.

"It meant so many things, America!" Simone de Beauvoir would write later about that postwar period. "Its jazz, cinema and literature had nourished our youth. . . . America was also the country which had sent our deliverance; it was the future on the march; it was abundance, and infinite horizons; it was a crazy magic lantern of legendary images."[15]

It was Richard Wright, more than any other contemporary American writer, who seemed to these existentialists to be writing the "committed literature" they were advocating for the postwar world. Wright was concerned with questions of freedom, oppression, individual choice. Like them, he was interested in the interface of literature, psychoanalysis, and sociology. As de Beauvoir would write in the *New York Times*, Richard Wright's *Black Boy* was about an "individual consciousness and an individual liberty. . . . The struggle of a man against the resistances of the world is depicted. And it is just this which today in France appears to us to be the true mission of the writer."[16]

THE NEXT DAY, JACQUES LAURENT BOST, ONE OF THE YOUNGER MEMBERS OF THE *Temps Modernes* group, told Sartre and de Beauvoir he had seen Richard Wright sitting on the terrace of the Café de Flore. He had gone up and introduced himself. "Wright laughed in his face," de Beauvoir noted in her diary. "Apparently he always laughs, but it's his way of avoiding contact with people."[17]

It took Wright no time at all to find the Flore and the Deux Magots (he spelt it "Deux Maggots"), those famous Saint-Germain cafés. During the war, Sartre and de Beauvoir had spent hours each day writing in these cafés. Their own rooms were unheated. And they liked the bustle of human activity around them.

Wright had discovered the answer to a question he had often asked himself. Why do French people spend so much time in cafés? The hotel the Wrights were staying in was drab. The walls were thin. The shared toilet, down the corridor, was a hole in the ground with two raised platforms for one's feet. From what Wright had seen so far, most Parisians lived in modest and rather dreary circumstances.[18]

So much was strange in France. "The knobs were in the center of the doors! Waiters ladled you your change out of bulging, sagging pockets. Sandwiches were a rough slab of meat flanked by two oblong chunks of bread. Hot milk was used in coffee instead of cream."[19] The women were beautiful and unashamed of being women, Wright observed. The material they wore was cheap, compared with American fabrics, yet they looked so smart in their simple dresses, shoes, and perky hats.

Wright loved the narrow cobblestone streets, the symmetry of the architecture, the trees everywhere. At night the streets seemed magic. With the dim yellow lighting they looked like an "underlit stage set."[20] He enjoyed walking in the Luxembourg Gardens, past the splaying fountains and statues of writers. There was an openness in France. People sauntered along, pausing to look at things or chat with the vendors at the outdoor stalls. And yet there was an intensity too. The talk in the cafés was animated.

Best of all was to be able to forget for hours at a time that he was black. He could walk into a bar or a café without pausing on the threshold and wondering whether he dared go in. He was told that there were some twenty thousand black people in Paris, mostly from Africa and the West Indies. Five hundred or so were black Americans, mostly ex-army men studying under the GI Bill of Rights.[21]

Wright saw no sign of racial hatred. But he was disconcerted that French Negroes always seemed to be together, in groups of two or three. He worried that the Germans and Americans might have left race prejudice in their wake. Some weeks later, Léopold Senghor, the Senegalese poet, assured him that they preferred each other's company. They came from the colonies. They shared the same language, values, and culture.

Wright would realize that black Americans and black Africans had grown up in very different conditions. The African brothers were not nearly as prone to self-hatred as the black Americans. They did not feel the same wariness of each other. They had no wish to avoid each other's company.[22]

THOSE FIRST FEW WEEKS IN PARIS INVOLVED A GREAT DEAL OF "HANDSHAKING, DIN-
ners, and what not."[23] Gaston Gallimard, head of the publishing house,
welcomed Wright to Paris at a glittering reception. Marcel Duhamel,
Wright's translator, ushered him around, acting as interpreter. Gertrude
Stein was there in a brown tweed suit and hat. American expatriates
mingled with French writers and journalists.

A few days later, Albin Michel, who was publishing *Uncle Tom's
Children* and *Native Son*, hosted a more modest party. There were
other receptions,[24] and several interviews with French newspapers. In
October Wright spoke at the famous Club Maintenant. These occasions
made him anxious, but he was flattered that the French were going out
of their way to make him feel welcome.

It soon became clear to him that the welcome he had received from
the American embassy was less sincere. At a cocktail party in the first
couple of weeks, an American official took him aside and said to him in
an urgent voice: "Listen, for God's sake don't let these foreigners make
you into a brick to hurl at our windows!"[25] Wright realized that the U.S.
government was worried about what he might say about racism in
America. He heard that the American embassy in Paris was constantly
receiving protest phone calls and letters from French people who read
about racial incidents in the United States. "We give folks a stick to beat
us over the head with," Wright told Dorothy Norman.[26] He intended to
take full advantage of his influential position in Europe. Had he not
always said: "Our mission as writers is to tell the truth at whatever cost?"[27]

In May 1946, two weeks after Wright arrived in France, *Samedi Soir*
published his first, very positive, impressions of France, translated into
French.[28] A week later, the same newspaper published his short story
"Long Black Song." In June *Paris Matin* printed Wright's account of his
train trip through the Jim Crow South in the summer of 1940.[29] French
friends warned Wright that these were tabloid publications. (*Samedi
Soir* regularly printed scurrilous gossip about Sartre and the great "Sar-
treuse," as it liked to call de Beauvoir.) Wright took the view that this
was snobbery. He did not care if his stories appeared on street pillars,
he retorted, as long as the French learned something about the reality
of American racism.

———

"DICK AND FAMILY ARE SO HAPPY THEY ABOUT ARE BURSTING WITH IT," GERTRUDE Stein reported to Carl Van Vechten four days after she met them at the station. "The French have been very good to him, we have been a lot together."[30] Hobbling on a cane, she had walked with the Wrights down the little lanes in the Luxembourg Gardens, explaining the intricacies of life in Paris. She invited the family to lunch at the rue Christine, where they met Alice B. Toklas and were shown the famous collection of Cézannes, Picassos, Matisses, Braques, Légers. The Wrights bought a small landscape painting by the British painter Francis Rose. But Stein and Toklas did not warm to Ellen, and they found the exuberant little Julia a trial. After the Wrights had been in Paris five weeks, Stein wrote to Carl Van Vechten in New York:

> About the Wrights, it is a long and also complicated story, he interests me immensely, he is strange, I have a lot of theories about him and sometime when it all gets straightened out I'll tell you, of course there was a bit of difficulty on account of the wife and child, she is rather awful, and the child terribly spoiled, and we had finally to sort of give it up, it was too fatiguing, but then in spite of giving it up it just has gone on, he has made quite clear to me the whole question of the Negro problem, the black white the white black, are they white or are they black, is Dick white or is he black, in his particular case it is very interesting, more so than in any of the others I have ever met.[31]

Though the Wrights were not aware of it, seventy-two-year-old Gertrude Stein was seriously ill. Her patience, never a strong point, was thinner than usual. Wright thought her one of the most "hot and bothered" people he had ever met. Julia called her "Grapefruit Stein," which her parents thought wonderfully apt.

For several weeks, Wright stuck to his belief that Stein was a "salty old dog,"[32] with an unusual understanding of black people and their culture. He would gradually discover that though she held firm views about race in America, they rarely converged with his. He noticed that though she had never written about being Jewish, it seemed important to her now. The Holocaust seemed to have frightened her a great deal.

She had always expressed the "spirit of her people," she told him. Was he trying to express the spirit of his race? He did not dare tell her that such talk held no meaning for him.

Stein had always made ambiguous statements about race in America. Wright had chosen to believe the more positive interpretation. The previous year, Ben Burns, a white journalist, had turned up at rue Christine to interview Stein for the black newspaper the *Chicago Defender*. It was the occasion on which she called Wright "the best American writer today."[33] She also said that the "nonsense of race" was incomprehensible to her. She neither understood the white notion of racial superiority nor did she understand Negro defensiveness. Wasn't it whites who suffered from a lack of racial pride when one hundred white families allowed themselves to be driven out of a street by one black family moving in?

Personally, she thought that Negroes had an advantage over whites. "They are the only people in America who are still pioneering. In the last fifty years they have pioneered up from the South. . . . If you pioneer, you're alive."

She was more worried about the persecutor than the persecuted, she said. "The white man is sinking deeper into the mire trying to hold the Negro by the leg. . . . Don't worry about the Negroes. They holler a little but they take care of themselves. Being pushed around makes them strong."

In that interview, Stein criticized Paul Robeson for "playing the role of Negro." But she was now finding herself disconcerted that Wright did not play that role. At the end of June she tried to explain herself to Carl Van Vechten:

> [Wright] is having a huge success here, being very feted by all the French all the salons and the intellectuals, having a perfectly fine time, and do I like him, well I don't know, there is a strange materialism about him that is not at all Negro, in fact he does not seem to me very Negro. . . . You see I kept saying his books were not Negro, that is what I liked in them so much, but now when he isn't, do I like it so much?[34]

ONE AFTERNOON, WRIGHT TALKED TO STEIN ABOUT HER LATEST BOOK, *BREWSIE and Willie*, subtitled *A Discussion of the GIs and Their Problems and*

Hopes. He had arranged to review it for *PM*, but after talking to Stein that afternoon he decided to discard his "pale notes" and write an account of their conversation instead.[35]

Stein, he wrote, had a "lean face, twinkling deep-set eyes, a forceful voice and ceaselessly moving hands." She struck him as a practical woman. "It is as though she feels that being modern in her art is enough, and that, in her daily, regular living, she should cling to the accepted and the familiar."

Stein had talked to dozens of young American GIs, she told him, and found them lost and sad, old-fashioned, and strangely conservative. Above all, they were scared. She could not understand it, for they had nothing to lose. All they seemed to want was a job. "I told them to be pioneers again, as Americans were once pioneers." Wright wrote:

> My impression of Gertrude Stein is this: perhaps more than any other mind of our time, she has realized acutely the difference between Yesterday and Today, the difference between living in a feudal society and in a modern industrial one. And she has realized the difference which that difference makes in the personalities of men and women.
>
> Gertrude Stein received the GIs like a mother. She talked with them and learned to know them with an objectivity which, perhaps, few people in America can muster. I think that I can say that really she saved them, lifted some of them up by the scruff of their necks and made them into straight talkers, straight thinkers and hard workers. I think that she made some of them into men devoid of petty prejudices and petty fears.

Twice, on Sunday afternoons, Wright called in alone, without the family, to see Stein. This was "salon" time at the rue Christine; there were always others present. Stein would sit on the horsehair sofa in front of Pablo Picasso's portrait of her over the mantel, with her large, white poodle, Basket, at her feet, and dominate the conversation. But Wright sensed no warmth in those beautiful rooms.

The only person he ever heard Stein talk about affectionately was Sherwood Anderson. "For Hemingway she had nothing but scorn and acid-like hate," he told Dorothy Norman later. "For Picasso an amusing kind of contempt. For everybody there were hard, scornful words, with Alice standing in the background and urging her on. At first, you laughed at these stories, and then you began vaguely to wonder what she would say about you as soon as you left."[36]

By making gaffes, Wright learned the rules. Stein's favorite word was "No." She would close her eyes and shake her head and say "No, no, no, no, no, no." Everybody in the room would become silent. Once or twice Wright argued with her. He saw immediately how much this annoyed her.

The last time he saw her—it was a Sunday salon at the rue Christine—the atmosphere was stranger than usual. Behind Stein's powerful restlessness, Wright sensed a constant probing for affirmation and for confirmation of her own ideas. That day, she interrupted the talk several times, making oblique remarks that were beside the point. Finally she left the room. When she came back she threw up her hands and said: "All right, it's time for dinner. Everybody go now." Everybody left, fast. Was she in pain? Wright wondered afterwards, when he found out she was ill. Or was she simply bored?

WHEN, IN EARLY JUNE, WRIGHT WROTE HIS *PM* ARTICLE IN PRAISE OF GERTRUDE Stein, he meant what he said. A month later, his essay embarrassed him. It was only half the story, he wrote to Dorothy Norman. He had come to see other things in Stein. "There's good in her and there is downright evil. I'm not used to seeing such things lying side by side in the same person."[37]

By then he had had an ugly rupture with Stein, provoked by her friend Christopher Blake. That first day in Paris, when Blake had come to their hotel room to see if he could do anything to help, Wright had asked where they could find an icebox. They had brought six hundred thousand units of penicillin from New York in case Julia, prone to tonsillitis, developed one of her bad throats. The medicine needed to be kept on ice. Blake had said: "I know the place." Wright had gone with him to the nearby Hotel Mascotte, where they packed a little chest with penicillin, butter, and juice bases and placed it on ice.

In the first few weeks Stein used to ask Wright how things were going, and he would tell her he had been running around organizing this and that, and she would say: "You dope, don't run yourself like that. Let Blake do it for you." But Wright did not like to ask favors. Meanwhile, Blake asked him for a loan; he and his boyfriend needed twenty-five thousand francs to secure an apartment on the Ile de la Cité. It was a considerable sum. Wright was spending fifty thousand francs a month to live in the hotel. He and Ellen discussed it. "Blake was Gerty's friend." They decided they would trust him.

One morning in June Ellen wanted a can of orange juice base from the icebox. Wright walked over to the Mascotte and found the chest almost empty. He phoned Blake, who was now living in a fashionable Ile de la Cité apartment. Blake burst out laughing. Maybe the barman had taken it, he said. Wright went back and talked to the barman. He said Mr. Blake had taken the things. Wright called Blake back. Blake said the barman was crazy and he did not want to talk about it and who the hell was Wright to accuse him?

Finally, the Wrights, both of them, went to speak to the owner of the hotel, who interrogated the barman. It emerged that Christopher Blake was known for lying, thieving, and black market dealings, and his boyfriend was a criminal. The Wrights were now concerned about their money. After more discussion, they decided that Wright should call Gertrude Stein. He told Dorothy Norman:

> I call Gerty and before I can tell her what has happened, she starts in in a wild scolding of me, telling me that I'm responsible for myself here in Paris, that Blake is her friend (which I admit he is) and so on . . . I'm astonished. I don't get a chance to say a word (this takes place on the phone) and she hangs up when I try to tell her that she told me to trust this guy. That was the end of my knowing Gertrude Stein.[38]

Only now, through Jennifer Bradley, a Paris-based American literary agent who worked for both Stein and Wright, did Wright learn that Stein was ill—perhaps gravely. And only now did he discover the extent of Stein's political conservatism. She had been against Roosevelt and the New Deal. During the Spanish civil war she had been in favor of Franco. Over the last few years, her closest French friend had been Bernard Faÿ, a friend of Marshal Pétain. Faÿ was anti-Semitic, like Pétain. Nevertheless, during the Occupation he had offered protection to Stein and Toklas—two Jewish Americans hiding in the south of France. In the final days of the Occupation, the Germans entered Stein's apartment. It was probably due to Faÿ that the art collection was saved.[39] Bernard Faÿ was currently in prison, awaiting trial as a collaborator.

No sooner had Wright digested this news when, on 27 July 1946, Gertrude Stein died of stomach cancer in the American Hospital at Neuilly. "So ends a fantastic career, so ends a woman who was alive in an incredible and astounding sort of way," he wrote to Dorothy Norman four days later.

> I had not spoken to her or seen her in six weeks, not since that fantastic phone call I made to her during which she read me the riot act in defense of her little friend Blake. But when I'd heard that she was dead, I thought that death ended all petty things and I swallowed my pride and went by to see Alice to pay my respects. Lo, I was not received. I went back home, as full of wonder and bafflement as before.[40]

Wright's phone began to ring. Stein's friends wanted to know why they had fallen out. Friends he thought were close to her turned out not to be close at all. He began to form a new picture of Stein—a woman intensely alone among her acolytes. "It was a kind of palace she kept, with many people vying to get into the magic circle. . . . This week a certain group was in, and another out, and next week it would be changed." And yet behind this regal hauteur, Wright thought that what he had probably seen was a frightened woman whose furious control on life kept slipping away from her.

> In the end, and I think I'm right about this, she was consumed with fear, just plain human fear. This fear was back of all she ever did; there was above all her fear of not being really a great writer. She hungered for praise in an infantile sort of way. Everybody who met her had to praise her. . . . In private life she was an empress sort of woman, imperious, over-bearing, dominating. . . . I'm convinced that she regarded death more or less like she regarded people, that she felt that she could manage death, and that if she said No, no, no, no . . . that death would wait or go away.

Threatening letters passed between them, but the Wrights never got their money back from Christopher Blake.[41]

———

IT WAS A STRANGE SENSATION TO TRAVEL ACROSS THE WORLD AND BECOME AN American. To the French, Wright was an American before he was black. It was a little embarrassing. The French were fascinated by America, but they did not think much of Americans, and Wright could understand why. The GIs tended to behave like a bunch of rowdy boys, and the American civilians who had come to France since the end of the war liked to sit around and complain. Many of them never bothered to learn French. Wright told Ellison: "The Americans flock together, living huddled in hotels taken over for them by the government; they sit in them, cold, mad, hungry, and longing for home."[42]

He and Ellen prided themselves on living among the French. But even if they held themselves slightly aloof from American expatriate circles, they benefited from the privileges enjoyed by the American colony in Paris. The exchange rate was extremely favorable to the dollar. Whereas the French had very restricted access to gasoline, Americans (paying with dollars) were given generous rations. Americans had their own PX store, formally known as the American National Interests Store, which sold imported food, staple and fresh, much of it otherwise unavailable in France. Americans in Paris had their own hospital, daily newspapers, libraries, and bookshops, their own schools, banks, and churches. Wright, who for most of his life had been confined to black ghettoes, now found himself in a "golden ghetto" in Paris.[43] "Life is tough here for the French people, with food sky high. Only foreigners seem able to live well," he wrote to American friends.[44]

Paris had a worse housing shortage than New York and finding an apartment proved harrowing. For two and a half months the Wrights lived in a hotel. This was not unusual in France—Sartre and de Beauvoir had lived in hotels for years—but to the Wrights it did not feel like a home. Eating out, given the food shortages, was exorbitant. Eventually, on 11 July, they moved into a small furnished apartment at 38, boulevard Saint-Michel. The rent was twenty dollars a month. In New York, their Charles Street apartment was bringing in more than two hundred dollars a month. Financially it seemed a good idea to stay on in Paris while Wright wrote his next book.

An Italian publishing house had bought a collection of five short stories by Wright, *Five Men*, several of which had previously appeared in English-language magazines. Wright finished "The Man Who Killed a Shadow," which was published in French in *Les Lettres Françaises*. He was excited when the Italian film director Roberto Rossellini expressed interest in *Native Son*. Meanwhile he was taking eight hours of French every week. "I swear I'm getting dumber with each lesson," he grumbled to Dorothy Norman, "but my teacher tells me that all at once things will open out for me and I'll understand everything. I hope so. Maybe one's mutest hour is just before the flood of words come."[45]

Because of the language difficulty, their friends were either Americans or those few French intellectuals who spoke good English. They had lunch once with Sartre and de Beauvoir, with de Beauvoir interpreting. At the end of summer, Wright, with the help of his French teacher, read *The Respectful Prostitute*, Sartre's one-act play about racism in the American South. He typed five pages of notes and suggestions.[46] Privately he thought Sartre's perceptions on race more impressive than his talents as a playwright. He corrected minor details about the race code in the Deep South, but his main quibble was with the dramatic structure. The action in the middle "bogs down hopelessly," he wrote in his notes to Sartre, and made several suggestions for improvement.

ONE MORNING IN AUGUST, ELLEN WOKE WRIGHT AT 4 A.M., COMPLAINING OF severe pain in the stomach. They told each other it would surely disappear, but it became considerably worse. At 7 A.M. Wright tried to phone a doctor—in vain. It was August. Paris had closed down. By midday he was at the American Hospital, begging for them to send an ambulance. That evening, Ellen had an appendectomy.

A couple of weeks later, Wright persuaded Ellen to go south to convalesce, taking Julia and her young Alsatian nanny. They went to Saint-Jean-de-Luz. It was like a tropical island, Ellen told Wright on the phone, and she was growing stronger fast. She and Julia even ventured briefly over the border into Franco's Spain. (Julia's nanny, with her French passport, was not permitted across the border.) In mid-September, Wright joined them for ten days.

During that vacation, the Wrights decided to return to the States—at least for a time, until the situation improved in Europe. The parlor-floor apartment in their Charles Street house had unexpectedly been vacated, and they were losing money. Before renting it out again, Ellen was keen to organize some repairs and renovations. Wright had done almost no writing in France, and he blamed the postwar chaos. Everything took so long in France. He had planned to visit Africa, but for the time being, travel was virtually impossible. Even getting tickets for Saint-Jean-de-Luz had involved "outright bribery."[47] He had hoped to see *Native Son* published by now, but Duhamel, the translator, was still "toying with it." It all made Wright impatient. "It tires one out to hurry things here; they simply have no sense of time."

They booked first-class cabins on the *Queen Elizabeth* leaving from Southampton in January. "Don't tell anyone we are coming back," Wright wrote to Dorothy Norman. "I am just perverse enough to want to come suddenly and catch my friends and enemies red-handed."[48]

WRIGHT, HIGHLY PROTECTIVE OF HIS PRIVATE LIFE, HAD NEVER BEEN MUCH OF A letter writer. His only regular correspondent during those months in Paris was Dorothy Norman. This was partly because of his editorial responsibility with the magazine *Twice a Year* and partly because she had done so much to help him get to Paris. And Norman spoke French and knew a great deal about French culture.

Naomi Replansky urged him to write "for god's sake, if not for mine." She was hoping to come to France soon herself.[49] Ralph Ellison, after getting no reply from Wright for a month, wrote to Ellen to say he had married his girlfriend, Fanny. "Absorb enough France for us," he said.[50] Horace Cayton complained that he heard about Wright from everyone except Wright himself. "I hear many good things—that you're the most interviewed American in Paris, that most of your work is being translated into French, and that you handle the language like a veteran. For all these things I envy you, my friend, and am also happy that you are able to enjoy them."[51] He added that he was gradually winding up his psychoanalysis. "I think it'll take a year to realize whether it did much good or not but I don't shake so much in the morning—that is, unless I have a hangover."

ON THE WAY HOME, THE WRIGHTS SPENT THREE WEEKS IN ENGLAND. WITH ITS smoking chimney stacks, gloomy narrow streets, and hordes of tired, ill-dressed people making their way to the subway, London reminded

Wright of Chicago. Signs of the war were everywhere. Rationing was grim, and heating was sparse. In their expensive hotel, Wright found himself the object of hostile stares.

He was shocked by the starkness of British class distinctions. And he was shocked that any grumbling he heard was directed not toward Germany, which had caused the endless vacant lots and rubble, but America, which had too much of everything. "Already the millions America sent to save England are being referred to as 'the American army of occupation we had with us for a while,'" he reported.[52]

During those few weeks in London they saw quite a bit of George and Dorothy Padmore. A tall, thin, dark-skinned man, Padmore originally came from Trinidad. He had once been high up in Communist circles in Moscow but had left the Party in a cloud of hostility. These days, he was preoccupied with the anticolonial struggle. His wife Dorothy, a large, imposing white woman from a working-class London family, was equally committed to the struggle. Wright liked them, but found them earnest. "All political talk," he noted in his journal. "Nothing to lift the mind or the emotions."[53]

The Wrights also spent time with Peter Abrahams, an ambitious twenty-eight-year-old black South African writer whom Wright thought brilliant. Wright recommended his work to Aswell.

Padmore and Abrahams were members of the Colored Writers' Association in London. On 10 January, the day before they sailed to New York, Richard Wright addressed the group at a French restaurant in Soho. His after-dinner talk was about race relations in the United States.

Europeans—particularly the French—kept asking Wright why on earth he was going back to the United States after all he had told them about it. Wright, looking slightly melancholy, would answer: "My life is back there."[54]

20

EXPATRIATES

February 1947–April 1948

If he felt the way he did about Paris, why had he returned to New York? two journalists from *PM* asked Wright. It was early February 1947. They had been interviewing him in his Charles Street house in Greenwich Village.[1] The living room was freshly painted, with gray walls and a mauve fireplace. In the corner was a suitcase. Some paintings were stacked in the fireplace. Otherwise there were few signs of the recent turmoil in the Wrights' lives.

Wright had been telling the journalists that he had not encountered "one iota of racial feeling in France" and that the French could not understand American racism. He added: "Don't let anyone tell you that any Negro in America, no matter what success he attains, has gotten over the difficulties and disabilities of being a Negro."

Nevertheless, their question seemed to surprise him. "'I live *here*,' he said with soft-voiced emphasis. 'My work is here. . . . I was fashioned in this peculiar kind of a hell.'" And he laughed that laugh of his.

IN FACT, THINGS HAD BEEN DIFFICULT AS SOON AS THEY HAD LANDED. THE ATTORney who managed their house during their absence, Jacob Salzman, had been negligent. The tenants had left the house in a mess, and the financial transactions had not been properly recorded. Wright wrote Salzman a furious letter. "All I want is a written report of your steward-ship from the time of the purchase of the property until the date of your report. In other words, what out did you collect, what expenses did you have, with an itemization as to each of those items, all of which should be backed up by paid bills. If there is any money left, let me have it."[2]

America had changed. Wright was taken aback by the new material-ism. In France, he told friends, people wanted to know your opinions. In America, they were only interested in your income.[3] There was an abundance of food compared with Europe, but Wright was interested in food for the mind.

The new America, now in a position of global eminence, saw itself as white, Protestant, and wealthy, he observed. "Americanism" had become a kind of religion. Postwar Americans hated the Soviets, Com-munists, and the labor unions. And they hated the Japanese, Chinese, and blacks. Everyone talked as if war with Russia was inevitable, and the Hearst Press was doing its best to whip up the "red scare." The liberal-ism of the Roosevelt era had completely disappeared.

When Wright walked around in the Village, people muttered "nig-ger" as he passed. One day, he paused in front of a corner store near his house, dazzled by an abundance of citrus fruit such as he had not seen in many months, and a swarthy Italian darted out. "Whudda yuy want, boy?"

Constance Webb, who lived nearby, remembers walking in the Vil-lage with Wright one day.[4] "Richard was having a fine time describing France and England, the people he had met, assuming various identities as easily as a professional actor," she writes.[5] It was cold outside, and to warm up they plunged into a snackbar on the corner of Twenty-second Street and Ninth Avenue. Wright had been teasing Webb and was wear-ing his gleeful look. The waitress brought two cups of steaming coffee.

Webb was the first to push her cup away in disgust. Wright was the first to speak. He beckoned to the waitress, who was observing them from a distance. "There's salt in our coffee," he said to her quietly. "That's how we serve it," the woman said defiantly. "If you don't like it here, then go somewheres else." Behind her, in the kitchen, the cook was holding a heavy skillet and glaring. They left.

On another occasion, Constance Webb took Julia to Central Park. They were waiting on Fifth Avenue for a bus home when Julia announced an urgent need to go to the bathroom. They went into the nearest store, Bergdorf Goodman. A saleswoman pointed out the way. Then she looked down and saw that Webb was holding the hand of a little brown girl. "There are no rest rooms for *you!*" the woman hissed.

In the Village that spring, there were several violent incidents when gangs of Italian youths took it upon themselves to punish interracial couples.[6] Wright never allowed Ellen to take his arm in the street. St. Clair Drake and his white wife had also moved to Greenwich Village, and Elizabeth was pregnant. Whenever they walked out together, Drake was terrified that somebody would attack his wife's swollen belly.[7]

AT THE END OF JANUARY 1947, SIMONE DE BEAUVOIR LANDED IN NEW YORK. IT was her first trip to the United States, and she was staying five months. She was astonished at the friendliness and human warmth of America, the superabundance, the overheated rooms, the expensively dressed women. Wright and his friends were a relief from the political conservatism, racism, and puritanism that shocked and confounded her.

She wrote to Sartre that of all the people she met in New York, she felt closest to Richard Wright. His Charles Street apartment felt like a home away from home. De Beauvoir (who did not easily warm to children) fell in love with five-year-old Julia—that "merveilleuse petite fille."[8] Ellen was "kind and lively like no other American woman in the world."[9] De Beauvoir would dedicate her book *America Day by Day* to Ellen and Richard Wright.

Whenever she walked in the streets with Wright, de Beauvoir was conscious of the hostile stares. Once, when she and her French friend Nathalie Moffat stood beside him on a street corner, an old woman stopped in front of them. "What are you two doing with that Negro?" she said.[10] De Beauvoir realized that Ellen Wright lived with these things every day.

One evening the Wrights took de Beauvoir to the Savoy, the famous dance hall in Harlem. They had arranged to meet in the lobby of her midtown hotel. As soon as Richard Wright walked in, de Beauvoir felt the atmosphere change. She saw the hostile looks from people when they tried to hail taxis in the street, and the drivers who refused to stop for them.

Years later, she recalled an incident in Wright's apartment that surprised her at the time:

> While I was there he had the visit of a female friend who was rather plain and rough mannered, and she grabbed Julia who must have been six at the time and pretended to be fighting with her. Well, Dick rushed and snatched the little one in his arms and shouted: "No violence, no violence," with a passion which quite astounded me. He was certainly disturbed by physical violence and wanted to protect Julia from even a show of it.[11]

In mid-April, after two months touring the country, de Beauvoir returned to New York. Over a quiet dinner at Dorothy Norman's with Richard Wright, she recounted her trip down South. She had been horrified by Jim Crow segregation, and shaken by the race hatred. Wright told her he had meanwhile decided he could no longer live in New York. He was taking his family back to Paris.

At one party they stayed to watch the dawn come up over the East River. De Beauvoir wrote to Sartre: "Wright was marvelous as he can be when he really relaxes, which is rare. I like him more and more."[12]

De Beauvoir spent her last evening in New York with Richard Wright and the writer and jazz aficionado Bernard Wolfe.[13] They ate in Chinatown, then took a taxi along the East River, past the glittering lights of Brooklyn and Queens, to Harlem. Wright was in high spirits. First he imitated a radio sports commentator at a baseball game, then a radio personality giving advice to troubled souls. When they stopped, their black driver said admiringly: "He's quite a card, your friend." So as not to be outdone, he showed them how the windows in his car the latest model—went up and down automatically.[14]

IT TOOK TWO MONTHS FOR WRIGHT TO DECIDE TO GO BACK TO FRANCE. Dorothy Norman watched the idea become an obsession. She was one of the few, she says, who understood:

Several people who knew both of us begged me to try to change his mind. "Why doesn't he accept his place in America and write as a black man about the Negro? He will kill himself as an author, as a creative force, if he goes abroad to live." I understood the argument, but couldn't agree with it. . . . The disputes went on for weeks. I refused to attempt to dictate Wright's destiny. If he wanted to move to Europe, he should go. If he stayed here and was miserable, what good would it do? Would it improve his writing?[15]

Wright heard the same argument over and over. He heard it from black friends; he heard it from white friends; he heard it from friends who were themselves expatriates. Camus, who had left his native Algeria for France, had told him he must not stay in France; the struggle was in America. Over dinner in Anaïs Nin's apartment, Albert Mangones, who had left Haiti to live in the U.S., was adamant that Wright should not live in Europe. He was needed here, among his people.[16]

"I can only be useful as a writer," Richard Wright would explain time and again, "and as a writer here I am strangled by petty humiliations, and daily insults. I am obsessed with only one theme. I need perspective. I need to get away from my personal hurts, my personal irritations. I am so constantly disturbed I cannot even work. I need to live free if I am to expand."[17]

ONE EVENING IN EARLY SUMMER, A YOUNG FRENCH JOURNALIST, MARIA LE Hardouin, came to the house to interview Wright for the French newspaper *Combat*.[18] It was dusk: children were playing in the street, and women sat and talked on the stoops. Le Hardouin liked this district; the Village seemed so much more human than the center of Manhattan. She had been shocked by the racism she had seen in her brief time in the United States, the hotels and restaurants where "colored people" were clearly not welcome. Charles Street—parallel to West Tenth Street, off Bleecker Street—seemed to her novice eyes a modest little street. She could not help wondering, though she did not dare ask him, whether Wright would be able to live elsewhere in New York if he wanted.

A smiling young woman with chestnut-colored hair and a sprinkling of freckles on her nose opened the door. "I'm Wright's wife," she told Le Hardouin. "My husband has just gone out to get some cigarettes."

Inside, Le Hardouin found herself sitting on a floral divan in a large room crowded with trunks and suitcases. Ellen Wright was asking about her impressions of New York when Richard Wright came in. He was stocky, Hardouin observed, and casually dressed. He carried a bottle of California wine under his arm. He filled their glasses, and they started to talk as if they had known each other for years, as people did in America. "Wright jumped from one subject to another with disconcerting rapidity," Le Hardouin would write, "and asked questions without listening to the replies. Suddenly, he asked me, with an attentive look: 'What about Existentialism?'"

Le Hardouin admitted that she preferred the idea of eternal flames to the idea of nothingness. Wright started to talk about the existentialist concept of "choice." Le Hardouin was not convinced that she alone had chosen what she had become. "I'm personally convinced of it," said Wright. "It is impossible that certain desires, which come to us in our childhood with an irresistible force, are not already the result of a choice that we struggled with and made before we were even conscious of it."

Le Hardouin suddenly realized, with pleasure, that she was no longer feeling nostalgic for France. She felt at home with this American couple. "Will you be going back to Paris soon?" she asked.

"In August," Wright said. And their faces—his and Ellen's—lit up.

BY THE END OF MAY, THE WRIGHTS HAD HAD ENOUGH OF THE RACIAL HOSTILITIES in the Village. They put their house on the market, and packed up again. They were going to spend the summer at Wading River, where Dr. Frank Safford had several cottages on a nine-acre piece of land overlooking Long Island Sound. They had thought of going there before, but the cottage had been available for only a month, and they had gone to Quebec instead. This time, they were staying for two months.[19]

They drove there in their new black Oldsmobile sedan—automatic transmission, with a radio.[20] Wright had been taking driving lessons and had obtained his license. Their new companion was a pretty black and white kitten, acquired from the Society for the Prevention of Cruelty to Animals.

On Long Island, with few interruptions and no telephone, Wright wrote for hours each day. In two months, he wrote almost a hundred thousand words of a new novel. He dropped *Black Hope* once and for all. Reynolds had extended the contract for his novel (originally due in January 1947) to April 1948.

Wright's new protagonist, Cross Damon, was trying to forge a new identity. A Chicago postal worker, he let people think he had died in a subway accident, and he began a new life in New York, with a new name. Wright, too, was about to start again in a new city. He was no longer categorized as a Communist, and he hoped he would no longer be categorized as a "Negro." He wanted to be a human being—a citizen of the world.

Wright was happy in Wading River. He was "always ready to parry any argument and was often the life of the party," Frank Safford would recall later. In the evenings, there were endless "talk fests" with the various artists and intellectuals who were staying in the other cottages.[21] Julia played on the beach and was learning to read. The cat roamed the woods. A photograph shows a relaxed-looking Wright sitting on the beach in shorts and sunglasses, cigarette in the corner of his mouth, holding in his arms a cat that is wriggling to escape.

Horace Cayton came to stay for a few days. Constance Webb came for two weeks and gave Ellen driving lessons. Wright did not have sufficient calm for this job. "I had to banish him from the car after the first trip," Webb recalls. "He got so nervous and nagged her so much that she ran into a vacant lot trying to make a corner."[22] Webb also remembers Wright's behavior with the cat. "He tried patiently to teach it tricks, aggravating the poor animal beyond endurance until it would hiss and run under the bed."[23]

The Wrights made a hefty profit on the Charles Street home. The sad news was that after twelve years at Harper, Edward Aswell was going over to McGraw-Hill. Aswell had been the first person prepared to take the risk and publish Wright's work. He had always been encouraging. Even if Wright did not always take his advice, Aswell was a good and conscientious editor. They had a warm relationship. He had liked Wright's recommendations for new manuscripts, and Wright had

had a significant influence on Harper's lists. Wright wrote him a heart-felt letter. The normally restrained Southerner found himself deeply moved. "Almost unnerved," Aswell admitted.[24]

Wright's new editor at Harper was John Fischer, a Rhodes scholar from Texas who had studied Russian history and recently made a three-month journey through the Soviet Union. Harper had just published his book, *The Scared Men in the Kremlin*. An impassioned piece of Cold War propaganda, it could just as well have been written by the Department of Defense.

Reynolds and Wright agreed that he might have to change publishers. Reynolds suggested he meet Fischer and then decide. "We want to be sure you don't have a publisher who might be trying in small ways to censor what you wanted to say."[25]

YEARS LATER, LOOKING BACK ON HIS DEPARTURE FROM THE UNITED STATES, Wright would tell Ed Aswell: "In all of this pointless racial business, I found that my being a rather well known writer did not help me any. In fact, it hindered, for many whites felt that by refusing me they were 'putting me in my place.' I also discovered that liberals in America were all but useless. . . . I grew more embarrassed by appealing to them than they did."[26]

The Wrights returned to New York City four days before sailing on 30 July 1947. They stayed with George Davis, who now lived in a large brownstone on East Eighty-sixth Street. Davis had spent time in France. A Francophile, he perfectly understood their decision to go and live there.

Wright mailed money to his mother. (He frequently sent money and clothes to the family.) He gave Paul Reynolds power of attorney. He made arrangements for the car and took the cat to the vet for injections.

They had been back in the United States just six months. This time, they were saying good-bye indefinitely. They had booked a stateroom cabin on the SS *America*, the largest steamship in the country. That last afternoon, they held a dockside party in their cabin.[27] Champagne flowed. Then, after a final round of hugs, the friends repaired to the quay, and amid streamers and the booming of the ship's funnel the Wrights set off across the Atlantic a second time.

———

THAT EVENING, WHILE THE SHIP CLEAVED ITS WAY THROUGH THE DARK NIGHT toward the Old World, Wright sat in their cabin, took out his typewriter, and started another journal. "I hope to remain away from America this time as long as possible," he wrote. "Maybe not in France, but certainly away from America."

Both the portholes were open. Wright felt calmed by the quiet swish of the ocean. It had been a long, hot day. Ellen was watching a movie in the ship's entertainment rooms. Julia had fallen asleep. They had done so much in the final days. They had a car in the hold and a cat in the ship's kennel. In his briefcase was half a novel in first draft. In the last week or so, he had never let it out of his sight. His hand was sore from clutching that briefcase. He told himself he must make sure to work on his manuscript every day of the voyage. If only they could settle into a Paris apartment quickly. He did not want to lose momentum. Not again.

WRIGHT KEPT HIS JOURNAL FOR THREE MONTHS, FROM 30 JULY TO 23 SEPTEMBER 1947. He knew he was at another major turning point in his life.

During the ten-day voyage, he walked around the decks and looked for hostile stares from white Americans. He found them, of course. He told himself that Americans were raw, crude, and lacking in sensitivity. The French, on the other hand, were logical and reasonable. They might be naïve, but at least they were not superficial. "Had red wine with my dinner," he wrote. "How like France that was; it brought back a thousand memories." He wondered if the Dodgers had won back home. If only his little radio could pick up American news.

He lay in bed at night and worried about the future. During the day he had more immediate concerns. They were trying to book passage across the channel for themselves and the car at the same time. Would they have to wait around for days, or even weeks, in England? On the last two voyages Julia had broken out in hives; Ellen was giving her milk of magnesia to settle her. If their cat, Knobby, landed on English soil, he would have to be in quarantine for six months. The ship stopped first in Cherbourg; the Wrights were hoping to find someone to take him from Cherbourg straight to Paris. "It is not enough that I spend my damn time worrying about the human race. Goddammit, I must worry about the animal kingdom too!"[28]

He had wasted a great deal of time over the past year. There had been so much to organize, so much to worry about. "I ought to be able to give the best of my life to my work but it is impossible. Things get loused up, especially when I let other people do things for me. . . . But if I do everything myself I cannot work."[29]

He sat on deck and stared at the sea and thought about his novel. That summer he had been reading Kierkegaard's *The Concept of Dread*. "Dread is an alien power which lays hold of an individual, and yet one cannot tear oneself away," Kierkegaard wrote. Wright thought he would use that as the epigraph to his new novel. Dread had always lurked in the shadows of his existence.

He reread the draft he had written on Long Island and was pleased that it had "some pull and heat." But it needed considerable work. He was reading a manuscript Peter Abrahams had sent him about his South African childhood under apartheid. It reminded him of his own childhood in Mississippi. He had wired Pete, and hoped he would be in Southampton to meet them. He wanted to tell him how good it was.

Things turned out well. He managed to book an immediate channel passage. An Italian-American family getting off in Cherbourg agreed to take Knobby to Paris. And when the Wrights disembarked in Southampton on 6 August, Peter Abrahams was on the wharf to meet them.

Abrahams returned to London the next day, and Wright drove the family to Folkestone, with Ellen navigating. Driving on the left side of the road was less difficult than he had feared. He was even able to admire the beauty of the English countryside. That night, they stayed in the Grand Hotel, with a view of the Channel, misty and blue, through the window.

At Dover the following afternoon, they watched a giant crane hoist the car onto the ship. Onlookers made a fuss over Julia, and some Americans came up and spoke to Wright. How different things were when they were outside the "shameful and restricting atmosphere" of the States. Julia had developed hives again. On the crossing, while she and her mother rested, Wright stood on deck and gazed at the jellyfish in the blue-green water.

From Boulogne, they drove to Paris. As they entered the city, the last rays of light were caressing the ancient stone buildings. Wright felt as if he were in a dream, driving his own car in the streets of Paris.

They stopped once to ask for directions, but they were surprised how easily they found their way to the Faubourg Saint-Germain. "It was a rather breathless time when we saw the rue de Lille where we were to stay for four months," Wright observed.[30] Odette Lieutier's house, number nine, was a magnificent old house, with a splendid garden and fountain, just one block away from the Seine. Odette Lieutier managed the Librairie Bonaparte, a bookshop on the rue Bonaparte that specialized in theater and performance. She spoke good English and had many American friends. The Wrights planned to stay in her house until the end of the year. It would give them time to find their own apartment.

ODETTE LIEUTIER WAS NOT HOME, BUT THE SERVANT LET THEM IN. "HOW TIRED we were when we sat down." Then Odette turned up with a party of friends, and Wright and Ellen were obliged to have drinks and make conversation. They finally got to bed at 11 P.M. "My sleep was troubled," Wright wrote in his journal. "All my deep desires came out and I tossed, half asleep and half awake."

Their first full day in Paris, 9 August, was frenetic and frustrating. There was no hot water. Odette said it would be back on the next day, but it was off for a week, and Odette did not seem to consider it important. In the meantime, bathing involved lugging boiling water from the kitchen to the bathroom and washing with a facecloth. The gas stove did not light. They had to find milk for Julia (not easy), fetch Knobby, start to unpack, and try to get back their former maid, Alice. (She would sleep in the back room with Julia.) Everything seemed to involve endless driving around the streets of Paris. By the end of the day, Wright was "tired, tired, tired."

Conditions in Paris were worse, much worse, than the previous year. People were hungry. There had been strikes all year. Different sections of Paris were without electricity at any one time, a deliberate policy to save coal. The strikes and severe rationing of power were having a devastating effect on French industry. Gas and water were periodically cut off. Everyone was worried about the coming winter.

Wright had to pick up their seventeen trunks of food and clothing from the station. They had to renew their *cartes d'identité* and register Julia at the American School on the boulevard Raspail. Knobby ate chicken bones and had to be taken to the vet. Wright went to buy a tub for Alice to wash their clothes in and found he needed ration coupons. It was August, French employees were on vacation, and they could not get food rations from the American Post Exchange for another two weeks. Wright kept forgetting that Paris closed down on Mondays and that French stores closed for two or more hours over lunch.

They decided they would need to find another place to live as soon as possible. Nothing seemed to work in that house. It was dirty, and they suspected that Odette Licutier was on drugs. "Poor Ellen" was back on the hunt for apartments.[31]

The car made it easier to run errands and search for an apartment. But Paris drivers were careless, and parking was a problem. Friends warned them the car would be stolen unless they found a garage for it at night. And then things kept going wrong. First the gas gauge didn't work; then the vehicle wouldn't reverse; then the speedometer didn't work; then it had a flat tire. Wright couldn't make himself understood by French mechanics and was relieved when he eventually found an American garage.

It embarrassed him that the French stared at his huge American car. People stopped and stared and clucked their tongues admiringly, and he was never sure how to react. "I've never been able to take much pride in having a material advantage over other people," he wrote in his journal.[32] Driving a car at all in Paris was a statement of privilege. The French could get hold of gasoline only if they were doctors or taxi drivers or else managed to secure costly black-market coupons. Americans were given an almost infinite supply. The government needed their dollars.

Wright rented a small garret room in a hotel across the street. It cost him a hundred francs a day, which at the current exchange rate was about fifty cents. He furnished it with a folding bed, a table, a bookcase full of books, two typewriters, several reams of yellow paper, a phonograph with records for learning French. He also took a telescope and sometimes amused himself by peering through people's windows.

He had no appetite and wondered why. But he was glad he was losing weight. "I live alone," he wrote in his journal. "My deepest thoughts are communicated to no one. No one around me. I just think them and try to write them. How can I live free, freely? That is the question of my life."[33] It was also the question in his new novel. The old world was dissolving, and the new world was as yet unformed. It seemed to Wright that people would need a new set of feelings and attitudes to respond to it.

They had hired a cook from an agency. One evening, she prepared an entire meal of string beans. Wright "felt like a horse."[34] He tried to make bread, but Ellen had allowed Julia to play in the kitchen, and Julia had mixed sugar into the salt. Wright was embarrassed. "All of this in front of people who are almost starving."[35]

He was dreaming a great deal. "Dreamed last night that we were in an auto, but driving from the back seat; no one was in the front seat."[36] Life itself felt like a dream at the moment. "How odd and strange life is, it is like something that we ride and do not know what it is, yet we ride it each and every day. We live, live in some vast mystery, and it is not ours to say how it was started or how it must end."[37]

At the end of August they found an apartment at 166, avenue de Neuilly, near the Bois de Boulogne, for twenty-five thousand francs a month. They did not like this sedate, wealthy district on the outskirts of the city, but the apartment was elegant and spacious, and they were keen to get out of Odette Lieutier's clutches. They told themselves it was only for a year or until they found something suitable on the Left Bank. They took it.

CARSON AND REEVES MCCULLERS WERE LIVING IN PARIS. THEY HAD REMARRIED after the war. Wright was curious to see how they were coping. He took a taxi to their apartment (his car was being repaired) and found Carson ill again. She had had another stroke, could not see out of one eye, and her whole right side was numb. She and Reeves had been in Paris for seven months and had been hardly anywhere.

While Wright waited for Reeves to come home, Carson drank four bottles of beer and told Wright it was because she was so glad to see him. Eventually, they gave up on Reeves, and Wright took her out to dinner. She drank most of the bottle of red wine, then had a stiff cognac at home, while telling Wright that her doctor forbade alcohol. He was convinced she did not have long to live.[38]

Later that week, he and Ellen went out to dinner with Carson and Reeves. They were already drunk when the Wrights picked them up in the car. Ellen had to leave the table early to relieve their maid Alice from baby-sitting, and Reeves insisted on seeing her to a taxi. When Wright got home, Ellen told him Reeves had made a pass at her. "I've been trying to find a job for Reeves, but can you help a man to find a job when he molests your wife? Wright wrote in his journal "I'll not help him anymore and I'll keep away from both Carson and Reeves. Too bad."[39]

He would soften in the weeks to come. When the Wrights moved out, Carson and Reeves moved into their apartment at Odette's. It was much nicer than the place they were in.

ONE AFTERNOON, THE FAMILY WENT TO THE BOIS DE BOULOGNE. ELLEN RENTED A rowboat and took Julia out on the lagoon. They wanted Wright to join them. He refused, then felt bad about it. "I don't like physical exertion. And when others expect me to like it, I become terribly ashamed. I sometimes wish that my wife and daughter had a husband and father who could do the things they naturally expect and the things that a man ought to do. But I do hope that they love me for what I am, just a nervous, scared, but somehow brave man who tries his goddamnest to do his best."[40]

Ellen could not have failed to notice her husband's susceptibility to the charms of other women. The day after the dinner with the McCullerses, Dr. Polin, a female gynecologist, came for afternoon tea at Odette's. The Wrights were invited and so were the women tenants who lived on the top floor. When the others went into the garden, Wright and Dr. Polin remained inside and talked. He thought she spoke English "charmingly." She questioned him about America and amused him with stories about the sex lives of French women. After dinner she drove with him to a garage nearby, where he could park his car at night. He took her for drinks at the Deux Magots.

> While with Dr. Polin, who has green-grey eyes, and whose hair is cut rather short but whose face is sweet . . . and whose mouth shapely, I could not help but marvel at how intensely feminine and at the same time intellectual the French woman was. This combination of woman-ness and sharp thought is something almost unknown in America, and I

told her so, that that was why so many American men lost their heads over French women, and why American women were so afraid of French women. She laughed, delighted.[41]

Dr. Polin was leaving the next day for the south of France. "When she returns I'd like to get to know her better," Wright wrote in his journal.

AT THE END OF AUGUST THEY WERE PACKING UP ONCE MORE. NOT WANTING TO tempt the French removalists, Wright and Ellen stashed their American food into the wooden crates themselves. The truck arrived while they were still eating breakfast. The rest of the day, in Neuilly, was spent unpacking. "Ellen was superb," Wright wrote in his journal. Only Knobby did not like their new quarters. "He misses the woods of Long Island, the garden of Odette, and wants to do his business all over the house."[42] Wright decided to shut him in the kitchen with his pan of sawdust until he made up his mind to use it.

The new apartment was airy, clean, and spacious, and it even had an elevator. But they now needed furniture. This involved several trips to the Marché aux Puces. Sylvia Beach, the former manager of Shakespeare & Company, had been storing their icebox. When she returned from her summer vacation, Wright went to fetch it and found her glowing with health. He went out to buy ice, then had to lug fifty pounds of ice up eight flights of stairs. The elevator was out of order.

"I must hide this journal," he wrote on 1 September. "Ellen is looking at me as though she has read some of it." Two days later, on 3 September: "Ellen's birthday. I must kiss her, though I got her her flowers yesterday. I've not had the chance to buy her anything." Ellen had turned thirty-five.

The day after was his own birthday. "I'm 39 years old, and not much yet done," he worried in his journal. "I don't feel old, just tired from too much worry about petty things." He was still finding it impossible to settle down to concentrated work on his novel. All he seemed able to do was read. Sometimes he took a book and read under the trees in the Bois de Boulogne. This was where he read Camus's *The Stranger*—in English. He read it slowly, weighing each sentence. He admired

Camus's narrative style and liked the way he used fiction to express a philosophical idea. But the novel was "devoid of passion."[43]

In addition to Alice the maid, Ellen had engaged a cook, who would also look after Julia. The cook refused to ride in the elevator because her husband had once had a terrible accident in one of them. "We pooh-poohed the idea and finally she said that she would try to overcome her fear," Wright wrote in his journal. "We don't care if she wants to walk up and down, but we don't want Julia to walk up and down. That would be awful."[44]

The garbage collectors went on strike in Paris. When the festering piles of garbage became a severe health hazard, state troops protected scab workers as they struggled to remove them. In October the transport workers went on strike. There was no *métro* and no buses. For ten days, Wright took Julia to school and fetched her in the late afternoon and ran friends around Paris. He felt like a taxi service.

WRIGHT WAS HELPING SOME FRENCH-SPEAKING AFRICAN FRIENDS ESTABLISH A NEW journal: *Présence Africaine*. The first issue was to appear in November. Alioune Diop, from Senegal, was the editor. Richard Wright was on the editorial board, along with Aimé Césaire from Martinique and Léopold Senghor from Senegal. Gide, Sartre, and Camus were named as patrons. The group needed the support of prominent whites to protect them from the *Ministère des Colonies*, which could have them arrested and the magazine stopped.

Their aim was to make Africa a presence, rather than an absence, in the European mind. The journal celebrated *Négritude*—a term coined in the 1930s by Césaire and Senghor. The word *nègre* had been thrown at them as an insult; they turned it into something positive. The colonizers had always dismissed African culture; the *Présence Africaine* men wanted to show that black culture carried weight in the white world.

Wright was wary of the Afrocentric strain in the journal. He was no *Négritude* man; he was a Westerner, and in favor of racial assimilation. But he did care about fighting colonialism and racism. Because of him, the journal's horizons expanded to include black America. The first issue contained French translations of a story by Wright and a poem by the Chicago poet Gwendolyn Brooks. During its first year, the journal published essays (sometimes in English, sometimes translated) by Horace Cayton, C. L. R. James, E. Franklin Frazier, and Wright.

Wright identified with the sense these Western-educated men had of being "uprooted beings," straddled between two societies and out-siders in both. He had always liked Robert Park's suggestion that "mar-ginal men" could see more clearly.

AMERICANS WERE COMING AND GOING THE WHOLE TIME, AND EVERYBODY seemed to want to see Richard Wright. One morning early in Septem-ber, Edith Schroeder phoned. She was, she explained, a close friend of Naomi Replansky. She had not been in Paris long and was waiting for the American military authorities to give her permission to join her hus-band, Max Schroeder, in Berlin. Wright invited her around for tea that afternoon.

"She is terribly lonely," he wrote in his journal. He was incredulous that she had come to Paris with no more than $250. He asked her back the following evening, along with another American who had called earlier in the week.

> Edith Schroeder and Helen Weinstein came by after dinner. What a dif-ference there was between those two girls, both Jewish, from the Bronx, tall, lanky American types, intelligent, and lost and melancholy and unhappy, running away from their country and their families. Helen is rather ugly, a florid and moving face, talks a blue streak, and is never still. . . . Edith is silent, trying hard to understand, saying little, asking many questions when she does talk.[45]

A week later, Ellen and Julia went to the country for a few days. Wright spent the afternoon reading the papers and waiting for coal to be delivered. "It is quiet in the house with Ellen and Julia gone and very restful, but I miss them already." He went to bed early.

The next day, Friday, he invited Helen Weinstein to dinner. "We ate and listened to some blues and jazz records. Went to bed dead tired; I had too much cognac to drink."[46] On Saturday, Ellen phoned and said they were having a fine time and would stay till Tuesday. That evening, Wright invited Edith Schroeder to dinner. "Ate dinner with Edith, talked, played records and drove her home."

In his journal he writes that he slept for only three hours, and got up at nine. He was invited to lunch with Adrienne Monnier and Sylvia Beach. He was tired and forced himself to eat, hoping they didn't notice. As soon as he could, he left and drove to Edith's hotel. They went for a drive in the Bois de Boulogne.

On Monday Edith came to lunch. Wright had also invited a black French doctor, recently back from Africa. The three of them argued about politics. Wright wished they hadn't. Edith was a committed Communist, and they did not agree.

That evening, he and Edith were at the Café de Flore when Odette Lieutier turned up with American friends. He suggested they all have dinner together and immediately regretted it. The group ended up at the Tabou, a smoky, noisy jazz cellar in the rue Dauphine. Wright was known there and some French journalists started taking pictures, until he stopped them. He did not enjoy watching French youths trying to imitate an American New Orleans dancing style. A mood of depression settled on him, which he could not shake:

> I hated that place; it made me feel like I was living again those horrible
> days in Chicago when I was lonely and hungry and scared. I could not
> tell my friends what I was feeling, but simply said that I had gone off the
> track somewhere and wanted to go home. I didn't really want to go
> home, but I wanted something that would nourish me. That is what I am
> missing, nourishing experiences. . . . Home, taking Edith to her hotel,
> and feeling that I was driving in a dream.[47]

In her memoirs, *Love in Exile*, Edith Anderson (this is her unmarried name) writes that her friend "Deborah" (Naomi Replansky) "virtually forced" Wright's telephone number on her when she left for Europe.[48] Edith knew about the scandal Wright's *Atlantic Monthly* essay, "I Tried to Be a Communist," had provoked in Communist circles. She had not read it, but she knew Wright as a renegade who denounced the Party.

Edith was thirty-one. Her Jewish parents were distressed to see her going to the country of the Nazis to join a husband she scarcely knew. She spoke no German and only schoolgirl French. With money to last her three weeks, she had taken a boat to Paris, where she had to wait for permission to travel to occupied Berlin. Through American contacts, she had found a temporary job in Paris as a filing clerk at a Jewish philanthropic organization. The only reason she decided to phone Richard Wright was loneliness. "On Saturdays and Sundays I was so lonely I could have howled."[49]

According to her, she had turned up at the Wrights' apartment in Neuilly in a "white cotton summer dress printed with little smears of color like a painter's brush strokes." The opulence of the furnishings astounded her. The living room, with its stained-glass windows framed in wrought iron, seemed to her like a hotel lobby. Ellen was not at home. Wright introduced her to the cook, who was going home and looked disapproving.

Wright wanted to know whether Edith was a poet, like Naomi. She told him she had written some stories and was thinking about a novel. He asked about the theme. Embarrassed, she told him it was about love between women. "To my amazement he seemed delighted to hear this. He saw connections between the oppression of black people, women, and Jews and thought my topic immensely important. I had thought it immensely trivial."

When they talked, he listened intently, bending forward and looking keenly into her face. ("His questions were not casual," Anderson writes. "His interest proved never to be feigned.") She told him she had once met him in Harlem with his wife. She and her first husband had answered an advertisement for an upstairs apartment. "Oh, that must have been Dhimah," Wright said. Anderson could tell this was not a subject he cared to pursue.

She decided to tell him that she had almost not phoned, that she belonged to the Party, that in her eyes he was a class enemy. To her surprise, he showed no animosity at this. "Patiently, insistently, he set out to prove that I was wrong." She argued back. "Oh girl, we have a lot of talking to do," Wright said.

She remembers him seizing some binoculars from a sideboard and saying, "Ever try one of these?" He walked over to an open window and leveled the glasses across the street. "'I could watch for hours,'" he cried gleefully. 'Oh! Look at this! Come here! Try them!'" She was shocked.

What Anderson leaves out of her memoirs is that Wright tried to seduce her. She was not keen, and he ended up chasing her playfully around the apartment. It was obvious to her that he was not used to resistance. "It's my color, isn't it?" he said to her. Edith denied it. Privately she would always wonder whether it played a role. "Dick was in love with me because I said no," she says.[50] That one evening, however, she ended up in bed with him.

She came to dinner at the apartment shortly afterward, when Ellen was there. It was, Anderson writes, "a ghastly occasion".

> The little girl having been packed off somewhere, I found myself in her place at the middle of an endless table with Ellen at the head and Dick at the foot and a shouting silence in between. . . . After dinner [Ellen] retired to a sofa at the far north end of the salon, adjusted and readjusted herself with sensuous rustling sounds in the plush fittings, said something about just adoring Dostoyevsky and made even the opening of a book an acoustic performance.
>
> In our original two armchairs Dick and I were graciously left to whatever conversation we could make under the circumstances. I have no recollection of it, only the occasional whisper of Ellen's page turning.[51]

Wright did not invite Edith to the house again. He would drive over to her hotel and wait in the lobby for her to come home from work, whereupon he took her somewhere in the car. Most of their conversations took place in the car.

In October Wright had another of his severe bouts of grippe. He was in bed for a week, got up for two days, and was back in bed. Friends recommended a holiday on the Côte d'Azur. Ellen made reservations for him, and in mid-November Wright went for two weeks to Monte Carlo. He loved the town perched on the hill, the blue Mediterranean stretching away in the mist, the narrow streets, the pastel-colored houses, the palm trees, the cactuses.

As soon as he had unpacked his things, he wrote to Edith. Couldn't she come down? If she wired him, he would get her a room at a hotel. In this mild climate and fresh air, he was already feeling better. He had just taken his temperature. It was normal for the first time in two weeks. Then he dropped the casual tone.

> Listen, you Funny-Faced girl, I'm pretty good at untangling my own emotions, but what you evoke in me is something I've not yet felt for any other woman. I don't know what it is. Why do you haunt me so?

Why can't I just put you away somewhere like I do all other people? I've tried, but that face of yours, that look in your eyes, just keeps coming back. . . . Maybe you know why? I don't. I burn to know you; I really do. It is as though there is some answer for me in getting to know you. It's silly, but there it is. I'm no good at naming my feelings; forgive the incoherence. I'm thinking of you and want to see you. Love, Dick.[52]

He enclosed a five-thousand-franc note.

The next day he sat in the warm sun in the gardens and watched the pigeons circling and wheeling. He thought about his new novel. Ever since his burst of work that summer on Long Island he had made no progress. He felt he was on the brink of plunging in again. He called by Cook's to make inquiries about travel from Paris. He wrote to Edith again. The plane trip to Nice took less than three hours, he told her, and he would meet her in Nice.

He put a call through to her hotel. It was good to hear her voice, but the conversation left him depressed. It seemed unlikely that she would come:

Well, darling, if you do or not come—and there is a chill in my heart telling me that you won't come—I still think you are one of the nicest people I've ever known. The talk I had with you that rainy night in the car, the mood of it, is still with me. . . . Whether you come down or not, I've got, somehow and someway, to get some of the fever of you out of me; really, I must, for I'm letting you and the sense of you just fill me and that is not good, since you are you and I am I and we are apart. . . . I've got to take hold of myself firmly and try to see what it was in me that you stirred up so violently, try to learn what kind of hunger it was that made me leap and want you so badly, and then try to direct that hunger somewhere else, maybe in writing. . . . I've had to do that before; it is not easy; and you are really not to blame for this at all. It just happened to me. . . . Be good, Sweet. And try to write. I shan't worry you with more letters like this, for I feel that I'm being rather foolish and childish and dull to you and I never want to be that to anyone.

I love you and I'd like to talk to you about it, to try to find out what kind of love it is; there are many kinds of love, you know. Meanwhile, be good. As ever, Dick.[53]

He spent his days thinking about Edith, thinking about his novel, reading, drinking hot chocolate, and climbing up the hill to the movies. He was pleased to read in the paper that André Gide had won the Nobel Prize for literature. He had met Gide briefly at a Paris reception the previous year and thought him a courageous man — one of the few on the Left prepared to speak out in defense of individual freedom.

Two days later, on 20 November, he wrote Edith for the last time from Monte Carlo:

In my last letter I had already retreated into my ice-box and was trying to close the door; I've such a deep-seated pattern and complex of rejections that when I see or smell one coming I try to get ready for it; and then you came just before I could get the door closed and you slammed it. Now, darling, I'm not bitter. But, gosh, why do you use such queer words to say no? Here they are in part: "the implications of such a trip are too foreign to my chief desires." God! You'd think that you were one government and I was another, and that we were almost about to go to war! . . . I doubt if there is anything, Edith, about you which I could not understand and accept.

He had decided he would not see her for a month or so after he got back.

That ought to give me time to get myself in hand. . . . I must say that you are firm, and yet that very firmness makes me love you all the more. Now this is what I must do; I must take firmly in my mind this turgid passion I have and hold it present to my gaze until it melts back to me, to where it leapt from, and when that happens I shall feel lonely indeed, the worst kind of loneliness, for it is the kind that makes you know that what you wanted so badly was not in the world but in you, that there was some lack, some hunger, some burning desire that made one's feeling leap out and seize hold of another. But when that happens one wonders what life is about, why feel these things when there is no way to realize them?[54]

Just as he was about to leave, there was a general strike. The workers were angry: prices had increased by 50 percent and they were hungry.

The French Communist Party encouraged the strikes, hoping to provoke a crisis and destroy de Gaulle and his right-wing party, the *Rassemblement du Peuple Français*. Everything closed down—factories, coal mines, post offices, the telephone exchange, trains. The country was in pandemonium. It looked as if the franc would collapse.

Wright could not get a message through to Paris, and he was stranded. He went to the airport and tried to get on a plane. A storm was battering the south and another was on the way. All flights were canceled. An Englishman came in and said he had a six-passenger plane and was going to try to get through the storm. Wright said he would take the chance. So did five Frenchmen. They took off. Ten minutes later, a fire broke out in the cockpit. They put it out, but the storm got worse. Bumping and rocking, they returned to Nice. Waves from the ocean were breaking on the landing strip.

The men then hired a private car to get them to Paris.[55] They kept hitting walls of water and had to tow the car to a service station to dry the spark plugs. They decided to go through the mountains. It had snowed, but they told themselves that snow would be better than floods. From Lyon, they plowed through snow to Paris. The trip took twenty-six hours. Their teeth were chattering most of the way.

Wright, who had gone south to convalesce, returned with a sore throat. Within three weeks, he was feverish. On 18 December, the doctor sent him to the American Hospital. For days he was given penicillin injections.

Edith came to see him in his hospital bed. "He was subdued and would not tell me what was wrong with him. 'Just tired,' he said with no voice. It was strange to find him inert and uncommunicative, with his head on a pillow."[56] It was the last time she saw him. She was leaving for Berlin on Christmas Eve. Wright had promised to take her to the station with her bags. The day before she left, he phoned to say he was in no condition to help her. She was not pleased. A week later, she wrote and apologized for her "scared and tantrumy" behavior and for sounding "so helpless and betrayed."[57]

A few months after that, Edith wrote from Germany. She had written a novel. The idea had germinated one evening in his car. She would like him to read it. "This may or may not gladden your heart, but if it were not for you I would never have begun it."[58]

ALL AROUND THE WORLD, COMMUNISTS WERE ATTACKING RICHARD WRIGHT. IN Moscow, he was described as a "renegade" whose works were showing "ever-growing signs of the putrefaction common to American decadent literature."[59]

In the United States his old friend Ted Ward (who had loved *Native Son*) declared in the left-wing journal *Mainstream* that Wright had exerted a most unfortunate influence on contemporary black writers, whose books echoed Wright's "defeatism."[60]

In France the Communist critic Jean Kanapa attacked *Les Temps Modernes* for its celebration of Wright.[61] How many radicals had the journal included in its American issue? he asked. Not one. Instead, it had published reactionaries like Wright! And why did *Les Temps Modernes* promote Wright? Because when it came to despair and mystification he was its brother!

"Whatever we may think about Wright, . . . this piece of communist writing was one of the dirtiest things I ever read," de Beauvoir wrote disgustedly to Nelson Algren in Chicago.[62]

DE BEAUVOIR TROD CAREFULLY WHEN SHE WROTE TO NELSON ALGREN ABOUT Wright. Her man in Chicago thought Wright took himself too seriously.

From Algren's point of view, Wright had fallen on his feet yet again. He had been a best-selling writer in the United States, and now he was having an impact in Europe. He lived in the heart of Paris and seemed to have endless contacts, including de Beauvoir and other French intellectuals. Algren's own friends were mostly junkies. His latest book, *The Neon Wilderness*, had received very little attention. As de Beauvoir would point out in *America Day by Day*, Algren was an example of the "great intellectual solitude in which American writers live today."[63]

Despite her tactful reticence, de Beauvoir's letters to Algren give brief glimpses of enjoyable moments spent with the Wrights. She and Sartre visited their apartment in Neuilly ("a sad wealthy district"), listened to Louis Armstrong and Bessie Smith records, drank brandy, and talked— in English. ("I think you Americans are the most lazy or the most arrogant people in the world, not caring to know any language but your own.") Then they all went and ate couscous in a "lonely Arabian restaurant."

Julia continued to charm her. "The little girl is more and more beautiful, and so lively and eager: I should like to be a fairy and endow her with all possible gifts." As for Ellen: "I think she is a really nice woman, one of the best women I know."[64]

She and Sartre enjoyed Wright's talent for imitating people. "Really," she told Algren, "he is better than most French intellectuals, much more lively, gay, humorous."[65]

AFTER A QUIET CHRISTMAS—WRIGHT WAS ONLY JUST OUT OF THE HOSPITAL—THE family drove to Belgium. The shops were full of American goods, and Wright was disgusted that Belgium's wealth was largely due to uranium mines in the Belgian Congo—uranium that the Belgians sold to the United States. "The Belgians are fat, dull, and their minds are as narrow and devious as their winding streets," he told Dorothy Norman.[66]

Native Son had been published just before he arrived in France. Now *Uncle Tom's Children* and *Black Boy* appeared. The reviews were excellent. *Black Boy* won the French Critics' Award. Maurice Nadeau, the man who had greeted Wright at the station the previous year, called it a "world masterpiece."[67] Wright's reputation in Europe was on the rise. One of his stories was adapted for French radio. Another appeared in the prestigious magazine *Les Nouvelles Littéraires*, and "How 'Bigger' Was Born" came out in the small review *La Nef*. The play *Native Son* was playing in London's West End, and was about to be staged in Prague.

In February 1948 Wright went to Italy, where he met his publishers and translators and was taken sight-seeing. Despite the poverty, Wright was struck by the Italians' good spirits. In contrast to the dim Paris lanterns, the streets of Rome were drenched with light.[68]

Wright met a number of Italian writers and intellectuals and was surprised to find that they were all Communist sympathizers who deeply resented the Marshall Plan and the political influence it gave America in Europe. Wright was taken aback by phrases like "the march of American imperialism." How did they think Europe would manage without the Marshall Plan? he asked them. Did they want the Americans to withdraw completely from Europe?

But he had to admit the hypocrisy of the United States. The House Un-American Activities Committee had just announced its intention to "clean up" the Hollywood studios, publishing houses, radio, and print media. It was an anti-Communist purge. Ten Hollywood screenwriters and directors had been given a hellish time by the committee. The ludicrous exchanges in the courtroom were printed in *Les Temps Modernes.*

"Russia has her cultural purges," Wright wrote, " and so do we; only in Russia it is official, and with us it is the force and so-called moral power of the community. But the results in the end are the same, that is, the suppression of the individual."[69]

In an embattled world in which it was impossible to admire either camp, Wright, along with Sartre, Camus, and others on the non-Communist Left, was looking for a middle ground—a third way out. It was a position the right-wing Gaullists referred to scathingly not as the "*troisième force,*" but the "*troisième farce.*"

ELLEN CONTINUED TO LOOK FOR AN APARTMENT ON THE LEFT BANK. WRIGHT continued to be plagued by throat infections. It was finally determined that his tonsils had to come out. In April 1948, he went into the American Hospital in Neuilly.

They still wavered about returning to the United States. "I don't know when we are returning home," Wright wrote to Ellison. "We cannot make up our minds. Each letter I get from the States makes me feel that I'm better off over here. What do you think?"[70]

Then they found a beautiful apartment at the heart of the Latin Quarter, in the shadow of the Sorbonne, and decided to stay.

21

ARGENTINA

May 1948–December 1951

The Wrights rented the apartment at 14, rue Monsieur le Prince on a long-term lease. The narrow street wound from the Odéon to the Luxembourg Gardens. Their front rooms looked across to the aged limestone walls of the Sorbonne's École de Médecine. Chester Himes, who would arrive in Paris a few years later, viewed the Wrights' apartment with "envy and amazement":

> It occupied the entire fourth floor of the building, and to me it appeared sumptuously furnished. The first room to the right of the entrance foyer was his book-lined study, with two large modernistic paintings, dozens of copies of his own books, several typewriters, his desk, a tape recorder, and overstuffed leather armchairs—all the paraphernalia of a working writer. It was the inner sanctum to which only selected visitors were ever invited. Beyond it were the dining room, the living room, the master bedroom, and at the back the bath, all overlooking the street. On the other side were a storeroom, pantry, kitchen, and the children's bedroom and nursery—eight rooms, exclusive of the bath and water closets.[1]

At the end of June, Ellen, two months pregnant, flew to New York to sort out their belongings and ship remaining items of furniture, books, and papers. Six-year-old Julia stayed behind with her father and nanny. Later that year, the apartment was filled with the din of workmen clanging on old iron pipes: the Wrights were having central heating installed.

"Wright and his wife have got a fine place near Saint-Germain-des-Prés," de Beauvoir told Algren. "At dinner, there was a fried chicken and Dick ate the bones. Ellen explained that you can eat the bones of an American chicken because they are wholly cooked. So I am a bit disappointed in you," she teased. "I thought nobody else could do it."[2]

FINDING THE PERFECT CAFÉ IN THE NEIGHBORHOOD WAS, WRIGHT WROTE, "A matter of . . . tasting, testing." The chairs had to be comfortable, the lighting just right; the sun had to strike the terrace at the right hour; the *patron* must be friendly but not invasive.[3]

He and Ellen chose the Monaco, a friendly, unpretentious, slightly shabby café at the Odéon end of their street. The clientele was international. English, spoken with dozens of different accents, was heard there almost as much as French. In the afternoons and evenings a group of Frenchmen sat at one end playing cards, cigarettes dangling from their lips, apéritifs at their elbows; and at the other end, near the windows, the foreigners congregated. Wright would listen to ex-GIs discussing American politics at the next table and find himself transported back to New York or Chicago.

NOW THAT THEY WERE FINALLY SETTLED AFTER TWO YEARS OF CONSTANT PACKING and unpacking, Wright hoped to get back to serious writing. His half-written novel, *The Outsider*, had been put aside for a year now, and he had lost momentum completely. Since finishing *Black Boy*, he had rewritten and discarded *Black Hope* as well as another novel, *The Jackal*. He had never begun the *Anthology of Negro Writing* and had to pay back the advance.

"We are eager to hear how you are coming along with the new novel," his editor John Fischer wrote from New York.[4] Paul Reynolds sent avuncular admonishments. When Wright had grippe, he wrote: "I'm afraid you're not as vigorous as some people are in this world and the solution is to cut down on all the not too important things that tear down one's strength."[5] After Wright had his tonsils removed, shortly before they moved to the Latin Quarter, Reynolds was pragmatic: "What news about you and the new book? Life is to be lived but it is also to be written about and you don't want too long a period of time between each book. My tonsils were removed when I was a boy and yours probably should have been but they are gone now."[6]

The delivery date for the new novel was extended to 1 June 1951. But still Wright lacked the urge to write. In 1955 he would look back on an eight-year publishing hiatus—from *Black Boy* in 1945 to *The Outsider* in 1953—and tell his old publisher Edward Aswell: "The act of pulling up one's roots in one country and planting them in another is not an easy matter. For five years (and that is a long time!) I did not feel like writing . . . I did not want to force myself. To me, writing comes freely or not at all."[7]

What Wright really wanted to do was to make a movie. The cinema had always been a passion of his. Sadly, Roberto Rossellini had abandoned the idea of *Native Son*. It was becoming quite clear that a film criticizing the United States was a thorny proposition in any European country dependent on the Marshall Plan. In the United States, ten left-wing producers and screenwriters—the Hollywood Ten—had been given prison sentences. From now on, it was clear, censorship in the Hollywood film industry was going to be worse than ever before.

LIKE SARTRE, WRIGHT BELIEVED THAT EUROPE SHOULD REMAIN A NEUTRAL THIRD force, neither in the Russian camp nor the American. Early in 1948 a new left-wing movement had formed—the *Rassemblement Démocratique Révolutionnaire*—with Sartre as a prominent spokesman. Wright lent his voice in support. Why should Europeans look on passively, the RDR insisted, while Europe became a pawn between the superpowers?

In the summer of 1948 the Soviet blockade of Berlin created the most serious crisis since the war. The prospect of another world war— nuclear war, this time—terrified Europeans. Throughout the year, the RDR gained popular support. The high point was a meeting, held at the Sorbonne on 13 December 1948, called "The Internationalism of the

Mind." Among the speakers were Sartre, Albert Camus, André Breton, the Italian writer Carlo Levi, and Wright.

One after another, the writers denounced dictatorship, totalitarianism, and imperialism.[8] Simone de Beauvoir introduced Richard Wright to the audience and translated his speech. He pointed out that both America and Russia proclaimed that they represented liberty, and both denied intellectual freedom in their countries. "We must unite," he told his European audience. His words were greeted with enthusiastic applause.

RACHEL WRIGHT WAS BORN AT THE AMERICAN HOSPITAL ON 17 JANUARY 1949. "SHE is as pretty as a doll," Wright told Dorothy Norman. "Ellen and I are terribly happy about it, and Julia is as proud as can be; she talks eternally about her little sister."[9] To celebrate, he went out with Simone de Beauvoir to a favorite Algerian restaurant that specialized in couscous.

"He has just got a nice little girl," Beauvoir wrote to Nelson Algren, "and is very happy with it, but he does not seem to work much. He seems awfully tired by having settled in Paris and get a baby [sic], so he goes to Roma for a month."[10]

Wright went to Rome in mid-February—for two weeks, not four. *Uncle Tom's Children* and *Native Son* had just been published in Italian. After that he proceeded to Zurich, for the Swiss publication of *Uncle Tom's Children*.

"CAN THE PEOPLE BELIEVE IN THE EFFORTS OF THE US FOR DEMOCRACY AND FREEDOM when it is well known that the US does not support her own democratic institutions?" Wright asked in *Time* magazine.[11] In an article about the "Garry Davis affair," his photograph was featured, along with that of Albert Einstein and André Gide.

The twenty-six-year-old American Garry Davis—whom *Time* described as a "carrot–topped, pleasant, shrewd and slightly corny Air Forces veteran"—had made international news by going to the American embassy in Paris, handing in his American passport, and declaring himself a "world citizen." Gide, Camus, Sartre, and de Beauvoir spoke out in support of his gesture. Einstein commended the young American's break with "the old and outlived tradition" of nationalism. *Time* described Richard Wright as "another Davisite."

For years Wright had been worried by the breakdown of civil liberties in the United States. In January 1949 the European newspapers were full of the trial of twelve Communist leaders in New York. Among them were two blacks—Ben Davis, Jr., and Henry Winston (popularly known as "Winnie"). Under the Smith Act, the twelve were accused of belonging to a party that conspired to overthrow the United States government by force and violence. The trial was quite unconstitutional. Even the U.S. attorney general admitted there was no evidence that the Communist Party planned any such thing. Ben Davis likened the proceedings to the Reichstag fire frame-up.[12]

"It is odd to see the picture of Ben Davis staring back at me, for I knew him rather well in New York," Wright wrote to Dorothy Norman.[13] "I must confess that though, in principle, I'm opposed to that sort of a trial, I cannot feel any sympathy at all for Ben Davis. There was a time when I personally would have liked to have punished him, and now I see that the government is doing what I wanted to do, and there is in me a kind of grim satisfaction."

In April Wright came out with a long anti-Communist tirade in the *New York Herald Tribune*.[14] He was incensed by a series of articles by Anna Louise Strong, a Communist Party functionary he had known in New York who had just been expelled from Russia, allegedly as a spy, and was now appealing to the West. As Wright pointed out in an open letter to Strong, why should she expect the democratic hearing she had systematically denied others? For years she had silenced comrades who tried to have their democratic say, sacrificing them, "in good old Bolshevik style," to the Party:

> So what are you beefing about? Or do you claim some special metaphysical relationship to the universe that absolves *you* of such treatment? . . .
>
> Comrade Strong, during my ten years of membership of the Communist Party of the U.S.A., I never accused any one of any political crime, never had any one hauled up for trial, never found it necessary to inform upon any one. My energies were directed toward struggling against those who held state power and who were and are now responsible for the plight of the Negro in America. Yet, I assure you, that the opportunity for such cruelty was never lacking; indeed, time and again Ben Davis and Winnie Winston, those political scoundrels who are now being tried for treason in New York—and treason is the mildest charge they will

ever have to face—urged me many times to lend my name to the persecution of "erring" Negro and white comrades. And because I could never
do it, I was told that I would never make a good Bolshevik.

After his *Atlantic Monthly* essay, Wright had vowed never again to
write for or against Communism. "I felt that being anti-Communist was
as much a case of psychological slavery as being Communist," he
wrote.[15] Despite this resolve, when John Fischer, his editor at Harper &
Brothers, asked him whether he would be prepared to contribute the
same *Atlantic Monthly* essay to a volume of autobiographical sketches
by prominent ex-Communists, Wright consented. He might have been
swayed by the illustrious company he would keep: Arthur Koestler,
Ignazio Silone, Stephen Spender, and André Gide.[16]

The God That Failed was published simultaneously in London and
New York at the end of that year. The book was on the best-seller lists
for weeks.[17] Rebecca West was not the only reader to find Wright's
essay the most moving of them all.[18]

TWENTY-FOUR-YEAR-OLD JAMES BALDWIN HAD ARRIVED IN PARIS, WITH FORTY
dollars, and no French. On his first day there, a friend took him along
to the Deux Magots. There they found Richard Wright sitting with the
American editors of *Zero*, an English-language literary magazine about
to be launched in Paris. Wright greeted him warmly. "Hey, boy!" he
said. Baldwin thought he looked "more surprised and pleased and conspiratorial than ever, and younger and happier."[19]

The first issue of *Zero* appeared in the spring of 1949. It contained a
story by Wright, "The Man Who Killed a Shadow," and an essay by
Baldwin, "Everybody's Protest Novel." With this controversial essay
(reprinted a few months later in *Partisan Review*), James Baldwin
launched his writing career.

Baldwin's argument was that protest novels were not necessarily
subversive at all. The famous nineteenth-century protest novel, Harriet
Beecher Stowe's *Uncle Tom's Cabin*, was sentimental, self-righteous,
and "a very bad novel." Uncle Tom was not a flesh-and-blood character; he was a stereotype, "robbed of his humanity and divested of his
sex." *Native Son*, that twentieth-century protest novel, was flawed in
exactly the same way. Bigger was subhuman. By painting Bigger solely

in terms of hatred and fear, Wright had denied Bigger's humanity. "The failure of the protest novel lies in its rejection of life, the human being, the denial of his beauty, dread, power," Baldwin wrote.

Soon after *Zero* appeared in the bookstores and newsstands, Baldwin walked into the Brassierie Lipp. Wright was sitting in a corner. According to Baldwin, Wright called him over.

> Richard accused me of having betrayed him, and not only him but all American Negroes by attacking the idea of protest literature. . . . I was young enough to be proud of the essay and, sad and incomprehensible as it now sounds, I really think that I had rather expected to be patted on the head for my original point of view. . . . I had mentioned Richard's *Native Son* at the end of the essay because it was the most important and most celebrated novel of Negro life to have appeared in America. Richard thought I had attacked it, whereas, as far as I was concerned, I had scarcely even criticized it. And Richard thought that I was trying to destroy his novel and his reputation; but it had not entered my mind that either of these *could* be destroyed, and certainly not by me.[20]

Throughout the 1950s, Baldwin would remain in Paris. He and Wright rarely met. Baldwin was never invited to rue Monsieur le Prince. Over the years, Baldwin's comments about Wright—both in print and in private—would oscillate between adoration and ridicule. He was obsessed by Wright. He had loved *Native Son*, and yet he attacked it in print. He loved Richard Wright, yet he attacked him in print. After Wright's death, he would look back with sadness on the pain he had caused him. He tried to explain it as a father-son oedipal rivalry.

"What made it most painful," Baldwin wrote later, "was that Richard was right to be hurt. . . . He saw clearly enough, far more clearly than I had dared to allow myself to see, what I had done: I had used his work as a kind of springboard into my own. His work was a road-block in my road, the sphinx, really, whose riddles I had to answer before I could become myself."[21]

NELSON ALGREN, ANOTHER FRIEND TO WHOM WRIGHT HAD GIVEN CONSIDERABLE encouragement and editorial advice, arrived in Paris in the spring of

1949. He was staying with Simone de Beauvoir, whose studio apartment on the rue de la Bûcherie was just ten minutes from the Wrights'. Algren had just finished writing his novel *The Man with the Golden Arm*. He was in good spirits. He loved Paris. Years later, he looked back on these few months as the best time of his life.

He and Wright met just once. Wright said he hoped Algren would stay in Paris. Algren retorted that as a writer he could not afford to lose contact with his roots in the United States. Wright became defensive, and argued that some of the greatest novels, including Dostoyevsky's, had been written in exile. Algren argued pointedly that writers who were forced into exile were not in the same category as those who chose it.

It was the end of a friendship that had been teetering ever since the success of *Native Son*. As Algren's biographer, Bettina Drew, points out, ending friendships was to become "an Algren trademark."[22]

OUT OF THE BLUE, A MOVIE OFFER CAME FROM PIERRE CHENAL, A FRENCH DIRECtor who had been living in Argentina since the Occupation of France.[23] In the summer of 1949 he was briefly back in Paris. One day Chenal and a film producer from Uruguay, Jaime Pradès, were sitting in a café discussing possible projects. Chenal mentioned *Native Son*. Both men had seen the play in Buenos Aires and liked it. They met with Wright.

Their plan, they told Wright, was to shoot the exterior scenes in Chicago and the interior scenes in the Argentina Sono Film studios. General Perón wanted to build up the Argentine film industry, and they could count on some state sponsorship. The film would be in English, and they hoped to be able to distribute it in the United States. Wright would write the screenplay.

They started to discuss actors. Wright said Canada Lee had been superb on stage and could probably be persuaded to play Bigger on screen.[24] Chenal had another idea. During their conversation he was struck by a transformation in Wright. "While we were exchanging ideas about distribution and locations for shooting, I had the impression that Dick was metamorphosing into Bigger Thomas," he recalled later. "The character was talking out of the mouth of his creator. Strictly speaking, Wright was a bit too old for the role, but he looked younger than he actually was. His whole attitude, his curiously high-pitched voice, his jerky gestures, gave the impression of a tense man acting relaxed. I said to him point-blank: 'I see you very well as Bigger Thomas.' "[25]

Wright laughed his rolling laugh, and protested he would have to go to acting school. Chenal said: "Not at all. You just need to lose twelve kilos."[26]

Wright did not take much persuading. This was exactly the kind of opportunity he had been looking for. He wanted to do something different. He had no training as an actor, it was true, but nor had Canada Lee when he started out. At forty, he was too old to play eighteen-year-old Bigger, but that applied equally to Canada Lee, who was forty-one. He amused people with his impersonations. Why shouldn't he try his hand at acting?

ATILIO MENTASTI, HEAD OF THE ARGENTINA SONO FILM STUDIO, WAS DETERMINED that *Native Son* was going to be the biggest and best movie ever produced in South America. On 20 August 1949, Richard Wright took a ship to New York.

Ellen had a maid and a cook to help her, but three or four months was a long time to be without her husband. Seven-year-old Julia had been in the hospital twice that year with tonsillitis, and would surely miss her father. Rachel, just seven months old, would not recognize her father when he returned. They said sad farewells. Ellen could never have imagined that Wright would be away for nearly a year.

Wright told almost no one in the United States that he was on his way there. It was essential that the press did not get wind of the film, so the film crew could shoot in Chicago undisturbed by the authorities. They were filming without a license. They knew they would never get permission for such a movie.

In New York Wright saw Paul Reynolds, who was worried about the movie as a business proposition.[27] Wright had not been paid anything yet, and Reynolds was deeply wary of South American businessmen. Wright had to agree it was a risky business venture, but he was determined to see this movie made.

He went to Chicago a few days ahead of the film crew to arrange for the sale of his house. His mother and Aunt Maggie had gone back to live in Jackson, Mississippi. He saw friends and bought dozens of jazz and blues records. The South Side was more crowded than ever. And the racial discrimination was just the same.

He went along to the sumptuous offices of the new black magazine *Ebony* and signed a contract to write three articles, at five hundred dollars each. Ben Burns, the white assistant editor, suggested that he begin with a piece about Chicago—what it felt like to come back after all these years.

Wright would tell black Chicagoans exactly what he thought. "Truthfully, there is but one word for it: ugliness," he wrote in the article he sent from Argentina.[28] He called the essay "The Shame of Chicago." He missed the trees he had become accustomed to in Paris, and the dirt and litter reminded him of Paris during the 1947 general strike, when the garbage had piled up dangerously. In Paris, martial law had been introduced to create order. Why did Chicagoans accept these conditions? While in that city, he had encountered racism at his hotel, and he had seen white police take bribes from the filmmaking team. "Chicago," he declared, "was still Chicago."

ON 22 SEPTEMBER WRIGHT, BACK IN NEW YORK, RECEIVED SIX THOUSAND DOLLARS from Pradès, the Uruguayan film producer. That evening, he boarded the SS *Uruguay* for Buenos Aires. Shipboard photographs show him bare-chested and in shorts, working on a punching bag and a rowing machine. During the three-week voyage, he managed to trim himself down from 170 to 145 pounds. He worked on the film script and wrote "The FB Eye Blues." ("Everywhere I look, Lord/I see FB eyes/I'm getting sick and tired of gover'ment spies.")

They stopped at Port of Spain in Trinidad, where Eric Williams, the black historian, had arranged for Wright to give a talk. Williams, who had a Ph.D. from Oxford, was the author of *Capitalism and Slavery*. He told Wright that the independence movement on that British-governed Caribbean island was gaining force.[29]

In Montevideo, Uruguay, Wright was interviewed by the press. He commented that the Negro problem in America was getting worse. The local American consulate immediately wired the State Department in Washington.

Wright arrived in Buenos Aires on 11 October 1949. The cultural attaché in Buenos Aires informed Washington that he anticipated considerable interest in Wright's visit from the local press. "His personal manners are sufficiently charming to win him a considerable following here in Buenos Aires." He suggested that the State Department cable information on Wright's political background for him to send out to South American newspapers to offset the effect.[30] He would report any new developments to the department.

WE KNOW ALMOST NOTHING ABOUT WRIGHT'S LIFE DURING THOSE MONTHS IN Buenos Aires. He never wrote about it. Did he like the city? How did he respond to the Argentine landscape—the long white beaches, the grassy pampas stretching to the horizon? What was his experience of life under Perón? (Pierre Chenal had warned him not to make even guarded statements about political conditions in Argentina, neither to the press nor in letters home.) Three years later, in *Black Power*, Wright would cursorily compare the African aristocracy with that of Argentina. "I'd seen the same thing in Buenos Aires. There I'd had to consort with the decadent nobility who sat huddled and afraid in their huge houses, cursing, swearing that peons could not operate telephones, could not run railroads."[31]

It took time to get the cast together. Pierre Chenal imported four professional actors from Hollywood.[32] Mary Dalton was played by Jean Wallace, a twenty-six-year-old platinum blond with a pageboy haircut and dazzling smile, who was making a name for herself in Hollywood as a blond starlet in the tradition of Joan Crawford or Jean Harlow.[33] The rest of the cast were locals, who had never acted before. Pierre Chenal had a reputation for bringing out the best in actors, but he faced quite a challenge this time.

Chenal had not realized how difficult it would be to find black people for the South Side scenes. As opposed to other countries in Latin America, the population of Argentina was overwhelmingly European.[34] Local blacks spoke Spanish. Chenal had to dub their voices with those of local white Americans, who did their best to imitate black American ghetto speech.

Wright was not a bad actor, but as Bigger he was miscast. He could no longer pass for an eighteen-year-old. And try as he might to ram his baseball cap down on his head, walk with a slouch, and say "ain't" and "naw" and "yessum," he could not convey the rough slum edge. He looked too knowing, too worldly.

The thorniest problem was the subject matter. Chenal and Wright had agreed to keep the film as close as possible to the novel, but both knew this was not possible. Wright's novel had been published in 1940; this was 1950. Wright himself wanted to tone down the politics. (In the film, Jan Erlone is no longer a Communist; he's a "labor leader.") He felt obliged to tone down the racial hostility and the interracial eroticism as well.

There were endless delays. Shooting did not begin until the early months of 1950. In May the *New York Times* reported: "Wright spends so little time away from the set that he scarcely has time to write to his wife and children in Paris."[35]

Wright had time for a romance with the glamorous Jean Wallace, whose seven-year marriage to the actor Franchot Tone had just ended. By the end of his stay, Madelyn Jackson, a Latin American dancer with a one-line part in the film, had become Wright's constant companion. She had light-colored skin, a pretty smile, and long dark hair.

IN APRIL PAUL REYNOLDS WROTE TO ELLEN WRIGHT ABOUT FINANCIAL TRANSACtions. He added:

> I am sorry about the long time it is taking to make the picture. I hope when Dick finally gets back and gets a rest that he'll begin to be able to settle down to a new book. I don't want him to just be known as the author of *Native Son* and *Black Boy* and although the money on *Black Boy* has still many years to run, still it won't run forever. Authors are apt to forget that they, like the rest of us, have only so much time and energy and usually the wise thing is to try to spend one's time and energy on new work which adds to one's reputation.[36]

Ten months of loneliness is too long for a woman, Ellen Wright confided to Simone de Beauvoir over lunch in May 1950. She was tempted, she said, to find herself a lover. The women agreed it seemed an unusually long time for making a movie. Dick seemed convinced it was going to be good, Ellen said.[37] She showed de Beauvoir some photos he had sent. He was thinner and had let his hair grow. One still from the movie showed him walking half-naked through a cotton field. De Beauvoir thought he looked quite wild.

In mid-June, the two women met again for lunch. When de Beauvoir asked after Wright, Ellen burst into tears.[38] De Beauvoir was astonished. With Wright away, she had come to know Ellen better, and she liked her more and more. "A deep warm heart she has got, and not just superficial kindness," she told Algren.

Ellen, usually so discreet about family affairs, admitted she was no longer getting loving letters from Argentina. She had wanted to go there to see her husband, but he had forbidden her to.

De Beauvoir tried to comfort her. Then Ellen told her that back in February Wright had sent home a parcel of books and papers. Among them were some pages of journal, in a scrapbook. She had learned that Wright was in love with a woman called Madelyn. It seemed he had bought her a car. And that he was staying on in South America to be with her.

Back in February, she had been devastated, Ellen sobbed, but she told herself the affair would pass. Now Dick's letters were cold. She was terrified he would abandon the family. These days she was remembering the way he had suddenly gone off and married Dhimah.

They had been happy for ten years, she sighed. De Beauvoir admitted she had always thought them the only married people she knew who seemed perfectly happy.

BY JUNE 1950 THE FILMING WAS FINISHED. THE OTHER AMERICAN ACTORS HAD flown home.[39] Wright stayed on. He was in no hurry to leave, and he had business matters to sort out. Reynolds's concerns appeared to have been justified. There had been financial problems. Pradès, Mentasti, and Chenal were squabbling among themselves. Wright's contract had been stolen from his room and subtly altered. Now he was trying to find someone to defend his interests after he left. "People who have been up to the tricks that the Sono Film people have been up to . . . are not likely to suddenly become lambs," Reynolds remarked from New York.[40]

Wright boarded the SS *Argentina* on 7 July, bound for Trinidad, then Haiti. The *Chicago Defender* published a photograph of him on board ship, surrounded by young "socialites" who were seeing him off. On his right, wrapped in a mink coat, was Madelyn Jackson.[41]

Before the ship sailed, the young women descended the gang plank. Madelyn Jackson, it seems, remained on board. In Trinidad, Eric Williams took Wright to hear his first steel drum band. ("Such a beat!" Wright told local reporters.)[42] He then stayed two weeks in Haiti, Jackson's home base.

Wright had never seen such abject poverty as he encountered in Haiti, and he was shocked at the corruption of the black elite. But he thought the mountainous countryside spectacular, and the light "a marvel." This was important. He hoped to come back to Haiti to make a film about its national hero, Toussaint-Louverture, the slave who led a successful rebellion against Napoleon's troops and was lured back to France to die in exile. Wright intended to write the script and act the leading role.[43]

From Haiti, he and Madelyn Jackson traveled to New York. Wright took his companion to visit friends—including C. L. R. James (Nello) and Constance Webb. "Dick brought her to our apartment in the Bronx," Webb remembers. "She wore a very starched white dress which was becoming to her, with her dark hair and eyes, but it was before the days of mini skirts and her dress kept sliding up to her thighs. . . . I thought she was rather vulgar and showing off and trying to be sexy. Dick paid no attention. He was busy talking with Nello and me, and pouring out his experiences in Argentina."[44]

On 19 August 1950 Wright sailed for France. He planned to return as soon as possible to Haiti. The *Pittsburgh Courier* reported: "Thin and drawn after months of strenuous movie work in South America, Wright said the movie version of his book probably is one of the most elaborate film productions ever made in Latin America."[45]

Ellen confided in de Beauvoir that he came home without a look or a kiss for her or the children.[46] He merely seemed to want to get out of the house. Ellen became angry and told him she knew about his affair. Then he broke the news that he planned to return to Haiti for a year, and make a film there. If that plan did not eventuate, Madelyn would come to Paris in the winter, and he would live with her. He mentioned divorce.

Ellen pleaded with him to wait a year before he made up his mind. The other woman could come to Paris: he could even sleep with her, but couldn't he live at home? She reminded him that if he left, he would have two families to support. (Jackson, it seems, had two children from two previous marriages.) Wright said that the family had made it impossible for him to write in recent years.

"You are destroying my life," Ellen wept.

"It's your life against mine," Wright told her. "I choose mine."[47]

FROM JACKSON, MISSISSIPPI, CAME THREE PENCILED LETTERS FROM WRIGHT'S AUNT Maggie. She and Ella had moved. With the money she had managed to make during the war, Maggie had purchased an old frame house on Lynch Street—the street where their parents had lived in the 1920s. Maggie had her barbershop at the front. But the roof leaked. The city inspector had come and said she must replace it. It was going to cost five hundred dollars. She desperately needed a check from Wright.

"Richard please do this before the weather get bad we will freese here with no top on the house and it rains in on us," she wrote on 18 October. "Ella say she would like to see your children, kiss them for me send both their pictures let me hear from you as soon as you get this letter. . . . Please help me and God will Bless you."

She wrote again, the same day. "I dont have a thing after living expence is paid Now Richard please send the money at once I am doing all I can for us to live in our old days I havnt finished paying for it yet please help me and God will Bless you."

The third letter, three days later, was frantic. "I have written you to letters but I am writing a gain I am in distress if you don't send me some money at once I will loose my place. My Note is due on the 5th of December and I havent money enough to pay it. . . . Ella said she believe you would help us and I hope you will do so at once please do so this time I think I will have the others when they come due next year I am working but things are so high I cant make it all by my self . . . please dont fail me, love to you and the Kids and Wife from your Aunt Margaret Wilson."

At Wright's request, Paul Reynolds sent a check for five hundred dollars. His aunt wrote the next day. "I thank you veery much I am so happy to have the roof put on the house I will start it next week and so thankful to you, Ella is well she like the place so much she can see the cars passing and the Buss all day, Lynch Street is paved from one in to the other, solid conreat and the widest street in Jackson. Richard I want to see your children so bad when you come please bring them with you."[48]

AFTER A YEAR AWAY IN SOUTH AMERICA, WRIGHT REALIZED THAT HE WOULD NEVER feel at home in Paris. He loved the city, but it was alien to him. He would always be an outsider.

He was struck by the deepening of American influence in Paris. In the last few years—largely due to the Marshall Plan and the Atlantic pact—the number of his compatriots in Paris had greatly increased. The exchange rate was still low, and American commercial businesses did well. But these companies never hired black Americans. Apart from the black doorman at the embassy (whom white patrons mockingly called "George Washington"), U.S. government agencies almost never employed blacks. Wright was now hearing stories about white American tourists who were managing to persuade some French hotels to keep out black clients. Wright bemoaned the situation in both *France-Observateur* and the black American journal *The Crisis*.[49]

An American woman in Paris wrote to him privately, reproaching him for slandering Americans in the international arena. "I say let these questions be brought into the open," he wrote back. "If America is embarrassed . . . then, I say, let her shun those guilty actions which make her embarrassed. What right has a white American to demand that a Negro shut up about his problems?"[50]

But the Cold War was about propaganda, not truth. In an article for the progressive French weekly *Réforme* (which regularly published articles on racism in the United States), Dorothy Canfield Fisher tried to assure Europeans that the truth about American race relations was more complicated than they kept hearing. The title of her piece (translated into French) was "Le Racisme américain n'est pas toute la vérité."[51] It was unfortunate, she wrote, that "the enemies of our country" did not mention that many white Americans were sincerely ashamed of racial discrimination in the U.S., or that there were protests against racism in the American press. Canfield Fisher wished that the truth could be printed in large letters in every town and village in Europe: "To be free to criticize evil is one of the greatest liberties."

———

WITHIN WEEKS OF RETURNING FROM ARGENTINA, WRIGHT DECIDED TO FORM A black American organization to exert pressure on the white American community in Paris. "All other racial and national and minority groups in France have their organizations," one character tells another in Wright's unpublished Paris novel, *Island of Hallucination.* "The French government permits it. Only we American blacks are unorganized. . . . Let's build a little American island here and keep a sense of ourselves alive."

The first meeting was held in late October 1950, in a room over a workers' bistro in the Gobelins district. To avoid arousing the interest of the CIA, Wright had asked people to arrive separately or in pairs. James Baldwin turned up late, drunk and giggling with a male friend. In an essay written after Wright's death, he said that he felt as if he had just stepped into "one of the most improbable and old-fashioned of English melodramas."[52]

Wright explained what he had in mind. As a group, they would be in a better position to fight racial discrimination in the American colony in Paris. The group could also have a social and cultural function. They could invite prominent American visitors to come and speak to them about current developments in the United States. They might like to hear from prominent French writers and philosophers who were sympathetic to the problems of minority groups. He hoped they could help introduce black American culture to the French.

Some people in the American community were bound to call them Communists, Wright warned them. They would have to make clear that they were not against America or the ideals of the Marshall Plan. They were against America spreading racial discrimination to Europe.

The group elected officers. Wright was made president. After some discussion, they agreed to call it the Franco-American Fellowship. Some members thought the title should have the words "Negro" or "Afro-American" in it. Wright argued that they might, at a later date, allow white members into the group.

The Franco-American Fellowship held its inaugural reception in December, at the International Center. Wright had invited Jean-Paul Sartre to be a guest speaker, with de Beauvoir translating. The other speaker was Louis Fischer, a white American political commentator and one of the contributors to *The God That Failed*.[53]

The club was active for a year and provided a valuable opportunity for black artists and intellectuals to come together.[54]

BEFORE CHRISTMAS 1950 MADELYN JACKSON WROTE TO SAY THAT SHE WAS HAVING an affair with a Haitian political leader and was thinking of taking up the invitation of a rich Argentine ranch owner to go and live with him in Argentina. Ellen found the letter. She also found evidence that Wright was now having an affair with a French woman. Ellen told this to Simone de Beauvoir, and the two women ended up laughing.

"She sees Dick with new eyes," Beauvoir wrote to Algren, "discovers he is too selfish and interested in himself. She doesn't love him very much, is interested in a young man and wants much to sleep with him. I told her to try to get this young man, to have an affair with him and let Dick go to the devil."[55]

In mid-January 1951 Wright left for two weeks in Italy. He kissed Ellen when he left and said he would try to be a good husband when he came back. Ellen doubted it. Nor was she sure that she wanted to be a good wife anymore. But Wright had agreed they should not divorce. For the sake of the children and the sake of appearances, they would stay together.

WRIGHT GAVE TALKS IN TURIN, GENOA, AND ROME.[56] THE LOCAL AMERICAN embassies paid informers to report on each lecture. One informer took the view that it was good propaganda for America to be seen to be facing the race problem openly, since Europeans were acutely aware of the problem of racism in the United States. Others took the more conventional position that Wright's "biased and misleading picture" of American race relations resembled the rhetoric of "Soviet ruling propagandists." The reports were forwarded to the State Department in Washington.

THE WILLIE MCGEE AFFAIR HAD BLOWN UP WHILE WRIGHT WAS STILL IN Argentina, and had caused national and international protest. McGee was a thirty-six-year-old black truck driver in Laurel, Mississippi, the father of four children. A white woman, Mrs. Troy Hawkins, had claimed that he raped her. McGee had been arrested and tortured until he signed a confession, which he later repudiated. At his trial, the all-white jury took two minutes to declare him guilty. Outside the court-house, a lynch mob had gathered.

There was an appeal. Evidence came to light, which showed that Mrs. Hawkins had had an intimate relationship with McGee for four years. Her husband, a traveling salesman, had come back early, and it was then that the white woman accused McGee of rape.

Signatures were collected around the world. President Truman granted a stay of execution. But the governor of Mississippi prevailed. On 8 May 1951, in the face of worldwide protest, Willie McGee was strapped into the electric chair. "We recall those terrible words that the great black writer Richard Wright gives to one of his black heroes," Georges Altman wrote in the *Franc-Tireur*. "'You must always beware of white women.'"[57]

"What used to happen outside of the law now takes place with the sanction of the law," Richard Wright pointed out on the front page of the human rights newspaper *Le Droit de Vivre*. He explained that one of the reasons for the regular brutal lynchings in Mississippi ("the most backward of America's 48 states") was that blacks outnumbered whites in that state. Before World War II, intractable blacks were suppressed by mob lynchings. After the war, pressure from progressive forces at home and abroad made this practice more difficult, and legally sanc-tioned lynching had become the practice. This was nevertheless a step forward, Wright argued. "It places the actions of Mississippi whites squarely and responsibly before the bar of world opinion."[58]

"IT DEFINITELY HAS AN AMATEURISH QUALITY," PAUL REYNOLDS WROTE TO WRIGHT after seeing a private screening of the film *Native Son* in New York. "Max, I thought, was very poor, a very bad actor. . . . The courtroom scene seems a little like a farce and much of the latter part of the pic-ture seems just sentimentality." Reynolds hoped it would sell in the United States, though he could say here and now that it would never sell in the South. "I think the picture was worth doing," he said, "but I hope now you will be bothered as little as possible about the matter and will be able to settle down again to being a writer."[59]

In March 1951, *Native Son* screened at the Gran Rex, the largest cinema in Buenos Aires. The local press praised the film. Throughout South America, the reception was generally enthusiastic.

The film was handed to an American distributor, Walter Gould. But the New York censors refused to pass it. Without consulting Chenal or Wright, Walter Gould proceeded to cut thirty-two minutes out of the movie. The trial scene, the only explicitly political part of the film, disappeared. When Wright protested, Gould wrote back:

On the subject of the trial sequence, there was no political implication which prompted us to eliminate it. . . . We consulted with important buyers in this country, people who I believe had a finger on the public pulse and know what the general public wants by way of motion picture entertainment. They and many others felt that the trial sequence was slowing down the action and that it was impeding the telling of the story.[60]

The stunted new version got past the New York censors. From Buenos Aires, Pierre Chenal, who had not yet seen the damage, wrote to Wright in Paris: "They made terrific cuts. But as you must know, they were obliged to make them, otherwise the picture never would have been released in Democracy No. 1."[61]

Wright saw the mangled version at a private screening in Paris in May. He was shocked. But he was slightly appeased by the favorable reactions of many in the audience. Simone de Beauvoir was genuinely enthusiastic. She thought that Wright made a very good Bigger. "He can act, that man," she wrote to Algren. "My heart was hit many times with the views of Chicago. The director did a good job, too: you really feel this crummy monster of a town."[62]

When Walter Gould asked Wright for an official statement saying that he approved the cuts, Wright supplied it. "I want to tell you how pleased I was that the film followed so closely and faithfully the book," he wrote.[63]

A few days later, on 16 June 1951, *Native Son* opened at the Criterion in New York City. In the advertising poster, a black man was shown walking down stairs with a limp white woman in his arms. "At last on the screen!" the advertisement blazed. "The Dynamite-Loaded Story of a Negro and a White Girl!"

The interest of the film was mostly its star, Richard Wright. After they had satisfied their initial curiosity, New York audiences thinned quickly. In the first week, the Criterion's takc was seventeen thousand dollars, in the second week six thousand dollars. The film, which played only three weeks, was panned by the critics. Many found it an underhand stab at the U.S., while others pointed out that the politics at the center of the novel were nonexistent in the film.

Chenal was mortified. He wrote to Wright that they must make sure that the original, not the abridged version, was screened in Europe. He urged Wright to read the small print carefully before signing anything.[64]

Chenal underestimated the influence of the State Department and the CIA on American film distribution. CIA reports, since opened to the public, indicate that the government was particularly bothered by the image of American race relations abroad. One undercover CIA agent working in Hollywood at this time reported that he was trying to get casting directors to incorporate "well dressed negroes as a part of the American scene, without appearing too conspicuous or deliberate."[65]

Gould sold the mangled version to Europe. Chenal was furious. Nor could he understand why Wright went along with this compromised version. In late July he wrote to Wright that he would not agree to the cut version being screened in European cinemas. He had asked his Paris lawyer to do whatever was necessary to get his name off the film.[66]

"I shall not concern myself at all with what happens to the film over here," Wright told Reynolds in early August. "Frankly I don't think I shall see any money from it and the reviews make it plain that my reputation is not being done any good by the film being shown. . . . Gould told me that they were planning to enter the film in some kind of festival in Venice; I hope that they did not enter it. . . . People over here are more intelligent than Gould thinks and they will not be fooled into believing that the Negro problem in the USA is what the cut version of the film tries to pretend it is."[67]

Gould did arrange to have the film shown at the Venice Film Festival later that month. Wright decided to attend the screening and explain the situation to the audience. The audience was not overly enthusiastic, but they nonetheless applauded Wright. The obstacles encountered in the United States by a film attempting to criticize that country added to the film's mystique.

In the United States, Gould battled one lot of state censors after another, arranging showings of the film across the country. "The battle is not altogether won, but we have made wonderful progress," he told Wright in October. "As to Mr. Pierre Chenal, I think that he is a damn fool."[68]

Wright had been intensely proud of the film when he left Argentina. Now it had become an embarrassment. He blamed the American censors. He never acknowledged that he himself had greatly curtailed the film's punch before the censors even got to it. Financially, the venture was a failure. Wright did not come close to covering his expenses.

IN THE UNITED STATES, ANTI-COMMUNISM HAD SETTLED ON THE COUNTRY LIKE A thick fog. The clampdown extended to former Communists, fellow travelers, black radicals, and almost anyone who dared to speak out. Since the end of the summer of 1950, it was U.S. government policy to withhold a passport from anyone who was or once had been associated with the CP, anyone who criticized American foreign policy, or anyone whose conduct abroad was "likely to be contrary to the best interest of the United States."[69]

In June 1951 the U.S. Supreme Court ratified the conviction of the twelve Communists tried under the Smith Act. They were given five-year prison sentences and ten-thousand-dollar fines. From 1951 to 1955 Wright's one-time friend Ben Davis would find himself behind bars— and segregated—in a high-security federal prison at Terre Haute, Indiana. He would serve extra months for refusing to name names.

The eighty-three-year-old W. E. B. Du Bois was not a Party member, but he was arrested for belonging to the Communist-sponsored World Peace Council. "I have faced during my life many unpleasant experiences, the growl of a mob; the personal threat of murder; the scowling distaste of an audience," he would write later, but nothing has so cowed me as that day . . . when I took my seat in a Washington courtroom as an indicted criminal."[70]

Had Paul Robeson been a member of the Party, he would have been behind bars like Ben Davis. But he was a sympathetic fellow traveler. Nevertheless, Robeson, who had been making regular trips to Europe since the end of the war, was informed that summer that his passport was void. His lawyers were told that Robeson's criticism of the treatment of black people in the United States was not a matter to be aired abroad. It was a "family affair."[71]

The blacklisting of Robeson had begun in earnest. Tragically, the black community joined in. In 1951 the NAACP published a list of past recipients of the Spingarn Medal. The 1945 winner—Paul Robeson— was left conspicuously off the list.

In 1951 two thousand American Communists were sent by the Party into hiding. It was a deliberate policy, in order to save the Party from extinction. Abe Chapman, the Jewish friend who had welcomed Wright to New York in 1937, disappeared that summer. Wright would never know the story. One day, before dawn, Abe, his wife Bella, and their two young daughters left behind their Manhattan apartment and all their worldly goods, and Communist Party agents sent them under cover via Mexico to Czechoslovakia. For years they would live behind the Iron Curtain under the assumed name "Capkova." Until they emerged from their Cold War exile in 1963, not even their family knew where they were.[72]

IN JUNE 1951 RICHARD WRIGHT'S FRANCO-AMERICAN FELLOWSHIP RECEIVED considerable press coverage when it protested the total absence of black employees at the American Hospital in Paris. Miss Margaret McCleveland, a black nurse, had been accepted for work over the phone. She was well qualified and the administrative clerk told her they were short of nurses. When she turned up, the same administrator informed her there was nothing available. She asked how that could be. Eventually, the clerk and various other administrators explained that no Negro doctors or nurses had ever been employed in the American Hospital.[73] Some months later, after the press coverage initiated by Wright, the hospital would rethink its policy.

In November 1951 Dr. Elmer Carter visited Paris. Wright invited him to speak to the fellowship. Carter was a black conservative whom Wright knew from his New York days. Carter had presented him with his Spingarn Medal in Houston, Texas, in 1941. In May 1945 they had argued on different sides in a town hall debate in New York. The issue had been "Are We Solving America's Race Problem?" Carter had argued yes; Wright argued no. Carter was now working for the New York State Commission against Racial Discrimination.

Carter spoke to the Franco-American Fellowship. He and his wife, Thelma, were invited to dinner at the Wrights' apartment. Before he left Paris, Carter visited the American embassy. His report was dispatched to Washington. "Dr. Elmer Carter . . gave it as his opinion to the Embassy that Richard Wright is willing to go to any length in order to attract attention to the problem of racial discrimination in general and to its manifestations in the United States in particular." As Carter saw it, Wright saw it as his "moral duty" to publicize racial discrimination in any form. This resulted in the "whole-sale broadcast of exaggerations and even untruths about the United States."[74]

Back in New York, Elmer Carter wrote to thank Wright for his hospitality. "I will make recommendations . . . as to the increased participation of Negroes in the official government agencies," he assured Wright, "and will take up with some of the firms here which have offices in Paris the question of the employment of American Negroes in their Paris establishments."[75]

THE STATE DEPARTMENT HAD KEPT A CLOSE WATCH ON THE FRANCO-AMERICAN Fellowship since its inception. With the lure of cash rewards, several student members had proved willing to inform on the group. They assured the State Department that, yes, it was a "Communist front."

In November 1951 Wright resigned as president. He was aware that there were informers in the group; this may have influenced his decision. In his letter of resignation he told fellow members that he had set up the club and secured its legal status; its future direction was up to them. Personally, he thought it imperative to open the club to French people and to white Americans. Without Wright's leadership, the club lost its impetus and soon ceased to exist.

WHEN WRIGHT'S ESSAY "THE SHAME OF CHICAGO" HAD LANDED IN *EBONY*'s offices in Chicago in August 1950, Ben Burns wrote to Wright: "I think that it is a swell piece that ought to give some of our local folk a good swift boot in the posterior."[76] John H. Johnson, *Ebony*'s director, was horrified. Since its beginnings in 1945, *Ebony* had published stories of black prosperity and success. Wright's article risked alienating readers and putting off the magazine's advertisers, *Ebony*'s main source of income. Johnson rejected the essay. Ben Burns argued that they had contracted the article from Wright, and *Ebony* did not want to develop a reputation for censorship. He suggested that they write an editorial rebutting Wright's views.

It fell to Burns to write it. In his Communist past, Burns had made scathing attacks on various individuals, including Langston Hughes, for "stepping off the train." These days, he had changed his colors. "We have our slums to be sure," he wrote in the editorial, "but we also have blocks and blocks of fine Negro apartments and homes which are newer, more roomy and more modern than 90 per cent of the flats in Paris, of which Wright is such an avid admirer. . . . Go right down the line of what most people in the world consider the measure of better living—food, clothing, shelter, job security—and the Chicago Negro is better off than most Frenchmen. . . . Too often some of our race leaders have sacrificed truth on the altar of militancy."[77]

In his memoir, *Nitty Gritty* (1996), Burns blames the editorial on the ultraconservative John Johnson. "The scurrilous editorial was one that I wrote with a sickening sense of dejection," he claims.

"The Shame of Chicago" did not appear until December 1951. That month, Wright sent Burns the second of the three articles they had contracted. Burns had asked him to write about his life in Paris. ("We would like to hear what happens when a Negro goes overseas and suddenly finds the freedom he has long been seeking.") Wright wrote a piece called "I Choose Exile." In it, he declared: "I tell you frankly that there is more freedom in one square block of Paris than there is in the entire United States of America."

Wright had still not been paid for his first article, and he asked for his money. He also pointed out that five hundred dollars for an article was not much, and he could not help thinking he would get a lot more if he sent his articles elsewhere. "I don't mean to say that I'm welshing on a perfectly good contract which I signed. . . . But please realize that the cost of living has gone up greatly and that you ought to be generous enough to up my price a bit."[78]

He told Burns that he had heard "The Shame of Chicago" had caused a stir, and that Johnson had written an editorial disagreeing

with him. Would he please send a copy? "I'd like to see the magazine
I'm writing for." Burns never told him who actually wrote it.

John H. Johnson hated Wright's Paris essay even more than the
Chicago essay. Wright was not simply going after Chicago; this time, he
was going after America. It would ruin the magazine. He refused outright to publish it. But Burns sat on it for almost a year, after which
time Wright asked for it back.

Burns never sent it back. In August 1969, nine years after Wright's
death, Ben Burns, who no longer worked at *Ebony*, sold both Wright's
essay and Wright's letter to him to Kent State University for five hundred dollars.

WRIGHT WAS FEELING PRETTY MISERABLE. NOTHING AT ALL HAD COME OUT OF THE
months of hard work in Argentina. Edith Schroeder wrote from East
Berlin, behind the Iron Curtain. Her novel had been rejected by thirteen publishers. Would Wright be prepared to look at it and see what
he thought? She had a daughter now, and did not much like the
"housewife life." She wished Wright would write to her.

"Send the novel on and I'll read it and get an answer to you as soon
as I can," Wright wrote back. "You know that I do not write many letters. . . . I know words and know how badly they say what they have
to say." He added: "Much has happened to me since I last saw you, but
not much that is of the nature that can be put in a letter."[79]

Two months later, he wrote to Edith from the mountains of Haute
Savoie, near Geneva, where he, Ellen, and the children were having a
summer vacation. He asked her to write in future not to his home
address but care of the poste restante, rue des Saints-Pères.[80] "I'm at the
time of a hard and brutal crisis in my life and it does not do to talk
about it. Enough to say that I'm so lonely that I wish I was a dog so I
could go up to the top of a high hill at night and howl at the moon. It
would ease my soul."[81]

22

EXISTENTIAL DREAD

December 1951–May 1953

The Wrights are seated at the dining table in their apartment in the Latin Quarter. The tablecloth is linen; the glasses crystal. Beside Ellen's plate is a bell for calling the maid. On their plates are artichokes, which they will eat French-style, plucking off the leaves and dipping them in vinaigrette. Ellen wears a delicate shawl over her dress and has a glass of wine in her hand. She is saying something to Rachel, a pretty, curly-haired child in a pleated skirt and cardigan. Julia, who has a kind, slightly anxious expression, is smiling at her father, who is looking down at his plate. On his left, a maid in a crisp white apron hovers with a jug of water. A gleaming silver dinner service stands on the side buffet.[1]

The photograph appeared in an article on Wright in the glossy magazine *Ebony*. Other pictures show him talking to proprietor George Whitman in the American bookshop in Paris, strolling past secondhand bookstalls on the Left Bank, and drinking with friends in a sidewalk café.[2] He and Ellen smile good-bye as the maid escorts the girls to school. According to *Ebony*, the girls attend "one of the best private schools in France." In reality Julia attended the American School; later she would go to the Lycée Fénélon, a state school. Rachel was not yet at school age.

Wright's wardrobe is international, writes the black American journalist William Gardner Smith—"the tie from Rome, socks from England, suit from France, nylon shirt made in the United States and bought in Germany." On Sundays Wright likes to walk with his family in the Luxembourg Gardens. In the summer they "pack their bags and climb into their car and motor through the little villages of France, stopping whenever it takes their fancy."

Not long before, *Ebony* readers had shaken their heads in wonderment at photographs of Wright the film star, surrounded by adoring young women in Argentina. This time, Wright had metamorphosed into a devoted family man, enjoying the bourgeois life on the Left Bank. In case readers needed reminding just how far he had come, the article was entitled "Black Boy."

THE REALITY WAS LESS IDYLLIC. SINCE COMING BACK FROM ARGENTINA, WRIGHT felt as if his life were falling apart. It had been five years since he, Ellen, and Julia left the United States and six years since his last book. John Fischer had been patient about the abandoned projects and delays, but Wright was well aware that if he did not produce another book soon, he would go down in literary history as a passing comet who had flashed briefly then burst. All that talk from American friends about going into "exile" and how he would lose touch with his roots and lose his inspiration: it was beginning to look as if they were right. Nor would his money last forever. Royalties from translations had been good, but he needed to keep new books coming. Since 1945 he had taken six thousand dollars a year out of his *Black Boy* account. There was still twenty-five thousand dollars left, but that would last only four more years.

Family news from Mississippi was depressing. His mother was about to turn seventy and had lost her mental faculties. "I read the Bible to her at night when I get of [sic] from work and try to get her to pray, but her mind is not good enough to think," Maggie wrote.[3] She added that her hairdressing business was slow at the moment.

Wright tended to blame his writing paralysis on his family. But these days, the family was increasingly going its own way. Some time in 1951, de Beauvoir suggested to Ellen that she become a literary agent.

She proposed herself as Ellen's first client. Why didn't Ellen take over the business arrangements for her American translations?[4]

Ellen leaped at the idea. With a maid to do the cooking and a nanny for the girls, she had time on her hands. Three-year-old Rachel would soon be going to kindergarten. With her friend Hélène Bokanowski as a business partner, she set up an agency that sold French books to America and American books to France.

Hélène Bokanowski had translated a number of American books into French (including *Native Son* with Marcel Duhamel). Like Ellen Wright, she had good contacts. Her husband, Michel Bokanowski, was a government minister, close to de Gaulle. Their son, Thierry, was Julia's age. Despite their political differences, the Bokanowskis and the Wrights had been friends since the Wrights' first days in Paris.

THERE WERE TOO MANY DISTRACTIONS IN PARIS, WRIGHT TOLD HIMSELF. ENDLESS friends and acquaintances passing through. Endless requests. The family made demands. In order to bear down on his book, he would go to London for a few months.

Between February and April 1952 Wright sat in a small flat in southeast London and typed,[5] terrified that the story would escape him before he had committed it to paper. He had with him the manuscript he had begun on Long Island five years before. The question he had been grappling with in that novel—the meaning of individual freedom—seemed more pressing than ever in this Cold War world of clashing ideologies, covert intelligence agencies, spies, and informers. His hero, Cross Damon, was a man determined to be free—free of illusions, ideologies, and responsibilities.

CROSS DAMON WALKS THE STREETS OF NEW YORK AND TELLS HIMSELF THAT NOTH-ing means anything anymore. He feels like fleeing and starting over, but knows this is not the solution. "He had once done that and it had led to nothing, to the nowhere in which he now lived." He walks into a tavern, drinks a beer, and goes over to the pinball machine in the corner. He drops a coin in the slot, and begins thumping the small shining balls with the lever. The machinery clatters, balls leap and bounce, lights flicker, his scores flash up on the screen. He loses. He plays again and loses again. "What the hell was he doing?" he thinks to himself. "Was he so lost that he had to resort to this for distraction?"

Wright made Cross Damon a black intellectual who is incessantly thinking about the meaning of life and the absurdity of the human condition. He believed in a godless universe, where individuals make their own laws. In New York, where he goes to forge himself a new identity, he becomes entangled in the Communist Party.[6] He soon sees it as a tyrannical organization, and tells a friend: "The heart of Communism is the will to power." Damon himself goes around murdering people who try to impose their will on others.

Ely Houston, the New York City District attorney, is a white hunch-back who sees the world in a similar way. He spends his life hunting down criminals and admits to Damon that he feels sympathy for those who break the law. He sees civilization, fundamentally, as a jungle. Damon reflects that he and Houston are alike in that they are both drawn toward that which they dread.

AT THE END OF *THE OUTSIDER*, ELY HOUSTON BENDS OVER CROSS DAMON, WHO IS dying. Houston's voice is brotherly, sympathetic. "Damon, you were an outsider. . . . You lived apart. . . . Tell me, why did you choose to live that way?" He strains to catch Damon's words.

"I wanted to be free," Damon says. "To feel what I was worth." There is silence. Then he summons his last strength. "The search can't be done alone," he whispers. "Alone a man is nothing."

"Is there anything, Damon, you want me to tell anybody?"

Damon answers him in a faint whisper. "I wish I had some way to give the meaning of my life to others. . . . To make a bridge from man to man."

Then come the strange words: "Men hate themselves and it makes them hate others. . . . We must find some way of being good to our-selves. . . . Man is all we've got."

"I'm talking about *you*, your life," Houston presses him. "How was it with *you*, Damon?"

"It was . . . horrible."

Houston's voice comes again. "What was horrible?"

"All of it . . ."

"But why? *Why?* Try and tell me . . . "

"Because in my heart . . . I'm . . . I felt . . . I'm *innocent.*"

IN THE LATE AFTERNOONS OR EVENINGS, AFTER A DAY'S WRITING, WRIGHT WOULD sometimes visit George and Dorothy Padmore, whose tiny apartment in Cranleigh Street, north London, was a center of anticolonial agitation. George Padmore, six years older than Wright, was a formal, old-fashioned Trinidadian gentleman, always impeccably dressed, who eked out an income as a journalist and writer. Dorothy Padmore worked outside the house as a secretary during the day and in the evenings typed her husband's manuscripts and cooked for their endless stream of visitors.

Around the Padmores' wooden kitchen table, cluttered with George's papers and a typewriter, with the kettle hissing in the background, George Padmore and his African friends endlessly discussed the situation in the Gold Coast and what their man Kwame Nkrumah was up against. Nkrumah had lived two years in London, and had sat long hours at that very table, plotting African liberation. He had just become prime minister, and was doing his utmost to lead the country to independence. Padmore himself was writing a book called *The Gold Coast Revolution.*[7]

In 1956, in a preface to Padmore's book *Pan-Africanism or Communism*, Wright would call Padmore "the greatest living authority on the fervent nationalist movements sweeping Black Africa today."

> I have often been a guest in his home. I have seen him labor day in and day out, to the exclusion of all other interests, upon the one thing that really matters to him: freedom for black people. The kitchen in that apartment is George's office and workroom and through that kitchen have trooped almost all of the present day leaders of Black Africa.[8]

More than ever, Wright was eager to visit Africa himself.

SIMONE DE BEAUVOIR, WHO REGULARLY HAD LUNCH WITH HER FRIEND AND NOW literary agent, Ellen Wright, wrote to Nelson Algren: "Dick is working hard now, somewhere in a small house in London suburbs. He never lets alone for one minute his book-script—when he goes down to phone, he takes it with him, when he goes to London for a lunch, he takes it beneath his arm, and during the lunch if he goes to the man's room, he takes it with him, too. It seemed very funny to her; so it does to me. The more and more I live on, the more it seems to me there is only one wise person on earth. meaning me."[9]

BY THE END OF APRIL WRIGHT HAD FINISHED THE FIRST DRAFT OF *THE OUTSIDER.* His original plan was to return to Paris for a couple of weeks to deal with accumulated business, then go elsewhere to write maybe Africa,[10] In the end, he decided to stay in Paris for as long as it took to revise the novel. Too much was at stake, and Harper wanted the manuscript by September.

That summer, he traded in the Oldsmobile for a smaller, more economical Citroën, better suited for the narrow streets of Paris and less expensive to repair. He sent the novel to Paul Reynolds in July. "My hopes for it are not great," he wrote defensively. "I cannot conceive of anybody liking it, especially Americans."[11]

Ellen admitted to de Beauvoir that she thought the novel pretentious, overintellectual, and not very good.[12] When Paul Reynolds read the manuscript, he was dismayed. To Wright he ventured that it would probably sell well. To John Fischer, Wright's editor at Harper, he sent a note: "I would . . . like to talk to you after you've read the book."[13] He suggested lunch at the Century Club.

Over lunch, Reynolds and John Fischer agreed that the book needed "drastic cutting." They hoped this might bring out the meaning, which was not clear to either of them. The manuscript was 220,000 words. Fischer asked Wright to reduce it by a third, to 150,000 words. He hoped Wright would agree to cut whole episodes in the first third of the novel. "Paul also suggests that if you agree in general with our suggestions about cutting, you might prefer to have us perform the actual surgery here."[14]

Wright said he would do the cutting himself. But he did not want to cut whole scenes. He personally believed that the early episodes were important, both for atmosphere and for the development of Cross Damon's character. (Several critics would comment later that the early sections were the best part of the novel.)

Wright worked on the novel through August and September. He managed to reduce the 740-page manuscript by 120 pages. John Fischer had hoped for considerably more. He tried again to get Wright to remove an early episode he thought superfluous. Wright shortened it still further but did not want to cut it altogether.

In November 1952 Fischer wrote to Wright: "At Paul Reynolds' suggestion we have done a painstaking job of copy editing, weeding out an excess adjective here and there and shortening a few of the descriptive passages a little."[15] Wright received the galleys just before Christmas.

WRIGHT HAD RETURNED FROM LONDON AT THE END OF APRIL 1952 TO FIND A COPY of *Invisible Man* waiting for him. The critics were saying it was the best book ever written by a black American writer. "You don't know how happy I am to see the successful completion of your project," he wrote to Ellison. He added that he would not have time to read it until he had finished his own book, which was occupying him day and night.[16]

Not until he passed in *The Outsider* in October did Wright allow himself to read *Invisible Man*. This was the novel Ellison had begun in the summer of 1945; it had taken him seven years. Wright, on the other hand, had begun *The Outsider* in the summer of 1947, then put it aside until February 1952, and had finally written it in six months. Whether or not Wright admitted it to himself, the difference showed. *Invisible Man* was carefully crafted and far more sophisticated than *The Outsider.*

Nevertheless, Wright must have been struck by the similarities between the two novels. Even the titles carried a similar meaning. Ellison's narrator, the unnamed "invisible man," was also a bright young black American struggling with his identity in an alienating and racist world. Both novels were an indictment of the totalitarian practices of the Communist Party. Both novels had autobiographical elements. A jazz motif ran through *The Outsider* and a blues motif ran through *Invisible Man.* But whereas Wright's novel was permeated with nihilistic despair, Ellison's narrator concludes: "I'm a desperate man—but too much of your life will be lost, its meaning lost, unless you approach it as much through love as through hate." (Ten years later, Ellison would be criticized by black nationalists for lacking rage.)

"I've finally gotten around to reading your powerful novel and right off I want to say that I liked it, felt that you hit home hard and pure," Wright wrote to Ellison in October. "Boy, you must be having a time with the Party boys around Harlem after what you said about 'em. . . . The prose in your book is by far the best prose you've done. As writing, it'll stand as a mark for the boys to shoot at. . . . I felt that the sharpest writing and the best character drawing was in relation to the Brotherhood. The riot was a lulu. Damn powerful. The speech of the Harlemites was done to a turn. . . . I think you can be proud of what you have turned in, Ralph. You entered the ranks of literature with your book, and there is no doubt about it."[17]

He told Ellison that he had sent off his own manuscript. "I've waded right out into the question of the Negro's relationship to the Western world." His hero was even more savage than Bigger Thomas. "I have not the slightest notion what the critics will say about it. I know the Negroes will not like it, not one bit."

He asked when Ralph and Fanny were going to come and spend time in "one of the world's great cultures." Ellison's reply to that had a caustic edge to it. "I am getting a little sick of American Negroes running over for a few weeks and coming back insisting that its [sic] paradise. My answer to them is that my problems are not primarily racial problems, that they are the problems of a writer and that if a trip across to France would solve those, I would make it tomorrow."[18]

For the moment, Ellison's future looked dazzling. More so than Richard Wright's. But he would work on his second novel for the next forty years. When Ellison died in 1994 at the age of eighty, it was still unfinished.

SNOW WAS FALLING. IT WAS MID-NOVEMBER 1952. WRIGHT HAD ENDURED ANOTHER of his bouts of grippe, and had still not recovered fully. He was sitting in a bar, answering a letter.[19] Naomi Replansky's first volume of poetry—*Ring Song*—had just been published. She had written to Wright that she would like to come to Paris in the spring, but because of her former association with the Communist Party, her passport application had been rejected.

Wright's letter was brief. He was happy about her book, he said. He was relieved that he had been able to renew his own passport for two

more years while he was in London. He worried a lot about his passport these days. He told Replansky he would soon be correcting the
galleys of his new novel. "It is a hard book. It is full of blood, violence,
betrayal, deception, murder. It is how I feel." After the book had come
out, he intended to go away again. "I see practically nobody and so
there is no news to give." As he grew older, he had fewer and fewer
friends, he told her. He wished she could come in the spring. He
missed her more than she could know. "Well, this is about all that my
empty heart can say today."

AFTER ALL THOSE MONTHS AWAY FROM HOME, WRIGHT HAD LOST THE INTIMACY
he once had with his family. He was proud of Julia, who studied Latin
at school and was regularly at the top of her class. Everyone said she
was his spitting image. They got along well. But he could scarcely communicate with Rachel, who seemed to resent his presence. She did not
speak a word of English and "raised hell" (her mother says) whenever
the family spoke English at the dinner table.[20] Because of this, Ellen
and the girls spoke French together. Ellen's French was far from fluent,
and she retained a strong American accent, but it was better than
Wright's.

The Outsider carried the dedication: "For Rachel, my daughter who
was born on foreign soil." The discarded version read: "To my daughter Rachel who though born on alien soil, I hope will learn to speak
and love the English language."[21]

THE OUTSIDER WAS PUBLISHED ON 18 MARCH 1953. "RICHARD WRIGHT'S BOISTER-
ous new novel, 'The Outsider,' arrives like a band of brigands from the
hills with horses snorting, guns blazing, bent on shooting up the town,"
Arna Bontemps wrote in the *Saturday Review*.[22] He added that Wright
"had a roll in the hay with the existentialism of Sartre, and apparently
he liked it."

"What is Wright after? What is he trying to say? What answers to the
great questions of life in our time does he seek?" Lawrence Reddick,
Wright's old friend, asked, bewildered.[23]

The critics mostly shared Reddick's bewilderment. They agreed that
the novel was gripping, with "the hypnotic power of a bad dream."[24]

They could see that they were looking at a "new Richard Wright."[25] What they could not fathom was the point. And what was Wright's relationship to his brooding hero?

"DICK'S OUTSIDER, HE CAN TELL A STORY, BUT WHAT A MEANINGLESS, CRAZY, stupid story that is—don't you think so?" de Beauvoir wrote to Nelson Algren.[26] She thought it unfortunate that some critics liked it because it was against Communism.

"Dick Wright . . . I think he made . . . a very bad mistake," Algren observed in a *Paris Review* interview. "I mean, he writes out of passion, out of his belly, but he won't admit this, you see. He's trying to write as an intellectual, which he isn't basically. . . . He's trying his best to write like a Frenchman."[27]

After Wright's death, Ralph Ellison would comment that Wright had written better existentialist fiction in *Uncle Tom's Children*. "I could have gone to Paris and become involved in existentialist politics as Richard Wright did, but it didn't improve his fiction; in fact it helped encourage some very bad tendencies in his writing."[28]

James Baldwin wrote to William Cole, his editor at Knopf, that Wright did not seem able to decide whether his hero was right or wrong. Personally, he did not find Cross Damon remotely real. Wright clearly intended it to be read as a novel of ideas, but the ideas had nothing to do with the action. "Very often . . . it's a pretentious bore."[29]

WRIGHT TOLD HIS FRIENDS THAT THE IDEA FOR *SAVAGE HOLIDAY* CAME TO HIM when he was lying in bed, in November 1952, with a high fever. ("Later, when he had let me read the finished manuscript, I believed him," says Chester Himes.)[30] Wright wrote the short novel between Christmas 1952 and Easter 1953.

It was about a man—a white man this time—who murdered a young woman who reminded him of his mother. Wright dedicated the novel to Clinton Brewer, the man he had helped release from prison ten years earlier who had reemerged into the world and promptly killed a second woman. At the time Wright had associated the Brewer case with Frederic Wertham's book *Dark Legend*, a psychoanalytical case study of a young Italian immigrant who had stabbed his mother to death. In *Savage Holiday*, Wright, who for years had been fascinated by Freudian psychology, produced a novel that read like a case study.

For the first time, he made all his characters white. He did not want to fudge the psychological issues with race. Nevertheless, the novel's imagery is obsessively black and white. In a gleaming white kitchen, as the white light of dawn creeps through the window, Erskine Fowler, described as a tall, heavy man with a "jutting lower lip" and "shock of jet-black, bushy hair," lifts a butcher knife again and again into a naked white woman.

Why are there so many mangled, dead white women in Wright's fiction? James Baldwin, looking back on Wright's work after his death, believed that the root of the violence in Wright's fiction was Wright's own rage. It seemed to Baldwin to be "the rage, almost literally the howl, of a man who is being castrated":

> When in Wright's pages a Negro male is found hacking a white woman to death, the very gusto with which this is done, and the great attention paid to details of physical destruction reveal a terrible attempt to break out of the cage in which the American imagination has imprisoned him for so long.[31]

Wright once claimed that "all writing is a secret form of autobiography."[32] His fiction is obsessed with guilt. His fictional landscape is the landscape of nightmare. Against a background that is often white (mostly covered in snow), Wright's male protagonists (all of them black, except Fowler) toss people out of windows, batter or stab women to death, and either run from the police or give themselves up. Wright's male characters nearly all suffer from an all-powerful, inexplicable sense that somewhere in their past they have done something irredeemably wrong.

WRIGHT WAS REVISING *SAVAGE HOLIDAY* AND GETTING READY TO LEAVE FOR AFRICA when Chester Himes arrived in Paris in the middle of April 1953. He had written Wright one of those "what shall I bring" letters that Wright still regularly received from Americans about to brave the deprivations of the Old World. Wright had said drip-dry nylon shirts, pajamas, underwear, medications and toilet articles, an American can opener, and a small alcohol stove. He also asked Himes to bring his six complimentary copies of *The Outsider* from Harper. And would he bring two reams of bond typing paper?

Himes was fed up with America. His 1947 novel, *Lonely Crusade*, had been panned by American critics. In 1952 French critics had named it as one of the five best American books published in France that year. Himes's translator, Yves Malartic, had urged him to come and live in Paris. Wright, who had written a preface to the French translation, also encouraged him.

The two men had become friends in New York in 1945, after Wright had written a positive review of Himes's first novel, *If He Hollers Let Him Go.* Wright liked this thin and brooding, outwardly tough man who had served time in prison for armed robbery. He understood Himes's volcanic temper. He liked his "hard, biting style."[33] Himes admired Wright, but suffered from feelings of rivalry.

In the first volume of his autobiography, *The Quality of Hurt*, Himes describes his desolation and bewilderment when he stepped off the boat-train in Paris and Wright was not there to meet him. Himes, who had kicked his girlfriend just before leaving New York and had broken his big toe, was limping badly. It was his first time abroad, he spoke no French, and he was trying to maneuver far too much baggage. When he could not see Wright, he climbed into a taxi, showed the driver a letter with Wright's address on it, and headed straight to rue Monsieur le Prince. As it happened, Wright was looking for him at the station, and Ellen was out. When a passerby finally showed Himes how to press the button to release the carriage gates that opened into the courtyard, the concierge spied him from behind her lace curtains and threw him out.

Eventually he remembered the name of a hotel an American friend had told him about, run by an American army officer. He took a taxi there, and the receptionist, who spoke fluent English, said to him: "Oh, you're Mr. Chester Himes. Mr. Wright has reserved a room for tonight for you."

There was no phone in the room, so he couldn't call Wright. Instead, he drank half a pint of whiskey. The next morning, he was woken by a hammering on the door. It was Wright. They went to the Monaco for breakfast, which seemed to Himes to be full of hungover Americans. "Dick greeted everyone with boisterous condescension; it was obvious he was the king thereabouts." They spent the morning finding Himes a more permanent hotel room. Then Wright invited him home for lunch.

Ollie Harrington, the *Bootsie* cartoonist, was there. He looked stockier than Himes remembered him from Harlem days at the end of the war, when Harrington wore an officer's uniform.[34] Himes was surprised to see that Ellen, whom he had always found very attractive, had "a harried, dissatisfied look." She had lost weight and dyed her hair blond. "One of the first things she said to me was that she and Dick had gone completely French," Himes writes. "I noticed Dick look sort of sheepish but he offered no comment, and Ollie looked wise and indulgent and his eyes twinkled knowingly."[35]

After lunch Wright was impatient to pick up Himes's trunk, containing his copies of *The Outsider.* He drove Himes to the Saint-Lazare customs shed in his Citroën—which, Himes commented, seemed small by American standards. They collected the trunk and "blowing and panting" hauled it up two flights to Himes's hotel room.

> Before we could get our breath, Dick insisted on my opening it so he could get his books, and without stopping for another thing, he took me through the dark narrow streets (it was already black dark by that time) to the English Book Store, run by a young blond Frenchwoman named Gaité [sic], for her to put on display in her window. I noticed at the time that she paid far more attention to me as a male than to Dick's valued copies of *The Outsider,* but nevertheless the three of us stood outside the shop on the sidewalk for the next half hour listening to Dick discuss how the books could be displayed to their best advantage.[36]

These two were not destined for a close friendship. Himes saw quite a bit of Wright in the month before Wright left for Africa, and many things about him got on Himes's nerves. Wright's "gleeful curiosity" about sexual matters annoyed him. He noticed that Wright liked to tease people mercilessly. In public places he would talk loudly about intimate matters, as if no one in Paris could understand English.

On one occasion Himes accompanied Wright to Wright's black marketeer to change some money. "Pops," as Monsieur Paul Landau was known by local Americans, lived in a tiny studio on the third floor of a walk-up apartment on the Champs-Elysées. He serviced the American community in Paris and some French people who had access to American currency. His clients gave him checks drawn on American banks, and Pops sent the checks to a bank in Switzerland that gave him an excellent exchange rate.

The routine was to knock on the door, and Pops would inspect his visitor through the peephole, then he would undo the large locks. On this occasion, Pops was changing money for a Frenchman. While the two Americans were waiting, seated near the door, Wright told Himes loudly about the various deals he, Wright, had done there. After the French client had left, Pops turned to Wright, annoyed. "Mr. Wright, you must learn not to talk too much in France. . . . That man who just left is an inspector of the police."[37]

Shortly afterwards, one Sunday in late April, Himes was visiting 14, rue Monsieur le Prince when the doorbell rang. A fair-haired, boyish-looking character introduced himself as Mr. David Schine, from the U.S. State Department. He asked to come in. He proceeded to question Wright—mostly about someone else, a former member of the John Reed Club. Wright said he did not know the man. His reply seemed to infuriate Schine, who warned him that he and his colleague Roy Cohn had just had Langston Hughes up before the House Un-American Activities Committee in Washington, and they could do the same to him. He advised Wright to refresh his memory about his past, and left.

"That stupid son of a bitch thinks he can threaten me," Wright told Himes defiantly. "I'll never testify. I've written everything I have to say about my Communist affiliations."[38]

But he was shaken by the incident. He learned that Cohn and Schine worked for Joseph McCarthy in his Senate investigating committee, and they were on a two-week trip around Europe to inspect libraries in the United States Information Service (USIS). They had gone around Britain, Germany, Austria, and France plucking off shelves books they thought "Communistic." The list included Mark Twain and Dreiser, as well as Langston Hughes, Steinbeck, Lillian Hellman, and Wright.

"IN TIME I CAME TO REALIZE THAT DICK HAD BEEN CORRECT IN ACCUSING SO many various people of attacking him," Himes would write almost twenty years after these events. "They *were* attacking him. . . . On the American literary scene, the powers that be have never admitted but one black at a time into the arena of fame, and to gain this coveted admission, the young writer must unseat the reigning deity."[39]

Himes, who was not the first to make this point, was referring to an outburst he had witnessed between Wright and James Baldwin. That there was conflict between Wright and Baldwin is clear from Baldwin's essays. But we will never know what really transpired that evening in Paris in May 1953. All three participants—Wright, Baldwin, and Himes—would describe the incident later, and all three versions are different. Each makes himself look innocent in his own account.

In November 1960 Wright would tell a largely white audience in the American Church in Paris that he and Chester Himes were strolling in Saint-Germain one summer night, and decided to have a beer on the terrace of the Deux Magots. Who should "heave into view" but James Baldwin, accompanied by a white American woman, Mrs. Putnam. They pulled up chairs and Baldwin asked Wright what he thought of the article he had written about Wright eighteen months earlier.[40] Wright said the article had not made much sense to him. Baldwin accused him of treating him like a child. Wright laughed. Baldwin leaped to his feet and screamed: "I'm going to destroy you! I'm going to destroy your reputation! You'll see!" According to Wright, the white woman stood there and egged him on. Himes stood up in disgust and said he was going to take a walk around the block.

Baldwin's account of that evening was written in 1961, a year after Wright's death. "Once, one evening . . . Richard, Chester Himes, and myself went out and got drunk. It was a good night, perhaps the best I remember in all the time I knew Richard. For he and Chester were friends, they brought out the best in each other, and the atmosphere they created brought out the best in me."[41]

Himes told his version in his autobiography, *The Quality of Hurt*, published in 1972. According to him, he was at Wright's one afternoon when Baldwin phoned and asked to borrow five thousand francs. Wright arranged to meet him at the Deux Magots. Himes went with him, and they found Baldwin on the terrace.

> I was somewhat surprised to find Baldwin a small, intense young man of great excitability. Dick sat down in lordly fashion and started right off needling Baldwin, who defended himself with such intensity that he stammered, his body trembled, and his face quivered. I sat and looked

from one to the other. . . . Dick accused Baldwin of showing his gratitude for all he had done for him by his scurrilous attacks. Baldwin defended himself by saying that Dick had written his story and hadn't left him, or any other American black writer, anything to write about.[42]

The animation was such that various acquaintances came up, including Mrs. Putnam, an American whom all three men knew. Most of the onlookers, including Mrs. Putnam, sided with Baldwin—probably, Himes surmises, because he looked small and vulnerable, whereas Wright appeared condescending and cruel.

The crowd dispersed and the three men wandered down the road to a Martinican café. Baldwin and Wright were still arguing, and Himes, who was getting drunk (they had not eaten all evening), no longer followed the conversation. He does remember Baldwin saying: "The sons must slay their fathers."

After that, Chester Himes hardly saw Richard Wright, who was busy preparing for his trip to Africa.

ELLEN TYPED THE FINAL COPY OF WRIGHT'S SHORT NOVEL *SAVAGE HOLIDAY*, AND developed calluses from pounding the typewriter. From London, Dorothy Padmore sympathized: "Sometimes I think that the typewriter was invented to turn quite nice women into weary slaves. And men are so demanding."[43]

23

JOURNEY TO
THE GOLD COAST

April 1953–September 1953

It is Easter Sunday in the Wrights' Paris apartment. Wright sips his coffee and gazes at the stone walls of the University of Paris across the street. One of his guests, Dorothy Padmore, turns to him and says: "Now that your desk is clear, why don't you go to Africa?" Wright writes: "The idea was so remote to my mind and mood that I gaped at her a moment before answering. *'Africa?'* I echoed."

In this scene at the beginning of *Black Power*, Wright builds up a picture of a man rooted in the Western world who had hardly ever given Africa a thought. In reality, Dorothy Padmore's suggestion might have come as a gentle prod, but she was not planting anything new in his head. Wright had been wanting to travel to Africa ever since first coming to France in 1946. The book he most enjoyed reading during that initial Parisian sojourn was André Gide's *Travels in the Congo*. Gide, inspired by his childhood reading of *Heart of Darkness*, had traveled up the Congo River on a steamer, then set out into the interior with a party of African carriers. "Each day we sank a little further into strangeness," he wrote.

Wright had been disappointed when it proved impossible for him, in chaotic postwar conditions, to travel to Africa. A year later, back in France, his desire to go there was as strong as ever. "I must see Africa," he wrote in his journal. "I say here and now that I shall write the only book about Africa that will be written in my time."[1] And yet he did not go.[2]

In April 1953 he had just finished two novels that explored the "dark continent" within himself, and was wondering what to do next. As Dorothy Padmore reminded him, Nkrumah was about to table his plan for self-government in parliament. It was a historic moment. If Wright went there now, he would be glimpsing the future of Africa.

"You *must* go," Ellen said.

WRIGHT'S EXCITEMENT WAS TEMPERED BY "A VAGUE SENSE OF DISQUIET." AFRICA had to do with his own sense of identity. He was interested in the black nationalist struggle, but deep down, he was far more interested in discovering "the African." Would he feel a common bond with the "racial stock" from which he had sprung? How would Africans see him? Would they regard him as a lost brother who had returned? What would they have to say about the tragic transactions that took place during the slave trade? He himself found it unbearably painful to reflect that Negroes had often been sold to white slavers by their Negro brothers.

He wrote to Kwame Nkrumah, hoping for his cooperation. Nkrumah replied that "a continuous stream of people" was arriving to research and write about the Gold Coast, but he would nevertheless help out where he could. He added that since Wright's visit was not government sponsored, neither he nor his Party would be able to help with financial support. "I should be happy to do all I could to make your stay a pleasant, interesting and informative one."[3]

Early in May Wright flew to London to see what was holding up his visa. He got nowhere with the British authorities, and finally George Padmore asked Kwame Nkrumah to intervene. Nkrumah obliged with a "to whom it may concern" letter, stating that he had first met Richard Wright in the United States and had known him for many years. (In fact, they had met in 1940 in the U.S., but not since.) "Mr. Wright would like to come to the Gold Coast to do some research into the social and historical aspects of the country, and would be my guest during the time he is engaged in this work."

The letter cleared all obstacles. (Wright framed it, and would stand it on the dresser in his sundry lodgings in Africa.) On 28 May Wright flew to London to pick up his visa and to glimpse London in full coronation regalia. England was about to have a new queen.

He stayed a few days with the Padmores. One afternoon an Ashanti chief turned up with two attendants in tow.[4] Afterwards Wright watched the three men walk down the street in their colorful robes. It was neither raining nor sunny, and yet one of the attendants held an enormous umbrella above the chief's head. Wright turned to Padmore with a quizzical look. Padmore laughed and lit his pipe. A chief is sacred, he explained. The sun must not shine on his head, nor must the earth touch his feet. He always walks under an umbrella and always wears sandals.

"But *how* is he sacred?" Wright asked.

Padmore laughed. "Keep calm. It's not simple. It's all part of a vast, complex philosophy of life."

Joe Appiah dropped by. A short, slight, dark-skinned man, related on both sides of his family to Ashanti royalty, Appiah was Nkrumah's personal representative in Britain. He had been in England since 1943 and was about to be admitted to the bar. He had just announced his engagement to Peggy Cripps, the daughter of the late Sir Stafford Cripps, former chancellor of the exchequer. The British newspapers were full of it.

Wright quizzed Appiah about some of the more bewildering features of African mysticism. Did he believe in ghosts? Yes, Appiah replied. Dead people could reappear as ghosts; he himself had seen them. Wright was astonished that an educated man could entertain such notions.

What about polygamous marriages? he asked. Appiah answered that it saved the messy business of men running off and having affairs. Wright wanted to know how a man could manage five wives. He had read that 75 percent of women in America were dissatisfied sexually. "What do these Africans know that we don't know?"

"Technique," Appiah grinned. "An African, sexually, is superb. . . . White husbands in the West do not know anything about women."

When Wright went to see a London doctor for a final typhus injection, he asked whether African men could possibly have a higher sexual capacity than white men. The doctor said it was most unlikely.

The coronation of Elizabeth II took place on 2 June 1953. It was raining and the sky was gray. Having read about all the people who had slept in the streets to catch a glimpse of the young queen, Wright preferred to sit at home and listen to the radio broadcast. The next day he took the train to Liverpool,

On the platform at Euston station he found himself surrounded by "swarms of Africans" heading for Liverpool to board the *Accra*. He shivered in his thin London raincoat, and told himself, as he would tell himself time and again in Africa, that though his skin was black and his sympathies were with black people, he was in every respect a European.

And yet he hated what Europeans had done to black people. After dozing for a few hours, he looked through the train window at Liverpool's fine church spires and thought to himself: "The foundations of the city were built of human flesh and blood." He remembered what an Englishwoman had once said to him about the colonies. "I'm sorry, but they'll have to go it on their own. We've bled ourselves white to feed them, to lift them up; now they've got to stand on their own feet."

On the evening of 4 June he stepped inside his first-class cabin on the *Accra*. The next day he felt feverish. The typhus injections had made his temperature soar. He spent the first day in his cabin, and could manage only soup and a slice of toast. He nevertheless sat at his typewriter, composing a speech he was sure he would be asked to give while in Africa. Although he had told Nkrumah that he wanted the least possible publicity attached to his visit, he supposed that newspapermen would ply him with questions when he landed at Takoradi. It was best to be prepared.

"I am one of the lost sons of Mother Africa," he wrote. "There is something in me that never left this land." He mentioned Africa's "dark past" of slavery. He pointed out that the whole world had its eyes on the Gold Coast, and that Nkrumah, the champion of African freedom, had been educated at an American university.

He was acutely conscious that he must not be thought to be meddling in Gold Coast politics. "Make no mistake," he would tell the African people. "I do not come here to teach or advise; rather it is from you that I wish to learn." He added: "During the next few months, I shall move among you, asking myriads of questions, begging you to bear your hearts to me, and I pray that you will respond to me as one of your blood brothers."[5]

He was drenched with sweat. That night, by 4 A.M., he had taken six aspirins but he could not bring his fever down. By the time he began to feel better, several days later, they were in tropical waters, and the stifling heat exhausted him. Just out of Freetown, the sight of his first tropical sunset filled him with awe. "I knew that it was from feelings such as these floating in me now that man had got his sense of God."

There was no color line on the ship, he was pleased to see, though the two groups—the English and the Africans—mostly kept to themselves. He was the only American on board. At mealtimes he shared his table with a black judge from the Nigerian Supreme Court. Educated in England, the judge admired the British and was contemptuous of the African "natives." He did not believe Africa was ready for independence. Wright lay on his narrow bunk and reflected that he must tell the truth about the Gold Coast, whatever he encountered.

The voyage to Takoradi, the Gold Coast's only deepwater port at the time, took twelve days from Liverpool. "I wonder what you're going to make out of Africa," the judge remarked at breakfast, as Wright was about to disembark.

Wright, convinced that nothing could possibly be stranger than Mississippi, answered: "I don't expect to find too much there that's completely new."

HE WAS NOT PREPARED FOR THE OVERBEARING HEAT AND HUMIDITY. FEELING AS IF the flesh were melting from his bones, he stepped off the boat into a customs shed that was hotter still. To his relief, Nkrumah had sent a young man to meet him. This man guided him through customs and took him to the bus depot. No reporters turned up. No one seemed to notice Wright's arrival.

The bus trip to Accra lasted eight hours. It was hot and dusty. Wright stared out of the window and felt a sense of disorientation that verged on panic. The earth was rich red, and at times he could almost imagine he was back in the American South. But the tangled jungle, the villages of mud-thatched huts, the chaotic marketplaces, the naked children and the bare-breasted women washing clothes in the streams were disconcertingly strange to him. "There was nothing here that I could predict, anticipate, or rely upon." Another emotion welled up in him, just as strong. "A protest against what I saw seized me." Both these initial reactions would remain with him.

It was dusk when the bus got into the capital. Joyce Gittens, the prime minister's secretary—"a smiling but somewhat reserved mulatto woman"—was waiting at the terminal. Wright had met her several times at the Padmores' flat in London. She drove him to a government bungalow in the foothills—"Ministerial Bungalow No. 2"—and left him to settle in. The heat was more bearable at this slight elevation. Wright walked out onto the screened-in porch, and looked down the valley at the faint lights of Accra.

"Massa!"

I turned and saw a steward, dressed in white, black of face, bare-footed, his lips hanging open expectantly.

"What is it?"

"Massa want chop?"

"What?"

"Chop? Hot chop? Cold chop?"

The steward made eating gestures. "Chop," Wright realized, meant food. He was ushered into the dining room, where more young house-boys dressed in white stood at attention. "That pidgin English! I shuddered. I resented it and I vowed that I'd never speak it." To Wright it seemed "a frightful kind of baby talk."[6]

The next morning, 17 June, Wright took a taxi into the city. There were open sewerage drains. People walked around barefoot. The women carried heavy bundles on their heads and often had a baby strapped to their backs, and yet their walk was graceful. Beggars were everywhere, and Wright found himself repelled by their gruesome deformities. Children as well as adults plied trade in the streets. The water hydrants, Wright noticed, functioned as the city's "social clubs."

He called in at the U.S. Information Service (USIS) to introduce himself and read the recent newspapers from the States. On board ship he had developed hearing problems, and Bob Fleming from USIS drove him to the hospital to have his left ear irrigated. They were told to come back in the morning. There were not enough doctors in this country, Wright wrote in his journal.

He phoned the American consulate and spoke to the consul, William E. Cole, who seemed affable. By early afternoon he was giddy with the heat and returned to the bungalow. He stood on his porch watching "clouds of black buzzards circling slowly in the hazy blue sky." He fretted. The bungalow was clean and quiet, but he did not want to live in luxury in the foothills. "I have 100,000 words to set down about what I feel about the lives of these people," he wrote in his journal. "I'm not getting anywhere resting here in this sunny solitude. Do they think I came here for a vacation?"[7] He decided to move in a few days to a hotel in town. "Night fell," he writes in *Black Power*, "and suddenly out of the blue velvet dark came the sound of African crickets that was like an air-raid siren. Frog belches exploded. A soft, feathery thud, like that of a bird, struck the window screen. Reluctantly, I climbed into bed."

TWO DAYS LATER THERE WAS A BRIEF NOTICE OF WRIGHT'S ARRIVAL IN THE ACCRA *Daily Echo*. It was Friday, 19 June 1953, the day on which Julius and Ethel Rosenberg were executed in the United States. That morning, a phone call came from the prime minister's office. In the afternoon a chauffeur picked Wright up and drove him to Nkrumah's residence. It was a redbrick two-story house that reminded him of colonial mansions in Georgia or Mississippi.

Nkrumah came down the stairs. "Richard!" he greeted him. Wright handed him an armful of books he had brought from Padmore in England. He was introduced to Nkrumah's mother—"a tiny little black woman with an amazingly sharp and intelligent face." He could sense the influence she had over her son. He resolved to ask Nkrumah more about that.

They were going on a tour of the city, Nkrumah told him. Wright would see how the people responded to him and his Convention People's Party. Wright asked: "What's going to happen in July?" Nkrumah threw back his head and laughed. "You are direct," he said.

That "African laugh" was to disconcert Wright a great deal. "It was not caused by mirth," he noted. He thought it an evasive tactic, a false laugh, a mask, a means of avoiding saying something while nevertheless indicating friendliness.

They climbed into the prime minister's car. Wright sat on Nkrumah's left. A large escort of motorcyclists, dressed in scarlet uniforms, roared their motors, and the cavalcade set off. Hearing the din of motorbikes, people rushed out to wave and salute. "Freedom!" they called. "Kwame!" The prime minister smiled and raised his right hand. Bare-breasted women came up to the car doing a "snakelike, shuffling dance." Wright thought to himself that he had seen those same movements in storefront churches in the Deep South. What did that mean? He had always insisted that race was a social myth, not a biological fact, and that the very word "race" should be put in quotation marks. But how could he explain some of the characteristics he was encountering among Africans that reminded him so strongly of American Negroes? As well as the weaving dance, there was the "laughter that bent the knee and turned the head," and "that queer shuffling of the feet when one was satisfied or in agreement." He looked through the car window at the cheering throngs, and again he felt bewildered. "Was it possible that I was looking at myself laughing, dancing, singing, gliding with my hips to express my joy? . . . Had I denied all this in me?"

Back at the prime minister's house, Wright felt obliged to explain to Nkrumah that he had been a member of the American Communist Party for twelve years but he was no longer a Communist. He was for black people. It was the first time he had seen a mass movement with a black leader, and he wanted to understand it. He wanted to see how Nkrumah was organizing it.

Nkrumah, who seemed distracted, gave a "mechanical nod." At that point, a crowd of people entered the room. Nkrumah waved in the direction of Wright and introduced him as "a novelist." After that, Wright was ignored. The people talked in their native languages, and he found himself standing to one side. After some time, a band struck up downstairs. Wright wandered out onto the balcony and looked down to see the prime minister dancing on the lawn with a dozen or so women. It was the same solitary, weaving dance he had seen on the streets that afternoon.

At three in the morning, he met the prime minister coming into the living room. "I must go. I'm dead tired," Wright told him. They shook hands. A chauffeur drove Wright back to his bungalow in the hills.

———

A FEW DAYS LATER, NKRUMAH ASKED WRIGHT TO GIVE A SHORT TALK AT ONE OF his political rallies. Wright delivered the speech he had prepared on the ship. A reporter from the white-owned newspaper the *Daily Graphic* asked Wright for permission to run it the next day. Wright turned to Nkrumah for his consent. Nkrumah hesitated, then asked to see Wright's notes. "He took them, looked off solemnly, then folded them slowly. The reporter waited. I waited. Then the Prime Minister came close to me and pushed the notes into the top breast pocket of my suit; he said no word and I said no word." Wright decided not to ask questions, but he returned to his bungalow "in a deeply thoughtful mood."

Two days later, he was invited to accompany Nkrumah on a campaign tour to Cape Coast. They traveled in an open convertible car, the motorbike escort roaring beside them. A loudspeaker admonished the people: "Vote for the CPP! Vote for self-government now! Follow Nkrumah to victory!" Wright privately thought it "an emotional blitzkrieg." After a spicy lunch (Nkrumah warned him to be cautious), the cavalcade made its way to the center of town where Nkrumah gave a speech. Wright felt faint as he sat in the glaring sun. Listening to Nkrumah attack the opposition and watching the people roar their appreciation, he thought to himself: "It was politics *plus.* . . . It bordered upon religion."

That lunch—groundnut soup, hot red peppers, and spicy meat stew—made Wright sick for days. When he recovered, he went with Gene Sawyer from USIS to look at hotels. It turned out that there were only three in Accra, all owned by the same Greek family. He settled on the Seaview, which fronted onto Jamestown, a maze of alleys between tumbledown slums. This way, he told himself, he would see life in Accra.

The hotel turned out to be grimmer than he first thought. Mosquito netting covered his bed, but the windows were not screened, and he was bitten by mosquitoes. Ants and cockroaches shared his quarters. The walls were spattered with grease. From the open drains outside came the smell of human excrement. The mattress was damp; everything was damp. Within days his nail file was red with rust. Green mold formed on his nylon shirts. "It was the kind of hotel that one read about in a Joseph Conrad novel," he writes in *Black Power.*

He liked kenke (maize paste wrapped in dark green leaves) and fufu (a starchy dish of yams and plantains). But his stomach rebelled against spicy fried food. Wary of the local water, he drank beer, like the Africans and Europeans who crowded the Seaview's verandah. He fought against "a never-ending sense of enervation." Why did the food give him no strength? he wondered. Someone told him that vegetables grew so quickly in the heat they lacked their usual nourishment.

He walked around Accra taking photographs. He was hoping to include some in the book. There were no parks, no water fountains, no public benches under shady trees, no cafés where he could stop for a cup of tea. When he began to wilt from the heat, he would go back to the Seaview and write in his journal or develop photos.[8] From Paris he had brought with him several packets of darkroom chemicals, carefully weighed in advance, which he kept in the hotel's communal refrigerator, clearly labeled. One day he discovered that someone had drunk from the bottles. "Jesus," he wrote in his journal in a panic. "Would somebody be sick or die?" He was too tense to work that day. When he heard that an Indian woman was sick, he went to see her and gave her some of his supply of bismuth. To his relief, she recovered.[9]

He had been in Africa a week and the educated Accra elite did not seem to give a damn that he was in their city. He was entertained by USIS people. James Moxon, a portly Englishman from the British Information Service, invited him to dinner. Moxon's house felt like Paris transported to Africa and the food was marvelous. But Wright had not come to Africa to clink glasses with Westerners.

His journal was his sole confidant. 23 June: "I'm enervated, listless, and I find myself longing to take a ship and go home." 24 June: "I feel like chucking up the whole thing. . . . I had thought that the Prime Minister would surely have had a long talk with me, would have found time, etc. But so far he has not." 25 June: "I feel that I really have no friends here. . . . And that was the last thing that I would have dreamed would happen!" 30 June: "In the tropics I always wake up sleepy, and there's that white sky staring at me through the paneless window. I'd like right now to be back in Paris to sleep some. . . . "

The National Assembly was about to open and the political atmosphere was tense. Nkrumah was busy with ministerial affairs. Wright knew that Nkrumah was a man of indefatigable energy who rose at 4 A.M. and worked until midnight, and had little time for anything outside politics. But still he had hoped for some personal attention.

On 2 July the prime minister tabled what he called his "White Paper." Wright went along to the Assembly. The CPP people, aloof and smiling, seemed to be avoiding him, he told himself. Nkrumah had "shied off" from him. Had he said something to offend these people?

Parliament was modeled on the British House of Commons. It seemed to Wright that the ministers strutted around like British aristocrats, and when they addressed "Mr. Speaker" they pitched their voices so low he could hardly make out what was going on. "I lost all interest in the Gold Coast as I sat in that hushed room," he wrote in his journal. He left the Assembly feeling more alienated than ever.

"Ought I to call this effort to write about the Gold Coast off and go home? That's what I want to do." He had signed a contract with Harper & Brothers and had been given a three-thousand-dollar advance. Now that he was here no one seemed to want to know him. That night he did not sleep. "Africa! Where are you. Are you a myth? I seek you and cannot find you. I'm in despair."[10] The next day, 3 July, he made inquiries about ships going back. He was told that the earliest date he could leave was 2 September.

When he went to pick up his mail at the prime minister's office, Nkrumah's secretary, Joyce Gittens, asked: "How are you getting on?"

I felt depressed. She knew what was happening and I resented her asking me to tell her what she already knew.

"I feel like the Africans have put their *juju* on me," I muttered, trying obliquely to let her know that I was dissatisfied.

She swirled in her swivel chair and stared at me.

"You must be careful of *that*," she said in a deadly serious tone.

"What?" I exclaimed, coming fully aroused now.

"There's something to *juju*," she said to me sternly. . . .

I sank weakly into a chair and stared at her. I'd met this cool, intelligent, and efficient woman in London and Paris and we'd had long discussions about the state of the world; and I had respected her opinions. And now, here in this heat and humidity, she was hinting to me that *juju* was real and not just a psychological delusion.

"What do they do to people down here?" I asked her. I walked slowly out of the office, feeling defeated.

On 9 July, Wright read a long passage from *The Outsider* to a British and American audience at the Accra Dining Club. He could not tell what their reaction was. Eugene Sawyer, from USIS, drove him home. The next day Wright moved into Sawyer's house. He had had enough of the Seaview. In an American household he could eat plain food.

That same day—10 July 1953—Nkrumah delivered his "Motion of Destiny" address. There were vast crowds outside the Legislative Assembly. In a stirring speech, Nkrumah called on the British govern ment to give the Gold Coast independence as soon as the "necessary administrative arrangements" were made.

Wright congratulated Nkrumah, then left by himself. He wrote to the Padmores that Nkrumah's speech was "moving and eloquent," but he wondered why the British agreed to everything so readily. It worried him that Nkrumah wanted to go ahead with the plan to dam the Volta River, a project that the British seemed to want more than anyone else. "I distrust any situation which the British like and are willing to defend."[11]

It was a historic turning point. Nkrumah's Motion of Destiny was debated for several days, then carried unanimously. A general election, fixed for June 1954, was to bring in an all-African parliament. After that, Wright hardly saw Nkrumah.

"THE GOLD COAST IS A FABULOUS COUNTRY AND MAINLY BECAUSE OF THE BASIC spirit of the people." Wright was writing his first and only letter to the Padmores after a month in Accra. He suspected that his mail from the Gold Coast would be opened. And he knew that the Padmores were devoted to Nkrumah. "The Prime Minister took me for a ride in his car, with his official escort and everything. It was one of the most inspiring trips I've ever had; I saw a sea of emotion and loyalty. I never dreamed that the boys had organized such a streamlined, modern political organization."[12]

"I had hoped that I'd see this place solely from the point of view of the CPP, that is, I'd hoped that they'd show me the place," he told the Padmores. "But instead I've had to see it on my own. . . . I have, there- fore, had to alter the plan of my book. Instead of its being a study of the political situation in terms of human interest and appeal, I'm having to concentrate mostly on the life of the people."

He finished: "I guess you ought to be seeing Ellen soon, as she is taking the children to a camp in England."

———

WHY DID WRIGHT EXPECT NKRUMAH'S PERSONAL ATTENTION? AS HE MAKES CLEAR in *Black Power*, the challenge ahead of this one man was almost insuperable. "When I last saw him he looked tired unto death," he would write in his journal on 27 July. "How long can Kwame last physically under such an onerous burden?"

The Gold Coast—as it was aptly christened by the Europeans—was richly endowed with gold, diamonds, bauxite, cocoa, and timber. Nearly all trade and commerce were run by the British. Most of the African people lived in squalor; roughly 90 percent were illiterate, and few had useful skills. Because of poor nutrition and poor sanitation, disease was rife. The British had done little to build roads, rail, or schools. Behind the British civil servants who administered the colony were the British police, the British navy, and the British army. Their criminal investigation forces were everywhere, on the trail of subversion.[13] Nkrumah had already spent a year in jail for sedition, enduring appalling conditions at James Fort Prison in Accra.

Nkrumah also faced tribal divisions. The educated black aristocracy looked down upon him. He was not from the coastal elite, but from an illiterate rural family. He had not gone to Oxford or Cambridge to be educated, as the cream of the Gold Coast usually did, but instead he had gone to America for ten years. He had studied not at Harvard but at Lincoln University, the black university in Pennsylvania.[14]

By the time Wright arrived in the Gold Coast in June 1953, Nkrumah had been prime minister for a little more than a year. He was making impressive progress in an almost impossible situation. His enemies in Britain and Africa accused him of being pro-Communist. Others accused him of establishing a "black dictatorship." It was said that he made too many concessions to the imperialists. It was rumored that he was a British agent. Corruption was said to be rife in his party. Wright even heard that Padmore had accepted bribes. There was no end to the rumors and allegations.

IN *BLACK POWER*, WRIGHT IS DISARMINGLY HONEST ABOUT THE WAY PEOPLE IN Africa reacted to him. He was greeted with stares, giggles, or laughter. Even those Africans who had been educated in the West found him too direct, too intrusive. In his own narrative, Wright comes across as an awkward American blundering his way through the African landscape. He was, he admits, out of his depth. He wanted Africans to trust him, and they did not. "I was black and they were black," he writes, "but my blackness did not help me."

Wright was profoundly affected by this. But why should his African cousins trust him? He did not trust them. He saw himself as "western to the bone,"[15] and he was proud of it. He walked around in khaki pants, a T-shirt, a British Raj-style sun helmet, with two cameras slung over his shoulder, and wondered why Africans knew, before he opened his mouth, that he was American. On one occasion, he almost caused a riot when he focused his camera on the intricate rites of a funeral ceremony.

He approached this highly religious country as an unbending rationalist. To him, ancestor worship and West African juju were ludicrous "mumbo-jumbo" that needed to be eradicated—by force if necessary. He thought the tribal chiefs "preposterous" figures, with their "foolishly gaudy" huge umbrellas and their "outlandish regalia." He wrote in his journal: "Their claims about their ability to appease the dead is a fraud, their many wives are a seductive farce . . . their justice is barbaric, their interpretations of life are contrary to common sense." The sight of men holding hands in the streets or two men dancing together closely gave him "a sense of uneasiness . . . deeper than I could control." He did not think it was homosexuality. Nevertheless, he wrote, "my Puritan background makes me disturbed when I see anything like this so blatantly exhibited in public."[16]

Today's "multiculturalist" ethics were not prevalent in the 1950s. Wright did not see why he should adapt to new cultural assumptions and social codes. He assured himself there was no danger of his "becoming infected with the African's religious beliefs." But he did not worry about imposing Western ideas on a complex African heritage.

He believed that the evasiveness he constantly encountered was deliberate. "It was childlike. . . . Didn't Africans know that their elusiveness simply whetted people's curiosity the more?" He suspected they were purposefully wanting to confound him. "I found the African an oblique, a hard-to-know man who seemed to take a kind of childish pride in trying to create a state of bewilderment in the minds of strangers." It made him defiant. "They seemed to feel that that which they did not reveal to me I could never know, but nothing could have been more erroneous."[17]

He was alone a great deal of the time. He would walk around different parts of Accra, conjecturing and speculating. In poor areas, he kept seeing women squat down and urinate. Did Africans urinate more than most people, he wondered? And all this nudity! In the West, nudity was associated with sex. He could only assume that Africans were largely asexual. "Undoubtedly, these people had . . . chosen some aspect of their lives other than sex upon which to concentrate their passions." He had come full circle from his speculations on African virility in London.

One morning he had breakfast with Peter Abrahams, the black South African writer. Abrahams commented later that Wright was astounded by the casual attitude to sex. "There was, he had said, too much sex, too casually given and taken; so that it worked out as no sex, with none of the emotional involvement associated with sex in the western mind."[18] He presumably had had some experience of it.

Wright slept so badly he could scarcely tell anymore whether he was thinking or dreaming. It was making him desperate that he could not find the material he needed. "The heat, the humidity, the dead slow reactions of people—all make me ill in a mental sort of way. I long to leave here, long to be with my own."[19]

And yet he pushed himself hard. He interviewed politicians, journalists, writers, and academics. He hired a car and made short trips into the bush and neighboring villages:

> Being alone and with no knowledge of the language, I'd miss a lot that I'd want to know, but, being alone, unannounced, with no guide or interpreter, I'd catch the native African without warning; he would have no chance to dress up or pretend; the chiefs would have no opportunity to get out those big and ridiculous umbrellas.

By the beginning of August, he felt he had seen as much as he could in this way, and he decided to trek inland. The car rental agency informed him he would have to pay twenty pounds a month, plus a shilling-a-mile premium for taking the car on bush roads. He would have to pay for the gas and oil, the driver's salary, and, while they were on the road, the driver's food and lodging as well as his own. The jungle, it seemed to Wright, was the most expensive place on earth. "My money is melting under this tropic sun faster than I am soaking up the reality about me."

He did not know it yet, but he had a hernia. Exhausted all the time, he was frightened of falling seriously ill in the jungle. With him was had come a daunting little booklet called *Hints on the Preservation of Health in Tropical Africa*, which advised travelers how best to avoid bilharzia, dysentery, the tumbu fly (this lays eggs under the skin), yaws, sleeping sickness, blackwater fever, worms, typhus. He was careful to put germicide in his washing water and only drank boiled water.

It required considerable courage to journey into the interior. It was not something tourists did. There were no hotels outside the towns, and, as Wright puts it in *Black Power*, the town hotels were "of a sort to discourage the heartiest of travelers." He went to the prime minister's office for help and was told to go and talk to the people at the British Information Service. Wright "balked" at being "shunted into the hands of the British." He "brooded," he writes, for a couple of days. Finally, he went to see James Moxon, director of the British Information Service.[20] Moxon drew up an itinerary and arranged accommodation at government rest houses or else private homes of British businesspeople. Wright hired a chauffeur, an ex–middleweight champion called Kojo— a man who could, if need be, look after them both in the jungle. On 4 August, they set off in a vanguard saloon Chevrolet, with a trunk full of canned food, for the high rain forest country.

It was the rainy season. It rained and rained. Each day the sun would shine for about half an hour, then the sky would turn gray again. The thick jungle gave Wright a "hemmed-in feeling." In Koforidua, a town in the cocoa-producing region, he stayed in the modern home of the district manager of the British-owned United Africa Company, a "young man with English public school mannerisms," who held a cocktail party for him. Wright resented the fact that no one in Africa had ever heard of him, or seemed to care what he was doing there. A possible title for his book, he mused, was "A Stranger in a Strange Land."

He wandered around in the mud-hut villages. People stared at him, giggled, and vanished. Wright, contrary to the thrust of all his previous thinking, now began to ask himself whether Africans were "so biologically different" that their attitudes would remain unaltered whatever influences they were subjected to. "Is the African less adaptable than other races to change?"[21]

From Koforidua they drove to Kumasi, where Wright stayed in a "dank and musty African hotel." He could hear the dull throb of drums in the distance. He took photographs of the vast, chaotic marketplace. Enervated by the heat, he had to force himself to interview the editor of the *Ashanti Pioneer*, the leading opposition paper. He was a guest at a dinner for Otumfuo Sir Osei Agyeman Prempeh II, the king of Ashanti. At a private audience with him some days later, Wright was astounded to discover that the king seemed to want his people to change, and yet he was imprisoned by their superstitions and traditions.

One morning a young photographer came to his hotel, a man Wright had met at the Padmores', in London. A grandson of the royal Asantehene household, he agreed to act as Wright's interpreter. They set off for the village of Mampong, where they met the local chief. They waited to meet elders who never appeared, and the Queen Mother "saved the hour" by inviting Wright to her "castle" for a drink. Her castle reminded him of a tenement on Chicago's South Side.

As they sat in the Queen Mother's living room, men and women wandered in and out. Wright whispered to his photographer friend:

"Who are these people? Are they guests of the Queen Mother?"

"Oh, no."

"Are they friends?"

"No."

"Are they servants?"

"Well, no."

"They all live in the same household?"

"Yes."

"Are they paid?"

"Well, no; we don't pay them."

"But they work for her?"

"Yes."

"Can they leave when they want to?"

"They'd never want to leave."

"Are they slaves?" I asked him finally and bluntly.

He was irritated. He bit his lips and looked off.

"You don't understand," he said. "They wouldn't want to leave us.

They live with us all of their lives. If they left, they wouldn't have any-where to go. We feed them, clothe them; they live with us till they die. They are like members of the family; you see?"

"But other people would call them slaves, wouldn't they?"

"Yes; but that's not right. It's not the right word. It's not right to call them that."

It was slavery, all right, but it was not quite the Mississippi kind; it fit-ted in with their customs, their beliefs. . . . I stared at the slaves. I tried to swallow and I could not. The Asantehene's grandson seemed to be wor-ried at the impression I was getting and he said:

"We live differently; you see?"

Wright tells the story as an example of perverse African evasive-ness. It is typical of the exchanges he describes with one African after another. He would ask questions—rather hostile questions that were the product of his Western assumptions—and the African would not be able to find the words to explain an entirely different reality, and would finally become impatient with the trap Wright seemed to be set-ting. Wright, irritated, would record the dialogue as yet another exam-ple of the African's "chronic distrust."

In Samreboi, the world's largest timber mill owned by the United Africa Company, Wright stayed with an English couple. That evening, he was obliged to attend another party of company officials and their wives. His host introduced him as "Dr. Williams from the States," and Wright did not bother to correct him. The members of the group, forti-fied by cognac, scotch, and sherry, regaled each other with anecdotes about the natives. "One of those savages working at a saw this morning had an accident," one began. Another told a joke about a half-educated "African monkey" who had misinterpreted the word "titter." Another chimed in: "One bugger came in one morning . . ." Each story was greeted by loud explosions of laughter. Wright sat holding his drink, wondering if Nkrumah knew the kind of British friends he had.

Back in his room, he got ready for bed, then stood at the window looking out into the jungle. A terrible moaning broke the night air. At first it sounded like a baby crying; then it became a scream; then it dis-solved into a despairing hooting. Finally there was a return of the moaning, as if some animal were in excruciating pain. The next morn-ing he was told it was a tree bear.

Shortly after that, Wright told Kojo to "drive nonstop to Accra." After three weeks in the jungle, he was worn down by the heat and eternal rain; he was tired of rooms that were "as damp as an underground cave"; he was fed up with fat, corrupt chiefs and their sprawling houses full of wives and servants; he was sick of mud-hut villages, sick of chaos, sick of poverty and squalor, flies, filth, and foul odors.

Back in Accra, Wright wrote in his journal: "I've decided to cut my stay short. . . . I've so far spent more than two thousand dollars to see this country and its people. If I stayed another month, it might cost me another thousand dollars. That is too much."

He spent the day of 25 August running around in the heat, trying to organize his return trip. "I had a headache from morning till night. Now, at about seven o'clock, I was told that I could leave on the 2nd of September. A great weight of anxiety lifted from my mind. My headache left. I relaxed. If I stayed longer, it would mean that my family would suffer."[22]

He had intended to stay in Africa between four and six months. He was going home after two and a half.

WHAT PUZZLED HIM, WRIGHT WROTE IN HIS JOURNAL THE DAY BEFORE HE LEFT Africa, was that black Americans like Paul Robeson and Du Bois had come to Africa and written about it, and not one of them had told the truth about African life. ("Even Du Bois, for all his learning and strutting and expounding the problem of Africa, has failed to make clear the essential nature of the problem.") The truth that no one had ever dared to say was that there was something lacking in the African character. "There is no doubt that Europe has exploited Africa for centuries, but there is something that has caused the exploitation, and that is the essential soddenness of the African mentality."[23]

BLACK POWER ENDS WITH A TEN-PAGE OPEN LETTER FROM WRIGHT TO KWAME Nkrumah. "My journey's done," it begins. "My labors in your vineyard are over." As his ship pulled away from Africa, he tells Nkrumah, he had fought against "soft, sentimental feelings."

The tone of the letter then changes abruptly. "Kwame, let me put it bluntly." Wright pointed out what Nkrumah already knew: that the "hard-faced men of the West" were ready to pounce at any time upon Africa, that Nkrumah did not have Western-educated Africans on his side, that Nkrumah had a huge challenge ahead, and that his very safety was in jeopardy.

Westerners were often negative about Africa, Wright told Nkrumah. He added that he himself had found "too much cloudiness in the Africans' mentality, a kind of sodden vagueness." His recommendation for the Gold Coast was militarism. He argued that compulsory draft would be necessary to overcome "the stagnancy of tribalism." It was the only way the people of the Gold Coast would stand united against the British:

A military form of African society will atomize the fetish-ridden past, abolish the mystical and nonsensical family relations that freeze the African in his static degradation; it will render impossible the continued existence of those parasitic chiefs who have too long bled and misled a naïve people; it is the one and only stroke that can project the African immediately into the twentieth century!

Wright admitted that this solution would look to many like "Communism, Fascism, Nazism," but he himself was convinced that only a militaristic organization would bring cohesiveness to a divided society and keep foreign powers at bay. "Regarding corruption," he warned Nkrumah, "use fire and acid and cauterize the ranks of your party of all opportunists. *Now!*"

It was a strange admonishment to come from a man who had always placed individual freedom above all else. In *The Outsider* he had condemned the Communist Party for that sort of behavior. A few months later, he would be astonished when he interviewed a white, Indonesian-born Dutch journalist who declared that Indonesia needed a dictatorship. "To me," Wright writes in *The Color Curtain*, "his conviction that Indonesia needed a dictator, that the people were not ready for democracy, seemed to be the product either of a sense of pity for the plight of the Indonesians or of an attitude of scorn. It was like saying that a delinquent child needed a stern father."[24]

At the end of his letter, Wright assured Nkrumah of his own solidarity in his struggle for Gold Coast independence. "With words as our weapons, there are some few of us who will stand on the ramparts to fend off the evildoers, the slanderers, the greedy, the self-righteous! You are not alone."

AND YET THE DAY BEFORE WRIGHT LEFT ACCRA FOR TAKORADI BY WAY OF THE slave castles, he called in at the American consulate and spoke to the consul, William E. Cole.

Nkrumah had rebuffed him—or so Wright believed. The American government officials, on the other hand, had been welcoming and helpful. Bill Cole had entertained him in his home several times. On 4 July Wright was among the group celebrating Independence Day at the U.S. consulate.

More than he dared say in *Black Power,* Wright distrusted Nkrumah. His methods of organization seemed blatantly Communist. Wright was convinced that Nkrumah had slighted him because he feared that Wright, as a former Communist, might understand more than Nkrumah wanted him to know. Soon after their conversation that day, Cole wrote to the State Department in Washington:

> Mr. Wright has just left the Gold Coast, having spent the last three months here collecting material for a book which he has agreed to write for Harper Brothers. He arrived here with the backing of George Padmore and in the expectation of being well received by Kwame Nkrumah and other foremost figures of the CPP. Wright's intention was to write a book describing the political advances in the Gold Coast and especially the CPP, which he intended to portray in a favorable light. However, Wright found that he was not cordially received by the CPP. On the contrary he feels that he was ignored by them and that his reasonable requests for information were evaded. He is therefore unable to carry out his original intention with respect to the kind of book he will produce. The reason why he could not gain the confidence of the CPP is unknown, but it may have something to do with his Communist past or with CPP fears that, especially in view of his familiarity with Communism, he would be an alert and critical observer of CPP activities.
>
> In any event, Mr. Wright traveled considerably in the Gold Coast, had numerous conversations with everyone except CPP personalities, and departed with voluminous notes of his observations. Wright's past experiences appear to have endowed him with a high degree of ability at fer-

reting out obscure political situations, and it is believed the enclosure presents certain background information not easily available.[25]

The enclosure was a four-page memorandum, "made voluntarily by Richard Wright."

"I do not believe that the CPP has any direct relation or affiliation with any local or foreign Communist group," Wright asserted, "but the leading members of the Party openly admit that they have conscientiously modeled their organization upon the Russian Communist Party. In short, it is a Communist minded political party, borrowing Marxist concepts and applying them with a great deal of flexibility to local African social and economic conditions." He pointed out that Nkrumah slept with a large portrait of Lenin above his bed.[26]

From one of Nkrumah's enemies, Dzenkle Dzewu, Wright had learned that Nkrumah's "Secret Circle" of six men maintained constant contact with George Padmore and Joe Appiah in London.

> One of the means of communication is maintained through a woman, Lucy Siedel, who is employed in the Government Printing Office. Padmore's letters to Nkrumah are generally sealed within envelope within envelope and addressed to Lucy Siedel in a barely legible scrawl to mislead governmental censorship. I am led to believe that there are other postal routes through which this flow of communication is kept alive.[27]

Wright's statement could not have contained much that was new to the State Department, and Wright knew that. Nevertheless, it was an act of betrayal, and he knew that too. His fear that the Communists would infiltrate Africa was genuine, but Nkrumah was no pawn of Moscow, and George Padmore unequivocally shared Wright's hostility toward Communism.[28] And yet behind their backs, Wright was giving away black men's secrets.

IN MID-SEPTEMBER 1953, WRIGHT WAS BACK IN PARIS, WITH HUNDREDS OF PHOTO-graphs and pages of notes. Two weeks later, he was in the American Hospital undergoing an operation for a hernia.

His family and friends found him depressed. "I'm told that the Gold Coast is by far the best part of Africa," he told them. "If that is so, then, I don't want to see the worst."[29]

24

FROM BULLFIGHTS
TO BANDUNG

March 1954–April 1955

The old fire has come back to you," Paul Reynolds congratulated Wright after reading his Africa manuscript in March 1954.[1] "This book has the force and impact and hard-hitting qualities of *Native Son* and *Black Boy*."[2] For Wright, numb with fatigue after months of hard work, the words offered intense relief.

Reynolds's only criticism was the book's anti-Americanism.

You speak of the fear on the faces of any crowd of Americans. My own opinion, which is doubtless distorted and wrong, is there is a great fear in Europe and in Australia where I was and in other parts of the world but very little here.

. . .

The critics are going to realize that you have been out of this country for a good many years and I think you will get a better press and will have a more convincing book if you are willing to just cut out the dozen or so places where you go out of your way to take cracks at America.[3]

Wright's current editor at Harper, Frank MacGregor, wanted him to make a clear statement in the introduction that he was no longer a Communist. He also hoped Wright could be persuaded to soften his letter to Nkrumah. "The impression given is one of utter ruthlessness."[4] Wright sent off the revised manuscript in May 1954.

THESE DAYS HE WAS SEEING A LOT OF VIVIAN WERNER, A THIRTY-TWO-YEAR-OLD divorcée with two young sons, who had recently arrived in Paris. She had been introduced to Ellen Wright at the Café Tournon, and Ellen had invited her to dinner at the apartment. Vivian Werner was trying to write a novel and the Wrights were encouraging.

That spring Wright and Werner met most afternoons in one café or another. He drank tomato juice, because of his stomach. She drank coffee. "One day," Werner writes in her unpublished memoir, "Dick asked me to go to bed with him." Wright's photographer friend Gisèle Freund had lent him the keys to her apartment:

Dick was gentle but there was no passion either on his part or mine. Later Dick was sheepish and apologetic. "I'm so clumsy," he mumbled. We met again, two or three times, either at Gisèle's apartment or the one I moved to in the Boulevard du Montparnasse. But there was still no passion involved and that phase of our relationship ended, tapering off quietly and without rancor and we went back to seeing one another in those Left Bank cafés.[5]

What Werner mostly remembers about their café conversations was that Wright was always complaining. At first she was too lonely to care. After some months, it got on her nerves. She was struck by Wright's tender tone when once, fleetingly, he alluded to Ellen in the early days of their marriage. By the time she knew him, the marriage was little more than a façade. "Ellen and Dick never went out together. Ellen would call me and suggest the movies. She would sometimes ask to come over, and lie on my couch and talk. She was very uptight and tense. She seemed to be in a state of constant desperation."[6] Ellen did not realize that her friend Vivian was another woman who had slept with her husband.

———

ON 17 MAY 1954, THE UNITED STATES SUPREME COURT HANDED DOWN ITS HISTORIC *Brown v. Board of Education* decision. Race segregation in public schools was declared unconstitutional. The Voice of America beamed the news around the world. The United States Information Service portrayed it as a triumph for democracy. *Newsweek* called it "the most momentous decision in the whole history of the Negro struggle . . . in the United States."[7]

In Paris a few days later, the black American journalist Ollie Stewart came across Richard Wright in the Monaco. "He had his glasses off," he recalls, "and his eyes were lit up with excitement. He was so happy he accepted a beer, although he usually drank coffee. 'It took a long time,' he practically shouted, 'but . . . no matter what happens, the kids will have the law on their side from now on.'"[8]

FOR THE MOMENT WRIGHT DID NOT WANT TO WRITE FICTION. "THERE ARE SO many . . . exciting and interesting things happening now in the world that I feel sort of dodging them if I don't say something about them," he told Paul Reynolds.[9] He wanted to explore another culture. But where? Russia interested him. Friends suggested Israel, but he felt no affinity with the idea of a Jewish homeland. ("It would be like my claiming Africa for the American Negroes.")

Reynolds thought he should stick to colonized peoples—French Africa or India, Egypt or Madagascar. "I will say from a sales point of view it would be superficially better if you wrote about negro people. . . . However, that's only superficial and you shouldn't feel bound by it."[10] Wright did not feel bound by Negro themes—even though he personally believed that what his agent and publishers held against *Savage Holiday* was that he had crossed the color line and written about white people.[11]

In July, over dinner with Gunnar and Alva Myrdal, a new idea was seeded in his mind. Gunnar Myrdal, the Swedish political economist who had written *An American Dilemma*, was now working for the European Economic Commission in Geneva. His wife Alva worked at UNESCO in Paris, and the couple commuted between the two cities. They suggested that Spain would make a fascinating study. Isolated from the rest of Europe, it was in some ways scarcely Western at all. Catholicism played an important role in the culture, and Wright had always been interested in religion as a social phenomenon. It contained oppressed minorities: Prostestants, Gypsies, Basques, and Jews. There were the Muslim and Moorish influences. Why not study a land that hovered in so many ways between Europe and Africa?

Wright was excited. His publishers were not. "Harper . . . genuinely question whether a crusading book on Spain would sell to the public and whether you're the person to write such a book," Reynolds told Wright. He added: "I personally don't like the Spaniard or the South American. They would seem to me to have very little sense of what's honorable or square and yet have a colossal pride."[12]

Wright insisted he had no intention of ranting about Franco's tyrannical regime. He was interested in the people and the culture.

IN THE MIDDLE OF AN UNUSUALLY HOT AUGUST, WRIGHT LEFT ON A THREE-WEEK exploratory trip to Spain in his Citroën. "Do take care while you are there," Dorothy Padmore warned him. "You wouldn't feel too comfortable in one of Franco's jails."[13]

"For almost a decade I had ignored the admonitions of my friends to visit Spain," Wright would write in *Pagan Spain*—"the one country of the Western world about which, as though shunning the memory of a bad love affair, I did not want to exercise my mind." He felt more and more nervous as he approached the French border town of Le Perthus. He knew people who had died in the Spanish civil war fighting for freedom. Seventeen years later, Franco was still running the country as a fascist dictatorship. Wright worried that his Communist past (and the anti-Franco statements he had made in the 1930s) would be known to Spanish intelligence.

When he entered Spain, it seemed to him that the world darkened. "I edged my car along in the wake of the car ahead, circling around the snaky curves of the tilting mountain slopes, glancing now and then from the narrow road to plunging precipices that yawned but a yard from my elbow." He was unnerved by the civil guards dotted along the road, cradling machine guns. (Wright himself had a gun in his glove box, just in case.)[14] When he stopped at a gas station, a guard clapped him on the shoulder and spoke to him in rapid Spanish. "*This is it,*"

Wright told himself. He took out his passport, but the guard waved it aside, shaking his head. The man at the pump, who spoke French, explained that the guard wanted a lift down the road. Wright grinned with relief, and the guard clambered into the car with his machine gun. They talked, and laughed at their inability to understand each other. After a few minutes, the officer looked at his wristwatch and pumped his foot down on an imaginary pedal. Wright thought he was asking him to go faster. Obligingly, he accelerated. The officer looked anxious. "Finally he grew desperate and, walling his eyes, he shook his head. I got the point: he had been urging me to step on the brake." He would not let Wright drive him back. Waving and laughing, he staggered off with his gun.

The road climbed up into the mountains. Wright passed peasants with donkeys trudging by the roadside. At every small stone bridge, two civil guards stood with their gleaming machine guns. Why? Wright wondered. He slowed down each time, expecting them to stop and challenge him. They didn't. Two pairs of brown eyes scrutinized him, and he drove on, feeling "naked vulnerability" in the back of his neck.

At the next bridge, he acted on impulse. "Timidly, I lifted my right hand in a greeting, a shy, friendly, salute. And the two soldiers came to attention, smiled, and waved their hands at me in return. I sighed, relieved." These men in uniform had responded like human beings after all.

He passed a truck and started violently when a ferocious dog sprang forward and "spewed . . . a torrent of ear-splitting barks, his long white fangs showing, his gleaming red tongue hanging out. . . ." Wright discovered that all trucks carried guard dogs to protect their merchandise.

In Barcelona he went to change money and was shocked by the number of armed guards standing about in the dim interior of the bank. He walked in the streets, soaking up his first impressions. Finally he approached two young men standing on a street corner and asked, in French, whether they could recommend a pension that was clean and cheap. Yes, they would show him one, they answered in French. At his invitation, they climbed into his car. They passed a large cathedral and asked Wright to stop. "But where is the pension?" he asked. "Later," they answered. He wondered what was going on. Were they crooks? Had they misunderstood him?

They entered the obscure interior. The boys dipped their fingers into the holy water and crossed themselves, then touched each other's right hand with their damp fingers, then the taller of the two touched Wright's right hand. They kneeled and crossed themselves again. Wright stood and watched. "You are not Catholic?" the tall boy asked him in astonishment. "No," Wright whispered. Suddenly he felt self-conscious. "I was a stranger and they were taking me into their Christian fellowship even before they knew my name. . . . To these boys it was unthinkable that there was no God and that we were not all His sons."

He looked around at the figures praying ardently in the flickering candlelight. A barefoot girl in a ragged dress knelt next to a fashionably dressed woman draped in pearls. The boys led him into some side chapels. Then they returned, wordlessly, to the sunlight. "Maintenant, la pension?" Wright asked.

"Oui, Monsieur."

The pension was three blocks from Barcelona's main street, Las Ramblas. The price was sixty pesetas ($1.50) with three meals included—as opposed to the twelve dollars Wright had paid on the French Riviera. At his first hotel in Spain, just over the border, he had written in his journal: "I've got to adjust to these cheap prices. I overtipped the man who took my luggage to my room. I gave him 100 francs and his bow almost touched the floor."

The young men helped him with his luggage, and he gave them some packets of American cigarettes and invited them to a bar for a beer. André, the tall one, was twenty-one and a student of maritime science. Miguel, twenty-six, was a carpenter who earned three hundred pesetas ($7) a week. André had a fiancée. Over their drinks, the young men kept referring to "good women" and "bad women." If he wanted, they offered, they would show Wright where to find bad women.

"And every time you go with a 'bad' woman, you confess it?" Wright asked.

"Of course," André replied.

They did not seem to comprehend what it meant when Wright told them he was a writer. And they were even more astonished by his butane-gas lighter. But Wright was relieved to see they showed no racial consciousness.

He was, after all, a novelty in Spain. People stared at him. Twice he was asked if he was a boxer. Spaniards had heard of Sugar Ray

Robinson and Joe Louis. Wright, who had put on weight in recent years, answered by grabbing his stomach. "Me no fighter. Look!"

On his first Sunday in Barcelona, he was invited to André's family's for a midday meal. He found the building, located at the seedy end of the Ramblas, and trudged up four sets of dark, malodorous stairs to their apartment, clutching red roses for André's mother. The apartment was threadbare and dirty. The only decoration was a print of the Last Supper on the living room wall. There were no books or magazines. Wright presented the mother with the roses. She looked stunned, then began to weep quietly. André patted her shoulder and winked at Wright. His father offered Wright a big black cigar. He was about to refuse it, when he felt André's elbow in his ribs. André's sister, small and mousy, seemed hypnotized by Wright.

After the greetings, the atmosphere became awkward, and André briefly led Wright out onto the balcony to show him the view of the Ramblas. The doorbell rang. Wright heard greetings at the front door. A young woman entered the room. "Ma fiancée," André said. The dark-haired young woman was voluptuous, with a full, moist, rouged mouth. Wright shook her hand and bowed. She looked at him wonder-struck, with melting eyes.

> "She's a virgin," André whispered proudly to me.
>
> "Oh!" I said. André was clearly waiting for me to make some kind of response to this announcement, but I was at a loss as to what to do or say. Instinct urged me to reach out my right hand. He had been waiting for it and shook it solemnly.
>
> "*You are lucky,*" I told him, nodding my head gravely.
>
> "Yes, yes," he agreed readily. . . .
>
> "What does your fiancée do?" I asked him.
>
> Dumbfounded, he stared at me.
>
> "She's a virgin," he repeated.

Being a virgin, Wright concluded, was a profession in itself in Spain. This young woman was never allowed out without a member of her family to accompany her. She was waiting to get married, after which she could live a more or less normal life. What struck Wright forcibly was the sexual aura she exuded. "One could have scraped sex off her with a knife," he thought to himself.[15] He guessed that she thought of little else.

The afternoon was hot, and the meal was long and heavy. The men were served first, and then the women ate. Paella was followed by fried fish, then fried steak. Wright protested he could eat no more. André's mother insisted he would collapse if he did not eat. The father held forth about famous bullfighters, while chewing mouthfuls of food. Wright was staggered by the amount everyone ate—including André's fiancée. "The yearning virgin . . . loaded her fork, packed the food into her sensual mouth, and wolfed it down with open relish. She would take a long swig of red wine, swish it about her gums for a moment to clean up, and would swallow while her eyes roved the table, appraising the men."

After lunch the men sighed, grunted, and lit their cigars. Wright pretended to smoke. He was delighted when the old man lumbered off for his siesta and he could let his cigar go out. Time dragged and Wright was bored. It was a relief to climb down the smelly stairs and walk out into the balmy evening air.

WRIGHT THOUGHT BARCELONA ONE OF THE MOST IMPRESSIVE CITIES HE HAD SEEN in Europe. It was full of surprises. The wide, tree-lined Ramblas was as cosmopolitan in atmosphere as Paris or New York, and yet one day he saw a herd of sheep ambling along, led by a boy with a long staff. Parts of Barcelona were "garishly modern," and the narrow, dirty streets of the slum area, the Parallelo, belonged to another world entirely. Wright was drawn back and back to those chasmlike streets, shaded by pastel-colored apartment buildings six to seven stories high. Washing hung from the balconies; he could smell fried garlic. Dogs seemed to be copulating everywhere; cats skulked; half-naked children played with each other; whores stood in the doorways.

In the evening he drove up one of the mountains that surrounded the city and looked down at the lights. "The city breathes," he wrote. "Lights twinkle on the wharves. The sound of a hooting horn, hoarse and long, tells of a departing ship heading for the open sea."[16]

In the city itself, he could scarcely believe the noise level. Besides the trucks that lumbered through the streets, and the streetcars with their steel wheels and jangling bells, were the shouts of children, the roar of motorcycles, and the honking of horns. Wright was an early riser; it was when he worked best. But no one in this country kept the hours he did. In Spain the day seemed to begin at ten at night. All night, there would be animated talk in the streets, loud laughter, passionate arguments, clapping and shouting. Only in the early afternoon, when people were taking their siesta with the shutters closed against the heat, were the streets quiet. Wright privately thought there was no hope for a country that kept such hours. It would never enter the modern world.

It did not at all suit his digestion to eat a heavy meal at ten o'clock at night. His stomach reacted badly to Spanish food, which swam in olive oil. Others had the same problem, he concluded, since he often saw bicarbonate of soda beside the salt and pepper on meal tables.

His room in the pension was shabby and rickety, the plumbing primitive, and the electric light dimmed several times an hour, but whenever he was not out on the streets observing life, meeting people, taking photographs, and making notes, he was reading about Spain or typing up his observations. "It seems that I'm the wonder of the pension," he wrote in his journal. "I'm told that the other paying guests are amazed at the fact that my typewriter goes so fast and long, like a machine gun, the waiter said, hour after hour."[17]

Everywhere he went—hotel foyers, banks, cafés, barbershops, gas stations, and newsstands—the portrait of "Big Brother" Franco gazed down from the walls. "The material here is rich, rich, and the people are much friendlier than I found the Africans," he wrote to Paul Reynolds.[18]

IN HIS FIRST WEEK HE ATTENDED A BULLFIGHT AT THE PLAZA DE TOROS ARENAS DE Barcelona. It was his first bullfight since Mexico City, fourteen years before. "I went with an open mind," he wrote. "Blood *per se* does not upset me: I wanted to soak it all up and see what it did to my feelings. Well, at the end I was limp."[19]

A few days later, on Sunday, 22 August, he went to another. This time it was in a larger stadium, and the matador was the young Chamaco. Wright had invited André and his brother-in-law. They had told him about the Chamaco fight over dinner at André's, but tickets, they told him wistfully, cost sixty pesetas and upwards of two hundred. Wright had pulled out a thousand-peseta note, and said he would treat them. The bank note had caused an animated family discussion with much shaking of heads.

They drove to the stadium in his car. The young men hunched forward, speechless with excitement. The traffic was heavy. Everybody was going to the same place. "We came in sight of the arena," Wright writes in *Pagan Spain*, "and even I began to succumb to the contagion of bull fever."

The young men disappeared inside the ticket office and came back with a ticket costing 160 pesetas for Wright and cheap tickets for themselves. "We couldn't pay that much of your money for seats for us," André explained. "Papa said so."

Chamaco, a nineteen-year-old *novillero*, was considered the greatest novice bullfighter in Spain. Tourists were present in droves. Wright was besieged by peddlers selling trinkets, photographs, and booklets, in English, about bullfighting. He bought a photograph of Chamaco, thinking he might include it in his book. A small cushion was thrust upon him for a small fee. Soon he understood why. The usher took his ticket and led him to the shaded area at the barrier, close to the arena. When he stopped and indicated a ten-inch slab of concrete jammed between two other people, Wright thought there had been a mistake.

> I had to straddle my legs so that my kneecaps, when I eased down into a sitting position, touched both of the hips of a fat woman sitting directly ahead of me on a lower tier; and I could feel the fleshy legs of a woman behind me cushioning my back. . . . I could not crook my elbow or reach for my packet of cigarettes without colliding intimately with female anatomy.

A band began to play, and the bullfighters appeared. When the bull thundered through the gate into the ring, Wright felt pure admiration for his dignity, tenacity, and indomitable willpower in a battle he could not win.

Matadors, picadors, and banderilleros teased the bull with trembling capes, tortured him with barbed hooks of steel, coaxed him, goaded him, wore him down. Finally, a slender figure entered the ring, carrying a muleta and a sword. It was Chamaco. "I was stupefied to see how young he really was," Wright would write. "The contours of adolescence were still upon his dark, brooding face." Wright's neighbor explained to him, in French, that Chamaco came from a poor family in Andalusia, and that he had many brothers and sisters. "Pain caused by a bull's horn is far less awful than pain caused by hunger," he told Wright.

For two long hours, Wright was "revolted, but hungry for more." At one point the bull, bleeding now, reared and tried to leap over the barrier. Reporters ran for cover. The crowd near the barrier stood up, screaming and shouting. The matador ran forward, trying to induce him to turn back to the ring:

> I had stiffened when the bull had reared and placed his hoofs upon the barrier's railing, but I could not have moved had I tried, for the fat woman who sat directly in front of me and a few inches lower down had twisted her body about in convulsive terror and had flung her hands to her face, covering her eyes, and had pushed her face down into my lap, shuddering in horror. Stupefied, I stared down at her tumbling, glistening black locks and did not move.
>
> A moment later she lifted her head and peeped out toward the ring, seeing that the bull had been enticed back from the barrier. She straightened, gave a little orgiastic moan, and turned her body toward the ring again, not saying a word. . . . I sat awhile, filled with wonder. And then I felt as though I needed to go to confession. . . .

Finally Chamaco drove his sword into the bull's body. The spectators stood up, roared, and fluttered their white handkerchiefs. The stadium looked to Wright like "a ripe cotton field being lashed by wind." He watched the bull take a few more tottering steps, then sink to the ground.

A few days later, he went to see Chamaco fight again. "I'm growing more and more obsessed with bullfights. I wonder, what does that mean?"[20] This time, he could focus more on the crowd's reactions.

That evening, he was strolling in the working-class district of the city, the Parallelo, when he saw Chamaco, walking alone, trailed by a crowd of admirers. He was a modest-looking and slight young man, and yet, Wright thought to himself, he was like a king to these people. "This man was their Christ. He would do their dying for them." He took Chamaco's photograph out of his bag, walked over, and asked the young hero to sign it. "He glanced at me briefly with a stare that had in it a look of fantastic authority; no wonder; he lives with death."[21]

ANDRÉ AND MIGUEL HAD PROMISED TO SHOW WRIGHT SOME "BAD WOMEN." THEY took him to a smoky dive up an alleyway, where dozens of women sat around tables and at the bar. Soon, the women were sidling up to the three men, asking for cigarettes or a drink. André and Miguel, who acted as interpreters, looked strained, Wright thought.

Several of the women spoke English with an American accent. They had spent time with sailors from American battleships. Most of them seemed to consider their work temporary, until they met a man who would marry them. "They were all fleshy, had a look of something rotten about them," Wright wrote in his journal. "When I took hold of the arm of one of the girls my finger seemed to sink right through the flesh and to touch the bone. I shuddered."

IN MADRID PEOPLE STARED AT HIM FAR MORE THAN THEY HAD IN BARCELONA, AND he concluded that Madrid was far less cosmopolitan. At the central post office he stood waiting while the woman behind the counter counted peseta notes. Then she looked up. "Her lips parted, her expression became blank, and she quickly crossed herself."[22] Did these people take him for "a Moorish ghost suddenly risen from the dust?"[23]

He drove to Seville and Granada. He visited the Gypsy camps on the outskirts of Seville and was shocked by the stench, the open sewerage ditches, the flies. The clay houses reminded him of Africa. So did the dirt and disease. Through an interpreter, he spoke to the Gypsy queen in her filthy one-room hut. He was glad to get away.

In bars, he talked to flamenco dancers, many of whom sold their bodies. From his first day in Spain, Wright had been astonished that ardent Catholicism and worship of the Madonna existed side by side with the most widespread and flagrant prostitution he had encountered anywhere. "These trapped and unfortunate women have been referred to as a 'wall of flesh,'" he wrote. "That wall is everywhere: in bars, cafés, pensions, hotels, sidewalks, churches, parks, etc. Almost all these women are deeply religious and almost all of them have children to feed."

An American pimp explained to him that a woman earned at most seven hundred pesetas a month by working in a home, factory, or office, whereas she could earn almost that much in a single night on the streets. Wright was shocked to learn that the pimp took young girls, most of them illiterate, to brothels in North Africa, where white women fetched higher prices than Arab women. Wright had encountered white slavery.

Finally, he returned to Madrid, where he made a number of contacts through the United States Information Service and the British-American Club. Harry Whitney was an articulate twenty-eight-year-old American who had been in Spain for two years, learning bullfighting. Wright had been giving a great deal of thought to the phenomenon. He admired Hemingway's book *Death in the Afternoon*, but he himself was less interested in the technique than in the psychology of bullfighting. And whereas for Hemingway the hero was unequivocally the matador, for Wright it was also the bull. Whitney reinforced Wright's opinions. To experience a bullfight fully, Whitney agreed, the spectator had to identify with both the bull and the matador. For the bullfighter himself, it was akin to a religious experience. He had to be prepared to sacrifice his life to the bull. And yes, Whitney nodded, it struck him too that the wildest beast in the bullring was not the bull but the audience. The public clamored for danger.

Harry Whitney was about to go with a small group of bullfighters— toreros—to fight in Morata de Tajuna, a village near Madrid. He invited Wright along to observe the men behind the scenes. But it was Wright, more than the toreros, who attracted the villagers' attention. "I was stared at with a kind of fearful, blank, absorbed curiosity that one reserves for the unheard-of, the unnatural, the fantastic."

He was fascinated watching the young bullfighters put on their tight-fitting costumes in the changing room:

> They stripped down to their underwear and I saw that their bodies were a mass of mangled tissue, scars and gashes from previous gorings. First they struggled into narrow-legged trousers of raw silk brocaded with gold and adorned with tassels. Next they buttoned pleated and ruffled white shirts and tied little black bowties. Then came pink stockings, two pairs of them, one being put on over the other in the hope that a bull's horn would glide harmlessly off the leg.

After a full hour of dressing, the men opened a box and took out a
package wrapped in brown paper. It was a statue of the Virgin Mary.
They perched it on a table. One by one, except for Whitney, they knelt
before her, prayed, and crossed themselves. Then they gathered their
capes and swords and strode toward the bullring.

WRIGHT SPENT THREE WEEKS IN SPAIN. HE DROVE MORE THAN SIX THOUSAND
kilometers and typed more than a hundred pages of notes. In many
ways, the country was a revelation to him. For the first time, he had
seen poverty and oppression that was not connected with race. "Half
of Spain actually lives in a kind of slavery," he concluded.[24] Spanish
Protestants were discriminated against in the army and in the work-
force; it was difficult for them to buy property, and they were socially
ostracized. Wright called them "white Negroes." He thought the Gypsy
camps in Seville made Harlem look tame. And he was shocked by the
oppression of women. Spanish men might kneel humbly in front of the
Virgin Mary in their churches, but there was nothing exalted about the
way they treated their women at home. Wright kept wondering: "What
must an intelligent, free-minded, perceptive, and reflective Spanish
woman think of her position in Spain?" It would prove insuperably difficult for him to speak with such a woman alone.

Wright left Spain hoping that Harper would give him an advance for
a book on Spain. He wanted to come back. He would need at least
three or four more months to gather material.

BACK IN PARIS, HE SENT REYNOLDS AN OUTLINE AND HIS NOTES. HE THOUGHT THIS
might help persuade Harper that he was taking an original approach
on the subject.

"I personally think the book will be pretty difficult from the outline," Reynolds commented to the publishers.[25] One of Harper's editors, Simon Michael Bessie, was making a brief trip to Paris. The
director, Frank MacGregor, asked him to meet with Wright and report
back. Bessie spent several hours listening to Wright on the subject of
Spain. "It is probably pointless to try to get him on to any other book
project now. He seems very impressed with his vision of Spain and the

Spaniards and can talk of nothing else. He said he wants to do that book and then get back to fiction."[26]

Wright's next project was only one of his worries. The State Department had tightened its passport regulations, and the thirty thousand American residents in Paris were nervous. Anyone who publicly criticized the United States and whose presence abroad was considered "undesirable" by the State Department could have his or her passport confiscated and be sent home. Ollie Harrington was one of the many to have passport problems.

These days, the Paris embassy had a reputation for being one of the toughest embassies in Europe for Americans wanting to renew their passport. Agnes E. Schneider, the consul at the American embassy in Paris, was known by local Americans as "Spider Schneider." As Ollie Harrington wrote anonymously in the *Observateur*, the Spider would write to "undesirable" Americans, saying there seemed to be some problem regarding their papers. They would come into the embassy and hand her their passports, and she would put them in a drawer, snap the drawer shut, and say: "We will give you the necessary documents for the return voyage."[27]

It was well known that Schneider was assisted by some fifty or so plainclothes spies who patrolled cafés and restaurants, eavesdropping on their countrymen.[28] The result of all this, Ollie Harrington explained, was that Americans in Paris espoused different views in public and in private. If they read left-wing papers, they did so in the privacy of their homes. He was not talking about Communists. They were nearly all back in the United States, unable to leave. He was talking about anyone who was remotely left-wing.

On 16 September 1954 Agnes Schneider made Wright sign a sworn affidavit about his Communist past.[29] Wright had to wait six agonizing days to hear the State Department's verdict. Once again he was fortunate. His passport was renewed.

Wright was aware of the spies in Paris and knew that the FBI and CIA were watching him. He had not yet guessed the extent of the underground surveillance. Extracts from *Black Power* were published in *Encounter, Preuves,* and *Cuadernos*. All three of these European magazines (as well as *Der Monat,* in Berlin) were sponsored by an organization called the Congress for Cultural Freedom.[30] A group of European and American intellectuals had met in Berlin in June 1950 (just as North Korean troops were invading South Korea) and written the charter. "We hold it to be self-evident that intellectual freedom is one of the inalienable rights of man," they proclaimed. "Such freedom is defined first and foremost by his right to hold and express his own opinions, and particularly opinions which differ from those of his rulers."

Prominent members were Thomas Mann, André Malraux, Arthur Koestler, Stephen Spender, Ignazio Silone, Albert Camus, and Bertrand Russell.[31] Even if they guessed CIA influence, none of them knew that the entire funding came from the CIA, and that Michael Josselson, the executive director, was a CIA agent.[32] They nearly all believed it to be what it claimed to be: an independent international organization of free-thinking intellectuals who valued freedom and deplored totalitarianism.

Why did the Congress for Cultural Freedom give *Black Power* such exposure? Wright was a well-known black American writer, whose success reflected well on American society. Even his criticism of racism showed that America was open to criticism. He was on the left, but emphatically anti-Communist. In many ways, *Black Power* was a celebration of Western life. Nevertheless, his outspoken presence in Europe was risky. It seemed a good idea to befriend him, to provide a platform for his work, to pay him well. Wright would see that the West was open to his dissenting opinions. It was called co-optation.

WHILE HE WAS WAITING FOR A DEFINITE ANSWER FROM HARPER ABOUT THE SPANISH book, Wright decided to go to Geneva to look at data on Spain held by the European Economic Commission, where Gunnar Myrdal worked. Myrdal, back in Paris for the weekend, suggested they drive there together. Wright could come back on the train.[33] As they were saying good-bye to Alva, she recommended a stopover at the Hôtel de la Poste in Beaune. She had eaten marvelous lobster there, she told them.

They drove through the suburbs of Paris in lashing rain. Myrdal, peering with difficulty through the windshield of his Jaguar, asked Wright what he thought about the world situation. Did he think there would be another war?

Wright said he feared the worst. Russia and America seemed to talk endlessly about their buildup of nuclear weapons. He feared Soviet aggression and thought Soviet talk of peace was probably simply a tactic. "Remember the words of the 'Internationale,' " he reminded Myrdal. "The International Soviet shall become the human race." He added that wherever people were exploited they would listen to the Communists, and the colonial peoples in Africa and Asia made up a huge pool of exploited people.

Myrdal thought it a hopeful sign that the "hard-bitten revolutionaries" in Russia were being replaced by a younger managerial class that seemed more flexible. But he had to admit that his optimism was not always well-founded. "I was wrong about World War II. I didn't think men would kill themselves so wantonly."

The rain dashed against the windshield. The horizon was lost in the mist. They passed a nasty road accident. "But I was right about America and her race problem," Myrdal said. He was referring to the new desegregation ruling.

"I must say that I didn't think that white Americans would move on that question," Wright admitted. "I was pessimistic about the race problem in America. I was perhaps too close to it to have a perspective."

After lunch in a small village, Wright took over the driving. Late that afternoon, they arrived in Beaune and found the Hôtel de la Poste. They went up to the desk, and Wright asked for two rooms with baths. The woman thumbed through the book, looked at her assistant, and announced that there were no rooms left. But they did have an annex nearby.

Wright took the keys. Once they glimpsed the neon-lit annex, Myrdal said dully: "Let's go to another hotel."

They went to the Hôtel de la Cloche, the largest tourist hotel in town. The lobby was warm and luxurious. They walked up to the front desk together. This time Myrdal spoke. A young man opened the reservation book, skimmed through the list, looked up, glanced at a woman who had just come in, and informed them that there was nothing. Wright started to move toward the door. Myrdal said nothing, started to follow Wright, then suddenly whirled around.

He lifted his walking stick and brought it down with a shattering bang upon the desk, just under the nose of the young Frenchman. "You've gotten goddamned sophisticated, haven't you?" Gunnar shouted. "You don't want to offend your white American clients, do you?"

There was a profound silence. A waiter in a far doorway stood thunderstruck in his white apron. A client, looking very American, stood appalled. Gunnar reached inside of his coat pocket and drew forth his diplomatic passport and tossed it upon the desk, under the nostrils of the staring woman and the white-faced young Frenchman.

"You will hear from this," Gunnar shouted "what's happening to you people?"

"Monsieur, we have rooms for you: rooms with bath, if you want them. Oui messieurs."

They took the rooms and went to wash. After some time, Myrdal tapped on Wright's door: "Ready for dinner, brother?"

We went down into the spic-and-span dining room which was filled with American tourists. We sat and waiters hurried forward. We ordered, and sat, waiting. The dining room was as silent as a tomb. Gunnar pinched off a piece of French bread and launched into a tirade in a loud voice, as though he were a professor addressing a roomful of students in sociology. . . .

Frankly, I did not enjoy that meal, though the wine was the finest that France has to offer. Gunnar was bent, deadly bent, upon making them know that he knew. . .

BACK IN PARIS, A LETTER FROM PAUL REYNOLDS INFORMED WRIGHT THAT *BLACK Power* had come out in the United States on 22 September. Advance sales, Reynolds wrote, were "very bad."[34] The review in the *New York Times* was "very, very bad."

I hate to be a Gloomy Gus, but MacGregor of Harpers is very gloomy. He says he's afraid that you've written a very fine book saying things that Americans don't want to hear and hence won't go into the book stores and buy. Whatever happens to you and *Black Power*, that does not in my opinion affect what may happen in Spain and I hope your thoughts will be always directed to the future and not into the past. I'm sorry to be so gloomy. I'm very depressed myself at the advance sale. We must both try to be of stout heart.[35]

The "very, very bad" review in the *New York Times* was by Michael Clark, who attacked Wright purely on the grounds of his politics. Clark said nothing at all about the power of Wright's writing or the interest of a black American confronting his complex feelings toward Africa. Clark was affronted by Wright's view that the white man should leave the Gold Coast. He personally thought that the black inhabitants of the Gold Coast should feel gratitude to the British colonizers.[36] Clark was not the only American reviewer who simply could not accept Wright's critical attitude to the West.[37]

Several left-wing critics praised the book. The British novelist Joyce Cary admired the fact that Wright had made West Africa neither romantic nor exotic. He had worked in the British government's Africa service, and he agreed with Wright's recommendations. "Democracy . . . is impossible in any state where 90 per cent of the people are illiterate," he wrote. "It exists only in literate and industrialized nations with a powerful middle class and organized unions capable of standing up to central government. . . . Nkrumah will have to be a dictator whether he likes it or not."[38]

Wright had produced a kind of nonfiction—both subjective and objective—that was decades ahead of its time. One bewildered critic called it "a curious mixture of history, biographical sketches, exposition of social customs and political chicanery, and blistering jabs at British management of governmental affairs."[39] The black critic Saunders Redding (who abhorred the book's Marxist underpinnings) worried that Wright, "being primarily a writer of fiction," applied a similar visceral passion and similar narrative techniques to his nonfiction. "One is plunged into the dark complexity, not of the Gold Coast of Africa, but of Wright's . . . ambivalence," he complained.[40] Doris Lessing was one of the few to see Wright's depiction of his own ambivalence as part of the book's strength.[41] Most readers agreed that Wright had lost none of his "emotional persuasiveness and power."[42]

NOT SURPRISINGLY, *BLACK POWER* WAS NOT WELL REGARDED IN THE GOLD COAST. But George Padmore liked the book. He shared Wright's views. To Padmore, tribalism was leading Africa to its own decay.[43] Industrialization and a degree of dictatorship were the only ways to liberate Africans from their stultifying traditions and prejudices.

Dorothy Padmore thought Wright had captured their friend Nkrumah beautifully. She had recently visited Africa for the first time, and *Black Power* expressed many of her own thoughts and reactions. "You have tried so hard to get behind the surface of things and to explain West African man as he is caught today between the forces of his own religion and that foisted upon him by the West," she congratulated Wright. "My own impression after traveling round the country and going into villages . . . was of people who had not yet developed into individuals. I hadn't dreamed of anything like it. One reads and reads, and one talks about primitive conditions and poverty and misery. But you just can't imagine the realities until you come bang up against them. Those people are not just ignorant and illiterate in the way in which we understand it in the West. They are just a mass without, I would put it, even a thinking apparatus, upon which have been impressed superstitions and fears."[44]

George Padmore's Pan-Africanist friend W. E. B. Du Bois was not impressed. "Naturally I did not like Richard Wright's book," he answered Padmore. "Wright has great talent and his descriptions of West Africa are literature; but to write a book to attack Communism in Africa where there has been no Communism in Africa, and when the degradation of Africa is due to that Capitalism which Wright is defending—this is sheer contradiction."[45]

HARPER AGREED TO THE BOOK ON SPAIN, WITH AN ADVANCE OF TWENTY-five hundred dollars. At the beginning of November 1954, Wright drove back to Spain and stayed six weeks, returning to Paris for Christmas.

The Padmores came for Christmas dinner at rue Monsieur le Prince, along with a mutual North Vietnamese friend, Dang Chan Lieu. They had plenty to talk about. Dorothy had been in the Gold Coast at the time of the national election in June. The CPP had won triumphantly. And Nkrumah had done exactly what Wright had suggested in *Black Power*. The election had exposed dozens of rebels within his party, all of whom he had expelled from the ranks.

Much of the talk that Christmas Day was about the teetering colonial empires. France was in a state of shock. The French had suffered huge casualties in the Indochinese war, and the final humiliation had been the battle of Dien Bien Phu in May, when Vietnamese Communists had triumphed over a French colonial army.

France was also having to give up its protectorates in Tunisia and Morocco. But the French government was determined not to give up Algeria. Prime Minister Pierre Mendès-France argued that Algeria *was* France. Algeria was not a protectorate. Algeria's nine million Muslim Arabs thought otherwise. In November a nationalist rebellion had broken out. The rebels had formed the *Front de Libération Nationale*. France, it seemed, was about to engage in another dirty war.

Early in January 1955—the Christmas tree was still up—Wright was home alone one evening. He was thinking about Spain and the work he still had to do there. Idly, he picked up the evening newspaper. He was astounded to read that, at the end of April, twenty-nine independent nations of Asia and Africa were going to meet in Bandung, Indonesia, to discuss "racialism and colonialism."

"My God!" Wright exclaimed. "Who had thought of organizing such a meeting?" The nations listed were almost all ex-colonies. Some had been under the domination of Western Europe for centuries, some for decades. He got up and paced the floor, then sat down again and read the aims of the conference. "This smacked of something new," he told himself. "Something beyond Left and Right."

He knew he must get to that conference. It would mean putting aside the book on Spain for a few months, but this was important. Bandung, he told himself, was potentially one of the most significant historical events of the twentieth century. If it worked out, Bandung could be the beginning of a world alliance of colored people.

He was conscious that it was also a personal quest. More and more he saw himself as a part of a brotherhood of Western-educated men of color—people who were outsiders in two worlds.

HE AND ELLEN HAD FOUND AN OLD FARMHOUSE ON SEVERAL ACRES OF LAND JUST outside the village of Ailly, near Gaillon-sur-Eure, in Normandy. In January 1955 they bought it for five thousand dollars. Wright had always wanted to spend more time in the country. He also conceived it as a way of getting away from his family. "Instead of sending my wife and kids to England, I shall send them to the country now," he told Paul

Reynolds.[46] During the school year, when Ellen and the girls were in Paris, he intended to disappear for weeks at a time to write at the farm.

The Congress for Cultural Freedom agreed to pay Wright's fare to and from Indonesia, in addition to five hundred dollars for expenses. Wright was adamant that this sponsorship must not affect his independence as a writer. The director, Michael Josselson, reassured him. The congress merely asked for first rights to anything he wrote for its French magazine, *Preuves*.

On 21 February Wright made a final trip to Spain. Since he planned to go directly from there to Indonesia, he took the train. There was snow on the mountains. He spent a week in Madrid, then traveled to Barcelona. One Sunday morning he found himself strolling again through the dark and narrow streets of Barcelona's Parallelo district, this time over fresh snow. Women were hanging wet clothes from the iron balconies; he could smell garlic and olive oil. He puffed on his pipe. Quiet voices murmured "Americano."

Wright took the fast train to Valencia for the fire festival, *Las Fallas*, from 17–19 March. He had been told that the citizens made huge papier-mâché monuments (called "fallas") in which they lampooned politicians or churchmen, and then, on the last night of the fiesta, they set them alight. Wright hoped to discover something about the people's hidden fears and preoccupations. He found that he had to pay an exorbitant 120 pesetas for a room during festival time; flamenco music blared from loudspeakers, and the explosions of firecrackers kept him awake at night. He forced himself to photograph the elaborate floats and make notes.[47]

A slow train to Granada meant standing for eighteen hours in a train, with no water to drink, no ventilation, and a stinking toilet. He crossed to Tangier. In a Moorish restaurant, little boys danced to "weird music." "I must say that though the Arab has my sympathy, I cannot fall in love with this strange and static culture, and little boys dancing and wriggling themselves do not move me; they ought to be at home and in bed."[48] He was shocked by the poverty in Algeciras. "These people . . . are so poor, so ragged, so dirty and generally dispirited in manner that they don't seem to belong to the white race."[49]

He arrived in Seville for *Semana Santa*—Holy Week—beginning 3 April. The town was crowded with tourists and foreign cars. He ended up in a pension in a noisy working-class neighborhood. The landlady kept chickens in the living room, and his room was double its normal price. "This celebration of Christ rising from the dead is a most lucrative business."[50]

A series of American ships had come in during recent weeks, and in his old flamenco haunts Wright was taken aback to see the women dancers chewing bubblegum. "Not just chewing, but working their jaws in a violent manner, blowing gum as they danced, their mouths holding huge balloons."[51] Several prostitutes handed him love letters they had received from American merchant seamen and naval sailors. Wright, who was planning a novel about American GIs in Europe, had offered handsome payment. He found the letters touchingly romantic.[52]

The streets of Seville were thronged with white-robed figures wearing tall, pointed hoods that covered the face, except for two holes for the eyes. They looked just like the Ku Klux Klan. On 26 March Wright wrote irritably in his journal: "This bigoted Catholic Church with all of its flapdoodle, its grotesque religious processions, its cult of bull worship, its heritage of Inquisitor, its cheap thirst for adventure, its Ku Klux Klan regalia—all of this fits admirably into the Mississippi mentality."

He could not resign himself to the sight of young children begging. And he was thoroughly disconcerted by their knowledge of sex. A group of ragged young boys he talked to in a park told him which of the passing women sold themselves and for how much.

One afternoon he sat in the window of his hotel room with a book in his lap. The sun was dying. Children were playing in the square below. Then they noticed him, the *Americano*. They assembled below his window and started to beg. To attract his attention, a little girl of about eight hissed at him. ("That sound which I hate most of all the sounds in all Spain.") She gestured from her mouth to her stomach, indicating that she was hungry. Wright pretended to read. There was no doubt about the girl's future, he reflected. Eventually the children resumed their playing.

The next day he wrote in his journal:

This afternoon, as yesterday, the little girl of about eight years of age in the ragged blue sweater came under the balcony of my window and began making those frantic gestures to me, begging for a peseta. She upsets me. I shook my head at her; it is not that I don't want to give her anything, but I don't want to encourage this kind of begging in a tiny little girl who looks as though she would grow up into a pretty young woman. I tried not to look at her; I kept my eyes on my book. . . . Then she did something that made me ill somewhat; she lifted her tiny little dress and pointed to her vagina. . . . I rose and left my chair and remained out of her sight. . . . She knows everything. I'm hardboiled, but not that hard. . . . I can't take that.

On 8 April Wright left the delicate spring blossom of Seville and took the night express to Madrid. Already he had been away from home for six weeks, and he would not see Ellen, Julia, and Rachel for another month. From Madrid he was traveling to Bandung, Indonesia. He felt that he was flying "from the old world of Spain to the new world of Asia."

25

THE LONELY OUTSIDERS

April 1955–September 1956

From Madrid, Wright flew to Rome, where he boarded a KLM plane to Cairo with a group of French newspapermen who were also bound for the conference in Indonesia. "Through the hot night we flew high over Africa," he writes in his Bandung book, *The Color Curtain*. "Cairo was but a far-flung lake of shimmering lights when the plane landed for passengers and refueling. I heard an explosion of the French language; I turned my head and saw red-fezzed North Africans from Morocco, Algeria, and Tunisia climbing aboard: revolutionaries and nationalists from the turbulent areas of French rule." On the plane "a dark-faced man with a thin mustache" passed around photos of Arabs being driven from their homes in Palestine. Fury about Jewish aggression raged up and down the aisles. Wright, who could not make out much of the conversation above the din of the engines, thought to himself: "There's gonna be a hot time in old Bandung. . . ."

Before they landed in Baghdad for refueling, he chatted with a shy young Indonesian who had been studying sociology in Holland for the past four years. How did he enjoy his stay in the West? Wright asked him. "I didn't," the young man answered. In Karachi, they were joined by Sikhs with bushy black beards and Oxford accents. In Calcutta, a group of Hindus in Western clothes climbed on board. The face of colonialism was everywhere.

They flew at fifteen thousand feet, and Wright, trying to study the barren land below, could make out nothing beneath the roaring flames of the motors. He took Nembutal and slept until they landed in Bangkok, when more journalists came aboard. As the plane flew high over the Malaysian jungle, the passengers endlessly speculated about the forthcoming meeting. "Was it true that the Japanese were going to offer a public apology for their role in World War II? . . . Would Red China take advantage of the conference and use it as a propaganda tribunal? . . . What the hell did Nehru think he was doing flirting with Communist China's Chou En-lai?"

The Color Curtain dramatically conveys the Cold War atmosphere of tension and conjecture. Countries represented at Bandung stood for a billion and a half colored people—more than half the world's population. Westerners, except journalists, were excluded. Wright was struck by the football-game atmosphere of the two Cold War teams. "A group of American newspapermen had made a list of all the delegates going to Bandung and had checked them all off according to their political leanings and had come to the conclusion that the West would emerge victorious from its clash with China's evil genius, Chou En-lai," he wrote.

Prime Minister Nehru of India, the main force behind the Bandung conference, insisted he was "neutralist," but Washington was only too aware that Russia was wooing India. And Nehru had invited Premier Chou En-lai of "Red China" to the conference at a time in which the Eisenhower government was concerned about the possibility of atomic war with China over Formosa.[1]

One thing was certain: the U.S. State Department was keeping a close watch on the proceedings. The West was worried. If Wright himself did not know that his trip had been actually financed by the CIA, there were plenty of U.S. government agents there who knew exactly who had funded theirs.

After forty-eight hours in the air, Wright landed in Jakarta on the afternoon of 12 April 1955. The humidity felt worse than it had in the African jungle. As he went through customs and immigration, he observed that the "brown young men" seemed to be fumbling with the paperwork. He presumed that these bureaucratic jobs were among the many the Dutch colonials had previously done. Indonesia had been independent for less than six years.

He was met by Mochtar Lubis, a novelist and editor of the socialist daily newspaper the *Indonesia Raya*. They plunged into "a chaotic, Oriental city" that reminded Wright of Accra. Lubis's car wound its way between "strange contraptions that resembled huge tricycles." Young men pedaled, and their passengers—one or two—sat on a rickety seat in front. Wright was shocked that something that looked like a rickshaw could still exist. Lubis confessed that Indonesians were ashamed of their *betjas*, and many refused to ride in them. They passed Dutch-built canals. Wright saw people defecating beside them, washing clothes in them, and cleaning their teeth.

His hotel room was dark and damp. The electric light did not work, and there was no table for his typewriter. Lubis said he would try to find him lodgings in a private house. The next day Wright moved to the home of an Indonesian engineer and his wife in a beautiful district that used to be the European section of the city. His hosts were anti-Dutch and "ardent nationalists." And yet, Wright noticed, almost everything in the house was imported from Europe. After dinner, they took him on a tour of the city. Wright was surprised to see hammers and sickles everywhere. It was past 10 P.M. and Wright saw children walking along with books under their arms. There were not enough schools or teachers, his hosts explained, and these students were on the night shift. They drove past large bungalows. They were built on the profits of black-market operations, the engineer told Wright. A class of Indonesians had emerged who acted very much like the Dutch.

In the next few days, Wright hired a *betja* and explored the city. Struggling with the heat, he interviewed a number of Indonesian politicians and intellectuals. He was astonished to learn that even in Jakarta there was little contact between educated Indonesians and Westerners. It was partly cultural, the Indonesians explained. Whites met over drinks in bars, whereas the Indonesians, for religious reasons, rarely drank alcohol. Invariably, too, the Indonesians found Westerners condescending. "We are exotic children to them."

Inevitably the talk turned to a discussion of East versus West. The Indonesians talked about the menace of industrialization and the need for them to preserve their own values. Wright argued that they had either to industrialize their islands or be ruled by foreign powers. "They made me know that I too was Western. What bridges could be built between these two worlds?"[2]

It did not take him long to realize how wrong was his stereotype of the soft, passive Asian. "The Negro problem is as nothing compared to this boiling cauldron of racial hatred," he wrote in his journal.[3] "I had thought when I came here that I'd have much difficulty getting at what these people felt. How naïve I was. What they feel lies on the surface, is . . . poured into your face."

On several occasions Wright was talking to Indonesians when a European entered the room. He noticed that the conversation became constrained. That was why the Bandung Conference was necessary, he told himself. Here, in the mountains of Java, ex-colonials could at last be among themselves and say what they thought. "Whatever the Westerner *thought* he was doing when he entered these tropical lands," Wright would write in *The Color Curtain*, "he left behind him a sea of anger."

He was constantly reminded of the Gold Coast. Indonesia was rich with natural resources—oil, tin, and rubber—and yet 70 percent of the "natives" were illiterate, malaria and yaws were rife, and infant mortality was high. After 350 years of Dutch rule, the Indonesians had more or less to start from scratch. There was the same bustling roadside trade he had observed in Africa—"that frantic buying and selling of matches and soap and tinned sardines." He was again struck by the graceful bearing of the people. Bare-breasted young women walked along with sarongs tucked around their waists. Barefoot men carried bundles on poles slung over their shoulders.

Instead of a dense wall of jungle, he saw "terraced rice paddies filled with muddy water and rising in serried tiers toward blue and distant mountains." He saw white mosques. And people, brown-faced people, everywhere. The island of Java was more crowded than anywhere else on earth.

Mochtar Lubis drove him up the mountain slopes to Bandung—four hours from Jakarta. The air became cooler as they climbed into the volcanic mountain country, and Wright felt normal for the first time since he arrived. The city of Bandung was decorated with bright banners and the flags of the twenty-nine participating nations. The streets were lined by white-helmeted militia carrying guns.

On the morning of 18 April, Wright was in the press gallery, looking down with anticipation as the delegates came in. "This is the first international conference of colored peoples in the history of mankind!" President Sukarno greeted the audience. It was, he said, a gathering of people who had traditionally been voiceless.

Throughout the conference, Nehru struck Wright as "a great man," with a great deal of sophistication and suavity. Like India itself, he combined the East and the West. Wright had written to him from Spain, asking for an interview and enclosing a copy of *Black Power*. Soon after the conference began, he drove a rented car sixty kilometers to Nehru's villa on the outskirts of Bandung. His daughter, Indira Gandhi, opened the door. She complained to Wright that the American press never stopped attacking her father. "Don't they know that if they destroy my father, they will be opening the gates to anarchy, to Communism even?" Her father was not available, she said, but she took Wright's note with his hotel and phone number.

The morning after the conference ended, Wright drove back to the villa for an hour's interview. He ended up doing most of the talking himself. Nehru said he could not understand the fear of Communism that hung over the conference. Wright talked about anti-Communism in the United States, his view of the Gold Coast, and the West's fear of colored nations. Finally, Nehru rose, "We are going on," he said.[4]

Surrounded by voices speaking English in an array of different accents, Wright found himself wondering about the future of his native language. Soon, the majority of people speaking English around the globe would have a mother tongue that was not English. "We shall be hearing some strange and twisted expressions," he reflected. "But this is all to the good; a language is useless unless it can be used for the vital purposes of life, and to use a language in new situations is, inevitably, to change it."

The conference called for a renewal of the ancient Asian and African cultures and religions. Privately, Wright considered such resolutions "pathetic exultations of past and dead cultures."[5] But he did not say so in *The Color Curtain*. He went to Bandung with a press badge, and he felt it his duty to report rather than comment. On the whole, he tried to keep his own opinions out of the book.

Nevertheless, the last few pages of *The Color Curtain* were a plea to the West. In *Black Power*, written two years earlier, Wright was adamant that Westerners should keep out of their former colonies. During the Bandung Conference, he came around to George Padmore's view that Westerners should offer capital and technical assistance to Africa and Asia, and that this should be done "openly and selflessly." If America and Europe could not meet the challenge, he warned, Chou En-lai was waiting in the wings.

BANDUNG MEANT A GREAT DEAL TO WRIGHT. DESPITE THEIR DIFFERENCES ABOUT the question of industrialization, he felt a strong rapport with this group of Western-educated non-Westerners. His next book, *White Man, Listen!*, would be dedicated to "the Westernized and Tragic Elite of Asia, Africa, and the West Indies"—

> The lonely outsiders who exist precariously
> on the clifflike margins of many cultures—men who are
> distrusted, misunderstood, maligned, criticized
> by Left and Right, Christian and pagan—
> men who carry on their frail but indefatigable shoulders
> the best of two worlds—and who,
> amidst confusion and stagnation,
> seek desperately for a home for their hearts:
> a home which, if found,
> could be a home for the hearts of all men.[6]

Wright shared his room at the press hotel, Hotel Van Hengel, with Winburn T. Thomas, a white American missionary who had lived in Asia for almost twenty years and was married to a Japanese woman. Every day they ate at a large table with other press associates. Thomas said later: "The refraction of the Bandung conference through Richard's consciousness was more illuminating for me than the proceedings." He was impressed by the methodical way Wright took notes during the sessions, then typed up his notes in the evenings. They argued, of course. Wright told him what he thought of missionaries, and Thomas tried to tell him he was "unnecessarily harsh." But Thomas conceded that missionaries were "a tool of imperialism," and that they were often racist. The two men got on sufficiently well for Wright to stay in Thomas's house in Jakarta after the conference, sharing the lower bunk of a double-decker with the youngest of Thomas's two sons.[7] During the day he was gathering more information for his book.

Wright returned to Europe on the *Willem Ruys*, docking in Naples. He preferred boat travel, and it gave him time to work on *The Color Curtain*. He had been traveling with his typewriter for three solid months. It was tiring. In mid-June 1955—two months after the Bandung conference—he sent the manuscript to New York.

HARPER & BROTHERS REJECTED THE BOOK. MACGREGOR TOLD PAUL REYNOLDS THAT interest in the Bandung Conference would have waned by the time it was published. Reynolds sent it to World Publishing, where Donald Friede thought it "an important contribution to an understanding of a very important subject" and accepted it immediately.[8]

In August and September, extracts appeared in *Preuves*, *Encounter*, *Cuadernos*, and *Der Monat*—the magazines funded by the Congress for Cultural Freedom. The CCF editors agreed on the importance of "controversial articles" that invited discussion and counterattack. They were also well aware of the need to confront "burning colonial issues." The minutes of their June meeting in Paris note: "All the editors paid a call on Richard Wright who had just returned from South-East Asia. He reported at length on his impressions of the rise of Asian national-ism. . . . His manuscript is likely to run to some two hundred pages, with each of the editors free to make such selections as they like for one or more articles."[9] On behalf of the U.S. government, the Congress for Cultural Freedom editors were carefully mediating their presenta-tion of Wright's views.

The Color Curtain was first published in French in October 1955. It appeared in New York and London the following spring[10] with a rather tepid introduction by Gunnar Myrdal, who described the book as "a collection of snapshots," written from a "very personal" point of view. On the whole, the reviews were favorable, and the American edition went into two printings.

When Mochtar Lubis read an extract in *Encounter*, he wrote to the editor denying that Indonesians were as race conscious as Wright made out. Wright sought "color and racial feelings" behind every atti-tude he encountered, he complained. Race was not a problem for Indonesians.

Reading to Julia,
New York, 1944.
*Beinecke Library,
Yale University.*

Edith Anderson Schroeder.
*Photograph by Irving Chidnoff, New
York. Courtesy Cornelia Schroeder.*

Wright, Simone de Beauvoir (center), and her French friend Nathalie Moffatt, New York City, 1947. *Courtesy Nelson Algren Collection, Ohio State University Library.*

Wright with Dorothy and George Padmore, Paris 1947. *Beinecke Library, Yale University.*

On the ship to Argentina, trying to lose weight, October 1949. *Beinecke Library, Yale University.*

Bigger is interviewed by Mr. Dalton. Movie shot. Argentina, 1950. *Photograph by Segovia. Beinecke Library, Yale University.*

Socializing in Buenos Aires. Madelyn Jackson is on Wright's left; photographer Gisele Freund on his right. *Photograph by Kurt Waldmann. Beinecke Library, Yale University.*

Ellen, Julia, and Rachel Wright, Paris, early 1950s. *Photograph by Richard Wright. Courtesy Ellen Wright.*

Julia and Rachel Wright, Christmas 1956. *Photograph by Richard Wright. Courtesy Ellen Wright.*

Wright in Germany on
the cover of *Der Spiegel*,
24 October 1956.
*Reprinted with permission
of* Der Spiegel *magazine.*

Chester Himes.
*Photograph by Carl Van
Vechten. Van Vechten
Collection, Beinecke Library,
Yale University. Courtesy
Van Vechten Trust.*

Oliver Harrington in his studio. *Photograph by Gerhard Kindt. The Walter O. Evans Collection of African American Art, Detroit.*

Celia Hornung. *Courtesy Celia Hornung.*

Wright relaxing in the countryside. *Courtesy Celia Hornung.*

Wright's response to Lubis was printed in the same issue. He pointed out that the speeches at Bandung were "loaded with race." He added: "Think hard, my friend Lubis, and you will recall the discussions that took place in your car as we drove through the Java mountains."[11]

Wright was ready to leave Harper & Brothers. They had turned down *Savage Holiday* and *The Color Curtain* and it seemed that with each new book Wright had to work with a different editor. World Publishing Company wanted Wright to sign a permanent contract with them. But Wright wanted Ed Aswell back, and Aswell was at McGraw-Hill.

"The thought of working with you again fills me with the most pleasurable anticipations," Aswell wrote to Wright. But he was not willing to enter a new contract with the Bandung book. It was too topical, he explained to Wright. He asked for more details about his writing plans.[12]

Wright was impatient to get back to his book on Spain before he lost momentum entirely, and now he felt obliged to spend a large part of the summer dreaming up future writing projects that he hoped would impress Aswell. He and his family spent July and August in the farmhouse at Ailly. There were plenty of distractions, but they irked him less than those in Paris. He left the furnishing of the house mostly to Ellen, while he planted string beans, carrots, potatoes, corn, lettuce, strawberries. Seven cherry trees needed picking. The well went dry and he turned into a "drayhorse," hauling water in his car. "Ah, the bucolic life," he sighed to friends.[13]

How were the girls adjusting to the country? George Padmore wanted to know. "Watch the water they drink. Some parts of France are as primitive as Africa and I hate primitiveness."[14]

In his office overlooking the vegetable patch, Wright typed Aswell a thirty-eight-page letter. His plan, he explained, was a series of novels that would be connected thematically. The theme of this work, called *Celebration*, would be the conflict between individuality (spontaneous impulse and emotion) and society (authority, tradition, custom, government, the church). His intention was to link the novels with sections in free verse. The sample he sent Aswell was more ponderous than the worst writing in *The Outsider*.[15]

He produced a dull six-page plot summary of a novel called *A*

Strange Daughter, about a young white American woman with a sexual problem, who has several relationships with black men. After this, Wright told Aswell, there would be another section of free verse, and then a novel about Montezuma, king of the Aztecs, who was conquered by Cortés. He would write the narrative mainly from Montezuma's unworldly, superstitious point of view.

In early October he mailed the letter to Aswell and sent a carbon copy to Reynolds.

WRIGHT WAS BACK IN PARIS IN SEPTEMBER 1955 WHEN THE NEWS OF THE EMMETT Till case hit the front pages of newspapers around the world. Although Paul Reynolds was always telling him he had lost touch with America, it did not seem to Wright that much had changed in Mississippi.

Emmett Till was a fourteen-year-old boy from Chicago's South Side. In mid-August, he and his seventeen-year-old cousin had taken the train down South to stay with their granduncle. Till's mother had warned him to watch himself with whites. Things were different down South, she told him.

She was right. Three months earlier, Reverend George Lee, the first black man to register a vote in the county, had been shot in the face. A week before Emmett's arrival, another black voter had been shot to death. No arrests were made.

The boys arrived in Money, a dusty little settlement in the Mississippi Delta, and on Sunday, 21 August, their granduncle, a preacher, took them to church. While he was in the pulpit preaching, the boys stole away, driving his '41 Ford to the local store. They chatted with a group of boys hanging around outside. Emmett showed them a photograph of some white kids he'd gone to school with and boasted that one of the girls was his girlfriend. One of the local boys said, "There's a white girl in that store there. I bet you won't go in there and talk to her." Emmett went in and bought candy. As he was leaving the store, he called to the young, married white woman behind the counter: "Bye, baby."

The boys outside were aghast. There would be trouble, they predicted, when the woman's husband came back to town. The following Saturday, in the early hours of the morning, two white men—the woman's husband and his half brother—came to the house and took

Emmett from his bed. They warned his uncle that if he called the sheriff he would not live for long.

A few days later, Emmett Till's body was found in the Tallahatchie River. A cotton gin fan had been wrapped around his neck with barbed wire. His face was bloated and disfigured. One eye was gouged out. His forehead was crushed. A bullet was lodged in his skull.

The sheriff wanted the body buried fast. But Emmett's mother insisted on shipping the body back to Chicago where she held an open-coffin funeral, "so all the world can see what they did to my boy." The gruesome photograph of the corpse was published in *Jet* magazine. For once, the story of a lynching received national attention.

The trial took place in suffocating heat. Emmett's uncle, who had already been receiving death threats, showed extraordinary bravery by pointing out the two white men in a Southern court.[16] The courtroom was segregated. Every white man in the room openly carried a gun. The white men on the jury drank beer under the judge's nose. Their verdict took an hour. Not guilty.[17]

"In their ignorance, they believe they have scored a victory," Wright wrote in *France-Soir*. "In fact, they have won one battle and are about to lose a war. The world will judge the judges of Mississippi."[18] He told his friend Margrit de Sablonière: "Such wanton killings fill me with disgust, uneasiness, and a sense of dread."[19]

"I'VE GOT TO TELL YOU WHAT I THINK EVEN IF WHAT I THINK ISN'T TOO PLEASANT to hear," Paul Reynolds wrote to Wright. He had read the thirty-eight-page proposal. He told Wright that he was "very dubious" about Wright's project from a commercial point of view. There was no market for poetic prose. Nor did he like the Montezuma idea. He thought *Strange Daughter* had potential if Wright set the novel in Paris, not New York. Once again, he told Wright that he no longer knew his native country:

> I haven't any question about your ability to write many very fine novels. I have a lot of doubts as to whether a man who has been nine years away from this country can successfully write them laid in this country. America has changed in the last ten years. Maybe for the better or maybe for the worse, probably some of both although I think on the whole for

the better. People's attitudes have changed, dialogue has changed. . . . Nearly everyone felt about *Savage Holiday* that the book was badly dated.[20]

Wright was used to Reynolds stating his mind bluntly. But he was anxious, now, about what Aswell would say. For three months there was silence. At the end of January 1956, a letter arrived. "What you wrote about your plans constitutes a remarkable document," Aswell wrote. "You can be sure that I read it and reread it and pondered it and then read it again."[21]

Aswell wished they could talk in person. Was Wright thinking of returning to the United States for a visit in the near future? Otherwise, Aswell was intending to spend time in England in the autumn. Perhaps he could make a detour to Paris. He gradually got around to telling Wright what he had been thinking:

What it comes down to, as I see it, is my belief, even my conviction, that these novels which you outlined for me at such length are not really the right things for you to tackle. There is no aspect of my career as a publisher that has given me greater satisfaction than my association with you during what has been up till now your most creative period. The question I want to get at if I can—and it seems to me the matter can be explored only in conversation—is: Why was that the most creative period in your life up till now, and why, since then, have the sources of your creativeness seemed to dwindle? The words, as I utter them, somehow sound harsh; yet I do not mean them to sound so. All I mean is that I am, frankly, puzzled by a mystery to the solution of which you and you alone hold the clues. . . . As I see it, there is something the matter, and your outline of these possible future novels underscores the point. It seems to me—and of course I am only guessing now—that as you have found greater peace as a human being, living in France and not made incessantly aware that the pigmentation of your skin sets you apart from other men, you have at the same time lost something as a writer.

Wright could not have been anything other than devastated. He had wasted his summer. Far worse than that, Aswell was implying he had wasted the last few years. It was obvious that Aswell had doubts about everything he had written since they had worked together on *Black Boy*. Not for the first time, Wright must have asked himself anguished questions. Had he really lost his creativity? Was it to do with leaving America? Or had it simply left him?

Wright abandoned his grandiose plan on the spot. He now suggested a novel about a young man brought up in Mississippi who went to France and made a mess of things.

Aswell thought this a far more promising subject. "This is something that you can write about with intuitive knowledge and something with which you can make effective use of your own experience—even though your experience, happily, is not at all the same as that of this young man."[22] There was no mention of a contract.

FIRST, WRIGHT HAD TO FINISH THE BOOK ON SPAIN, FOR WHICH HE HAD A CONtract with Harper & Brothers. He spent most of the winter alone at the farmhouse in Ailly, heating just two ground-floor rooms for the sake of economy.

He was back in Paris at the end of February 1956 when Khrushchev denounced Stalin in his sensational "secret speech." A few days later, in an article on Richard Wright, "They're Not Uncle Tom's Children," Ben Burns wrote in *The Reporter*: "Down deep inside of him there manifestly burns a relentless insatiable loathing for white people and America that erupts whenever he sits down at a typewriter. And Wright's venom . . . has succeeded in poisoning European thinking about racial problems in America."[23]

It was Burns who back in 1951 had written the editorial attacking Wright's *Ebony* article, "The Shame of Chicago." Now he made the same point he had made then: France was no better than the United States. He wrote that in the fall of 1953 he had talked to Wright in a Paris café and asked him about the situation for Arabs in France.

> Suddenly Wright was talking in whispers that contrasted immensely with his usual loud, sure tone.
>
> "You can say or write just about anything you want over here, but don't get started on France's colonies," he admitted. "Whoop, the police will be on your neck and out you go in forty-eight hours. There's no explanation—just out you go!"

Burns had reported a private conversation. He could have caused Wright to be deported. Wright considered suing him, but Reynolds's lawyer advised him against it. Even if a lawsuit were successful, he would get nothing much in damages.

Burns was "morally crooked," Wright fumed, and he wanted nothing more to do with him.[24] "It is simply foolish to say that I poisoned the mind of Europe; if that is true, I am more powerful than either Moscow or Peking."[25]

"I am outraged by the article in *The Reporter*," Gunnar Myrdal wrote to Wright. "It is worse because *The Reporter* is a liberal periodical read by good people.... What can be done? Could I do anything?"[26]

BURNS'S ARTICLE APPEARED ON 8 MARCH 1956. A FEW DAYS LATER, PERHAPS PARTLY with self-protection in mind (his passport was up for renewal again that year), Wright went to visit the American embassy.

The members of *Présence Africaine* were planning a "Second Bandung," to be held in Paris in September 1956. Richard Wright had agreed to be on the executive committee and help organize the American delegation.[27] He had missed several meetings while he was in Ailly, finishing *Pagan Spain*. When he returned to Paris he was taken aback to find that the executive committee had developed a significant Communist faction. There was talk of inviting Paul Robeson and W. E. B. Du Bois.

Wright knew how this would go down with the State Department, and he wanted to disassociate himself from any such moves. After his visit, the American embassy in Paris sent a five-page dispatch to the State Department in Washington. "On his own initiative, Mr. Wright called at the Embassy to express certain concerns over the leftist tendencies of the Executive Committee for the Congress," the report noted. "He thought there was a distinct danger that the Communists might exploit the Congress to their own ends.... To counteract such a tendency, Mr. Wright wondered if the Embassy could assist him in suggesting possible American negro delegates who are relatively well known for their cultural achievements and who could combat the leftist tendencies of the Congress."[28]

Wright returned to the American embassy on several occasions to discuss ways in which they could "offset Communist influence."[29] Why did he go behind the back of his African co-organizers? Mostly, no doubt, for the same reasons he would give to the Communist organizers of a cultural festival in London in 1959:

> I'm an American Negro. We American Negroes who live abroad live under tremendous political pressure. . . . For me to be present at such a gathering places me in a position to be called harsh names by my American colleagues. I suffer from enough disabilities as a Negro; for me to associate myself with the festival entails my shouldering still another disability which will amount to being blacklisted. . . . My right to fight for Africans as I see fit will be taken away from me.
>
> I'm alone. I belong to no gang or clique or party or organization. If I'm attacked there is nobody to come to my aid or defense. Hence I must keep clear of entanglements that would stifle me in expressing myself in terms that I feel are my own.[30]

AT THE BEGINNING OF APRIL WRIGHT SENT *PAGAN SPAIN* TO PAUL REYNOLDS. "I'M glad that this awful grind is over," he told Margrit de Sablonière, his Dutch translator. "Now, I want to start a novel, but not right away. I've got to get the kinks out of my brain." His nonfiction had not been a success commercially; nor had it done anything to enhance his reputation as a writer. It seemed, he wrote, that readers "like their facts floated to them on the syrup of imagination."[31]

Reynolds did not like *Pagan Spain*. Nor did Harper & Brothers. They thought it overwritten, too long, and too contentious. They had expected 100,000 words; Wright's manuscript was 150,000 words.

Reynolds told Wright that MacGregor was hesitating about publishing the book at all. Wright felt he had no choice other than to give his consent to major cuts. He believed he knew the reason: his book was in some respects critical of Spain, and America now had an important treaty with Franco. But he remained convinced that his original version was better and felt strongly enough about the matter to make trips to Italy, Germany, and England the following year to try to get the original version published. He was successful in Italy and Germany. The English edition, though it would be more skillfully edited than the American edition, was cut even more severely.

In fact, Wright's Spanish manuscript contains some of his most evocative, vigorous writing. His problem, once again, was that he was a good decade ahead of his time. In the 1950s, a personal travel narrative was considered "mere journalism"; creative writers were supposed to write novels. As he had done in *Black Power*, Wright was using techniques traditionally associated with fiction. *Pagan Spain* contains absorbing stories, interesting characters, first-rate dialogue. More than simply a travel essay, it is personal, subjective, and controversial. We see Spain through Wright's eyes. His narrative voice—personal, honest, wry, humorous, and occasionally self-mocking—in many ways resembles the voice of "New Journalism" in the mid-1960s. Had the cutting and rearranging been done by an inspired editor, *Pagan Spain* could have been an outstanding work of nonfiction. John Appleton, Wright's latest editor at Harper, cut colorful scenes and left in twenty-five pages of dull quotation from the Falangist catechism.

It was the end of Wright's seventeen-year partnership with Harper. World Publishing offered Wright a five-thousand-dollar advance for his next novel. But Wright wanted Ed Aswell. Then, in the summer of 1956, came the shocking news that Aswell had been fired from McGraw-Hill.

Aswell had not told Wright that he was under considerable pressure at McGraw-Hill. He had gone there from Harper in 1947 to head the trade book division. In eight years he had published no one of extraordinary distinction, and nothing that made much money. As he understood it, his dismissal was for financial reasons. Fortunately for him, he was quickly snapped up by Doubleday. Wright had fresh hope that Aswell might take on the new Mississippi novel.

Paul Reynolds, who lived on the same street as Aswell in Chappaqua, New York, told Wright: "He would like to publish you . . . but I'm ninety percent certain that he wouldn't advance $5,000 to $6,000, at least not without seeing a fair portion of the book and being very excited about it. He would say to me that . . . your past record didn't justify an advance of such money."[32]

Reynolds was wrong. By the end of July Aswell had advanced six thousand dollars for Wright's next novel and told Wright he felt a "very special pride and joy" in being able to resume their old relationship.[33]

As I understand it, this new novel . . . is to be about an American Negro born in the South and now living in France. Thus the theme will lie within your own experience; and even though the novel may not be autobiographical, you will certainly know deep in the marrow of your bones, what such an experience for such a man must mean. As I told Paul, I think it is wonderful that you will thus, in a sense, be returning to the essence of your own living which you have drawn upon so richly in the past.

Wright was hugely relieved to have Aswell back. He was aware that he needed a good editor. His writing was uneven, and he was not a good judge of his own work. He had a tendency to overwrite, and he often labored points. Ironically, Aswell and Reynolds were anxious to bring him back to the emotionally charged, visceral writing that had brought him success in the 1940s. Other critics, ignoring the fact that much of Wright's 1950s writing had moved away from the personal, complained that Wright was unable to step outside himself. "What is your opinion of Negro writers?" William Faulkner was asked when he visited Japan in the mid-1950s.

"There was one that had a great deal of talent, named Richard Wright," he answered. "He wrote one good book and then he went astray, he got too concerned with the difference between the Negro man and the white man and he stopped being a writer and became a Negro."[34] The comment was published in both *Esquire* and the black American press.

THE FIRST INTERNATIONAL CONGRESS OF NEGRO WRITERS AND ARTISTS CONFERence opened on 19 September 1956 at the Sorbonne. The poster, portraying the head of an African, was designed by Picasso. Wright was a highly visible presence. James Baldwin wrote afterward, in his report on the Congress for *Encounter*: "Wright had been acting as liaison man between the American delegation and the Africans and this had placed him in rather a difficult position, since both factions tended to claim him as their spokesman."[35]

After the opening session, a message was read out that caused a considerable stir. It came from the eighty-nine-year-old W. E. B. Du Bois, the author of several groundbreaking books, the founder of the Pan-African Congress, and the cofounder of the National Association for the Advancement of Colored People in America. "I am not present at your meeting today because the United States Government will not grant me a passport for travel abroad," he wrote bluntly. "Any Negro-American who travels abroad today must either not discuss race conditions in the United States or say the sort of thing which our State Department wishes the world to believe. The government especially objects to me because I am a Socialist and because I believe in peace with Communist States like the Soviet Union."[36]

The French audience cheered and applauded. The U.S. delegation felt under personal attack.[37] On the first evening, in a closed session, Wright remarked: "We had a message today that hurt me."[38] He assured the French audience that the Americans participating in the conference could speak their minds freely, and that he would be doing so in the next few days. He added: "When my role [is] finished in this conference, I would appreciate it if you would tell me what governments paid me." Several times during the conference he referred to Du Bois's message, complaining that it made the Americans look like "agents of some kind."

The following days would see heated debate. James Baldwin found himself wondering whether there was any meeting point between these black men from all over the world. He decided there was. "What they held in common was their precariousness, their unutterably painful relation to the white world."[39]

Wright had never felt comfortable with the *Négritude* movement and its racial mysticism. He deplored Senghor's idea that the Negro was intuitive, whereas the European was Cartesian. Nor could he understand Senghor's enthusiasm for the ancestor cult religion. Wright had more in common with Frantz Fanon of Martinique, author of *Black Skin, White Masks* (1952), who believed that violent revolution would be necessary to end the repression of colonialism. Fanon, who worked as a psychiatrist in Algeria, was allied with the Algerian liberation movement.

Three years earlier, Wright had written a warm introduction to George Lamming's autobiography, *In the Castle of My Skin*, about Lamming's childhood in Barbados and the shock of moving to England. But after inviting him home to dinner and observing the animated conversation between him and Ellen, Wright took a dislike to this good-looking West Indian. Later that week, when Wright got back to the house one evening, Ellen was not there. Wright, in a sudden frenzy of jealousy, asked Vivian Werner to call Lamming's hotel to check on his whereabouts.[40]

By Friday evening, when Wright was to give his speech, he was defensive. When he wrote his talk in Normandy that summer, he had imagined an audience of secular black men like himself. But during the conference, religion had cropped up constantly. So had black nationalism. The Africans were highly skeptical about assimilation into white culture. Wright tried to point out that it was different for American Negroes: "We do not oppose the West; we want the effective application of Western principles of freedom."[41]

Since his travels in Spain, Wright had been more conscious of women as an oppressed group. In the preamble to his speech, he made the remark: "I don't know how many of you have noticed it. There have been no women functioning vitally and responsibly upon this platform helping to mold and mobilize our thoughts. . . . In our struggle for freedom, against great odds, we cannot afford to ignore one half of our manpower, that is, the force of women. . . . Black men will not be free until their women are free."

In the speech itself Wright argued that the ideas of the West had to some extent freed the Africans and Asians from their "stultifying traditions and customs." He wished only that Europe had not introduced these ideas by means of colonization, murder, and slavery.[42]

> My wholehearted admiration would have gone out to the spirit of a Europe that had had the imagination to have launched this mighty revolution out of the generosity of its heart, out of a sense of lofty responsibility. Europe could then stand proudly before all the world and say: "Look at what we accomplished! We remade man in our image!"

His speech was long and muddled. It was the end of a long day. The participants must have wondered if they had understood him rightly. James Baldwin (who also felt a gulf between him and his African brothers) thought Wright both wrongheaded and insensitive.[43] The Nigerian journal *Black Orpheus* would express incredulity that Wright virtually thanked European powers for the destruction of African cultures.[44]

Wright was disappointed that there was almost no discussion of his

views. But the verdict was clear enough. The conference's main resolu-
tion (just as it had been at the Bandung Conference) was that black
cultures had been "systematically misunderstood, underestimated, sometimes destroyed," and that the aid of writers, thinkers, scientists, and
technicians was necessary to revive and develop these cultures. Black
people did not want to be defined by others; they wanted to define
themselves.

A few days after the conference, Wright told a friend that it was "a
success of a sort" but that it had left him "terribly depressed."[45]

"THERE IS A STORY, A RUMOR, ABOUT YOU THAT IS GOING ABOUT," THE AMERICAN
writer Kay Boyle wrote to Wright. "It was first told me in late August,
and it was repeated to me, from another source, the day before yesterday. It is told by American visitors returning from Paris, and they say
that you are known to be working with the State Department, or the
FBI, I don't know which, and that you give information about other
Americans to these powers in order to keep your own passport and be
able to travel."[46]

Kay Boyle, who had known Wright in Paris, was back in the United
States, living in Connecticut. In the early 1950s, she and her husband
had been accused of being Communists. It had been a harrowing time,
but these accusations were common in McCarthy's America. The
rumors about Wright, on the other hand, were disconcerting to Boyle
and upsetting for Wright. These, evidently, were the motives imputed
to his actions by the people at the embassy. And they had talked about
him to others.

26

"I AM NOBODY"

September 1956–December 1959

With the Algerian war, the atmosphere in Paris was tense. There was palpable hatred toward Arabs. The French police could often be seen harassing swarthy street vendors or demonstrators. Black men no longer felt comfortable on the streets late at night. Wright was strongly in favor of Algerian independence and was horrified by the stories of slaughter, rape, and torture practiced by the French army in Algeria. But if he wanted to remain a guest in France, he could not criticize the government.[1]

France remained "an alien land." In the only novel Wright set in Paris, his unpublished *Island of Hallucination*, Fishbelly, from Mississippi, feels detached from his surroundings:

> In Paris he went in and out of bars, offices, cafés, hotels, and restaurants free of that dogging racial constraint that had been his all his life.
>
> Yet he was not at ease. Beneath his daily bantering there ebbed a secret tide of melancholy that he could not stay. He had not an iota of homesickness, but, deep down, he had to admit that he was not truly *in* or *of* France; he knew that he could never be French even if he lived in

France a million years. He loved France and the French, yet France was always psychologically distant in his mind. Had he come too late?

With his few French friends—Rémy and Colette Dreyfus, Michel and Hélène Bokanowski—Wright spoke English. At home he spoke English—except with Rachel, who, at seven, still refused to speak her parents' language. Julia was doing well at school, and though she still had three years to go before her baccalaureate, her parents were encouraging her to think in terms of Cambridge University. They were thinking it might be a good idea for the family to move to England.

"I don't think you'd really like to live in England, though I know that there are many irritations from your Gauls," Dorothy Padmore wrote from London. "You'd find more in brushing up against the Anglo-Saxons." She added: "I think it's rather odd that you should be thinking—even vaguely—about sending Julie to Cambridge. It seems to me to be such a dead place. Our feeling is that the English universities—especially the older ones—are so conservative and prejudiced."[2]

Dorothy did not add that racism had become far more evident in England. Signs were often to be seen on the front of boardinghouses: "No rooms for Coloured." After the war, Britain's ravaged economy had desperately needed cheap labor from the Commonwealth countries. Now, a few years further on, the influx of colored people from the West Indies, India, Pakistan, and Africa was widely resented.

IN OCTOBER 1956 WRIGHT WAS IN GERMANY, WHERE *BLACK POWER* HAD JUST BEEN published by Claassen Verlag in Hamburg.[3] German critics praised the honest account of his illusions and delusions as a black man searching out his African roots. His face was on the cover of *Der Spiegel*.[4] Wrapped in a warm scarf, coat collar upturned, a cigarette dangling from his lips, he looked world-weary and sad.

He was back at the country house in Normandy when the news came over the radio that British and French troops had landed in Egypt. Wright was dismayed. As far as the French were concerned, this was part of the Algerian War. Nasser openly supported the North African independence movements and was sending arms to Algerian rebels. While the world was preoccupied with the Suez crisis, Soviet tanks rolled into Hungary. On several occasions, Wright was asked to add his name to petitions against the Soviet invasion. He said he would sign only if they also protested against the Anglo-French invasion of Egypt.

At the end of November he went on a six-lecture tour of Scandinavia organized by his Swedish publisher, Albert Bonnier. *The Outsider* had just been published in Stockholm and was selling well. Wright had always been popular in Scandinavia. *Black Boy* had sold sixty-five thousand copies, *Native Son* seventy-five thousand. His talks aroused such interest that Bonnier suggested he write them up as a book.

It rained the whole time he was in Copenhagen, and Wright caught a cold. He disliked the place, which seemed full of pale-faced, beer-swilling people. They stared at him. It seemed to him that racism seethed beneath the surface. On the train home, he began a humorous story about a black man's encounter with the manager of a Copenhagen hotel. Paul Reynolds sold "Big Black Good Man" to *Esquire* for six hundred dollars. Martha Foley would include it in the *Best American Short Stories 1958*.

Over Christmas, when he looked again at the lectures he had given in Europe over the last couple of years, Wright decided they did indeed form a coherent whole. They were his personal views—"admittedly explosive and blatantly unacademic," as he wrote in his introduction to *White Man, Listen!*—on relations between the West and the East, between black people and white people.

The first essay in the book, "The Psychological Reactions of Oppressed People," contained valuable insights into the psychological effects of oppression and colonization.[5] It was a delicate subject, and Wright knew he annoyed colored people by telling what they considered their secrets. But he believed it was his mission as a writer to break the silence, to explode the myths.

White Man, Listen! landed on Paul Reynolds's desk in mid-January 1957. Reynolds thought Wright was "a little severe at times as to the motives of the white man," but assured Wright that the essays were powerful. "They are the old Richard Wright."[6]

Aswell also praised them. He came up with an advance of fifteen hundred dollars and a list of suggestions for edits. Wright wrote back: "Your letter was like a window opening out upon the world after being closed for many years."[7]

———

AT LAST HE COULD SETTLE DOWN TO HIS MISSISSIPPI NOVEL, *THE LONG DREAM*. Apart from occasional days in Paris with the family, he planned to stay in Ailly for the next few months and write. Alone in the house, he could lose himself in his own world. He was often surprised by the long stretches he was able to work—eight to ten hours at a time. Then he would take the car and relax by driving along the narrow, winding roads, stopping in an auberge for a beer or coffee. His favorite destination was Rouen. He loved that old city.

His head was already filled with thoughts of Mississippi when bad news arrived from Jackson. His Aunt Maggie had died on 8 January 1957. Wright had known since he came back from Denmark that she had cancer and had immediately cabled three hundred dollars for an operation. Her death still came as a shock. In his childhood memories, his mother's spirited younger sister stood out as a bright spark.

Three weeks before she died, Maggie had written a will. She requested that her house be sold. One-half of her net estate should be divided between her surviving brothers and sisters and her niece Maggie Hunt, who had come to look after her in her final illness.[8] The other half was to be divided into three portions, and put in a trust fund for her young nieces, Julia Wright, Rachel Wright, and Deborah Wilson. It was, she specified, primarily intended for their education.[9]

The house at 1085 Lynch Street was valued at $9,500. Maggie Wilson, as a black woman with little education and no husband to help her, had done extraordinarily well.

Correspondence about the will arrived in Paris from a Jackson bank, addressed to "Wright." They were not going to say "Mr." to a black man, Wright complained to Reynolds. As he plunged into his Mississippi novel, he told himself once again that hardly a damn thing had changed in Mississippi. He was forever grateful that his daughters had never had to experience that place. "Their minds and emotions would be crippled in such an atmosphere."[10]

"I WAS SINCERELY TOUCHED TO FIND THE DEDICATION TO ALVA AND MYSELF," Gunnar Myrdal wrote to Wright when he got around to reading *Pagan Spain*. "The book I read with great interest. I think you are on an important track. But if you will permit me to offer a criticism, my feeling is that this is really only a preface to the serious, penetrating and enlightening analysis of the Spanish situation which you should write. What you give are flashes of insight, incisive impressions by the stranger. . . . I want you to write a bigger and deeper book. Do not forget that this is meant as praise, both for your present installment and, still more, for your potentialities of human analysis!"[11]

Pagan Spain was published in New York in February 1957 to more consistent acclaim than any of Wright's books since *Black Boy*. "This is Richard Wright's Spain, which means that it is fascinating, intense, subjective, emotional," Herbert Matthews wrote in the *New York Times*. "The talent displayed is enormous, as one would expect. Everybody who writes about Spain describes a bullfight, but few can describe one like this author. . . . This is a provocative, disturbing, and, at times, sensational book. Spaniards will hate it; Roman Catholics will be dismayed, but other readers will have an exciting time. Mr. Wright does not disappoint his fans."[12]

In the *Times Literary Supplement* Wright was praised for his understanding of modern Spain. According to the reviewer, the quality of Wright's writing, his powers of observation, and his love of humanity put the book in a class by itself.[13]

"Some Americans were shocked to see a Negro comment upon white affairs," Wright commented. "I was reversing roles: until then, it was whites who would go to Asia or Africa in order to comment on native problems."[14]

IN HIS NORMANDY FARMHOUSE, WRIGHT WROTE LIKE A MAN OBSESSED. BY APRIL he realized that his novel was about Fishbelly in Mississippi, not France. He was plunging back into his own past. Forgotten episodes floated to the surface, things he had not mentioned in *Black Boy*.[15] He thought about his mother and the moments they had shared in his early childhood before she became ill. In *The Long Dream*, young Fishbelly likes being sick because he can briefly enjoy his mother's attention.

> The comfort he drew from her was sensual in its intensity, and it formed
> the pattern of what he was to demand later in life from women. When

he was a man and in distress, he would have to have them, but his need of them would be limited, localized, focused toward obtaining release, solace; and then he would be gone to seek his peculiar, singular destiny, lonely but affable, cold but smiling, and strongly insulated against abiding relationships.

Wright decided he would have to write another novel about black Americans in Paris. He explained this apologetically to Aswell and hoped he would not mind. Aswell said he was not at all disappointed. He suggested that Wright make the Paris novel a sequel that could stand on its own, with Fishbelly retained as a character.

When Wright finished *The Long Dream* at the end of June 1957, after six months of intensive writing, he admitted he had been feeling anxious. So much seemed to depend on this book. "I would rather die than let you down," he told Aswell.[16]

"DO YOU EVER SEE RICHARD WRIGHT IN PARIS?" LANGSTON HUGHES WROTE TO Ollie Harrington. "The rumor in Harlem is that he is being divorced but I hope it is not true, especially with such a nice family of children."[17] Harrington, who knew how fast gossip spread in Harlem, did his best to quench the flames:

Yes, I do see Dick Wright very often. As for rumors of impending divorce I can only say that the rumors there in Harlem are so fantastic that one wonders how in the hell they got started. A couple of years ago someone wrote to ask if it was true that Dick was confined in an insane asylum! Talk about bad-mouth! Actually Dick is very happy and works with tremendous energy. They recently bought a beautiful old Normandy farmhouse surrounded by softly rolling woodland and with a lovely stream winding lazily through the meadows. Both Dick and Ellen have been industriously and happily supervising the remodeling of the house and outbuildings. Dick's only problem, that I can see, seems to be in his inability to act like a loud-talking father to his youngest daughter, who speaks only French. Dick's French sounds more like a cockney bus conductor trying to talk Harlem jive! So the mischievous daughter turns to her mother and too blandly asks, "Mommy, what did he just say?" Perhaps that's where the asylum rumor got started because at these times his eyes do seem to roll wildly and jerkilly [sic]![18]

OLLIE HARRINGTON WAS AMERICA'S FOREMOST BLACK CARTOONIST. IN PARIS HE lived largely off the *Bootsie* cartoons he sent home to the *Pittsburgh Courier*. Bootsie, syndicated throughout the African-American press, was a black, cigar-smoking, wise fool, always in trouble with his white landlord, the white cops, and with women. Through Bootsie, Harrington mounted a stinging attack on racism.

A genial, light-skinned man (his father was black; his mother was a Hungarian Jew), Ollie Harrington used to sit in the corner of the Café Tournon smoking his pipe, drinking coffee or a dry martini, and observing the world. Chester Himes thought of him as a brown Spencer Tracy. He had the "same twinkling eyes puckered at the corners, strong broad shoulders and devil-may-care air." He also had legendary success with women. "Women like pipe smokers, I am told," Himes writes in his autobiography. "It makes men look virile, fatherly and profound."[19]

The Café Tournon had taken over from the Café Monaco as the major meeting place for the soul brothers. Wright would often drop by in the afternoon to have a coffee and play the pinball machine. In the summer he would join friends at one of the small round tables on the terrace, under the yellow awning. A rather garish café, with paintings of the Luxembourg Gardens on the walls, it was at the top of the rue Tournon, across from the Luxembourg Gardens. The owners, Monsieur and Madame Alazar, seemed to enjoy their international clientele. Madame, plump and motherly, doted on Richard Wright. It was rumored that she had been a "*collabo*" during the war and that her hair was shaved off at the Liberation of Paris, but her clients did not hold this against her.

The Tournon was the first place that visiting black Americans headed when they arrived in Paris; it was the place to find out where to locate Richard Wright, and the place to exchange news about America. When Chester Himes was in Paris (he was often in the south of France), he appeared at the Tournon most days. His relationship with "the Richard Wrights," as he referred to them, had cooled considerably.

Ellen had little time for Himes's "floozies," as she had been heard to call them, and she once accused Himes of trying to pull her husband down in the gutter with him. Himes had annoyed Wright by suggesting he should write about something he knew about. All this Africa and Spain stuff was getting him nowhere. The Africans had hated *Black Power*; Wright had offended the Spaniards with his book on Spain. Why didn't he write a romping good story that would entertain?[20]

In the second volume of his autobiography, *My Life of Absurdity*, Himes writes that the black men who frequented the Tournon were all with white women, and usually more than one. "All of us vocal blacks collected there to choose our white woman for each night, and the white women gathered about us and waited our selection. . . . There were always numbers waiting to go home with Ollie, each trying to outlast the others."[21]

Leroy Haynes, a black ex-GI who had set up a soul food restaurant near the Place Pigalle with Gaby, his French wife, recalls that over fried Georgia catfish, barbecued pig feet, chitterlings, collard greens, and Southern fried chicken, he and Wright used to talk about desirable "bitches" and "getting pussy."[22] It is how the black expatriates talk in Wright's novel *Island of Hallucination*.

This Paris novel contains only one admirable character, Ned Harrison. Slightly rotund, smiling, and unusually self-possessed, Harrison is clearly based on Ollie Harrington. He was the only man Wright trusted these days, and their mutual enemies brought them closer. With the escalation of the Algerian War, they had become aware that there were spies at the Tournon. "There was one man," Harrington recalled later, "an Algerian, who obviously had lived in France for a long time, studied probably at the Sorbonne, who was always wonderfully dressed and he was always trying to get Dick or myself to write articles in favor of the Algerian revolution. I don't know what kind of idiots he thought we were. . . . And we obviously always refused to do that. . . . We were sympathetic to the Algerians, but we couldn't mention it."[23]

For several years Ollie Harrington had lived in a small top-floor studio in the rue de Seine, where he had spread out his paintings, antiques, and African sculptures. In the summer of 1956 he went to Sweden for a few months and sublet his apartment to the black American journalist Richard Gibson. When Harrington returned, Gibson refused to move out. They had a fistfight on the terrace of the Tournon.

Harrington was a left-winger with passport problems. As an illegal resident in France, he could not afford to risk police intervention. Gibson knew this. He stood firm, and Harrington was obliged to find another place to live. When Harrington turned up at the apartment one day to reclaim his record player, Gibson greeted him with loud abuse: "Communist! Spy! Traitor!" Harrington, usually the most peaceful of men, punched him in the head. This time, Gibson was in the hospital for a week.[24]

On Harrington's behalf, Wright went to the American embassy. He explained that Harrington had never been a Communist and that the source of these rumors was probably Richard Gibson and Bill Gardner Smith, black journalists from Philadelphia who worked for Agence France-Presse. Not only did they accuse Harrington of being a red. They also went around saying that he, Wright, worked for the FBI.

The black community in Paris took sides. Ollie Harrington was a much-loved figure. No one trusted Richard Gibson, with his shifty manner and glib talk. He had played a dirty trick on a fellow black man. And there were more dirty tricks to come.

"FRANCE IS SINKING EACH DAY, EACH HOUR," WRIGHT COMMENTED IN AUGUST 1957.[25] The family had definitely decided to move to London. They would keep the farmhouse at Ailly for vacations, and give up the Paris apartment. Wright would be back in an English-speaking country, and they hoped Julia would attend Cambridge University.

But Wright's application for immigration had received no acknowledgment. When he phoned the British embassy in Paris, he was given evasive replies. Wright did not want to move countries unless he could be assured that his residency application was likely to succeed. He guessed—and he was right—that there was a great deal of cabinet discussion about race and the need to stem the influx of colored immigrants. Britain was seeing the first tightening of immigration controls since 1906.

That summer Wright had gone to London and discussed his case with John Strachey, the ex-Communist radical who was now a Labor MP. Strachey wrote to Reginald Butler, the home secretary.[26] While Wright waited to hear from the British Department of Immigration, Ellen and the girls went to London to look for a house. Wright

remained in Paris and wrote two radio plays for Hamburg radio—
"Man, God Ain't Like That" and "Man of All Work." On the surface they
were humorous; underneath they were biting indictments of ignorance
and racism.

ON 30 SEPTEMBER, *LIFE* PUBLISHED AN ARTICLE THAT ARGUED THERE WOULD BE
political and economic chaos in Algeria when France left the colony to
its own devices.[27] Three weeks later, the magazine printed a letter
about the article, in which the writer vigorously denounced French
colonialism.[28] It was signed "Ollie Harrington, Paris, France." Two similar letters appeared in the London *Observer*, with Harrington's name on
them. Harrington had never written any of them.

Wright and Harrington immediately suspected Richard Gibson and
Bill Gardner Smith, and surmised that the two journalists must be
working for American or French intelligence, or both. The atmosphere
at the Tournon was tense with accusations and counteraccusations.

Harrington, who by this time had assembled a dossier on Gibson,
managed to secure the help of a prominent French criminal lawyer,
Jacques Mercier, who had been active in the Resistance. Bill Gardner
Smith, who had helped Gibson write the letters, now became scared
and turned on his friend. He even smuggled a sample of Gibson's
handwriting out of the Agence France-Presse as evidence.

The French police wanted Harrington to sign a complaint that
would put Gibson behind bars. Harrington refused. "I can't think of
two blacks fighting each other in a French court," he told them. "I
won't sign it." The police thought he was mad.

In *The Outsider*, which Wright wrote in 1952, Cross Damon looks
around at the network of Communists and anti-Communists who sur-
round him and muses: "What a system of life! Spies spying upon spies
who were being spied upon!"[29] In 1958, Wright had Fishbelly thinking
along similar lines. "All his life he had seen his people, pinned in their
squalid racial prisons, killing, burning, cheating, and framing their own
kind; and here, in this distant and lovely Paris . . . that same sodden
drama was unfolding with new scope and intensity."

Wright's friends mocked what they called his "paranoia." Even Harrington used to laugh at his friend's wild fantasies. "I know I am para-

noid," Wright would retort. "But you know, any black man who is not paranoid is in serious shape. He should be in an asylum and kept under cover."[30]

He joked about it, but it was frightening to live in a world in which a friend, one's landlord or concierge, a delivery boy, a hotel maid, a man in sunglasses at a nearby table, a woman in a car parked across the street—everyone was a potential informer.

In fact, the "paranoid" Wright was one of the few who realized that behind these single traitors there lurked a powerful network. This was not hallucination; this was the Cold War. Just how far his enemies were prepared to go, he did not know. And he never would.

WRIGHT'S BOOK OF FOUR ESSAYS—BASED ON TALKS HE HAD GIVEN IN EUROPE— was to come out in mid-October 1957. Aswell was effusive in his enthusiasm for *White Man, Listen!*: "I can hardly wait for the first reviews, to get a line on the public reaction."[31] As he pointed out, recent events in the American South made the essays particularly timely. He meant the crisis in Little Rock, Arkansas, where nine black schoolchildren had attempted to enroll at Central High School and two hundred white people had screamed at them while troops from the Arkansas National Guard prevented them from entering the building. He was also referring to an incident in his own hometown, Nashville, Tennessee, in which the Hattie Cotton Elementary School had been destroyed in a dynamite blast for admitting one black child among 388 whites. "That such things can occur gives no ground for optimism," Aswell sighed.

White Man, Listen! was commended for its convincing argument. Wright was praised for his courage and frankness, his "reasoned passion" and "trenchant prose."[32] One reviewer recommended the book for colleges and universities. But the book did not sell well. The white man did not want to listen. Wright told himself that whether he liked it or not, he would have to stick to fiction for some time to come. There was no point in writing books no one wanted to read.

Thomas Diop, from the *Présence Africaine* group, was struck by Wright's understanding of the psychology of oppression. Léopold Senghor congratulated Wright on his courage and lucidity. "You have said some salutary truths to whites and blacks, even if these are sometimes not pleasant to hear. We can accept these truths because we feel, throughout the book, a great spirit of human brotherhood."[33]

PAUL REYNOLDS WAS DELIGHTED WITH *THE LONG DREAM*. "THIS IS A VERY MUCH better piece of work than your recent novels."[34] He added that some passages were "a wee bit on the dull side"; it would need tightening. And he hated to say this, but the vulgar language needed to be toned down.[35] "You certainly have every right to be tired out and should have a rest and vacation before starting another long work," he told Wright.[36]

Three months passed before a response came from Aswell. On the day before Christmas 1957, a six-page letter arrived in Paris. "I am tremendously impressed," Aswell wrote. He thought the novel had "the ring of truth throughout." But it needed "a great deal of work."[37] The manuscript was 767 typed pages. He wanted Wright to cut it to 500 pages. The narrative dragged in places; the dialogue was sometimes long-winded; there was too much explanation where none was needed; and some of the jokes were dirty without being funny. He enclosed several pages of offensive words, wanting them omitted or replaced.

Wright worked hard on the revision. He liked this book and had high hopes for it. A daring novel, it showed black complicity in white oppression. Fishbelly's father, Tyree, a prominent member of the black community in a small Southern town, makes his money by exploiting and betraying his own people. He tells his son he *has* to buy protection through bribes. "If we niggers didn't buy justice from the white man, we'd never git any." But Tyree discovers that not even money can buy justice for a black man in Mississippi. As a result of his success, he is lynched by whites. His son, Fishbelly, is thrown into prison, falsely accused of raping a white woman. At the end of the novel, Fishbelly is on an airplane bound for Paris.

WITH *THE LONG DREAM* COMPLETED, WRIGHT FELT GLOOMY; IT WAS A RECURRING word in his correspondence. The world seemed devoid of hope. In the American South, desegregation was proceeding painfully slowly. President Eisenhower urged black leaders to be patient. In Indonesia, a newly independent nation, Sukarno was turning his "guided democracy" into a brutal dictatorship. The war in Algeria was intensifying. In February 1958 French aircraft bombed the Tunisian border village of Sakiet Sidi Youssef on market day, horrifying Wright and causing an international outcry. "France, we see, is creating another Viet Nam in North Africa," Dorothy Padmore wrote from Ghana.[38] Just as the Wrights were hoping to move to London, the Padmores had packed up their London flat and moved to Accra.

The Wrights had still not heard from the British immigration authorities. Builders were making changes to the farmhouse at Ailly so the family could live there more comfortably when they came back to France for vacations. The walls between the house, the stables, and the hayloft had been knocked down, creating a spacious living room with a high wooden-beamed ceiling.

The uncertainty of their future was unsettling for the family. Julia, a young woman now, was under considerable pressure at school, preparing for her baccalaureate. The long hours of work and cramming made her nervous and bad-tempered, and she worried her parents. She seemed to have inherited her father's anxious temperament.

Nine-year-old Rachel—tall and springy—was a difficult child. She and Julia were not close; the seven-year age gap was too wide. Above all, Rachel knew how to annoy her father. Perhaps because he had been absent a great deal during her early years and was always talking about his next trip, she behaved as if she did not want his affection.

In May 1958 France was on the verge of civil war. It was rumored that the right-wing Algerian army, led by French Algerians, planned to invade Paris and establish a military government. De Gaulle, who had not held public office since 1946, was asked to assume control of the republic.

"What are you going to do now it seems pretty certain that de Gaulle will be coming in the saddle?" Dorothy Padmore asked the Wrights at the end of May. "I must say that here in Accra, in this bungalow in which we live right off the Castle Road, in its own grounds, with blossoming trees and singing birds, we seem a long way off from what is today's world of reality."[39]

On 1 June 1958, de Gaulle became president. Wright was relieved. It was better than a military government.

———

ISLAND OF HALLUCINATION, UNPUBLISHED TO THIS DAY, PAINTS A GRIM PICTURE OF the Paris world Wright was eager to flee. Apart from Ned Harrison, there is not one appealing character in this black American expatriate world. The characters were based loosely on people Wright knew. The narrative contains an incriminating and falsely signed letter to *Life*, a fight outside the Tournon, an incident where an effeminate homosexual character goes to prison for stealing a hotel sheet. (Wright was thinking of Baldwin.)[40] "Everything in the ms. happened," Wright wrote to Paul Reynolds, "but I've twisted characters so that people won't recognize them."[41]

In this island of hallucinations, black men might have the illusion of freedom—at least as far as white women are concerned—but they are surrounded by informers. Paris is a Cold War center, with UNESCO and NATO bases in the city. The drive against Communism has created a huge, international spy business. "Goddam! This town crawls with serpents," Fishbelly exclaims.

Aswell read the first hundred pages in June 1958 and was encouraging. "I know you are going to have a fine and very interesting book, about aspects of life which so far as I know have not been observed or related by anyone else. My warmest congratulations."[42]

WRIGHT'S MISSISSIPPI NOVEL *THE LONG DREAM* WAS PUBLISHED IN NEW YORK IN October 1958. On the cover it was hailed as a powerful novel of Negro life in the Deep South, comparable to *Native Son*. Advertisements promised: "Even more explosive than his *Native Son!*"

It *was* a good novel—perhaps better than *Native Son*. But the reviews, with two or three exceptions,[43] were negative. People resented Wright's dismal portrait of corruption (white and black) in a black community in the South. Wright had "abandoned all respect for his own people," the critics said.[44] One after another they claimed that "expatriate Wright" had lost touch with his homeland. "He shows no awareness of what has happened to America—and even to Mississippi—during this decade," the black critic Ted Poston asserted in the *New York Post*.[45] "*The Long Dream* proves that Wright has been away too long," Saunders Redding lamented. "He has cut the emotional

umbilical cord through which his art was fed, and all that remains for it
to feed on is the memory, fading, of righteous love and anger. Come
back, Dick Wright, to life again!"[46]

WRIGHT'S DEDICATION TO *THE LONG DREAM* READ: "TO MY FRIENDS EDWARD C.
Aswell and Paul R. Reynolds, whose aid and counsel made this book
possible." Two weeks after publication, Edward Aswell died in his sleep
at his home in Chappaqua, New York. He was fifty-eight. Wright was
mentioned in the obituaries, along with Thomas Wolfe and Kay Boyle.

Wright had lost a friend, a supporter, and the most encouraging,
thorough, and painstaking editor a writer could hope for. After the shock
of this death and the negative reception of *The Long Dream*, he was
losing heart for its sequel. "If *Island of Hallucination* gets the same
press that *The Long Dream* did, then I must seriously think of abandoning writing for a time," he told Reynolds. "One has to be realistic."[47]

Timothy Seldes, who replaced Aswell as Wright's editor at Doubleday, made it clear that he thoroughly disliked what he had seen of the
first draft. "Much too much didactic material and too little plot and
character development," he told Wright.[48] Seldes was not at all sure it
could be salvaged.

IN NOVEMBER 1958 CHESTER HIMES WAS AWARDED THE *GRAND PRIX DE LA LITTÉRA-
ture Policière* for his detective novel *La Reine des Pommes*. (He wrote
in English, and his books were translated into French.) There were
interviews and photographs. "I became a person comparable to Richard
Wright," he writes in his autobiography.[49]

Time magazine published an article, "Amid the Alien Corn," about
black American artists and writers in Paris. "Some Negro artists have
done impressively well," the article stated, and mentioned Chester
Himes, Harold Cousins, a sculptor, and the painter Beauford Delaney. A
brief paragraph on Richard Wright came later in the piece:

> Richard (*Native Son*) Wright, the dean of Negro writers abroad, says
> bluntly: "I like to live in France because it is a free country. Then there
> are my daughters. They are receiving an excellent education in France."
> What of the danger of getting out of touch with U.S. life? Snaps Wright:
> "The Negro problem in America has not changed in 300 years."

Wright was furious. He had never said those things to any reporter from *Time*. He wired the magazine. "Quotations attributed to me in your article completely false and fabricated. Astounded at *Time*'s journalistic ethics. Did not see your reporter. Are you aping communist tactics of character assassination? Richard Wright."[50]

A New York lawyer wrote to the magazine on Wright's behalf, demanding compensation. But he advised Wright not to sue. It would cost too much.

Time magazine claimed that Gisèle Freund, the photographer, had interviewed him. Wright, furious, phoned Freund. She agreed that she had done no such thing. He got her to write a formal statement emphatically denying she had interviewed him.

Time did nothing. Ultimately, there was nothing Wright could do. He was convinced it was a CIA ruse to undo his reputation in the United States, and he linked it to the letter-forging "Gibson affair." His friends (including Gisèle Freund) could not understand why Wright made such a fuss about a statement he might well have said had he been interviewed. For Wright, that was not the point. If he was going to be quoted as saying things he did not say, there was no end to this dirty business.

ON 13 JANUARY 1959, AT LEON'S HOME IN CHICAGO, WRIGHT'S MOTHER DIED. THE immediate cause of death was given as left cerebral apoplexy. She had been living with Leon's family for eighteen months. From Paris, Wright had continued to send monthly checks.

He had feared his mother's death since he was ten. For almost as long as he could remember, she had been an invalid. And yet, Ella had outlived her robust younger sister Maggie. On her death certificate Leon recorded her birthdate as "unknown" and her age as "about 65." In fact, Ella Wright was seventy-five years old when she died.

Wright had not seen his mother for some fifteen years. She had no idea of his life, except for the glamorous articles friends showed her in *Ebony* magazine.

ON 6 FEBRUARY 1959 DR. MARTIN LUTHER KING, JR., VISITED WRIGHT'S APARTMENT in rue Monsieur le Prince. He and his wife, Coretta, were traveling to

India with Wright's old friend Lawrence Reddick, curator of the Schomburg Center in Harlem. Reddick had just finished writing King's biography, *Crusader Without Violence*. "I would like very much for you and King to meet," he had written to Wright from New York.[51]

Unfortunately none of the four participants have left any record of the meeting. Julia's is the only recorded memory of the occasion. She was studying in her room at the back of the apartment. After some time her father called her in to his study to meet the famous civil rights leader. She was seventeen and shy, and didn't know what to say. Her father said to Dr. King: "Remember what we talked about, Martin? I want you to do that for Julia." And Dr. King unbuttoned his shirt and showed her a nasty red scar across his chest where, a few months earlier, a mentally deranged black woman had struck him with a letter opener as he autographed books in a Harlem store. "This is what happens to people in the States who speak up for their rights," Wright told his daughter. Then he nodded, she remembers, to indicate she could leave now.[52]

THREE YEARS EARLIER WRIGHT HAD GONE TO SEE LOUIS SAPIN'S FOLK COMEDY, *Papa Bon Dieu*, and thoroughly enjoyed it. Performed by a company of black actors (the first in Europe), it was a playful satire on cult religion and superstition. It reminded Wright of Southern black communities.

With Sapin's permission, he had translated and adapted the play for the American stage, transporting the action to the American South. He called it *Daddy Goodness*. Paul Reynolds had not managed to find an interested director in New York or London.

It looked as if the American Theatre Association of Paris would put it on that summer. In the spring, for several weeks, Wright was diverted by rehearsals. Several professional actors were hired. Daddy Goodness was played by Leroy Haynes, who ran the soul food restaurant in Montmartre. Wright liked going along to rehearsals. It felt like old times.

But the organizers were unable to find sufficient backing to carry on. In the end, there was just a reading of the play at the end of May 1959. The *American Theatre Association of Paris Newsletter* called it "one of the warmest, most delightful plays to come along in many years."

———

WRIGHT WAS STILL STRUGGLING WITH THE BRITISH DEPARTMENT OF IMMIGRATION. In November 1958 his friend John Strachey had taken up his case in the House of Commons.[53] Wright wrote a formal statement for Strachey to pass on to the Home Office officials. "In the event that I am granted the right to reside in England, I shall not participate in British politics or racial problems in any shape, form or manner. This is the attitude I have maintained during my twelve years residence in France. I feel that this is the minimum courtesy which a guest should display to the host country in which he resides."[54]

Reginald Butler, the Home Secretary, maintained there were no objections to Wright's coming to live in the United Kingdom with his family, provided Wright could provide evidence of financial assets. "Subject to that, and assuming there is no significant change of circumstance in the meantime, Mr. Wright will then be free to enter the United Kingdom and the immigration officer is likely to grant him leave to land for an initial period of stay not exceeding twelve months."[55]

Strachey argued that this was too vague, but Butler was firm. Foreigners had to complete four years of conditional residency. After that, if they proved satisfactory, the Wrights, like anyone else, would be accepted as permanent residents of the United Kingdom.[56]

Wright found the whole saga insulting and humiliating. Ellen decided to proceed with her plans. She and the girls moved to London in July 1959, on temporary visas. Julia would complete her baccalaureate at the French lycée in Kensington, and Rachel, who was ten, would go there too. Ellen had found a house nearby, in Chelsea, she wanted to purchase, but for the time being they rented a house on Cromwell Road, southwest London.[57]

Wright promised the family he would move as soon as he heard definite word from the British Immigration Department. After that, he hoped to set out again for Africa. He wanted to visit French West Africa and write about the Western-educated black elite. Dorothy Padmore told him that conditions in French West Africa were even harsher than those in Ghana, but Wright was not deterred. He planned to leave in the summer or fall of 1959, and stay away for six to nine months. Reynolds managed to organize an advance of twenty-five hundred dollars from Doubleday.

After Ellen and the girls left for England, Wright was able to spend more time with Celia Hornung. She had a room in the Hôtel Casimir Delavigne, around the corner from Wright's apartment in rue Monsieur le Prince. Sometimes, she says, on these summer evenings when the windows were open, she could hear Richard Wright's booming laughter a whole block away.

Celia Hornung was German Jewish, blue-eyed and bottle-blond. As a refugee from Nazism, she had been living in London since she was fourteen. She was now thirty-eight. She had arrived in Paris in June, and Wright met her shortly afterwards, on the terrace of the Tournon. They had a mutual friend, Hornung whispered to him; Sonia Courtenay, whose maid he had had an affair with.

He asked her if she had ever slept with a black man before. She hadn't. He asked her if she had ever been in the Communist Party. He seemed relieved to hear she hadn't. He told her he was tired of Communist women who wanted to prove they were not prejudiced.

Hornung spoke no French and had no job. She had received some compensation from the German government, and she also received a small allowance each month from an admirer in Australia—a married man, an Austrian, who had gone to Melbourne to establish a chocolate business. He hoped to marry her when he managed to extricate himself from his present wife, but Hornung was not keen on living in Australia.

"I don't remember ever loving anybody," she says today.[58] Her childhood in a well-to-do Jewish family in Berlin was lonely and unhappy. Her younger brother was mentally retarded and put away in an institution. Her mother committed suicide when Celia was six. In 1937, when Celia was fourteen, her father remarried and her stepmother did not want an adolescent girl around the house, so she was sent to boarding school in Berkshire, England. In 1939 her father and stepmother got out of Berlin just in time. They left Celia's brother to his inevitable fate.

Hornung liked the atmosphere in the Tournon. There were at least half a dozen black men who were regulars, and she liked them all. She was flattered to be courted by the famous writer among them. She had a soft spot for Ollie Harrington: everyone did. And while she was with Richard Wright, Bill Gardner Smith, Wright's archenemy, vigorously pursued her. "I want to sleep with you," he kept telling her. "What do I have to do? Rape you?"

On weekends Wright would sometimes take Celia Hornung for a drive in the country. Occasionally they stayed in an inn somewhere in Normandy. During the week they saw each other in the afternoons or evenings. Never in the mornings, when Wright worked. She did not stay overnight. In the late evening he would open the door to the street—sometimes he was naked, which embarrassed her—and she would go back to her hotel. They never went to the theater or movies. Occasionally they went out to eat. Generally, Wright preferred to cook at home. She remembers magnificent steaks, pierced with garlic.

When Wright "held forth" about something, he became beautiful, she says. But Hornung, who prided herself on her well-to-do background, was irritated by what she considered his lack of sophistication. He let the peas fall off his fork. He put his knife in his mouth. He spoke too loud. He held his cigarettes like a nonsmoker. A favorite expression was "Hot Dog!" He would say to her: "Let's pull faces!" Or "Let's fuck!"

She wanted to be a writer, but she had never read anything by him. He lent her *Black Boy*. She took ages to read it, she remembers. He would say, "Have you read it yet?" She didn't like it. His poverty shocked her. They never discussed his books.

Wright often talked about being short of money, she says. It amazed her that he washed his own sheets, rather than taking them to the laundry. The Wrights' former maid came once to spring-clean the apartment. Hornung remembers this because Wright told her afterwards he had tried to seduce her, without success. Hornung decided he had a thing about maids.

Wright liked to tell her about seducing other women. He would describe the scene in graphic detail. Hornung was never jealous—personally she did not think him much of a lover—but she thought it bad taste. Sometimes he bought pornographic photos at Pigalle, and they used to look at them together. He preferred to take his own. Hornung enjoyed being his model.

The London-Paris domestic situation seemed to be working out. Ellen continued to work as a literary agent[59] and also worked for a women's organization around the corner from where she lived. The girls had adapted well to their new school.

Wright had taken out a novel he began in the 1940s, *The Jackal*, and turned it into a short story, "Rite of Passage." He was getting together a collection of his short stories, to be called *Eight Men*. Then, suddenly, without any warning, he became ill. On 22 August, he went into the American Hospital. The diagnosis was amoebic dysentery. The doctors thought he had probably caught the amoebas from contaminated food in West Africa, a high-risk area. But he could have caught them in Asia, South America, Spain, or even during his childhood in the American South. Stress was often the factor that transformed a carrier into a sufferer.

It was a debilitating disease. The symptoms were intermittent fever, a tender and enlarged liver, abdominal cramps and discomfort, dehydration, and fatigue. The heavy medication was known to make patients weaker still. In addition to sulfa, penicillin, bismuth, and arsenic, Wright was given injections of emetine hydrochloride. The drug was potentially cardiotoxic, and patients were advised to remain in bed while under treatment. They hardly felt like doing anything else.

After coming out of the hospital, Wright saw less of Celia Hornung. She recalls that he sweated a great deal and sometimes had trouble getting up from the sofa. In September, when George Padmore came back to London for tests on his liver, Wright struggled over the channel on the ferry. At Boulogne, the British authorities took him aside—he was the only colored person in the group and the only one they singled out—and informed him they would have to keep his passport until he reached Folkestone. They had never done this before, though Wright had been to England and back at least a dozen times since 1946.[60] At Folkestone, he was kept waiting for more than an hour, then interrogated. "Why are you coming to England?" "How long do you intend staying?" "You won't attempt to reside here?"

Wright answered "Not at this time." But he was alarmed. The next day, he phoned John Strachey and told him the story. But he lacked the energy to fight. For most of his stay in England, he lay on his bed, too weak to go out.

He returned to Paris on 21 September. He had scarcely had time to put his bags down when Ellen phoned to say that Padmore was in a coma with only a few days to live.

Padmore died two days later. He was fifty-six. Wright flew to London on 28 September, and was again held up by the immigration people. The funeral, at Golders Green crematorium, was attended by some two hundred friends and admirers. Padmore's ashes were flown to Ghana.

"When I saw the urn in which George's ashes had been placed, I thought how strange that the remains of so tremendous a personality, so great a man could be put into so small a compass," Dorothy Padmore wrote to Wright afterwards from Ghana. Do our efforts and our strivings and our acts that we think so important, after all boil down to so little?"[61]

She told him how much of a struggle it had been for Padmore in the last couple of years in Ghana. As a West Indian in Africa, he was regarded as an impostor, even though he had devoted himself to African freedom for most of his life. His influence on Nkrumah was widely resented.

In October 1959 Wright gave up the idea of living in England. The immigration authorities were not prepared to grant him more than a trial period of twelve months. Wright took it as racism. "Self-respect as much as anything else compelled my withdrawal," he wrote to John Strachey. For himself, it no longer mattered, he said, but there were larger issues at stake. "Dammit, we've got to live in this Western world together. Can the white West afford this kind of behavior? Do white Britons realize the cultural consequences of such actions?"[62]

Wright was worried about money these days, and they were now running two households. With a great deal of sadness, he sold the farmhouse in Ailly, and he and Ellen gave up the large apartment in rue Monsieur le Prince. With the proceeds from Ailly, Wright bought a modest one-bedroom apartment on a tiny, quiet street—4, rue Régis—amid the art galleries and antiques shops of Saint-Placide. It was still close to the Luxembourg Gardens and only fifteen minutes by foot from rue Monsieur le Prince. He moved there on 30 October 1959.

It was the end of his affluent lifestyle. It was also the end of his marriage. He and Ellen both were highly discreet about it. Only close friends knew. Dorothy Padmore understood that the marriage was "not completely harmonious," though neither Ellen nor Richard ever broached the subject with her.[63]

The official story was that British racism had forced the family to live separately. Perhaps Wright told himself, as he sat writing, ill and depressed, in his dark apartment in the rue Régis, that it was not such a bad thing. He had never liked England. And he preferred to live alone. "Have you taken solitude for your friend?" he asked Margrit de Sablonière. "I have. When I'm alone and wake up in the morning, with my world of dream close by me, I write without effort. By noon, I've done a day's work."[64]

In *White Man, Listen!* he had publicly embraced his rootlessness and solitude. "I declare unabashedly that I like and even cherish the state of abandonment, of aloneness; it does not bother me; indeed to me it seems the natural, inevitable condition of man. . . . I can make myself at home almost anywhere on this earth and can, if I've a mind to and when I'm attracted to a landscape or a mood of life, easily sink myself into the most alien and widely differing environments."

Celia Hornung complained in her journal: "I've never had an affair that sparkled less." Wright was not spending much time with her. He was planning a trip to French Africa. "I don't know whether I'm included in his immediate plans or not, or whether I want to be. Yes, so I can reject them."[65]

Sanders, her suitor in Australia, was pressuring her to spend time in Melbourne. She had not seen him for four years and thought she probably should. She felt a need to be adored, and Sanders was good at that. Wright did not want her to go and took the opportunity to be scathing about Australia. Why didn't she come with him to Daniel Guérin's artist colony, La Ciotat, overlooking the bay near Marseille? She confided to her journal: "If I could see the slightest chance of being happy with Richard I'd go with him to Marseille. In Australia there's no stimulation."

THE DOOR TO WRIGHT'S APARTMENT IN THE RUE RÉGIS OPENED STRAIGHT INTO the living room, with its books, modern paintings, and green velour divan. Through an arched opening was the bedroom. Through another arch was Wright's study, lined with books. On the desk, next to his sturdy Underwood typewriter, was a neat pile of typed pages.

These days, Ollie Harrington lived outside Paris with a girlfriend, but whenever he came to the city, he called by to see Wright. Wright would bring in a steaming coffeepot or a bottle of scotch, and they would sit and talk. Every few minutes Wright would dash into his study. "Have you seen this?" he would ask. "Have you heard of that?"

His mind seemed constantly running like a terrier sniffing for a still warm rabbit's tracks. He was constantly making plans and, though in his work he was painfully meticulous and his notes and other reference material were tremendously organized, in these plans there seemed to be a complete lack of organization. Certainly there was a zeal but it was the erratic zeal of a mischievous truant. He planned another trip to Africa. He was curious about Cuba and perhaps he'd go there. Then there was China where something of unimaginable magnitude was taking place and he must go there. His hungry mind was already on ten voyages.[66]

Wright's mind was far more active than his body. He was regularly consulting a specialist in gastroenterology, Vladimir Schwarzmann, a Russian Jew in his late thirties who had studied medicine at the Sorbonne and published articles on diseases of the liver.[67] Schwarzmann, Wright assured dubious friends, was one of the top intestinal and liver specialists in France. He also spoke English.

Schwarzmann lived with his father in a spacious apartment on avenue George V, off the Champs-Elysées. When Wright went there for the first time, Schwarzmann had a copy of *White Man, Listen!* on his coffee table. Had Wright written that? he asked. He insisted he would not charge Wright for his services. He admired his writing.

Schwarzmann was a firm believer in oral bismuth salts. He told Wright he would need to take bismuth constantly for at least two years. Bismuth therapy was popular in France. Almost nothing was known at that time about heavy-metal poisoning. Ten years later, oral bismuth preparations would be withdrawn from the market in most Western countries.[68] By then it was known that ingestion of oral bismuth can cause poisoning within a matter of weeks. Symptoms include lethargy, sleeplessness, depression, sweating and thirst, nausea, vomiting, diarrhea, abdominal cramping, and paranoid delusions. Bismuth poisoning can also cause kidney and liver failure.

On 5 November Wright left to tour some American army camps south of Paris. He wanted to fill out the picture of GI life in his novel in progress, *Island of Hallucination*. On 10 November, he phoned Celia Hornung, asking her to join him in Tours. She caught the train there. He was on the platform to meet her, she recalls, wearing a beret and holding a gaudy box of chocolates. They stayed at the three-star Grand

Hôtel. She saw little of Tours. They spent most of the next day in bed. Then they drove back to Paris via Chartres and Malmaison. She was on edge. "How could anyone but a peasant live with such a man?" she asked herself in her journal. She did not like his clothes, and noticed they were not as clean as they might be. She thought him "utterly imaginative." It amused her that he was always observing other people, and that he liked to attribute imaginary motives to their behavior. She noticed that he looked into every mirror they passed. She wondered what he saw.

She did not like women, she announced one afternoon; they had no dignity. Wright agreed with her. Hornung pointed out that, nevertheless, when Ellen was in town, he depended on her. "I can't affirm or deny this," Wright answered. "I don't seem to know myself very well."[69]

They returned to Paris on 13 November. Ten days later, Wright left with Ollie Harrington for Germany. "Sometimes I think you don't like me at all," he said to Hornung.

"I don't," she said.[70]

While Wright was away, Bill Gardner Smith danced attendance on Hornung. Just before Christmas, she left for Australia. She did not know when she would be back.

In mid-December Wright went to Moulin d'Andé, an old flour mill not far from Rouen, which had been converted into guest accommodation for writers and artists. The Seine flowed through the oldest part of the mill. The surroundings were low hills covered in woodland. Wright desperately needed the peace of the countryside. His intestines felt raw. Psychologically he was "damnably sensitive."[71] He listened to the radio, ate, slept, and took drives in his car. He had no energy at all.

Since being in the American Hospital in August, he had been writing haikus, reading haikus, and reading about haikus. He was possessed by these tiny Japanese poems. He loved their fragility—"like spider webs."[72] A form of meditation, they gave Wright a modicum of inner peace in the worst period of despair and self-doubt he had ever known.

During the day he would lie on his bed or sit quietly, like an old man. Several of his haikus carry the refrain: "How lonely it is." At night he was haunted by memories.

A slow autumn rain
The sad eyes of my mother
Fill a lonely night.

His gentle, wistful haikus could hardly have been more different from his hard-edged, raunchy novel *Island of Hallucination*. They contain no trace of anger. The poems are about loss, transience, fleeting moments of joy. In them, Wright allowed himself to be sensuous and whimsical.

Just enough of rain
To bring the smell of silk
From the umbrellas.

Images of Normandy fog, church bells, scarecrows, and cows tangle with images of magnolias, cornstalks, and cotton from Wright's Mississippi childhood. Where the poems contain human figures, which is rare, they are desolate figures: prostitutes, blind men, peg-legged men, hunchbacks, newspaper boys plying their trade in the wind.

The "I" in the poems is sleepless and anguished—"yearning for what I never had/And for what never was." One poem sketches a sickbed with an indented pillow. In another the narrator reflects that the other inhabitants of his room, the cockroaches, should share the rent. Otherwise, a solitary figure finds himself in a cold, pitiless landscape filled with buzzards, cawing crows, hooting owls, and sinking suns. All-pervasive is a sense of departure, ending, and death. The show is over.

Empty autumn sky:
The bright circus tents have gone,
Taking their music.

"It does seem odd that you should be indulging in poetry," Dorothy Padmore wrote from Accra. "That always seems to me a youthful indulgence."[73] Among Wright's friends, only Margrit de Sablonière had any idea that he was seriously ill and trying to hold terrible anguish at bay. It seemed to Wright that he had failed in life, that the bright promises of his early adulthood were mocking him.

I am nobody:
A red sinking autumn sun
Took my name away.

In his worst moments, he would sometimes think to himself: "If somebody could stop this old earth, I'd like to get off of it."[14]

27

STEPPING OFF
THIS OLD EARTH

February 1960–November 1960

Ellen came to Paris early in February 1960 to sort out and sell bits of furniture. Wright sent Celia Hornung a brief letter from the "awful Tournon." "My wife is here. I'm afraid the next few weeks will be a kind of hell for me."[1]

Despite his weakness, Wright had written almost four thousand haikus. *Eight Men*, his new volume of short stories, had been accepted by William Targ at World Publishing, with an advance of one thousand dollars.[2] But then came bad news from New York. On 17 February 1960, a theatrical adaptation of *The Long Dream* opened on Broadway. The scriptwriter was Ketti Frings. The previous year she had won the Pulitzer Prize and the New York Drama Critics' Circle Award for her stage adaptation of Thomas Wolfe's novel *Look Homeward, Angel*. *The Long Dream* lasted five performances. Wright's portrait of a shoddy and corrupt Southern community was unfavorably compared with Lorraine Hansberry's *A Raisin in the Sun*, which portrayed a lovable and united black family struggling against the evils of racism. Hansberry's play had been running for a year—the first commercially successful African-American drama in American stage history.

Wright heard a rumor that the government had played a role in the closing of the play. "They hate the idea of an independent Negro living in a foreign country and saying what he likes," he told Paul Reynolds. "I'm about the only 'uncontrolled' Negro alive today and I pay for it."[3]

Soon afterwards, he suffered a relapse. According to Schwarzmann, the tests showed he was clear of microbes and his liver functioned normally. Nevertheless, Wright felt as "weak as a kitten."[4] For three weeks, he did not dare to go out, drive his car, or do the simplest errands. He plunged into depression. It seemed he would never get better. "As long as I feel I'm making just a little progress, I'm content. But when I reach the point where I'm scared to go out of doors, then I go to pieces."[5] Since falling ill the previous August, he had lost eighteen pounds.

A young Danish girl who had written a thesis on *Black Boy* wrote to Wright confiding her sense of worthlessness and powerlessness in a world that seemed to her quite inhuman. She wanted to end her life. He wrote her several letters, kind and encouraging, pleading with her to value her life. "For God's sake, don't let anybody make you feel that you have no worth. If I, a black man from Mississippi, made my way, then you surely can make yours."[6] Wright was stricken when she committed suicide in mid-March 1960.

Despite his gloom, Wright wrote warm and thoughtful introductions to two books by foreigners on aspects of black American life. In both cases—Englishman Paul Oliver's book on the blues and Frenchwoman Françoise Gourdon's novel about racism in North America—Wright was impressed that the writers had managed to get inside a world that was alien to them.[7] The collection of blues in Oliver's book—some 350 fragments—allowed him to reflect on the themes, moods, and range of images of those old "devil songs." He was freshly astonished that, despite their "burden of woe and melancholy," the blues songs transformed themselves—"through sheer force of sensuality"—into "an almost exultant affirmation of life."

By mid-March, after a three-week treatment of vitamin injections and sedatives, he could at least get back in his car. "I'm lacking about 50 percent of my old energy," he told Margrit de Sablonière. "What I need to do now is measure my strength and try to work out a way of living with what I've got. In terms of physical energy, I'm not rich any more."[8] His doctor had told him the relapse was caused by colic, and he would take at least two years to heal. The more he rested, the quicker he would recover.

The least thing gave him stomach spasms. He had given up alcohol, fried foods, and spices, and was cutting down on smoking. He had cut out milk and even dropped the café au lait he loved so much. He rarely went out anymore in the evenings. It was not worth feeling exhausted the next day. Though he felt tired the whole time, he had to take tranquilizers to get to sleep.

His illness seemed to frighten his friends, he observed. They did not know what to do. "People are such children," he remarked to de Sablonière.[9] Harrington and Himes continued to believe he had a severe case of hypochondria. Harrington would chide him that he was "one of the most vitally alive brimming-over-with-health healthiest cats in the world." Wright would smile. "Yeah. But man, one never knows, does one?"[10]

Only one person in the world understood how ill he was and did not shrink from this reality, and she lived far away—in Holland. Wright had met Margrit de Sablonière briefly in 1954, when he went to Leiden. That was the year she had translated *The Outsider*. When Wright's Dutch publisher, Sijthoff, wanted to cut eighty pages to save costs, she quietly persuaded the printer to put one more line on every page instead. Since then, she had translated all Wright's books as they came out. She wrote to him regularly, asking for explanations of words or phrases (her English was far from perfect), and praising his latest work. In January 1960 they finally dropped the "Mlle de Sablonière" and "Mr. Wright" and became "Margrit" and "Richard."

For years de Sablonière had devoted herself to Wright's work, and now she devoted herself to him. She became Wright's confidante. With her, he did not have to pretend to be stronger than he felt. She worried about the drugs he was taking and asked him whether he had had his liver tested recently. She sent him parcels of soothing teas, a syrup called "Karvan," and baby biscuits. ("*Now don't strive against. It is a must.*")[11] She knitted him girdles, two different sizes, to keep his intestines warm. She knew what sore intestines felt like; she took sulfa herself. "Thank you for being you," he said to her, gratefully. It was like having a sister. He had never had a sister.

She worried about his living on his own, separated from his daughters. He tried to reassure her. "I'm proud, but before I let go of my last breath, I'll give vent to a loud scream, to be sure. . . . I'm used to living alone and I do manage. . . . Tension is what kills me. I do not want any tension now. Of course, it is sad about the children, but they are all right for the moment, in school, studying, etc. Rachel is harder and tougher than Julia, who I'm sure, does a bit of melancholy brooding over things."[11]

De Sablonière, a left-winger who did not underestimate the seriousness of the Cold War, was worried about his safety. His response—that he was probably in less danger than when he was born—was not reassuring.

> I'm not exactly unknown here and I have personal friends in de Gaulle's cabinet itself. I don't want anything to happen to me, but if it does, my friends will know exactly where it comes from. . . . So far as the Americans are concerned, I'm worse than a Communist, for my work falls like a shadow across their policy in Asia and Africa.[13]

Wright was quite clear these days that if his life was in danger, it was not from the Communists but the American government. He was grateful to his "protectors," the Bokanowskis. Michel Bokanowski was minister of Post and Telecommunications in de Gaulle's government. Hélène Bokanowski, who for a brief period had been Ellen's partner in the literary agency, had recently translated *The Long Dream* into French. Wright dedicated *Eight Men* to the Bokanowski family, "whose kindness has made me feel at home in an alien land."

These days, more information was coming out about the McCarthy era. Joe McCarthy had been dead for several years, and "McCarthyism" was on the wane. In June 1958 the Supreme Court had ruled that it was unreasonable to deny passports to its citizens on the basis of their beliefs, and that the passport division had no right to make applicants sign an affidavit about their membership in the Communist Party. American citizens who had been confined at home for most of the decade were suddenly free to travel, and some of the details about the impact of McCarthyism on their daily lives were beginning to emerge. Over the years, Wright had not shown much sympathy for Paul Robeson or W. E. B. Du Bois. These days, he realized more fully what it had meant to be an outspoken black in the United States, targeted from all angles.

He lent de Sablonière a book on Clarence Darrow—"the quintessence of all that was good and great in an America that is no more."[14]

———

WHAT DID SHE THINK, WRIGHT ASKED DE SABLONIÈRE IN EARLY APRIL 1960, OF HIS coming to Leiden for a couple of days? His doctor planned to attend a medical conference in Noordwijk, the seaport near Leiden. Schwarz-mann was driving there with his father, and had invited Wright to go along too. "What do you think? . . . The doctor swears that I'm all right, that I'm healing fast, etc. Maybe I ought to get into more action? I don't feel like it. But he says so."[15] Wright confessed to de Sablonière that he was puzzled by the invitation. Schwarzmann had told him there was nothing for him to learn at the conference, but that he wanted to see an American doctor who was going to give him money for research. Wright didn't know what to make of it.

On 17 April Wright sent de Sablonière a telegram, asking her to reserve three rooms in a Leiden hotel—for himself, the doctor, and his father. She managed to secure one single and one double room, and hoped the doctor and his father would not mind sharing. On 20 April Wright thanked her for his room. "The doctor is able to find something for himself in some neighboring town: he has loads of friends in and about Holland."

The trio left Paris on Friday morning, 22 April. That evening Wright called de Sablonière from The Hague and said they were looking for rooms for the doctor and his father and they would not be in Leiden before 11 P.M. Could she meet them at the hotel where she had booked him a room? De Sablonière got there in time to see Wright struggling with abundant quantities of luggage, including his typewriter, while the doctor and his father looked on. She was shocked by Wright's appear-ance. He had lost weight and looked wretchedly tired. He told her he had done all the driving. They had come in his car. She told him to go to bed at once.

Wright spent the next day in de Sablonière's light and airy apart-ment, with a canal flowing past the windows. He had brought her a necklace and a silver filigree pillbox. And he brought letters and vari-ous documents concerning Richard Gibson and Bill Gardner Smith to show he was the victim of a plot. In case something happened to him, he wanted to leave the papers in her safekeeping. "What if something should happen to *me*?" she asked him. "Should these papers be sent back to you?"[16] Wright wrote the name and address of Hélène Bokanowski on an envelope.

He talked and talked.[17] Seeing how exhausted he was, de Sablonière tried to persuade him to stay another day, go back by train, and let the doctor drive his car back. He told her he had to get back to lecture at the University of Nancy.

Before the drive back, de Sablonière invited the doctor and his father for Sunday lunch. The old man was pleasant and sociable. The doctor, a slight young man with gray-blue eyes, ignored his hostess completely. Was he homosexual? De Sablonière wondered. Or was he extremely introverted? She asked him if the medical congress had been helpful. He told her he had not gone; there was nothing for him to learn there. She thought it a strange reply. Why then had he come? It was an international conference (she had checked on that): was there really nothing he could learn from it?

Most of all, she was struck by the change in Wright when the doctor was in the room. He ignored her as well. He talked to the doctor the whole time, with that smile of his which he had once told her was his armor against whites. She disappeared to make Wright a drink of egg white and orange juice and Karvan, and thought to herself that his laughter sounded uneasy—almost afraid.[18]

The next day Wright phoned to thank her and tell her he had arrived safely, having driven all the way once again. Soon afterwards, he wrote to her.

I'm stumped about one thing: why in all hell did I deprive the doctor and his father of their hotel rooms? Was I reacting unconsciously to something in the doctor? I've puzzled over this for hours since I've been back. I can read; I read that part of the letter in which you told me that you had gotten me a room, but failed to read the other part. That must have been intentional; it could not have been otherwise. . . . yet the doctor and his father are friends of mine and only wish me well; I'M CONVINCED OF THIS. And this is not the first time that I've felt this deep unconscious aversion to people without knowing exactly why. There is something between me and the doctor that creates tension, but I don't know what it is. . . . I must be a strange man. I wish somebody could tell me exactly *who* I am. No, I'm not mad.[19]

The lecture at the University of Nancy was canceled, with a flimsy excuse. It had been organized by an American exchange professor, and Wright had agreed to it because he needed the five hundred dollars. Instead, he got a fifty-dollar cancellation fee. He asked Hélène Bokanowski to investigate who might be behind the cancellation; he suspected the CIA.

Fishbelly, the handsome French edition of *The Long Dream* translated by Hélène Bokanowski, was published in France in April. The book did well. (Later in the year it was a success in Germany and Holland.) In interviews in the French press, Wright pointed out that despite the Supreme Court decision six years earlier fewer than 6 percent of black children had been integrated into white schools. "A black child cannot enter the American school system without being crucified psychologically."[20]

He pointed out that the Cold War was suppressing black literature in the United States. The "Negro problem" was an embarrassment. He did not know how long he himself would continue to be published in the States. "I am willing to die for my country, but I refuse to be forced to lie for it," he told Maurice Nadeau, the journalist who had been on the platform to meet him when he had first arrived in France in 1946.[21] "When America practices suppression in an underhanded way while proclaiming in broad daylight the benefits of freedom, it places itself on the same level as the Communists."

In June Georges Charbonnier recorded a long interview with Wright for the radio. They spoke in French. The interview would be broadcast in seven brief episodes in October and November. Wright seemed uninhibited, but his command of French was poor and his accent strong. The broadcasts were made more palatable with music and a mellifluous French voice reading passages from his works.[22]

WITH THE HELP OF FRIENDS, WRIGHT WAS SORTING THE PRODIGIOUS QUANTITIES of books and papers stored in the basement of his apartment building. It made him think about times past. "I'm amazed at what has happened to me in my life; so many things came and went."[23]

Julia came to Paris for Father's Day in May, and she and her father had a long heart-to-heart talk. It came out that Julia felt he had abandoned her. He did his best to reassure her. It struck him afterwards that his children were more influenced by him when they were away from him than when they were with him.

He had dinner with Schwarzmann and found him "stranger than ever." The doctor spent the entire meal talking about his own problems. Wright told himself that at the end of the month he would return to his old doctor, who had been away from Paris. But he stayed with Dr. Vladimir Schwarzmann, whom he always, even to Margrit de Sablonière, called "Dr. Schwartzmann"—misspelled. He seemed strangely in the sway of the intense Russian doctor.

De Sablonière asked him to have a sample of his blood tested and to send her the results. He did. The report was the same as it had been at the American Hospital, a little high in white blood cells. "I read it to Schwartzmann and he said that I could send it along, that there was nothing wrong really. The trouble lies in my intestines, which are still spastic when I'm tired."[24] In June, tests indicated a "slow liver." Schwarzmann assured him it would pass.

"I've promised Dr. Schwartzmann to show him the documents I left with you," Wright told de Sablonière. "Maybe this fall, when I'm back in Paris, you could send them to me, registered mail, express, and then I could return them to you. Or maybe Dr. Schwartzmann would like to visit me while I'm in Normandy. If that happens, you could mail them to me there. But I'll send them back to you. I want those documents in the hands of somebody I trust."[25]

Wright was trying to select the best of his haikus, reducing their number to a quarter for publication. He found the process agonizing. The pressure of it all made him feverish and nervous. Writing, he told himself, was more than mental and emotional work; it was physical too—far more so than most people realized. He worried that the poems were worthless.

In early June he sent them to New York. His publisher, William Targ at World Publishing, said no. "You do have the poetic gift. . . . But after reading a few hundred, a quiet monotony sets in," he wrote to Wright. "I should say that a fine little book could be produced from a careful selection; but frankly, I don't have the courage to undertake such a publication, publishable though it be. Commercially speaking it simply would not get off the ground."[26] Wright was keenly disappointed.

In mid-June Wright left for the Moulin d'Andé. "I saw Doctor Schwartzmann last night and he said that my intestines are healed, but that they were still sensitive and that I must continue to take bismuth. My medication has been reduced in other cases, but bismuth must be kept up for at least a year longer," he wrote to de Sablonière.[27] He hoped that in the country he would be able to sleep for ten or twelve hours each night, and work steadily, getting some air and sun during the day.

Instead, he fell into a depression. He was bereft that the haikus could not find a publisher; he fretted about his writing, his lack of income, and his lack of energy. The weather was bad. It rained day after day, and the sun rarely appeared. He stayed in bed most days until noon. "By doing that, I'm not too tired. But that is only half living," he told de Sablonière. "I ought to be in Africa. NOW!"[28]

He listened to the Voice of America and the Voice of Peking and tried to make sense out of the world. The African countries, one after the other, were proclaiming their independence. Wright worried that America would bring the Cold War to Africa, and he did not underestimate the role of Western secret agents. "The Americans have their fingers everywhere."[29]

A postcard arrived from Havana. "Greetings from revolutionary Cuba—a really free and democratic and progressive land that has dared to shake off the shackles of American imperialism. Sartre is coming back in Oct.—perhaps you would like to come and see for yourself? Best Wishes, Richard Gibson."[30] Was the revolutionary card from Cuba yet another attempt to make Wright look suspicious?

At the beginning of July Ellen and the girls crossed the channel to Paris. Wright returned to give the car to Ellen, who was taking the girls on a holiday to Italy. For a couple of days, Rachel slept on his sofa, Julia stayed with the Bokanowskis, and Ellen with a friend of hers.

Back at the Moulin d'Andé, Wright started a new novel. "I'm pounding on the machine morning and night," he told de Sablonière. "It makes me feel much better. You know I think that writing with me must be a kind of therapeutic measure. . . . I'm free, with white sheets of paper before me, and a head full of wild ideas."[31] By mid-August he had written three hundred pages. "The theme . . . has me by the throat."

The novel, *A Father's Law*, was about guilt. The main characters were a policeman father and his son. The son, Tommy, had been about to get married when he and his girlfriend went for their Wassermann tests and he learned that she had four-plus syphilis. He dropped her brutally, then started to murder people. Wright was remembering Marion Sawyer, the woman he had almost married twenty-one years earlier, before he discovered she had congenital syphilis. He felt sick about it. What had happened to her?

At the end of August, from Normandy, Wright wrote to Celia Hornung at Colombo, one of her ports of call. She had been away for nine months, and was returning from Australia by boat. He told her he would be back in Paris to meet her off the train. "I'm waiting impatiently for you! Come and make life exciting again!" He had bought some photographs at Pigalle, he told her, and was looking forward to setting up his darkroom again. He had written three hundred pages of a novel, and had 150 to 200 pages to go. "I'm as scared as hell that it is not worth a damn."[32]

Dorothy Padmore passed through Paris for two days at the beginning of September. She was shocked to see Wright, and privately thought he looked just like her husband in the last weeks of his life. She could see he was extremely tired—physically and also, she sensed, spiritually.[33] He told her he was worried about not being able to finance the family's separate establishments in London and Paris. He said that Ellen did not understand why, for the sake of his personal dignity and integrity, he could not accept the conditions of the British Home Office. He also told Dorothy he was the victim of a plot aimed to destroy him, and that he had evidence to prove it.

Dorothy Padmore did not say so to Wright, but she personally was suspicious of Schwarzmann. On her second evening in Paris, Wright took her to his doctor's apartment. First he had a formal consultation, and then the three of them went to dinner at Leroy Haynes's soul food restaurant. Dorothy Padmore, who thought Wright was taking "far too many drugs," did not understand how this Russian doctor could live in such spacious and luxurious accommodation while having so few patients. She thought it most bizarre that Schwarzmann was encouraging an obviously sick man to take another trip to Africa—with Schwarzmann and his father. Wright explained to her that Schwarzmann knew someone who owned an airline, so the travel would not cost anything.

JULIA WRIGHT HAD DECIDED NOT TO GO TO CAMBRIDGE UNIVERSITY AFTER ALL. She saw no point in studying French in England, and now that her father was staying in Paris, she wanted to return. Cambridge required a third language, and though she had studied Italian that summer (and traveled to Italy with her mother and sister), she had not managed to get the language up to standard. Instead she enrolled at the Sorbonne.[34]

Her father was delighted to have her back in Paris. He found her a room across the river with the Valabrègue family, friends of the Bokanowskis. Julia coached the children in Latin, Greek, and mathematics. She was pleased to be able to help her father, who she could see was not at all well. She came to see him at least twice a week.

Sometimes she was bewildered by things he said. One day he told her to be aware that some of her friends might use her to get to him. Another day she turned up to his apartment limping. She had arrived late at a crowded lecture and while she was squeezing past other students on the steep stairs of the amphitheater, she had missed a few steps and sprained her ankle. "You know Julia, you should stop that studying," Wright told her. He worried that the academic path was throttling her imagination and curiosity. He wanted her to remain open-minded. He hoped she would become a journalist.[35]

In September Wright, who had just seven hundred dollars left in the bank,[36] took on the job of writing liner notes for blues record jackets. Nicole Barclay, the director of a recording company in Paris, hired him to write about Big Bill Broonzy, Louis Jordan, and Luc Barney. A few weeks later, some black American musicians threatened to boycott the company if Wright continued. It is not clear what they objected to. Was it Wright's politics? Once again Wright wondered at the lack of solidarity between blacks. He gave up the job.

The passing years had not healed old rivalries. Nelson Algren had been in Europe since mid-February, staying with Simone de Beauvoir in her apartment and traveling with her in Europe, but he did not once meet Wright. In August de Beauvoir left him her apartment while she traveled to Brazil with Sartre. Algren went to London, where he had a brief romance with Ellen Wright.[37]

At the end of September Wright enjoyed a reunion with Arna Bontemps and his wife Alberta. Bontemps had not seen Wright since visiting his apartment in Brooklyn, early in Wright's marriage to Ellen. Everything had been going so well in those days. Now Bontemps found him living in a small apartment, with his wife Ellen living in London. Bontemps did not pry into these matters. He knew Wright would not have told him anything anyway.

Wright talked with pride about Julia. Bontemps, who was head librarian at Fisk University, suggested Julia might like to spend some time there. Wright reminisced about his trip to Fisk, and, remembering his old film script on the Jubilee Singers, suggested they collaborate on a new one. Bontemps, who had also written on the subject, was keen.

With Ollie Harrington and his girlfriend, they went to Haynie's soul food restaurant in Montmartre. Bontemps noticed that Wright would always dissolve a powder in water and drink it before he ate. Wright explained it was because of stomach problems due to amoeba he had caught in Africa. Apart from that, Bontemps thought Wright "more outgoing and joyous" than he had ever seen him.[38] He speculated that his buoyant mood might have something to do with the large publicity placard of *Eight Men* he had seen in Wright's living room.

The Bontempses were on their way to Africa. Wright was envious. "Crazy, I'm hankering to get back to Africa. The place haunts me."[39]

A few weeks later, in late October, he wrote to the Bontempses in Uganda. He had talked to Julia about Fisk, and she was keen to spend time there. "She hopes that, in two years time, she will visit America, going as far south as Mexico; then, on her way back, she can stop off at Fisk. Maybe she can be an exchange teacher or something. . . ." He was looking forward to seeing Arna and Alberta again on their return from Africa. "Keep well, work hard, and hurry back."[40]

IN LATE SEPTEMBER CELIA HORNUNG WAS BACK IN PARIS. THE REUNION WAS NOT A success. One afternoon in early November, Wright said to her: "I have to give a speech at the American Church. What would you want to know about me?"

"Nothing," she said.

They had a date that evening, but Wright did not turn up. He never phoned her again and never saw her again.[41] Celia did not mind. She was now going out with the man Wright believed was spying on him— Bill Gardner Smith.

In October 1960 Wright learned—it is not clear how—that the Congress for Cultural Freedom was organized and financed by the CIA.[42] "The Americans now do all of their important work through the non-communist left," he wrote to de Sablonière[43]—"an anti-communist left which they have bought and which they control."[44] She had told him about a ferocious newspaper attack on him in the Dutch papers by a Dutch-Indonesian woman he had met at Bandung. He answered that she was bound to be a member of the Congress for Cultural Freedom.[45]

"My attitude to Communism has not altered," he told Paul Reynolds's new assistant, Oliver Swan, "but my position toward those who are fighting Communism has changed. I find myself constantly under attack—both me and my books—by the white West. I lift my hand to fight Communism and I find that the hand of the Western world is sticking knives into my back." He added bitterly: "The Western world must make up its mind as to whether it hates colored people more than it hates Communists or does it hate Communists more than it hates colored people."[46]

Because of his illness, he had turned down two opportunities for travel (to Tolstoy conferences in Venice and India) sponsored by the Congress for Cultural Freedom. Now he wanted nothing more to do with this CIA front organization.[47] It was painful to realize that for all these years in which he had prided himself on his independence from any party, he had in fact been a propaganda tool for the CIA.

In October Richard Crossman, editor of that famous collection of essays by former Communists, *The God That Failed*, wrote to Wright saying that ten years after publication he wanted to do a book of interviews with the contributors of the book. He thought it would be interesting to see how their views had developed in the interim. Wright sent him a furious letter. He wrote that the book had clearly been intended as Cold War propaganda against Communism. Recently he had been shocked to discover that the Congress for Cultural Freedom could insult and corrupt the human spirit by offering dollars as inducements to join the American camp.[48] Did Crossman have any idea how the CIA and its spies were disrupting the expatriate Paris community? He would not contribute to Crossman's anniversary edition![49]

ON THE EVENING OF TUESDAY, 8 NOVEMBER, WRIGHT SPOKE AT THE AMERICAN Church, on the Quai d'Orsay. He liked the minister, Clayton Williams, and had spoken at the church before. The title of his talk was "The Position of the Negro Artist and Intellectual in American Society."

Never before had Richard Wright sounded so disillusioned about the effect of white supremacy on the black world. He was not talking about Bigger Thomases this time. He was talking about black artists and intellectuals. He was talking about his own friends and acquaintances. He described the world they inhabited as a "nightmarish jungle."

Whites who wanted to destroy blacks did not need to dirty their own hands, he told the audience bitterly. There were always blacks who would do the dirty work for them. Because black artists and intellectuals depended on white publishers, sponsors, and markets, and because the white world only ever made room at any one time for one "pet nigger" (he was using Zora Neale Hurston's phrase), it created a vicious rivalry among blacks. Like crabs in a bucket, they pulled each other back. Time after time, Wright had seen black people bring down their more successful brothers—by snide insinuations, verbal abuse, physical violence, or ostracism.

Sometimes this rivalry would take the form of a "deadly fight," Wright said. He added that he spoke from experience. He mentioned the occasion when he and Chester Himes had gone to dinner with Ralph Ellison in Paris, soon after Ellison had won the National Book Award for *The Invisible Man*. Over cocktails, Chester Himes had said to Ellison: "Well, son, you found the formula." Ellison was annoyed. Himes continued to bait him. Finally, Ellison became so mad that he flicked open a knife and threatened to kill Himes. Wright mentioned the argument he had had with Baldwin, and the fistfight between Richard Gibson and Ollie Harrington on the terrace of the Tournon.

Look at Paul Robeson, he said. As soon as Robeson became an enemy of the state, he was ostracized by his own people. "All Negro churches (with the exception of a very few) closed their doors to him. All concert halls in the Black Belts refused him. Any dinner or testimonial at which Robeson was present was shunned. Robeson, a man whose income had averaged nearly $100,000 a year, found himself earning less than $2,000 a year. The hand of the white man was effective, but invisible."[50] It was the first time in more than a decade that Wright had mentioned Robeson sympathetically. Did he reflect, as he denounced those blacks who had turned their backs on Robeson, that he himself had joined the anti-Communist fervor?

It was a long, rambling, bitter speech. Because he knew there would be government spies right there in the church, Wright did not hold back. "It went over big," he told de Sablonière. "The people were sort of stunned at what I had to say."[51] He intended to revise his notes for publication as soon as he felt better.

Shortly afterwards, he became seriously ill. His intestinal tract was extraordinarily sensitive. The doctor called it grippe. For two weeks Wright was in bed with high fever. He had planned to go back to the Moulin d'Andé in Normandy. Instead, he stayed on in Paris, taking antibiotics. He could not sit at his desk and type without breaking into a sweat. He had dizzy spells. "Julia has been a great help," he told de Sablonière. "I feel that she likes to help me. . . . She's wonderful."[52] Julia was taken aback when she went to pick up more bismuth and the pharmacist said to her: "No wonder your father is so ill, taking so much of this."[53]

Margrit de Sablonière was sure the drugs were poisoning him. "Richard, they are killing you, or you are killing yourself. Stop it and come to me. Come to Holland," she urged him on the phone.[54] He was too ill to go anywhere.

His stomach could not tolerate food. He brought it up. He had nausea, diarrhea, fever, sweating, and a fast heartbeat. Knowing what we now know about bismuth, it was probably liver poisoning.[55] Schwarzmann was giving him penicillin injections for flu. On 23 November Wright wrote to de Sablonière: "Tonight I take the third million units of penicillin [sic]. It makes me weak and I feel dizzy. I keep to the house. . . . I'll let you know how I progress. Thanks for your phone call. You are a dear. I am too weak to work now. Hell, I don't seem to have any luck this year at all." It was the last letter he would write to his friend.

Three days later, on Saturday afternoon, 26 November, Richard Wright was dressed to go to the Eugène Gibez clinic. It was his first time there; he usually went to the American Hospital. Schwarzmann had apparently chosen the small private clinic because it was close by. He told Wright he wanted him to have more tests and a rest.

While waiting for Schwarzmann to drive him to the clinic, Wright was lying on his bed. The doorbell rang. Julia was with him, and they both assumed it was Schwarzmann. Julia opened the door to Langston Hughes. A few weeks before, Wright had written to him in Harlem:

"Say, guy, what with all the current sweep forward of Africa and our people in general, we ought to keep in closer touch." And here was the man himself, standing in the doorway.

Julia led him inside. Hughes was disconcerted to see Wright, fully clothed in a gray suit and tie, flat on his bed. "Man! You look like you are really in good glow!" Hughes exclaimed. They laughed and shook hands. Wright said he was fine. It was an old stomach ailment, caught in Africa. The medicine, he explained, was worse than the ailment.[56]

As they talked, Wright became animated. Hughes was struck that he started to look just like the young Dick Wright he had known in Chicago before he became famous—"vigorous, questioning, very much alive, and with a big warm smile." Wright asked about Harlem. "I'd like to see it again." Hughes recalled later:

As we talked his doctor arrived with the car to take him to the hospital. Wright swung briskly out of bed and handed me the manuscript of a play he had adapted from the French, *Daddy Goodness*, which he asked me to bring to New York. He hoped, he said, some little theatre might be interested in it. Then with daughter Julia's help, he slipped into his top-coat, meanwhile apologizing to me for having to walk out on a guest. I left the house as he headed for the hospital. "But I'll write you soon," he said.[57]

It was cold when Julia ventured out to see her father the next day. The leaves had fallen, and the trees were bare. The clinic was shabby and her father's room small. She found him sitting up in bed, surrounded by books. He looked tired, she thought, but he was wearing his gleeful expression. "He looked as if he had something up his sleeve."[58] Her father told Julia he would call her on Monday night, when the test results came through. Schwarzmann had told him he would probably go home on Wednesday.

On Monday evening, 28 November, Julia waited for a phone call from her father. None came. It made her uneasy. "When he promised something he always kept his promise."

According to the nurse later, Wright had a brief visit from a woman that evening. For years, people would wonder whether this woman—a Hungarian, it was rumored—might have given him a deadly injection. It was not Celia Hornung, who was out that evening with Bill Gardner Smith. Vivian Werner says that Wright's money changer, Pops Landau, told her it was a prostitute friend of Wright's, who was delivering five hundred dollars that Pops had changed into francs.[59]

Wright rang for the night nurse at 9 P.M. The nurse said later that he seemed cheerful. Two hours later, his bell rang again. By the time she got to his bedside this time, he was dead. The clinic files record the time of death as 2300 hours. Dr. Vladimir Schwarzmann gave the cause as obstruction of the coronary artery—in other words, a heart attack. Wright was fifty-two.

Wright had given Hélène Bokanowski's phone number in case of an emergency. It fell to her to phone Ellen, in London.

The following morning Ollie Harrington returned to Paris from Normandy to find a telegram from Wright. "Ollie please come to see me as soon as you get this." Harrington had never heard of the clinic. He phoned immediately. A nurse informed him Monsieur Wright had died the previous night.

Harrington was grief-stricken. And he was frightened. Wright's note left him highly suspicious. Wright had more than once said to him that if anything happened to him, he would like Harrington to get his urine or vomit tested. Had Wright suspected foul play?

Ollie Harrington arrived at the clinic and was led down to the basement. There was Richard Wright on a long board, laid out, with a bare lightbulb dangling over his corpse. "It was really the most terrible experience I had ever had."[60] That same morning, eighteen-year-old Julia was faced with the same spectacle.

FOR SEVERAL DAYS, WRIGHT'S BODY LAY AT THE CLINIC. FINALLY ELLEN PLACED A first edition of *Black Boy* in Wright's arms—the book that carried the dedication "For Ellen and Julia who live always in my heart"—and the coffin was sealed.

The funeral was held at the Père Lachaise Cemetery on the morning of Saturday, 3 December. Ellen Wright had arranged for a closed service. At the last minute, Ollie Harrington and Chester Himes managed to persuade her to have a small commemorative service, open to the public. But it was too late for most people to hear about it.

It was a bitterly cold day. A small gathering of Wright's friends huddled forlornly in the chapel. Julia and her mother sat together. Rachel remained in the car, outside. Ellen asked Wright's Senegalese friend Thomas Diop, one of the few in the *Présence Africaine* group who spoke English, to give the funeral eulogy. Friends rose to say a few words.

When the coffin slid into the flames, there was an unnerving crackling sound. Leroy Haynes whispered to Ollie Harrington: "Just like Old Dick. He's grumbling to the very end." The two men laughed.[61]

AFTERWARD, OLLIE HARRINGTON AND CHESTER HIMES WENT WITH ELLEN AND JULIA for a drink at a café along the quai. Rachel didn't join them. Over lunch, at Leroy Haynes's soul food restaurant, Ollie Harrington told Ellen he did not believe that Wright had died from natural causes. Ellen began to wish she had insisted on an autopsy. They were not common in France at the time, and Schwarzmann had not asked for one.

Not until 1977—two years after the revelations about CIA interference in Western cultural life—did Ollie Harrington make his suspicions publicly known. Writing for the left-wing *Daily World*, he implied that the diagnosis of a heart attack was a dubious cover for a more sinister death, probably associated with the FBI or CIA.[62] In a speech in Detroit in 1991, Ollie Harrington did not stop at hints. "I've never met a black person who did *not* believe that Richard Wright was done in," he said. "By whom, I don't know. . . . There are so many possibilities."[63]

Julia Wright is equally convinced that her father's death was not natural. It is a point of contention between mother and daughter. Ellen Wright believes that her husband's premature death was probably caused by the strain and tension in his life.

"If I haven't written you until now, it's just that I haven't had the courage," Ellen wrote to Constance Webb in January 1961. "Somehow the act of answering letters and telegrams had the effect of making Dick's death a reality, something I still find hard to accept. It's so difficult to adjust to the idea of a future without him. He was so very much present, and it happened so suddenly. And while he's left behind a body of work attesting to his mighty dedication to the cause for freedom, it's so hard to believe that all that remains of the physical Dick is encompassed in a small urn cemented into a niche in a Parisian cemetery."[64]

EPILOGUE

The Père Lachaise Cemetery is a walled city within the working-class eastern suburbs of Paris. Elevated from the surrounding noisy streets, it could almost be a small town in Normandy. Shaded cobbled lanes stretch up and down the hill. On each side are tiny chapels, crumbling in disrepair. Swallows dart through the chestnut trees.

This ghost town is haunted by memories. Wright's ashes are on the site of a famous struggle for freedom. The cemetery was one of the last strongholds of those famous proletarian revolutionaries, the Paris Communards. Paris was smoldering; there had been savage fighting for a week. At dawn on Whitsunday, 28 May 1871, the final battle occurred between these marble and granite tombstones. Government soldiers lined up the 147 survivors against a wall in the eastern corner, shot them one after the other, and threw the bodies into an open grave.

Molière is buried here, also Balzac, Proust, and Colette. There's a joint tomb for Simone Signoret and Yves Montand. Abelard and Héloïse are here. And there are expatriates who chose to be buried in France. Gertrude Stein, once part of the lure of Paris for Wright, shares a headstone with Alice B. Toklas. Bill Gardner Smith, whose urn is in the Columbarium, was among those who had made this city into an "island of hallucination" for Wright.

The crematorium, known as the Columbarium, is in a corner of the cemetery. Four stone shelters, with round arches, slate roofs, and Corinthian pillars, make up the corners of a large square that opens into a garden containing a domed gray edifice. It could be a church, except for the two chimney stacks.

In each of these corner monuments, elegant concrete staircases lead up to the mezzanine level. From a distance, the reflection of light on the black, cream, and gray tiles looks like a proof sheet of photographs. It's quiet in this walled world of vertical graves, apart from the shuffling of pigeons on the slate roof.

In the southeast corner, on the ground floor, partly hidden by a staircase, is a black tile with gold writing: "Richard Wright: 1908–1960."

NOTES

1: MISSISSIPPI

1. Any evidence of Richard Wilson's postwar activity is lost in the mists of time. In *Black Boy,* Wright greatly exaggerates his grandfather's action during the Civil War. He claims he joined the army at the outbreak of the war. Surviving letters from Richard Wilson to the Bureau of Pensions indicate that he joined the navy just before the end of the war.

2. The marriage date is given in his pension documents.

3. *Black Boy,* p. 56.

4. The 1912 Natchez City Directory gives the address of Richard and Maggie Wilson as 20 Woodlawn Avenue. Richard Wilson's 1912 Declaration for Pension gives it as 20 Woodlawn Street. The City Directory is more likely to be correct.

5. Wilson's pension applications are among the Horace Cayton papers, Vivian G. Harsh Collection of Afro-American History and Literature, Chicago Public Library. Originals (No. 41.594) are in the National Archives, Washington, D.C. Richard Wilson died in Jackson, Mississippi on 8 November 1921. His widow, Margaret Wilson, continued to apply for a widow's pension under the same act, without success.

6. *Black Boy,* p. 163.

7. Their names (and that of their owner, John Rucker) are on the Muster Rolls and Regimental Description Records, 58th Colored U.S. Infantry, Record Group 94, National Archives, Washington, D.C. (See Ronald L. F. Davis, *The Black Experience in Natchez 1720–1880* [Mississippi: Natchez Historical Park, 1994], p. 156.) According to

the records, George and James Wright, twenty-eight and twenty-four respectively, deserted in October 1863 and returned in June 1865.

8. Nathaniel Wright, the father, is buried in a tiny cemetery in a clearing among straggling conifers and elms, stone lambs, and Greek vases, on Hood Fork Road, not far from the small town of Roxie. His dates are not on his tomb. Several of Nathaniel's brothers and sons are also here. (Nathan Wright, who died in the 1950s, is apparently buried farther up the road in the church cemetery, in an unmarked grave.) Information on the tombstones is haphazard. Nathan's youngest brother, George, is the only one to have his years on his tombstone: 3 March 1887–29 January 1958. Solomon's year of death is given as 1942. He married Sallie, whose dates are given as 1880–1937.

9. The boll weevil, which had already appeared in other parts of the South, was first seen in Adams County in 1908.

10. Early draft of *Black Boy.*

11. Early draft of *Black Boy.*

12. *Black Boy,* pp. 19–20.

13. *Black Boy,* p. 21.

14. Erskine Fowler, in *Savage Holiday,* wishes he could remain ill all his life. When his mother goes back to work, he spends his time thinking of ways to make her feel his resentment (p. 39).

15. *Black Boy,* p. 39.

16. *Black Boy,* p. 34.

17. "Memories of My Grandmother," unpublished essay. Wright papers, box 6, folder 118.

18. *Black Boy,* p. 44.

19. *Black Boy,* pp. 45–46.

20. This is actually Wright's description of Aunt Lulu, his mother's sister, in Wright's unpublished novel *Tarbaby's Dawn.* She is clearly modeled on Aunt Maggie.

21. *Black Boy,* p. 63.

22. Because white communities covered up the evidence and because lynching records relied on newspaper reports or letters to the black press from local blacks, they are unrealistically low. Eliza Steelwater (Project HAL lynching database, Bloomington, Indiana) kindly checked in both the NAACP and Project HAL database for Arkansas and could not find any record of Hoskins's lynching. As she points out, the database uses a conservative definition of lynching: the murder must be at the hands of three or more persons. This might well have been a murder by one or two local policemen.

23. Wright wrote the poem in 1934, and it was published in *Partisan Review* (July–August 1935).

24. Fred Hoskins to Richard Wright, 11 April 1945.

25. Richard Wright to Fred Hoskins, 23 April 1945. Copy in Wright papers.

26. Early draft of *Black Boy.*

27. *Black Boy,* p. 116.

28. *Black Boy,* p. 130.

29. "Memories of My Grandmother."

30. *Black Boy,* p. 119.

31. Early draft.

32. "Memories of My Grandmother."

33. *Black Boy,* pp. 125–27.

34. Early draft.

35. "Memories of My Grandmother."

36. *Black Boy,* p. 137.

37. *Black Boy,* p. 141.

38. Joe Brown to Constance Webb, 4 January 1967. Fabre private papers.

39. Author's interview with Essie Lee Ward, Chicago, 22 and 27 March 1997

40. Joe Brown to Constance Webb, 28 January 1967. Fabre private papers.

41. As an adult, Wright would feel bad about that boy. In *The Long Dream,* a group of schoolboys bashes up a boy who has a sweet smile and mincing walk. "We treat 'im like the white folks treat us," one of them observes in a moment of insight.

42. Wright describes these weapons and gang warfare in an early draft.

43. Joe Brown to Constance Webb, 28 January 1967.

44. *Black Boy,* p. 168.

45. Early draft

46. *Black Boy,* p. 160.

47. *Black Boy,* p. 181.

48. Joe Brown writes about Barrett and his water hole in a letter to Constance Webb, 28 January 1967. Fabre papers.

49. Wright writes about the episode in his early draft, *Black Confession.* He left it out of the final version.

50. Early draft of *Black Boy.*

2: THE WHISPER OF LIBERTY

1. *Black Boy,* p. 192.

2. Joe Brown to Constance Webb, 28 January 1967. Fabre private papers.

3. Author's interview with Essie Lee Ward, Chicago, 22 March 1997.

4. Joe Brown to Constance Webb, 28 January 1967.

5. The school closed in 1971, in the days of desegregation. These days, the school is a museum that documents the struggles and achievements of African Americans in Mississippi. It contains a small display on Richard Wright, the school's most famous pupil.

6. In *Caste & Class in a Southern Town* (New York: Doubleday, 1937), John Dollard makes the point that white Southerners could mostly manage to say "Professor," whereas they could never bring themselves to say "Mister."

7. Essie Lee Ward told this to Margaret Walker in 1983 (Walker, *Richard Wright: Daemonic Genius,* p. 29). She told the same story to me on 22 March 1997.

8. Joe Brown to Constance Webb, 28 January 1967.

9. Joe Brown to Constance Webb, 28 January 1967.

10. Joe Brown to Constance Webb, 28 January 1967.

11. Minnie Farish interview with David Bakish, 23 December 1969. Bakish papers.

12. Early draft.

13. This is how Essie Lee Davis describes her.

14. Early draft.

15. Joe Brown to Constance Webb, 28 January 1967.

16. Wright talks about this in untitled and unpublished notes. Wright papers, (box 6, folder 129).

17. See Michel Fabre, *The Unfinished Quest,* p. 49.

18. Michel Fabre was told that Ray Robinson was a married man with two children. (See Fabre, *The Unfinished Quest,* p. 51.)

19. *Black Boy,* p. 203.

20. Early draft of *Black Boy.*

21. There are echoes of the famous 1951 Willie McGee case in the "Chris" episode. In the novel, Wright makes it the white woman who wanted the affair, and it had lasted two years. Then she turned him in.

22. Joe Brown to Constance Webb, 28 January 1967. Fabre private papers.

23. *Black Boy,* pp. 206–7.

24. *Black Boy,* p. 217.

25. Allison Davis, Burleigh B. Gardner, and Mary R. Gardner, *Deep South: A Social Anthropological Study of Caste and Class* (Chicago: University of Chicago Press, 1941), p. 23.

26. See Dollard, *Caste & Class in a Southern Town,* pp. 46–47.

27. *Black Boy,* p. 228.

28. In *Black Boy,* Wright does not name his two friends. Joe Brown says they were the Hubert boys, the sons of the president. (Joe Brown to Constance Webb, 17 January 1967.) Ralph Ellison independently confirmed this. Maryemma Graham and Amritjit Singh, eds., *Conversations with Ralph Ellison* (Jackson, MS: University Press of Mississippi, 1995), p. 325.

29. This is the ending of Wright's story "The Man Who Was Almost a Man," in *Eight Men.* The seventeen-year-old protagonist, Dave, has jumped on a boxcar, hoping to make his way to freedom. A constant theme in Wright's fiction is that a black man in the South could never aspire to be a man, in the true sense of the word.

30. *The Long Dream,* p. 23.

31. It was 570 Beale Avenue. The Memphis City Directory indicates that Wiley Walls, a carpenter, lived here with his wife, Rosa, and daughter, Rosa.

32. *Black Boy,* p. 246.

33. *Black Boy,* p. 248.

34. *Black Boy,* p. 257.

35. *Black Boy,* p. 263.

36. He mentions this in "Memories of My Grandmother."

37. Dewey W. Grantham, *The South in Modern America* (New York: Harper-Perennial, 1994), p. xvi.

38. *Black Boy,* p. 290.

39. *Black Boy,* p. 293.

40. H. L. Mencken, *A Book of Prefaces* (New York: Knopf, 1917), p. 214.

41. H. L. Mencken, *A Book of Prefaces,* pp. 217–18.

42. H. L. Mencken, *A Book of Prefaces,* pp. 275–76.

43. *Black Boy,* p. 295.

44. "Down by the Riverside" was one of Wright's earliest stories, and was published in *Uncle Tom's Children* (New York: Harper & Brothers) in 1938. "Silt" was published in the *New Masses* in 1937 and reprinted in *Eight Men* with the new title: "The Man Who Saw the Flood" (New York: World Publishing Co., 1961).

45. *Black Boy,* p. 302.

3: THE SOUTH SIDE OF CHICAGO

1. *12 Million Black Voices: A Folk History of the Negro in the United States* (New York: Viking Press, 1941).

2. "Skyscraper" was defined by the *Dictionary of American Slang* in 1891 as "a very tall building such as are now being built in Chicago." The famous Merchandise Mart, which opened in 1929, was the world's largest building at the time

3. *Lawd Today* (1963, reprint, Boston: Northeastern Press, 1991), p. 138.

4. Horace R. Cayton, *Long Old Road* (New York: Trident Press, 1965), pp. 177, 184.

5. Arna Bontemps, *The Old South* (New York: Dodd, Mead, 1973), pp. 17–18.

6. *12 Million Black Voices,* p. 121.

7. Nicholas Lemann, *The Promised Land: The Great Black Migration and How It Changed America* (New York: Vintage Books, 1991), p. 65.

8. *Black Boy,* p. 311.

9. *Black Boy,* pp. 318–19.

10. In fact, Wright's remarks about the lives of these white women are remarkably similar to a passage earlier in *Black Boy* where he muses about the shallowness of black life. "How lacking in genuine passion we were, how void of great hope, how timid our joy, how bare our traditions . . . and how shallow was even our despair." Over the years, this passage has proved the most controversial in the whole book.

11. *White Man, Listen!* (1957; reprint, New York: HarperPerennial, 1995), p. 108.

12. *Black Boy,* p. 313.

13. *Black Boy,* p. 199.

14. *Black Boy,* p. 332.

15. Early draft of *Black Boy.*

16. The details in this paragraph come from an early draft of *Black Boy.*

17. Early draft of *Black Boy.*

18. Wright also admired Crane's Civil War novel, *The Red Badge of Courage,* in which a young soldier, keen to be a hero, adopts a swaggering façade to overcome his fear.

19. Harry Bernstein, "Post Office Nights," *The Anvil,* no. 7 (July–August 1934). The story confirms Wright's picture of conditions in the post office.

20. *Black Boy,* p. 335.

21. *Black Boy,* p. 328.

22. Author's interview with Len Mallette, Chicago, 29 March 1997.

23. *Black Boy,* p. 339.

24. *Black Boy,* p. 340.

25. The newly formed Negro forum was modeled on the white forum known as the "Bug Club" at the south end of the park.

26. Early draft. The published version is more moderate.

27. Early draft of *Black Boy.*

28. Early draft of *Black Boy.*

29. He describes the novel in an early draft of *Black Boy.*

30. *12 Million Black Voices,* p. 131.

31. Harold D. Lasswell and Dorothy Blumenstock, *World Revolutionary Propaganda: A Chicago Study* (New York: Alfred A. Knopf, 1939).

32. Early draft of *Black Boy.*

33. Early draft of *Black Boy.*

34. Mary Wirth to Michel Fabre, 22 September 1963. Fabre private papers.

35. Richard Wright, introduction to Nelson Algren's *Never Come Morning* (New York: Harper & Brothers, 1942).

36. Richard Wright to Miss Florence M. Seder, Social Work Publicity Council, 4 April 1940. Michel Fabre private papers.

37. Early draft of *Black Boy.*

38. *Black Boy,* p. 358.

39. *Black Boy,* p. 366.

40. Dr. George Cleveland Hall was an African American, a renowned surgeon, and one of the founders of the Chicago Urban League. He persuaded the Jewish philanthropist Julius Rosenwald to donate the land on which the library was built.

41. Vivian Harsh, born in 1890, was to commit suicide in 1960, at the age of seventy.

42. Joe Brown to Constance Webb, 28 January 1967. Fabre papers. The quotations in the rest of the chapter are from this letter.

43. In future years, Arthur Leaner posed as "Reverend Arthur B. Leaner" and made money out of that. Then he transformed his sacred quarters into a recording studio and, under the name Al Benson, became one of the best-known swing disc jockeys on the Chicago airwaves. "Yes, Rev. Leaner (Al Benson) is a plutocrat," Joe Brown would write to Dick Wright in March 1948, "but still a jack-ass." Wright papers.

4: WORDS AS WEAPONS

1. Like most members of the Party, Aaron wrote under a pseudonym. His was Tom Butler.

2. *Black Boy,* p. 372.

3. In the original draft of *Black Boy,* Wright gives "Gr·mm" his real-life name: Gilbert Rocke.

4. Edith Lloyd to Richard Wright, 7 April 1940: "Remember the poetry you brought to the Reed the first time you came? The love letter to a capitalist and the one about liberals?" Correspondence "L," Wright papers.

5. Early draft of *Black Boy.*

6. Abe Aaron to Jack Conroy, 24 November 1933. Conroy papers, Newberry Library, Chicago.

7. Abe Aaron to Jack Conroy, 13 January 1934. Conroy papers.

8. This is also what he told Conroy in their correspondence.

9. Bettina Drew interview with Abe Aaron, 4 August 1984. See Drew, *Nelson Algren: A Life on the Wild Side* (New York: G. P. Putnam's Sons, 1989), pp. 52–53.

10. *Black Boy,* p. 293.

11. Richard Wright, "Rest for the Weary," *Left Front,* no. 3 (January–February 1934): 3.

12. This was actually in a forthcoming issue. (Eugene Leslie, *Left Front,* vol. 1, no. 2 [September–October 1933].)

13. Nelson Algren, *Somebody in Boots* (New York: Vanguard Press, 1935).

14. Among Wright's friends, Sam Ross, originally Sam Rosen, was born in the

Ukraine and came to the U.S. as a young boy; Herbert Kline was originally Klein; Abraham Chapman, whose Ukrainian family name was Chipiniuk, had spent several years in Jerusalem and spoke fluent Hebrew; Nelson Algren's last name was actually Abraham.

15. *Black Boy,* p. 381.

16. In a draft of *Black Boy,* Richard Wright wrote: "I looked at the white comrades; they kept deadpan faces." In the published version he writes: "Some of the more intelligent ones were striving to keep deadpan faces."

17. *Black Boy,* p. 388.

18. "Reflections on Richard Wright: A Symposium on an Exiled Native Son," in *Anger, and Beyond: The Negro Writer in the United States,* ed. Herbert Hill (New York: Harper & Row, 1966), pp. 196–97.

19. Mary Wirth to Edward Margolies, 24 March 1963. Margolies private papers.

20. 4804 St. Lawrence Avenue.

21. Jane Newton to Michel Fabre, 22 February 1964. Fabre private papers.

22. Fern Gayden interview with Horace Cayton, 4 November 1968. Cayton papers.

23. *The Outsider* (1953; reprint, New York: HarperPerennial, 1991), pp. 17–24.

24. *The Long Dream,* p. 84.

25. Early draft of *Native Son.*

26. *The Outsider,* p. 21.

27. Early draft of *Black Boy.* His grandmother's death was left out of the published version.

28. Margaret Wilson's death certificate, reg. no: 23209. Vital Records Office, Chicago. She was cremated at Restvale Cemetery, Worth, Cook County.

29. This paragraph is a summary of Wright's thoughts in "Memories of My Grandmother."

30. Early draft of *Black Boy.*

31. "Memories of My Grandmother."

32. Scrap of paper among the Wright papers, box 84, folder 972.

5: BASTARD INTELLECTUAL

1. Early draft of *Black Boy.*

2. Other participants were Joyce Gourfain, Ben Gerschwin, Peter Pollack, Stuart Engstrand, Virginia Scott, Irving and Sylvia Eisenstein.

3. She had died after a botched illegal abortion.

4. Writing in 1968, Lipton thought the episode took place in late fall 1931, but this is not possible. Wright was not yet moving in white circles.

5. Lawrence Lipton, "Richard Wright: The Agony of Integration," *Los Angeles Free Press,* 26 April 1968, Living Arts section, pp. 18–19.

6. *Black Boy,* p. 401.

7. "How 'Bigger' Was Born" (New York: Harper, 1940), in *Native Son* (New York: HarperPerennial, 1991), p. 516.

8. *Black Boy,* p. 401.

9. Thomas Lee Philpott, *The Slum and the Ghetto: Neighborhood Deterioration and Middle Class Reform, Chicago, 1880–1930* (New York: Oxford University Press, 1978), p. 322.

10. Richard Wright interview in the *New York Sun,* 4 March 1940.

11. Richard Wright, "How 'Bigger' Was Born."

12. *The Slum and the Ghetto,* pp. 322–23.

13. *Native Son* (1940; reprint, New York: HarperPerennial, 1991), p. 340.

14. Horace Cayton interview with Fern Gayden. Cayton papers.

15. Author's interview with Susan Woodson, Chicago, May 1997. Dorothy Farrell used the same word, "plain," and commented on Joyce's ready jealousy of attractive women. (Author's interview with Farrell, New York, 10 July 1997.)

16. Horace Cayton interview with Joyce Gourfain. Cayton papers.

17. Horace Cayton interview with Joyce Gourfain. Cayton papers.

18. Langston Hughes to Michel Fabre. Hughes papers, Beinecke Library, Yale University, box 57.

19. Horace Cayton interview with Joyce Gourfain. Cayton papers.

20. Virginia Scott to Richard Wright, 1 May 1940. Wright papers.

21. Front-page article with photograph in the *Chicago Defender,* 22 December 1934.

22. Chicago *Herald & Examiner,* 19 December 1934. After the hearing, Jane Newton repaired to the International Labor Defense Headquarters to celebrate. The Hearst reporter comments: "Mrs. Newton was surrounded by people of her political faith . . . the faith of the sickle and the hammer. Communism, brash and unashamed. They swarmed around her, colored and white, among them a few whose race was somewhat indistinguishable through horror of the bathtub."

23. Jane Newton to Michel Fabre, 22 February 1964. Fabre private papers.

24. Local black preachers had asked the police to drive away the "agitators" who used to speak in the small Negro forum in Ellis Park. (The main forum for black speakers was in Washington Park.)

25. Edith Margo, "The South Side Sees Red," *Left Front,* vol. 1, no. 4 (May-June 1934).

26. Jane Newton to Michel Fabre, 22 February 1964. Fabre private papers.

27. *Black Boy,* p. 391.

28. Taken from Richard Wright's notes on Poindexter, "Biography of a Bolshevik." Wright papers.

29. In *Black Boy,* Poindexter is called "Ross," and Oliver Law "Ed Green."

30. James Yates, *Mississippi to Madrid: Memoir of a Black American in the Abraham Lincoln Brigade* (Seattle: Open Hand Publishing, 1989), p. 138.

31. *Black Boy,* p. 419.

32. Harry Haywood, *Black Bolshevik: Autobiography of an Afro-American Communist* (Chicago: Liberator Press, 1978).

33. Claude Lightfoot, a black Chicago Communist who observed the Wright-Haywood relationship, comments that Haywood "tormented" Wright. Mark Solomon, *The Cry Was Unity: Communists and African Americans, 1917–1936* (Jackson, MS: University Press of Mississippi, 1998), p. 269.

34. William Patterson, *The Man Who Cried Genocide* (New York: International Publishers, 1971), p. 149.

35. *Black Boy,* p. 424.

36. *Black Boy,* p. 432ff. (This includes the quotations in the next few paragraphs.)

37. Claude Lightfoot, another witness, gave a very different account of the trial in an interview in 1974. According to him, there was a lot of support for Poindexter in the hall. He had numerous admirers, particularly women. He responded to the charges with his usual persuasive rhetoric. "If I soiled Communist principles while leading the unemployed, while fighting for relief, while standing at the citadels of power and demanding justice for the working class—while [voice rising] comrade Haywood was studying at the Lenin School, so be it, so be it," Haywood decided, in view of Poindexter's "sell criticism," to withdraw the charges. (Solomon, *The City Was Unity*, p. 161.)

38. *Black Boy*, p. 414.

6: CROSSING THE DIVIDE

1. Wright tells this story in his review of Gertrude Stein's *Wars I Have Seen*, *PM*, 26 July 1946. Quoted in Michel Fabre, *Richard Wright: Books and Writers* (Jackson, MS: University Press of Mississippi, 1990), pp. 247–49.

2. James Henle to Richard Wright, 29 May 1935. Wright papers.

3. William Targ to Paul Reynolds, 20 June 1961. Harper & Brothers papers, Rare Books and Manuscripts, Firestone Library, Princeton University.

4. Ellen Wright to Paul Reynolds, 4 July 1961. Wright papers.

5. When some white postal workers come into the room, Bob whispers: "Here comes some white cunt." This was changed to "Here comes some white piece." This was a typical change.

6. Gwendolyn Brooks, review of *Lawd Today!*, *Chicago Sun-Times*, 28 April 1963.

7. James Baldwin interview with Wolfgang Binder, Cannes, 23 October 1980. *Revista/Review Interamericana* 10 (Fall 1980), pp. 326–41; reprinted in *Conversations with James Baldwin*, eds. Fred L. Standley and Louis H. Pratt (Jackson, MS: University Press of Mississippi, 1989), p. 204.

8. His poem "Red Leaves of Red Books" was in the issue of the *New Masses* being sold at the doors.

9. Herbert Kline, "Invitation to a Harlem Party," in *New Theatre and Film, 1934–1937* (New York: Harcourt Brace Jovanovich, 1985), pp. 112–13.

10. And Wright did try to produce a one-act play at this time. Draft fragments among his papers show that he tried to recast the opening scene of his novel *Cesspool* (*Lawd Today!*) as a drama. But Kline gave him only three months to do it in. At the time, Wright was more interested in revising his novel for publication.

11. Clifford Odets's plays *Waiting for Lefty* and *Awake and Sing* were hailed as ushering in a new era of social drama in the United States. *Tobacco Road* was a highly successful dramatization by Jack Kirkland of Erskine Caldwell's novel about white sharecroppers in Georgia. *Till the Day I Die* was a one-act anti-Nazi play. *Black Pit*, by Albert Maltz, was about a coal miner who betrays his class in a strike.

12. Richard Wright to Mrs. Mary Wirth, 10 May 1935. Horace Cayton papers, Vivian G. Harsh Collection, Chicago Public Library.

13. Essie Lee Davis in conversation with Michel Fabre, 19 June 1964. See Fabre, *The Unfinished Quest* (1973; reprint, Urbana and Chicago: University of Illinois Press, 1993), p. 545, n. 4.

14. It was one of Wright's favorite inscriptions when friends asked him to sign their copies of his books.

15. In March 1936 Henry G. Alsberg, the national director of the Federal Writers' Project, wrote to all state directors, asking them how many colored writers were employed. Mississippi employed none. WPA papers, National Archives, Washington, D.C.

16. "Ethnological Aspects" is dated December 1935. This and the "Bibliography" are in the Vivian Harsh Collection, in the Carter Woodson branch of the Chicago Public Library. The essay on the Urban League, dated 8 January 1936, is in the main location of the WPA papers, Library of Congress.

17. "A Survey of the Amusement Facilities of District #35" (Wright's Indiana Avenue apartment was in this district) and "Amusements in Districts 38 and 40." WPA papers, Library of Congress, box 875.

Of the poolrooms, Wright wrote: "Unsuspecting strangers are lured in and filched of their money through various schemes and rackets." It was the same world that he was writing about in his novel *Lawd Today!*.

18. See Chris Mead, *Champion: Joe Louis: Black Hero in White America* (New York: Charles Scribner's Sons, 1985).

19. Richard Wright, "Joe Louis Uncovers Dynamite," *New Masses,* 8 October 1935.

20. Arna Bontemps, "A Symposium on an Exiled Native Son," in *Anger, and Beyond,* p. 199.

21. Richard Wright, review of *Black Thunder, Partisan Review and Anvil* (April 1936): 31.

22. Alfred Kreymborg, Lewis Mumford, and Paul Rosenfeld, eds., *The New Caravan* (New York: W.W. Norton, 1936).

23. Wright intended to write a second part, in which Tarbaby becomes a prizefighter like his hero Jack Johnson, then suffers from incipient paralysis and ends up drunk, sick, and alone. But he never wrote this second part. *Tarbaby's Dawn* remains the story of Tarbaby's formation in the South.

24. There are two short essays of his in the Federal Theatre Collection, Performing Arts Room, Library of Congress. "Outdoor Theatre in Chicago" is dated 5 January 1936 and "Playwrights in Chicago" is dated 28 January 1936.

25. *Black Boy,* p. 430.

26. *Black Boy,* p. 432.

27. This was Robert J. Dunham. (See John O'Connor and Lorraine Brown, eds., *Free, Adult, Uncensored: The Living History of the Federal Theatre Project* [Washington, D.C.: New Republic Books, 1978], p. 29.)

28. Richard Wright probably intended the article for the *New Masses,* but it was never published. Wright papers, box 5, folder 106.

29. Haile Selassie's army had fought barefoot, with spears and muskets, against a well-equipped modern fascist army using air bombings and mustard gas.

30. Richard Wright, "Two Million Black Voices," *New Masses,* 25 February 1936, p. 15.

31. The quotations from Margaret Walker in this section are taken from her book *Richard Wright: Daemonic Genius.*

32. Frank Marshall Davis, *Livin' the Blues: Memoirs of a Black Journalist and Poet* (Madison: University of Wisconsin Press, 1992).

33. Two friends of Wright's from the post office—Barefield Gordon and Len Mallette—occasionally came.

34. Walker, *Richard Wright: Daemonic Genius,* p. 71.

35. Davis, *Livin' the Blues,* p. 240.

36. Bone calls Wright the "towering figure." Bill V. Mullen (*Popular Fronts: Chicago and African-American Cultural Politics 1935–46* [Urbana, Il.: University of Illinois Press, 1999]) argues (not convincingly, in my opinion) that Wright's influence has been exaggerated.

Some critics use the term "second Chicago Renaissance," to differentiate that period of black productivity from the Dreiser and Carl Sandburg period in the early decades of the twentieth century.

37. Generally included are Arna Bontemps (*Black Thunder,* 1936), William Attaway (*Blood on the Forge,* 1941), Willard Motley (*Knock on Any Door,* 1947, which was substantially influenced by *Native Son),* Frank Marshall Davis (author of four collections between 1935 and 1948), Margaret Walker (*For My People,* 1942), and Gwendolyn Brooks (*A Street in Bronzeville,* 1945). Brooks was to be the first African-American writer to win the Pulitzer Prize, with her 1949 volume of poetry, *Annie Allen.*

38. Len Mallette said this to the author. (Author's interview with Len Mallette, Chicago, 29 March 1997.) Frank Marshall Davis commented that Walker was "hopeful of marriage with Dick." (Frank Marshall Davis to Keneth Kinnamon, 24 October 1964.)

39. Wright told Margaret Walker that he was in love with Marian Minus until he found out that she was a lesbian. Walker, *Richard Wright: Daemonic Genius,* p. 91.

40. Walker, *Richard Wright: Daemonic Genius,* p. 80.

41. Davis, *Livin' the Blues,* pp. 248–49.

42. Walker, *Richard Wright: Daemonic Genius,* p. 80.

43. Jack Conroy, "A Reminiscence," in D. Ray and R. Farnsworth, eds., *Richard Wright, Impressions and Perspectives* (Ann Arbor: University of Michigan Press, 1971), p. 33.

44. Jack Conroy to Richard Wright, 14 November 1936. Wright papers.

45. Walker, *Richard Wright: Daemonic Genius,* p. 73.

46. Walker, *Richard Wright: Daemonic Genius,* p. 90.

47. Margaret Walker 1993 interview with Madison Davis Lacy for his documentary: *Richard Wright: "Black Boy,"* Mississippi Educational Television/Fire Thorn Productions, 1994. Lacy private papers.

48. Margaret Walker to Richard Wright, undated, January 1938. She worried about being one of his "meaningless entanglements," as he once described them to her.

49. *White Man, Listen!,* p. 92.

50. Walker, *Richard Wright: Daemonic Genius,* p. 77.

51. Margaret Walker 1993 interview with Madison Davis Lacy. Lacy private papers.

52. Richard Wright letter to the editors, *Partisan Review and Anvil* (June 1936): 30.

53. Jane and Herbert Newton had just left for several months in Soviet Russia, and were intending afterwards to settle in New York. Herbert Kline and his brother Mark Marvin were now living in New York, heavily involved in the theater scene. Abe and Belle Chapman lived in New York. Marian Minus, the woman Wright was courting, was about to return to New York, her hometown, to help her friend Dorothy West with the journal *New Challenge.*

54. Richard Wright to Essie Lee Davis, 26 February 1938. Fabre private papers.

55. Essie Lee Davis to Richard Wright, 20 March 1938. Wright papers.

56. Abe Chapman to Richard Wright, 11 December 1936. Wright papers.

57. These are the words of Edwin Seaver in the *Daily Worker,* 18 November 1936, p. 7. The *Saturday Review* called Wright one of the "discoveries" of the anthology, and the *New York Times* commented on his "unusual dramatic talent."

58. Abraham Chapman to Richard Wright, 19 January 1937. Wright papers.

59. Sterling Brown's correspondence with Wright (March and April 1937) is in the WPA papers, National Archives, Washington, D.C. Just as Wright was about to leave, some good black creative talent joined the Project: Katherine Dunham (the dancer-choreographer), Gwendolyn Brooks, Willard Motley, and Frank Yerby. Arna Bontemps came on board in 1937—the only other black to be employed as a supervisor.

60. He was borrowing the phrase from Stein's "Melanctha." Wright's letters to Chapman have not survived, but Chapman quotes Wright in his 19 January 1937 letter to Wright.

61. Abe Chapman to Richard Wright, 19 January 1937. Wright papers.

62. Abe Chapman to Richard Wright, 24 May 1937. Wright papers.

63. Margaret Walker to Richard Wright, 7 June 1939. Wright papers.

64. Nelson Algren, "Remembering Richard Wright," *The Nation,* 28 January 1961.

7: CHANGE OF FORTUNE

1. Richard Wright, "The barometer points to storm." Unpublished report on the congress. Wright papers, box 5, folder 75.

2. *Writers Take Sides: Letters about the War in Spain from 418 American Authors* (New York: League of American Writers, May 1938).

3. Haywood made a series of impetuous tactical errors in Spain. When he returned to the U.S., he would be out of favor with the Party for good.

4. James Farrell to Richard Wright, 9 February 1937. Wright papers.

5. The *Daily Worker* (28 April 1938) and the *New Masses* (3 May 1938).

6. Richard Wright to Fern Gayden, 28 June 1937. Cayton papers.

7. Richard Wright to Ralph Ellison, 2 November 1937. Ellison papers, Library of Congress.

8. In the summer of 1932, the relief stations in Georgia had closed and Herndon led a protest march of hungry black and white workers. He was charged with "incitement to insurrection." Wright probably had Herndon in mind when he wrote his short story "Fire and Cloud," about a hungry black community that eventually decides to march with the Communists.

9. "What Happens at a Communist Party Branch Meeting in the Harlem Section?" *Daily Worker,* 15 August 1937.

10. He calls it this ("jokingly") in an interview in the *New York Sun,* 4 March 1940.

11. James W. Ford, "A Disservice to the Negro People," *Daily Worker,* 5 September 1944, p. 6.

12. Ralph Ellison, "Remembering Richard Wright," in *The Collected Essays of Ralph Ellison,* ed. John F. Callahan (New York: Modern Library, 1995).

13. Abe Aaron to Richard Wright, 25 August 1937. Wright papers.

14. He first lived at the Douglas Hotel, 809 St. Nicholas Avenue, then moved to a rooming house where he was able to use the family kitchen. It is not clear whether this was at 230 West 136th Street or 268 West 153rd Street. It seems that he lived briefly at both these addresses.

15. Richard Wright to Ralph Ellison, 2 November 1937. Ellison papers.

16. Richard Wright, untitled, unpublished article on the Negro and the war [1941?], Wright papers, box 6, folder 126. Although Tuskegee was situated in Alabama, no representative from the school uttered a word of protest against the savagely racist court trials of Angelo Herndon and the Scottsboro boys in the 1930s in Alabama.

17. Ralph Ellison, "Remembering Richard Wright." The unattributed Ellison quotes in the next few paragraphs come from this essay.

18. Ralph Ellison to Richard Wright, 11 May 1940. Wright papers.

19. Ralph Ellison to Richard Wright, 8 November 1937. Wright papers.

20. Ralph Ellison to Richard Wright, 8 November 1937. Wright papers.

21. James Henle, president of Vanguard Press, to Richard Wright, 30 March 1937. Wright papers.

22. James Henle to Richard Wright, 12 April 1937. Wright papers.

23. Saxe Commins, Random House, to Richard Wright, 21 July 1937. Wright papers.

24. Simon & Schuster to Richard Wright, 1 November 1937. Wright papers.

25. David Zablodowsky, Viking Press, to Richard Wright, 14 July 1937. Wright papers.

26. David Zablodowsky to Richard Wright, 23 September 1937. Wright papers.

27. Margaret Walker to Richard Wright, 21 December 1937. Wright papers.

28. See Henrietta Weigel, "Personal Impressions," *Richard Wright: Impressions and Perspectives,* p. 71. Weigel, a married woman, became Wright's confidante and lover for a time. Trounstine was also Arna Bontemps's agent. For some reason, in September 1940, John J. Trounstine legally changed his name to John B. Turner.

29. He was also the agent for Langston Hughes, Erskine Caldwell, and Meridel Le Sueur.

30. Maxim Lieber to Richard Wright, 6 May 1937. Wright papers.

31. Howard Fast, *Being Red* (Boston: Houghton Mifflin, 1990), pp. 65–66.

32. Abe Aaron to Richard Wright, 8 November 1937. Wright papers.

33. Claude McKay to Dorothy West, 12 January 1936. Dorothy West papers, Schlesinger Library, Harvard University.

34. Wallace Thurman to Dorothy West, 2 September 1934. See Adelaide M. Cromwell's afterword in Dorothy West's *The Living Is Easy* (Old Westbury, NY: Feminist Press, 1982).

35. "What are you doing about the girls' girls?" Ellison joked from Ohio. Ellison to Richard Wright, 27 October 1937. Wright papers.

36. Richard Wright to Langston Hughes, 29 May 1937. Hughes papers.

37. Richard Wright to Langston Hughes, 29 May 1937. Hughes papers.

38. *Daily Worker,* 8 June 1937.

39. Wright had organized black writing groups in Chicago, New York, San Francisco, and Detroit, and he had written to Alain Locke, at Howard University, to see if he knew anyone who would set one up in Washington, D.C.

40. Adelaide M. Cromwell, afterword to Dorothy West's *The Living Is Easy.*

41. There was considerable ambivalence about the editorial hierarchy. On the *New Challenge* notepaper at the time, Dorothy West is sole editor, with Minus and Wright as "associate editors." Dorothy West papers.

42. Wright had asked Alain Locke to review Claude McKay's autobiography, which he had heard Locke disliked. "I do hope you will feel free to enter the ring with both hands loaded when you review MacKay [sic]," he wrote him. "Since you know that Harlem school so thoroughly, we felt that you were the only possible person to handle such a book." Richard Wright to Locke, 8 July 1937. Alain Locke papers, Howard University.

43. James Dugan, "New Negro Quarterly," *Daily Worker,* 25 October 1937.

44. Richard Wright to Ralph Ellison, n.d. [September 1940]. Ellison papers, Library of Congress.

45. "A Memoir by Dorothy West as Told to David Evanier," *Boston Review* (August 1983): 7–10.

46. Wright and Minus may have argued about it. In the magazine's galley proofs, Marian Minus signed her review with her full name; in the printed version, she used her initials, "M.M." The galley proofs are among the Dorothy West papers at the Schlesinger Library.

47. Richard Wright, "Between Laughter and Tears," *New Masses,* vol. 25, 5 October 1937, pp. 22, 25.

48. Margaret Walker to Richard Wright, 18 February 1938. Wright papers.

49. *Story* files, Firestone Library, Princeton University.

50. Abe Aaron to Richard Wright, 24 December 1937. Wright papers. Probably because of this secrecy, Abe Aaron would develop the theory—very hurtful to Wright—that Wright had somehow rigged the prize.

51. Margaret Walker to Richard Wright, 14 February 1938. Wright papers.

52. *New York World-Telegram,* 15 February 1938.

53. *New York Amsterdam News,* 26 February 1938.

54. *Story* files.

55. Harry Scherman briefly favored *American Primitive,* but came around to giving Wright his first vote.

56. Lewis Gannett, *New York Herald Tribune,* 25 March 1938, p. 17.

57. Richard Wright described that first meeting in his last lecture: "The Position of the Negro Artist and Intellectual in American Society," speech at the American Church in Paris, 8 November 1960.

58. Ed Aswell to Richard Wright, 19 February 1957. Wright papers.

59. See Edward Aswell in *The Quindecennial Report, Harvard Class of 1926,* Harvard University Archives. Also: *Twentieth Anniversary Report* (1946) and *Twenty-Fifth Anniversary Report* (1951).

60. Mary Aswell Doll to the author, 27 November 1998.

61. Richard Wright to Ed Aswell, 5 July 1957. Harper & Brothers papers. Firestone Library, Princeton University.

62. *New York World-Telegram,* 15 February 1938.

63. Richard Wright to Millen Brand, 26 February 1938. Millen Brand papers, Columbia University Rare Books and Manuscripts.

64. Margaret Walker to Richard Wright, 4 March 1938. Wright papers.

65. Richard Wright to Margrit de Sablonière, undated, 1960. Schomburg Center, New York.

66. "White Fog," *Time,* 28 March 1938, pp. 63–64.

67. Fred T. Marsh, "Hope, Despair and Terror," *New York Herald Tribune Books,* 8 May 1938, p. 3.

68. Eleanor Roosevelt, "My Day," *New York World-Telegram,* 1 April 1938, p. 25.

69. Sterling Brown, "From the Inside," *The Nation,* 16 April 1938, p. 448.

70. Anon., "A Chatugu Can Look," *by him Family News,* 16 April 1930, p. 6.

71. Robert Van Gelder, "Four Tragic Tales," *New York Times Book Review,* 3 April 1938, pp. 7, 16.

72. Zora Neale Hurston, review of *Uncle Tom's Children, Saturday Review,* 2 April 1938. She added: "Mr. Wright's author's solution, is the solution of the PARTY—state responsibility for everything and individual responsibility for nothing, not even feeding one's self. And march!" This was unfair, given that there was only one Communist story in that first edition.

73. She was the wife of Franklin Folsom, the secretary of the League of American Writers.

74. Ann Watkins to Richard Wright, 27 January 1938. Wright papers.

75. See Paul R. Reynolds, *The Middle Man: The Adventures of a Literary Agent* (New York: William Morrow, 1972).

76. Richard Wright journal, 18 January 1945. Wright papers.

77. Author's conversation with Mary Folsom, Amherst, 15 December 1997.

78. In the 1950s, Paul Reynolds took on the blacklisted Howard Fast. Later he also represented Malcolm X and Alex Haley. Howard Fast, who left the Party but remained on the Left, speaks of Paul Reynolds in glowing terms. Fast was able to get past the stiff exterior, and they became close friends. Reynolds, says Fast, was "a wonderful human being. He was scrupulously honest. He had great understanding and depth. His mind was not rigid. He was conservative, but he was not an anti-Communist." Fast recalls him speaking warmly of Richard Wright. (Author's phone interview with Howard Fast, 28 September 2000.)

79. Richard Wright to Henrietta Weigel, 3 June 1938. Fabre private papers.

80. Richard Wright to Millen Brand, 5 March 1938. Millen Brand papers.

81. Among the white writers working on the New York Project at the time were the poets Willard Maas, Maxwell Bodenheim, and Kenneth Fearing, and critics Lionel Abel and Philip Rahv.

82. Wright worked with Claude McKay's original material, and he was helped by Arnold DeMille, but the Washington director, Henry G. Alsberg, thought Wright's by far the most vivid writing. (Alsberg to Ruth Crawford, 18 July 1938, WPA papers, Library of Congress.)

When *New York Panorama* was published in late 1938, Alain Locke, the Harlem Renaissance scholar, complained that Wright's treatment of Harlem vacillated between "superficial flippancy and hectic propagandistic exposé." (*Opportunity,* 17 February 1939, pp. 36–42.)

83. Richard Wright to Henrietta Weigel, 3 June 1938. Quoted in Fabre, *The Unfinished Quest,* p. 555, n.18.

84. Margaret Walker to Richard Wright, 11 February 1939. Wright papers.

85. Author's interview with Helen Yglesias, New York, 6 May 1999.

86. Barbara Kline interview with Jean Blackwell Hutson, 10 and 16 March 1978. Oral History Collection, Butler Library, Columbia University.

87. Jerre Mangione, *An Ethnic at Large* (New York: G. P. Putnam's Sons, 1978), pp. 263–64.

88. Ted Ward to Constance Webb, undated, quoted in Constance Webb, *Richard Wright: A Biography* (New York: G. P. Putnam's Sons, 1968), p. 181.

89. These few details about Marion Sawyer come from Jane Newton's letter to Michel Fabre, 18 March 1964. Fabre private papers. Newton believed Marion was illiterate. She was not. Marion Sawyer handwrote and signed the note to say the marriage was indefinitely postponed. Jane Newton's daughter, Dolores Newton, still has the note.

90. The WR test is no longer used. It is nonspecific, and the rates of false positive results have been variously reported as between 5 and 40 percent. Positive results could in fact indicate other diseases entirely—viral infections, measles, glandular fever, and hepatitis. But a license to marry was contingent on a clean health slate.

91. Jane Newton to Michel Fabre, 18 March 1964. Fabre private papers.

92. The telegram is among the letters (either from unidentified sources or not considered worthy of a file of their own) in the "S" correspondence file in the Wright papers.

93. Horace Cayton interview with Ralph Ellison, New York, 8 September 1968. Cayton papers.

94. Richard Wright to Henrietta Weigel, 3 June 1938. Fabre private papers.

95. When a Southern preacher from his mother's church visits Bigger Thomas in his prison cell, Bigger is reminded of his mother's religious diatribes to him in his youth. He reflects: "The preacher's face was black and sad and earnest and made him feel a sense of guilt deeper than that which even his murder of Mary had made him feel. He had killed within himself the preacher's haunting picture of life even before he had killed Mary; that had been his first murder."

8: GRAPPLING WITH BIGGER

1. "How 'Bigger' Was Born."

2. These imagined reactions come from "How 'Bigger' Was Born."

3. As Keneth Kinnamon points out, Ernie's Kitchen Shack was a slight fictional disguise for the Chicken Shack, at 4647 Indiana Avenue, owned by Ernie Henderson. "Native Son: The Personal, Social, and Political Background" in *Richard Wright's Native Son,* ed. Richard Abcarian (Belmont, CA: Wadsworth Publishing, 1970).

4. This article, "Brick Slayer Is Likened to Jungle Beast" (5 June 1938), was the model for the article in the *Chicago Tribune* that Bigger reads in his cell.

5. Nixon's contradictory confessions, nearly all repudiated later, were almost certainly extracted by means of police brutality. His defense lawyers claimed he had been hung naked, by the ankles, then beaten and kicked until he signed the confession paper. Wright did not bring this element into *Native Son,* though he has the state attorney visit Bigger in prison and persuade him, with false promises, to sign a false confession. In fact, Wright gave Bigger Thomas a far easier time in prison than Robert Nixon had.

6. Wright borrowed the pamphlet from the Chicago Library on Margaret Walker's

card. He also took out Maureen McKernan's *The Amazing Trail of Loeb and Leopold* (1924).

7. This is part of Wright's dedication in the Newtons' copy of *Native Son,* which he signed on 27 June 1940. Dolores Newton private papers.

8. Jane Newton to Michel Fabre, 18 March 1964. Fabre private papers.

9. Richard Wright to Paul Reynolds, 23 October 1938. Harper & Brothers papers, Princeton University.

10. Paul Reynolds to Richard Wright, 25 October 1938. Wright papers.

11. "Plans for Work," application to John Simon Guggenheim Memorial Foundation. John Simon Guggenheim Foundation archives, New York.

12. Apart from Eleanor Roosevelt, they were playwright Clifford Odets, Malcolm Cowley (editor and writer), Harry Scherman (president of the Book-of-the-Month Club), Lewis Gannett *(Herald Tribune),* Martha Foley and Whit Burnett from *Story,* Professor Lawrence Martin and Professor Robert M. Lovett (Chicago academics who had encouraged him), Claude Barnett (Associated Negro Press in Chicago), Alain Locke (Howard University scholar and critic), Henry G. Alsberg (director of the Federal Writers' Project), Edward Aswell, Granville Hicks (editor of the *New Masses*), and Genevieve Taggard, poet and critic at the *New Masses.*

13. Richard Wright to Millen Brand, 10 November 1938. Brand papers.

14. See *Daily Worker,* 30 May 1938, pp. 1, 4; and "The Negro People March," *Sunday Worker,* 14 August 1938, magazine section.

15. The husband's name, according to Newton, was Arthur Ffun.

16. Jane Newton to Michel Fabre, 22 February 1964. Fabre private papers.

17. Stan Brakhage, *Film at Wit's End* (New York: McPherson, 1989). (See his chapter on Marie Menken.)

18. Norman Rosten to Richard Wright, 3 April 1940. Wright papers.

19. See Ann Kimmage, *An Un-American Childhood* (Athens, GA: University of Georgia Press, 1996).

20. Kathleen Currie interview with Marvel Cooke, October and November 1989. Cooke said the same to Gerald Horne in an interview she had with him on 6 April 1988. See Gerald Horne, *Black Liberation/Red Scare: Ben Davis and the Communist Party* (Newark, DE: University of Delaware Press, 1994), p. 339, n. 38. For more about Marvel Cooke, see Rodger Streitmatter, *Raising Her Voice: African-American Women Journalists Who Changed History* (Lexington, KY: University Press of Kentucky, 1994), pp. 84–94.

21. Walker, *Richard Wright: Daemonic Genius,* p. 123.

22. Ted Ward to Constance Webb, 7 December 1966. Bakish papers.

23. Jane Newton to Michel Fabre, 22 February 1964. Fabre private papers.

24. Richard Wright to Margaret Walker, undated. Walker says the letter was written in the spring of 1939. Quoted in Ray and Farnsworth, eds., *Richard Wright: Impressions and Perspectives,* p. 62.

25. Margaret Walker to Richard Wright, 11 February 1939. Wright papers.

26. Jane Newton to Michel Fabre, 22 February 1964.

9: MARRIAGE

1. Paul Reynolds to Richard Wright, 28 February 1939. Wright papers.

2. Paul Reynolds to Richard Wright, 8 March 1939. Wright papers.

3. Ed Aswell to Richard Wright, 15 March 1939. Wright papers.

4. The Guggenheim Committee had awarded fellowships to progressives before—for example, to Langston Hughes in 1934 and to Jack Conroy in 1935.

5. Eslanda Goode Robeson to Richard Wright, 19 April 1939. Wright papers.

6. Joe Brown to Richard Wright, 20 March 1939. Wright papers.

7. Gwendolyn Bennett to Richard Wright, 27 March 1939. Wright papers.

8. The remark was published in *The Commentator* (NY), October 1938. See Monty Noam Penkower, *The Federal Writers' Project* (Chicago: University of Illinois Press, 1977), pp. 195–97.

9. The League of American Writers was the American branch.

10. Ed Aswell to Richard Wright, 21 June 1939. Harper & Brothers papers.

11. Interview with Ed Aswell by Dr. Harlan B. Phillips, 10 April 1956. McGraw-Hill Publishing Company Oral History, Butler Library, Columbia University.

12. Jane Newton to Michel Fabre, 18 March 1964. Fabre private papers.

13. Ellen Wright interviewed by Constance Webb, September 1963. Webb papers, Schomburg Center, New York.

14. Jane Newton to Michel Fabre, 18 March 1964. Fabre private papers.

15. It seems the hotel was named after a "Mr. Douglas," not the renowned Frederick Douglass.

16. Report on Third American Writers' Congress, *New York Amsterdam News,* 17 June 1939.

17. Richard Wright, untitled, undated article [1939–40]. Wright papers, box 6, folder 124.

18. Margaret Walker to Richard Wright, 11 February 1939. Wright papers.

19. Walker, *Richard Wright: Daemonic Genius,* p. 131.

20. Walker, *Richard Wright: Daemonic Genius,* p. 88.

21. Walker, *Richard Wright: Daemonic Genius,* p. 127.

22. Walker, *Richard Wright: Daemonic Genius,* p. 131.

23. Walker, *Richard Wright: Daemonic Genius,* p. 135.

24. The reported accusations are taken from Walker's letter of apology to Wright, 7 June 1939. Wright papers.

25. Margaret Walker to Richard Wright, Wednesday, 7 June 1939. Wright papers. She says she realizes she comes over like "a common gossip" and adds: "I hope to God I have learned my lesson!" Not entirely, it seems. Her biography of Wright portrays him, without any evidence, as "kinky." About Jane Newton (who invited her over to Brooklyn), she writes: "She told me how she had courted Herbert Newton, how she had put her contraceptives in her purse and gone to see him. I learned from her something of the aggression of Jewish women, so unlike the passive southern black woman who allows herself to be reacted against and acted upon. . . . I knew then I would be forever black" (p. 145). But Jane Newton was not Jewish.

26. Langston Hughes to Richard Wright, 21 June 1939. Wright papers. Hughes signed it "Original Lyric by the 66 Trio Harlem, Sugar-Hill, N.Y."

27. Madison Davis Lacy interview with Margaret Walker, Jackson, 1994. Lacy private papers.

28. Author's interview with Ellen Wright, Paris, 17 June 1995.

29. Constance Webb interview with Ellen Wright, September 1963. Webb papers.

30. Author's interview with Ellen Wright, Paris, 17 June 1995.

31. Ted Ward to Constance Webb, 7 December 1966. Webb papers.

32. Ted Ward to Langston Hughes, 29 August 1939. Hughes papers.

33. Jane Newton to Michel Fabre, 18 March 1964. Fabre private papers.

34. Constance Webb interview with Ellen Wright, September 1963. Webb papers.

35. Arna Bontemps to Langston Hughes, 21 August 1939. Hughes papers.

36. Hughes papers.

37. Langston Hughes to Arna Bontemps, 9 September 1939. Charles H. Nichols, ed., *Arna Bontemps–Langston Hughes Letters 1925–1967* (New York: Dodd, Mead, 1980).

38. Nelson Algren to Richard Wright, 9 December 1939. Wright papers.

39. Peter Goldsmith private papers, Cleveland.

40. *Morning Telegraph,* 15 May 1928.

41. Nickolas Muray, *Dance Magazine,* February 1929.

42. Mignon Verne, "The Dance," *New Theatre,* vol. 3, no. 2 (January 1934): 15.

43. See the *Dance Observer,* vol. 2, no. 2 (February 1935). 22, and the *American Dancer* (February 1935): 18. Dhimah sailed on 3 January on the S.S. *Manhattan.* "Her first recital will be given in Moscow at the end of February and frequent recitals will thereafter intersperse her organizing activity. She expects to remain in Russia for two years and at the end of that time will import a Russian troupe trained by her" *(Dance Observer).*

44. Dhimah, "I Dance for Moscow," *New Theatre* (New York) vol. 2, no. 10 (October 1935): 24–26.

45. When Dhimah married her third husband, Arthur Goldsmith, Peter Wollman became Peter Goldsmith.

46. Michel Fabre refers to this conversation in *The Unfinished Quest of Richard Wright,* p. 561, n. 17. He told me that the unnamed "former mistress" in his book was Henrietta Weigel.

47. Ted Ward to Constance Webb, 10 January 1967. Bakish private papers.

48. Theodore Ward to Langston Hughes, 29 August 1939. Hughes papers.

49. Horace Cayton interview with Ralph Ellison, 8 September 1968. Cayton papers.

50. *Black Boy,* p. 244.

51. Dhimah Meidman stated on her marriage certificate that the divorce had been granted in October 1937. Her divorce certificate gives it as 10 August 1939.

52. Edith Anderson, *Love in Exile: An American Writer's Memoir of Life in Divided Berlin* (South Royalton, VT: Steerforth Press, 1999), p. 33.

53. A sign of the changing times was Ben Gitlow, who lived farther up Paulding Lane. Gitlow had been influential in the Party in the 1920s. His mother, Kate Gitlow, a Russian Jew who worked in the New York garment industry, had been one of the Party matriarchs. Gitlow was a man with an independent mind and considerable integrity. In the late 1920s, in Russia, he had the courage to defy Stalin. By the time Wright came to the Mohegan Colony, Gitlow no longer believed it was possible to enjoy basic human freedoms within a Communist system. He was shortly to testify against the Party in front of the House Committee on Un-American Activities. His 1940 book, *I Confess: The Truth about American Communism,* would be the first of the anti-Stalinist memoirs. *Black Boy* (the unabridged version) followed the same pattern.

10: FAME

1. Interview with Roy Wilder in the *Herald Tribune,* 17 August 1941, sec. vi., p. 4.

2. See Irving Howe and Lewis Coser, eds., *The American Communist Party* (New York: Frederick A. Praeger, 1962), p. 387.

3. Ralph Ellison to Richard Wright, 22 April 1940. Wright papers.

4. On Finland, too, Wright echoed the Party's rhetoric: "The Finnish situation is being used by the big imperialist powers as a smoke screen for involving the whole world in war." Angelo Herndon article on Richard Wright in the *Sunday Worker,* 11 February 1940, p. 7. See *Conversations with Richard Wright,* eds. Keneth Kinnamon and Michel Fabre (Jackson, MS: University Press of Mississippi, 1993), pp. 25–27.

5. Ed Aswell to Richard Wright, 22 August 1939. Wright papers.

6. The three readers' reports for *Native Son,* by Harry S. Scherman, Graham Bates, and Rebecca Lowrie, are among the Book-of-the-Month Club papers in the Manuscript Division, Library of Congress, Washington, D.C.

7. Henry Canby, a former Yale English professor, edited the *Saturday Review of Literature.* Heywood Broun and Christopher Morely were writers and columnists. William Allen White edited the Kansas *Emporia Gazette.*

8. On 24 August (*after* Aswell wrote to Wright about the club's interest in the book) Dorothy Canfield Fisher wrote to the club secretary: "Yes, I've read it, enormously interested by it, not at all sure what I'd think of it as a choice. <u>Can you tell me something about the author?</u> I'd like very much to know his background, etc." Dorothy Canfield Fisher to Meredith Wood, 24 August 1939. Canfield Fisher papers, Book-of-the-Month Club correspondence, University of Vermont.

9. Louis M. Starr, "An interview with Dorothy Canfield Fisher," Book-of-the-Month Club papers, Oral History Collection, Columbia University.

10. Canfield Fisher was proud of the Quaker background she shared with Henry Seidel Canby. She believed this made them particularly scrupulous about the morality of the books they selected.

11. Ed Aswell to Richard Wright, 22 August 1939. Wright papers.

12. Kit Schryver to Richard Wright, 19 September 1939. Wright papers.

13. Only since 1991, when the Library of America published the text that was originally sent to the Book-of-the-Month Club in galley form, have we been able to read the narrative as Wright intended it.

14. In terms of sexual realism, Wright was some twenty-five years ahead of his time. *Portnoy's Complaint* was published in 1969.

15. Arnold Rampersad, "Too Honest for His Own Time," in *The Critical Response to Richard Wright,* ed. Robert J. Butler (Westport, CT: Greenwood Press, 1995), p. 165.

16. Richard Wright to Willard Maas, undated, probably November 1939. Willard Maas papers, Harry Ransom Center, University of Texas at Austin.

17. Ed Aswell to Richard Wright, 11 January 1940. Wright papers.

18. Wright told Canfield Fisher that the Book-of-the-Month Club showed "courage and manliness" in choosing the book. Richard Wright to Canfield Fisher, 4 March 1940. Canfield Fisher papers, University of Vermont Library.

19. Richard Wright to Dorothy Canfield Fisher, 4 March 1940. Canfield Fisher papers.

20. Wright took the story from the end of his unpublished novel *Tarbaby's Dawn.*

21. Arna Bontemps to Langston Hughes, 21 January 1940. Hughes papers.

22. The previous September, he and Dhimah had made a trip to Chicago, where he had spoken at the Chicago Festival of Negro Culture. He had looked over the property at that time. Formerly a home for old people, it consisted of a front and rear building on 4011 Vincennes Avenue.

23. Richard Wright to Paul Reynolds, 17 February 1940. Harper & Brothers papers, Firestone Library, Princeton University.

24. Lawrence Martin, "Life among the Escapists," *The American Mercury* (February 1940).

25. Richard Wright to Lawrence Martin, 27 January 1940. Fabre private papers.

26. Richard Wright to Lawrence Martin, 5 February 1940. Fabre private papers.

27. Richard Wright to Paul Reynolds, 6 February 1940. Harper & Brothers papers.

28. Paul Reynolds to Richard Wright, 14 February 1940. Wright papers.

29. Wright asked lawyer and doctor friends to tell him whatever they knew about arsenic use to lighten skin. "Am told colored girls use arsenic," Ulysses Keys scrawled at the bottom of a letter. "Was given names, one died. One is leader of a 'white' orchestra." Ulysses Keys to Richard Wright, 2 May 1940. Wright papers.

30. Untitled and unpublished piece Wright wrote about his Chicago trip. Wright papers, box 5, folder 78.

31. Wright would sign Frank Marshall Davis's copy of *12 Million Black Voices:* "To Frank Marshall Davis, who opened my eyes to the joy of photography."

32. Bonnie Hansen to Susan Cayton Woodson, 13 February 1993. Woodson private papers.

33. Coincidentally, Hansen worked as a social worker in the very relief office (44th and Prairie) to which Wright turned up in a desperate plight. Her supervisor was Mary Wirth.

34. The photos are not in *Life*'s archives—perhaps because the article was never run. My attempts to reach Hart Preston were unsuccessful.

35. Wright signed the papers on 28 February 1940. I am grateful to Wendy Plotkin for locating the file of documents at the Office of the Recorder of Deeds, Chicago.

36. *New York Amsterdam News,* 9 March 1940. (Allison Davis was a Chicago social scientist, who would later write controversial psychoanalytical portraits of Wright and Du Bois, among others. He contended that Wright despised his own race.)

37. Ed Aswell to Richard Wright, 29 February 1940. Wright papers.

38. *Book-of-the-Month Club News* (February 1940), pp. 2–3.

39. Louis Starr's interview with Dorothy Canfield Fisher (1956), Oral History Collection, Butler Library, Columbia University.

40. Mike Gold, "Change the World," *Sunday Worker,* 31 March 1940.

41. Sterling A. Brown, "Insight, Courage, and Craftsmanship," *Opportunity* (June 1940): 185–86.

42. Ralph Ellison, "Recent Negro Fiction," *New Masses,* 5 August 1941, pp. 22–26.

43. Lillian Johnson, "'Native Son' Is Personal Triumph, but No Value to a Nation," *Baltimore Afro-American,* 13 April 1940.

44. Unidentified clipping from the first issue of an Afro-American newspaper. The article, without a byline, is called "Native Son Fades." Wright papers.

45. Langston Hughes to Richard Wright, 29 February 1940. Wright papers.

46. Langston Hughes, "The Need for Heroes," *The Crisis* (June 1941): 184–86.

47. Shirley Graham to W. E. B. Du Bois, 6 March 1940. Unpublished correspondence, Du Bois papers, Special Collections, W. E. B. Du Bois Library, University of Massachusetts, Amherst.

48. W. E. B. Du Bois to Shirley Graham, 12 April 1940. Du Bois papers.

49. Langston Hughes, *New York Age,* 22 May 1946.

50. David Bradley describes his evolving relationship with the book over the years in his essay "On Rereading *Native Son,*" *New York Times Magazine,* 7 December 1986, pp. 68–79.

51. They sailed on 22 March 1940, traveling via Havana and the Yucatán to Veracruz in the Gulf of Mexico. The voyage took a week.

11: CUERNAVACA

1. He and Dhimah had been trying, in vain, to get their passports renewed by the State Department. The good thing about Mexico was that Americans did not need a passport to go there.

2. Lawrence Martin to Michel Fabre, 12 July 1964. Fabre private papers. (Mabel Dodge Luhan, now in her sixties, was famous for her Greenwich Village bohemianism in the 1910s when she was the lover of John Reed, and more recently for her passion for New Mexico and her tormented friendship with D. H. Lawrence and his wife, Frieda. She had come to Mexico City with her fourth husband, Antonio Luhan, a Pueblo Indian, who was attending a conference.)

3. Richard Wright to Paul Reynolds, 7 April 1940. Harper & Brothers papers.

4. Richard Wright to Nelson Algren, 21 May 1940. Algren papers, Ohio State University Library.

5. Richard Wright to Willard Maas, n.d. 1940. Willard Maas papers.

6. Richard Wright to Willard Maas, n.d. Willard Maas papers.

7. Richard Wright to Ralph Ellison, n.d. [April 1940]. Ellison papers.

8. Richard Wright to Willard Maas, n.d. Willard Maas papers.

9. Richard Wright, "I Bite the Hand That Feeds Me," *Atlantic Monthly* (June 1940): 826–28.

10. Richard Wright to Joe Brown, 29 April 1940, *Letters to Joe C. Brown* (Kent, OH: Kent State University Libraries, 1968). Wright was not alone in this verdict. In 1954 Howard Fast and his family were to go to Cuernavaca to escape McCarthyism. The place was full of American Communists, all there for the same reason. Nevertheless, writes Fast, "We were bored to distraction. We had planned to spend three months in Cuernavaca; at the end of two months, we had all of it that we could tolerate" (Fast, *Being Red,* p. 334).

11. Richard Wright to Willard Maas, n.d. Willard Maas papers.

12. Wright was horrified to read that the United States Army had even issued an order, "Secret Information Concerning Black American Troops," which urged French military authorities not to be too friendly to black American officers and soldiers or to praise them too highly, for fear of offending white American military officers and soldiers. (Richard Wright, review of *Black Manhattan* in *Chicago News,* 22 May 1940, p. 10.)

13. Richard Wright to Ed Aswell, n.d. Quoted in *New York Times Book Review,* 26 May 1940, p. 2.

14. Richard Wright to Ralph Ellison, n.d. From Lawrence Martin comes the tale that Dhimah cried in the bathroom after being attacked by the scorpion, and Wright did not go to her rescue. He was supposed to have told the Martins: "She was mean to me. At last she found a beast that stood up to her." Lawrence Martin to Fabre, 2 August 1964. Fabre private papers.

15. Richard Wright to Willard Maas, n.d. Willard Maas papers.

16. Richard Wright to Ralph Ellison, n.d. [May 1940]. Ellison papers.

17. Ulysses Keys to Richard Wright, 2 May 1940. Wright papers.

18. Ralph Ellison to Richard Wright, 22 April 1940. Wright papers.

19. The presence of these Communists—nearly all white—was resented by many in the NNC, which prided itself on being a black united front, independent of the CP.

20. Ralph Ellison to Richard Wright, 11 May 1940. Wright papers.

21. Ralph Ellison interview with Horace Cayton, 8 September 1968. Cayton papers.

22. Author's interview with Ellen Wright, Paris, 17 June 1995.

23. Richard Wright to Ralph Ellison, n.d. Ellison papers.

24. Ralph Ellison to Richard Wright, 14 April 1940. Wright papers.

25. Ted Ward to Richard Wright, 23 May 1940. Wright papers.

26. New York *Sunday Worker,* 14 April 1940, pp. 4, 6.

27. Ellison commented to Wright that Ben Davis is "a broad scholar of deep perception after Berry and Bassett." He meant Abner Berry and Ted Bassett. (Ralph Ellison to Richard Wright, 22 April 1940. Wright papers.)

28. Ben Davis, Jr., *Sunday Worker* (New York), 14 April 1940. Herbert Newton was one of the many who wrote to congratulate Ben Davis on the "swell job" he made of a difficult review. He clearly did not care for the novel that had been written under his roof.

29. Mike Gold, "Change the World," open letter to Richard Wright, *Daily Worker,* 29 September 1940. (Wright evidently saw or heard about his remarks much earlier than September.)

30. Richard Wright to Mike Gold, n.d. Draft in Wright papers, box 98, folder 1354.

31. In 1944, Cohn, a white Mississippi writer, would write two articles in the *Atlantic Monthly,* effectively defending racial discrimination in the South. Arna Bontemps described the first essay ("How the South Feels") as a "perfectly KKK article." (Bontemps to Langston Hughes, 10 January 1944. Nichols, ed., *Arna Bontemps–Langston Hughes Letters,* p. 151.)

32. David Cohn, review of *Native Son* in *Atlantic Monthly* (May 1940): 659–61.

33. Richard Wright to Ralph Ellison, n.d. Ellison papers.

34. Richard Wright to Ralph Ellison, n.d. [April 1940]. Ellison papers.

35. Edward Weeks to Richard Wright, 19 April 1940. Wright papers, correspondence "W."

36. Ralph Ellison to Richard Wright, 11 May 1940. Wright papers.

37. Ted Ward to Richard Wright, 23 May 1940. Wright papers.

38. Joyce Gourfain to Richard Wright, 17 August 1939. (She wrote this before the book came out.)

39. Drew, *Nelson Algren: A Life on the Wild Side,* p. 121.

40. Nelson Algren to Richard Wright, 12 March 1940. Wright wrote back: "I think you reacted more honestly than anybody I know. But, really, I wasn't trying to

frighten anybody or make anybody angry. I just wrote as I felt." (Richard Wright to Algren, 21 May 1940. Algren papers.)

41. Margaret Walker interview with Madison Davis Lacy, Jackson, 1994. Lacy private papers.

42. Walker, *Richard Wright: Daemonic Genius,* p. 145.

43. Richard Wright to Nelson Algren, 21 May 1940. Algren papers.

44. Ralph Ellison to Richard Wright, 15 May 1940. Wright papers.

45. Richard Wright to John Houseman and Orson Welles, 19 May 1940. Welles papers, Lilly Library, Indiana University, Bloomington, IN.

46. John Houseman to Richard Wright, 25 May 1940. Wright papers.

47. Richard Wright to Paul Green, 22 May 1940. Green papers, Southern Historical Collection, Library of the University of North Carolina at Chapel Hill.

48. *Heart of Spain* (1937), *Crisis* (1939), and *Lights Out in Europe* (1940).

49. Herbert Kline, "On John Steinbeck," *Steinbeck Quarterly,* vol. 4, no. 3 (summer 1971): 80–88.

50. Richard Wright to Ralph Ellison, n.d. Ellison papers.

51. Richard Wright to Willard Maas, n.d. Willard Maas papers.

52. Nelson Algren to Richard Wright, 25 May 1940. Wright papers.

53. *New Masses,* 25 June 1940.

54. Richard Wright to Ralph Ellison, n.d. Ellison papers.

55. Fabre wrote to her, and Dhimah replied, but she never wrote to him again. Married to Arthur Goldsmith, she was living in Cleveland and had become an amateur painter. She became an invalid in the last years of her life and died in 1974.

56. Author's interview with Peter Goldsmith, Cleveland, 17 and 19 December 1999.

57. St. Clair Drake and Horace Cayton, *Black Metropolis* (New York: Harcourt, Brace, 1945), pp. 138–39.

58. This was her marriage to the twenty-eight-year-old Arthur Faber, an artist. They both give their address as 119 East 23rd Street, NYC. His parents were born in Austria, hers in Russia. She gives her birthplace as Cairo, Egypt. Municipal Archives, NYC Department of Records. Social Security Record: no. 124–30-3798, dated 23 September 1943.

59. Dhimah told her son she had four husbands. In fact, she had three. She was never married to the boy's father. Among Ellison's papers at the Library of Congress is a letter to Dhimah from Bill Wollman, dated 22 December 1940. In it, Bill beseeches Dhimah to let him see the boy. "It is over a year since I begged you in tears not to take my son completely from me," he writes. (Ralph Ellison and his wife were sharing an apartment with Dhimah at the time. Somehow the letter became mixed up with Ellison's papers. I am grateful to Arnold Rampersad, Ellison's biographer, for drawing my attention to it.)

60. All quotations in the next few paragraphs come from "How Jim Crow Feels," *Negro Digest* (January 1947): 44–55. The essay was first published in French translation in *Paris Matin* (27 June–2 July 1946).

61. In Wright's FBI file it is reported that his passport, no. 614947, was removed from him at the Mexican border. Wright wrote to the passport office on 17 September 1940 asking for it back. He wanted to travel to the Soviet Union.

62. "How Jim Crow Feels."

63. "How Jim Crow Feels."

64. *Black Boy,* pp. 40–41.

65. The quoted passages in the next paragraphs are all from "How Jim Crow Feels."

12: BACKSTAGE AND ONSTAGE: THE DRAMA OF *NATIVE SON*

1. Green papers.

2. Paul Green to Harper & Brothers 6 May 1940. Green papers.

3. Richard Wright to Paul Green, 22 May 1940. Green papers.

4. Richard Wright to John Houseman and Orson Welles, 19 May 1940. Welles papers.

5. Jennie T. Hall interview with Paul Green, Chapel Hill, North Carolina, 8 February 1970. The interview is included as an appendix to her M.A. thesis from the North Carolina State University at Raleigh: *A Change in Philosophy—Richard Wright's* Native Son *to Paul Green and Richard Wright,* Native Son, A Play in Ten Scenes.

6. Elizabeth Lay Green, *The Paul Green I Know* (Chapel Hill: North Caroliniana Society Imprints, 1978), Paul Green papers.

When Langston Hughes had visited the University of North Carolina in 1931, possibly as the university's first black speaker, he was billeted with a black businessman. A white professor who taught a course on black culture admitted to him that when it came to accommodating a black guest overnight, "most of us white folks are either too hypocritical or crowded, or both." (Guy B. Johnson to Langston Hughes, 27 October 1931. Langston Hughes papers. See Arnold Rampersad, *The Life of Langston Hughes, vol. I: 1902–1941, I, Too, Sing America* [New York, Oxford: Oxford University Press, 1986], p. 224.)

7. Wright made a trip to New York to see it. As he said later, the play cut both ways: black actors were given some scope at last, and white audiences could not complain about the subject matter. Richard Wright, "Negro Tradition in the Theatre," *Daily Worker,* 15 October 1937.

8. John Houseman, *Unfinished Business: A Memoir* (London: Chatto & Windus, 1986), pp. 230–31.

9. Houseman remembers the car trip as having taken place at the end of Wright's five-week writing period in Chapel Hill. In fact, it took place after the three men's initial two-day discussion. In his memoirs, Houseman writes about Paul Green with consistent hostility. But back in 1940, he wrote and thanked Paul Green for his hospitality, adding: "I cannot tell you how pleased I was with the apparent understanding between you and Richard Wright." (27 June 1940, Green papers.)

In the Jennie T. Hall interview, Paul Green would comment that Houseman's book "lambasted me up and down the land."

10. John Houseman, "*Native Son* on Stage," in Ray and Farnsworth, eds., *Richard Wright: Impressions and Perspectives,* pp. 89–100.

11. Langston Hughes to Richard Wright, 21 June 1940. Wright papers.

12. It was the successor to Jack Conroy's *Anvil.*

13. The event was organized by his attorney friend Ulysses Keys.

14. Harold Woodson interviewed by Madison Davis Lacy, Chicago, 1993. Lacy private papers.

15. A memorable photograph, taken at the exposition, shows Wright standing with Arna Bontemps, Langston Hughes, Claude Barnett, Horace Cayton, and Frank Marshall Davis. It was published in New York's *Sunday Worker,* 14 July 1940, sec. 2, p. 2.

16. Green had been in trouble with the university administrators for organizing a party at his house for the visiting writer James Weldon Johnson. The year before Wright came to Chapel Hill, Zora Neale Hurston had spent the summer in town, teaching drama at the North Carolina College for Negroes. Once or twice she came to the University of North Carolina in her little red roadster to see Green. He was terrified the students would drive her off the campus. (Jennie T. Hall interview with Paul Green.)

17. Paul Green journal entry, 12 August 1940. (A retrospective entry.) Green papers.

18. These observations are based on five photographs taken by the Raleigh *News & Observer,* held in the North Carolina Division of Archives and History.

19. National Public Radio interview with Paul Green, 30 April 1975. (Interviewer unidentified.) Green papers.

20. Jennie T. Hall interview with Paul Green. Green papers.

21. National Public Radio interview with Paul Green, 30 April 1975. Green papers.

22. Paul Green to Doris Abramson, 24 September 1965. Green papers.

23. Paul Green to Doris Abramson, 24 September 1965. Green papers.

24. Unidentified interview with a "Mr. Bower," 1941. Kinnamon and Fabre, eds., *Conversations with Richard Wright,* pp. 40–42.

25. Jennie T. Hall interview.

26. Interview with Paul Green in *The Rebel* (East Carolina College), vol. 3, no. 2 (winter 1960): 4. Green papers.

27. Paul Green, "Pleasure and Pain in Art," essay. Green papers.

28. Paul Green quotes Jefferson in his essay "Of Heroes and the Making of Nations." Green papers.

29. Paul Green, "What I Believe," 21 April 1947. Green papers.

30. Laurence G. Avery, ed., *A Southern Life. Letters of Paul Green 1916–1981* (Chapel Hill, NC: University of North Carolina Press, 1994), p. 248.

31. Paul Green to Richard Wright, 7 February 1941. Wright papers.

32. Ouida Campbell, "Bigger Is Reborn," *The Carolina Magazine* (October 1940): 21–23.

33. Author's phone interview with Ouida Campbell Taylor, Colorado, 19 September 1998.

34. Campbell, "Bigger Is Reborn."

35. Richard Wright, "The Problem of the Hero." Wright papers, box 83, folder 946.

36. Author's phone interview with Ouida Campbell Taylor.

37. This story is from the Jennie Hall interview.

38. Paul Green to Constance Webb, 9 May 1967. *Native Son* folder, Green papers.

39. Jennie Hall interview.

40. Daphne Athas, a former friend of Ouida Campbell's, met Wright in the late 1950s in Paris, and they talked about the incident. (Phone conversation with Daphne Athas, Chapel Hill, 6 September 1998.)

13: ELLEN POPLOWITZ

1. The address was 343 Grand Avenue, Brooklyn.

2. Michel Fabre and Constance Webb interview with Ralph Ellison, 3 February 1963. Fabre private papers.

3. Ralph Ellison interview with Horace Cayton, 8 September 1968. Cayton papers.

4. June Newton to Michel Fabre, 22 February 1964. Fabre private papers.

5. Richard Wright to Ralph Ellison, n.d. Ellison papers.

6. Author's interview with Ellen Wright, Paris, 17 June 1995.

7. Sponsors included Orson Welles, Eleanor Roosevelt, Langston Hughes, Paul Robeson, and Richard Wright.

8. Ralph Ellison describes one such agency to Wright in a letter to Mexico, 22 April 1940. Wright papers.

9. Ella Baker and Marvel Cooke, "The Bronx Slave Market," *The Crisis* (November 1935): 330–32.

10. Wright describes these interviews in an undated piece among his papers, box 21, folder 330.

11. Arna Bontemps to Langston Hughes, 26 January 1941. Hughes papers.

12. Ed Aswell to Paul Reynolds, 15 August 1940. Harper & Brothers papers.

13. Paul R. Reynolds, Jr., *The Middle Man: The Adventures of a Literary Agent* (New York: William Morrow, 1972), pp. 133–34.

14. Richard Wright review of Carson McCullers's *The Heart Is a Lonely Hunter* in the *New Republic,* 5 August 1940, p. 195.

15. Richard Wright review in *Chicago Daily News,* 4 December 1940.

16. Privately, Wright could not forget that Du Bois had pressed blacks to fight in WWI, arguing that it would bring them full recognition in their own country. Wright saw it as "some of the most disgusting war propaganda released in America." Wright papers, box 6, folder 124.

17. *New Republic,* 24 October 1940, p. 600.

18. Ellen Wright interviewed by Constance Webb, September 1963. Webb papers.

19. Ellen Wright interviewed by Constance Webb, September 1963. Webb papers.

20. Isidor Poplowitz was born in Warsaw in 1870. He arrived in the U.S. on 18 March 1912. He had two children from his previous marriage: Max was fifteen and Lena was twelve when they immigrated to the U.S. with Isidor's ex-wife and her new husband in 1914. The two families lived in Brooklyn, but they had almost nothing to do with each other.

21. Rose Poplowitz (née Goldfarb) was born on 10 March 1887.

22. Author's interview with Ellen Wright, Paris, 17 June 1995.

23. Author's interview with Ellen Wright, Paris, 17 June 1995.

24. John Ehle, "Reflections on Paul Green," in *Paul Green's Celebration of Man* (Chapel Hill, NC: Human Technology Interface, 1994).

25. Richard Wright to Paul Green, 3 October 1940. Green papers.

26. John Houseman to Paul Green, 24 December 1940. Green papers.

27. John Houseman to Paul Green, 24 December 1940. Green papers.

28. Paul Reynolds to Richard Wright, 4 December 1940. Wright papers.

29. Paul Reynolds to Richard Wright, 4 December 1940. Wright papers.

30. It was 467 Waverly Avenue, off Fulton Street.

31. Harry Birdoff (husband of Berthe Hibble) in Ray and Farnsworth, eds., *Richard Wright: Impressions and Perspectives,* p. 81ff.

32. It was 411 Grand Avenue.

33. Helen Deaton (née Sattler) to author, 6 January 1999.

34. Richard Wright to Claude Barnett, 5 February 1941. Claude Barnett papers, Chicago Historical Society.

35. Claude Barnett to Richard Wright, 8 February 1941. Barnett papers.

36. Louise Rosskam in Nicholas Natanson, *The Black Image in the New Deal* (Knoxville: University of Tennessee Press, 1992), p. 244, n. 66.

37. The photographers included Walker Evans, Ben Shahn, Russell Lee, Dorothea Lange, Jack Delano, and Marian Post Wolcott.

38. Wright's use of "we" was a rhetorical ploy that irritated some readers. Nicholas Natanson argues that by blending twelve million black voices, Wright was "treating the black millions as a monolithic mass," just as whites always tended to do. See Natanson, *The Black Image in the New Deal,* p. 247. Natanson calls it "presumption" and a "fundamental act of cultural suppression."

39. Richard Wright to Paul Green, 3 February 1941. Green papers.

40. Richard Wright to Paul Green, 12 February 1941. Green papers.

41. Richard Wright to Claude Barnett, 5 February 1941. Barnett papers.

42. "Richard Wright Wins 1940 Spingarn Medal." Press release, 31 January 1941. Press Service of the National Association for the Advancement of Colored People. NAACP papers, Library of Congress.

43. "Dime a Dozen Awards," *Pittsburgh Courier,* 15 February 1941, pp. 1, 4.

44. Wright was sitting at the main table with Clifford Odets, Anna Louise Strong, Lillian Hellman, Dashiell Hammett, and others. Robert E. Elias described the scene to Dreiser biographer Thomas Riggio on 10 August 2000. Riggio private papers.

45. Ed Aswell to L. Arnold Weissberger, 31 March 1941. Harper & Brothers papers.

46. *New York Herald Tribune,* 30 March 1941.

47. Robert Francis, *Brooklyn Daily Eagle,* 8 June 1941.

48. See Jean Rosenthal, "Native Son—Backstage," *Theatre Arts* (June 1941): 467–70.

49. Harry Birdoff to Horace Cayton, 9 May 1960. Cayton papers.

50. John Houseman, *"Native Son* on Stage," in Ray and Farnsworth, eds., *Richard Wright: Impressions and Perspectives,* p. 97.

51. John (Jack) Berry interviewed by Patrick McGilligan, in *Tender Comrades: A Backstory of the Hollywood Blacklist,* eds. Patrick McGilligan and Paul Buhle (New York: St. Martin's Press, 1997), p. 64.

52. "Theatrical Folk Seem Queer to the Author of *Native Son.*" *New York World-Telegram,* 22 March 1941.

53. "Nothing Too Big For 'Bigger,'" article on Canada Lee in *Current Biography,* December 1944.

54. Paul Green to Paul Reynolds, 3 March 1941. Green papers.

55. Paul Green to Paul Reynolds, 10 March 1941. Green papers.

56. Western Union telegram, 12 March 1941. Green papers.

57. It was aired on radio, WNYC, 8 April 1941. See Curtis R. Scott, "The Dramatization of *Native Son," The Journal of American Drama and Theatre,* vol. 4, no. 3 (fall 1992).

58. I did not manage to find out where Wright filed for a divorce from Dhimah. It was not Manhattan, Brooklyn, or the Bronx. It was not Chapel Hill, North Carolina, or Greensboro, South Carolina, or Reno, Nevada. Ellen Wright claims not to know.

59. Wright would have heard from Ellen about the pass Ellison made at her in Washington and would certainly have seen this as a betrayal. This was likely to be one reason why he had distanced himself from Ellison.

60. *New York Amsterdam Star-News,* 22 March 1941, p. 11.

61. Houseman, *Unfinished Business,* pp. 233–34. Houseman uses his memoir to demolish Paul Green, Orson Welles, and various others—in the most urbane manner possible.

62. Paul Green interview with Jennie T. Hall.

63. Brooks Atkinson, *New York Times,* 25 March 1941.

64. Sidney B. Whipple, *New York World-Telegram,* 25 March 1941.

65. *New York Amsterdam Star-News,* 22 March 1941, p. 13.

66. Wolcott Gibbs, "Black Boy," *New Yorker,* 5 April 1941, pp. 33–34.

67. The retrospective entry is marked "March 13 to April 16."

68. Paul Green to Paul Reynolds, 4 April 1941. Wright papers.

69. Wright was disappointed and annoyed that only 15 percent of the audience was black. Among other strategies, he proposed a meeting with the theater editors of the three leading national black newspapers. His argument was to throw responsibility onto the black community. (Richard Wright, "Blueprint for an Emergency," Welles papers.)

70. Quoted by John Houseman in *"Native Son* on Stage," in Ray and Farnsworth, eds., *Richard Wright: Impressions and Perspectives,* pp. 89–100.

71. *Native Son* was the judges' third choice.

72. "The Pulitzer Prizes," *New Masses,* 13 May 1941, p. 21.

73. Paul Green to Paul Reynolds, 13 December 1942. Green papers.

14: THE WEATHERCOCK TURNS

1. Nothing had come of Hart Preston's photographs for *Life* the year before. The other new photo-documentary magazine, *Look,* had beaten *Life* to the draw, with a six-page photo spread of Harlem slums, called "244,000 Native Sons." (*Look,* May 1940.)

2. Edwin Rosskam interview with Richard K. Doud, 3 August 1965. Transcript at Archives of American Art, Washington, D.C. The photos are in the FSA collection at the Library of Congress. Several photos that are not included in *12 Million Black Voices* are in Nicholas Natanson's *The Black Image.*

3. Wright wrote an essay that was published two years later as a publicity brochure: "The Negro and Parkway Community House." (The center had changed its name.)

4. Wright would recollect the episode in his 1960 lecture: "The Position of the Negro Artist and Intellectual in American Society."

5. Billie Kyle Mitchell, "Chicago's Mayfair," *Pittsburgh Courier,* 19 April 1941.

6. Arna Bontemps to Langston Hughes, 21 April 1941. Nichols, ed., *Arna Bontemps–Langston Hughes Letters 1925–1967,* p. 80.

7. Claude Barnett to secretary of state, 10 April 1941. Barnett papers.

8. Richard Wright to Department of State, 13 May 1941. Wright papers.

9. R. B. Shipley, passport division, to Richard Wright, 24 June 1941. Wright papers.

10. *Philadelphia Record,* 11 May 1941.

11. Langston Hughes, on the other hand, well known for over a decade as a "fellow traveler," was being given a hard time. Without his permission, the *Saturday Evening Post* had reprinted "Goodbye Christ," an antireligious and pro-Communist poem Hughes had written in 1932. In an America now swell-chested with war patriotism, the poem was an embarrassment. Hughes, who already struggled to make a meager income as a black writer, defensively insisted that it no longer represented his views. The Party was calling him a turncoat and a renegade.

12. Abe Aaron to Richard Wright, 1 June 1941. Wright papers. Shortly after being a witness at Wright's marriage, Aaron had shocked Wright by voluntarily enlisting in the army.

13. Joyce Gourfain came to the congress. Her husband, Ed, stayed in Chicago, looking after the children. She was upset because Wright did not take her to see *Native Son.* In fact, he didn't see much of her at all. These few days were the last time she saw him. (Gourfain interview with Horace Cayton, 13 November 1968. Cayton papers.)

14. Frank Folsom, *Days of Anger* (Boulder, CO: University Press of Colorado, 1994), p. 226.

15. John Hammond to Michel Fabre, 24 December 1963. Fabre private papers.

16. Michel Gordey interview with Richard Wright, *Les Etoiles,* 22 October 1946. (See Keneth Kinnamon and Michel Fabre, eds., *Conversations with Richard Wright,* pp. 92–98.) A. Philip Randolph was awarded the Spingarn Medal the year after Wright, in 1942.

17. *Opportunity* was the National Urban League's magazine.

18. Spingarn Medal papers, Library of Congress.

19. Wright refers to his speech in untitled and undated notes about the Negro, the war, and the Communist Party (probably written in 1943 or 1944). Wright papers, box 87, folder 1023.

20. Ed Aswell to Richard Wright, 9 July 1941. Harper & Brothers papers.

21. "Memories of My Grandmother."

22. *New York World-Telegram.* Undated clipping in Herbert Newton's FBI file, opened February 1941. (Newton was arrested on 18 July 1941.) Courtesy Dolores Newton.

23. Beth McHenry, "Negro Leaders Hit Police Terror," *Daily Worker,* 9 November 1941.

24. See Michel Fabre, "From Tabloid to Myth: 'The Man Who Lived Underground,'" in Fabre, *The World of Richard Wright* (Jackson, MS: University Press of Mississippi, 1985), pp. 93–107.

25. Frederic Wertham to Richard Wright, 27 May 1942. Wright papers.

26. Richard Wright Introduction to Morris U. Schappes, *Letters from the Tombs* (New York: Schappes Defense Committee, 1941).

27. They stayed with Louis Shapiro, a Communist acquaintance, who had a cottage there. A wealthy art collector from Boston, he was a friend of Willard Maas and Marie Menken who admired Wright's work. Marie Menken joined them on the weekend.

28. Paul Reynolds to Richard Wright, 12 September 1941. Wright papers.

29. Howard Taubman, *New York Times,* 30 November 1941, sec. 9, p. 6.

30. Elliott Grennard, *New Masses,* 20 January 1941.

31. Leo J. Margolin, "Paroled Musician Enjoys the World After 19 years in New Jersey Prison," *PM,* 22 August 1941.

32. Jane Cabot, "Youth Makes Good Use of Time in Prison; Ready for Musical Career." *Journal & Guide* (Norfolk, Virginia), 2 August 1941, p. 14.

33. Dan Burley, "Dick Wright's Bigger Thomas Comes to Life in Clinton Brewer," *New York Amsterdam News,* 11 October 1941.

34. Richard Wright to Frederic Wertham, 24 October 1941 (quoted in Fabre, ed., *Richard Wright: Books and Writers,* p. 171.

35. Richard Wright to Willard Maas, 15 November 1941. Willard Maas papers.

36. Richard Wright journal, 7 January 1945. Wright papers.

37. Clair Goll, *Love Poems* (Brooklyn: Hemispheres, 1947). See Fabre, ed., *Richard Wright: Books and Writers,* p. 62.

38. Richard Wright journal, 25 March 1945. Wright papers.

39. "Ofay" is African-American slang for a white person.

40. Arna Bontemps to Langston Hughes, 5 November 1941. Nichols, ed., *Arna Bontemps–Langston Hughes Letters,* p. 94.

41. It was a boom time for photo-documentary books. One month earlier, *Let Us Now Praise Famous Men* was published, with photographs by Walker Evans and narrative (about poor, white Alabama sharecroppers) by James Agee. Because of the timing—more or less exactly when the U.S. declared war—sales were low (six hundred copies). When it was reissued in 1960, *Let Us Now Praise Famous Men* sold sixty thousand copies.

42. Nevertheless, a decade after *12 Million Black Voices,* J. Saunders Redding would begin his book *On Being Negro in America* by insisting that *his* book did not pretend to speak for others: "I remember my anger at the effrontery of one who a few years ago undertook to speak for me and twelve million others. I concurred with practically nothing he said." Saunders Redding was born into a middle-class black family in Delaware; his father worked in the postal service; his brother went to Harvard; he went to Brown University in Providence. Wright was not writing about privileged blacks like Redding.

43. *Sunday Worker,* 9 November 1941.

44. Beatrice M. Murphy, "Wright's new book biased, depressing," *Baltimore Afro-American,* 22 November 1941.

45. Ralph Thompson, *New York Times,* 18 November 1941, p. 29.

46. Willard Maas to Richard Wright, n.d. Wright papers.

47. Ralph Ellison to Richard Wright, 3 November 1941. Wright papers.

48. Gordon Parks, *Voices in the Mirror: An Autobiography* (New York: Doubleday, 1990).

49. *New Masses,* 16 December 1941.

50. Richard Wright to Joe Brown, 28 September 1940. *Letters to Joe C. Brown* (Kent, Ohio: Kent State University Libraries, 1968), p. 11.

51. Wright refers to the incident in his journal, 30 January 1945. Wright papers.

52. Richard Wright to Arthur Upham Pope, 21 December 1941; Richard Wright to Paul Green, 21 December 1941 (Green papers).

53. They were Guy Glover, Norman McLaren, and Ernest Borneman.

54. Ernest Borneman to Richard Wright, 10 February 1942. Wright papers.

55. Richard Wright to John Grierson, n.d. [1942]. Wright papers.

56. Richard Wright journal, 21 January 1945. Wright papers. (Wright quotes Grierson's statement, made years earlier.)

57. Richard Wright to Paul Reynolds, April 1941. Wright papers.

58. Ralph Ellison to Kerker Quinn, 29 May 1942. Ellison papers.

59. Undated memorandum from Edwin Seaver to Harry Scherman. Wright papers.

60. See 20 October 1942 issue of *New Masses* devoted to Negroes and the war.

61. Ellen Wright interview with Constance Webb, September 1963. Webb papers. New American Communist Party materials at the Library of Congress show that the Wrights were quite right: oppressed Negroes were important to the Party and targeted as recruits. And yet the Party did almost nothing for them during the war.

62. Wright's FBI file.

63. Paul Reynolds to Richard Wright, 13 April 1942. Wright papers.

15: WARTIME BROOKLYN

1. Ellen Wright interview with Constance Webb, September 1963. Webb papers. The details in the next two paragraphs are also taken from this interview.

2. Benjamin Appel, in Ray and Farnsworth, eds., *Richard Wright: Impressions and Perspectives,* p. 76.

3. Ellen Wright interview with Constance Webb, September 1963. Webb papers.

4. Louise Rosskam, phone conversation with author, 10 March 1999. She and Ed had left Washington and were living at the time in Greenwich Village.

5. C. L. R. James was author of *The Black Jacobins* (1938), about Toussaint-Louverture, who led a successful Haitian slave revolt against the French military forces.

6. The following description comes from an unpublished draft Constance Webb originally intended to be the introduction to her 1968 biography of Wright. (Constance Webb private papers.)

7. Benjamin Appel, in Ray and Farnsworth, eds., *Richard Wright: Impressions and Perspectives,* pp. 75–76.

8. *The Diary of Anaïs Nin, 1939–1944,* vol. 3 (New York: Harcourt Brace & World, 1969), p. 281. The poet Paul Muldoon (a friend of Davis's) refers to the incident in his poem "Carson" in *Meeting the British* (London: Faber & Faber, 1987). "When the Richard Wrights moved in the super/moved out, unwilling, it seemed to draw and hew/and tend the furnace for fellow Negroes."

9. A few months later, the story was selected for *O'Henry Award Prize Stories of 1940* (Harry Hansen, ed., [New York: Doubleday, 1940]).

10. George Davis to Richard Wright, 3 October 1940. *Harper's Bazaar* file, Wright papers.

11. Davis's novel, *The Opening of a Door,* set in Paris, was published by Harper & Brothers in 1931.

12. Truman Capote, "A House on the Heights" (1959), *A Capote Reader* (New York: Random House, 1987), pp. 597–99.

13. *The Diary of Anaïs Nin,* vol. 3, p. 270.

14. Gypsy Rose Lee was in her late twenties at the time. A famous stripper in the 1930s and 1940s, she was one of the first to make stripping into an art form, perfecting the aspect of "teasing."

15. Other fleeting residents had been Paul and Jane Bowles, Benjamin Britten, and Golo Mann, the youngest son of Thomas Mann. Some of these connections

came through Auden, a homosexual himself, who had married Golo's sister Erika Mann in 1936 so that she could get a British passport and leave Germany. Auden had made a documentary with music by Benjamin Britten.

16. Langston Hughes, at Yaddo that year, told Arna Bontemps she was "about the most anti-cracker cracker you ever saw." (Langston Hughes to Arna Bontemps, n.d. [August 1942], Nichols, ed., *Arna Bontemps Langston Hughes Letters 1925–1967*, p. 109.)

17. *The Diary of Anaïs Nin*, vol. 3, p. 279.

18. In 1951, after Kurt Weill died prematurely of a heart attack, George Davis would marry the bereft Lotte. It was a companionable marriage, not romantic. Davis continued to have affairs with men. In 1957, aged fifty-one, he, too, died of a heart attack.

19. See Fabre, *Richard Wright: Books and Writers,* p. 101.

20. *The Diary of Anaïs Nin,* vol. 3, p. 279–81.

21. *The Diary of Anaïs Nin,* vol. 3, p. 283. Nin inscribed Wright's copy of her 1939 novel *Winter of Artifice:* "For Ellen and Richard Wright, with gratitude for being initiated by 'Native Son' to the deepest, most tragic and most lovable people of America. Anaïs Nin." (Fabre, *Richard Wright: Books and Writers,* p. 117.)

22. Author's interview with Naomi Replansky, New York, 28 March 1999.

23. *The Diary of Anaïs Nin,* vol. 3, p. 279.

24. *The Diary of Anaïs Nin, 1947–1955,* vol. 5 (New York: Harcourt Brace Jovanovich, 1974), p. 206.

25. *The Diary of Anaïs Nin,* vol. 3, p. 281.

26. Helen R. Crawford to Mrs. Franklin D. Roosevelt, 5 July 1942. Wright papers, box 105, folder 1582.

27. Helen Crawford told Mrs. Roosevelt that her twenty-three-year-old son had almost finished his Ph.D. at M.I.T., but insisted he could not remain in an ivory tower while the rest of the world was dying in a desperate struggle with the fascists, and he was now with an engineering corps in Virginia. She herself was an air-raid warden in Brooklyn. Her husband, a copyreader at the *New York Times,* was helping with a war-bond drive.

28. Wright seemed to think Becky Crawford's letter was responsible. On 7 August 1942, he wrote to Aswell: "The story of me and my draft board is something which I'll have to relate to you in person sometime. It involves an ironic comment upon the democratic process: when a guy's neighbor is allowed to decide if he is to go into the army or not, strange things happen. If the guy happens to be a Negro writer of strange views, then stranger things happen. But I'm hoping to resolve things eventually." Wright papers.

29. Reynolds, *The Middle Man: The Adventures of a Literary Agent,* p. 117ff.

30. Horace Cayton to Truman K. Gibson, 9 July 1942. Wright papers.

31. "Alas, My Old Favorite Brooklyn Barbershop." Unpublished essay. Wright papers.

32. Chandler Owen, *Negroes and the War* (Washington, D.C.: Office of War Information, 1942).

33. The letter, dated 13 October 1942, is included in Richard Wright's FBI file.

34. 8 December 1942, Wright's FBI file.

35. Robert A. Hill, ed., *The FBI's RACON* (Boston: Northeastern University Press, 1995), p. 75.

36. Naomi Replansky, "Even the Walls Have Ears," in Replansky, *The Dangerous World* (Chicago: Another Chicago Press, 1994).

37. Richard Wright journal, 7 January 1945. Wright papers.

38. Undated note. Wright papers. (Another letter to Dick and Ellen, signed "love Naomi," is dated July 1943. She had just moved to Greenwich Village.)

39. Author's interview with Naomi Replansky, New York, 30 December 1997.

40. Ed Aswell to Richard Wright, 30 March 1943. Harper & Brothers papers.

41. Horace Cayton to Richard Wright, 26 March 1942. Wright papers.

42. Horace R. Cayton, *Long Old Road* (New York: Trident Press, 1965), p. 234.

43. Horace Cayton, "The Curtain," *Negro Digest* (December 1968). The story in the following paragraphs is also taken from this short memoir.

44. *The Autobiography of W. E. B. Du Bois* (New York: International Publishers, 1968), p. 121.

45. Horace Cayton interview with Joyce Cooper Arkhurst, Chicago, 3 December 1968. Cayton papers.

46. "Richard Wright Describes the Birth of 'Black Boy,'" *New York Post,* 30 November 1944, B6.

47. Charles S. Johnson to Richard Wright, 22 April 1943. Wright papers.

48. Telegram sent 12 April 1943 from Chicago. Wright papers.

49. "Richard Wright describes the birth of 'Black Boy,'" *New York Post,* 30 November 1944, B6.

50. Unpublished notes on the genesis of *Black Boy,* undated. Wright papers, box 15, folder 262.

51. See Robin D. G. Kelley, *Race Rebels: Culture, Politics, and the Black Working Class* (New York: Macmillan and Free Press, 1994).

52. Mark Schubart, "Richard Wright Feels Grip of Harlem Tension," *PM,* 3 August 1943, p. 8.

53. Author's conversation with Sol and Frieda Rabkin, Brooklyn Heights, 27 December 1997.

54. A close friend of both Wright's and George Davis's, Willard Maas had the same proclivities, though in his case he did the beating up. He and Marie Menken, the filmmaker, lived nearby, on Montague Street. Somehow their marriage had survived Willard's endless succession of sadomasochistic relationships with men. In 1943–44 he and Menken were working together on a documentary film, *Geography of the Body,* which set close-ups of naked male bodies to poems by Willard's lover of the time, the British poet George Barker.

55. Richard Wright journal, 14 August 1947. Wright papers. This was written three years later, in Paris, but Wright's wariness does not appear to be new.

56. William Gardner Smith, "Black Boy in Brooklyn," *Ebony* (November 1945): 26–27.

16: A TROUBLINGLY DELICATE MATTER

1. Paul Reynolds to Ed Aswell, 27 December 1943. Harper & Brothers papers.

2. Reynolds asked Aswell to send a check immediately for a thousand dollars so that Wright could include it in the current financial year. With the royalties for *Black Boy,* Reynolds came up with an income-spreading arrangement, whereby Harper would pay Wright royalties in payouts of five hundred dollars a month, beginning the month after publication.

3. Richard Wright to Ed Aswell, 14 January 1944. Harper & Brothers papers.

4. Harriet F. Pimple from Greenbaum, Wolff & Ernst to Edward Aswell, 10 March 1944. Harper & Brothers papers.

5. This typed statement among Wright's papers does not have a date (box 87, folder 1032). It may have been written earlier, or later. But since Wright mentions induction it is likely to have been at this time. Such a statement was not entirely unusual among black intellectuals. Langston Hughes wrote on his registration form. "I use this opportunity to regret as a citizen of the United States the dissolving of the brigade of the armed forces of the United States into white and Negro units thereby making colored citizens the only group so singled out for Jim Crow treatment, which seems to me contrary to the letter and spirit of the constitution and dangerous to the moral [sic] and well being of not only the colored citizens of this country but those of our darker allies as well." (This is quoted in Hughes's FBI file.)

6. Malcolm X, eighteen in 1943, writes about the mentally deranged performance he put on in order to get a 4F classification. It worked. A 4F card came to him in the mail. (*The Autobiography of Malcolm X as Told to Alex Haley* [New York: Ballantine Books, 1964], p. 121ff.)

7. New York FBI report, 8 July 1944. It's possible that Wright's friend Frederic Wertham was willing to reinforce this verdict. Wertham's literary executor would not permit me to see Wright's correspondence to Wertham in the Wertham papers at the Library of Congress.

8. Louis M. Starr interview with Dorothy Canfield Fisher, 1956. Oral History Collection, Butler Library, Columbia University.

9. The deleted passage was a conversation that took place in Jackson between Wright and his white employer:

"Richard, how long is your thing?" he asked me.

"What thing?" I asked.

"You know what I mean," he said. "The thing the bull uses on the cow."

I turned away from him; I had heard that whites regarded negroes as animals in sex matters and his words made me angry.

"I heard that a nigger can stick his prick in the ground and spin around on it like a top," he said, chuckling. "I'd like to see you do that. I'd give you a dime, if you did it." (Early draft. Wright papers.)

10. In fact, the Chicago section was not published in book form during Wright's lifetime. In 1977, long after Aswell's and Wright's deaths, Harper & Row published the Chicago section under the title *American Hunger*. In 1991 the Library of America published the whole book—"Southern Night" and "The Horror and the Glory"—under the title *Black Boy*. This was finally the book as Wright intended it. What is not yet clear is which version publishers will choose in the future.

11. Richard Wright to Ed Aswell, 25 June 1944. Harper & Brothers papers.

12. Dorothy Canfield Fisher to Richard Wright, 29 June 1944. Canfield Fisher papers.

13. Richard Wright to Dorothy Canfield Fisher, 6 July 1944. Wright papers.

14. Dorothy Canfield Fisher to Richard Wright, 12 July 1944. *Keeping Fires Night and Day: Selected Letters of Dorothy Canfield Fisher,* Mark J. Madigan, ed. (Columbia, MO: University of Missouri Press, 1993), pp. 234–35.

On the same day, she told Aswell: "As far as the Book-of-the-Month Club judges go, I'm sure they never would dream of making any difficulties about the book as it now stands, for it certainly is excellent. I have ventured once more to re-state my case, to re-explain my idea that it would add greatly to the maturity of his book if [Mr. Wright] puts in it only two or three words acknowledging the existence of Americans who have other ideas about racial discrimination than those of the South. . . . I'm so eager for American Negroes to make the very best showing that they possibly can, I had hoped that he might feel capable of adding this one, round-ing-out note. But it's no matter if he doesn't." (Did Aswell pass this news on to Wright?)

15. Richard Wright to Ed Aswell, 20 July 1944. Harper & Brothers papers.

16. Richard Wright to Dorothy Canfield Fisher, 20 July 1944. Canfield Fisher papers.

17. Dorothy Canfield Fisher to Richard Wright, 23 July 1944. Mark J. Madigan, ed., *Keeping Fires Night and Day.*

18. Ed Aswell to Dorothy Canfield Fisher, 24 July 1944. Harper & Brothers papers.

19. Dorothy Canfield Fisher to Ed Aswell, 24 July 1944. Harper & Brothers papers.

20. Richard Wright to Ed Aswell, 10 August 1944. Harper & Brothers papers.

21. Wright told Aswell he thought the title "autobiography" said too much. Richard Wright to Ed Aswell, August 1944. Harper & Brothers papers.

22. Editor Edward Weeks paid him six hundred dollars for the essay.

23. "Negro Author Criticizes Reds as Intolerant," *New York Herald Tribune,* 28 July 1944, p. 11.

24. In April 2000, the FBI's Departmental Review Committee released to me thirty-nine newly declassified pages of Richard Wright's file. On 8 August 1944, Spe-cial Agent E. E. Conroy, from the New York office, transmitted a document with a taped phone conversation to Hoover, in Washington. The conversation occurred at 2:10 P.M. on 28 July 1944. On my declassified copy, Ben Davis's comments are repro-duced in full; his respondent's replies are completely blocked out. The two Commu-nists were worried about Wright's forthcoming essay in the *Atlantic Monthly,* which they hadn't yet seen. About Wright, Davis told his friend: "I regard him as a casualty of the struggle for Negro rights. . . . To enter into a polemic with this guy is simply going to prolong that period during which they are going to try and exploit every-thing he can say against the Communists."

25. Benjamin J. Davis, *Daily Worker,* 6 August 1944.

26. Horace Cayton, "The Communists," *Pittsburgh Courier,* 26 August 1944, p. 7.

27. Benjamin J. Davis, "What Makes Mr. Cayton Tick," *Daily Worker,* 3 Septem-ber 1944.

28. Notable predecessors were Fred Beal's essay "I Was a Communist Martyr," which appeared in *American Mercury* in September 1937, and Benjamin Gitlow's memoir, *I Confess: The Truth about American Communism,* published in 1940.

29. Ted Ward to Ken Kinnamon, 8 July 1965. Kinnamon private papers.

30. Richard Wright to Ralph Ellison, 1 September 1944. Ellison papers.

31. Richard Wright to Frieda Lewis, Canada, 24 July 1944. Wright papers.

32. Richard Wright to Ellison, n.d. Ellison papers.

33. Ed Aswell to Richard Wright, 28 August 1944. Harper & Brothers papers.

34. Richard Wright to Dorothy Canfield Fisher, 1 September 1944. Canfield Fisher papers.

35. Robert Minor, "Mr. Wright Didn't Discover It," *Daily Worker,* 15 August 1944.

36. James Ford, "A Disservice to the Negro People," *Daily Worker,* 5 September 1944, p. 6.

37. James Farrell to Richard Wright, 31 July 1944. Wright papers.

38. George S. Schuyler, "Views and Reviews," *Pittsburgh Courier,* 12 August 1944, sec. 2, p. 7.

39. Richard Wright to Ralph Ellison, 1 September 1944. Ellison papers.

40. Langston Hughes had just been added to the Security Index, no doubt because of his vocal attacks on segregation in the armed forces.

41. J. Edgar Hoover to Special-Agent-in-Charge, New York, 4 August 1944. Wright's FBI file.

42. Richard Wright to Ed Aswell, 27 November 1944. Harper & Brothers papers.

43. Ed Aswell to Richard Wright, 6 December 1944. Harper & Brothers papers.

44. Wright's income for 1944 was thirty-eight hundred dollars. In 1945, with sales of *Black Boy* and foreign royalties on *Native Son,* Reynolds anticipated that it would be around fifteen thousand dollars. It was surely much higher.

45. Richard Wright journal, 18 January 1945. Wright papers.

46. Michael Carter's real name was Milton A. Smith. He later went back to this name.

47. Richard Wright journal, 1 January 1945. Wright papers.

17: DAILY LIFE

1. Other contributors they hoped to get were the Trotskyist writer C. L. R. James, the Chicago sociologist E. Franklin Frazier, and J. Saunders Redding, writer and literary critic. The University of North Carolina Press had just published a series of essays by black intellectuals called *What the Negro Wants.* The publisher was a conservative white Southerner named W. T. Couch, who had also written an insulting, racist introduction. This book was partly conceived as a response to Couch's book. But the project was dropped.

2. Cayton was having analysis four times a week at the time.

3. The Lafargue Clinic was opened in March 1946 in a Harlem parish house basement. Wright wrote about it in "Psychiatry Comes to Harlem," *Free World* (an international magazine for the United Nations), vol. 12 (September 1946). Wertham (born Wertheimer) came to the U.S. in 1922 and taught psychiatry for seven years at Johns Hopkins University in Baltimore, where he became a friend of Clarence Darrow. Wertham was the only psychiatrist Darrow could find to testify in Negro court cases. In 1932 Wertham came to New York, to the Bellevue Mental Hospital. In 1945–46 Wright would sometimes visit Frederic and Florence Wertham in their Gramercy Park home. Wertham was associated with the Party.

4. Ethol Sexton Kossa was another writer he helped promote.

5. The middleman proved unreliable, and Wright eased himself out of the project.

6. Marshall Field also made money from real estate. It is possible that Wright had him in mind when he created Mr. Dalton, in *Native Son.*

7. Richard Wright journal, 17 January 1945. Wright papers.

8. *Negro Digest* to Richard Wright, 11 January 1945. Wright papers.

9. See Kathryn Talalay, *Composition in Black and White: The Life of Philippa Schuyler* (New York: Oxford University Press, 1996). There is a complete draft of

Sacrifice among Wright's papers at Yale. It was never published—probably because the play would have been highly libelous. Strangely, Wright almost predicted the Schuylers' plight. Philippa Schuyler was killed in a tragic accident, and two years later, her mother committed suicide.

10. Horace Cayton to Richard Wright, 6 June 1945. Wright papers.

11. Letter written on 5 March 1945. Wright papers.

12. W. E. B. Du Bois, "Richard Wright Looks Back," *New York Herald Tribune,* Weekly Book Review, 4 March 1945, p. 2.

Wright struck back in the *Afro-American.* "It is obvious that Du Bois is a nineteenth century idealist. . . . Since Du Bois is a sociologist, the things described by me should be well known to him. I wonder what he has been teaching his pupils for all these years." (Michael Carter, "Richard Wright Talks to the AFRO," *Afro-American,* 24 March 1945.)

13. Horace Cayton, "Frightened Children of Frightened Parents," *Twice a Year,* 12–13 (spring–summer/fall–winter 1945): 262–69.

14. Wright read his friend's essay that summer. "It is the best writing you've done to date," he told Ellison. "I'd say that if your novel does not pan out as you plan it, then switch without blinking to non-fiction and go to town. I don't think I've read any sharper non-fiction prose by a Negro." He had only one objection to the essay. It was the suggestion that he had been influenced by the blues. It was not because it was "a Negro expression form" that he objected. He simply did not think it had played much of a role. (Richard Wright to Ralph Ellison, 25 July 1945. Ellison papers.)

15. Richard Wright to Gertrude Stein, 27 May 1945. Stein papers, Beinecke Library, Yale University.

16. See also: Franklin Folsom, *Days of Anger, Days of Hope* (Boulder, CO: University Press of Colorado, 1994), pp. 253–54.

18: PREPARING TO LEAVE

1. In mid-February 1945 Wright had gone to a writers' group meeting in Greenwich Village. A young woman in the group, Esther Carlson, told him about Jimmy Baldwin, who had come to a meeting and read a chapter from his novel, *Crying Holy.* Wright said he would like to meet him. (Lesley Conger, "Jimmy on East 15th Street," *African American Review,* vol. 29, no. 4 [1995]: 557–66.) It seems that Esther Carlson went with him to Wright's, though Baldwin leaves her out of his account of the meeting.

2. See Julius Lester, "James Baldwin—Reflections of a Maverick," *New York Times Book Review,* 27 May 1984, pp. 1, 22–24 (reprinted in Standley and Pratt, eds., *Conversations with James Baldwin*); and James Baldwin, "Alas, Poor Richard," in Baldwin, *Nobody Knows My Name* (1961; reprint, New York: Vintage International, 1993).

3. Baldwin, "Alas, Poor Richard."

4. James Baldwin to Richard Wright, 27 December 1945. Wright papers.

5. Esther Carlson to Richard Wright, 18 May 1946. Wright papers.

6. Wright met Ollie Harrington at the same party, in December 1944. Hughes was living with his aunt, Toy Harper, in Sugar Hill.

7. Richard Wright, "Two Novels of the Crushing of Men, One White, One Black," *PM,* 25 November, 1945, pp. m7–m8.

8. Undated letter [1945]. Wright papers.

9. Gwendolyn Brooks to Richard Wright, 25 February 1945. Wright papers.

10. Richard Wright to Ed Aswell, 18 September 1944. Harper & Brothers papers.

11. Richard Wright to Ida Guggenheim, 3 July 1945. Guggenheim papers, Schomburg Center, New York.

12. Richard Wright to Ida Guggenheim, 20 July 1945. Guggenheim papers. Wright was not alone to make this type of comment about Ben Davis and James Ford. In *Being Red,* Howard Fast calls Davis a "rigid Leninist." Ben Gitlow, an ex-Communist of undisputed integrity, knew Ford in the Soviet Union. He commented: "He had . . . a canny ability to take advantage of situations that had to do with his own advancement. . . . His rise to Communist fame and high position has been rapid. I doubt that he ever had an independent thought. Yet Ford is paraded not only in the United States, but throughout the world, as the outstanding champion for the *liberation* of the Negro people." (Gitlow, *I Confess: The Truth about American Communism* [New York: E. P. Dutton, 1940], pp. 454–56.)

13. Richard Wright to Carl Van Vechten, July 1945. Van Vechten papers, Beinecke Library, Yale University.

14. Richard Wright to Carl Van Vechten, July 1945. Van Vechten papers.

15. The quotes from the court records are taken from Michel Fabre's essay " 'The Man Who Killed a Shadow': A Study in Compulsion," which examines the source material in detail. Michel Fabre, *The World of Richard Wright* (Jackson, MS: University Press of Mississippi, 1985), pp. 108–21.

16. Several years later, in 1953, Wright would give the name "Houston" to the white district attorney in *The Outsider,* the only admirable man in the novel. It was a small tribute to the great black civil rights lawyer Charles Hamilton Houston, who died in 1950, aged fifty-four.

17. Joe Brown to Richard Wright, 25 June 1945. Wright papers.

18. Richard Wright to Joe Brown, 9 August 1945. *Letters to Joe C. Brown* (Kent, OH: Kent State University Libraries, 1968), p. 15.

19. In his 1946 reelection campaign, Senator Bilbo would argue: "Do not let a single nigger vote. If you let a few register and vote this year, next year there will be twice as many, and the first thing you know the whole thing will be out of hand." (James W. Loewen and Charles Sallis, eds., *Mississippi: Conflict & Change* [New York: Pantheon Books, 1974], p. 239.)

20. *Congressional Record,* 91, pt. 5, 27 June 1945.

21. Dorothy Norman published the article in *Twice a Year* (fall–winter 1946–47). (Richard Wright, "Urban Misery in an American City: Juvenile Delinquency in Harlem.")

22. St. Clair Drake, however, was critical. His introduction to the 1962 revised edition reveals that he had strong reservations about Wright's essay. "Here is Richard Wright at his provocative and challenging best, deliberately picking the words he knows will hurt and propounding ideas certain to shock his readers, while taking full advantage of the artist's prerogative to overstate his case. He was, undoubtedly, deriving immense satisfaction from wielding the verbal sledge-hammer and twisting the literary stiletto."

23. Richard Wright to Ida Guggenheim, 20 July 1945. Guggenheim papers.

24. Richard Wright to Ralph Ellison, 11 August 1945. Ellison papers.

25. Richard Wright to Ed Aswell, 12 August 1945. Harper & Brothers papers.

26. Richard Wright to Ralph Ellison, 11 August 1945. Ellison papers.

27. Ralph Ellison, "Richard Wright's Blues," *Antioch Review* (summer 1945).

28. Richard Wright journal, 12 February 1945. Wright papers.

29. Richard Wright journal, 17 January 1945. Wright papers.

30. Bill Targ at World Publishing also lived in the Village. He and Wright became friends.

31. Paul Reynolds to Richard Wright, 21 August 1945. Wright papers.

32. Richard Wright to Mr. Scanton, 15 June 1946. Fabre private papers.

33. Julia Wright to Richard Wright, Wright papers, box 108, folder 1698. The letter is undated, but was almost certainly written while Wright was on this tour.

34. Cayton, *Long Old Road,* pp. 262–63.

35. Paul Reynolds to Richard Wright, 29 November 1945. Wright papers.

36. Richard Wright to Carl Van Vechten, 20 December 1945. Van Vechten papers.

37. Richard Wright journal, 28 January 1945. Wright papers.

38. Carl Van Vechten to Gertrude Stein, March 1945. Donald Gallup, ed., *Flowers of Friendship: The Letters of Gertrude Stein and Carl Van Vechten 1913–1946* (New York: Columbia University Press, 1986), p. 768.

39. Gertrude Stein to Carl Van Vechten, 2 May 1945, Gallup, ed., *Flowers of Friendship,* p. 771.

40. Gertrude Stein to Richard Wright, 22 April 1945. Oddly, there is no copy among Wright's papers. (Ellen Wright believes the Stein letters were stolen from her before she sold Wright's papers to Yale.) Wright copied the letter for Dorothy Norman, and this copy is among Norman's papers at the Beinecke Library.

41. Richard Wright to Gertrude Stein, 27 May 1945. Stein papers, Beinecke Library.

42. Richard Wright to Gertrude Stein, 29 October 1945. Stein papers.

43. *Chicago Defender,* 27 October 1945, p. 11.

44. William Faulkner to Richard Wright, Tuesday, undated [probably September 1945]. Wright papers. Also in Joseph Blotner, *Selected Letters of William Faulkner* (London: Scolar Press, 1977).

45. Leon Wright to Constance Webb, 16 January 1967. Webb papers.

46. Leon Wright to Constance Webb, 4 February 1967. Webb papers.

47. Quoted in Michel Fabre, "Paris as a Moment in Consciousness," *The Black Columbiad,* eds. Werner Sollors and Maria Diedrich (Cambridge: Harvard University Press, 1994), p. 125. Countee Cullen died in January 1946 at the age of forty-two. Wright was a pallbearer at his huge funeral in Harlem.

48. James Baldwin, *Just above My Head* (New York: Dial, 1979), p. 468. Quoted by Fabre, "Paris as a Moment in Consciousness."

49. Richard Wright to Gertrude Stein, 28 March 1946. Stein papers.

50. Sartre, "Ce que j'ai appris du problème noir," *Le Figaro,* 16 June 1945.

51. Author's phone interview with Lionel Abel, New York, 29 August 1997.

52. Richard Wright to Gertrude Stein, 28 March 1946. Stein papers.

53. Richard Wright to Gertrude Stein, 28 March 1946. Stein papers.

54. The interview, which took place in March or April, was published several months later in *Les Etoiles,* 22 October 1946. (See Kinnamon and Fabre, eds., *Conversations with Richard Wright,* pp. 92–98.) Gordey's real name was Michel Rappaport. He was to interview Wright again in Paris. They would remain friends over the years in Europe.

55. Complete interview is translated by Michel Fabre in Kinnamon and Fabre, eds., *Conversations with Richard Wright.*

19: CROSSING THE ATLANTIC

1. Richard Wright, "I Choose Exile." Unpublished, undated essay written in 1950. Wright papers.

2. Richard Wright to Dorothy Norman, 4 April 1946. Norman papers, Beinecke Library, Yale University.

3. Richard Wright to Ralph Ellison, 4 May 1946. Ellison papers.

A female French passenger was horrified by the racist attitude of the Americans on board, and commented that when Wright sat down in the smoking room, several people near him would ostentatiously get up and leave. (Aline Caro-Delvaille, L'Amérique sans Hollywood [Paris: Editions Emile-Paul Frères, 1949], p. 179.)

4. Janet Flanner, 22 May 1946. Paris Journal 1944–1955 (New York: Harcourt Brace Jovanovich), p. 56.

5. Richard Wright to Gertrude Stein, 28 March 1946. Stein papers.

6. Richard Wright to Dorothy Norman, 12 May 1946. Norman papers.

7. Maurice Nadeau, "There's No Black Problem in the USA, but a White Problem, the Black Writer Richard Wright Tells Us," Combat, 11 May 1946, p. 1. (Kinnamon and Fabre, eds., Conversations with Richard Wright, pp. 87–89.)

8. Douglas Schneider, France–Etats Unis (December 1960). (See Fabre, Unfinished Quest, p. 302.)

9. Richard Wright to Roger Pippett, 13 July 1946, in PM, 26 July 1946, pp. 15–16.

10. Richard Wright to Dorothy Norman, 23 July 1946. Norman papers.

11. Le Courrier de l'Etudiant, 15 May 1946.

12. Richard Wright to Dorothy Norman, 23 July 1946. Norman papers.

13. This story is taken from an article Wright wrote that was translated into French for a French newspaper. Richard Wright, "A Paris les GI Noirs ont appris à connaître et à aimer la liberté" [In Paris, black GIs have learned to know and like freedom], Samedi Soir, 25 May 1946, p. 2. Unpublished in English.

14. Richard Wright to Dorothy Norman, 12 May 1946. Norman papers.

15. Simone de Beauvoir, Force of Circumstance (New York: G. P. Putnam's Sons, 1964), p. 17.

16. Simone de Beauvoir, "An American Renaissance in France," New York Times Book Review, 22 June 1947, pp. 7, 29. Les Temps Modernes would publish Wright regularly over the next few years. In addition, Sartre referred to Wright in his essays "Portrait of the Anti-Semite" and "What Is Literature?" De Beauvoir, in America Day by Day, painted a vivid picture of Richard Wright and his family in New York. In The Second Sex (Paris: Gallimard, 1949), she made several allusions to Wright's work.

17. De Beauvoir, Force of Circumstance, p. 82.

18. Richard Wright, "There's Always Another Café," The Kiosk (Paris), no. 10 (1953): 12–14.

19. These are actually Fishbelly's reflections in Wright's unpublished novel Island of Hallucination.

20. Richard Wright to Dorothy Norman, 13 September 1946. Norman papers.

21. The GI Bill paid them twenty-two thousand to thirty-six thousand francs a month.

22. See James Baldwin, "Encounter on the Seine: Black Meets Brown" (1950), Notes of a Native Son (1955; reprint, Boston, MA: Beacon, 1984).

23. Richard Wright to Ida Guggenheim, 6 June 1946. Guggenheim papers.

24. Other receptions were held by the *Société des Gens des Lettres,* Pen Club, and the Ministry of Foreign Affairs.

25. Richard Wright, "I Choose Exile." Unpublished, undated essay. Wright papers.

26. Richard Wright to Dorothy Norman, 26 August 1946. Norman, *Encounters: A Memoir,* p. 199.

27. "Entravista con Richard Wright," *Revista Branca* (Buenos Aires), 1960. See Fabre, *Richard Wright: Books and Writers,* p. 141.

28. Richard Wright, "A Paris les GI Noirs ont appris à connaître et à aimer la liberté," *Samedi Soir,* 25 May 1946, p. 2.

29. *Paris Matin,* 27 June–2 July 1946. The essay did not come out in English until November that year in *True Magazine.*

30. Gertrude Stein to Carl Van Vechten, 14 May 1946. Gallup, ed., *Flowers of Friendship,* pp. 820–21.

31. Gertrude Stein to Carl Van Vechten, 14 June 1946. Gallup, ed., *Flowers of Friendship,* pp. 822–23.

32. This is how Wright described Stein to Dorothy Norman after three days (12 May 1946). Norman papers.

33. Ben Burns, *Nitty Gritty* (Jackson, MS: University Press of Mississippi, 1945), p. 77ff. The quotations in the next three paragraphs come from this book.

34. Gertrude Stein to Carl Van Vechten, 27 June 1946. Gallup, ed., *Flowers of Friendship,* p. 827.

35. "American GIs' Fears Worry Gertrude Stein," *PM,* 26 July 1946.

36. Richard Wright to Dorothy Norman, 31 July 1946. Norman papers.

37. Richard Wright to Dorothy Norman, 23 July 1946. Norman papers. Details of the icebox story are taken from this letter.

38. Richard Wright to Dorothy Norman, 23 July 1946. Norman papers.

39. For a detailed account of Stein's complicity with Faÿ, see appendix IX in Edward Burns and Ulla E. Dydo with William Rice, eds., *The Letters of Gertrude Stein and Thornton Wilder* (New Haven: Yale University Press, 1996), pp. 401–21.

40. Richard Wright to Dorothy Norman, 31 July 1946. Norman papers. The quotations in the following two paragraphs are from this letter.

41. In October Ellen Wright would write Blake a note, requesting their money back. His reply read: "Mr. Wright, If I see your wife or any of your relations anywhere near my place, I know perfectly well what I have to do. . . . I will not tolerate blackmail from Mrs. Wright." Another threatening letter followed, giving his lawyer's address. Wright papers.

42. Richard Wright to Ralph Ellison, 6 June 1946. Ellison papers.

43. The term is Joseph Barry's: *The People of Paris* (New York: Doubleday, 1966), p. 125.

44. Richard Wright to Owen Dodson, 9 June 1946. (See Ray and Farnsworth, eds., *Richard Wright: Impressions and Perspectives,* pp. 140–42.) Wright had not let the French government pay his first month's expenses after all. He had understood that Lévi-Strauss's kind offer (from the French embassy in New York) was basically to impress the U.S. State Department that Wright's invitation to France was formal and "official."

45. Richard Wright to Dorothy Norman, 23 July 1946. Norman papers.

46. Richard Wright, "Reactions to the script of *La Putain Respectueuse*." Wright papers.

47. Richard Wright to Dorothy Norman, 30 September 1946. Norman papers.

48. Richard Wright to Dorothy Norman, 30 September 1946. Norman papers.

49. Naomi Replansky to Richard Wright, 18 June 1946. Wright papers.

50. Ralph Ellison to Richard Wright, 23 September 1946. Wright papers.

51. Horace Cayton to Richard Wright, 11 October 1946. Wright papers.

52. Richard Wright to Dorothy Norman, 31 December 1946. Norman papers.

53. Richard Wright journal, 18 August 1947. Wright papers.

54. Raphael Tardon, "Richard Wright Tells Us: The White Problem in the United States," *Action,* 24 October 1946, pp. 10–11. (Kinnamon and Fabre, eds., *Conversations with Richard Wright,* pp. 99–105.)

20: EXPATRIATES

1. *PM's Sunday Picture News,* 16 February 1947, pp. m5–6. (See Kinnamon and Fabre, eds., *Conversations with Richard Wright.*)

2. Richard Wright to Jacob A. Salzmann, 14 February 1947. Wright papers.

3. Taken from various 1947 interviews in Kinnamon and Fabre, eds., *Conversations with Richard Wright.*

4. Webb had meanwhile married C. L. R. James, but the FBI was tailing James, and the marriage was under considerable pressure.

5. Constance Webb tells these stories in her biography of Wright, admitting only in the endnotes that it was she who was Wright's anonymous "friend." (See Webb, *Richard Wright,* ch 20.)

6. Constance Webb recalls: "In April or May roving gangs of armed Italian youths were terrorizing Village residents. A cab driver, stopped for a light at the corner of Eighth Street and Sixth Avenue, was pulled from his taxi and beaten for carrying an interracial couple. The passengers, a Negro girl and a white man, were knocked to the ground and kicked by teenagers. On two different occasions, gangs entered the Howard Johnson's on Sixth Avenue and the Humpty-Dumpty on Fourth Street, dragged two Negro men who were eating with white women into the street and beat them." (Webb, *Richard Wright,* p. 260.)

7. St Clair Drake interview with Horace Cayton, 1969. Cayton papers.

8. Simone de Beauvoir to Jean-Paul Sartre, 14 April 1947. De Beauvoir, *Lettres à Sartre,* Sylvie Le Bon de Beauvoir, ed. (Paris: Gallimard, 1990), p. 344.

9. Simone de Beauvoir to Jean-Paul Sartre, 16 April 1947. *Lettres à Sartre,* p. 349. (Author's translation.)

10. De Beauvoir, *America Day by Day,* p. 276.

11. Michel Fabre interview with Simone de Beauvoir, 24 June 1970, in Fabre, *The World of Richard Wright.*

12. Simone de Beauvoir to Jean-Paul Sartre, 8 May 1946, *Lettres à Sartre,* p. 356.

13. De Beauvoir was very partial to Wright's friend Bernard Wolfe, a writer of Russian Jewish heritage who had gone to Mexico at the age of twenty-one to be Trotsky's secretary. He was passionate about jazz, blues, and hip black language. With Mezz Mezzrow he had cowritten a book, *Really the Blues,* about Mezzrow,

a white Jewish jazz musician who had immersed himself in black street culture. (Mezzrow called himself "a voluntary Negro.") One evening Wolfe took de Beauvoir to hear Louis Armstrong play at Carnegie Hall.

14. De Beauvoir, *America Day by Day*, p. 352.

15. Dorothy Norman, *Encounters: A Memoir* (New York: Harcourt Brace Jovanovich, 1987), p. 199.

16. *The Diary of Anaïs Nin, 1944–47,* vol. 4 (New York: Harcourt Brace Jovanovich, 1971), pp. 212–14.

17. Anaïs Nin quotes Wright in *The Diary of Anaïs Nin*, vol. 4, pp. 212–14.

18. Maria Le Hardouin, "Richard Wright parmi les siens," *Combat,* 11 July 1947, pp. 1–2. (Author's translation.)

19. The previous summer, the newly married Ralph and Fanny Ellison had stayed there. And in the winter, Chester Himes had gone there with his wife, Jean, to finish his novel *Lonely Crusade.*

20. The car cost $2,677.

21. Frank K. Safford, in Ray and Farnsworth, eds., *Richard Wright: Impressions and Perspectives,* p. 80.

22. Madison Davis Lacy interview with Constance Webb, San Francisco, 18 December 1993. Lacy private papers.

23. Constance Webb, unpublished introduction to her biography of Wright. Webb private papers.

24. Ed Aswell to Richard Wright, 10 July 1947. Harper & Brothers papers.

25. Paul Reynolds to Richard Wright, 16 June 1947. Wright papers.

26. Richard Wright to Ed Aswell, 21 August 1955. Wright papers.

27. Among the friends were Ralph and Fanny Ellison, C. L. R. James and Constance Webb, Marie Menken and Willard Maas, Bernie Wolfe, Chef and Ethel Kossa.

28. Richard Wright journal, 31 July 1947. Wright papers.

29. Richard Wright journal, 2 August 1947. Wright papers.

30. Richard Wright journal, 8 August 1947. Wright papers.

31. Richard Wright journal, 14 August 1947. Wright papers.

32. Richard Wright journal, 15 August 1947. Wright papers.

33. Richard Wright journal, 9 August 1947. Wright papers.

34. Richard Wright journal, 23 August 1947. Wright papers.

35. Richard Wright journal, 20 August 1947. Wright papers.

36. Richard Wright journal, 21 August 1947. Wright papers.

37. Richard Wright journal, 19 August 1947. Wright papers.

38. She lived twenty more years, to the age of fifty.

39. Richard Wright journal, 17 August 1947. Wright papers.

40. Richard Wright journal, 23 August 1947. Wright papers.

41. Richard Wright journal, 17 August 1947. Wright papers.

42. Richard Wright journal, 1 September 1947. Wright papers.

43. Richard Wright journal, 6 September 1947. Wright papers.

44. Richard Wright journal, 4 September 1947. Wright papers.

45. Richard Wright journal, 11 September 1947. Wright papers.

46. Richard Wright journal, 19 September 1947. Wright papers.

47. Richard Wright journal, 22 September 1947. Wright papers.

48. Edith Anderson, *Love in Exile: An American Writer's Memoir of Life in Divided Berlin* (South Royalton, VT: Steerforth Press, 1999), p. 27.

49. Anderson, *Love in Exile,* p. 27.

50. Author's interview with Edith Schroeder (Anderson), Berlin, 22 June 1997.

51. Anderson, *Love in Exile,* p. 38.

52. Richard Wright to Edith Schroeder, 14 November 1947. Schroeder private papers.

53. Richard Wright to Edith Schroeder, 18 November 1947. Schroeder private papers.

54. Richard Wright to Edith Schroeder, 20 November 1947. Schroeder private papers.

55. Richard Wright to Ralph Ellison, 12 January 1948. Ellison papers.

56. Anderson, *Love in Exile,* p. 48.

57. Edith Anderson to Richard Wright, 6 January 1947. Wright papers.

58. Edith Anderson to Richard Wright, 11 April 1948. Wright papers.

59. Joseph Newman, "Russia Looks at American Authors," *Saturday Review of Literature* (New York), 10 April 1948.

60. Theodore Ward, "Five Negro Novelists: Revolt and Retreat," *Mainstream,* vol. 1, no. 1 (winter 1947): 100–10. He referred to William Attaway, Carl Ruthaven Offord, Chester Himes, Ann Petry, and Frank Yerby.

61. Jean Kanapa, "Petite Anthologie des Revues Américaines," *Poésie* 47, no. 41 (November 1947): 115–33, and "Il y a deux littératures Américaines," *Les Lettres Françaises,* 5 February 1948, p. 3.

62. Simone de Beauvoir to Nelson Algren, 6 February 1948. De Beauvoir, *A Transatlantic Love Affair: Letters to Nelson Algren* (New York: New Press, 1998), p. 162.

63. De Beauvoir, *America Day by Day,* p. 103.

64. Simone de Beauvoir to Nelson Algren, 26 January 1948. De Beauvoir, *A Transatlantic Love Affair.*

65. Simone de Beauvoir to Nelson Algren, 28 February 1948. De Beauvoir, *A Transatlantic Love Affair.*

66. Richard Wright to Dorothy Norman, 28 February 1948. The letter was published in *Art & Action* (1948).

67. Maurice Nadeau, *Gavroche,* 4 February 1948.

68. Richard Wright to Dorothy Norman, 28 February 1948. *Art & Action* (1948).

69. Richard Wright to Dorothy Norman, 9 March 1948. *Art & Action* (1948).

70. Richard Wright to Ralph Ellison, 28 April 1948. Ellison papers.

21: ARGENTINA

1. Chester Himes, *The Quality of Hurt: The Autobiography of Chester Himes,* vol. I (New York: Doubleday, 1972), pp. 197–98.

2. Simone de Beauvoir to Nelson Algren, 3 August 1948. De Beauvoir, *A Transatlantic Love Affair.*

3. Richard Wright, "There's Always Another Café," *The Kiosk* (Paris) no. 10 (1953), pp. 12–14. Reprinted in *Richard Wright Reader,* eds. Ellen Wright and Michel Fabre (New York: Harper & Row, 1978), pp. 55–57.

4. John Fischer to Richard Wright, 3 March 1949. Wright papers.

5. Paul Reynolds to Richard Wright, 25 November 1947. Wright papers.

6. Paul Reynolds to Richard Wright, 26 May 1948. Wright papers.

7. Richard Wright to Ed Aswell, 21 August 1955. Wright papers.

8. The organizers were David Rousset, an ex-Trotskyite who had survived Buchenwald, and Georges Altman, editor of the left-wing paper *Franc-Tireur.*

9. Richard Wright to Dorothy Norman, 29 January 1949. Norman papers.

10. Simone de Beauvoir to Nelson Algren, 19 January 1949. De Beauvoir, *A Transatlantic Love Affair,* p. 260.

11. "The Little Man," *Time,* 10 January 1949, pp. 13–14.

12. Horne, *Black Liberation/Red Scare,* p. 209.

13. Richard Wright to Dorothy Norman, 29 January 1949. Norman papers.

14. Richard Wright, "Comrade Strong: Don't You Remember?" *New York Herald Tribune,* 4 April 1949.

15. Richard Wright, "Comrade Strong."

16. Crossman wanted an American contributor. Hemingway had refused. Crossman considered Whittaker Chambers (the ex-Communist who had recently informed on Alger Hiss), but decided he was too controversial.

17. See Frances Stonor Saunders, *The Cultural Cold War: The CIA and the World of Arts and Letters* (New York: New Press, 1999).

18. Rebecca West, "Roads to Communism and Back: Six Personal Histories," *New York Times Book Review,* 8 January 1950, pp. 3, 29. Rebecca West had become a virulent anti-Communist by this time.

19. Baldwin, "Alas, Poor Richard," p. 195.

20. Baldwin, "Alas, Poor Richard."

21. Baldwin, "Alas, Poor Richard."

22. Drew, *Nelson Algren,* p. 324.

23. Wright's old Communist Party friend Mark Marvin (the brother of Herbert Kline) had hoped to produce the film in France with Canada Lee as his coproducer. Paul Reynolds made discreet inquiries and was told they were an unreliable team, and so was their budget. Mark Marvin had once bought the stage rights for *Black Boy,* but nothing had come of it.

24. It is not clear whether Canada Lee would have taken the part or not. On 10 December 1948 Paul Reynolds wrote to Wright that he believed Lee would play the role, whoever the director was. It is possible that by the time the movie came to be made, Lee had other commitments. Or perhaps he did not want to be associated with a film that was likely to cause him even more trouble with the House Committee on Un-American Activities.

25. Pierrette Matalon, Claude Guiguet, Jacques Pinturault, eds., *Pierre Chenal: Souvenirs du Cinéaste* (Paris: Editions Dujarric, 1987), pp. 185–86. (Author's translation.)

26. Johannes Skancke Martens, "A Black Writer Becomes a Movie Actor," *Aftenposten* (Oslo), 9 November 1950, p. 3. See Kinnamon and Fabre, eds., *Conversations with Richard Wright,* pp. 148–50.

27. Reynolds had bought Wright's share of the movie rights from Paul Green, Welles, and Houseman for six thousand dollars. The arrangement was that Wright would get the same money (six thousand dollars) from Chenal and Pradès, and 20 percent of the gross takings from movie showings throughout the world (except for Argentina, Paraguay, and Uruguay).

28. Richard Wright, "The Shame of Chicago," *Ebony* (December 1951).

29. In 1956 Williams established the Peoples' National Movement and became prime minister of Trinidad and Tobago.

30. Resident Agent, Montevideo, to Secretary of State, Washington, D.C., 13 October 1940. State Department files, National Archives, Washington.

31. Through Gisèle Freund, the German-Jewish photographer, Wright met Victoria Ocampo, the novelist, feminist, and cultured Argentine aristocrat who edited *Sur,* Latin America's foremost literary and cultural journal. During the French Occupation, it was Ocampo who had arranged a ticket to Argentina for Gisèle Freund, who was hiding at the time in the South of France.

32. Nicholas Joy played Mr. Dalton; Charles Cane the chief detective; Willa Pearls Curtiss, who had been a house servant in *Gone With the Wind,* played Bigger's mother; Jean Wallace played Mary Dalton.

33. In 1951 Wallace would marry Cornel Wilde and costar with him in *The Big Combo.* In *Sword of Lancelot,* Wallace would play Guinevere. She died in 1990, at the age of sixty-six.

34. In October 1974, *Ebony* would send down a reporter to investigate why Argentina was the "land of the vanishing blacks."

35. Virginia Lee Warren, "Argentina Doubles as Chicago Locale for 'Native Son,' " *New York Times,* 21 May 1950, sec. 2, p. 5.

36. Paul Reynolds to Ellen Wright, 26 April 1950. Wright papers.

37. Simone de Beauvoir to Nelson Algren, 23 May 1950. De Beauvoir, *A Transatlantic Love Affair.*

38. The incident is related in de Beauvoir's letter to Algren, 20 June 1950. De Beauvoir, *A Transatlantic Love Affair.*

39. In May 1950, Gloria Madison married her boyfriend in Chicago—a white man, Robert Algmin.

40. Paul Reynolds to Richard Wright, 17 March 1950. Wright papers.

41. *Chicago Defender,* 2 September 1950.

42. *Haitian Journal,* 28 July 1950. See Fabre, *The Unfinished Quest of Richard Wright,* p. 600, n. 14.

43. In the early 1930s, the Russian director Sergey Eisenstein had hoped to make a Toussaint-Louverture film with Paul Robeson as star, but the plan had never come off.

44. Constance Webb to author, 20 January 1998.

45. *Pittsburgh Courier,* 2 September 1950.

46. Ellen told this to de Beauvoir, who told Algren, 7 October 1950. De Beauvoir, *A Transatlantic Love Affair.*

47. This is reminiscent of the passage in *Native Son* when Bigger decides to kill Bessie. "He couldn't take her and he couldn't leave her; so he would have to kill her. It was his life against hers."

48. Margaret Wilson to Richard Wright, 18 October 1951 (two letters), and 21 October, 31 October. The address was 1085B Lynch Street, Jackson. The originals are with Ellen Wright. Copies are in the Webb papers.

49. *France-Observateur,* 3 May 1951; *The Crisis* (June–July 1951): 381–83.

50. Richard Wright to Mrs. Shelton, 9 October 1951. Wright papers.

51. *Réforme,* 13 May 1950, pp. 1, 3.

52. Baldwin, "Alas Poor Richard."

53. Wright had urged both speakers not to be too political. Sartre spoke first. Then Fischer launched into a vehement attack on the Soviet Union. Sartre became irritated and pointed out that it was the U.S. who had used the atom bomb. The members of the fellowship started to wonder what exactly the group was about.

54. Among the members were Gordon Parks, the photographer; Leroy Haynes, an ex-GI who had set up a soul food restaurant in Montmartre; Jean Maho, an artist; Bill Rutherford and Ollie Stewart, both journalists. Some of the invited speakers were Roger Baldwin, the civil liberties leader; Charles Delaunay, the black American jazz musician; Jean Cocteau, the French film director; and Daniel Guérin, a French sociologist who had just written *Whither the American People?* about racism in the U.S.

55. Simone de Beauvoir to Nelson Algren, 14 December 1950. For reasons of discretion, Sylvie Le Bon changed the Wrights' names halfway through this volume of letters to Algren, to Bob and Tamy Guld. I have changed them back again in this one passage.

56. He was invited by the Italian Cultural Association, which belonged to the umbrella group the Congress for Cultural Freedom—an anti-Communist organization.

57. Georges Altman, "Cette Lèpre, le Racisme," *Franc-Tireur,* 17 April 1951.

58. Richard Wright, "Derrière l'affaire McGee" [Behind the McGee Case], *Le Droit de Vivre,* Paris, 15 May 1951, p. 1.

59. Paul Reynolds to Richard Wright, 16 November 1950. Wright papers.

60. Walter Gould to Richard Wright, 5 September 1951. Wright papers.

61. Pierre Chenal to Richard Wright, 1 April 1951. Wright papers. (This letter was in English. Generally Chenal wrote to Wright in French.)

62. Simone de Beauvoir to Nelson Algren, 15 May 1951. De Beauvoir, *A Transatlantic Love Affair.*

63. Richard Wright to Walter Gould, 11 June 1951. Wright papers.

64. Pierre Chenal to Richard Wright, 1 April 1951. Wright papers.

65. Saunders, *The Cultural Cold War: The CIA and the World of Arts and Letters,* p. 290.

66. Pierre Chenal to Richard Wright, 29 July 1951. Wright papers.

67. Richard Wright to Paul Reynolds, 6 August 1951. Wright papers.

68. Walter Gould to Richard Wright, 16 October 1951. Wright papers.

69. David Caute, *The Great Fear: The Anti-Communist Purge under Truman and Eisenhower* (New York: Simon & Schuster, 1978), p. 245.

70. *The Autobiography of W. E. B. Du Bois,* p. 379. Du Bois wrote the draft of this autobiography in 1958–59. It was published posthumously in 1964 and 1965 in China, the USSR, and East Germany.

71. Martin Duberman, *Paul Robeson: A Biography* (New York: New Press, 1989), p. 389.

72. See their daughter's account of their exile: Kimmage, *An Un-American Childhood.*

73. The American Hospital of Paris, in Neuilly-sur-Seine, opened in 1910. During both wars it served as a military hospital.

74. Foreign Service Dispatch, 26 November 1951. U.S. embassy in Paris to Department of State, Washington, D.C. State Department records (NND852917), National Archives, Washington, D.C.

75. Elmer Carter to Richard Wright, 29 October 1951. Wright papers.

76. Ben Burns to Richard Wright, 22 August 1950. Wright papers.

77. "Return of the Native Son," *Ebony* (December 1951): 100. Burns, *Nitty Gritty,* p. 168ff.

78. Richard Wright to Ben Burns, 4 December 1951. Burns papers, Kent State University, Ohio.

79. Richard Wright to Edith Schroeder, 1 June 1951. Schroeder private papers.

80. From now on, he told all female correspondents to write to him at the poste restante address.

81. Richard Wright to Edith Schroeder, 25 July 1951. Schroeder private papers.

22. EXISTENTIAL DREAD

1. William Gardner Smith, "Black Boy," *Ebony* (July 1953). The article was written in 1953, so I appear to be jumping ahead, but the Wrights' domestic situation was the same in 1951. Unfortunately, it is *Ebony* policy not to release their photographs for publication, so I could not include any of these in the book.

2. He is talking to Mercer Cook, Jr. (son of the Howard University professor), Ollie Harrington (cartoonist with the *Pittsburgh Courier*), and two unidentified women, one Canadian and one French.

3. Margaret Wilson to Richard Wright, 27 February 1952; 1 April 1952; 9 June 1952. Webb papers.

4. De Beauvoir's American publications would prove very lucrative over the years.

5. He first stayed at the Regent Palace Hotel in Piccadilly Circus, then 28 Glenluce Road, SE London, then 45 Rosenthal Road, Catford, SE London.

6. Damon falls in love with a woman called Eva. When he tells her the truth about himself, she is so horrified she jumps out of a sixth-floor window. Wright probably had Anna Damon vaguely in mind. (The name "Cross Damon" also suggests this.) In May 1944, Anna Damon, the daughter of a wealthy Chicago family and a prominent member of the Party, jumped to her death from the window of a Manhattan hotel. Wright would have known her. She was a friend of Angelo Herndon, the black militant whom Wright knew well. (See Bella V. Dodd, *School of Darkness* [New York: P. J. Kenedy & Sons, 1954], pp. 171–73.) "Gil Blount" might have been partly inspired by Gil Green, a white New York Party leader who was indicted at the Smith Act trial.

7. *The Gold Coast Revolution* would be published in 1953 (the same year as *Black Power*), by the left-wing British publisher Dennis Dobson.

8. George Padmore, *Pan-Africanism or Communism? The Coming Struggle for Africa* (London: Dobson, 1956). Padmore inscribed Wright's copy: "Your eulogistic foreword makes me feel guilty of the cult of the personality. Well, we shall wait and see the public reactions. Yours ever, George. London, July 26, 1956."

9. Simone de Beauvoir to Nelson Algren, 4 May 1952. De Beauvoir, *A Transatlantic Love Affair*.

10. Richard Wright to Edith Schroeder, 19 April 1952. Shroeder private papers.

11. Richard Wright to Paul Reynolds, 28 June 1952. Harper & Brothers papers.

12. Simone de Beauvoir to Nelson Algren, 2 July 1952. Some of Wright's sentences, cut by the publishers, were poor imitations of the worst excesses of Sartrean existentialist philosophy. One example (which has been restored in the recent Library of America edition) describes Damon's state of mind: "Imprisoned he was in a state of consciousness that was so infatuated by its own condition that it could not

dominate itself; so swamped was he by himself with himself that he could not break forth from behind the bars of that self to claim himself."

13. Paul Reynolds to John Fischer, 21 July 1952. Harper & Brothers papers.

14. John Fischer to Richard Wright, 31 July 1952. Wright papers.

15. John Fischer to Richard Wright, 10 November 1952. Wright papers.

16. Richard Wright to Ralph Ellison, 27 May 1952. Ellison papers.

17. Richard Wright to Ralph Ellison, 21 October 1952. Ellison papers.

18. Ralph Ellison to Richard Wright, 21 January 1953. Wright papers.

19. Richard Wright to Naomi Replansky, 18 November 1952. Replansky private papers.

20. Author's interview with Ellen Wright, Paris, 19 April 2000.

21. One particularly awkward version of the dedication read: "To my daughter Rachel who, though born on alien soil, I hope will learn to speak and love the English language; but I pray that in her acquiring of it that her heart be spared the shock of dismay, for English, more than any other modern language, has the dubious honor of having given to the world the most elaborate theories and justification of racial hatred."

22. Arna Bontemps, *Saturday Review,* 28 March 1953, pp. 15–16.

23. L. D. Reddick, "A New Richard Wright?" *Phylon,* 14 (second quarter, 1953): 213–14.

24. Milton Rugoff, *New York Herald Tribune Book Review,* 22 March 1953, p. 4.

25. This was the title of Reddick's review.

26. Simone de Beauvoir to Nelson Algren, 24 March 1954. De Beauvoir, *A Transatlantic Love Affair.*

27. Nelson Algren, "The Art of Fiction," interview, *Paris Review* (winter 1955).

28. Ellison interview with Allen Geller (1963), Graham and Singh, eds., *Conversations with Ralph Ellison,* p. 84.

29. James Baldwin to William Cole, 13 April 1953. Baldwin papers, Lilly Library, Indiana University, Bloomington.

30. Chester Himes, *The Quality of Hurt: The Autobiography of Chester Himes,* vol. 1 (New York: Doubleday, 1972), pp. 190–91.

31. Baldwin, "Alas, Poor Richard."

32. Richard Wright, "On Literature," unpublished essay. Wright papers.

33. Richard Wright review, *PM,* 25 November 1945, pp. m7–m8.

34. Harrington had been in Paris since 1951. He and Wright had met briefly in Harlem in the mid-1940s, at one of Langston Hughes's parties. In 1940 he had illustrated *Native Son,* serialized in the black newspaper *The People's Voice.* The series was canceled when readers complained Wright's language was obscene.

35. Himes, *The Quality of Hurt,* pp. 179–80.

36. This was Gaïte Frogé's small "English Bookshop" at 42 rue de Seine. Wright was also a regular at George Whitman's Librairie Mistral, facing Notre Dame Cathedral, which sold English and other foreign-language books.

37. Himes, *The Quality of Hurt,* p. 209.

38. Himes, *The Quality of Hurt,* pp. 198–99.

39. Himes, *The Quality of Hurt,* p. 201.

40. Baldwin, "Many Thousands Gone," *Partisan Review* (November 1951).

41. Baldwin, "Alas, Poor Richard."

42. Himes, *The Quality of Hurt,* p. 200.

43. Dorothy Padmore to Ellen Wright, 19 June 1953. Wright papers.

23: JOURNEY TO THE GOLD COAST

Any quotations in this chapter whose sources are not given come from the published version of *Black Power.*

1. Richard Wright journal, 16 September 1947. Wright papers.

2. In 1950 he had just returned from Argentina when John Grierson contacted him. Grierson, who had resigned from the Canadian Film Board and was now working at the United Nations in Paris, had just been to Africa, and was "damned excited," he told Wright. "I propose to do a film in Africa next year, I want you with me if you can manage." (Grierson to Richard Wright, 2 October 1950.) Wright did not go—presumably because he had projects of his own he needed to get on with.

3. Kwame Nkrumah to Richard Wright, 16 April 1953. Wright papers.

4. The following quotations are taken from the original draft of *Black Power* in Wright's papers. ("Africa journal.") The story about the chief's visit was published in French in *Preuves,* in November 1954.

5. Africa journal, 5 June 1953. Wright papers. (Wright used this both as his private journal and an early draft of *Black Power.* Sometimes he gives dates. Much of the time he does not.)

6. In an essay on *Black Power,* the African scholar Kwame Anthony Appiah (son of Joe and Peggy Appiah) suggests that Wright felt "a palpable anxiety about redescending into the ancestral mire." ("A Long Way from Home: Wright in the Gold Coast," in *Modern Critical Views: Richard Wright,* ed. Harold Bloom [New York: Chelsea House, 1987], p. 188.)

In *Black Power,* Wright broaches this subject himself. "I understood why so many American Negroes were eager to disclaim any relationship with Africa. . . . So long had Africa been described as something shameful, barbaric, a land in which one went about naked, a land in which his ancestors had sold their kith and kin as slaves—so long had he heard all this that he wanted to disassociate himself in his mind from all such realities." Wright denied that this applied to him.

7. Africa journal. Wright papers.

8. His African photographs are among his papers at Yale.

9. Africa journal. Wright papers.

10. Africa journal, 30 June 1953. Wright papers.

11. Richard Wright to Padmores, 16 July 1953. Wright papers.

12. Richard Wright to Padmores, 16 July 1953. Wright papers.

13. Richard Wright, "The Miracle of Nationalism in the African Gold Coast," *White Man, Listen!* (1957). Wright was able to be more forthright about the problems Nkrumah faced in this essay, published after Ghana had won its independence.

14. Ironically, the inspiration for Nkrumah's Pan-Africanism had come from America and the West Indies: from Marcus Garvey, W. E. B. Du Bois, and George Padmore.

15. Africa journal. Wright papers.

16. Africa journal. Wright papers.

17. *Black Power,* p. 85.

18. Peter Abrahams, "The Blacks," in *An African Treasury,* ed. Langston Hughes (New York: Crown, 1960), pp. 42–55.

19. Africa journal, 21 July 1953. Wright papers.

20. Dorothy Padmore, remaining in Accra after George Padmore's death, would

write to Wright about "a fellow called Moxon in the Ministry of Information who should have been chucked out ages ago. . . . We all loathe him and George despised him." (31 October 1959)

21. Africa journal. Wright papers.

22. Africa journal, 25 August 1953. Wright papers.

23. Africa journal. Wright papers.

24. Richard Wright, *The Color Curtain* (1956; reprint, Jackson, MS: University Press of Mississippi, 1994), p. 31.

25. William E. Cole, American Consulate General, Accra, to the Department of State, Washington, 15 September 1953. State Department files, National Archives, Washington, D.C.

26. Wright stated that during his stay he had met only one self-avowed Communist: Mr. Bankole Renner, a man who had been imprisoned along with Nkrumah and had since broken away from the CPP. He said that Renner held a weekly Marxist study group in his home, and that he had attended one of these meetings. "They are concentrating their activities on educating young Africans and urging them to infiltrate the ranks of the Convention People's Party. In short, it is the tactic known as boring from within. They can easily accomplish this tactic because of ideological and emotional similarities between the Communist Party and the Convention People's Party."

27. He added: "A West Indian businessman living in London seems to be the business contact between the Secret Circle and foreign business firms. This man's name is McDermot. DD indicates that the profits derived from commissions are banked in free currency zones."

28. "No self-respecting African wishes to exchange his British masters for Russian ones," Padmore would write in his book *Pan-Africanism or Communism?*, pp. 339–40.

29. Richard Wright to Paul Reynolds, 4 September 1953. Wright papers.

24: FROM BULLFIGHTS TO BANDUNG

Any unattributed quotations in this chapter are from *Pagan Spain* (1956; reprint, New York, HarperPerennial, 1995).

1. Paul Reynolds to Richard Wright, 10 March 1954. Wright papers.

2. Paul Reynolds to Richard Wright, 23 March 1954. Wright papers.

3. Paul Reynolds to Richard Wright, 10 March 1954. Wright papers.

4. Frank MacGregor to Richard Wright, 9 April 1954. Wright papers.

5. Vivian Werner private papers. Author's phone interviews with Werner, Lenox, Massachusetts, 16 December 1997 and 12 March 1998.

6. Author's phone interview with Werner, 16 December 1997.

7. *Newsweek,* 24 May 1954.

8. Ollie Stewart, "The Richard Wright I Knew," *Ave Maria,* 6 May 1961, pp. 9–11.

9. Richard Wright to Paul Reynolds, 30 May 1954. Harper & Brothers papers.

10. Paul Reynolds to Richard Wright, 2 June 1954. Harper & Brothers papers.

11. In fact, they thought it a "thoroughly bad novel." (John Fischer to Frank MacGregor, 19 May 1953, Harper & Brothers papers.) Reynolds thought it would be a mistake to publish it, for the sake of Wright's reputation. With Reynolds's agreement, Harper refused it. Since Wright was not prepared to abandon the book, Reynolds sold it to Avon, an inexpensive paperback publishing house. The book was scarcely noticed, and received no reviews in the U.S. at all. It was translated into French, Ital-

ian, Spanish, and Dutch, but received little attention. Wright's Danish publisher, Otto Lindhardt, was shocked by the poor quality of the book. "I feel that we would be doing the author a gross disservice if we were to permit a translation to appear here," he wrote to Harper. (Lindhardt to Simon Michael Bessie, 7 February 1955. Harper & Brothers papers.)

12. Paul Reynolds to Richard Wright, 21 July 1954. Harper & Brothers papers.

13. Dorothy Padmore to Richard Wright, 25 October 1954. Wright papers.

14. Wright occasionally kept a diary in his Spanish journal, which served both as a first draft and a personal notebook. Once again, he does not always date the entries.

15. Spanish journal, 21 August 1954. Wright papers.

16. Spanish journal, 21 August 1954. Wright papers.

17. Spanish journal, 21 August 1954. Wright papers.

18. Richard Wright to Paul Reynolds, 22 August 1954. Wright papers.

19. Spanish journal, 19 August 1954. Wright papers.

20. Spanish journal, 24 August 1954. Wright papers.

21. Spanish journal, 22 August 1954. Wright papers.

22. Spanish journal, 26 August 1954. In *Pagan Spain,* Wright places this incident in Barcelona. In his journal, which was written at the time, it occurred in Madrid. In *Pagan Spain,* arranged by theme, Wright jumbles dates and places, and sometimes conflates several different characters into one.

23. Spanish journal. (During the Spanish civil war, there had been unfortunate incidents in which African and African-American soldiers fighting on the Loyalist side had been shot at by Loyalists who mistook them for Moors fighting for Franco.)

24. Spanish journal. Wright papers.

25. Paul Reynolds to Frank MacGregor, 21 September 1954. Harper & Brothers papers.

26. Simon Michael Bessie to Frank MacGregor, 13 October 1954. Harper & Brothers papers.

27. Harrington's article was published in *L'Observateur,* 25 February 1954, and in *Labor Action* (U.S.), 15 March 1954, p. 4.

28. Guy Henriques, "Paris Diary," *Tribune* (London), 14 May 1954, p. 3.

29. The outline of Wright's 1954 statement is given in a long document in Wright's FBI file, dated April 1958.

30. *Encounter* was a London monthly edited by Stephen Spender and an American, Irving Kristol. *Preuves* was edited by François Bondy in Paris. *Cuadernos* was a Spanish-language magazine published in Paris.

31. See Peter Coleman, *The Liberal Conspiracy: The Congress for Cultural Freedom and the Struggle for the Mind of Postwar Europe* (New York: Free Press, 1989).

32. Michael Josselson, a white Russian émigré who spoke four languages without an accent, had become a U.S. citizen in the 1930s. (See Frances Stonor Saunders, *The Cultural Cold War: The CIA and the World of Arts and Letters* [New York: New Press, 1999].) In his autobiography, *Out of Step* (1987), Sidney Hook writes that he, "like almost everyone else," knew that the CIA was making some contribution.

33. This story comes from an unpublished essay Wright wrote a few months later about their trip: "The heart, for reasons that reason does not know, is on both sides." Wright papers.

34. Advance sales were four thousand. *The Outsider* had sold fourteen thousand advance copies.

35. Paul Reynolds to Richard Wright, 23 September 1954. Wright papers.

36. Michael Clark, "A Struggle for the Black Man Alone?" *New York Times Book Review,* 26 September 1954, p. 3. Some weeks later, a letter to the editor began: "May I suggest that author Richard Wright is not so easily spanked as Michael Clark's indignant review . . . would indicate?" Henry F. Wilson lamented "Mr. Clark's typically Western arrogance," and regretted that Clark would no doubt shoo readers away from "a brilliantly absorbing if bitterly frank book." (*New York Times Book Review,* 31 October 1954, p. 44.)

In 1959 Clark, a *New York Times* correspondent in North and West Africa, would write a book on the Algerian revolution in which he did not mention French atrocities. These reports were, he believed, largely Communist propaganda. "Several 'liberal' reviewers gagged on *Algeria in Turmoil* so completely that it was beyond their power to give the book a kind word," he complained in a postscript to his preface in the 1960 second edition.

37. Another was the black American scholar Saunders Redding, who ridiculed the book's politics in the *Saturday Review of Literature* ("Two Quests for Ancestors," *Saturday Review of Literature,* 23 October 1954, p. 19).

38. Joyce Cary, *The Nation,* 16 October 1954, pp. 2–4.

39. Fred R. Conkling, "Wright Sees West Africa in Turmoil," *Fort Wayne News Sentinel,* 9 October 1954.

40. Saunders Redding, "Two Quests for Ancestors," *Saturday Review of Literature,* 23 October 1954.

41. Doris Lessing, "Africa Illuminated," *Daily Worker,* September 1956. (Lessing was a Communist at the time.)

42. "An indictment of Western Colonialism," *Newsday,* 25 September 1954. Ralph Ellison, asked by Wright's publishers to provide a comment, stated that *Black Power* was "of great interest, not only as a travel book but as the attempt of a passionate intellectual to come to grips with the perplexing problem of Africa and modern power politics." See advertisement for *Black Power* in *New York Times Book Review,* 3 October 1954, p. 16.

43. Padmore pointed out that the colonial powers had done nothing to dismantle tribalism. For them it had the advantage of maintaining disunity and separatism among the people.

44. Dorothy Padmore to Richard Wright, 19 October 1954. Wright papers.

45. W. E. B. Du Bois to George Padmore, 10 December 1954 and 27 January 1955. He added: "I don't like Wright. The Communists of America started him on his career. It is quite possible that some of them presumed on his help and tried to push him around. They, like most human beings, are often narrow and ignorant. But because of that to slur Communism as such, to slander Russia and above all, to spit on American Negroes is too much for an honest artist." (*The Correspondence of W. E. B. Du Bois,* vol. 3, 1944–1963, ed. Herbert Aptheker [Amherst: University of Massachusetts Press, 1978], pp. 374–75.)

46. Richard Wright to Paul Reynolds, 4 February 1955. Harper & Brothers papers.

47. This section was cut from the published book.

48. Spanish journal, 22 March 1955. Wright papers.

49. Spanish journal, 24 March 1955. Wright papers.

50. Spanish journal. Wright papers.

51. Spanish journal, 1 April 1955. Wright papers.

52. He included several extracts in *Pagan Spain*. These were published in the 1958 French translation, but not in the American or British editions.

25: THE LONELY OUTSIDERS

Any unattributed quotations in this chapter come from *The Color Curtain*, (1956; reprint, Jackson, MS: University Press of Mississippi, 1994)

1. The United States supported Chiang Kai-shek's exiled government on Formosa (later Taiwan).

2. Richard Wright, Indonesia journal, Wright papers.

3. Indonesia journal, Wright papers.

4. Indonesia journal, Wright papers.

5. Unpublished draft of Wright's 1960 introduction to *Black Metropolis.*

6. The book was also dedicated to his friend Eric Williams, who now headed the newly independent government in Trinidad.

7. Winburn T. Thomas, "Reminiscences," in Ray and Farnsworth, eds., *Richard Wright: Impressions and Perspectives,* pp. 151–53. Thomas told Wright that he worried about the racism his sons might encounter if the family returned to the U.S. After Bandung, he and Wright wrote to each other occasionally, and Thomas visited the Wrights in Paris in 1958.

8. Donald Friede to Paul Reynolds, 18 July 1955. Wright papers.

9. Melvin J. Lasky, "Report on 3rd Editorial Meeting," 2 June 1955. Congress for Cultural Freedom papers, University of Chicago Library. I thank Frances Stonor Saunders for sending me this report.

10. The French translation was published by Calmann-Lévy. In England the publisher was Dennis Dobson.

11. *Encounter* (March 1956): 73.

12. Ed Aswell to Richard Wright, 11 August 1955. Wright papers.

13. Richard Wright to Whit Burnett, 28 July 1955. *Story* files.

14. George Padmore to Richard Wright, undated [autumn 1955]. Wright papers.

15. "For the fullness of time is every day and every hour; and of time I sing, time that seeks fulfillment.

And yet no song am I; my music is unheard; there is no pulse that can feel my rhythms;

And yet nearer to music am I than to anything amidst the millions of whirling suns. . . .

And no flesh am I, and no blood. . . ."

The next nine pages described the growth and death of a plant. "Consciousness dawned slowly in the form of knowing that it had a dull feeling of pulpy oblongness and roundness in the cold and dead black of the earth, yet peripheral sensations of pleasurable dampness enclosed it all around. . . ."

16. The two men admitted to abducting the boy. The jury asserted that the body was too mangled to be identified. Later, in an extraordinary parody of justice, the two men told their story to the press for four thousand dollars. They were never convicted.

17. See Henry Hampton and Steve Fayer, with Sarah Flynn, eds., *Voices of Freedom: An Oral History of the Civil Rights Movement from the 1950s through the 1980s* (New York: Bantam Books, 1990).

18. Richard Wright, "Cette parodie de justice est tout de même une victoire pour les noirs," *France-Soir,* 27 September 1955.

19. Richard Wright to Margrit de Sablonière, 28 November 1955. Schomburg Center.

20. Paul Reynolds to Richard Wright, 25 October 1955. Harper & Brothers papers.

21. Ed Aswell to Richard Wright, 24 January 1956. Wright papers.

22. Ed Aswell to Richard Wright, 9 February 1956. Wright papers.

23. Ben Burns, "They're Not Uncle Tom's Children," *The Reporter,* 8 March 1956, pp. 21–23.

24. Richard Wright to Paul Reynolds, 14 March 1956. Wright papers.

25. Richard Wright to Paul Reynolds, 13 April 1956. Wright papers.

26. Gunnar Myrdal to Richard Wright, 3 April 1956. Wright papers. *The Reporter* was in fact funded by the CIA.

27. Wright suggested Langston Hughes, Ralph Ellison (currently in Rome on a fellowship), Chester Himes and William Gardner Smith (both in Paris), J. A. Rogers (a historian from New York), Carl Rowan (a journalist who was at Bandung), and Melvin Tolson (a professor of English whose son lived in Paris). Later, in May 1956, Wright added to his list St. Clair Drake, E. Franklin Frazier, Arna Bontemps, L. D. Reddick, Ira D. A. Reid, Rayford Logan, Mercer Cook, and Horace Mann Bond.

28. The report was not written until 8 May 1955. It went on to say that *Présence Africaine* was "definitely to the left" in orientation. Committee members included the poet Aimé Césaire, a "Communist Deputy from Martinique," and René Depestre, from Haiti, "also alleged to be a member of the Communist Party." Its subsidy from the French government had been discontinued because of the "leftist anti-colonial and generally irresponsible nature of its editorial policy."

29. Paris Embassy dispatch to the Department of State, 17 May 1956.

30. Richard Wright to James Holness, 7 July 1959. Fabre private papers.

31. Richard Wright to Margrit de Sablonière, 2 April 1956. Schomburg Center.

32. Paul Reynolds to Richard Wright, 5 July 1956. Harper & Brothers papers.

33. Ed Aswell to Richard Wright, 7 August 1956. Wright papers.

34. Interview with Faulkner at Tokyo American Cultural Center, August 1955. (Robert A. Jelliffe, ed., *Faulkner at Nagano* [Tokyo: Kenkyusha, 1956], p. 171.) It was reprinted in *Esquire* and *Jet* in December 1958.

35. James Baldwin, "Princes and Powers," *Encounter* (January 1957), reprinted in *Nobody Knows My Name* (New York: Dial Press, 1961).

36. Du Bois's letter was printed in full in the June–November 1956 issue of *Présence Africaine.* So was Wright's speech.

37. The five-man delegation from the United States included two men Wright had suggested: Dr. Horace Mann Bond (president of Lincoln University) and Mercer Cook (professor of French at Howard University). But the group was not at all what Wright originally had in mind. This team consisted of academics and administrators; they were not famous writers.

38. Wright had hoped his comments were for a closed session only. They were in fact published in the conference issue of *Présence Africaine* (June–November 1956).

39. Baldwin, "Princes and Powers."

40. Author's phone interview with Vivian L. Werner, 16 December 1997.

41. Interview with Richard Wright, *L'Express,* 18 August 1960. (See Kinnamon and Fabre, eds., *Conversations with Richard Wright.*)

42. His talk was one of the essays published in *White Man, Listen!* It is called "Tradition and Industrialization."

43. Baldwin, "Princes and Powers."

44. Janheinz Jahn, "World Congress of Black Writers," *Black Orpheus* (September 1957), 39—46.

45. Richard Wright to Daniel Guerin, 29 September 1956. See Fabre, *The Unfinished Quest of Richard Wright,* p. 441.

46. Kay Boyle to Richard Wright, 5 October 1956. Wright papers.

26: "I AM NOBODY"

1. In January 1971 Ellen Wright received a warning from the French Préfecture de Police. (At that time she was a Paris contact for the Black Panthers.) The letter (12 January 1971) reads: "I remind you that in exchange for the hospitality and the great freedom that is accorded foreign nationals, it is required of them to respect neutrality during their stay on French territory.

I have found myself obliged to issue you with a warning, and to make it clear to you that if you do not abide by these rules in the future, then I will have to consider a more serious administrative sanction, which could extend to expulsion from French territory." (Author's translation.) Ellen Wright private papers.

2. Dorothy Padmore to Ellen Wright, 13 April 1956. Wright papers.

3. *Black Power* did very well in Germany. It also sold well in Italy and Scandinavia.

4. *Spiegel,* 24 October 1956.

5. With the work of Frantz Fanon, Octave Mannoni, and Albert Memmi, there was new interest in this subject. In the early 1950s, Fanon had written the groundbreaking *Black Skin, White Masks.* In 1956 (when it came out in English translation), Wright reviewed Mannoni's *Prospero and Caliban: The Psychology of Colonization* for *The Nation.* Albert Memmi had just published *Portrait du colonisé* (1957), which Wright had heard about, though he could not read it.

6. Paul Reynolds to Richard Wright, 28 January 1947. Wright papers.

7. Richard Wright to Ed Aswell, 19 February 1957. Wright papers. The letter has not survived, but Aswell refers to it, and he quotes this line in his letter to Wright of 19 February 1957.

8. Maggie Hunt was the daughter of Thomas Booker Wilson, the eldest brother in the family. He had died. The surviving siblings were Ella, Charlie (Toledo, Ohio), Edward (Los Angeles), Addie and Lawrence (both lived in Chicago).

9. Margaret Wilson's will, case #51,899. Chancery Court, Jackson, MS.

10. Richard Wright to Margrit de Sablonière, 20 August 1958. Schomburg Center.

11. Gunnar Myrdal to Richard Wright, 15 April 1957. Wright papers.

12. Herbert L. Matthews, "How It Seemed to Him," *New York Times Book Review,* 24 February 1957, p. 7.

13. Anon. "Red Rag to Spain," *Times Literary Supplement,* 15 April 1960.

Inevitably, there were those who could not take nonfiction seriously. Nor could they take seriously a black man writing about white culture. In a review subtitled "He Should Stick to Fiction," the black critic Roi Ottley made the comment: "When a novelist of Richard Wright's stature pauses in his fictional chores to turn journalist and report on a foreign nation's social fabric, one always wonders whether he merely is indulging himself in a writing exercise. . . . This distinguished writer's gifts and insights as a novelist might be better served in reporting such dramas as now unfold in Montgomery, Tallahassee, and Clinton, Tenn." (*Chicago Tribune,* 3 March 1957.)

14. Richard Wright interview in *L'Express,* 18 August 1960. (Kinnamon and Fabre, eds., *Conversations with Richard Wright.*)

15. Wright had taken his 1937 novel, *Tarbaby Dawn,* out of his filing cabinet, and he worked in episodes from that.

16. Richard Wright to Ed Aswell, 5 July 1957. Wright papers. (The letter has disappeared. It was cited by Aswell in a letter to Wright, 11 July 1957.)

17. Langston Hughes to Ollie Harrington, 14 March 1957. Hughes papers.

18. Ollie Harrington to Langston Hughes, 15 April 1957. Hughes papers.

19. Chester Himes, *My Life of Absurdity: The Autobiography of Chester Himes,* vol. 2 (New York: Doubleday, 1976), p. 58.

20. Author's phone interview with Lesley Himes, New York, 21 March 2000.

21. Himes, *My Life of Absurdity,* p. 37.

22. David Bakish interview with Leroy Haynes, Paris, 8 July 1968. Bakish private papers.

23. Madison Davis Lacy interview with Ollie Harrington, Detroit, Michigan, 19 April 1991. Lacy private papers.

24. Madison Davis Lacy interview with Ollie Harrington, 19 April 1991. Lacy private papers.

25. Richard Wright to Margrit de Sablonière, 28 August 1957. Schomburg Center.

26. John Strachey to Reginald Butler, 16 August 1957. Wright papers.

27. "Hopeful Plan for Algeria," *Life,* 30 September 1957.

28. *Life,* 21 October 1957, p. 10.

29. *The Outsider* (1953; reprint, New York: HarperPerennial, 1993), p. 453.

30. Madison Davis Lacy interview with Ollie Harrington, 19 April 1991. (Frances Stonor Saunders writes: "When Ernest Hemingway complained to his friends that he was under surveillance by the FBI, they thought he was losing touch with reality. His file, released in the mid-1980s, confirmed Hemingway's suspicions: he was followed, taped, and harassed by Hoover's men for over twenty-five years." (Saunders, *The Cultural Cold War,* p. 195.)

31. Ed Aswell to Richard Wright, 11 September 1957. Wright papers.

32. Roi Ottley, "Reasoned Passion Against Racism," *Chicago Sunday Tribune,* 10 November 1957, book sec., p. 11.

33. Léopold Senghor to Richard Wright, 21 July 1959. Wright papers. Author's translation.

34. Paul Reynolds to Richard Wright, 30 September 1957. Wright papers.

35. Paul Reynolds to Richard Wright, 8 October 1957. Wright papers.

36. Paul Reynolds to Richard Wright, 23 September 1957. Wright papers.

37. Ed Aswell to Richard Wright, 23 December 1957. Wright papers.

38. Dorothy Padmore to Ellen Wright, 19 March 1958. Wright papers.

39. Dorothy Padmore to Dick and Ellen Wright, 29 May 1958. Wright papers.

40. In his essay "Equal in Paris," published in 1955, Baldwin writes about spending eight days in a French prison during Christmas 1949, accused of stealing a hotel sheet. Wright was disdainful that Baldwin wept on his way to jail.

41. Richard Wright to Paul Reynolds, 16 February 1959. Wright papers.

42. Ed Aswell to Richard Wright, 25 June 1958. Wright papers.

43. In *The Nation,* Robert Hatch pointed out: "Wright is an advocate, not a judge; he sees race from the viewpoint of the Negro, and one does not look to him for any withdrawn, balanced appraisal of issues. But he is not bemused, either, by the sufferings of his people. He does not think that suffering is ennobling or that the Negro is a pure creature in an evil land. Corruption is corruption and Wright exposes it." ("Either Weep or Laugh," *The Nation,* 25 October 1958, pp. 297–90.)

Irving Howe was the only other critic to defend Wright. There was plenty to admire about *The Long Dream* on literary grounds alone, he wrote. The dialogue was marvelous, the scenes vividly painted: "Negro boys edging into a circus, the central figure, Fishbelly, collecting rents on a Saturday morning from a Negro slum, a bang-up burial for victims of a dance hall fire. And Wright has created one superb and memorable figure, Tyree, a Negro undertaker who half the time is a shuffling good nigger and the other half rages with hatred for everything white." Howe concluded: "There may be two or three other Negro writers in America who are more polished than Wright, but beside him they seem, inevitably, like boys looking up to a man." (Irving Howe, "Books," *Partisan Review* [winter 1959]: 133–34.)

44. Phillip Bonosky, "Man without a People," *Mainstream* (February 1959): 49–51.

45. Ted Poston, "Wright: He's Out of Touch," *New York Post,* 26 October 1958.

46. "The Way It Was," *New York Times Book Review,* 26 October 1958, pp. 4, 38. Wright was upset by the review.

47. Richard Wright to Paul Reynolds, 16 February 1959. Wright papers.

48. Timothy Seldes to Richard Wright, 11 November 1959. Wright papers. (Seldes was referring to a conversation they had had about the book months before.)

49. Himes, *My Life of Absurdity,* p. 181.

50. The draft of the telegram is in Wright's papers at Yale.

51. Lawrence Reddick to Richard Wright, 14 January 1959. Wright papers.

52. Madison Davis Lacy interview with Julia Wright, Paris, 1994. Lacy private papers.

53. See Hansard Report for 20 November 1958.

54. Richard Wright to John Strachey, 18 January 1959. Ellen Wright private papers.

55. Reginald Butler to John Strachey, 29 January 1959. Wright papers.

56. Reginald Butler to John Strachey, 26 February 1959. Wright papers.

57. It was 2 Brompton Lodge, 9–11 Cromwell Road, London SW 7.

58. The details are from several interviews that I conducted with Celia Hornung Sanders in Melbourne, Australia, from June 1995 to October 1996.

59. Hélène Bokanowski had dropped out of the business after a year or so. It was an amicable separation.

60. Wright relates this story in a long and bitter letter to Strachey in October 1959. The draft is among Wright's papers.

61. Dorothy Padmore to Richard Wright, 31 October 1959. Wright papers.

62. Richard Wright to John Strachey, 12 October 1959. Wright papers.

63. Dorothy Padmore to Michel Fabre, 13 March 1963, in Fabre, *The World of Richard Wright,* pp. 256–61.

64. Richard Wright to Margrit de Sablonière, 8 April 1960. Schomburg Center.

65. Celia Hornung journal, 30 October 1959. Hornung private papers.

66. Oliver Harrington, "The Last Days of Richard Wright," *Why I Left America and Other Essays,* Thomas Inge, ed. (Jackson, MS: University Press of Mississippi, 1993), p. 7.

67. His Sorbonne thesis, completed in 1951, was titled "Contribution à l'étude physiopathologique de l'ascite cirrhotique." The following year he published a book on the subject, along with J. Caroli and A. Paraf: *Traitements Nouveaux de l'ascite cirrhotique et leurs bases pathologiques* (Paris: Vigot Frères, 1952).

68. France was slower to withdraw the drug from the market than most Western countries. One thousand cases of bismuth toxicity were reported in France between 1973 and 1980, before it was withdrawn from sale. (See: K. A. Winslip, "Toxicity of Bismuth Salts" in *Adverse Drug Reactions and Acute Poisonings Review,* vol. 2 [1982]: 103–21.)

69. Celia Hornung journal, 14 November 1959. Hornung private papers.

70. Hornung journal, 24 November 1959. Hornung private papers.

71. Richard Wright to Margrit de Sablonière, 8 April 1960. Schomburg Center.

72. Richard Wright to Margrit de Sablonière, 28 March 1960. Schomburg Center.

73. Dorothy Padmore to Richard Wright, 16 February 1960. Wright papers.

74. In his last speech, at the American Church in Paris in November 1960, Wright attributes the saying to "a friend."

27: STEPPING OFF THIS OLD EARTH

1. Richard Wright to Celia Hornung, 2 February 1960. Fabre private papers.

2. The collection spanned twenty years of writing. In 1944, after he had finished *Black Boy,* Wright had planned a collection called *Seven Men.* In 1951, five of the stories were published by Mondadori in an Italian edition, *Cinque Uomini.* At first, Wright had wanted the collection to be *Ten Men* and to include the story "Rite of Passage" (from his old novel *The Jackal*) and his short novel *Savage Holiday* under the title "Man and Boy." Reynolds had persuaded him to leave out the last two.

3. Richard Wright to Paul Reynolds, 23 February 1960 and 2 March 1960. Wright papers.

4. Richard Wright to Paul Reynolds, 10 September 1959. Wright papers.

5. Richard Wright to Margrit de Sablonière, 28 March 1960. Schomburg Center.

6. Richard Wright to Bente Heeris, March 1960. See Fabre, *The Unfinished Quest of Richard Wright,* p. 514. She killed herself on 18 March 1960. Her mother came to visit Wright in October 1960 to thank him for a correspondence that had been important to her daughter.

7. François Gourdon, *Tant qu'il y aura la peur* (Paris: Flammarion, 1960) and Paul Oliver, *Blues Fell This Morning* (London: Horizon Press, 1960). See Wright's reviews in Fabre, ed., *Richard Wright: Books and Writers.*

8. Richard Wright to Margrit de Sablonière, 24 March 1960. Schomburg Center.

9. Richard Wright to Margrit de Sablonière, 22 March 1960. Schomburg Center.

10. Oliver Harrington, "The Mysterious Death of Richard Wright," in Harrington, *Why I Left America and Other Essays.*

11. Margrit de Sablonière to Richard Wright, 23 February 1960. Schomburg Center.

12. Richard Wright to Margrit de Sablonière, 22 March 1960. Schomburg Center.

13. Richard Wright to Margrit de Sablonière, 30 March 1960. Schomburg Center.

14. Richard Wright to Margrit de Sablonière, 27 April 1960. Schomburg Center.

15. Richard Wright to Margrit de Sablonière, 7 April 1960. Schomburg Center.

16. De Sablonière told this story to Constance Webb, 26 December 1966. Webb papers. Several years after Wright's death, de Sablonière sent the papers to Julia Wright who had married a Frenchman and was working for Nkrumah in Ghana.

17. Margrit de Sablonière to Michel Fabre, May 1952. Fabre private papers.

18. Margrit de Sablonière wrote this later to Constance Webb, 16 December 1966. Webb private papers.

19. Richard Wright to Margrit de Sablonière, 26 April 1960. Schomburg Center.

20. See the various 1960 interviews in Kinnamon and Fabre, eds., *Conversations with Richard Wright.*

21. Interview with Maurice Nadeau, *Les Lettres Nouvelles,* April 1960. (Kinnamon and Fabre, eds., *Conversations with Richard Wright.*)

22. A CD called *Trois Américains à Paris* has Wright talking to Charbonnier (1960), Chester Himes talking in English to Michel Fabre in 1970, and James Baldwin speaking excellent French with Eric Laurent in 1975. It is an RFI production, in a series called "Les Voix de L'Ecriture." Michel Fabre wrote the notes.

23. Richard Wright to Margrit de Sablonière, 31 May 1960. Schomburg Center.

24. Richard Wright to Margrit de Sablonière, 29 April 1960. Schomburg Center.

25. Richard Wright to Margrit de Sablonière, 9 June 1960. Schomburg Center.

26. William Targ to Richard Wright, 6 July 1960. Wright papers.

27. Richard Wright to Margrit de Sablonière, 9 June 1960. Schomburg Center.

28. Richard Wright to Margrit de Sablonière, 3 July 1960. Schomburg Center.

29. Richard Wright to Margrit de Sablonière, 23 July 1960. Schomburg Center. He was quite right. In January 1961 the Congo independence leader Patrice Lumumba would be murdered—allegedly by Katanga separatists. We now know that the CIA had a hand in it.

30. Richard Gibson to Richard Wright, 6 July 1960. Wright papers.

31. Richard Wright to Margrit de Sablonière, 2 August 1960. Schomburg Center.

32. Richard Wright to Celia Hornung, 27 August 1960. Hornung private papers.

33. Dorothy Padmore to Michel Fabre, 13 March 1963, in Fabre, *The World of Richard Wright.*

34. Stunned by her father's death, Julia did not continue with her studies. She never got a university degree.

35. Madison Davis Lacy interview with Julia Wright, Paris, 1994. Lacy private papers.

36. Julia Wright said this in "Richard Wright Deeply Wounded, Daughter Says," Memphis *Commercial Appeal,* 4 September 1995, B2. In an interview with the author, Ellen Wright confirmed this figure.

37. It seems this was a long-term attraction. On 4 May 1952, de Beauvoir had written to Algren about her lunch with Ellen Wright. "It happened we talked about you. It always happens with her because *she* talks about you. No kidding, I think she got a romantic womanly feeling for you; she speaks in a dreamy, regretful way of what a great writer and a nice man you are; she asks reproachfully why you don't come here." (De Beauvoir, *A Transatlantic Love Affair*)

38. Arna Bontemps to Constance Webb, 24 January 1967. Webb papers.

39. Richard Wright to Langston Hughes, 8 October 1960. Hughes papers.

40. Richard Wright to Arna and Alberta Bontemps, 24 October 1960. Bontemps papers, Syracuse University.

41. Author's series of interviews with Celia Hornung, Melbourne, 18 June 1995–30 October 1996.

42. See Thomas W. Braden, "I'm Glad the CIA is 'Immoral,'" *Saturday Evening Post,* 20 May 1967, pp. 10–14.

43. Richard Wright to Margrit de Sablonière, 24 November 1960. Schomburg Center.

44. Richard Wright to Margrit de Sablonière, 23 November 1960. Schomburg Center.

45. Beb Vuyk attacked Wright in the weekly *Vrij Nederland.*

46. Richard Wright to Oliver Swan, 24 October 1960. Wright papers.

47. The Venice conference at the end of June 1960 was to celebrate the fiftieth anniversary of Tolstoy's death. It was planned to coincide with a celebration of Tolstoy in the Soviet Union. Cass Canfield, ex-director of Harper, who was associated with the CIA, wrote to organizer Nicholas Nabokov (23 December 1958): "Tolstoy basically was the embodiment of the concept of individual freedom and I have no doubt that the Soviets will celebrate the anniversary in a manner to prove that Tolstoy anticipated the ideas and practices of Lenin, Stalin & Co. Therefore it strikes me that it would be most effective if a western celebration of Tolstoy represented this great man as he really was in a convincing manner. The contrast between the two presentations would be obvious to any independent thinker and this ought to make excellent propaganda for us." (Congress for Cultural Freedom papers, University of Chicago Library.) There was another conference planned for New Delhi in December 1960.

48. I was unable to find a copy of Wright's letter to Crossman, and am surmising the content from Crossman's reply and from comments Wright made in an unpublished article written around this time: "Am I an American?"

49. Ollie Harrington remembers Wright's fury with Crossman. (See Harrington, "The Mysterious Death of Richard Wright.") Crossman replied on 31 October 1960: "Thank you for your extremely interesting—and painful—letter, which comes as a great shock to me." He added: "I certainly didn't regard the book, when I edited it, as a propaganda work against Communism. On the contrary, what virtue the book possessed was the integrity of the authors and the determination to state the truth about themselves, pleasant or unpleasant." (Wright papers.) In *The Cultural Cold War,* Frances Stonor Saunders demonstrates that Crossman *had* intended the book as propaganda, and the CIA helped distribute it. Wright was quite correct.

50. Richard Wright, "The Position of the Negro Artist and Intellectual in American Society," speech delivered at the American Church, Paris, 8 November 1960.

51. Richard Wright to Margrit de Sablonière, 20 November 1960. Schomburg Center.

52. Richard Wright to Margrit de Sablonière, 20 November 1960. Schomburg Center.

53. Margrit de Sablonière to Constance Webb, 16 December 1966. Webb private papers.

54. Margrit de Sablonière to Constance Webb, 16 December 1966. Webb private papers.

55. Not until 1969 did the first medical article on bismuth poisoning appear in a French medical journal.

56. Hughes had just come from newly independent Nigeria. Nnamdi Azikiwe had invited him, all expenses paid, to attend his inauguration ceremony. Du Bois and his wife, Shirley Graham, were also there, as was the Reverend Martin Luther King, Jr. Now Hughes was excited to be back in Paris, which he had not seen since 1938.

57. Langston Hughes, "Richard Wright's Last Guest At Home" in *Ebony,* February 1961, p. 94. Hughes papers.

Wright must have been very relieved that he had declined to review the second volume of Langston Hughes's autobiography, *I Wonder as I Wander,* a few years before. "Hughes' book is the work of an amiable, grownup child," he had told Robert Evett at the *New Republic.* "If I reviewed this book as I should and gave my honest reactions, I'd hurt Langston Hughes terribly, and he is a man whom I know personally and against whom I harbor no ill will whatsoever." He added that he preferred not to review books by American blacks. "The Negro intellectual world in America is small and protectively glued together like a can of squirming worms, and any objective criticisms directed toward any one of them is accepted as having been hurled at all of them." (Richard Wright to Robert Evett, date unknown. Wright papers.)

58. Madison Davis Lacy interview with Julia Wright, Paris, 1994. Lacy private papers.

59. Author's phone interview with Vivian Werner, Lenox, Massachusetts, 16 December 1997.

60. Madison Davis Lacy interview with Ollie Harrington, Detroit, Michigan, 19 April 1991. Lacy private papers.

61. Madison Davis Lacy interview with Ollie Harrington, Detroit, 19 April 1991. Lacy private papers.

62. Harrington, "The Mysterious Death of Richard Wright," Harrington, *Why I Left America and Other Essays.*

63. Ollie Harrington, "Why I Left America," speech given at Wayne State University, Detroit, 18 April 1991, in Harrington, *Why I Left America and Other Essays,* p. 109.

64. Ellen Wright to Constance Webb, 16 January 1961. Webb papers, Schomburg Center.

SELECTED BIBLIOGRAPHY

PUBLISHED WORKS BY RICHARD WRIGHT

The following are first publications; editions cited in the endnotes are given last.

Uncle Tom's Children: Four Novellas. New York: Harper, 1938.

Uncle Tom's Children: Five Long Stories. New York: Harper, 1940; restored text established by the Library of America, New York: HarperPerennial, 1993.

Native Son. Introduction by Dorothy Canfield Fisher, New York: Harper, 1940; restored text established by the Library of America, introduction by Arnold Rampersad, New York: HarperPerennial, 1991.

How "Bigger" Was Born: The Story of Native Son. New York: Harper, 1940.

Native Son (The Biography of a Young American): A Play in Ten Scenes. With Paul Green. New York: Harper, 1941.

12 Million Black Voices: A Folk History of the Negro in the United States. Photo direction by Edwin Rosskam. New York: Viking Press, 1941; New York: Thunder's Mouth Press, 1992.

Black Boy: A Record of Childhood and Youth. New York: Harper, 1945; restored and complete text established by the Library of America, introduction by Jerry W. Ward, Jr., New York: HarperPerennial, 1993.

The Outsider. New York: Harper, 1953; restored text established by the Library of America, introduction by Maryemma Graham, New York: HarperPerennial, 1993.

Savage Holiday. New York: Avon, 1954; afterword by Gerald Early, Jackson, MS: Banner Books, University Press of Mississippi, 1994.

Black Power: A Record of Reactions in a Land of Pathos. New York: Harper, 1954; introduction by Amritjit Singh, New York: HarperPerennial, 1995.

The Color Curtain: A Report on the Bandung Conference. Foreword by Gunnar Myrdal. New York: World Publishing Co., 1956; afterword by Amritjit Singh. Jackson, MS: Banner Books, University Press of Mississippi, 1994.

Pagan Spain. New York: Harper, 1957; introduction by Faith Berry, New York: HarperPerennial, 1995.

White Man, Listen! New York: Doubleday, 1957; introduction by Cedric Robinson, New York: HarperPerennial, 1995.

The Long Dream. New York: Doubleday, 1958; New York: Perennial Library, Harper & Row, 1987.

Posthumous Publications

Eight Men. New York: World Publishing Co., 1961; introduction by Paul Gilroy, New York: HarperPerennial, 1996.

Lawd Today! New York: Walker, 1963; unexpurgated edition, foreword by Arnold Rampersad, Richard Yarborough, ed., Boston: Northeastern University Press, 1993.

Letters to Joe C. Brown. Thomas Knipp, ed., Kent, OH: Kent State University Libraries, 1968.

American Hunger. (Continuation of *Black Boy.*) Afterword by Michel Fabre, New York: Harper & Row, 1977.

Conversations with Richard Wright. Keneth Kinnamon and Michel Fabre, eds., Jackson, MS: University Press of Mississippi, 1993.

Rite of Passage. Afterword by Arnold Rampersad, New York: HarperCollins, 1994.

Haiku: This Other World. Yoshinobu Hakatuni and Robert L. Tener, eds., New York: Arcade, 1998.

MOTION PICTURE

Native Son. Directed by Pierre Chenal, produced by James Pradès, screenplay by Richard Wright. Argentina Sono Film, 1950. American and European Distribution: Walter Gould Presentation. Released through Classic Pictures, 1951.

BOOKS ON RICHARD WRIGHT
(Includes books containing major essays on Wright.)

Biographical Works

Michel Fabre, *The Unfinished Quest of Richard Wright.* New York: Morrow, 1973.

Addison Gayle, *Richard Wright: Ordeal of a Native Son.* New York: Doubleday, 1980.

Margaret Walker, *Richard Wright: Daemonic Genius.* New York: Amistad, 1988.

Constance Webb, *Richard Wright: A Biography.* New York: Putnam's, 1968.

Criticism

David Bakish, *Richard Wright.* New York: Ungar, 1973.

James Baldwin, "Everybody's Protest Novel" and "Many Thousands Gone," in *Notes of a Native Son.* Boston: Beacon, 1955.

——— "Alas, Poor Richard" in *Nobody Knows My Name,* New York: Dial Press, 1961.

Harold Bloom, ed., *Richard Wright.* New York: Chelsea House, 1987.

Robert Bone, *Richard Wright*. Minneapolis: University of Minnesota Press, 1969.

Russell C. Brignano, *Richard Wright: An Introduction to the Man and His Works*. Pittsburgh: University of Pittsburgh Press, 1970.

Robert J. Butler, ed., *The Critical Response to Richard Wright*. Westport, CT: Greenwood Press, 1995.

Charles T. Davis and Michel Fabre, *Richard Wright: A Primary Bibliography*. Boston: G. K. Hall, 1982.

Ralph Ellison, "Richard Wright's Blues," The World and the Jug," and "Remembering Richard Wright," in *The Collected Essays of Ralph Ellison*. Preface by Saul Bellow, ed. John F. Callahan. New York: Modern Library, 1995.

Michel Fabre, *The World of Richard Wright*. Jackson, MS: University Press of Mississippi, 1985.

———— ed., *Richard Wright: Books and Writers*. Jackson, MS: University Press of Mississippi, 1990.

Robert Felgar, *Richard Wright*. Boston: Twayne, 1980.

Henry Louis Gates, Jr. and K. A. Appiah, eds., *Richard Wright. Critical Perspectives Past and Present*. New York: Amistad, 1993.

Paul Gilroy, *The Black Atlantic: Modernity and Double Consciousness*. Cambridge, MA: Harvard University Press, 1993.

Yoshinobu Hakutani, ed., *Critical Essays on Richard Wright*. Boston: G. K. Hall, 1982.

Joyce A. Joyce, *Richard Wright's Art of Tragedy*. Iowa City: University of Iowa Press, 1986.

Keneth Kinnamon, *The Emergence of Richard Wright*. Urbana, IL: University of Illinois Press, 1972.

———— *A Richard Wright Bibliography: Fifty Years of Criticism and Commentary, 1933–1982*. Compiled by Keneth Kinnamon with the help of Joseph Benson, Michel Fabre, and Craig Werner. Westport, CT: Greenwood Press, 1988.

Edward Margolies, *The Art of Richard Wright*. Preface by Harry T. Moore. Carbondale, IL: Southern Illinois University Press, 1969.

Dan McCall. *The Example of Richard Wright*. New York: Harcourt, Brace & World, 1973.

John M. Reilly, *Richard Wright: The Critical Reception*. New York: Franklin, 1978.

A NOTE ON PRIMARY SOURCES

For future Wright scholars I feel bound to add a general word on sources and gaps.

It has been forty years since the first generation of Wright scholars began research on Richard Wright. Michel Fabre, Constance Webb, Ken Kinnamon, David Bakish, and Edward Margolies have generously shared with me correspondence and interviews from their private archives.

In 1976 the Beinecke Rare Book and Manuscript Library at Yale University purchased the Richard Wright papers from Mrs. Ellen Wright. It consists of manuscripts, letters, photographs, journals, newspaper cuttings, jazz records, video clips, and other miscellaneous material.

There are letters from Wright in various library collections around the country, and important new correspondence has surfaced in the last few decades. For the most part, my efforts to find new Wright correspondence in private hands met with frustration. Wright's papers at Yale contain intimate letters from his Chicago friends Abe Aaron and Abe Chapman, written in the 1930s and '40s, but Wright's side of the correspondence has not survived. Abe Aaron's brother, Chester Aaron, believes that Abe destroyed letters from his former leftist friends during the McCarthy period. Abe Chapman, his daughter points out, left all his papers and possessions behind when the family fled New York in 1951 to a life of exile behind the Iron Curtain.

Horace Cayton and Wright wrote to each other between 1940 and 1951. Wright kept Cayton's letters; Cayton did not keep Wright's. In 1968, Cayton began a biography of Wright. The work was curtailed by his death in Paris in January 1970. Apart from brief notes, Cayton left recorded interviews with several of Wright's friends and colleagues in Chicago. The audiotapes are in the Cayton papers, in the Vivian G.

Harsh Research Collection of Afro-American History and Literature, in the Carter Woodson branch of the Chicago Public Library.

The Padmore side of the Wright-Padmore correspondence (1947–1960) is intact. Wright's letters to George and Dorothy Padmore seem to have disappeared.

I was fortunate to interview Edith Schroeder in Berlin in June 1997 and see the eight letters she had received from Wright. When she died, in April 1999, the letters went to the Stiftung Archiv der Akademie der Künste der Länder Berlin und Brandenburg, in Berlin.

Celia Hornung Sanders, Wright's last girlfriend, who lives in Melbourne, Australia, has some dozen or so letters from Wright in her possession. He wrote them in 1960, when she was in Australia visiting her future husband.

Before he died, Wright entrusted to Margrit de Sablonière documents that he believed were evidence of a plot against him. In the mid-1960s, Sablonière sent the package to Julia Wright, then living in Accra with her husband, Henri Hervé, and their baby daughter. Presumably, Julia Wright still has these documents. Julia Wright's long-awaited memoir about her father, *Daughter of a Native Son,* is to be published by Random House.

Wright's letters to Margaret Walker (1937–1941), held by Jackson State University, are not yet open to the public. Nor are Wright's letters to the psychiatrist Frederic Wertham, held in the Wertham papers at the Library of Congress.

I hoped to benefit from new gains made in recent years by legal suits against the FBI under America's Freedom of Information Act (1966). When I first started work on Wright, in August 1995, I wrote to the FBI and asked for his file. Two months later, I received the partially released file that Addison Gayle had seen in 1978. I submitted an appeal. I also asked for files on George Padmore, Oliver Harrington, William Gardner Smith, Celia Hornung, and Dhimah Meidman Goldsmith.

In January 1997 I received Gardner Smith's file. (Like Wright's file, it came relatively quickly, since it had already been declassified for a previous scholar.) The few unblacked-out sections in Gardner Smith's file were mostly so blurred as to be illegible. The FBI insisted that this had nothing to do with the photocopying process. (However, I have noticed on several occasions that the same document that is illegible when sent by the FBI is impeccably clear in the State Department files.)

My appeal on the Wright file was accepted in July 1997. In December 1997, with the help of a lawyer, I wrote a letter pointing out the FBI's failure to comply with the stated guidelines for release of FBI material. This resulted in several phone calls from the FBI and assurances that the matter would be followed up with more reasonable speed.

In March 1998, I was informed that there were no records for Celia Hornung. In June 1998, an FBI employee called to say that Wright's file was in the declassification unit and she would do her best to hurry the process along. In September 1998, I was told that the Padmore file had been "assigned" and I should receive it any day now. In October 1998, I heard that Oliver Harrington's file was in the declassification unit, on its way to me. (Later I was informed in a telephone conversation that there were no records on him, which is almost certainly not true.)

In November 1998, I received material on George Padmore. As it turned out, of the 159 pages in the packet, only 38 were pages of Padmore's actual file and these were almost entirely blacked out. The rest were FBI "search sheets" and "deleted page information" sheets. In September 1999 two pages arrived on "Dhima Goldsmith." An investigation by the Cleveland bureau in 1959 verified her status as a housewife, married to Arthur Goldsmith, and revealed no political activity. (There is no mention of Wright.)

In April 2000, four and a half years after submitting my appeal, the FBI's office of Information and Privacy released to me thirty-nine pages of newly declassified material on Wright. They contain little of interest. One two-page document from the American embassy in Paris to the FBI in Washington (3 March 1952), heavily blacked out in the previously released file, was now slightly less so—though one name was blacked out that had not been before. In the meantime, I had seen the same document, uncensored, in the State Department files. It concerned Wright's friendship with the Russian-born French journalist Michel Gordey.

There are forty-two pages on Wright in the State Department files at the National Archives in Washington. Having been declassified, on 7 May 1988, these documents were left intact, without blackings out. Some pages overlap with material in Wright's released FBI file; other pages indicate surveillance of Wright that is not hinted at in his released FBI file. A careful examination of the declassified material in both the FBI files and the State Department files gives some impression of the extent of state-sponsored espionage into Wright's activities.

ACKNOWLEDGMENTS

First and foremost, I am indebted to Ellen Wright, who consented to several interviews with me in Paris over the years and who granted permission to quote from Wright's unpublished writings. I am grateful to her for giving me the freedom to interpret Wright's life as I construed the evidence before me.

Michel Fabre has been encouraging and unwaveringly generous with his help. In addition to his files of unpublished correspondence, his published collections of Wright's interviews and his annotated bibliographies of Wright's personal library and Wright's published and unpublished writings have been indispensable to me. As the intrepid pioneer of Wright studies, Fabre represents an inspiring model of personal courage.

Constance Webb Pearlstien knew Wright, his family, and many of his friends personally. I have enjoyed her colorful e-mails and appreciated her help. David Bakish kindly let me pore over the handwritten notes he took when he interviewed Wright people in the late 1960s. Ken Kinnamon, whose exhaustive *Richard Wright Bibliography* has been invaluable, sent me letters. Madison Davis Lacy, whose video documentary *Richard Wright: Black Boy* was first broadcast on PBS-TV on 4 September 1995, let me read transcriptions of the interviews he conducted in 1993–94. Ed and Claire Margolies have been magnanimous with their help and hospitality.

I am grateful to those people in the United States, Europe, and Australia who gave me their recollections of Wright and his circle: Chester Aaron, Lionel Abel, Mary Doll Aswell, Daphne Athas, Sanora Babb, Christopher Blake, Hélène Bokanowski, Margaret Burroughs, Marvel Cooke, Suzette and Schofield Coryell, Adelaide

Cromwell, Essie Lee Ward Davis, Helen Sattler Deaton, Rémi Dreyfus, Dorothy Butler Farrell, Howard Fast, Mary Elting Folsom, Herbert Gentry, Richard Gibson, Peter Goldsmith, Rebecca Goldsmith, Helma Harrington, Herbert Hill, Lesley Himes, Ann Kimmage, Stephen Maas, Len Mallette, Ed Mashberg, Betty Milhendler, Albert Murray, Dolores Newton, Constance Webb Pearlstien, Jean Pouillon, Sol and Frieda Rabkin, Naomi Replansky, Robbin Reynolds, Louise Rosskam, Leonard Rubin, Celia Hornung Sanders, Edith Anderson Schroeder, Roger Shattuck, Dorothy and Reuben Silver, Ouida Campbell Taylor, Studs Terkel, Anna Tyler, Vivian Werner, Susan Cayton Woodson, Charles Wright, Helen Yglesias.

In different ways and in different degrees, many people have helped make this book a reality. I extend my warm thanks to the following: Sue Aitkin, Brian Boyd, Paul Buhle, Edward Burns, John F. Callahan, Frank Campbell, Trevor Code, Morris Dickstein, Bettina Drew, Mary Dudziak, Gerald Early, Brent Edwards, Emory Elliott, Paul Gilroy, Julie Flanagan, Maryemma Graham, Benjamin Harris, Clive Harris, Richard Hobbs, Gerald Horne, Rosemary Jones, H. J. Kaplan, Kathryn Karipides, Madison Davis Lacy, Paul Lauter, David Leeming, Helena Lewis, Rosemary Lloyd, Jock McCulloch, Tracy McNeal, James A. Miller, Toril Moi, Bill Mullen, Richard Munday, Andrew Patner, Cleo Paturis, Wendy Plotkin, Dorothy Porter, Arnold Rampersad, Della Rowley, Derrick and Betty Rowley, Martin Rowley, Frances Stonor Saunders, Amritjit Singh, Werner Sollors, Eliza Steelwater, Odile Baron Supervielle, Christina Thompson, Irene Tomaszewski, David Walker, Jerry Ward, Howard Zinn.

I am grateful to the Beinecke Rare Book and Manuscript Library for awarding me the Donald C. Gallup Fellowship in American Literature at the Beinecke Rare Book and Manuscript Library in January 1997. I am beholden to the International Forum for U.S. Studies for awarding me a Rockefeller Humanities Fellowship at the University of Iowa from 1 February to 31 April 1997. IFUSS codirectors Jane Desmond and Virginia Dominguez provided excellent working conditions and stimulating interaction with scholars in related fields.

The W. E. B. Du Bois Institute for Afro-American Research at Harvard has provided me with an ideal working environment in Cambridge, Massachusetts, and I am grateful to its director, Henry Louis Gates, Jr., for enabling me to enjoy this privilege. Richard Newman, W. E. B. Du Bois Research director, has been particularly encouraging and helpful, and I am much obliged to him for reading my final manuscript so carefully. I finished the manuscript while I was a fellow at the Radcliffe Institute for Advanced Study at Harvard University. I would like to thank my Radcliffe colleagues for their support of my scholarship.

I am grateful to the estate of Richard Wright for permission to quote excerpts from Wright's correspondence and unpublished manuscripts; HarperCollins, New York and Random House, UK for permission to quote from *Black Boy*. For other copyright permissions I thank Harcourt (extract from *Black Metropolis*); the Paul Green Foundation; the Estate of Gertrude Stein; Robbin Reynolds; Princeton University Library; Gunther Stuhlmann (Anaïs Nin estate); Dolores Newton; Diana Fleischmann (John Houseman Estate); Lesley Himes c/o Roslyn Targ Literary Agency; Helma Harrington; William Morris Agency (Ralph Ellison Estate); Frederick Courtright (Estate of W. E. B. Du Bois); Susan Cayton Woodson; University of Vermont; Watkins/Loomis Agency for the Estate of Kay Boyle; Harold Ober Associates for the Estate of Arna Bontemps; Sylvie Le Bon de Beauvoir for the Estate of Simone de

Beauvoir; Eileen Ahearn (James Baldwin Estate); Helga Schmidt, Steerforth Press, for permission to quote from Edith Anderson's *Love in Exile;* Peter Steinberg at Donadio & Ashworth for quotations from Nelson Algren.

I thank the following librarians, archivists, and institutions for their help: Stephen Jones, Lynn Braunsdorf, Maureen Heher, Ngadi Kponou, and Pat Willis, curator of American Literature, at the Beinecke Library, Yale University; Margaret Sherry, Rare Books and Special Collections, Princeton University Library; Richard Faber, Chicago Public Library, Patricia Mikkelich and Andrea Telli, Special Collections, Chicago Public Library; Michael Flug, curator of the Vivian G. Harsh Research Collection of Afro-American History and Literature, Carter Woodson branch of the Chicago Public Library; Special Collections, Joseph Regenstein Library, University of Chicago; Alice Birney and Fred Bauman, Manuscript Division, Library of Congress; Joy Holland, Brooklyn Collection, Brooklyn Public Library; Dave Stein, archivist, Kurt Weill Foundation for Music; Rebecca Cape, Lilly Library, Indiana University, Bloomington; Jeffrey Marshall, curator of manuscripts, University of Vermont; Alice Cotton, reference historian, North Carolina Collection, University of North Carolina; Steven Niven and John White, Southern Historical Collection, University of North Carolina at Chapel Hill; Robin Van Fleet, Manuscripts, Moorland-Spingarn Research Center, Howard University; Katie Salzmann, Southern Illinois University, Carbondale; Manuscript Division, Newberry Library; Chicago Historical Society; Oral History Collection, Butler Library, Columbia University; G. Thomas Tanselle, John Simon Guggenheim Foundation; Jim Hatch, Hatch Billops Collection; Manuscript Section, Schomburg Center, New York Public Library; Elva Griffith, Rare Books and Manuscripts, Ohio State University Library, Columbus; Sylvia Kennick Brown, special collections librarian, Williams College; Terry Keenan, Special Collections, Syracuse University Library; National Archives at College Park, Maryland; Linda Seidman, Special Collections and Archives, W. E. B. Du Bois Library, University of Massachusetts, Amherst; Mark Brown, Brown University Library; Mary Ellen Rogan, senior archivist, Billy Rose Theatre Collection, New York Public Library for the Performing Arts; Beth Howse, Special Collections, Fisk University Library, Nashville; Nancy Birk, Kent State University; Jennifer Ford, Special Collections, University of Mississippi Library; Mary Miller, Historic Natchez Foundation; Tony Bliss, Bancroft Library, University of California, Berkeley; Carol Turley, Department of Special Collections, University of California, Los Angeles; Françoise Cochaud, director, Alliance Française, Buenos Aires; Victoria Peters, Archives, Modern Records Centre, University of Warwick Library, Coventry; Cathy Henderson, chief archivist, Harry Ransom Humanities Research Center, University of Texas at Austin.

I particularly thank Elaine Bernard, Beverly Tucker, and James Alan McPherson for their encouragement and sustained interest in my work. Countless discussions with Carlos Brossard stimulated me to go further and deeper, I am also inordinately grateful for his help when computer problems arose.

I am grateful to the *New York Times* for placing a notice that resulted in several useful contacts. I thank Jack Macrae, at Henry Holt, for his editorial insights, and his assistant, Katy Hope, for her helpfulness. I feel immensely fortunate to have Denise Shannon as my agent.

Finally, my warm thanks go to a special friend who lives across the world in Adelaide, South Australia. No one knows better than Ann Timoney Jenkin the ups and downs I have gone through during the writing of this book. In anguished times, she has been as solid as a lighthouse. Unstinting with her time and imaginative with her pencil, she has read my manuscript and made suggestions with the commitment most writers give only to their own work.

INDEX

ABOUT THE AUTHOR

Hazel Rowley is the author of *Christina Stead: A Biography,* a 1994 *New York Times* Notable Book, described in the *Times* as "everything a literary biography should be." She has taught at Iowa University and Deakin University in Melbourne. During the writing of this book, she was a Rockefeller fellow at the University of Iowa and a Bunting fellow at Radcliffe College, Harvard University. She lives in Cambridge, Massachusetts.